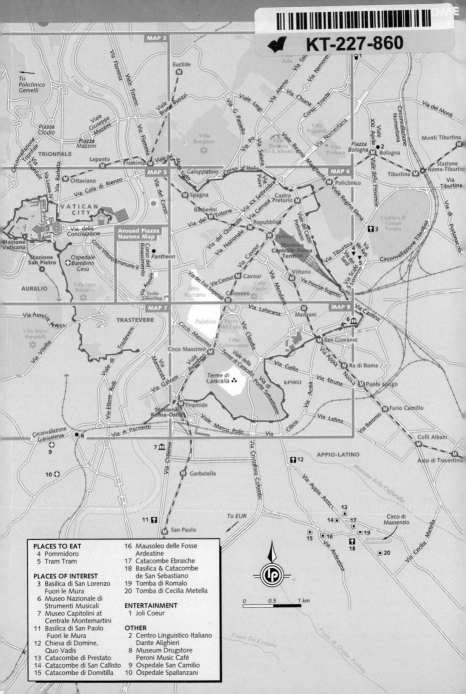

KT-227-860

PLACES TO EAT
4 Pommidoro
5 Tram Tram

PLACES OF INTEREST
3 Basilica di San Lorenzo
  Fuori le Mura
6 Museo Nazionale di
  Strumenti Musicali
7 Museo Capitolini at
  Centrale Montemartini
11 Basilica di San Paolo
  Fuori le Mura
12 Chiesa di Domine,
  Quo Vadis
13 Catacombe di Prestato
14 Catacombe di San Callisto
15 Catacombe di Domitilla

16 Mausoleo delle Fosse
  Ardeatine
17 Catacombe Ebraiche
18 Basilica & Catacombe
  de San Sebastiano
19 Tomba di Romalo
20 Tomba di Cecilia Metella

ENTERTAINMENT
1 Joli Coeur

OTHER
2 Centro Linguistico Italiano
  Dante Alighieri
8 Museum Drugstore
  Peroni Music Café
9 Ospedale San Camillo
10 Ospedale Spallanzani

0   0.5   1 km

Rome
1st edition – July 1999

Published by
Lonely Planet Publications Pty Ltd A.C.N. 005 607 983
192 Burwood Rd, Hawthorn, Victoria 3122, Australia

Lonely Planet Offices
Australia PO Box 617, Hawthorn, Victoria 3122
USA 150 Linden St, Oakland, CA 94607
UK 10a Spring Place, London NW5 3BH
France 1 rue du Dahomey, 75011 Paris

Photographs
Many of the images in this guide are available for licensing from
Lonely Planet Images.
email: lpi@lonelyplanet.com.au

Front cover photograph
Fontana Trevi (Simon Bracken)

ISBN 0 86442 626 7

Rome

Helen Gillman
Stefano Cavedoni
Sally Webb

LONELY PLANET PUBLICATIONS
Melbourne • Oakland • London • Paris

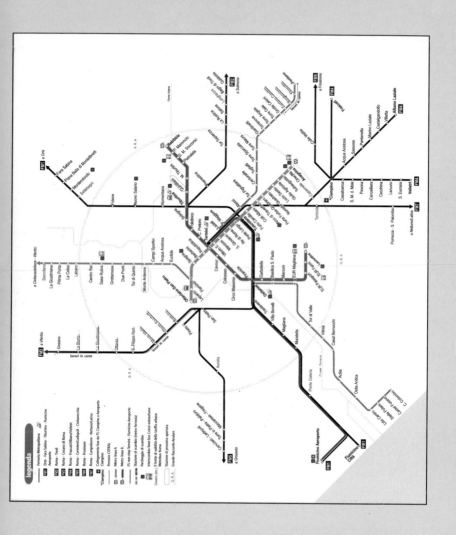

Contents – Text

2 Contents – Text

The Authors

Helen Gillman & Stefano Cavedoni

Helen works as a writer and editor, based in Italy. For many years she worked as a journalist in Australia (her country of birth), before moving to Italy in 1990. Helen is the coordinating author of this book, as well as the coordinating author of Lonely Planet's *Italy* and *Walking in Italy* guides. She has also written the Italy chapter in LP's *Mediterranean Europe* and *Western Europe* shoestring guides. On all of these guides, she works closely with her husband, Stefano Cavedoni.

Stefano is an actor and writer. In the late 1970s, while still a university student, Stefano's career in the Italian entertainment industry was launched with a bang when his rock band, *Skiantos*, became a major success. After this he wrote and performed humorous one-man shows. But while on stage, he was secretly thinking about travel, forests and mountains. He has worked with Helen on the LP *Italy* guides since the 1st edition and researched and wrote many of the walks in the *Walking in Italy* guide.

Sally Webb

Sally Webb was born and brought up in Melbourne, Australia, but has spent many years living in both the UK and Italy and has travelled throughout Europe, the USA and Asia.

In a former life she was an art historian, having studied at Melbourne University and at the Courtauld Institute of Art in London from where she graduated in 1990 with an MA in Art History. Deciding it was time for some radical changes in her life, she moved from London to Italy in 1994, and became a journalist and travel writer.

Sally currently lives in Trastevere in the heart of Rome where, when not writing LP guides, she works as a journalist and editor for *Wanted in Rome*, an English-language fortnightly magazine. She is a regular contributor to the *Australian Gourmet Traveller* and has written for several other Australian publications, including the *Qantas Club* magazine and Ansett Airline's *Viva*. She also contributes to publications in the USA and Italy. She recently updated the Malta chapter for LP's *Mediterranean Europe* and is currently working on the 4th edition of *Italy*.

FROM THE AUTHORS

Helen Gillman & Stefano Cavedoni It might sound like a cliché, but this book literally wouldn't have been possible without the help of various friends and colleagues. Thanks especially to Carla Landi for her input and advice on the shopping chapter – her in depth knowledge and experience has helped give the chapter a real insider's perspective. Laura Clarke was a great help and her translation of Stefano's Rome Walks chapter (originally written in Italian) was first-rate. Thanks also to Barbara Walsh, and to Daniela Fiorelli and the helpful staff of the Comune di Roma. As always, the energetic and enthusiastic support of Fulvia and Pierluigi at Enjoy Rome was greatly appreciated.

Sally Webb First and foremost I would like to thank Mary Wilsey, Maggie Mason and Sabina Triulzi at Wanted in Rome, all of whom shouldered a significant extra burden while I was writing this book. Thanks also to the following for invaluable information and assistance: Nicholas Rigillo, Adrian Arena, Claire Hammond at The Corner Bookshop, Sarah Yates, Claudio and Rocco at Babele, Anna Quartucci at COIN, Signora Ziroli and Signor Cerroni at ATAC-Cotral, and Roberto Faidutti. Our editor Ada Cheung also deserves special thanks for her contribution to the music and history sections when she already had plenty to do.

On a personal note, I would like to thank Orla Guerin, Sari and Alessandro Taddei, Alfie Fabbroncini, Jeremy Hall-Smith, Celia and Markus Bockmuehl, Gillian Abbott, Helen Dixon and all my houseguests over the past few years (the list is too long to print) whose Roman holidays made my ongoing research even more enjoyable. Finally, I would like to thank my family for love and encouragement from afar and in particular my parents, Geoff Webb and Noey Webb, whose support knows no limits.

This Book

This is the 1st edition of LP's Rome city guide. It incorporates material written by Helen Gillman for the 3rd edition of the *Italy* guide. Helen Gillman coordinated this book, and wrote the Introduction and the Shopping and Excursions chapters. Stefano Cavedoni wrote the Rome Walks chapter. Sally Webb wrote Getting There & Away; Getting Around; Things to See & Do; Places to Eat; and Entertainment. Helen Gillman and Sally Webb co-wrote the Facts about Rome and Facts for the Visitor, as well as the Places to Stay chapter.

From the Publisher

This book was edited and proofed by Ada Cheung, Wendy Owen, Rebecca Turner, Helen Yeates and Chris Wyness. Katie Cody helped with the proofing. Quentin Frayne provided the language section. Ann Jeffree coordinated the mapping and design, assisted by Csanad Csutoros and Adrian Persoglia; cover design by Simon Bracken. The illustrations were drawn by Trudi Canavan and Ann Jeffree. Layout assistance was rendered by Tim Uden.

Foreword

ABOUT LONELY PLANET GUIDEBOOKS

The story begins with a classic travel adventure: Tony and Maureen Wheeler's 1972 journey across Europe and Asia to Australia. Useful information about the overland trail did not exist at that time, so Tony and Maureen published the first Lonely Planet guidebook to meet a growing need.

From a kitchen table, then from a tiny office in Melbourne (Australia), Lonely Planet has become the largest independent travel publisher in the world, an international company with offices in Melbourne, Oakland (USA), London (UK) and Paris (France).

Today Lonely Planet guidebooks cover the globe. There is an ever-growing list of books and there's information in a variety of forms and media. Some things haven't changed. The main aim is still to help make it possible for adventurous travellers to get out there – to explore and better understand the world.

At Lonely Planet we believe travellers can make a positive contribution to the countries they visit – if they respect their host communities and spend their money wisely. Since 1986 a percentage of the income from each book has been donated to aid projects and human rights campaigns.

Updates Lonely Planet thoroughly updates each guidebook as often as possible. This usually means there are around two years between editions, although for more unusual or more stable destinations the gap can be longer. Check the imprint page (following the colour map at the beginning of the book) for publication dates.

Between editions up-to-date information is available in two free newsletters – the paper *Planet Talk* and email *Comet* (to subscribe, contact any Lonely Planet office) – and on our Web site at www.lonelyplanet.com. The *Upgrades* section of the Web site covers a number of important and volatile destinations and is regularly updated by Lonely Planet authors. *Scoop* covers news and current affairs relevant to travellers. And, lastly, the *Thorn Tree* bulletin board and *Postcards* section of the site carry unverified, but fascinating, reports from travellers.

Correspondence The process of creating new editions begins with the letters, postcards and emails received from travellers. This correspondence often includes suggestions, criticisms and comments about the current editions. Interesting excerpts are immediately passed on via newsletters and the Web site, and everything goes to our authors to be verified when they're researching on the road. We're keen to get more feedback from organisations or individuals who represent communities visited by travellers.

Lonely Planet gathers information for everyone who's curious about the planet – and especially for those who explore it first-hand. Through guidebooks, phrasebooks, activity guides, maps, literature, newsletters, image library, TV series and Web site we act as an information exchange for a worldwide community of travellers.

Research Authors aim to gather sufficient practical information to enable travellers to make informed choices and to make the mechanics of a journey run smoothly. They also research historical and cultural background to help enrich the travel experience and allow travellers to understand and respond appropriately to cultural and environmental issues.

Authors don't stay in every hotel because that would mean spending a couple of months in each medium-sized city and, no, they don't eat at every restaurant because that would mean stretching belts beyond capacity. They do visit hotels and restaurants to check standards and prices, but feedback based on readers' direct experiences can be very helpful.

Many of our authors work undercover, others aren't so secretive. None of them accept freebies in exchange for positive write-ups. And none of our guidebooks contain any advertising.

Production Authors submit their raw manuscripts and maps to offices in Australia, USA, UK or France. Editors and cartographers – all experienced travellers themselves – then begin the process of assembling the pieces. When the book finally hits the shops, some things are already out of date, we start getting feedback from readers and the process begins again …

WARNING & REQUEST

Things change – prices go up, schedules change, good places go bad and bad places go bankrupt – nothing stays the same. So, if you find things better or worse, recently opened or long since closed, please tell us and help make the next edition even more accurate and useful. We genuinely value all the feedback we receive. Julie Young coordinates a well travelled team that reads and acknowledges every letter, postcard and email and ensures that every morsel of information finds its way to the appropriate authors, editors and cartographers for verification.

Everyone who writes to us will find their name in the next edition of the appropriate guidebook. They will also receive the latest issue of *Planet Talk*, our quarterly printed newsletter, or *Comet*, our monthly email newsletter. Subscriptions to both newsletters are free. The very best contributions will be rewarded with a free guidebook.

Excerpts from your correspondence may appear in new editions of Lonely Planet guidebooks, the Lonely Planet Web site, *Planet Talk* or *Comet*, so please let us know if you *don't* want your letter published or your name acknowledged.

Send all correspondence to the Lonely Planet office closest to you:

Australia: PO Box 617, Hawthorn, Victoria 3122
USA: 150 Linden St, Oakland, CA 94607
UK: 10A Spring Place, London NW5 3BH
France: 1 rue du Dahomey, 75011 Paris

Or email us at: talk2us@lonelyplanet.com.au

For news, views and updates see our Web site: www.lonelyplanet.com

HOW TO USE A LONELY PLANET GUIDEBOOK

The best way to use a Lonely Planet guidebook is any way you choose. At Lonely Planet we believe the most memorable travel experiences are often those that are unexpected, and the finest discoveries are those you make yourself. Guidebooks are not intended to be used as if they provide a detailed set of infallible instructions!

Contents All Lonely Planet guidebooks follow roughly the same format. The Facts about the Destination chapters or sections give background information ranging from history to weather. Facts for the Visitor gives practical information on issues like visas and health. Getting There & Away gives a brief starting point for re-searching travel to and from the destination. Getting Around gives an overview of the transport options when you arrive.

The peculiar demands of each destination determine how sub-sequent chapters are broken up, but some things remain constant. We always start with background, then proceed to sights, places to stay, places to eat, entertainment, getting there and away, and getting around information – in that order.

Heading Hierarchy Lonely Planet headings are used in a strict hierarchical structure that can be visualised as a set of Russian dolls. Each heading (and its following text) is encompassed by any preceding heading that is higher on the hierarchical ladder.

Entry Points We do not assume guidebooks will be read from beginning to end, but that people will dip into them. The tradi-tional entry points are the list of contents and the index. In addition, however, some books have a complete list of maps and an index map illustrating map coverage.

There may also be a colour map that shows highlights. These highlights are dealt with in greater detail in the Facts for the Visitor chapter, along with planning questions and suggested itin-eraries. Each chapter covering a geographical region usually begins with a locator map and another list of highlights. Once you find something of interest in a list of highlights, turn to the index.

Maps Maps play a crucial role in Lonely Planet guidebooks and include a huge amount of information. A legend is printed on the back page. We seek to have complete consistency between maps and text, and to have every important place in the text captured on a map. Map key numbers usually start in the top left corner.

Although inclusion in a guidebook usually implies a recommen-dation we cannot list every good place. Exclusion does not necessarily imply criticism. In fact there are a number of reasons why we might exclude a place – sometimes it is simply inappropriate to encourage an influx of travellers.

Introduction

'I now realise all the dreams of my youth,' wrote Goethe on his arrival in Rome in the winter of 1786. Perhaps Rome today is more chaotic, but certainly no less romantic or fascinating. In this city a phenomenal concentration of history, legend and monuments coexists with an equally phenomenal concentration of people busily going about everyday life. It is easy to pick today's tourists because they are the only ones to turn their heads as the bus passes the Colosseo.

Rome has always inspired wonder and awe in its visitors – from pilgrims to historians, artists, writers and plain old tourists. Its ruined, but still imposing, monuments represent a point of reference for a city which, through the imperial, medieval, Renaissance and Baroque periods, has undergone many transformations. As such, the cultured and well-to-do Europeans who, from the mid-17th century onwards, rediscovered Rome, found in the Eternal City a continuity from the pagan to the Christian worlds. In fact, from the time of the Roman Empire, through the development of Christianity to the present day – a period of more than 2500 years – Rome has produced an archaeological archive of Western culture.

Rome is a city on many levels. The historical sites are merely the tip of the iceberg. Tourists wandering around the city with their eyes raised to admire its monuments should know that about 4m under their feet exists another city, with traces of other settlements deeper still. The Basilica di San Pietro stands on the site of an earlier basilica built by Emperor Constantine in the 4th century over the necropolis where St Peter was buried. Castel Sant'Angelo was the tomb of Emperor Hadrian before it was converted into a fortress. The form of Piazza Navona is suggestive of a hippodrome and, in fact, it was built on the ruins of the emperor Domitian's stadium. To know all this can help you interpret and understand this chaotic and often frustrating city.

The most important event in Rome's contemporary history is the Holy Year or Jubilee which will take place in 2000. For Roman Catholic pilgrims this is a once in a lifetime chance to visit Christianity's most important cities and bear witness to their faith (see the boxed text 'A pilgrim's progress').

However, for the vast majority of Romans the preparations for the Jubilee have created nothing but havoc. The city's traffic – at best chaotic and at worst intolerable – has worsened considerably as roads have been widened, underpasses dug and tunnels deepened so that the millions of extra visitors will be able to move around the city. Tourists haven't fared much better; the city's most beautiful monuments, churches, palazzi, bridges and fountains have been shrouded from view by scaffolding and tarpaulins as they undergo major cosmetic surgery.

Fortunately, by the time you read this book, much of the cleaning, conservation and restoration will have finished. The national and municipal heritage authorities have made enormous efforts to reopen museums and cultural sites that had long been languishing in disrepair. Between summer 1997 and summer 1998 several major museums were inaugurated (or reopened their doors after lengthy restorations) including the world-famous Museo e Galleria Borghese, and two new seats of the Museo Nazionale Romano.

Although end of millennium Rome has no great architectural genius who can leave a mark on the city the way Michelangelo and Bernini did, what this period does mark is a greater understanding and respect for the city's existing cultural patrimony, and laudable efforts to show it to its best advantage while at the same time preserving it for future generations.

When in Rome do as the Romans do. This is a city for the senses, where the minutiae of daily life possess a charm unimaginable in other capitals. Get your cultural fill but make sure to leave time for other concerns. Eat till you can eat no more; get drunk on wine, architecture and sunshine. Shameless hedonism is a way of life in Rome.

Romans tend to have a love/hate relationship with their city, but at the end of the day few of them would choose to live elsewhere. When you're sipping a chilled *aperitivo* at an outdoor *caffè* in a magnificent baroque piazza, basking in the fading sunlight of a balmy summer's day, you'll understand why.

Facts About Rome

HISTORY
Legendary Beginnings

Nearly 500 years after Aeneas arrived in Italy, the twins Romulus and Remus were born after the war god Mars took a fancy to a Latin princess.

Like Moses, the infants were set adrift in a reed boat, but on the Tevere (river Tiber) rather than the Nile, and they were adopted by a she-wolf. Later raised by shepherds, the boys grew up, gave their wicked uncle his come uppance, and claimed their right to rule. The brothers decided to build separate cities, with Romulus choosing a site on the Palatino (Palatine Hill). When his walls were partially complete, Remus tauntingly jumped over them. He got more than he bargained for when Romulus killed him.

This date, 21 April 753 BC, became Rome's official starting point, with historians counting the years *ab urbe condita* (AUC), from the foundation of the city in 1949 it was discovered that the Palatine was the earliest inhabited area of the city, and that the huts dated from the 8th century BC.

Romulus disappeared, either taken up by the gods, or, more gruesomely, secretly murdered by senators who dismembered the body. The next seven kings were elected from the ranks of the nobles. Most notably, Numa Pompilius is credited with establishing the state religion; and the Etruscan Servius Tullius built the first walls around the city state and established the basic organisation of the political and military system. See also the 'Etruscans' boxed text in the Excursions chapter.

Servius Tullius was assassinated by a rival, Tarquinius Superbus (Tarquin the Proud), who became notorious for raising a delinquent son who, in 509 BC, broke all rules of hospitality and good manners by raping his host's wife when her husband was out of the city. Lucretia was so mortified that she committed suicide after telling the story to her male relatives. One of them, Lucius Junius Brutus, decided that enough was enough, and incited the overthrow and expulsion of the Etruscan royal house. The Roman Republic was born, and the first temple was built on the Campidoglio (Capitoline Hill).

The Republic

Although the Romans never developed a written constitution, the success of their unique government was such that it became the model on which the American Constitution was based.

Polybius, a Greek historian writing in the late 2nd century BC to explain Rome's remarkable 50-year rise to Mediterranean dominance, suggested that the Romans combined the best of all the known systems, held in a state of equilibrium. Monarchy was represented by the two consuls who were also

---

Beginnings
1180 BC
   Aeneas lands in Italy
   after the fall of Troy.
753
   Foundation of Rome
   by Romulus.
700-396
   Etruscan civilisation.

715-673
   Numa Pompilius
   becomes the first
   Etruscan king of Rome.
   State religion established.
578-535
   Servius Tullius reforms
   the social and military
   structure.

509
   Rape of Lucretia and
   the expulsion of the
   monarchy.
   Dedication of the
   Capitoline temple.
501
   Senatorial appointment
   of the first Dictator.

The Capitoline Wolf, an Etruscan animal with Renaissance additions

the alternating commanders-in-chief; oligarchy came from the Senate, to which all the higher magistrates, including the consuls, belonged; and democracy came from the direct election to almost all political offices. To keep the magistrates in check, all offices were strictly annual; re-election was originally forbidden, then later allowed only after a 10-year gap. No man was permitted to stand for high office until he had progressed through the sequence of junior posts, and all magistracies were held jointly, with the 'no' vote – the *veto* – given precedence. The exception was the Dictator, appointed along with a subordinate Master of the Horse for six months during periods of crisis. Unlike American presidents, Roman magistrates were immune from prosecution while in office, but could be called to account once the year was over.

The Romans also developed a unique system for dealing with the other peoples (eg the Sabines and Etruscans to the north, the Oscans, Samnites, Hernici, and Greek colonies to the south) in the region. Defeated city states were not taken over, but became allies. Allowed to retain their own government and lands, they were required to provide troops to serve alongside Roman soldiers in future wars.

450 BC
Law of the Twelve Tables.
390
Sack of Rome by the Gauls.
396
The Etruscan stronghold of Veio captured.

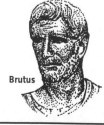

Brutus

338
Rome subsumes the Latin League.
386-5
Defeat of the Latins, Volsci, and Hernici.
312
Construction of the Via Appia begun.

Pius Aeneas

In Homer's version of the Trojan war, Aeneas only has a bit part. According to Roman legend, he was the son of the goddess Venus and a mortal Trojan. When Troy was destroyed, Aeneas escaped from the captured city, taking his father, his son, and the shrine containing their household gods.

After various adventures, including a trip to the underworld and a tragic affair with Dido, Queen of Carthage (set up by his mother, the goddess of love, and broken off by order of Jupiter himself, after which Dido committed suicide), Aeneas fulfilled his divine mission by reaching central Italy and founding a new Troy. Defeating a tribe who objected to the new arrivals, he forged a marriage alliance with one of the native kings of Latium, thus founding the line of kings of Alba Longa.

As well as in Vergil's epic *Aeneid*, 'Father Aeneas' appears throughout Roman art and literature. He is often depicted fleeing Troy, holding his small son's hand and carrying his elderly father on his shoulders while the old man cradles the *palladium*, their household shrine. He is also portrayed on the west side of the Ara Pacis, sacrificing a sow in thanksgiving for his arrival in Latium. Aeneas embodies the great Roman virtue of Pietas – not so much 'piety' as Duty shown towards the Gods, the State, and one's family, without regard for the self.

This naturally increased Rome's military strength, and the protection offered by the Roman hegemony induced many cities to become allies voluntarily.

The civic structure was also expanding. In 450 BC the existing laws were codified as the 'Law of the Twelve Tables', which remained in force for the next thousand years. Construction of the Via Appia began in 312 BC, and in 244 BC the road was extended to the eastern port of Brindisi.

Not everything, however, went the Romans' way. In 390 BC the Gauls who swept down from the north besieged Rome. The populace retreated to the Campidoglio, which was saved on one occasion when the geese sacred to Juno alerted the defenders to a nocturnal attack. The invaders were finally bought off with a massive bribe.

Hannibal

The other Mediterranean power during this period was Carthage, a kingdom of traders based in north Africa (modern Tunis). Since Rome was still an agricultural society, it was not inevitable that these states come into conflict.

The First Punic War (264-241 BC) was the result of the internal politics of Messina, a Greek colony in Sicily. One faction,

---

Republic		
264-241 BC	**216**	**146**
First Punic War.	Roman defeat at	Carthage completely
218-202	Cannae.	destroyed.
Second Punic War.	**214-205**	**144**
217	First Macedonian War.	Construction of the
Roman army defeated	**192-189**	Aqua Marcia.
and the consul killed at	Syria defeated.	**142**
Lake Trasimeme.	Roman client kingdoms	First stone bridge over
	established in the East.	the Tevere.

thrown out of the city, invited Carthaginian support. The besieged party appealed to Rome. During the resulting 23-year war the Romans learned the lesson of naval power. Eventually victorious, they forced the Carthaginians to abandon their colonies in western Sicilia and, for good measure, the Romans also seized Sardegna.

One of the defeated and aggrieved Punic generals was Hamilcar Barca, who turned to building a personal fiefdom in southern Spain, where he taught his sons, Hannibal and Hamilcar, to view Rome with a profound hatred. Hannibal inherited the command, and provoked war in 219 BC by attacking Saguntum. This city lay within the agreed Carthaginian area, but, like the Messina faction, it appealed to Rome for help. In 218 the Roman Senate declared war on Carthage again.

With the Romans controlling the seas, Hannibal daringly crossed into Italy by leading his army over the Alps. Despite losing up to half his troops and almost all of his war elephants in the crossing, the Punic general was able to inflict several crushing defeats on the Romans at Ticinus, Trebia and Lake Trasimeno in 217, and at Cannae in the following year. The Romans were also hampered by the system which had the command alternating daily between the two consuls; Hannibal waited until the less able consul was in command before he attacked. Had he attacked Rome in 216 BC, the city would have fallen. Instead, he chose to consolidate his position in southern Italy.

During this stalemate, the Romans discovered a military genius of their own to match Hannibal – Publius Cornelius Scipio. He was unprecedentedly granted military command before he had held any public office, the 23-year-old struck first at Hannibal's power base in Spain and then, in 204 BC, attacked Africa itself, forcing the Carthaginians to recall Hannibal to defend their own capital. Scipio won the battle of Zama in 202 BC; Hannibal committed suicide in exile some 20 years later.

Philip V of Macedon had been Hannibal's ally, and through the subsequent Macedonian Wars the Romans came into contact with the splendour (and wealth) of the Hellenistic empire left by Alexander the Great. Since a Roman politician alternated between military and civilian offices, the astute and the ambitious quickly made the connection between the prestige – and money – won in overseas conquest, and electoral success at home. Using the same system of alliance rather than direct conquest, Rome established a series of 'client kingdoms' ruled by local princes who understood that their bread was buttered on the Roman side.

From Republic to Empire

Gaius Marius' innovation of a standing army of volunteers which looked towards the individual generals rather than the Senate for their reward made civil wars inevitable. Roman politics was also increasingly polarised into two factions, linked as much by marriage as by policies: the Optimates, who upheld the primacy of the Senate; and the Populares, who preferred to take their bills before the people's assemblies. This split in political methods was the

---

Late Republic

107 BC
  Gaius Marius consul.

82
  Sulla marches on Rome; judicial murders follow

81
  Sulla becomes Dictator.

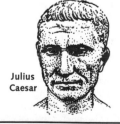
Julius Caesar

73-71
  Revolt of Spartacus.

70
  Marcus Crassus and Pompey the Great consuls.

60-54
  First Triumvirate.

cause of civil conflict between the supporters of Marius, a Popularis, and his erstwhile lieutenant Cornelius Sulla, an Optimate.

Sulla twice threatened Rome with his troops, and in 82 BC, after he committed a string of political murders, the Senate gave in to his demands, voting him Dictator for the extraordinary period of 10 years.

One of Sulla's protégés was Gnaeus Pompeius Magnus, Pompey the Great. Against his own legislation, Sulla allowed Pompey to leapfrog his way up the political ladder. In 71 BC the fabulously wealthy Marcus Licinius Crassus was finally mopping up the dramatic slave rebellion led by the gladiator Spartacus, which had been running amok through Italy the last eight years; 6000 slaves who did not die in battle were crucified along the Via Appia. Crassus and Pompey together campaigned (and bribed) their way to the consulships of 70 BC. Pompey then took an army as far east as Syria. Meanwhile, Crassus was cementing his alliance with a young aristocrat who had already bribed his way to the post of Pontifex Maximus, Chief Priest.

Gaius Julius Caesar was running for the consulship of 59 BC, and made a deal with Crassus and the newly returned Pompey. In return for their electoral and financial support, Caesar as consul would ensure that his allies' interests would be looked after despite Optimate opposition. This was reinforced by Pompey's marriage to Caesar's daughter, Julia. After his consulship, Caesar left to win military glory in Gaul. The so-called First Triumvirate was renewed in 56

BC, and with Caesar's electoral support, Crassus and Pompey shared another consulship in 55 BC. Things soured when Julia died in 54 BC, and Crassus was monumentally defeated and killed in Parthia the following year.

With Pompey increasingly under the influence of Optimates who wanted to impeach Caesar for irregularities in Gaul, civil war began when Caesar crossed into Italy with his army of devoted veterans in 49 BC. Pompey and his supporters evacuated Italy for Spain, Africa and Greece, where their main force was defeated by Caesar at Pharsalus a year later. Pompey fled to Egypt, where he was assassinated.

In 47 BC Caesar returned to Rome, where he began to institute a series of reforms, including the overhaul of the calendar and the Senate. Of his extensive building program, the Curia (Senate House) and the Forum Giulia remain. Initially declared Dictator for one year, Caesar had this extended to 10 years and then, in 44 BC, was proclaimed Dictator for life. This accumulation of power fatally alienated even those who had initially supported him, and Caesar was famously assassinated in the portico of the Teatro di Pompeo (Theatre of Pompey) on the Ides of March, 44 BC.

The Liberators, as Caesar's assassins called themselves, found that they had severely underestimated Caesar's popularity with the soldiers and the general populace; the people regarded the dead Dictator as a new god. Caesar's lieutenant, Marcus Antonius – Mark Antony – took command of the city, aided by the troops under the command of Lepidus.

Transition to Empire
40-45 BC
 Civil war between
 Caesar and Pompey.
44
 Caesar assassinated.
42
 'Liberators' defeated at
 Philippi.

Augustus

40-31
 Second Triumvirate.
27
 Pantheon built.
23
 Augustus' constitutional
 position regularised.
19
 Death of Vergil.

Caesar's will had declared the adoption of his great-nephew as his son and heir; the 18-year-old Octavianus, then studying in Greece, returned to Rome to claim his inheritance.

Now calling himself Gaius Julius Caesar Octavianus, the young man first sided with the Liberators against Antony, then promptly switched sides and fought with Antony when Brutus and Cassius were defeated at Philippi. The orator Cicero, who had attacked Antony in a series of speeches and then underestimated Octavian, became a victim of the political murders which followed.

Lepidus was quickly frozen out of the Second Triumvirate, and the Roman world was divided in two, with the new Caesar raising troops in the western half while Antony administered the wealthy provinces and client kingdoms of the east. Although Antony married Octavian's sister, the situation inevitably deteriorated again into civil war, with Octavian making brilliant propagandistic use of Antony's affair with Cleopatra VII, the queen of Egypt. The enormous Mausoleum of Augustus near the Tevere was part of this struggle; it was constructed precisely when the rumour went round that Antony had renounced Rome by officially marrying Cleopatra and wanted to be buried in Egypt, where his heart was.

Octavian's general Marcus Agrippa defeated Antony and Cleopatra in a naval battle off the coast of Actium in 31 BC, and the famous couple committed suicide in Alexandria the following year when they were beseiged by Octavian's army.

The Empire

Octavian was left the sole ruler of the Roman world, but, remembering Caesar's fate trod very carefully. In 27 BC he officially surrendered his extraordinary powers to the Senate, which promptly gave most of them back. Four years later his position was regularised again, with the Senate voting him the unique title 'Augustus' – Your Eminence.

The new era of political stability allowed the arts to flourish. Augustus was exceptionally fortunate in having as his contemporaries the poets Vergil, Horace and Ovid, as well as the historian Livy. He also encouraged the visual arts, restoring existing buildings and constructing many new ones. Agrippa built the original Pantheon; Augustus himself dedicated the Teatro di Marcello in honour of his nephew, Marcellus, and commissioned the Ara Pacis, the Altar of Peace, explicitly to commemorate his achievement. He boasted in his memoirs that 'he found Rome in brick, and left it in marble'.

Augustus succeeded because instead of trying to re-invent the political system, he simply made room for himself at the top. He never called himself a king or an emperor, but only 'princeps' – the leading man. The 'Republic', from the consuls down, continued as usual. He died aged 76 after a 40-year reign.

Tiberius' reign (14-37 AD) was stable but dour, and he ruled from his villa in Capri for the last decade. Gaius Caligula (37-45 AD) had little time for the political niceties which the Senate expected; his increasingly extravagant and bizarre behaviour led to his assassination by an officer of the Praetorian Guard, the imperial bodyguard.

A return to Republican government was contemplated, but the Praetorians, with an eye on job security, declared Claudius, Gaius' uncle, emperor. In one version, he was discovered hiding behind a curtain in the imperial residence on the Palatino. Despite his unexpected elevation, Claudius proved to be a conscientious ruler. He extended the port facilities at Ostia and constructed a new aqueduct, the Aqua Claudia, to service the growing population of Rome. He also strengthened Rome's hold on Britain, first invaded by Caesar.

Probably poisoned in 58 AD by his wife, Agrippina, Claudius was succeeded by Nero, her 17-year-old son by a previous marriage. Nero gradually showed his preference for Gaius Caligula's style of government. In the ultimate act of youthful rebellion, he had his mother assassinated, then began to impose his passion for all things Greek on an increasingly resentful Roman aristocracy. With revolt spreading amongst the provincial governors – who commanded armies – in 68 AD, the Senate declared Nero a public enemy, and he committed suicide while on the run. In the 'Year of the Four Emperors' which followed, Galba, Otho and Vitellius came and went in quick succession.

Stability was restored when Vespasian, sent to Judaea to crush the Great Rebellion of 66 AD, was proclaimed emperor by his troops, and the exhausted Senate agreed. A practical man, Vespasian (69-79 AD) made a point of rebuilding the temple on the Campidoglio, which had been burned down during the civil wars, and constructing a huge amphitheatre in the grounds of Nero's Domus Aurea. The Colosseo takes its popular name from the colossal statue erected in front of it; originally of Nero and destined for his entrance hall, Vespasian had it re-dedicated to Apollo, the sun god.

Rather like Augustus, he celebrated the return of normality by building the Forum di Pace (Forum of Peace). Titus' brief reign (79-81 AD) is chiefly remembered for the catastrophic eruption of Vesuvio, which buried Pompeii and Herculaneum. He did find time to construct public baths, as well as the Arco di Tito, which commemorates him as the captor of Jerusalem.

Domitian, his younger brother, built the Forum Transitorio (for which his successor took the credit and the name, calling it the Forum di Nerva) and greatly extended the palace complex on the Palatino; he had the corridors lined with highly polished stone to allow him to detect lurking assassins. This paranoia was justified in 96 AD when he was murdered in a palace plot.

After the brief reign of Nerva (96-98 AD), the elderly stop-gap emperor, came Trajan, an experienced general of Spanish birth. His victories over the Dacian tribes are depicted on the column erected in the forecourt of his forum, which also contained separate Greek and Latin libraries. Other public works included his market, and the Via Traiana linking Benvenuto with Brindisi. Trajan was the first Roman general to conquer Parthia, the traditional eastern enemy. He died while on campaign

Zenith
79 AD
  Eruption of Vesuvio.
80
  Dedication of the
  Colosseo.
92
  Palatino palace complex
  completed.

Trajan

116
  Parthia conquered.
118-25
  Pantheon rebuilt.
174
  Meditations of Marcus
  Aurelius.
193
  Civil war.

in 117, and his ashes were buried in the base of his column.

Hadrian (117-138) is known as a prodigious traveller, but, also a keen architect, he remodelled the Pantheon in its current form, generously retaining the original inscription which gives the credit to Agrippa. The Castel Sant'Angelo was originally his mausoleum, and his holiday villa at Tivoli is very well preserved.

This era was the peak of the Roman empire, when stability on the borders was matched in internal politics. By 100 AD, the city of Rome had more than 1.5 million inhabitants, and was the true capital of an empire, its wealth and prosperity obvious in the rich mosaics, the marble temples, public baths, theatres, circuses, and libraries. The extensive network of aqueducts fed not only the baths, but also provided private houses with running water and flushing toilets.

The reigns of Antonius Pius (138-161) and the philosopher-emperor Marcus Aurelius (161-180) were stable, but the latter ominously spent 14 years fighting northern invaders, with his victories commemorated on his column.

A slow decline began with the disturbed Commodus (180-192), and with his assassination, the events of 68-69 repeated themselves. Pertinax, Didius Julianus, and Pescennius Niger came and went before Septimius Severus (193-211), born in north Africa, defeated the other challengers. Serious cracks were beginning to appear in the empire.

Severus was jointly succeeded by the brothers Caracalla and Geta, with Caracalla predicably having his sibling assassinated. Despite financial problems, his building programme included refurbishing the roads as well as his monumental public baths.

When Caracalla was throttled in 213, chaos gradually took over. Some 24 assorted emperors and pretenders violently rose and fell until Diocletian (284-305) realised that increasing instability on the borders made central government impossible, and so he divided the empire in half. Diocletian looked after the east, and allocated the west to Maximian, who based himself no longer in Rome, but in Milano.

In 305 Maximian and Diocletian abdicated simultaneously. A four-way tug of war continued, until, in 312, Constantine faced Maxentius, his last rival, just outside Rome at Saxa Rubra. Constantine claims ot have seen a vision of the Christian monogram superimposed over the sun, and heard the command 'with this sign you will conquer'. He placed the symbol on his banners, and, sure enough, won. More prosaically, Christianity was by now the religion of many army officers and aristocrats, men whose support Constantine needed.

Whether his inspiration was divine or political, Constantine kept his side of the bargain. In 313 the Edict of Milan enshrined religious freedom in law, and Constantine founded San Pietro, San Lorenzo Fuori le Mura, gave to the pope the place which became San Giovanni in Laterano, and built Santa Croce di Gerusalemme to house the great relic recovered in Jerusalem by his deeply religious mother, Helena. Although he determined to move the capital of empire to Byzantium, he kept with tradition and erected the Arco di Constantino.

Decline and Fall

211-16
    Construction of the Baths of Caracalla.

271
    Aurelian Wall begun.

285
    Division of the Empire between East and West.

Christian monogram

313
    Christianity legalised.

330
    Constantinople founded as the new capital.

382-420
    Vulgate Bible produced.

455
    Vandal sack of Rome.

Dark Ages

Pope Damasus (333-384) made the first concerted effort to Christianise Roman culture. As part of his programme, he commissioned his secretary, Eusebius Hieronymous (St Jerome), to render the Bible in elegant, but accessible Latin; the Vulgate Bible has remained in use ever since.

Rome became increasingly insignificant to the Byzantine empire. In 408 a Gothic army commanded by Alaric surrounded Rome, and was let into the city in 410. Some districts were sacked and many temples destroyed, but the intercession of Pope Innocent I averted a massacre. This act of papal heroism was repeated even more dramatically in 440 when Leo I persuaded Atilla the Hun not to attack Rome. Less fortunately, the city was thoroughly plundered 15 years later by the Vandals, whose name became a byword for wanton destruction. Normality returned quickly, however, and church construction flourished, including Santa Sabina, Santa Maria Maggiore, and San Stefano Rotundo.

The last 'emperor', Romulus Augustulus, was deposed in 476. The Ostrogoth ruler Theodoric, though, was no barbarian, and repaired both the Colosseo and the imperial palaces. By 500, however, the aqueducts feeding into Rome had been deliberately cut by invaders, or had been looted for the lead piping; the swamps created by the leaking water were to last until the 20th century.

In 536 Justinian sent Belisarius to recapture Rome for the Byzantine empire, which he did – briefly. During the plague which swept through the city in 590, Pope Gregory I saw a vision of the Archangel Michael hovering above the mausoleum of Hadrian, sheathing his sword. This was interpreted as a sign that the plague was over, and a chapel was built on the mausoleum, which came to be known as the Castel Sant' Angelo.

Gregory I (the Great) had converted his family palace on the Celio into the Benedictine monastery of St Andrew and, as pope, founded San Giorgio in Velabro and Santa Maria in Via Lata. A true Roman, he could not understand the attractions of Constantinople over Rome, and had no qualms about defending the Church from the emperor himself. He set the pattern of Church administration which was to guide Catholic services and rituals throughout history, and made a concerted effort to convert the English tribes to Christianity.

After Gregory's death Rome was threatened first by waves of barbarians, then, from the mid 7th century, by the Islamic armies which swept through the Mediterranean world. To make matters worse, relations between Rome and Constantinople deteriorated to the extent that Martin I was held under house arrest in San Giovanni in Laterano for over a month before being taken to Constantinople to be humiliated and flogged.

It seems that Pepin, the Merovingian king, offered to conquer Lombard territory for Pope Stephen II in return for papal recognition of the legitimacy of his line of succession. The relationship between the

Church and the Frankish kings was further cemented in 774 when Leo III, continuing in the footsteps of Hadrian I, crowned Charlemagne as Holy Roman Emperor during Christmas Mass in San Pietro.

In 846 a Saracen fleet sailed up the Tevere and attacked Rome, sacking the graves of Sts Peter and Paul. In response, Leo IV had the Leonine Wall built to protect il Vaticano.

Medieval Rome

In 1300 Boniface VIII proclaimed the first Holy (Jubilee) Year, with the promise of a full pardon for those who made the pilgrimage to San Pietro and San Giovanni in Laterano. It is said that there were 200,000 pilgrims in Rome at any one time during that year. Dante was among them, and made Holy Week 1300 the central point in his *Divina Commedia*.

Boniface also used his power to continue his family feud with the Colonna clan. When he was preparing the excommunicate King Philip of France, the Colonna family helped French forces to break into the papal palace at Anagni and threatened the life of the pope. Boniface died a month later, and the next eight popes based themselves in Avignon.

During this period goats and cows grazed on the Campidoglio and in the Foro Romano, and residential support for the city's many churches and cathedrals disappeared. Ancient marble was burned to make lime for cement. The city became a battleground for the struggles between the powerful Orsini and Colonna families. The ruling families challenged the papacy's ongoing claim to be temporal rulers of Rome and the Papal State began to fall apart.

After the failed attempt of Cola di Rienzo, a popular leader, to wrest the control of Rome from the nobility in 1347, Cardinal Egidio d'Albornoz managed to restore the Papal State with his Egidian Constitutions, thereby enabling Pope Gregory XI to return to Rome in 1379. When he found a ruined and almost deserted city, Gregory transferred the papal residence from the Lateran Palace to il Vaticano because it was fortified close to the formidable Castel Sant'Angelo. When Gregory died a year after returning to Rome, Roman cardinals tried to ensure their continuing power by electing as pope the unpopular Urban VI, sparking off a renegade movement of cardinals, mainly French, who, a few months later, elected a second pope, Clement VII, who set up his claim in Avignon. So began the Great Schism which continued until 1417.

The election of Nicholas V as pope in 1447 marked the beginning of a new era for Rome, at the time when the Renaissance was flowering in Firenze. The prestige of the papacy was restored under such popes as Sixtus IV, who built the Capella Sistina (Sistine Chapel) and initiated an urban plan which was to link the areas that had been cut off from one another during the Middle Ages. The artists Donatello, Sandro Botticelli and Fra Angelico lived and worked in Rome at this time.

In 1471, Sixtus IV effectively created one of the oldest museums in the world, the

---

Renaissance

1309-1379
  Papacy based in Avignon.
1425
  San Giovanni in Laterano rebuilt by Martin V
1471
  Museo Capitolino and Capella Sistina founded.

Il Vaticano

1500
  Pietà sculpted by Michelangelo.
1505
  Julius II hires 200 Swiss mercenaries.
1506
  Rebuilding of San Pietro begun.

Museo Capitolino, when he handed over to the people of Rome a selection of bronzes. At the beginning of the 16th century Pope Julius II opened Via del Corso and Via Giulia and ordered in 1506 that the old Basilica di San Pietro be demolished, commissioning Bramante to build a new church. In 1508, Raphael started painting the rooms in il Vaticano which are now known as Le Stanze di Raffaello, while in 1508 Michelangelo began work on the vaults of the Cappella Sistina (Sistine Chapel).

All the great artists of the epoch were influenced by the ever more frequent discoveries of marvellous pieces of classical art, such as the Laocoön (now in the Musei Vaticani), found in 1506 in the area of Nero's Domus Aurea. Rome had 100,000 inhabitants at the height of the Renaissance and had become the major centre for Italian political and cultural life. Pope Julius II was succeeded by Pope Leo X, a Medici, and the Roman Curia (or Papal Court) became the meeting place for learned men such as Baldassar Castiglione and Ludovico Ariosto.

But the papacy was also deeply involved in the power struggles that kept Europe in turmoil. In 1527 Pope Clement VII was forced to take refuge in Castel Sant'Angelo when the troops of Charles V sacked Rome, an event that is said to have deeply influenced Michelangelo's vision of the Last Judgment, which he began for Clement VII only two years later.

Rome owes much of its present splendour to 16th century popes Paul III and Sixtus V, who altered the urban plan, opening up straight avenues, raising obelisks and laying out grand piazzas. In 1538 Paul III asked Michelangelo to lay out the Piazza del Campidoglio, which included the placement of the bronze statue of the emperor Marcus Aurelius in its centre. Under Sixtus V, the dome of San Pietro was completed.

The Counter-Reformation

By the third decade of the 16th century, the broad-minded curiosity of the Renaissance had begun to give way to the intolerance of the Counter-Reformation. This was the response of the Catholic Church to the Reformation, a collective term for the movement led by Martin Luther that aimed to reform the Church and led to the rise of Protestantism in its many forms.

The transition was epitomised by the reign of Pope Paul III (1534-49) who promoted the building of the classically elegant Palazzo Farnese in Roma but who also, in 1540, allowed the establishment of Ignatius Loyola's order of the Jesuits and the organisation in 1542 of the Holy Office. This was the final (and ruthless) court of appeal in the trials which began to gather momentum with the increased activities of the Inquisition (1232-1820), the judicial arm of the Church whose aim was to discover and suppress heresy.

Pope Paul III's opposition to Protestantism and his purging of clerical abuse, as he saw it, resulted in a widespread campaign of torture and fear. In 1559, the Church published the Index Librorum Prohibitorum, the Index of Prohibited Books, and the Roman Church's determination to

1508	1532	1555
Cappella Sistina frescoes begun.	Henry VIII repudiates papal authority.	Paul IV establishes the Ghetto in Rome.
1517	**1540**	**1585**
Martin Luther begins the Reformation.	Foundation of the Society of Jesus (Jesuits).	Accademica di Santa Cecilia established.
1527	**1547**	**1600**
Sack of Rome by Charles V of Spain.	Michelangelo appointed architect of San Pietro.	Giordano Bruno burned for heresy.

regain papal supremacy over the Protestant churches set the stage for the persecution of intellectuals and free thinkers.

Two great Italian intellectuals who felt the force of the Counter-Reformation were Giordano Bruno (1548-1600) and Galileo Galilei (1564-1642). Bruno, a Dominican monk, was forced to flee Italy for Calvinist Geneva, from where he travelled extensively throughout Europe before being arrested by the Inquisition in Venezia in 1592. A statue of Bruno now stands on the site in the Campo de' Fiori where he was burned at the stake in 1600.

An advocate of Aristotelian science, Galileo was forced by the Church to renounce his approval of the Copernican astronomical system, which held that the earth moved round the sun rather than the reverse. But where Bruno had rejected the Catholic Church, Galileo never deviated from the faith which rejected him.

However, the latter years of the 16th century were not all counterproductive. Pope Gregory XIII (1572-85) replaced the Julian calendar with the Gregorian one in 1582, fixing the start of the year on 1 January and adjusting the system of leap years to align the 365-day year with the seasons.

The Chiesa del Gesù was the prototype of Rome's great churches of the Counter-Reformation, built to accommodate huge congregations. In the 17th century, under the popes and grand families of Rome, the theatrical exuberance of the Baroque found masterful interpreters in Bernini and Borromini. The designs of Piazza Navona and Piazza San Pietro, and the sculptures in Rome's churches and museums confirm Bernini's genius as architect and artist.

Over the centuries the popes had acquired a group of provinces in central Italy that was known as the Papal States, with Rome as their capital. They constituted a strategic prize that Napoleon set out to win as he made his bid for power in Europe. In 1796 he forced a humiliating armistace on the Pius VI, including the choice of any 100 works of art and 500 manuscripts to be taken to France. In 1805 Napoleon crowned himself king of Italy and later named his infant son king of Rome, and three years later demanded the abdication of the pope, and annexed Rome.

Goethe's 1816 account of his travels in Italy, Italian Journey, opened the way for a flow of literary and artistic visitors to Rome, which became the principal destination for cultivated travellers on the Grand Tour.

Risorgimento

After Napoleon's defeat, action to unify Italy under a modern Roman Republic took the form of revolt in 1849. Patriot Giuseppe Mazzini and soldier Giuseppe Garibaldi led an assault on Rome that failed miserably after a few initial successes. But the Risorgimento (Resurgence) movement proved irresistible. At the head of a band of militia, Garibaldi took Sicily and Naples. In 1861 the Kingdom of Italy was declared and Victor Emmanuel II was proclaimed king. But the pope, supported by the French, was still sovereign of Rome.

In 1870, the French were busy defending themselves from the Prussians, and Italian

1610 Death of Caravaggio. **1624** Bernini commissioned to create the baldacchino in San Pietro. **1680** Death of Gian Lorenzo Bernini.	**1723** Construction of the Scalinata di Spagna. **1763** Creation of the Fontana Trevi. **1796** Napoleon annexes papal lands, forces armistice.	**1848** Garibaldi and Mazzini begin the Risorgimento. **1870** Victor Emmanual enters Rome. **1922** Mussolini marches on Rome.

troops breached Rome's city walls at Porta Pia. King Victor Emmanuel entered the city and Pope Pius IX, who had rejected war with Austria, an Catholic country, retired behind the walls of il Vaticano, refusing to recognise Italy.

At last Rome was capital of the newly united kingdom of Italy. The city was transformed by a scandal-ridden building boom, land speculation and an influx of bureaucrats, politicians and labourers.

Fascism & WWII

Discontent and social unrest after World War I favoured the rise of Benito Mussolini, who founded the Fascist Party in 1919 with its hallmarks of the black shirt and Roman salute. These were to become the symbols of violent oppression and aggressive nationalism for the next 23 years. In 1921 the party won 35 of the 135 seats in parliament. In October 1922, Mussolini staged the March on Rome by 40,000 members of his Fascist militia. King Victor Emmanuel III invited him to form a government. In April 1924, following a campaign marked by violence and intimidation, the Fascist Party won the national elections and Mussolini created the world's first Fascist regime. By 1925 the term 'totalitarianism' had entered the language. By the end of 1925 Mussolini had expelled opposition parties from parliament, gained control of the press and trade unions and had reduced the voting public by two-thirds.

In 1929, Mussolini and Pope Pius XI signed the Lateran Pact, whereby Catholicism was declared the sole religion of Italy and the Città del Vaticano was recognised as an independent state with extra-territorial rights to the patriarchal basilicas of Santa Maria Maggiore, San Giovanni in Laterano and San Paolo Fuori le Mura, among other sites.

With the intent of glorifying Rome's imperial past, Mussolini's regime initiated radical, often destructive, public works. Via dei Fori Imperiali and Via della Conciliazione were laid out, parks were opened at the Colle Oppio and Villa Celimontana, the Imperial Fora and the temples at Largo Argentina were excavated, and the monumental Foro Italico sports complex and the EUR district were built.

Dreams of imperial glory also led Mussolini to invade Abyssinia (present-day Ethiopia) in 1935, and to form the Rome-Berlin Axis with Hitler in 1936. In 1940, from the balcony of Palazzo Venezia, Mussolini announced Italy's entry into W WII to a vast, cheering crowd. Declared an open city, Rome was largely spared from destruction during the war, although many members of the city's Jewish community were deported and killed in the Nazi death camps. Although there were many acts of individual heroism, the official silence from il Vaticano during the Holocaust continues to be controversial, especially with the rumoured plans to canonise Pius XII.

One of the worst atrocities of WWII in Italy occurred in Rome. In March 1944, urban partisans blew up 32 German military police in Via Rasella. In reprisal, the Germans rounded up 335 people who had

20th Century
1929
  Mussolini and Pius XI
  sign the Lateran Treaty.
1936
  Rome-Berlin Axis.
1944
  Fosse Ardeatine
  massacre.

Mussolini

1946
  Italian monarchy
  abolished.
1960
  Olympic Games in Rome
  Fellini makes *La Dolce Vita*.
1962-65
  Second Vatican Council.

no connection with the incident, and shot them at the Fosse Ardeatine, just outside the city. A monument was constructed at the site.

In a 1946 referendum the Italian people voted to abolish the monarchy and adopt a republican form of government. The first president of Italy was installed in Palazzo del Quirinale, former residence of popes and kings. Rome was the scene in 1953 of the signing of the Treaty of Rome, which established the European Economic Community and laid the groundwork for the present European Union.

Rome's population continued to grow, and the city expanded. Rome was the centre of Italy's film industry from 1948 to the early 1960s, centred on Rome's version of Hollywood, the Cinecittà studios. Federico Fellini's film La Dolce Vita made a modern legend of the lifestyle of the rich and famous in Rome during that period. In 1960, the city was host to the Olympic Games.

Protest & Terrorism

The late 1960s were marked by student revolt in 1967-68. Influenced by similar events in France, university students in Rome and throughout the country rose up in protest, ostensibly against poor conditions in the universities, but in reality in broader protest against authority and what they saw as the impotence of the left. The movement resulted in the formation of many small revolutionary groups which attempted to fill what the students saw as an ideological gap in Italy's political left wing.

But as the new decade began, a new phenomenon – terrorism – began to overshadow this turbulent era of protest and change. By 1970, a group of young left-wing militants had formed the Brigate Rosse (Le BR). While the Brigate Rosse were the most prominent of Italy's terrorist groups, they were by no means the only terrorists operating in the country during the Anni di Piombo (Years of the Bullet) from 1973-80.

The most notorious of a chain of political inspired killings in those years was the 1978 kidnap-murder of former prime minister Aldo Moro. During the 54 days that Moro was held captive by the BR, his colleagues laboured over whether to bargain with the terrorists to save his life, or to adopt a position of no compromise. In the end, they took the latter path and the BR killed Moro on 9 May 1978, leaving his body in the boot of a car parked in Via Caetani in the centre of Rome, precisely half-way between the headquarters of the Communist Party and that of the Christian Democrats.

In 1981, a Turkish assassin severely wounded Pope John Paul II, in front of a crowd in Piazza San Pietro.

GEOGRAPHY

The Comune di Roma covers an expanse of roughly 150,000 hectares, of which 37% is built-up urban area, 15% is parkland and 48% is under agricultural use.

Rome's best known geographical features are its seven hills: the Palatino (Palatine), Campidoglio (Capitoline), Aventino (Aventine), Celio (Caelian), Esquilino (Esquiline),

---

1975
Death of Pasolini.
1978
Murder of Aldo Moro.
1981
Attempted assassination of John Paul II.
1990
World Cup held in Rome.

Pope John
Paul II

1994
Restoration of the Cappella Sistina frescoes completed.
1998
John Paul II celebrates 20 years as Pope.
2000
Jubilee Year.

Viminale (Viminal) and Quirinale (Quirinal). Two other hills, the Gianicolo (Janiculum), which rises above Trastevere, and the Pincio, above Piazza del Popolo, were never actually part of the ancient city.

The Gianicolo is, in fact, a good vantage point from which to survey Rome's geography. From there it is possible to identify each of the seven hills, although two of them – the Viminale and Quirinale – are swallowed up by the city sprawl and seem not much more than gentle slopes. From here you can see how the Tevere (Tiber River) winds through town, a handy thing to understand since the river is a good point of reference for navigating your way around the city centre.

The Tevere, which has its source in the Apennines north of Arezzo (in Tuscany) and runs into the sea at Ostia, is subject to sudden flooding. Until the late 19th century this caused significant problems for the areas bordering the river, including Trastevere. There were 46 devastating floods on record up to 1870. The problem was solved in 1900 by raising the level of the river's embankments. It is still possible to see markers around Trastevere denoting the water level reached by various floods. The ancient Romans built a major sea port, Ostia Antica, at the mouth of the Tevere, but the harbour silted up long ago. Today the area is Rome's closest beach resort, known as Lido di Ostia.

In ancient times, the city covered roughly what is now called the *centro storico* (historical centre) and was enclosed by defensive walls. The earliest wall was, according to tradition, built by Romulus around the first settlement on the Palatino. As the city grew during the Republican era, it was divided into four *regiones* (regions, or city wards) known as the Palatino, the Suburra, the Esquilino and the Collina, which were surrounded by the Mura Serviane (Servian Wall) started in 378 BC following a surprise attack by the Gauls. Today only traces of the wall and its 12 entrances, known as *porte*, remain.

The emperor Aurelian started to build a second wall in 271 AD to defend the growing city, which by then had about one million inhabitants, from barbarian attack. The huge wall, which was 19km long, had not been completed in 275 AD when Aurelian died, and was finished by his successor, Probus. Much of the Aurelian Wall is still standing, as well as many of its entrances, including the Porta Maggiore, Porta San Giovanni, Porta Latina, Porta San Sebastiano, Porta San Paolo, Porta San Pancrazio, Porta del Popolo and Porta Pia. Many of these entrances are still in use.

Over the centuries the wall was frequently consolidated and adapted for military use In 536 the Byzantine emperor Justinian sent his general Belisarius, who arrived in Rome from Constantinople to snatch Italy from the reign of the Goths. His officials counted 383 towers, 7020 battlements, 14 main entrances, 116 latrines and 2066 external windows in the Mura Aureliane. In 1870, the Savoyards breached the wall near the Porta Pia entrance and took Rome from Pope Pius IX to the capital of Italy.

Also enclosed by defensive walls is the Città del Vaticano (Vatican City), actually an independent state with its own legal and postal systems, and even currency. This enclave was established in 1929 with signing of the Lateran Treaty between Mussolini and Pius XI, giving the pope full sovereignty over this small territory within the city of Rome.

Modern Rome is divided into 22 *rioni*, 35 *quartieri* and six *suburbi*. The rioni, which are all in or near the city centre, trace their origins back to the regiones of the city of theRoman Republic. The regiones evolved into rioni during the Middle Ages and by the late 16th century there were 14 of them. Another eight rioni were declared in 1921. Based on what might be called neighbourhoods, some of the rioni still retain a strong sense of history and tradition, notably Monti, the area incorporating the Esquilino, Viminale and Celio; Borgo, next to San Pietro and il Vaticano; and Trastevere, bordered by the Gianicolo hill and the Tevere.

CLIMATE

Spring and autumn are the best times to visit Rome, when the weather is warm and generally sunny. In September it is often still warm enough to head for the beach and well into October you'll be able to sit comfortably at an outside table while drinking your cappuccino. In a good year, mild weather can continue right up to December, punctuated by occasional days of icy winds which blow in from northern Europe. However, in a bad year, you might strike heavy rain in October. July and August are generally extremely hot, with temperatures hovering around the high 30°s for days on end. This is a very unpleasant time for sightseeing, particularly if you are travelling with children. Romans desert their city in droves, heading for the beaches or the mountains, which means that tourists (and the few remaining residents) can enjoy the light traffic and semi-deserted footpaths.

From November through to February the weather can be unpredictable, with heavy rain, particularly in November, and icy winds a hindrance to enjoyable sightseeing. However, if you rug up with a good, heavy coat, a hat and scarf, you can take advantage of being among the few tourists in the city.

Rome's sunniest months are May, June and July; its hottest months are June, July and August; its coldest are December, January and February; and its wettest are October, November and December.

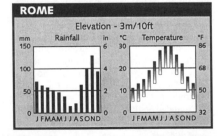

ECOLOGY & ENVIRONMENT
Cleaning Up

Any large city can seem chaotic and claustrophobic and Rome is certainly no exception. Its traffic problems are appalling and the air pollution caused by all of those vehicles idling in traffic jams can be choking at times, just ask anyone riding around on a motorino! Efforts have increased in recent years to steer the traffic away from the city's historic centre and its main monuments, and only holders of special permits are allowed to drive in certain restricted areas of the centre. However, many of the city's most important monuments, the Colosseo included, remain at risk from pollution.

At the same time, there has been a massive clean-up and restoration effort, partly in preparation for the Jubilee Year (celebrated in Rome as a combination of the new millennium and as a Holy Year by papal declaration), but also as part of a major effort by the Comune di Roma to modernise the city for the new millennium. The effort has seen many of Rome's historic churches and palaces emerging from behind scaffolding with their façades finally cleaned of the dirt and grime built up over centuries.

Much as when Michelangelo's ceiling in the Cappella Sistina was revealed in all its glorious colour, many Romans have expressed some shock at seeing so many dazzling white marble buildings, after becoming so accustomed to their former dirty grey colour. Among the highlights of these restorations has been the opening of the restored Museo e Galleria Borghese in the Villa Borghese, and the opening of the Palazzo Altemps and Palazzo Massimo as two new seats of the Museo Nazionale Romano.

Preparations for the Jubilee Year and the new millennium have included a huge public works programme, mainly concentrated on improving roads, public transport and other infrastructure. Works are underway to create an integrated railway network, to further develop the subway and tram lines and to create a new plan for traffic and pedestrian areas.

Oh Poo!

Just a short note on another 'pollution' problem which tourists will doubtless encounter in Rome: dog poo! Literally, no footpath is without it, so watch your step.

A brief effort by the Comune at public awareness raising on this issue came and went with little effect and while the law provides for L200,000 fines of the owners of offending pooches, no-one seems to worry much, not least the *vigili urbani* (urban police) who do little to enforce the law.

In this important process, the challenge is to modernise the city while preserving its extraordinary historical, architectural and artistic heritage. In Rome, where there is such an incredible concentration of monuments – many yet to be excavated – the Comune has regularly fallen foul of the Sovrintendenza dei Beni Culturali (the body responsible for protecting and maintaining the city's art and architectural patrimony). Several public works projects were halted by the Sovrintendenza when it was discovered that they could have interfered with monuments, including a proposed underpass next to the Castel Sant'Angelo and a rail link to Ciampino airport. The Sovrintendenza said the former would have caused the Castel Sant'Angelo to slide into the Tevere and that the latter would have cut right through a Roman villa.

The Sovrintendenza also vetoed plans by Rome's mayor to hang a gigantic clock on the Colosseo showing the countdown to the millennium. while Romans have appreciated the mayor's energetic dedication to dragging the city into the 21st century, this incident demonstrated that there is fortunately a limit!

Parks

Rome has an extensive network of parks, many of which were the former private gardens and parklands of the city's nobility. According to figures provided by the Comune di Roma, 64% of the territory of the comune is 'green', although this includes agricultural land, as well as parkland. The Villa Borghese, just north of the city centre, was once the estate of Cardinal Scipione Borghese, whose villa now houses the Museo e Galleria Borghese. The Villa Doria Pamphili in Trastevere is Rome's largest park. It was the private estate of Prince Camillo Pamphili, whose uncle was Innocent X, and it features a number of different environments, including a small forest of *pini domesticii* and a large lake. Other large parks include the Villa Ada and Villa Glori, north of the city, and the Villa Celimontana, on the Celio.

FLORA & FAUNA
Flora

Most of Rome's parks were formerly the private gardens of the city's aristocrats and they were designed and planted according to the fashion of the relevant periods. Accordingly, they generally contain a wide variety of exotic species – plants indigenous to the city were rarely considered fashionable.

But long before the nobles started to plant their spectacular gardens, the Etruscans and ancient Romans had been chopping down trees, trampling the native vegetation and importing exotic species. The stone pine (*pino domestico*), considered a symbol of the city, was in fact imported, probably by the Etruscans, from the Middle East and botanists debate whether or not it should be considered indigenous to Rome.

Despite thousands of years of interference, Rome still manages to host almost 1300 native plants. Typical trees include about 10 species of oak (*quercia*), including the holm oak (*leccio*) and the cork oak (*sughera*), both of which grow spontaneously in small forests in the Roman countryside.

Rome's archaeological sites provide an ideal environment for the caper (*cappero*). This plant, which usually grows only in the hot, dry climate of the country's south, has found ideal conditions in the rocks of

Fellini's Felines

While animal rights is not a major consideration for the average Roman, the welfare of the city's huge stray cat population is a fascinating exception. Most of the city's feline residents are semi-wild, although it can be hard to pick the strays from the pets just out for a stroll.

The strays are often just as well-fed and contented, thanks to the army of women who feed them with leftover pasta. There are an estimated 10,000 cat colonies in Rome, many located in archaeological areas, such as the Colosseo, Foro di Traiano and in Largo Argentina. Some 500 of these colonies are under veterinary supervision, either by private animal welfare groups or by the city's own services.

Since the introduction of an extraordinarily humane law in 1988, Rome's stray cats are guaranteed the right to live where they're born – which means that locals can't chase them away, whatever problems they cause. This right is also included in the model for national legislation.

Rome's ruined monuments. In spring the caper forms cascading, puffy bushes which in June become masses of pink flowers. You will see them growing in areas including the Palatino, the Terme di Caracalla, the Mura Aureliane and on the Ponte Rotto near the Isola Tiberina.

Rome's native plants also find an ideal environment along the banks of the Tevere. These include the willow (*salice*) and the poplar (*pioppo*). In the uncultivated areas of the countryside, there are hundreds of species of daisies, grasses, grains and clover.

Rome's botanical gardens (*orto botanico*) are at the base of the Gianicolo hill in Trastevere, at Largo Cristina Svezia. Originally part of the grounds of the Palazzo Corsini, the gardens were handed over to the University of Rome in 1883. There are more than 7000 plant species from around the world in the gardens and the collection of orchids is particularly notable.

Fauna

The animals you are most likely to observe in Rome are cats, dogs and perhaps the odd rat, although you might be lucky to spot a squirrel or fox in one of Rome's numerous parks. However, in the parks and even while walking around the city streets, you can observe a surprising variety of birdlife. More than 100 different types of birds are said to nest in Rome's parks and rooftops, including kingfishers, kites, woodpeckers, kestrels, barn owls and horned owls. You'll have no trouble spotting red robins, sparrows, finches, tits, swallows and seagulls, as well as ducks, moorhens and swans on lakes. Some of the lakes in Rome's parks are also occasional refuges for cormorants and grey herons.

If you have a particular passion for birdwatching, you might like to pick up the *Atlante degli uccelli nidificanti a Roma* (Atlas of nesting birds in Rome), by Bruno Cignini and Mario Zapparoli (L50,000).

GOVERNMENT & POLITICS

Rome's municipal government is located on the Campidoglio (Capitoline Hill), which has been the seat of the city's civic government since the late 11th century. The city has a *sindaco* (mayor) elected by the public, who appoints a *giunta*, a body of councillors called *assessori* who hold ministerial positions as heads of municipal depart-ments. The assessori are appointed from the consiglio comunale, a body of elected officials, much like a parliament.

Rome's mayor until 2001 is Francesco Rutelli, a left-leaning former member of parliament. Elected in 1993 as a representative of the Verdi (Green) Party, he was re-elected with an overwhelming majority in 1997. He leads a left-leaning consiglio comunale. Rutelli's term as mayor has been something of a renaissance for Rome. It has been a period marked by furious modernisation activities and extensive public works programmes (see Ecology & Environment) which are beginning to have a positive effect on the city's previously extremely neglected services and facilities. Rutelli's term has also been notable for Rome's bid for the 2004 Olympics. Although unsuccessful, the bid went a long way towards ensuring his re-election in '97.

It is interesting to note that, unlike in other parliamentary democracies, politicians in Italy are not required to be exclusively local or national. For instance, Gianfranco Fini, Member of Parliament and leader of the right-wing Alleanza Nazionale, is also a member of the Rome consiglio comunale. Fini was defeated by Rutelli in the 1993 mayoral elections.

Rome is also the seat of national government. A parliamentary republic, Italy is headed by a president, who appoints the prime minister. The parliament consists of two houses – a Senate and a Chamber of Deputies – both with equal legislative power. Following a referendum in 1946, the republic replaced the former constitutional monarchy and operates on the basis of a constitution which came into force on 1 January 1948.

The president resides in the Palazzo del Quirinale, on Rome's Quirinale hill, the Chamber of Deputies sits in the Palazzo di Montecitorio, just off Via del Corso, and the Senate sits in the Palazzo Madama, near Piazza Navona.

Italy's electoral system generally forces the formation of unstable coalition governments. Since the declaration of the republic in 1946 there have been 57 governments with an average lifespan of 11 months.

In April 1996 was formed a coalition government which for the first time included the Communist Party. Led by Bolognese university professor, Romano Prodi, this centre-left coalition, known as the Olive Tree coalition won 50% of the seats in the Senate and 45% in the House of Deputies. As Prime Minister, Prodi worked hard to ensure that Italy joined Europe's economic and monetary union (EMU) in the first intake in 1998. However, he was not as successful in his efforts to ensure that his government would serve a full five-year term.

In a classic example of the Byzantine workings and mysteries of Italian politics, Prodi's government fell in late 1998, only to be replaced by basically the same faces – but with a new leader, Massimo D'Alema, the former leader of the Olive Tree's biggest coalition partner, the Democratic Party of the Left. D'Alema had long been suspected of merely waiting for the right moment to take over the prime ministership. He is Italy's first ex-communist prime minister, although he has a much cosier relationship with the right wing than did his predecessor.

ECONOMY

As the new millennium approaches, Rome is in a period of significant transformation: physically, politically and economically. Before Romans elected Francesco Rutelli as their mayor in 1993 (see Government & Politics), the city seemed to be in a state of torpor, its infrastructure functioning poorly and many of its monuments and museums badly maintained or closed to the public. Rutelli ushered in a pre-2000 renewal with a speed which has taken many Romans' breath away. Now residents are more likely to complain about the disruption caused by the many public works projects underway, than about the city's services not functioning. It is with some surprise that a Roman might note that 'things' are actually beginning to work in Rome.

Public facilities and services, as well as Rome's considerable architectural and artistic attractions have been targeted. The new local government on the Campidoglio has initiated a massive public works programme to improve the city's infrastructure and clean-up and restore its cultural and historic patrimony (see Ecology & Environment).

More than L2000 billion have been invested in conjunction with the Ferrovie dello Stato to improve the city's rail network, as well as the facilities to accommodate the new high speed trains serving the country. As well, L1,800 billion has been invested in laying fibre optic cables to modernise the city's telecommunication network. Funds have been invested by the European Union in projects to restore monuments and museums and the Comune di Roma is working to improve facilities for tourists. There are plans to increase the number and quality of hotels, improve sporting and entertainment facilities and events, and develop theme parks, as well as offer incentives to tourists and business travellers to visit the city out of season.

While Rome's new local government has been very proactive in attracting investment from outside sources for these numerous projects, the mainstays of its budget are the annual 'garbage tax' paid by residents (a form of municipal tax) and its share of taxes paid to the national government. In comparison to other cities, Rome receives a fairly low share of the tax pool – L290,000 annually per capita – while Milano receives L449,000 and Napoli L1,015,000 for every resident.

Unemployment in Rome was running at 12.8% in 1991, although the figure is much higher for people aged between 14 and 29 years – around 22%. The Comune itself is one of the city's biggest employers and a good proportion of Romans employed in the private sector are self-employed.

POPULATION & PEOPLE

The Comune di Roma (City of Rome) has a population of some 2.6 million people. The Provincia di Roma (Rome province) – which encompasses areas including Ostia south west of the city, the Castelli Romani and Colli Albani to the south east, Tivoli to the east, Cerveteri and Lago di Bracciano to the north east, and the Monti Sabini to the north – has a population of 3.8 million. The Regione Lazio (Lazio region), which comprises the provinces of Roma, Rieti, Viterbo, Latina and Frosinone, has a total population of 5.2 million.

Of the Roman population, 17.1% are under 20 years old, 65.5% are aged between 20 and 64, and 17.4% are over 65. The ageing population echoes the demographic trend throughout Italy, which is the only country in the world where the old outnumber the young. Demographic estimates suggest that by 2040, those over 65 will represent 41 per cent of Italy's population.

In the Lazio region in 1997 there were 47,172 births and 48,807 deaths, following national trends. Italy has had a negative birth rate for the past five years and in 1997 there were -0.4 births for every 1000 people. In fact Italy's current birth rate is the lowest in the world and the lowest in its history. International demographers have warned that if the current levels of generation replacement remain, the Italian population will become extinct in 200 years. The trend is unlikely to reverse itself in the short term. A recent survey conducted by a leading women's magazine found that more than half of the young women in Italy do not want to have children. For those between the age of 16 and 24 a staggering 52% claimed already to have decided against having children. Only 19% were in favour of having children and of those most wanted only one child.

However, the population of the Lazio region actually increased in 1997 thanks to the arrival of around 30,000 immigrants.

Estimates of the number of foreigners in Rome vary, although it is thought that one fifth of the total number of immigrants in

Italy live in Rome. The official number is around 211,000 (or around 8% of the city's population). However, there are also around 33,000 illegal immigrants living in the city. Of the foreigners in Rome, around 21% are in the city for religious reasons.

Around 11% of the foreigners in Rome come from the Philippines, 6% from Poland, 4.2% from the USA, 3.8% from India, 3.7% from Bangladesh and 3.7% from Spain. The majority of immigrants (35.5%) come from other countries in Europe (EU, central and eastern Europe) followed by Asia (29.4%), the Americas (17.2%) and Africa (16.9%). The immigrant population is essential to the Italian economy, as the immigrants do jobs such as domestic work, manual labour and seasonal agricultural jobs, which Italians are increasingly less willing to take on.

EDUCATION

The Italian state-school system is free of charge and consists of several levels. Attendance is compulsory from the ages of six to 14 years, although children can attend a *scuola materna* (nursery school) from the ages of three to five years before starting the *scuola elementare* (primary school) at six. After five years they move on to the *scuola media* (secondary school) until they reach the age of 14.

The next level, the *scuola secondaria superiore* (higher secondary school), is voluntary and lasts a further five years until the student is 19 years old. It is, however, essential if young people want to study at university. At this level there are several options: four types of *liceo* (humanities-based school), four types of technical school, and teacher-training school.

The government is in the process of reforming the education system. The standards of education in the state-run system compare well with those in other countries, although the system does have its problems, compounded by relatively low standards in teacher-training and poor government management. Officially at least, only 3% of Italians over the age of 15 are illiterate.

Private schools in Rome are run mainly by religious institutions, notably the Jesuits. There are also 21 private international schools, which provide education for English, French, German, Spanish and Japanese speaking children.

In Rome there are three state universities, one private university, several Catholic universities and several international universities (see Universities in the Facts for the Visitor chapter). The largest Italian university, La Sapienza, has around 150,000 students. Courses are usually from four to six years, although students are under no obligation to complete them in that time. Students in fact often take many more years to fulfil their quota of exams and submit their final thesis. Attendance at overcrowded lectures is optional and for scientific courses, practical experimentation is done. Students therefore tend to study at home. All state-school and university examinations are oral, rather than written.

Italy produces far fewer graduates per capita than most other countries in the West. Of the 65% of Italian secondary school students who enrol at university, only a third ever actually graduate. Despite that, unemployment among graduates is estimated at higher than 40%.

ARTS
Architecture

Pre-Roman There are archaeological and architectural remains dating back to the 4th millennium BC in Italy, but the earliest well-preserved Italian art and architecture dates from the 1st millennium BC. It comes from three cultures: Latin and Roman culture in Lazio; Etruscan culture, from what is now northern Lazio and southern Toscana (see Excursions chapter); and the culture of Magna Grecia, in southern Italy and Sicilia, where city states were founded in the 8th and 7th centuries BC by Greek colonists who settled alongside the Italic peoples.

Like the Greeks, the early Romans built temples of stone. Whereas the Greek temples (of southern Italy and Sicilia) had steps and colonnades on all sides, the

Roman variety had a high podium with steps and columns only at the front, forming a deep porch. The Romans also favoured fluted Ionic columns with volute capitals and Corinthian columns with acanthus leaf capitals (rather than the Greek Doric columns with cushion-like capitals). Examples still standing today in Rome include the Republican Tempio di Ercole Vincitore and the Tempio di Portunus by the Tevere near Piazza della Bocca della Verità and, though not so well preserved, the temples in the Area Sacra di Largo Argentina.

Roman The Romans' great achievement was in perfecting existing construction techniques and put these skills to use in the service of the Republic and later the Empire. For example, they learnt how to build roads and bridges from the Etruscans, and used these skills to create aqueducts and arches on a grandiose scale, the likes of which had never been seen before.

From the 1st century BC the Romans, using volcanic sand, made a quick-curing, strong concrete for vaults, arches and domes. It was used especially in Rome to roof vast areas like the Pantheon, which was until the 20th century the largest poured concrete dome in existence. Pumice was used in the concrete at the top to reduce the weight. Huge vaults covered the hot baths and other rooms in complexes such as the Terme di Caracalla built in 217 AD.

Brick-faced concrete was also used for *insulae* (multi-storey apartment blocks) and basilicas such as the massive Basilica di Costantino (completed in 315 AD). Dry-stone masonry was used for some temples, aqueducts and for the vaulted substructures to support the seating of theatres and amphitheatres such as the Teatro di Marcello and the Colosseo.

Marble was a popular building material in both Republican and Imperial Rome and was used from the 2nd century BC. As Rome's power grew, new buildings were needed to reflect the city's status in the Mediterranean world. The Romans developed complexes used for both commercial and political activities such as the Foro e Mercati di Traiano. Building projects became more and more ambitious. Artistic concerns took second place to size and impressive engineering, evident in structures such as the massive Terme di Diocleziano (built in 298 AD).

In the 4th century, an ambitious building programme financed by Constantine saw the erection of several places of worship, most of which followed the basilican style of late antiquity, although little of the original buildings remain. A notable exception is the domed baptistry of San Giovanni in Laterano, built by Constantine between 315 and 324 and remodelled into its present octagonal shape in the 5th century; it became the model for many baptistries throughout the Christian world.

Middle Ages Early medieval architecture in Italy (around 600 to 1050 AD) involved mainly the construction and decoration of Christian churches and monasteries, much of which took place outside Rome, notably in Ravenna. Among the most important churches in Rome of this period were Santa Maria in Cosmedin, built in the 8th century, and the 9th century Santa Prassede.

The basilican style survived into the so-called Romanesque period (11th to 13th centuries) which saw a revival of buildings whose size and structure resembled those of the Roman Empire. Many Romanesque basilican churches were built throughout Italy with rounded arch forms echoing those of classical and late antiquity.

Late medieval Gothic architecture, influenced by northern European styles of pointed arches and vaults, never took off in Rome the way it did in northern Italy. The city's only Gothic church is the Chiesa di Santa Maria sopra Minerva.

Renaissance Almost all the architectural and artistic activity of the early Renaissance was in Toscana and Venezia. However, with the revival of the papacy, Rome was on course to take over the limelight. The popes of the 15th century saw that the best way to

STEFANO CAVEDONI

Sea nymphs getting some exercise in the Piazza Navona

QUENTIN FRAYNE

Simonetti's grand staircase in the Musei Vaticani

Bernini's Fontata dei Fiumi in the Piazza Navona

People-watching in the Piazza Navona

The easiest way to get a park in Rome – Piazza Cairoli

ensure political power was to rebuild the city and the leading artistic and architectural masters were summoned to Rome. The Venetian Paul II (1464-71) commissioned many works including Palazzo Venezia, Rome's first great Renaissance palazzo, built in 1455 when he was still a cardinal and enlarged when he became pope in 1464. The pontificate of Julius II (1503-13) marks the true beginning of the high Renaissance in Rome.

Domes, vaults and arches and the model of classical Rome provide the key to Renaissance architecture. The first such buildings were by Donato Bramante (1441-1514) who had already made a name for himself in Milano when he arrived in Rome. Impressed by the ruins of ancient Rome, he created a refined classicism that embodied the concerns of the Renaissance more fully than any previous architecture. Bramante's respect for the ancients and understanding of Renaissance ideals can be seen in his Tempietto (1502), next to the Chiesa di San Pietro in Montorio on the Gianicolo, and in the perfectly proportioned cloister (1504) of the Chiesa di Santa Maria della Pace near Piazza Navona. The circular Tempietto, surrounded by 16 Doric columns, was the first building to depend entirely on the proportions of the classical orders and the most sophisticated attempt that had yet been made to combine the highest ideals of faith and art in order to create a perfect temple.

In 1506 Bramante was commissioned by Julius II to start work on the Basilica di San Pietro, the reconstruction of which under Nicholas V had virtually ground to a halt 50 years earlier. Bramante's original design was on a Greek cross plan topped by a huge central dome and flanked by four smaller cupolas. Bramante died in 1514 at which time the four central piers and the arches of the dome had been completed.

The Basilica di San Pietro occupied most of the other notable architects of the high Renaissance including Raphael (1483-1520), Giuliano da Sangallo (1443-1517), Baldassarre Peruzzi (1481-1537) and

Antonio da Sangallo the Younger (1483-1546). Commissioned by Paul III, Michelangelo Buonarotti (1475-1564) took over the task and created the magnificent light-filled dome, 42m wide, based on Brunelleschi's design for the Duomo cupola in Firenze, the first major architectural achievement of the early Renaissance.

Paul III also commissioned Michelangelo to create a new civic square on the Campidoglio, for which he adapted the vocabulary of classicism to suit his own ends, creating columns and pilasters that rose through two or more storeys of the palazzi façades.

Counter-Reformation During the Counter-Reformation both art and architecture were entirely at the service of the Church. A costly building programme was begun, largely under the direction of the Jesuits, to create massive and impressive churches to attract and overawe worshippers.

Giacomo della Porta (1539-1602) was the leading architect of the age and the last of the Renaissance tradition. He designed the mannerist façade of the main Jesuit church in Rome, the Chiesa del Gesù (1568-75). In a move away from the style of earlier Renaissance churches, the façade has pronounced architectural elements which create a contrast between surfaces and a play of light and shade. The building's exterior, as well as the interior – a wide nave and side chapels instead of aisles – was widely copied throughout Italy. Della Porta also designed the Chiesa di Sant' Andrea della Valle in 1591 and the Palazzo della Sapienza, which was the seat of Rome's university until 1935.

The end of the 16th century and the papacy of Sixtus V (1585-90) marked the beginning of major urban planning schemes as the city became a symbol of the resurgent Church. Domenico Fontana (1543-1607) and other architects created a network of major thoroughfares to connect previously disparate parts of the sprawling medieval city and erected obelisks at various vantage points. Fontana also designed the large-scale but uninspiring Palazzo Laterano (1607) next to the Basilica di San Giovanni.

In his design for the façade of the Chiesa di Santa Susanna (1603), Fontana's nephew, Carlo Maderno (1556-1629) created his masterpiece, which was regarded as a forerunner of the Baroque.

Baroque The two great artistic figures of 17th century Rome are the architect Francesco Borromini (1599-1667) from Lombardia and the Neapolitan-born architect and sculptor Gian Lorenzo Bernini (1598-1680).

No other architect before or since has had such an impact on a city as Bernini did on Rome. His patron was the Barberini pope, Urban VIII, who appointed him as the official architect of San Pietro from 1629. Bernini designed towers for Carlo Maderno's façade (which were structurally problematic and later demolished) and the *baldacchino* or altar canopy above St Peter's grave, for which ancient bronze was stripped from such places as the Pantheon.

Under Urban VIII's patronage, Bernini had an opportunity, afforded to no other man before or since, to transform the face of the city, and his churches, palaces, piazzas and fountains are Roman landmarks to this day. However, things soured for a short time on the death of Urban VIII in 1644 and the accession of Innocent X, who wanted as little contact as possible with the favoured artists and architects of his detested predecessor. Instead he turned to Borromini, Alessandro Algardi (1598-1654) and Girolamo and Carlo Rainaldi.

The son of an architect and well versed in stone masonry and construction techniques, Borromini created buildings involving complex shapes and exotic geometry. Distinctive features of his designs were windows, often oval-shaped, positioned for maximum illumination. His most memorable works are the Chiesa di San Carlo alle Quattro Fontane (1634), which has an oval-shaped interior, and the Chiesa di Sant'Ivo alla Sapienza, which combines a unique arrangement of convex and concave surfaces and is topped by an innovative spiral campanile.

Stories abound about the rivalry between Bernini and Borromini. Certainly, the latter was envious of Bernini's early success. Bernini came back into favour with his magnificent design for the Fontana dei Quattro Fiumi (1651) in the centre of Piazza Navona opposite Borromini's church of Sant'Agnese in Agone. It is said that Bernini's figure of the Nile is holding up his arm to shield his eyes from the sight of Borromini's church. In fact the fountain was built several years before the church so the story, while engaging, doesn't stand up. What is true is that together they were the dominating architectural forces of the baroque period.

Like Michelangelo, Bernini thought of himself first and foremost as a sculptor, and his best known works fall somewhere between sculpture and architecture. He was responsible for the setting for the throne and tombs for Urban VIII and Alexander VII in the Basilica di San Pietro and the magnificent sweeping colonnade in Piazza di San Pietro (1656-67) as well as the Chiesa di Sant'Andrea al Quirinale (1658). His most endearing works include the small obelisk set on the back of an elephant in Piazza della Minerva near the Pantheon and the angels set on the parapets of the Ponte Sant'Angelo bridge over the Tevere.

Late 17th to 20th Centuries The early 18th century saw a brief flurry of surprisingly creative architecture such as the Scalinata di Spagna (Spanish Steps) built between 1723 and 1726 by Francesco de Sanctis, which provided a focal point for the many Grand Tourists who came to Rome to rediscover its classical past. The rococo Piazza di Sant'Ignazio designed by Filippo Raguzzini (1680-1771) in 1728, with its curved façades, gives the Chiesa di Sant'Ignazio, the second Jesuit church of Rome, a theatrical setting.

Carlo Fontana (1634-1714) was the most popular architect at the tail end of the Baroque era who designed various palazzi and churches.

The baroque love of grand gesture continued with the Fontana di Trevi, one of the city's most exuberant and enduringly popular monuments, which was designed in 1732 by Nicola Salvi (1697-1751) and completed three decades later.

The beginning of modern architecture in Italy is epitomised in the late 19th century iron and glass-roofed shopping galleries in Milano, Napoli, Genova and Torino, but this fashion never quite made it to Rome, which instead got the massive white marble monument – the so-called wedding cake or typewriter – to Victor Emanuel II built between 1885 and 1911. Its enormous colonnade alludes to ancient precedents.

There was still time for flights of fancy such as the wonderfully frivolous Art Nouveau palazzi of Coppedè, north east of the city centre near Via Salaria before Mussolini and the Fascist era made its architectural mark with grandiose building schemes such as the Foro Italico sports centre at the foot of Monte Mario (1928-31) and EUR (Esposizione Universale di Roma), a complete district on the outskirts of Rome which has a classicising, axial monumentality, massive statues and under-utilised museums.

Other than rather hideous and anonymous apartment buildings in the outer suburbs of the city, Rome has seen little new architecture in the second half of the 20th century. Exceptions are the Stadio Flaminio built for the 1960 Olympics, the Stadio Olimpico built for the 1990 World Cup, the mosque in the Parioli area designed by Paulo Portoghesi and the new auditorium north of the city centre designed by Renzo Piano, well under construction at the time of writing. But with the exception of the last, none of these are particularly interesting buildings.

However, world-class contemporary architecture might return to Rome in the near future. At the time of writing a church was being built in Tor Tre Teste, a suburb east of the city centre. Its inspirational design is by the American architect Richard Meier, and it is meant to be the symbolic new church of the new millennium. If

bureaucratic obstacles are removed, another design by Meier – for a new museum complex for the Ara Pacis in Piazza Augusto Imperatore in the centre of Rome – might be realised in the not-too-distant future. This is an exciting project and, if and when it is completed, it will be the first major architectural intervention in the historic centre of Rome for about 60 years.

Painting and Mosaics

Roman The Romans used painting and mosaic work, both legacies from the Greeks and Etruscans, to decorate houses and palaces from at least the 1st century BC. Although very little decoration of this type survives, there are some magnificent examples in the Museo Nazionale Romano collection at Palazzo Massimo alle Terme.

Roman wall-paintings, including those of the catacombs, were in true fresco technique with water-based pigments applied to wet plaster. The frescoes represent four styles: the first imitates stone-work; the second creates illusions of architectural settings and dates to the last century BC; the third has a pattern of delicate architectural tracery combined with imitations of panel paintings; and the fourth, from the mid-1st century, combines features of the second and third styles and is the most common. Later frescoes, to be found at Ostia Antica and in the catacombs, tend towards simpler decoration and are often on a white ground.

Christian At first, black and white mosaic cubes were used for floors; later coloured stones were employed. By the 4th century, glass tesserae were used to splendid effect in the apses of the early Christian churches of Rome including the Chiesa di Santa Costanza, the Chiesa di Santa Pudenziana, the Chiesa di SS Cosma e Damiano and the Basilica di Santa Maria Maggiore.

During the 5th and 6th centuries the only art permitted was Christian art, which changed little in style but broadened its subject matter, including scenes from the Old Testament and the Passion of

Hidden Treasures

Few tourists know that within Rome's medieval churches are some of the most beautiful Byzantine mosaics in Italy. Most of these mosaics decorate the apses of the city's important churches, such as Santa Maria Maggiore, Santa Maria in Trastevere and San Clemente. The oldest mosaics date from the 4th century (Mausoleo di Santa Costanza and Chiesa di Santa Pudenziana), the period in which the Roman art of mosaic-making was evolving into the early Christian and Byzantine styles. Those depicting Santa Costanza retain some characteristics of Roman mosaics: a white background, geometric composition and ornamental motifs.

During the reign of Constantine, who decriminalised the Christian religion, many churches were being built and ornamental mosaic became the main form of decoration. Often used to cover vast areas of wall inside these new churches, they were a form of architectural tapestry which, with their uneven tesserae of coloured glass and gold, brilliantly reflected light to create strong effects and sharp contrasts of colour.

Rome's early Christian mosaics also illustrate the progression from the naturalism of Roman art to the symbolism of Christian art, reflected, for example, in the various ways in which Jesus Christ was represented. A very early Christian mosaic, in a mausoleum under the Basilica di San Pietro, shows Christ in the form of Apollo. In Chiesa di Santa Pudenziana (390 AD) he is enthroned between the apostles, but his magisterial air is reminiscent of Jupiter and the apostles are dressed as Roman senators. By the 9th century, as in Chiesa di Santa Prassede, he has become the Lamb and the faithful his flock.

The mosaics of Rome's medieval churches are a fascinating and often overlooked treasure for the tourist who might not have time to visit Ravenna or Monreale. The following is a suggested itinerary of some of the lesser known churches. The mosaics in major churches are described in the Things to See & Do chapter.

The **Mausoleo di Santa Costanza** was built in the mid-4th century by Constantia, daughter of Constantine, as a mausoleum for herself and her sister Helen. This round church is in the same grounds as **Basilica di Sant'Agnese Fuori le Mura**, on Via Nomentana, a few kilometres north of the centre (catch bus No 60 from Piazza Venezia). As well as the fascinating paleochristian mosaics on the barrel-vaulting of the ambulatory, the 7th century mosaic of St Agnes and Popes Symmachus and Honorius I in the apse of the basilica are also worth a look.

Christ. The tradition of mosaic decoration of churches continued from the 7th to the 9th century in the Chiesa di Santa Prassede and the Basilica di Santa Cecilia in Trastevere, and the influence of imported Byzantine mosaic artists who created images against a gold background, began to be more widespread.

Middle Ages Local artists were used to decorate churches and palaces when Rome started building again in the 12th century. The most famous decorative artists of the day were the Cosmati, originally a single family of artisans, but eventually a name for a whole school.

The Cosmati revolutionised the already well established art of mosaic by reusing fragments of coloured glass from the ruins of ancient Rome. They also sliced up ancient columns of coloured marble and other precious stones into circular slabs, which were used to create intricate patterned pavements, altars, paschal candle-sticks, pulpits and other decoration. Their work is referred to as 'Cosmati' and can be found in churches all over Rome.

Some of the Cosmati school eventually

Hidden Treasures

According to tradition, **Chiesa di Santa Pudenziana**, one of the oldest churches in Rome, was founded on the site of a house where St Peter was given hospitality. The structure actually incorporated the internal thermal hall of the house. The mosaic in the apse dates from 390 AD and is the earliest of its kind in Rome but, unfortunately, was partially destroyed by a 16th century restoration. The church is in Via Urbana.

Basilica di SS Cosma e Damiano, on Via dei Fori Imperiali, harbours magnificent 6th-century mosaics on the triumphal arch (Christ as the Lamb enthroned, surrounded by candlesticks and angels, as well as the symbols of the evangelists) and in the apse of Cosma and Damian being presented to Christ by Peter and Paul and, underneath, Christ as the Lamb, with the 12 apostles also represented as lambs. Bethlehem and Jerusalem are represented on either side.

The 9th century **Chiesa di Santa Prassede**, in Via Santa Prassede, was founded in honour of St Praxedes, sister of St Pudentiana, by Pope Paschal I, who transferred the bones of 2000 martyrs there from the catacombs. The rich mosaics of the apse date from the 9th century and feature Christ in the centre of the semi-dome, surrounded by Sts Peter, Pudentiana and Zeno (to the right) and Sts Paul, Praxedes and Paschal (to the left). Underneath is Christ the Lamb and his flock.

The **Cappella di San Zenone** (Chapel of St Zeno), inside the church, is the most important Byzantine monument in Roma, built by Paschal I as a mausoleum for his mother. Known as the Garden of Paradise, the chapel has a vaulted interior completely covered in mosaics, including the *Madonna with Saints*, *Christ with Saints* and, in the vault, *Christ with Angels*. The pavement of the chapel is one of the earliest examples of *opus sectile* (polychrome marble), and in a small niche on the right are fragments of a column brought from Jerusalem in 1223 and said to be the column at which Christ was scourged.

Across the Tevere, in Piazza dei Mercanti, is the **Basilica di Santa Cecilia in Trastevere**, built in the 9th century by Paschal I over the house of St Cecilia, where she was martyred in 230. The impressive mosaic in the apse was executed in 870 and features Christ giving a blessing. To his right are Sts Peter, Valerian (husband of St Cecilia) and Cecilia herself. To his left are Sts Paul, Agatha and Paschal. The holy cities are depicted underneath.

---

became accomplished sculptors, architects and mosaicists, such as Pietro Vassalletto (died 1186) who built the cloisters at the Basilica di San Giovanni in Laterano and the Basilica di San Paolo Fuori le Mura, two of the best surviving examples of Cosmati decoration in Rome.

One of the greatest Roman artists of the Middle Ages, and a precursor of the Renaissance, was Pietro Cavallini (c 1250-1330) who switched effortlessly between fresco painting (for example in the Basilica di Santa Cecilia in Trastevere) and mosaic work (in the Basilica di Santa Maria in Trastevere).

Renaissance The main artistic activity of the early Renaissance took place in Firenze, Siena and Venezia. However, painting flourished once again as Rome was rebuilt after the papacy was restored in the 15th century.

Between 1481-83 some of the country's greatest painters were employed by Sixtus IV to decorate the walls in his newly rebuilt Cappella Sistina in il Vaticano. The frescoes, of the lives of Moses and Christ and portraits of popes, were done by Perugino

(1446-1523), Sandro Botticelli (1444-1510), Domenico Ghirlandaio (1449-94), Cosimo Rosselli (1439-1507) and Luca Signorelli (c 1441-1523). These artists were assisted by members of their workshops, including Pinturicchio (1454-1513), who subsequently frescoed the Borgia apartments between 1492 and 1494, Piero di Cosimo (1462-1521) and Bartolomeo della Gatta (1448-1502).

The decoration of the official apartments of Pope Julius II (the so-called Stanze di Raffaello), marked the beginning of the brilliant Roman career of Urbino-born Raphael (Raffaello Sanzio, 1483-1520) who arrived from Firenze in 1508. In the true spirit of the Renaissance, he absorbed the manner of classical Rome and became the most influential painter of his time.

Raphael was also adept at portraiture and mythological paintings, and there are wonderful frescoes in this vein in the Villa Farnesina in Trastevere which he painted between 1508 and 1511. Other leading artists who worked on the villa designed by Baldassarre Peruzzi were Sebastiano del Piombo (c 1485-1547), Sodoma (1477-1549), and Giulio Romano (c1492-1546), one of the few native Roman artists of the Renaissance.

The greatest achievement of the period was by Raphael's contemporary, Michelangelo Buonarotti (1475-1564) on the Cappella Sistina ceiling (1508-12). The dramatically foreshortened figures are the most striking examples of the Mannerist style of the 16th century. The ceiling is the most moving and original combination of art and faith in Renaissance Rome, and one of the greatest artistic achievements of all time – by an artist who didn't think of himself as a painter. (See also boxed text 'Michelangelo in Rome' in the Things to See & Do chapter.) Three decades later, after the Sack of Rome, Michelangelo returned to il Vaticano to adorn the altar wall of the Cappella Sistina with the *Giudizio Universale* (Last Judgement), between 1535 and 1541.

Counter-Reformation Both painting and sculpture hit a low point in the late 16th century, although there were some highlights at the very end of the century. Annibale Carracci (1560-1609) left his mark on Rome with the magnificent frescoes of mythological subjects in the Palazzo Farnese done between 1597 and 1603, and the inside of the dome of the Basilica di San Pietro was covered in mosaics based on designs by the technically proficient, if uninspiring, Cavalier d'Arpino (1568-1640).

The arrival in Rome of Michelangelo Merisi da Caravaggio (1573-1610) heralded a move away from the confines of the high Renaissance towards a new naturalism. In Caravaggio's case, his naturalism was often regarded as being just a little too 'real' and his paintings, using street urchins and prostitutes as models for biblical subjects, were often rejected. However, his innovative sense of light and shade and supreme draughting ability meant that he was courted by contemporary collectors and was influential for centuries. See also boxed text 'On the Caravaggio Trail' in the Things to See & Do chapter.

More successful in their day although less highly revered afterwards were the dryly academic painters Guido Reni (1575-1642) and Domenichino (1581-1641) who were considered by their contemporaries and immediate successors to be on a par with Raphael and Michelangelo.

Domenichino was a native of Bologna and a pupil of Annibale Carracci. He was one of the most prodigious and admired masters in early 17th century Rome and, for a time at least, so in favour with the aristocratic clergy of the day that he received innumerable commissions. His best works were his fresco cycles which adorn nine churches in Rome.

Baroque Michelangelo had started a fashion for ceiling frescoes which continued well into the 17th century. Pietro da Cortona (1596-1669) was one of the most sought-after decorators of Baroque Rome. His fresco on the ceiling of the Salone Grande of Palazzo Barberini, begun in 1632, paved the way for numerous other commissions including the ceiling frescoes in the Chiesa Nuova and in many private palaces. Many other painters tried, but failed, to match his talent.

The Jesuit artist Andrea dal Pozzo (1642-1709) made a name for himself creating *trompe l'oeil* perspectives on ceilings and walls in the many Jesuit churches and buildings being erected in Rome, while serene landscapes were being produced by Salvator Rosa (1615-73) and the Italianised French painters Nicolas Poussin (1594-1665) and Claude Lorrain (1600-82).

The 18th to 20th Centuries By the 18th century Rome's artistic heyday was over; the attention of the many foreign artists who settled in Rome turned to the antique. The widely-disseminated etchings of the city and its ancient ruins by Giovanni Battista Piranesi attracted Grand Tourists and artists alike. The Swiss-born Angelica Kauffmann was just one example of a foreign artist who settled in the Eternal City and produced proficient, if uninspiring, academic art.

Painting and sculpture since Italian unification in 1870 is most readily found in the Galleria Nazionale d'Arte Moderna. The end of the 19th century saw the emergence of Italian post-Impressionism with the so-called *Macchiaioli*, who produced a version of pointillism using thousands of dots of pure colour to build up the picture, and of the Italian Symbolists.

The Italian Futurists were inspired by urbanism, industry and the idea of progress. Umberto Boccioni (1882-1916) and Giacomo Balla (1871-1958) aligned themselves with the Futurist manifesto (1909) of the writer Emilio Marinetti, and Carlo Carrà (1881-1996) had much in common with Cubists like Pablo Picasso. Giorgio Morandi (1890-1964) consistently depicted bottles and jars as forms rather than objects, while the Surrealist Giorgio De Chirico (1888-1978) painted visionary empty streetscapes with elements disconcertingly juxtaposed, often incorporating allusions to classical antiquity.

Amedeo Modigliani (1884-1920) spent most of his adult life in Paris. However, his art – mainly arresting portraits and sensuous reclining female nudes – was firmly rooted in the tradition of the Italian Renaissance and Mannerist masters.

Important post-WWII artists include Burri, Colla, Manzoni and Pascali, and the Transavanguardia whose exponents include Enzo Cucchi, Francesco Clemente (1952-), Mimmo Paladino and Sandro Chia (1946-), many of whom have worked and gained success both in Italy and abroad.

Sculpture

Etruscan Most evidence of Etruscan art has come from their tombs, richly furnished with carved stone sarcophagi, fabulous gold jewellery, ceramic and bronze statues and utiltarian objects, as well as frescoes, fine examples of which are displayed in the Villa Giulia. The Etruscan artists learned Greek artistic techniques and transformed them into a unique style of their own.

The Etruscans were famous for metalwork, such as the bronze *Lupa Capitolina* in the Musei Capitolini, although such large pieces rarely survive. The figures of Romulus and Remus, though, are a much later addition, made to measure in the Renaissance. Most of the surviving Etruscan pieces are smaller figurines and household items such as engraved mirrors; the techniques used to make the amazingly intricate filigree work which decorates Etruscan gold jewellery were only rediscovered in the 20th century.

Roman During both the Republic and the Empire, sculpture was very much at the service of the Roman state (and the emperor), and more than any other art form provides a compelling record of the city's history.

The first 'Roman' sculptures were actually made by Greek artists brought to Rome or were copies of imported classical Greek works. An exception was Roman portrait sculpture, derived from the Etruscans who aimed for naturalism and the honest representation of the subject. A popular form of sculpture for the Romans was to have statues made of themselves in the guise of Greek gods or heroes. However, the most interesting Roman sculpture was that of the 1st and 2nd centuries AD which commemorated the history of the city and its citizens or which was made for specific architectural settings such as the Villa Adriana at Tivoli.

The emperor Augustus was an expert at exploiting the possibilities of sculpture as a propaganda tool. One of the most important works of Roman sculpture is the Ara Pacis (9 BC) made to celebrate the peace which he had brought to the empire – and established at home. The reliefs, exemplified by clarity and classical restraint, mark the point at which Roman art gained its own identity. The so-called Prima Porta statue of Augustus himself, now in the Musei Vaticani, is another masterpiece of intricate symbolism combined with idealised portraiture.

Later commemorative works include the early 2nd century AD Colonna di Traiano, erected to celebrate Trajan's military achievements in the Dacian campaigns, and the Colonna Antonina (180-196) built to commemorate Marcus Aurelius' victories over the Germans and Sarmatians between 169 and 176 AD.

In the 3rd and 4th centuries there was little public sculpture, although a notable exception is the 4th century statue of Constantine, a 10m colossus which stood at his basilica in the Foro Romano. Pieces of it (namely the head, a hand and a foot) are in the Musei Capitolini.

Christian The early Christian period saw an almost total rejection of sculpture, except for carved decoration on Christian sarcophagi. The carved wooden panels depicting scenes of the Passion of Christ on the doors of the Basilica di Santa Sabina dating from the 5th century are a significant but rare exception.

Sculpture took centuries to recover and longer to do so in Rome than in other parts of the country where stonemasons and sculptors carved notable church porticos, pulpits and façade decorations.

Arnolfo di Cambio (c 1245-1302) is best known for his work in Firenze but, together with his pupils, he created a number of interesting works in Rome in the late 13th century including a bronze statue of St Peter in the Basilica di San Pietro, tombs in the Chiesa di Santa Prassede and the Basilica di San Giovanni in Laterano, and wall tabernacles at the Basilica di San Clemente and the Basilica di San Paolo Fuori le Mura.

Renaissance Michelangelo Buonarroti (1475-1564) already had an established reputation as a sculptor when he arrived in Rome from Firenze at the end of the 15th century. His staggeringly beautiful *Pietà* now in the Basilica di San Pietro, was sculpted when he was only 25 years old and amazed the Roman public.

Julius II immediately put him to work on the massive project to create a tomb for the pope, involving 40 pieces of sculpture. The tomb occupied the artist for his entire career but was never completed, and, despite the fact that Michelangelo regarded himself above all as a sculptor, in Rome his greatest legacy was as a high Renaissance painter and architect. (See the boxed text 'Michelangelo in Rome' in the Things to See & Do chapter).

Baroque In Rome, the Baroque meant one thing: Gian Lorenzo Bernini. A visit to the Museo Borghese, which houses many of Bernini's early and best works, gives a clear idea of the sculptor's astounding talent.

Bernini could do things with marble that no one before or since has managed. He could make the cold hard stone appear to be soft flesh and a solid static figure seem to be dynamic. Not only was he a virtuoso carver but he also took risks using the marble blocks, breaking all sorts of unwritten sculptors' rules about wasting expensive stone by creating an outflung arm or leg or a figure that genuinely appears to be in motion.

Baroque sensibilities gave a new importance to exaggerated poses, cascading drapery and primacy of emotions and Gian Lorenzo Bernini was an unequalled master. His were not sculptures but rather theatrical and emotional spectacles set in stone which unfolded before the viewers' eyes. His *Davide*, *Il Ratto di Proserpina* and *Apollo e Dafne*, all in the Museo Borghese and the *Santa Teresa trafitta dall'amor di Dio* (The Ecstasy of St Teresa) in the Chiesa di Santa Maria della Vittoria are cases in point.

Bologna-born Alessandro Algardi (1595-1654) was one of the few sculptors in Rome not totally overshadowed by Bernini, his great rival. He received commissions from Pope Innocent X and noble Roman families and his bronzes and marbles grace several Roman churches and palazzi. His white marble monument to Pope Leo XI (1650) is in the Basilica di San Pietro.

The 18th to 20th Centuries The Neoclassicism of the late 18th and early 19th centuries was a reaction to the excesses of the Baroque and a response to the renewed interest in the classical world which had been sparked by the excavations of Pompeii and Herculaneum.

The Neoclassical sculptural style was best represented by Antonio Canova (1757-1822). He was an accomplished modeller but his work is sometimes devoid of obvious emotion. His most famous work is a daring sculpture of Paolina Bonaparte Borghese as a reclining *Venere Vincitrice* in the Museo Borghese. Her diaphanous drapery leaves little to the imagination and is typical of the mildly erotic sculptures for which Canova became known. One of his best works in Rome is the majestic *Ercole* in the Galleria Nazionale d'Arte Moderna, where every muscular ripple of the dynamic, straining figure of Hercules is clearly evident.

The Sicilian-born sculptor Mario Rutelli (1859-1941), great-grandfather of Rome's current mayor, left his mark on the city with a series of fountains, monuments and equestrian statues, mainly in an academic style, including a statue of Anita Garibaldi on the Gianicolo. One of his most visible and delightful works is the Fontana delle Naiadi (1901) in Piazza della Repubblica

God's Choirmaster

Palestrina's musical career began as a choirboy at Santa Maria Maggiore, and he later served as organist and singing teacher in the Cathedral of Palestrina. When the Bishop, Cardinal Giovanni Maria del Monte, was elected pope as Julius II, he took Palestrina to Rome with him as the new director of the papal choir.

Two popes later, Paul IV was scandalised to find that a married man was directing his choir, and Palestrina was sacked. He moved on to San Giovanni in Laterano, and, six years later, came full circle to become maestro at Sant Maria Maggiore. He spent the last twenty years of his long life again as the choirmaster to the pope, and was buried in a (now lost) chapel in San Pietro.

Palestrina's greatest contribution was his ability to combine complex polyphonic music with the requirements laid down by the Council of Trent that the words of liturgical music must be clearly heard – the Council had even considered banning polyphony from scared music until they heard Palestrina's *Messa Papae Marcelli* (Mass for Pope Marcellus).

which has just been beautifully cleaned and restored.

Giacomo Manzù (1908-91) revived the Italian religious tradition. His best known work is a bronze door (to the left of the central Holy Door) in the Basilica di San Pietro which he was awarded after a competition in 1949.

Music

The Italians have played a pivotal role in the history of music: they invented the system of musical notation in use today; a 16th century Venetian printed the first musical scores with movable type; Cremona produced immortal violins; and and Italy is the birthplace of the piano.

Not surprisingly, the medieval and Renaissance popes had a strong influence on music in Rome. The Church was by far the most stable employer for talented musicians, and individual popes established the great musical institutions, many of which have survived. It is unlikely that Gregory I actually had any hand in creating the liturgical music known as Gregorian Chant, but this certainly provided the basis for the uniform liturgical music still in use. Sixtus IV greatly increased the status of the papal choir, not the least by having a new chapel commissioned – the Cappella Sistina.

The greatest musicians of the day served as papal choirmasters, including Giovanni Pierluigi da Palestrina (c 1525-1594) and Domenico Scarlatti (1685-1757), while Girolamo Frescobaldi (1583-1643), who was admired and studied by the young J.S. Bach, was twice an organist in San Pietro.

The papal choirs, originally composed of priests, were closed to women, and the high parts were originally taken by men singing in falsetto. The *falsetti* were gradually supplanted by *castrati*, boys surgically castrated before puberty to preserve their high voices for life. Although castration was punishable by excommunication, the Cappella Sistina and other papal choirs contained castrati as early as 1588; the last known castrato, Alessandro Moreschi (1858-1922), had been a member of the Cappella Sistina choir. Moreschi even made a primitive recording in 1903, the very year that Pius X banned castrati from the papal choirs. Boy sopranos were introduced in the 1950s.

As well as liturgical singing, castrati, whose unique voices combined a female register with lung power of a man, were also in demand for the operatic stage and are known to have taken female roles even before Sixtus V, worried about public morals, banned women from performing in public. The castrati were the pop stars of their day, with voices described as 'the singing of angels'.

The Cappella Sistina choir now consists of 20 men and 30 to 40 boys. It is regarded as the pope's personal choir and accompanies him whenever he celebrates a papal mass (3 or 4 times a month). The choir also sings at any festivities on the church calendar, such as beatifications, canonisations, funerals, and papal anniversaries.

In 1585 Sixtus V formally established the Accademia di Santa Cecilia, originally called the Congregazione dei Musici di Roma and established as a support organisation (perhaps even an early trade union) for papal musicians. From its 17th century role in supervision musical education and the publication of sacred music it developed a teaching function (Arcangelo Corelli was an early maestro of the instrumental section in 1700), and in 1839 it reinvented itself as an Accademia with wider cultural and academic goals – including even the admission of women! It is today one of the most highly respected conservatoria in the world, with its own orchestra and chorus.

Ottorino Respighi (1879-1936) came to Rome from Bologna as Professor of Composition at Santa Cecilia, and later served as the Director of the Accademia. His works include three sets of tone poems evoking various features of his adopted city: *Pini di Roma* (Pines of Rome), *Fontane di Roma* (Fountains of Rome), and *Feste Romane* (Roman Festivals).

Outside the precinct of il Vaticano, music publishing came to Rome very soon after its birth in Venice; music was printed in Rome from 1510, and Roman music publication was the first to replace movable type with copperplate engraving.

See also the Entertainment chapter later in the book.

Opera Ballet and opera developed in Rome as they did in Firenze and Venezia – out of the lavish musical entertainments which diverted the nobility. The Barberini were particularly noted for the extravagance of their 17th century spectacles, held either in their new palace at Piazza Barberini, or in the Cardinal's residence in the Palazzo della Cancelleria.

The melodramatic story of Giacomo Puccini's opera *Tosca* takes place entirely in Rome, during the Napoleonic occupation. The first act taking place in the Chiesa di Sant'Andrea della Valle, the second in the Palazzo Farnese, and the final act set at Castel Sant'Angelo from which of which Tosca jumps to her death. Neither the diva Floria Tosca nor her revolutionary lover Mario Cavaradossi existed, but the villainous Chief of Police, Baron Scarpia, may well have been based on Baron Sciarpa, a Bourbon officer. In 1992 an Emmy Award-winning television broadcast was made of the opera (starring Catherine Malfitano and Placido Domingo), shot on location and at the precise times specified by the libretto.

Tenor Luciano Pavarotti (1935-) is still the best known of Italian opera singers, though he is well past his prime. Current operatic talents include home-grown mezzo superstar Cecilia Bartoli, Barbara Frittoli, Cecilia Gasdia, Anna Caterina Antonacci, Luciana Serra, Sonia Ganassi, Ruggero Raimondi, Renato Bruson, Ferruccio Furlanetto and Giuseppe Sabbatini, many of whom regularly sing in Rome.

Due to mismanagement and inconsistent artistic direction, the Teatro dell'Opera di Roma has a reputation as the poor cousin of the country's premier opera theatres such as La Scala in Milano, San Carlo in Napoli, the Teatro Nuovo in Torino, and (before it burnt to the ground in 1997) La Fenice in Venezia. The Rome opera season runs from December to June, with special outdoor performances during summer (see the Entertainment chapter); full details are available at www.comune.roma.it/cultura/musica/opera/opera.html.

Contemporary Music Few modern Italian singers or groups have made any impact outside Italy. The best vocalist to emerge since the war is probably Mina. During the 1960s she cut dozens of records. Many of her songs were written by Giulio Rapetti, better known as Mogol, the undisputed king of Italian songwriters.

The 1960s and 1970s produced various *cantautori* (singer songwriters), vaguely reminiscent of some of the greats of the UK and USA. Lucio Dalla, Vasco Rossi and Pino Daniele have been successfully hawking their versions of protest music since the early 1970s. While not of the stature of, say, Bob Dylan, the strength of their music lies in lyrics occasionally laced with venom portraying the shortcomings of modern society. Daniele, whose Neapolitan roots are clearly on display, brings an unmistakably bluesy flavour to his music.

Much softer and less inclined towards social critique, but highly popular since the end of the 1960s, was Lucio Battisti who died in 1988. Some of the early music will make your hair stand on end (*very* 1970s), but Battisti was highly regarded, even by younger generations.

Zucchero (Adelmo Fornaciari) is a phenomenon on the Italian music scene. Starting out as a session musician with the likes of Joe Cocker, he has aimed at both the Italian and international market as few other Italians have, earning a lot of sour grapes along the way. He sings many of his songs in Italian *and* English, and is known in the UK and USA as Sugar and was clever enough to earn further fame by doing *Senza una Donna* with Paul Young.

Other names to look out for include Luca Carboni, Francesco de Gregori, Antonello Venditti, Fiorella Mannoia, Claudio Baglioni and the group RAF. Since the early 1990s, Eros Ramazzotti has been one of the country's top male artists.

For what it's worth, Italian hip-hop and house productions are much appreciated by connoisseurs, and there is a flourishing market in home-grown rap. A particularly popular exponent of the latter is Jovanotti. Other home-grown hip-hop bars include Neffa, Frankie-Hi-Nrg, Space One, Spaghetti Funk, Solo Zippo, Chief & Soci and La Famiglia. There are also some decent Indie-style bands in circulation, such as Litfiba. A lighter sound comes from Pooh, a band which appeared in the mid-90s.

Latin Literature

Instead of attempting a potted history of 500 years of Latin literature, the following is a selective examination of some representative figures. All of the works mentioned are readily available in translation as well as on websites such as classics.mit.edu/index.html and www.perseus.tufts.edu/Texts.html.

Republic Marcus Tullius Cicero (106-43 BC) stands out as the pre-eminent prose author of the Republic. A 'new man' without consuls in his family tree, Cicero won his way to the consulship of 63 BC through his brilliance as a barrister. As well as his philosophical works, he tidied up many of his notable speeches for publication, and his secretary later published many of his letters to family and friends. Fancying himself as the senior statesman, Cicero took the young Octavian under his wing, and attacked Mark Antony in a series of 14 speeches, the *Philippics*; these soon proved fatal when Octavian changed sides and joined up with Mark Antony, who then demanded – and got – Cicero's head.

Cicero on Mark Antony

You, with those jaws, those sides, that gladiator's body, drank so much wine at Hippia's wedding that you were forced to vomit the next day in the sight of the Roman people. A disgusting thing to hear about, let alone see! If this had happened to you at dinner with those enormous wine cups of yours, who would not have been revolted? But a man holding public office in an assembly of the Roman people, the Master of the Horse to whom it should have been disgraceful to burp, vomiting down his toga, the whole tribunal wet with what he had eaten, reeking of wine!

Philippics II.25

Golden Age Latin This era centred around the reign of Augustus. With the *Aeneid*, Vergil (70-19 BC) transformed the various Aeneas legends into the great foundation myth of Rome. This blend of myth, history, and moral instruction immediately became a school text, and remained one for the next 1700 years or so. The *Aeneid* acquired such an aura that a popular method of fortune telling involved interpreting the significance of a randomly selected passage – the same process used by some with the Bible.

Rome's imperial mission

... Others, I believe, will beat out breathing bronze more delicately,
Will draw living forms from marble,
Will plead their cases better,
Or will trace the path of heaven with a rod and predict the rising of the stars:
Remember, O Roman, yours is to rule the nations;
These are to be your arts: to impose the law of peace,
To spare the defeated, and conquer the proud.

Aeneid VI.847-854

Silver Age Latin As Roman society changed over a century, so too did the Latin language, and the people who used it. While Livy, Vergil's contemporary, had written the history of Rome's glorious past, Tacitus (c 56-116 AD) viewed more recent history with a decidedly colder eye.

The real conquest of Britain

[The Britons] were led to the causes of vice: the portico, the bath, and the elegant banquet. This in their ignorance they called civilisation when it was a part of slavery.

Agricola 21

Emperors were not, however, just written about but, in the tradition of Julius Caesar's *Commentaries* on his various wars, left their own versions of history. As well as his autobiography, the scholarly Claudius produced volumes of Etruscan, Carthaginian and Augustan history, and Agrippina, Nero's mother, wrote her own autobiography. All of these are, unfortunately, lost. Only the philosophical *Meditations* of Marcus Aurelius has survived.

Italian Literature

Middle Ages From before the final collapse of Rome until well into the Middle Ages, creative literary production declined, kept barely alive in western Europe by clerics and erudites who debated theology, wrote histories and handbooks of rhetoric, translated or interpreted classical literature and used Latin as their lingua franca. The 12 century *Mirabilia Romae* were effectively the first guidebooks to the monuments of the ancient city.

Although the 13th century popes wrote great books and sermons and issued laws and official acts, the removal of the papacy to Avignon in 1309 meant that for the rest of the 14th century literary activity in Rome was less noteworthy. Throughout the Italian peninsular, Latin had already ceased to be a living language. Firenze was the most productive centre, and the period was marked by the production of literature in Italian, in the highly influential work of Dante, Boccaccio and Petrarch.

Dante (1265-1321) was probably the greatest figure in Italian literature. His *Divina Commedia* is an allegorical masterpiece that takes his protagonist on a search for God through Hell, Purgatory and Paradise. It confirmed the Italian vernacular (in its Tuscan form) as a serious medium for poetic expression, and was highly influential on subsequent writers. Dante's Latin work *De Monarchia* reflects his preference for a return of imperial power and his vision of a world where the roles of pope and emperor complemented each other.

Even more influential than Dante was the Tuscan humanist Petrarch (Francesco Petrarca, 1304-74). Petrarch was the most important Latinist of his day and was crowned poet laureate in Rome in 1341 after earning a reputation throughout Europe as a classical scholar. He had sought to win recognition through his Latin writings but in fact the reverse happened. His lyrical works in the Tuscan vernacular, such as his epic poem, *Africa*, and the sonnets of *Il Canzoniere* have had a permanent influence on Italian poetry.

Another Florentine, Giovanni Boccaccio (1313-75), is considered the first Italian novelist. The 100 short stories that make up his *Il Decamerone* are told by 10 young nobles who had escaped from their plague-ridden city.

The humanist movement that swept Italy and Europe in the 14th and 15th centuries put Rome in the spotlight. After centuries when thought and writing were dominated by the religious beliefs of Christianity and the Catholic Church, scholars and intellectuals became more interested in the essentially secular aspects of antiquity, and the idea of classical Rome began to play a crucial role in the evolution of western culture.

Flavio Biondo (1392-1463) was a disciple of Petrarch and the founder of modern archaeology. His *Decades*, a history of Christendom from the fall of Rome to the 1440s was effectively the first history of the Middle Ages.

Lorenzo Valla (1407-1457) was greatest Roman humanist. He bravely challenged the Church administration and was sceptical about various aspects of papal primacy. He also produced a humanist commentary on the New Testament, pioneering a new critical attitude to the text, and at times he was branded a heretic because of his philosophy. He was renowned for his vigorous mind and sharp tongue and an expert command of Latin – exhibited in his *Opus elegantiarum linguae Latinae* – to which hardly any of his contemporaries could aspire.

Renaissance By the end of the 15th century, Rome was a kind of cultural capital of Europe due to the enormous number of Latinists employed in the city and the papal and ecclesiastical patronage of artists and architects. However, much of the most significant literary activity of the 14th and 15th centuries actually took place outside Rome in the courts of Milano, Ferrara, Mantova and in the Kingdom of Naples, and the Roman humanists were, on the whole, less significant figures and less original thinkers than those in northern Italy.

In the 16th century the qualities inherent in the Petrarchian and Neo-Platonic tradition became more pronounced. Although he was better known as a painter, sculptor and architect, Michelangelo Buonarotti (1475-1564) was also one of the greatest poets of the time. At an early age in the Florentine court of Lorenzo de' Medici he was exposed to Neo-Platonist writers as well as important sculptors and painters. He began writing poetry in his youth, although his finest works – mainly sonnets and madrigals – were composed in Rome the last 20 years of his life. Michelangelo's poems are regarded as the finest poems written in Italian since Petrarch and Dante (in whose praise Michelangelo wrote two sonnets).

It is indeed through one of Michelangelo's sonnets that we learn exactly some of the difficulties he encountered in painting the ceiling of the Cappella Sistina:

My beard turns up to heaven; my nape falls in
Fixed on my spine: my breast-bone visibly
Grows like a harp: a rich embroidery
Bedews my face from brush-drops thick and thin

His writing was not actually published until 1623 when his great-nephew released the poems in a slightly edited version, suppressing the fact that many of them were written for a young man, Tommaso Cavalieri (with whom Michelangelo fell in love in 1532), and that they explored the dilemma of a homosexual whose moral beliefs conflict with his sexuality. It was mistakenly thought for several centuries that they were love poems for the Roman noblewoman, Vittoria Colonna.

Vittoria Colonna (1490-1549) was a member of the noble Roman Colonna family. She spent much of her early life on Ischia, an island in the Golfo di Napoli, but visited Rome and Napoli regularly. Her unusual intellectual abilities won her a considerable reputation and she formed friendships with many outstanding writers, reformers and religious figures. After the loss of her philandering husband, she wrote a series of around 100 poems lamenting his death and idealising his character. Later in her life she wrote poems on sacred and spiritual themes. Her poetry – skilful but not strikingly original – was written in the Petrarchan and Neo-Platonic vein. Her relationship with Michelangelo was a truly 'Platonic' friendship, marked by frequent exchanges of philosophical sonnets and letters. Michelangelo was at her bedside when she died in 1549, .

Giorgio Vasari's *Vite dei Più Eccellenti Pittori* (1550 and republished in 1568, translated as Lives of the Painters) a treatise on the lives of his artist contemporaries and predecessors, remains one of the most informative works of Renaissance art history. Vasari was a close contemporary of Michelangelo and spent several years in Rome as chief architect of San Pietro (to which he was appointed in succession to Michelangelo).

The sculptor and goldsmith Benvenuto Cellini (1500-71) began writing his famous autobiography, *Vita*, in 1558. A native of Firenze, Cellini spent many years in Rome and worked for important ecclesiastical figures including popes Clement VII and Paul III. In his autobiography, Cellini used an uninhibited spoken manner, which was unparalleled for several centuries. It has been described as a narrative made up of fact, fiction, self-justification and technical information. The story reaches its dramatic climax with the Sack of Rome in 1527 and the author's escape in 1538 from Castel Sant'Angelo, where he had been imprisoned.

Censorship became institutionalised with the publication in 1554 (under Paul IV) of the Roman Index of Prohibited Books. The publication of the list, which concerned itself not only with faith but also morals, was accompanied by public book-burnings in Rome and elsewhere, and many printers were forced to flee the city.

Giordano Bruno (1548-1600) was one of the earliest champions of freedom of speech and thought. His fiery temperament brought him into conflict with one form of Counter-Reformation establishment after another. Originally a Dominican priest, his interests included natural magic, cosmology and astrology – one of his assertions was that the earth was not the centre of the universe. Among the orthodox Church doctrines that he questioned was the notion of the Immaculate Conception. He spent many years in exile outside Italy, returning only in 1591. In 1600, after an eight year trial, he was branded a heretic and burnt at the stake in Campo de' Fiori. In 1603 all Bruno's books were placed on the Index of Prohibited Books.

The absence of free speech in Counter-Reformation Rome is one explanation for the lack of significant literature from that period; anything of which the Church and State disapproved was suppressed. But in 17th century Rome an 'underground' literary form emerged, in the posting of anonymous satirical writings or *pasquinades* (named after the first person who was identified as having written one) which criticised the Church and authoritative figures. One of the most popular places for such notices to be left was on the torso of a Roman statue, near Piazza Navona (in a small square today known as Piazza Pasquino). The epigrams were usually posted in the dark of night and then gleefully circulated around town the following day.

The 18th Century The 18th century is marked not by Italian literature but by the writings of the many historians and Grand Tourists from northern Europe. Edward Gibbon penned his influential *The History of the Decline and Fall of the Roman Empire* between 1776 and 1778. Johann Wolfgang von Goethe, already a celebrated poet when he arrived in Rome in 1786, found the city an inspiration for his literary and artistic travails. His *Italian Journey* captures better than any other text the elation of the northern travellers as they discovered the ruins of ancient Rome and the colours of the modern city. 'In Rome I found myself for the first time,' he wrote.

Rome was also a magnet for the English Romantics. Keats, Byron, Shelley, Mary Shelley and other writers all spent time in the city. Byron claimed Rome as the city of his soul even though he only visited it fleetingly. John Keats came to Rome in 1821 in the hope that it would cure his ill health but he died of tuberculosis in his lodgings at the foot of the Scalinata di Spagna after only a few months in the city.

Percy Bysshe Shelley (1792-1822) wrote his most important works in Italy between 1818 and 1822, including the powerful verse drama *The Cenci*, based on the true story of Beatrice Cenci, a tragic young Roman woman who was dominated and abused by her father, killed him and then was put to death herself for the murder.

The 19th Century Italy's home-grown Romantic, Giacomo Leopardi (1798-1837) was less inspired by the wonders of Rome than his northern counterparts and he spent only a few months in Rome in 1822-23.

Nathaniel Hawthorne lived in Italy from 1857 to 1859. *The Marble Faun*, published in 1860, recreates the author's impressions of Rome in a narrative context. In 1869 Henry James made the first of his 14 trips to Italy, which inspired his enduringly popular classic, *Portrait of a Lady*, and his book of essays, *Italian Hours*.

Romans are particularly proud of their most famous local poets, Gioacchino Belli (1791-1863), Carlo Alberto Salustri (1871-1950), better known as Trilussa, and Cesare Pescarella (1858-1940), all of whom wrote in the Roman dialect.

Belli started his career with conventional and undistinguished verse but found the medium for his expression in the crude and colourful dialect of the Roman people, making use of its puns and obscenities. He was a savage satirist and outspoken in his attacks on all classes and institutions. He often painted vulgar caricatures of important Risorgimento figures.

The 20th Century Gabriele D'Annunzio (1863-1938) is the most flamboyant literary figure of the turn of the 20th century and into the modern era. Born in Pescara, D'Annunzio settled in Rome in 1881. An ardent nationalist, his often virulent poetry was perhaps not of the highest quality, but his voice was a prestige tool for Mussolini's Fascists.

Italy's richest contribution to modern literature has been in the novel and short story, and two of the most popular figures were closely tied to the capital.

Alberto Moravia (1907-90) grew up in the residential area east of the Villa Borghese. He describes Rome and its people in his prolific writings. Novels such as *La Romana* (A Woman of Rome) convey the detail of place and the sharp sense of social decay that make his story-telling so compelling. The alienated individual and the emptiness of Fascist and bourgeois society are common themes in his writing. *Racconti romani* (Roman tales), published in 1954, and *Nuovi raconti romani* (New Roman tales), published four years later, offer amusing sketches of the lives of Roman characters including plumbers, servants and hoodlums.

The novels of Elsa Morante (1912-85), characterised by a subtle psychological appraisal of her characters, can be seen too as a personal cry of pity for the sufferings of individuals and society. Her 1974 novel *La storia* (History: a Novel) follows the fortunes of a half-Jewish woman in occupied Rome.

Pier Paolo Pasolini (1922-75) moved to Rome 1950 in the wake of a sex scandal in his native Friuli. Rome gave him an opportunity to explore both his homosexuality and different ways of writing. His first novel, *Ragazzi di Vita* explores the violent, temperamentally and linguistically explosive, sordid but vital world of the dilapidated suburbs of Rome in which theft, card-sharping, prostitution and murder are commonplace. These were subjects Pasolini returned to in later works such as *Una vita violenta* and in many of his films, which were often controversial.

Rome is a continual source of inspiration for foreign writers. It is becoming increasingly fashionable for many contemporary novelists to use ancient and modern Rome as a backdrop for their stories.

Cinema

Rome has always played a major role in Italian cinema, both as a subject and as a production centre. Born in Torino in 1904, the Italian film industry originally made an impression with silent spectaculars. By 1930 it was virtually bankrupt and Mussolini began moves to nationalise the industry. These culminated in 1940, when Rome's version of Hollywood, Cinecittà, was ceded to the state. Set up in 1937, this huge complex was fitted out with the latest in film equipment. Half the nation's production took place here – 85 pictures in 1940 alone – and in its glory days it was labelled 'Hollywood on the Tiber'.

Abandoned later in the war, Cinecitta only went timidly back into action in 1948, although its absence had not bothered the early neo-realist directors. In 1950 an American team arrived to make *Quo Vadis?*, and for the rest of the 1950s film-makers from Italy and abroad moved in to use the site's huge lots.

Major American productions included William Wyler's *Ben Hur* (1959) with Charlton Heston, Stanley Kubrick's *Spartacus* (1960) with Kirk Douglas, and Joseph Mankiewicz's *Cleopatra* (1963) with Elizabeth Taylor and Richard Burton. By the early 1960s, however, this symbol of Italian cinema had again begun to wane as location shooting became more common. The main moneymakers for the Italian film industry in the 1960s and 70s were Sergio Leone's 'spaghetti westerns' shot near Viterbo.

In the three years following the close of hostilities in Europe, Roberto Rossellini (1906-77) produced a trio of neo-realist masterpieces. The first and most famous of these was *Roma Città Aperta* (Rome Open City), made in 1945, set in German-occupied Rome and starring Anna Magnani. It was filmed in the working-class district of Via Prenestina east of the city centre. For many cinophiles the film marks the true beginning of Neo-Realism, uniting a simplicity and sincerity peculiar to Italian film-making; often heart-rending without ever descending into the bathos to which so many Hollywood products fall victim.

Vittorio de Sica (1901-74) kept the neo-realist ball rolling in 1948 with another classic set in Rome, *Ladri di Biciclette* (Bicycle Thieves), the story of a man's frustrated fight to earn a crust and keep his family afloat. It was filmed in the outskirts of the city where the ugly purpose built suburbs meet the countryside.

Federico Fellini (1920-94) took the creative baton from the masters of neo-realism and carried it into the following decades. Some of his best known films were set in Rome, his adopted home (he lived for many years in Via Margutta). His disquieting style demands more of audiences, abandoning realistic shots for pointed images at once laden with humour, pathos and double-meaning – all cleverly capturing not only the Rome of the day, but the human foibles of his protagonists. Fellini's greatest international hit was *La Dolce Vita* (1968), starring Marcello Mastroianni and Anita Ekberg, with memorable scenes set in the Fontana di Trevi (for which a Cinecittà set was actually used) and Via Veneto. *Roma* (1972) could almost be described as a surreal and poetic documentary about Rome. It satirised the Church and used relatively unpicturesque parts of Rome as a backdrop, including the Grand Raccordo Annulare, the city's motorway ring road.

Pier Paolo Pasolini (1922-75) used his local neighbourhood, Pietralata, in his films and books. Homosexual, Catholic, and Marxist, Pasolini's films reflect his ideological and sexual tendencies and are a unique portrayal of Rome's urban wasteland. In his earlier work he was preoccupied with the condition of the subproletariat in films like *Accattone* (1961), set in the forgotten suburbs of Rome, and *Teorema* (1968). Later he became obsessed with human decay and death as reflected in *Il Decamerone*, *I Racconti di Canterbury* and *Il Fiore delle Mille e Una Notte*. Pasolini was murdered in mysterious circumstances in 1975.

Nanni Moretti (1953-), who first came to the silver screen in the late 1970s, has proved to be a highly individualistic actor-director. *Caro Diario* (Dear Diary), his whimsical, self-indulgent, autobiographical three-part film won the prize for best director at Cannes in 1994. A major part of the film involved a camera recording Moretti driving through the streets of Rome on a Vespa.

A wonderful homage to film-making is *Nuovo Cinema Paradiso* (1988), by Giuseppe Tornatore (1956-). Tornatore was back in 1995 with *L'Uomo delle Stelle* (The Starmaker), the story of a fraud touring around Sicilia and peddling hopes of a screen career in Cinecittà.

According to recent press reports, the glory days of Italian cinema are back and the future for Cinecittà looks rosy with increased private investment in state-of-the-art digital technology and special effects equipment. There has also been a revival of interest in ancient Rome by leading Hollywood directors. At the time of writing, Steven Speilberg was planning to shoot a film set in pre-Republican Rome about the last Etruscan king, Tarquin the Proud.

RELIGION

Some 85% of Italians professed to be Catholic. Of the remaining 15%, there were about 500,000 evangelical Protestants, about 140,000 Jehovah's Witnesses, and other, small groups, including a Jewish community in Rome, which has re-established itself after virtually being anhiliated by the Nazis (see the 'Anti-Semitism in Rome' boxed text in the Things to See & Do chapter). There are also communities of orange-clad followers of the Bhagwan Rajneesh, known in Italy as the *arancioni*.

The big surprise on this front is the growth of the Muslim population, currently estimated at 700,000, and thus the second largest religious community in Italy after the Catholics. A fitting symbol fordemographic shift in the heart of Christendom was the inauguration in 1995 of the first mosque in Rome.

Although the fabric of life is profoundly influenced by the presence of the Church, surprisingly few Italian Catholics practise their religion. Church attendance is low – an average of only 25% attend Mass regularly – and many children are never baptised. But a child's first communion remains a popular event, the majority of Italian couples prefer to be married in a church, and religious festivals never fail to attract a large turnout. Most Italians are also generally familiar with saints' feast days and legends, and they keenly follow the activities of the pope.

A Pilgrim's Progress

In 2000, an estimated 20 to 30 million Roman Catholic pilgrims are expected to descend on Rome. It is an extremely important event for devout Catholics, as Holy Years (or Jubilees) are celebrated only every 25 years and this one coincides with the end of one millennium and the beginning of the next.

The practice of making pilgrimages began with the early Church, when believers started to visit the holy lands of Judaea and Rome. Jubilee years themselves were adapted from a Jewish custom based on instructions in *Leviticus*.

Pope Boniface VIII instituted the first Christian Jubilee in 1300, when pilgrims visited the major religious sites in Rome. For their efforts the pilgrims were granted indulgences, which would effectively annul the time in purgatory due for sins committed during their lifetimes.

Pilgrims traditionally visited seven Roman churches: the four patriarchal basilicas (San Pietro, Santa Maria Maggiore, San Giovanni in Laterano and San Paolo Fuori le Mura), and three minor ones (San Lorenzo Fuori le Mura, Santa Croce in Gerusalemme and San Sebastiano). They also visited the catacombs, the shrines of Christian martyrs and the places where important Christian relics were kept. Pilgrims also had to attend confession and participate in a communion Mass.

In the Middle Ages indulgences were sold, which was one of Martin Luther's objections; today the Church is a little stricter about what constitutes a plenary (full) indulgence for all sins. According to a Papal Bull issued at end of 1998, pilgrims to Rome in 2000 will be granted a plenary indulgence for the following: confession of sins and attendance at communion; saying prayers for the Pope; visiting the basilicas in Rome, and cathedrals in the Holy Land and other dioceses; doing charitable work; visiting the ill and incarcerated; helping abandoned children, the elderly and immigrants; doing volunteer work; giving up smoking and not drinking alcohol for one day; fasting or other acts of penance.

However, 20 million pilgrims to be fed, housed and entertained, in addition to Rome's annual millions of regular tourists, is a significant number. To reduce the strain on resources, the official travel agency for the Jubilee is encouraging pilgrims to spend the minimum amount of time possible in the city. Accommodation options are being suggested outside Rome, including Italy's least holy town, the seaside party resort of Rimini which has a over 1200 hotels.

The Jubilee's official website is: www.Jubil2000.org, which includes information on the computerised 'Pilgrim Card' designed to facilitate travel and accommodation details.

The agency has even published a book warning of disasters that befell past pilgrims. In the Jubilee of 1300, for instance, Ponte Sant'Angelo collapsed because of overcrowding and many pilgrims perished. In the 1450 Jubilee there were food shortages and 172 pilgrims were killed by stampeding crowds. In 1750 Leonardo da Porto Maurizio, a famed preacher (later beatified) was almost trampled to death in the Colosseo, where he had set up the Stations of the Cross. Only time will tell what happens in 2000.

Facts for the Visitor

WHEN TO GO

Rome's mild climate makes it visitable year-round, but you will be likely to strike unpleasantly hot weather in July and August, and briskly cold weather from December to February when icy winds blow in from northern Europe. Spring and autumn are without doubt the best times to visit, with generally sunny skies and mild temperatures, although late autumn (November) can be rainy (see Climate in the Facts about Rome chapter).

The main tourist season starts at Easter and runs until October, building to peak periods in spring and autumn, when the tour buses pour in and tourists are herded around like cattle at the main sights. In July and August it is almost heartbreaking to observe the suffering of heat-exhausted travellers as they drag screaming, dehydrated kids around the historic centre. Temperatures can soar to the high 30°s Celsius and humidity is often close to 100% in Rome during those months, but there are some advantages: Romans desert the city for the beaches and mountains, which means very light traffic and a consequent reduction in air pollution, as well as a much less crowded city centre. In summer there are also numerous outdoor festivals and concerts (see Public Holidays & Special Events and Entertainment). If you must visit in summer, try hitting the sights early, take a long lunch and a nap and then head out again around 6 pm to take advantage of the cooler evening.

While November is noted for heavy rain and December to February can bring icy weather, in recent years there has been unseasonably warm weather right up to Christmas. In any case, Rome is hardly Moscow! In fact, the city is less crowded with tourists and there are some fun events around Christmas time, including the traditional Christmas market held in Piazza Navona.

ORIENTATION

Rome is a vast city, but the historic centre is relatively small, defined by the twisting Tevere (Tiber) river to the west, the sprawling Villa Borghese park to the north, the Foro Romano (Roman Forum) and Palatino (Palatine Hill) to the south and the central railway station, Stazione Termini, to the east. Most of the major sights are within a reasonable distance of the railway station. It is, for instance, possible to walk from the Colosseo, through the Foro Romano and the Palatino, up to Piazza di Spagna and across to the Vatican in one day, although such a crowded itinerary is hardly recommended even for the most dedicated tourist.

One of the great pleasures of being in Rome is wandering through the many beautiful *piazzas*, stopping now and again for a caffè and *pasta* (pastry). Make sure you use a map. While it can be enjoyable to get off the beaten track in Rome, it can also be very frustrating and time-consuming.

Most new arrivals in Rome will end up at Stazione Termini, the terminus for all international and national trains. The station is commonly referred to as Termini. The main city bus station is in Piazza dei Cinquecento, directly in front of the station. Many Intercity buses depart from and arrive at Piazzale Tiburtina, in front of Stazione Tiburtina, accessible from Termini on the Metropolitana Linea B. Buses serving towns in the region of Lazio depart from various points throughout the city, usually corresponding to stops on the subway lines. See Getting There & Away, as well as Excursions for details.

The main airport is Leonardo da Vinci (commonly referred to as Fiumicino airport) at Fiumicino – about half an hour by the special airport-Termini train, or 45 minutes to one hour by car from the city centre. A second airport, Ciampino, south of the city on the Via Appia Nuova, serves most charter flights to Rome. It is not as easily accessible as Fiumicino (see Getting Around) from the city centre.

If you're arriving in Rome by car, invest in a good road map of the city beforehand so as to have an idea of the various routes into the city centre. Rome is encircled by a ring road, called the Grande Raccordo Anulare (GRA), which is connected to the A1 autostrada (the main north-south route in Italy, extending from Milan to Reggio di Calabria. The main access routes from the GRA into the city centre of Rome include Via Salaria from the north, Via Aurelia from the north-west and Via Cristoforo Colombo from the south.

Normal traffic is not permitted into the city centre, but tourists are allowed to drive to their hotels (you will need a booking and your hotel will give you a special pass.) Without a pass your car could be towed away. There is unsupervised parking available along the Lungotevere (beside the Tevere river) and on the periphery of the historic centre at L2000 per hour (you will need coins to obtain parking tickets from the vending machines placed every 100m or so along the road). The main car park is at the Villa Borghese. (See the Getting Around section.)

The majority of cheap hotels and *pensioni* are concentrated around Stazione Termini, but if you are prepared to go the extra distance, it is not much more expensive and definitely more enjoyable to stay closer to the city centre. The area around the train station, particularly to the west, is seedy, but the sheer number of hotels makes it the most popular area for budget travellers and tour groups.

MAPS

Invest L6000 in the street map and bus guide simply entitled *Roma*, which is published by Editrice Lozzi in Rome; it is available at any newspaper stand in Termini. It lists all streets, with map references, as well as all bus routes. There is also an excellent free map, called *Roma Centro*, which details the city's public transport routes, including buses, trams and the subway. It also has a reasonable map of the city centre. Information is in English and Italian. Pick it up at the tourist office, or at the Atac booth in Piazza dei Cinquecento in front of Stazione Termini.

City maps are available at good bookshops (like Feltrinelli) or newspaper stands. Excellent city plans and maps are published by the Istituto Geografico de Agostini, the Touring Club Italiano and Michelin. Another option is to pick up a map before coming to Rome. One excellent map, available outside of Italy is called *Streetwise Rome*. This is a plastic covered, fold-out map, perfect for sightseeing. It costs $5.95 in the US, $9.99 in Australia and £3.99 in the UK.

TOURIST OFFICES
Local Tourist Offices

As with most things in Rome in the run up to the Jubilee Year in 2000, the city's tourist information service, the APT, was in a state of flux at the time of writing. There were plans for new information offices and new services, such as web sites and email addresses, however, no definite information was available at the time of writing.

There is an information office in the central hall at Stazione Termini, which is open daily from 8.15 am to 7.15 pm (Map 6, ☎ 06 487 12 70). The main APT office (Map 6, ☎ 06 48 89 92 55) is at Via Parigi 5 and is open Monday to Saturday from 8.15 am to 7.15 pm. Walk north-west from Stazione Termini through Piazza dei Cinquecento and Piazza della Repubblica; Via Parigi runs to the right from the top of the piazza, about a five minute walk from the station. The office has information on accommodation, museums, festivals and concert seasons, as well as details on local and intercity transport. Brochures and, sometimes, maps and hotel lists for other Italian cities are available at this office. There is a branch office (☎ 06 65 95 44 71) in the arrivals hall at Fiumicino airport.

A good alternative is Enjoy Rome (Map 6, ☎ 06 445 18 43; fax 06 445 07 34; info@enjoy rome.it), Via Varese 39, which is a privately-run tourist office a few minutes walk north-east of the train station brimming with information about the city and its surrounds. It offers a free hotel reservation service and can also organise alternative accommodation, such as rental apartments. It can also organise accommodation in some other parts of Italy. Enjoy Rome organises guided walking tours in Rome (see Organised Tours in the Getting Around chapter), as well as in Firenze and Venezia. Information about all of these services is available on the web at www.enjoyrome.it.

There's always someone who speaks English in the office and staff are very keen to help. The office is open Monday to Friday from 8.30 am to 2 pm and 3.30 to 6.30 pm and on Saturday from 8.30 am to 2 pm. Enjoy Rome publishes a very useful city guide called *Enjoy Rome*, with lots of practical information.

Tourist information booths can also be found at Largo Corrado Ricci, opposite the entrance to the Foro Romano (Map 6); Largo Goldoni, on Via del Corso at the end of Via Condotti (Map 5); and next to the Palazzo del Esposizione in Via Nazionale (Map 6). There is also a booth in Trastevere, in Piazza Sonnino (Map 7), and in il Vaticano (Map 5)

Tourist Offices Abroad

Italy has a national tourist board, with offices throughout the world. Known in Italy as ENIT and overseas as the Italian State Tourist Office, it has a world wide web site (www.enit.it) with updated addresses, phone numbers and email addresses for its offices, as well as details on museum opening hours and some information about places to visit in Italy. The Rome office of ENIT is at Via Marghera 2 (Map 6; ☎ 06 49 711; fax 06 44 63 379; email sedecentrale .enit@interbusiness.it).

Information on Rome and Italy is available from the Italian State Tourist Office in the following countries:

Australia
    Alitalia, Orient Overseas Building, Suite 202, 32 Bridge St, Sydney 2000 (☎ 02-9247 1308)
Canada
    1, Place Ville Marie, Suite 1914, Montreal, Quebec H3B 3M9 (☎ 514-866 7667; initaly@ican.net)

Denmark
    Gammel Mont 12, 4, TV, Copenhagen DK 1177 (☎ 45-33 14 03 60; italien@nethotel.dk; www.sima.dk/italien)
France
    23 Rue de La Paix, Paris 75002 (☎ 1-42 66 03 96; 106616.131@compuserve.com)
Germany
    Goethestraße, 20, München 80336 (☎ 89-531 317)
    Karl Liebknecht Str., 34, Berlin D10178 (☎ 30-247 83 97; Enit-berlin@t-online.de)
    Kaiserstrasse, 65, Frankfurt 60329 (☎ 69-259 332; Enit.ffm@t-online.de)
Japan
    Minami Aoyama Minat5o-Ku, Tokyo 107-2-7-14 (☎ 813-408 1524; enittky@cd.mbn .or.jp)
Netherlands
    Stadhouderskade, 2, Amsterdam 1054 ES (☎ 020-616 66 84)
Spain
    Gran Via, 84, Edificio Espagna, Madrid 28013 (☎ 91-559 97 50)
UK
    1 Princess St, London W1R 8AY (☎ 0171-408 1254; Enitlond@globalnet.co.uk)
USA
    630 Fifth Avenue, Suite 1565, New York, NY 10111 (☎ 212-245 4822; enitny@ bway.net)
    12400 Wilshire Blvd, Suite 550, Los Angeles CA 90025 (☎ 310-82 02977)
    401 North Michigan Ave, Suite 3030, Chicago, IL 60611 (☎ 312-644 0990)

CIT (Compagnia Italiana di Turismo), is an international network of travel agencies which promotes tourism in Italy. It has offices throughout the world which can provide extensive information on travelling in Italy and will organise tours, as well as book individual hotels. CIT can also make train bookings, including sector bookings (such as Rome-Napoli), and sells Eurail passes and discount passes for train travel in Italy. CIT offices include:

Australia
    263 Clarence St, Sydney 2000 (☎ 02-9267 1255; fax 02-9261 4664; fkernot@cittravel.com.au)
    Level 4, 227 Collins St, Melbourne 3000 (☎ 03-9650 5510; fax 03-9654 2490; www.cit travel.com.au)

Canada
    1450 City Councillors St, Suite 750, Montreal, Quebec H3A 2E6 (☎ 514-845 4939; fax 514-845 9137; citmil@videotron.ca)
    80 Tiverton Court, Suite 401, Markham, Ontario L3R 0G4 (☎ 905-415 1060; fax 905-415 1063; cittours@interlog.com)

France
    3 Boulevard des Capucines, Paris 75002 (☎ 01-44 51 39 51; fax 01-445 13 967)

Germany
    Geibelstrasse 39, Düsseldorf D-40235 (☎ 0211-690030; fax 211-6900319)

UK
    Marco Polo House, 3-5 Lansdowne Rd, Croydon, Surrey CR9 1LL (☎ 0181-686 0677; 0181-686 0328; ciao@citalia.co.uk; www.citalia.co.uk)

USA
    15, West 44th St, 10th floor, New York, NY 10036 (☎ 212-730 2121; fax 212-730 4544; citnewyork@msn.com)
    6033 West Century Blvd, Suite 980, Los Angeles, CA 90045 (☎ 310-338 8615; fax 310-670 4269; citlax@email.msm.com; www.cit-tours.com)

The Italian cultural institutes based in major cities throughout the world have information on opportunities to study in Rome and other cities throughout Italy.

Other Information

Magazines and booklets which provide a weekly guide to what's on in Rome, as well as general, up-to-date information about the city include: (in English) *Wanted in Rome*, available at selected newsstands in the city centre and at all English-language bookshops, and *Enjoy Rome*, available at the Enjoy Rome information office. If you speak Italian, pick up a copy of *Roma C'è*. The Italian daily newspaper, *La Repubblica*, publishes useful phone numbers and information on entry fees and opening hours of Rome's major monuments. Each Thursday, the newspaper comes with *Trovaroma*, a good source of information on what's happening in the city.

DOCUMENTS
Passport

Citizens of the 15 European Union member states can travel to Italy with their national identity cards alone, and now that Italy is a member of the Schengen Area, EU citizens can enter the country without passport controls. People from countries that do not issue ID cards, such as the UK, must carry a valid passport. All non-EU nationals must have a full valid passport.

If you've had the passport for a while, check that the expiry date is at least some months off, otherwise you may not be granted a visa (if you need one). If you travel a lot, keep an eye on the number of pages you have left in the passport. US consulates will generally insert extra pages into your passport if you need them, but others tend to require you to apply for a new passport. If your passport is nearly full when you are preparing to leave home, do yourself a favour and get a new one before you leave.

Visas

EU citizens require only a passport or ID card to stay in Italy for as long as they like. Citizens of many other countries, including the US, Canada, Australia, New Zealand, Japan and South Africa, do not need a visa if entering as tourists for up to three months. Since passports are often not stamped on entry, that three-month rule can generally be interpreted flexibly, since no-one can prove how long you have been in the country.

The only time you are likely to have your passport stamped is when you arrive by air – although even at Rome's airport there's a good chance they won't stamp it. If your passport has been stamped and you wish to stay longer, you can play safe by leaving the country and re-entering – in that case you will have to make sure a new entry stamp goes into the passport, as it's likely you won't be stamped out either.

If you are entering Italy for any reason other than tourism (for instance, study) or if you plan to remain in the country for an extended period, you should insist on having the entry stamp. Without it you could encounter problems when trying to obtain a *permesso di soggiorno* – in effect, permission to remain in the country for a nominated period – which is essential for everything from enrolling at a language school to applying for residency in Italy (see under Permesso di Soggiorno).

EU Citizens EU citizens do not require any permits to live or work in Italy. They are, however, required to register with a *questura* (police station) if they take up residence and obtain a permesso di soggiorno (see later in this section). A loophole in Italy's new immigration laws, introduced in 1998, has meant that non-EU foreigners are favoured over EU citizens in being able to obtain an unlimited permit to remain in Italy. This permit, known as a *carta di soggiorno*, is issued if non-EU foreigners can satisfy certain conditions and prove that they have been in the country for more than five years.

However, EU citizens are still required to present themselves every five years to have their permits renewed by the police. The Italian government was to review the law regarding EU citizens sometime in 1999.

Study Visas Non-EU citizens who want to study at a university or language school in Italy must have a study visa. These visas can be obtained from your nearest Italian embassy or consulate. It should be noted that you will normally require confirmation of your enrolment, payment of fees and proof of adequate funds to support yourself before a visa is issued. The visa will only be the period of the enrolment. This type of visa is renewable within Italy but, again, only with confirmation of ongoing enrolment and proof that you are able to support yourself – bank statements are preferred.

Travel Insurance

Don't, as they say, leave home without it. It will cover you for medical expenses, luggage theft or loss, and for cancellation of and delays in your travel arrangements. Cover depends on your insurance and type of ticket, so ask both your insurer and ticket-issuing agency to explain where you stand. Ticket loss is also covered by travel insurance, but keep a separate record of your ticket details (see the Photocopies section later). Buy travel insurance as early as possible. If you buy it the week before you fly or hop on the bus, you may find, for example, that you are not covered for delays to your trip caused by strikes or other industrial action.

Travel insurance papers, and the international medical aid numbers that generally accompany them, are valuable documents, so treat them like air tickets and passports. Keep the details (photocopies or handwritten) in a separate part of your luggage.

Paying for your ticket with a credit card often provides limited travel accident insurance, and you may be able to reclaim the payment if the operator doesn't deliver. Ask your credit card company what it will cover.

Driving Licence & Permits

If you plan to drive while in Rome, you will need to carry your driving licence. Either an international driving licence or a translation of your licence (available from Italian State Tourist Offices – see earlier in this chapter) might be useful, but is not necessary. EU citizens and foreigners who have held residency in Italy for one year or more are required to have an Italian licence. If you are driving your own car, you must carry an International Insurance Certificate, known as a Green Card, and the car's registration papers.

Hostel Card

A valid HI hostelling card is required in all associated youth hostels (Associazione Italiana Alberghi per la Gioventù, AIG) in Italy. You can get this in your home country or at the youth hostel in Rome. In the latter case you apply for the card and must collect six stamps in the card at L5000 each. You pay for a stamp on each of the first six nights you spend in the hostel. With six stamps you are considered a full international member.

Student & Youth Cards

An ISIC (International Student Identity Card) or similar card will get you discounted entry prices into some museums and other sights and is an asset for other purposes. It can help for cheap flights out of Italy and can also come in handy for such things as cinema and theatre and other travel discounts.

Similar cards are available to teachers (ITIC). They are good for various discounts and carry a travel insurance component.

If you're aged under 26 but not a student you can apply for a FIYTO (Federation of International Youth Travel Organisations) card or Euro 26 card (known in the UK as the Under 26 Card), which gives much the same discounts as ISIC.

These student cards are issued by student unions, hostelling organisations and some youth travel agencies (like Campus Travel in the UK). They don't always automatically entitle you to discounts, but you won't find out until you flash the card.

In Rome, the office of the Centro Turistico Studentesco e Giovanile (CTS) will issue ISIC, ITIC and Euro 26 cards.

Seniors' Cards

EU citizens aged over 65 are often entitled to discount or free entry to museums and monuments. The Italian railways also offer discounts train fares (see Getting Around).

Other Documents

Permesso di Soggiorno Visitors are technically obliged to report to a questura if they plan to stay at the same address for more than one week, to receive a permesso di soggiorno (permission to remain in the country). Tourists who are staying in hotels are not required to do this, because hotel owners are required to register all guests with the police.

A permesso di soggiorno only becomes a necessity if you plan to study, work (legally) or live in Italy. Obtaining one is never a pleasant experience. It involves enduring long queues and the frustration of arriving at the counter (after a two hour wait) to find that you don't have all the necessary documents.

The exact requirements, such as documents and official stamps (marche da bollo), can change from year to year. In general, you will need: a valid passport, containing a visa stamp indicating your date of entry into Italy; a special visa issued in your own country if you are planning to study; four passport-style photographs; and proof of your ability to support yourself financially.

It is best to go to the questura (police headquarters) to obtain precise information on what is required. Sometimes there is a list posted, otherwise you will need to join a queue at the information counter.

The main Rome questura, in Via Genova (Map 6), is notorious for delays and best avoided if possible. This problem has been solved by decentralisation: in Rome it is now possible to apply at the police station closest to where you are staying.

Work Permits Non-EU citizens wishing to work in Italy will need to obtain a permesso di lavoro (work permit). If you intend to work for an Italian company and will be paid in lire, the company must organise the permesso and forward it to the Italian consulate in your country – only then will you be issued an appropriate visa.

If non-EU citizens intend to work for a non-Italian company or will be paid in foreign currency, or wish to go freelance, they must organise the visa and permesso in their country of residence through an Italian consulate. This process can take many months, so look into it early.

In any case it's advisable to seek detailed information from an Italian embassy or consulate on the exact requirements before attempting to organise a legitimate job in Italy. Many foreigners, however, don't bother with such formalities, preferring to work 'black' in areas such as teaching English, bar work and seasonal jobs. See the section on Work later in this chapter

Photocopies

Make photocopies of all important documents, especially your passport. This will help speed replacement if they are lost or stolen. Other documents to photocopy might include your airline ticket and credit cards. Also record the serial numbers of your travellers cheques (cross them off as you cash them).

All this material should be kept separate from the documents concerned, along with a small amount of emergency cash. Leave extra copies with someone reliable at home. If your passport is stolen or lost, notify the police and obtain a statement, and then contact your embassy or consulate as soon as possible.

EMBASSIES & CONSULATES
Italian Embassies & Consulates Abroad

The following is a selection of Italian diplomatic missions abroad. Bear in mind that Italy maintains consulates in additional cities in many of the countries listed below:

Albania
  Ruga Deshmoret e 4 Shkurtit, Tirana (☎ 42-34045; fax 64343; ambittia@icc.al.eu.org)
Algeria
  18 Rue Ouidir Amellal, El Biar (☎ 2132-922 330, 922 550; fax 925 986; ambitalgeri @ist.cerist.dz)
Australia
  Embassy: 12, Grey Street Deakin ACT 2600 (☎ 02-6273 3333; fax 6273 4223; ambital2 @dynamite.com.au; www.netinfo.com.au/ italembassy
  Consulate: Level 43, The Gateway, 1 Macquarie Place, NSW 2000 (☎ 02-9392 7900; fax 9252 4830; itconsyd@armadillo.com.au)
Austria
  Metternichgasse, 13, Vienna 1030 (☎ 01-712 5121, fax 7139719, ambitalviepress@via.at)
Bosnia-Hercegovina
  Ulica Cekalusa, 39, 71000, Sarajevo (☎ 771-441 867, 533 765 533 484; fax 659 368; ambsara@bih.net.ba)
Canada
  Embassy: 21st floor, 275 Slater St, Ottawa, Ontario KIP 5H9 (☎ 613-232 2401, fax 613-233 1484, ambital@trytel.com; www.try tel.com /~italy)
  Consulate: 1200 Burrard Street, Suite 705, Vancouver BC V6Z 2C7 (☎ 604-684 5575; fax 685 4263)
Croatia
  Meduliceva Ulica 22, Zagreb 41000 (☎ 051-48 46 386; fax 051-48 46 384; veleposlanstvoital ije@zg.tel.hr)

France
  7 rue de Varenne, Paris 75007 (☎ 1-49 54 03 00, fax 45 49 35 81; stampa@dial.oleane.com)
Germany
  Karl Finkelnburgstrasse 49-51, Bonn 53173 (☎ 0228-822 0; fax 0228-822 155; italia.ambasciata.bonn@t-online.de; www.iei.pi.cnr.it/ bonn/ambasciata/italia)
Greece
  Odos Sekeri 2, Athens 10674 (☎ 01-361 7260; fax 01-361 7330;ambaten@hol.gr)
Ireland
  63 Northumberland Road, Dublin (☎ 01-660 1744; fax 366 82759; italianembassy@tinet.ie; homepage.tinet.ie/~italianembassy)
Israel
  4 Weizman Street Asia House, Tel Aviv (☎ 3-696 4223; fax 691 8428; italemb@netvision .net.il; www.italian-embassy-israel.org)
Japan
  Mita 2-chome Minato Ku 5/4, Tokyo 108-8302 (☎ 03-34 53 52 91; fax 03-34 56 23 19; itemb tky@gol.com, embittky@gol.com; SunSite .sut.ac.jp/embitaly)
Malta
  5 Vilhena Street Floriana, Valletta 5 (☎ 356-233 157, 238 147; fax 235 339, 239 217; ambitalia@vol.net.mt)
Netherlands
  Alexanderstraat, 12, The Hague 2514 JL (☎ 070-346 9249; fax 070-361 4932; italemb @worldonline.nl)
New Zealand
  34 Grant Rd, Thorndon, Wellington (☎ 04-473 53 39; fax 04-472 72 55; ambwell@xtra .co.nz)
Slovenia
  Embassy: Snezniska Ulica 8, Ljubljana 61000 (☎ 061-126 21 94; fax 061-125 33 02)
Spain
  Calle Lagasca 98, Madrid 28006 (☎ 01-577 6529; fax 01-575 7776;ambital.sp@nauta.es; www.area.fi.cnr.it/spagna/ambit.htm)
Switzerland
  Elfenstrasse 14, Bern 3006 (☎ 031-352 41 51, fax 031-351 1026; ambitaal.bema@spectra web.ch; ambital.berna@spectraweb.ch)
Tunisia
  3 Rue de Russie, Tunis (☎ 01-32 18 11, fax 01-35 41 55, Emb-Italy-tun@emb-italy.intl.tn)
UK
  14 Three Kings Yard, London (☎ 0171-312 2209; fax 0171-312 2230;emblondon@emb italy.org.uk; www.embitaly.org.uk)
  Consulate: 32 Melville Street, Edinburgh EH3 7H (☎ 0431-226 3631, 220 3695; fax 226 6260; consedimb@consedimb.demon.co.uk

USA
Embassy: 1601 Fuller St, NW Washington DC 20009 (☎ 202-328 5500; fax 202-328 5593; itapress@ix.netcom.com; www.italyemb.org)
Consulates: 690 Park Ave, New York 10021/5044 (☎ 212-737 9100; fax 212-249 4945; ItalConsNY@aol.com; www.italconsul nyc.org)
Suite 300,12400 Wilshire Blvd, West Los Angeles 90025 (☎ 213-820 06 22;fax 213-820 0727; cglos@aol.com; www.conlang.com)
Yugoslavia
Bircaninova Ulica 11, Belgrade (☎ 938111-659 722, 659 743; fax 324 9413; italbelg@eunet.yu)

Foreign Embassies & Consulates in Rome

Albania
Embassy: Via Asmara 3 (☎ 06 86 21 03 80)
Consulate: Via Asmara 5 (☎ 06 86 20 58 56)
Australia
Via Alessandria 215 (Map 4, ☎ 06 85 27 21)
Austria
Embassy: Via Pergolesi 3 (☎ 06 844 01 41)
Consulate: Viale Liegi 32 (Map 4, ☎ 06 855 29 66)
Bosnia & Hercegovinia
Embassy: Via Bazzoni 3 (Map 3, ☎ 06 372 85 48).
Canada
Embassy: Via G B de Rossi 27 (Map 4, ☎ 06 44 59 81)
Consulate: Via Zara 30 (Map 4, ☎ 06 44 59 81)
Croatia
Via Luigi Bodio 74/76 (☎ 06 36 30 73 00)
France
Embassy: Piazza Farnese (Map: Around Piazza Navona, ☎ 06 68 60 11)
Visas: Via Giulia 251 (Map: Around Piazza Navona, ☎ 06 68 80 21 52)
Germany
Via San Martino della Battaglia 4 (Map 6, ☎ 06 492 131)
Greece
Embassy: Via Mercadante 36 (Map 4, ☎ 06 855 85 89)
Consulate: Via Stoppani 10 (Map 4, ☎ 06 808 20 30)
Ireland
Piazza Campitelli 3 (Map: Around Piazza Navona, ☎ 06 697 91 21)
Israel
Via Michele Mercati 14 (Map 4, ☎ 06 322 15 42)
Japan
Via Sella 60 (Map 6, ☎ 06 48 79 91)

Malta
Lungotevere Marzio 12 (☎ 06 687 99 90)
Netherlands
Via Michele Mercati 8 (☎ 06 322 11 41)
New Zealand
Via Zara 28 (Map 4, ☎ 06 441 71 71)
Slovenia
Via L Pisano 10 (Map 4, ☎ 06 808 10 75)
Spain
Embassy: Largo Fontanella Borghese 19 (Map 5, ☎ 06 68 32 168)
Consulate: Via Campo Marzio 34 (Map 5, ☎ 06 687 14 01)
Switzerland
Embassy: Via Barnarba Oriani 61 (Map 4, ☎ 06 80 95 71)
Consulate: Largo Elvezia 15 (Map 4, ☎ 06 808 83 61)
Tunisia
Embassy: Via Asmara 5-7 (☎ 06 860 30 60)
Consulate: Via Egadi 13 (☎ 06 87 18 80 06)
UK
Via XX Settembre 80a (Map 6, ☎ 06 482 54 41)
USA
Via Vittorio Veneto 119a-121 (Map 6, ☎ 06 467 41;www.usis.it)

For other diplomatic missions in Rome, look under 'Ambasciate' or 'Consolati' in the telephone book. The tourist offices will also generally have a list.

CUSTOMS

People from outside Europe can import, without paying duty, two stills cameras and 10 rolls of film; a movie or TV camera with 10 cartridges of film; a portable tape recorder and 'a reasonable amount' of tapes; a CD player; a pair of binoculars; sports equipment, including skis; one bicycle or motorcycle (not exceeding 50cc); one portable radio and one portable TV set (both may be subject to the payment of a licence fee) and personal jewellery. Limits on duty free imports include: up to 200 cigarettes; 50 cigars; 2L of wine and 1L of liquor.

Visitors who are residents of a European country and who enter from an EU country can import a maximum of 300 cigarettes, one bottle of wine and half a bottle of liquor. There is no limit on the amount of lire you can import.

MONEY

The best thing to do is to take a combination of travellers cheques and credit cards.

Currency

From January 1, 2002, Italy will have a new currency. It is one of 11 EU countries in the first intake for European Monetary Union (EMU) – basically the introduction of a single currency, the *euro*. The euro became currency in the financial sense (it can be traded on international exchanges) from January 1999. The actual notes and coins will be phased in over the first six months of the year 2002.

Italy's present currency is the lira (plural: lire). The smallest note is L1000. Other denominations in notes are L2000, L5000, L10,000, L50,000, L100,000 and L500,000. Coin denominations are L50, L100, L200, L500 and L1000. Remember that like other Continental Europeans, Italians indicate decimals with commas and thousands with points.

Exchange Rates

country	unit		lira
Australia	A$1	=	L1132.51
Canada	C$1	=	L1178.12
euro	€1	=	L1936.27
France	1FF	=	L295.18
Germany	DM1	=	L990.00
Japan	¥100	=	L1499.10
New Zealand	NZ$1	=	L958.10
United Kingdom	UK£1	=	L2908.23
USA	US$1	=	L1777.70

Exchanging Money

You can change money in banks, at the post office or in a *cambio* (exchange office). Banks are generally the most reliable and tend to offer the best rates. However, you should look around and ask about commissions. These can fluctuate considerably and a lot depends on whether you are changing cash or cheques.

While the post office charges a flat rate of L1000 per cash transaction, banks charge L2500 or even more. Travellers cheques attract higher fees. Some banks charge L1000 *per cheque* with a L3000 minimum, while the post office charges a maximum L5000 per transaction. Other banks will have different arrangements again, and in all cases you should compare the exchange rates too. Exchange booths often advertise 'no commission', but the rate of exchange can often be inferior to that in the banks.

Balanced against the desire to save on such fees by making occasional large transactions should be a healthy fear of pickpockets – you don't want to be robbed the day you have exchanged a huge hunk of money to last you weeks!

Cash There is little advantage in bringing more than a small amount of foreign cash with you. True, exchange commissions are often lower than for travellers cheques, but the danger of losing the lot far outweighs such petty gains.

It is worth bringing some lire with you into the country (especially if you're arriving by air) to avoid the hassles of changing money on arrival.

Travellers Cheques These are a safe way to carry money and are easily cashed at banks and exchange offices in Rome and throughout Italy. Always keep the bank receipt listing the cheque numbers separate from the cheques and keep a list of the numbers of those you have already cashed – this will reduce problems in the event of loss or theft. Check the conditions applying to such circumstances before buying the cheques.

If you buy your travellers cheques in lire (which you should only do if your trip is to be restricted to Italy alone), there should be no commission charge when cashing them. Most hard currencies are widely accepted, although you may have occasional trouble with the New Zealand dollar. Buying cheques in a third currency (such as US dollars if you are not coming from the USA), means you pay commission when you buy the cheques and again when cashing them in Italy. Get most of the

Introducing the Euro

On 1 January 1999 a new currency, the euro, was introduced in Europe. It's all part of the harmonisation of the European Union (EU) countries. Along with national border controls, the currencies of various EU members are being phased out. Not all EU members have agreed to adopt the euro, however: Denmark, Greece, Norway, Sweden and the UK rejected or post-poned participation. The 11 countries which have participated from the beginning of the process are: Austria, Belgium, Finland, France, Germany, Ireland, Italy, Luxembourg, the Netherlands, Portugal and Spain.

The timetable for the introduction of the euro runs as follows:
On 1 January 1999 the exchange rates of the participating countries were irrevocably fixed
    to the euro. The euro came into force for 'paper' accounting and prices could be displayed
    in local currency and in euros.
On 1 January 2002 euro banknotes and coins will be introduced. This ushers in a period of
    dual use of euros and existing local notes and coins (which will, in effect, simply be tem-
    porary denominations of the euro).
By July 2002 local currencies in the 11 countries will be withdrawn. Only euro notes and coins
    will remain in circulation and prices will be displayed in euros only.

The euro will have the same value in all member countries of the EU; the €5 note in France
is the same €5 note available in Italy and Portugal. There will be seven euro notes. In different colours and sizes they come in denominations of 500, 200, 100, 50, 20, 10 and five euros.
There are eight euro coins, in denominations of two and one euros, then 50, 20, 10, five, two

cheques in largish denominations to save on per-cheque exchange charges.

Travellers using the better known cheques, such as Visa, American Express and Thomas Cook, will have little trouble in Rome. American Express, in particular, has offices in all the major Italian cities and agents in many smaller cities. If you lose your Amex cheques while in Rome, you can call a 24-hour toll free number (☎ 167-87 20 00).

Take along your passport when you go to cash travellers cheques.

Credit/Debit Cards & ATMs Carrying plastic (whether a credit or ATM card) is the simplest way to organise your holiday funds. You don't have large amounts of cash or cheques to lose, you can get money after hours and on weekends and the exchange rate is better than that offered for travellers cheques or cash exchanges. By arranging

for payments to be made into your credit card account while you are travelling, you can avoid paying interest.

Major credit cards, such as Visa, Master-Card, Eurocard, Cirrus and Euro Cheques cards, are accepted in Rome and throughout Italy. They can be used for many purchases (including in many supermarkets) and in hotels and restaurants (although pensioni and smaller trattorie and pizzerie tend to accept cash only).

Credit cards can also be used in ATMs (*bancomat*) displaying the appropriate sign or (if you have no PIN number) to obtain cash advances over the counter in many banks – Visa and MasterCard are among the most widely recognised for such transactions. Check charges with your bank but, as a rule, there is no charge for purchases on major cards and a 1.5% charge on cash advances and ATM transactions in foreign currencies.

Introducing the Euro

and one cents. Each participating state will be able to decorate the reverse side of the coins with their own designs, but all euro coins can be used anywhere that accepts euros.

So, what does all this mean for the traveller? It is somewhat uncertain exactly what practices will be adopted between 1999 and 2002, and travellers will probably find varying degrees of 'euro-readiness' between different countries, between individual towns within the same country, or between different establishments in the same town. It is certain, however, that euro cheque accounts and travellers cheques will be available.

Credit card companies can bill in euros, and shops, hotels and restaurants might list prices in both local currency and euros. Travellers should check bills carefully to make sure that any conversion from local currency to euros has been calculated correctly. The most confusing period will probably be between January 2002 and July 2002 when there will be two sets of currency.

Luckily for travellers, the euro should make everything easier. One of the main benefits will be that prices in the 11 countries will be immediately comparable, avoiding those tedious calculations.

Also, once euro notes and coins are issued in 2002, you won't need to change money at all when travelling to other single-currency members. Banks may still charge a handling fee (yet to be decided) for travellers cheques but they won't be able to profit by buying the currency from you at one rate and selling it back to you at another, as they do at the moment. However, even EU countries not participating may price goods in euros and accept euros over shop counters.

There are many Web sites dealing with the introduction of the euro but most are devoted to the legal implications and the processes by which businesses may adapt to the single currency and are not particularly interesting or informative for the traveller.

It is possible to use your own ATM card in machines in Rome and throughout Italy, to obtain money from your own bank account. This is without doubt the simplest way to handle your money while travelling.

If an ATM rejects your card, don't despair or start wasting money on international calls to your bank. Try a few more ATMs displaying your credit card's logo at major banks before assuming the problem lies with your card rather than with the local system.

If your credit card is lost, stolen or swallowed by an ATM, you can telephone toll-free to have an immediate stop put on its use. For MasterCard the number in Italy is ☎ 167-870 866, or make a reverse-charges call to St Louis in the USA on ☎ 314-275 66 90; for Visa, phone ☎ 167-877 232 in Italy. If, by chance, you have a credit card issued in Italy call ☎ 167-822 056 to have it blocked.

American Express is also widely accepted (although not as common as Visa or MasterCard). Amex's full-service offices (such as in Rome and Milano) will issue new cards, usually within 24 hours and sometimes immediately, if yours has been lost or stolen. Some American Express offices have ATMs that you can use to obtain cash advances if you have made the necessary arrangements in your own country.

The toll-free emergency number to report a lost or stolen American Express card varies according to where the card was issued. Check with American Express in your country or contact American Express in Rome on ☎ 06 7 22 82, which itself has a 24-hour cardholders' service.

International Transfers One reliable way to send money to Rome is by 'urgent telex' through the foreign office of a large Italian bank, or through major banks in your own country, to a nominated bank in Rome. It is important to have an exact record of all details associated with the money transfer, particularly the exact address of the Italian bank to where the money has been sent. The money will always be held at the head office of the bank in the town to which it has been sent. Urgent-telex transfers should take only a few days, while other means, such as telegraphic transfer, or draft, can take weeks.

It is also possible to transfer money through American Express and Thomas Cook. You will be required to produce identification, usually a passport, in order to collect the money. It is also a good idea to take along the details of the transaction. It is inadvisable to send cheques by mail to Italy, because of the unreliability of the country's postal service.

A more recent and speedy option is to send money through Western Union (☎ 1670-13839 toll free). This service functions in Rome through a number of different outlets and it is best to call the toll-free number in order to get the address of the closest outlet. The sender and receiver have to turn up at a Western Union outlet with passport or other form of ID and the fees charged for the virtually immediate transfer depend on the amount sent.

Costs

A *very* prudent traveller could get by on L70,000 per day, but only by staying in a youth hostel, eating one hot meal a day (at the hostel), buying a sandwich or pizza by the slice for lunch and minimising the number of galleries and museums visited, since the entrance fee to most museums is cripplingly expensive at around L12,000. You can save on transport costs by buying tourist or day tickets for the city bus and Metro services. Museums and galleries usually give discounts to students, but you will need a valid student card which you can obtain from CTS offices if you have documents proving you are a student.

One step up, you can get by on L100,000 per day if you stay in the cheaper pensioni or small hotels, and keep sit-down meals and museums to one a day. Lone travellers may find even this budget hard to maintain, since single rooms tend to be pricey.

With a generous budget, you'll find your niche in Rome. There's no shortage of luxury hotels, expensive restaurants and shops. Realistically, a traveller wanting to stay in comfortable lower to mid-range hotels, eat two square meals a day, not feel restricted to one museum a day and be able to enjoy the odd drink and other minor indulgences should reckon on a minimum daily average of L200,000 to L250,000 a day.

A basic breakdown of costs during an average day could be: accommodation L25,000 (hostel) to L200,000; breakfast L3000 (coffee and croissant) to L20,000 (sit-down at an outdoor caffè; lunch L5000 (sandwich and mineral water) to L50,000 (sit-down in a mid-range restaurant; public transport (day pass for bus and Metro) L6000; entry fee for one museum L12,000; a sit-down dinner L25,000 to L100,000.

Tipping & Bargaining

You are not expected to tip on top of restaurant service charges, but it is common to leave a small amount. If there is no service charge, the customer might consider leaving a 10% tip, but this is by no means obligatory. In bars, Italians often leave any small change as a tip, often only L100 or L200. Tipping taxi drivers is not common practice, but you should tip the porter at higher class hotels.

Bargaining is common in flea markets, but not in shops. At the Porta Portese market in Rome, for instance, don't hesitate to offer half the asking price for any given item. Don't be deterred by stallholders who dismiss you with a wave of the arm: the person at the next stall will be just as likely to accept your offer after a brief (and obligatory) haggle. While bargaining in shops is not acceptable, you might find that the proprietor is disposed to give a discount if you are spending a reasonable amount of money.

It is quite acceptable to ask if there is a special price for a room in a pensione if you plan to stay for more than a few days.

Taxes & Refunds

Value-added tax, known as IVA (Imposta di Valore Aggiunto) is slapped on to just about everything in Italy and hovers around 19%. Tourists who are residents of countries outside the EU may claim a refund on this tax if the item was purchased for personal use and cost more than a certain amount (L300,000 in 1998). The goods must be carried with you and you must keep the fiscal receipt.

The refund only applies to items purchased at retail outlets affiliated to the system – these shops display a 'Tax-free for tourists' sign. Otherwise, ask the shopkeeper. You must fill out a form at the point of purchase and have the form stamped and checked by Italian customs when you leave the country. You then return it by mail within 60 days to the vendor, who will make the refund either by cheque or to your credit card. At major airports and some border crossings you can get an immediate cash refund at specially marked booths.

Receipts Laws aimed at tightening controls on the payment of taxes in Italy mean that the onus is on the buyer to ask for and retain receipts for all goods and services. This applies to everything from a litre of milk to a haircut. Although it rarely happens, you could be asked by an officer of the *Guardia di Finanza* (fiscal police) to produce the receipt immediately after you leave a shop. If you don't have it, you may be obliged to pay a fine of up to L300,000.

POST & COMMUNICATIONS

Italy's postal service is notoriously slow, unreliable and expensive. Don't expect to receive every single letter sent to you, or that each letter that you send will reach its destination.

Postal Rates

Stamps *(francobolli)* are available at post offices and authorised tobacconists; look for the official *tabacchi* sign: a big 'T', often white on black. Since letters often need to be weighed, what you get at the tobacconist's for international air mail will occasionally be an approximation of the proper rate. Tobacconists keep regular shopping hours.

Information about postal services can be obtained on ☎ 160. Rome's main post office is at Piazza San Silvestro 18/20 (Map 6). It is open Monday to Friday from 8.30 am until 6 pm. On Saturday it is open from 8.30 am to 2 pm and on Sunday from 9 am until 2 pm. The post office at Via di Porta Angelica (Map 5), opposite the entrance to il Vaticano, is open the same hours.

There are local post offices in every district of the city. The opening hours are usually 8.30 am to 1.50 pm on Monday to Friday and 8.30 to 11.50 on Saturdays. All post offices close two hours earlier than normal on the last business day of each month.

The cost of sending a letter air mail *(via aerea)* depends on its weight and wheredestination. Letters up to 20g cost L1400 to Australia and New Zealand, L1300 to the USA and L800 to EU countries (L900 to the rest of Europe). Postcards cost the same. As only a small percentage of postcards sent to, from or within Italy are ever delivered, it's a good idea to put your postcards in envelopes and send them as letters. Aerograms are a cheap alternative to letters and cost only L900 to send anywhere in the world. They can be purchased at post offices only.

Sending letters express *(espresso)* costs a standard extra L3600, but may help speed a letter on its way.

If you want to post more important items by registered mail *(raccomandato)* or by insured mail *(assicurato)*, remember that they will take as long as normal mail. Raccomandato costs L4000 on top of the normal cost of the letter. The cost of assicurato depends on the value of the object being sent (L6,000 for objects up to L100,000 value) and is not available to the USA.

Sending Mail

An air-mail letter can take up to two weeks to reach the UK or the USA, while a letter to Australia will take between two and three weeks. Postcards will take even longer because they are low-priority mail. One of the authors of this book sent a postcard from Australia for Christmas – it got tangled up in the Italian postal system and did not arrive until September of the *following* year.

The service within Italy is not much better: local letters take at least three days and up to a week to arrive in another city. Past surveys on postal efficiency in Europe have found that next-day delivery does not exist in Italy. Sending a letter express (see Postal Rates above) can help.

Parcels *(pacchetti)* can be sent from any post office. You can buy posting boxes or padded envelopes from most post offices. Stationery shops *(cartolerie)* and some tobacconists also sell padded envelopes. There are some strange regulations about how parcels should be sealed, and these appear to vary from one post office to another.

Don't tape up or staple envelopes – they should be sealed with glue. Your best bet is not to close the envelope or box completely and ask at the counter how it should be done. Parcels usually take longer to be delivered than letters. A different set of postal rates apply.

Express Mail Urgent mail can be sent by the post office's express mail service, known as *posta celere* or CAI Post. Letters up to 500g cost L30,000 in Europe, L46,000 to the USA and L68,000 to Australia. A parcel weighing 1kg will cost L34,000 in Europe, L54,000 to the USA and Canada, and L80,000 to Australia and New Zealand. CAI post is not necessarily as fast as private services. It will take three to five days for a parcel to reach the USA, Canada or Australia and one to three days to European destinations. Ask at post offices for addresses of CAI post outlets.

Vatican Post Many people, both Romans and tourists, choose to use the Vatican postal system instead of the Italian one. There is a post office in Piazza San Pietro (Map 5) next to the information office and another one inside the Musei Vaticani. Rates are similar to those of the Italian postal system. The Vatican post is run in association with the Swiss postal service and is considered to be significantly more reliable than the Italian system, especially for overseas mail.

However, this is not always the case. A letter sent by one of the authors via Vatican post from Rome to Australia took five months to reach its destination. Also, the Vatican post offices don't accept poste restante mail.

Couriers Several international couriers operate in Italy: DHL has three offices in Rome and two others at Fiumicino and Ciampino airports and a 24-hour toll free phone line ☎ 167-345 345; Federal Express is located centrally in Via Barberini 115 and has a toll free number ☎ 167-833 040; for UPS call toll-free ☎ 167-822 054. Note that if you are having articles sent to you by courier in Italy, you might be obliged to pay IVA of up to 20% to retrieve the goods.

Receiving Mail

Poste restante is known as *fermo posta* in Italy. Letters marked thus will be held at the counter of the same name in the main post office. Poste restante mail sent to Rome should be addressed as follows:

> John SMITH,
> Fermo Posta,
> Posta Centrale,
> Piazza San Silvestro,
> 00186 Roma

You will need to pick up your letters in person and present your passport as ID.

American Express card or travellers cheque holders can use the free client mail-holding service at the American Express office, Piazza di Spagna 38 (Map 6). You can obtain a list of other branches throughout Italy from American Express offices inside or outside Italy. Take your passport when you go to pick up mail.

Drinking fountain in the Ghetto area

Mounted police in front of the Pantheon

Temple of Antoninus and Faustina

A doorway to high fashion

Hadrian's version of Egypt at Tivoli

The gorgeous ceiling of the Galleria delle Carte

Checking the quality of the produce

Telephone

The state-run Telecom Italia is the largest telecommunications organisation in Italy, and its orange public pay phones are liberally scattered throughout Rome. The most common accept only telephone cards *(carte/schede telefoniche)*, although you will still find plenty that accept cards and coins (L100, L200 and L500). Some card phones now also accept special Telecom credit cards and even ordinary credit cards. Among the latest generation of pay phones are those that also send faxes. If you call from a bar or shop, you may still encounter old-style metered phones, which count *scatti*, the units used to measure the length of a call.

Telecom pay phones can be found in the streets, train stations and some big stores as well as in Telecom offices. Some of the latter are staffed, and a few have telephone directories for other parts of the country. Where these offices are staffed it is possible to make international calls and pay at the desk afterwards. There is a Telecom office at Stazione Termini and another near the Castro Pretorio metro station in Via San Martino della Battaglia (Map 6).

You can buy phonecards at post offices, tobacconists, newspaper stands and from vending machines in Telecom offices. To avoid the frustration of trying to find fast-disappearing coin telephones, always keep a phonecard on hand. They come with a value of L5000, L10,000 and L15,000.

Public phones operated by a new telecommunications company, Infostrada, can be found in airports and stations. These phones accept Infostrada phone cards (available from post offices, tobacconists and newspaper stands) which come with a value of L3000, L5000 and L10,000. Infostrada's rates are slightly cheaper than Telecom's for long-distance and international calls but you cannot make local calls from these phones.

Costs Rates, particularly for long-distance calls, are among the highest in Europe. The cheapest time for domestic calls is from 10 pm to 8 am. For international calls, the cheapest off-peak time is 11 pm to 8 am and most or all of Sunday, depending on the country called.

A local call *(comunicazione urbana)* from a public phone will cost L200 for three to six minutes, depending on the time of day you call. Peak call times are 8 am to 6.30 pm Monday to Friday and 8 am to 1 pm Saturday.

Rates for long distance calls within Italy *(comunicazione interurbana)* depend on the time of day and the distance involved. At the worst, one minute will cost about L580 in peak periods.

If you need to call overseas, beware of the cost – even a call of less than five minutes to Australia after 11 pm will cost around L12,000 from a private phone (more from a public phone). Calls to most of the rest of Europe cost about L800 per minute, and closer to L1200 from a public phone.

Travellers from countries that offer direct dialling services paid for at home country rates (such as AT&T in the USA and Telstra in Australia) should think seriously about taking advantage of them.

Domestic Calls Telephone area codes all begin with 0 and consist of up to four digits. The area code is followed by a number of anything from four to eight digits.

Area codes are now an integral part of all telephone numbers in Italy, even if you are calling within a single zone. If you are in Rome and are calling another Rome number, you still have to dial the area code ☎ 06 first.

Mobile phone numbers begin with a four-digit prefix such as 0330, 0335, 0347, 0368 etc. Free-phone or toll-free numbers are known as *numeri verdi*. The cost of ☎ 167 numbers are picked up by the company concerned, and ☎ 147 numbers are toll free. The latter are currently in the process of being changed over from 147 or 167 to 800. For directory enquires, dial ☎ 12.

International Calls Direct international calls can easily be made from public telephones by using a phonecard. Dial ☎ 00 to get out of Italy, then the relevant country and area codes, followed by the telephone number. Useful country codes are: Australia

Telephone Shakeup

Telecommunications in Italy had a serious shake-up in 1998. Telecom Italia's monopoly was broken for long distance and international calls and several new companies have entered the market, undercutting Telecom's exorbitant rates.

A new dialling procedure was also introduced. Area codes are now an integral part of the phone number, even if you are making a local call. So for any number you dial in Rome, you must first dial ☎ 06.

To call fixed lines in Italy from abroad, the initial 0 in the area code must be included after the country code for Italy (39). Conversely, when dialling a mobile phone number from abroad, the 0 of the prefix is dropped after the country code (39).

Further upheaval is in store. From December 2000 Italy's telephone numbers are scheduled to change again. The ☎ 06 currently dialled at the beginning of a number in Rome will become ☎ 46. (Numbers in Milano will begin with ☎ 42, numbers in Firenze ☎ 455, numbers in Napoli ☎ 481 and so on). Thus, the Rome telephone number ☎ 06 76 54 32 10 will become ☎ 46 76 54 32 10, and area codes as such will cease to exist.

However, as with many things in Italy, radical changes are often delayed. The 1998 introduction of the obligatory area code was postponed for six months even though over L40 billion had already been spent on advertising. So check with the tourist office, your hotel, the Italian embassy in your country or an international telephone operator for an update ... and happy dialling!

☎ 61, Canada and USA ☎ 1, New Zealand ☎ 64, and the UK ☎ 44. Codes for other countries in Europe include: France ☎ 33, Germany ☎ 49, Greece ☎ 30, Ireland ☎ 353, and Spain ☎ 34. Other codes are listed in Italian telephone books.

To make a reverse charges (collect) international call from a public telephone, dial ☎ 170. For European countries dial ☎ 15. All operators speak English.

Easier, and often cheaper, is using the Country Direct service for your country. You dial the number and request a reverse charges call through the operator in your country. Numbers for this service include:

Australia (Telstra)	☎ 172-10 61
Australia (Optus)	☎ 172-11 61
Canada	☎ 172-10 01
France	☎ 172-00 33
New Zealand	☎ 172-10 64
UK (British Telecom)	☎ 172-00 44
UK (British Telecom Chargecard Operator)	☎ 172-01 44
USA (AT&T)	☎ 172-10 11
USA (MCI)	☎ 172-10 22
USA (Sprint)	☎ 172-18 77
USA (IDB)	☎ 172-17 77

For international directory enquires call ☎ 176.

Calling Centres Cut-price calling centres are all over Rome, especially near Stazione Termini, il Vaticano and in the city centre. These are run by various companies and rates are significantly lower for international calls than Telecom pay phones. The other advantages are that it's usually a little less noisy than making a call from a pay phone in a busy street and you don't need a phone card. You simply place your call from a private booth inside the centre and pay for it when you've finished.

International Phonecards Several private companies now distribute international telephone cards, mostly linked to US phone companies such as Sprint and MCI. You call the number provided, which connects you with a US-based operator, through whom you can then place your international call at rates generally lower (by as much as 40% compared with standard peak hour rates) than the standard Italian rates. A recorded message will tell you before your call goes through how much time you have left on the card for that call. The cards come in a variety of unit 'sizes', and are sold in some bars and tobacconists – look out for signs advertising them.

Calling Italy from Abroad The country code for Italy is ☎ 39. You must always include the initial 0 in area codes. For example to call the number ☎ 06 777 77 77 in Rome you need to dial the international access code followed by ☎ 39 06 777 77 77. However, for mobile phones in Italy you should still drop the initial 0 of the prefix. For example, to call the mobile number ☎ 0335 77 77 77, you need to dial the international access code followed by ☎ 39 335 77 77 77.

Fax
There is no shortage of fax offices in Rome but the country's high telephone charges make faxes an expensive mode of communication. To send a fax within Italy you can expect to pay L3000 for the first page and L2000 for each page thereafter, plus L50 a second for the actual call. International faxes can cost L6000 for the first page and L4000 per page thereafter, and L100 a second for the call. You can imagine what this can mean with a slow fax machine at peak rates! Faxes can also be sent from some Telecom public phones.

Telegram
These dinosaurs can be sent from post offices or dictated by phone (☎ 186) and are an expensive, but sure, way of having important messages delivered the same or next day.

Email & Internet Access
If you are bringing your laptop to Rome and want access to the Internet you will need to have a server that operates in Italy

too. CompuServe has nodes in Rome and Milano as well as slow-access numbers in other towns. Some Italian servers can provide short-term accounts for Internet access. Flashnet (☎ 06 66 05 41) offers one-month subscriptions for L30,000 and three-month subscriptions for L90,000. Agora (☎ 06 699 17 42) has subscriptions for two months for L84,000. Both of these providers have English-speaking staff.

You will need to stay in hotels with a modern phone in the room and even then you will need to get advice before leaving home on measures to protect your modem – many hotel PABX phone systems can fry both modem and computer. Bear in mind that Italy has slower band rates than many other countries and local calls are metered and can get expensive. Net surfing is cheaper in off-peak times.

Rome has several Internet cafés. These allow you to surf the Net and in most cases permit you to send email. Some places also provide email accounts. If they don't, receiving email can be difficult, unless you have your own email account, such as Yahoo or Hotmail, to log on to.

Hackers (Map 5, ☎ 39 73 92 68), is a huge Internet café/restaurant near the Musei Vaticani in Via San Veniero 10-16. Internet access costs L8000 an hour or you can pay L50,000 for 10 hours. You can order a snack or a full meal by placing your order on the computer. It is open every day from 7.30 am until 1 am (with later closing on Friday and Saturday nights).

Bibli bookshop (Map 7, ☎ 06 588 40 97) in Trastevere is a popular Internet spot for foreign students in Rome. It is conveniently located around the corner from Piazza Santa Maria in Trastevere at Via dei Fienaroli 28 and is open Tuesday to Saturday from 11 am to midnight and from 5.30 pm to midnight on Monday. Internet access costs L50,000 for 10 hours or L100,000 for 25 hours. When you buy Internet time you automatically get your own email account.

The Netgate (Map: Around Piazza Navona, ☎ 06 689 34 45), Piazza Firenze 25, in the heart of the historic centre, offers

Internet access at L10,000 per hour including an email account. If you pay for 10 hours you get another six hours free and there are discounts for students. In summer it is open Monday to Saturday from 10.30 am to 10.30 pm. In winter it is open seven days a week from 10.40 am to 8.30 pm.

In the San Lorenzo area, the Internet café (Map 6, ☎ 06 445 49 53) offers Internet access for L10,000 per hour or L70,000 for 10 hours. Email boxes are available for an extra charge. Located in the heart of the university area at Via Marrucini 14, it's popular with students and is open Monday to Friday from 9 am to 2 am and from 5 pm to 2 am on Saturday and Sunday.

INTERNET RESOURCES

There is a page on Italy and one on Rome on Lonely Planet's website (www.lonely-planet.com). Another good place to start is Excite Reviews (www.excite.com). Call it up and key in Rome, Italy and it will give you a long selection of sites, as well as brief reviews and ratings. Alfanet (www.alfanet.it) has a Welcome Italy page, with a link to information about Rome. Planet Italy (www.planetitaly.com) has some interesting information.

Italy's leading student travel organisation, CTS, has a site Vivi Roma (www.cts.it). Other sites with tourism information are: Roma 2000 (www.roma2000.it), Giada InfoCenter Rome (giada.nexus.it) and Travel Italy (www.travel.it).

Roma's municipal government, the *comune*, has its own web page (www.comune.roma.it) which provides information about everything from rubbish collection, health and social services, education to cultural listings. The site is not updated as regularly as it should be and is geared towards people living in Rome rather than to tourists although there's a small amount of tourism info. Two sites emanate from the Vatican: www.vatican.va is the official homepage of the Holy See; and www.christusrex.org offers internet tours of the various Vatican museums and galleries.

The website of the fortnightly magazine *Wanted in Rome* (www.wantedinrome.com) has listings and reviews of current exhibitions and cultural events as well as informative articles on aspects of Rome and the surrounding region. It also has classified ads on-line which are helpful if you're planning a longer stay in the city and want to find a room in a shared apartment (see Newspapers and Magazines section below).

The *English Yellow Pages* is a useful directory of English speaking professionals, commercial activities, organisations and services in Rome. Its website (www.mondoweb.it/eyp) could be a good first stop and has lots of useful links.

BOOKS

Most books are published in different editions by different publishers in different countries. As a result, a book might be a hardcover rarity in one country while it is readily available in paperback in another. Fortunately, bookshops and libraries search by title or author, so your local bookshop or library is best placed to advise you on the availability of the following recommendations.

Lonely Planet

If Rome is not your only destination in Italy, consider buying Lonely Planet's *Italy*. Hikers who are planning to visit other parts of the country should definitely consult Lonely Planet's *Walking in Italy* guide. *Mediterranean Europe on a shoestring* and *Western Europe on a shoestring* include chapters on Italy and are recommended for those planning further travel in Europe. Also published by Lonely Planet, the *Italian phrasebook* lists all the words and phrases you're likely to need when travelling in Italy.

Guidebooks

The paperback *Companion Guide to Rome* by Georgina Masson is packed with historical detail and fascinating anecdotes. A revised and updated edition was recently published. The Blue Guide to *Rome* gives very good detailed information about the art and monuments of the city and surrounding region. If you can read in Italian you can't go past the excellent Red Guides to Rome and Lazio published by the Touring Club Italiano.

A. Claridge's *Oxford Archaeological Guide to Rome* is an extremely detailed guide to ancient Rome, with descriptions, maps, plans and photos of more than 150 archaeological sites.

Travel

There are endless books written by travellers to Italy, many of which describe sojourns in Rome. For a potted idea of how the great writers saw the country, it's worth reading *When in Rome: the Humorists' Guide to Italy* or the *Traveller's Literary Companion to Italy* by Martin Garrett.

Three Grand Tour classics are Johann Wolfgang von Goethe's *Italian Journey*, Charles Dickens' *Pictures from Italy*, and Henry James' *Italian Hours*. James also used Rome as a backdrop for part of *Portrait of a Lady*. D.H. Lawrence wrote three short travel books while living in Italy, now combined in one volume entitled *DH Lawrence and Italy*.

H.V. Morton's *A Traveller in Rome*, written in the 1950s, is still a useful guide to the city and its people. Morton also wrote *A Traveller in Italy* and *A Traveller in Southern Italy*.

History & Politics

If you want a first-hand account of life in ancient Rome, and can handle the ancient philosophers and writers, try Plutarch, Tacitus and Livy, all of whom are available in the Penguin Classics series. Edward Gibbon's 18th century *History of the Decline and Fall of the Roman Empire* (available in six hardback volumes, or an abridged, single-volume paperback) is as much a masterpiece of literature as history; for an overview of Rome from Romulus to Constantine, try M Carey & H.H. Scullard's *History of Rome. Rome: Biography of a City* by Christopher Hibbert is one of the most readable studies of

Rome's multi-layered history, and an excellent reference book.

Other history books include: *The Oxford History of the Roman World* edited by J Boardman et al; *The Oxford Illustrated History of Italy* edited by G. Holmes; *Daily Life in Ancient Rome* by J. Carcopino; *Italy: A Short History* by Harry Hearder; *Concise History of Italy* by V. Cronin; *History of the Italian People* by G. Procacci; *The Oxford Dictionary of Popes* compiled by J.N.D. Kelly; *The Penguin Historical Atlas of Ancient Rome* by C.s Scarre; *Rome in the Dark Ages* by P. Llewellyn; and *The Transformation of the Roman World AD 400-900* edited by L. Webster and M. Brown.

A History of Contemporary Italy: Society and Politics 1943-1988 by Paul Ginsburg, is an absorbing and very well written book which will help Italophiles place the country's modern society in perspective. *Modern Italy: A Political History* by Denis Mack Smith is a complete and absorbing account of the fate of Italy from Risorgimento to the present. Mack Smith is widely regarded as the most authoritative historian on the subject writing in English.

Art

Useful references are *A Handbook of Roman Art*, edited by Martin Henig; *Roman Architecture* by Frank Sear; and *Art and Architecture in Italy 1600-1750* by Rudolf Wittkower. *The Penguin Book of the Renaissance* by J.H. Plumb, *Painters of the Renaissance* by Bernard Berenson, and Giorgio Vasari's *Lives of the Artists* should be more than enough on the Renaissance.

There is also a series of guides to Italian art and architecture, published under the general title World of Art. These include: *Roman Art and Architecture* by Mortimer Wheeler; *Palladio and Palladianism* by Robert Tavernor; *Michelangelo* by Linda Murray; and *Italian Renaissance Sculpture* by Roberta .J.M. Oleson.

General

People For background on the Italian people and their culture, as seen by an

Italian, there is the classic, *The Italians*, by Luigi Barzini. *Italian Labyrinth* by John Haycraft looks at Italy in the 1980s. Charles Richards' *The New Italians* is an absorbing account of modern Italy, its people and its political upheavals. *Italy* by Matt Frei, the BBC's Rome correspondent, challenges the notion of Italy as a disordered society and catalogues the changes it has undergone in the past decade.

Italian Neighbours by Tim Parks is an often hilarious account of the life of an expatriate in Verona. Parks' *An Italian Education* is in the same vein and looks at child rearing, bilingual style.

The Church *His Holiness* by journalists Carl Bernstein (of Watergate fame) and Marco Politi (*La Repubblica*) takes the reader behind the scenes in il Vaticano and examines the influence of Pope John Paul II on Church doctrine and Italian society; *Man of the Century* by Jonathan Kwitny looks at the life and times of John Paul II. *Saints and Sinners* by Eamon Duffy is an illustrated history of the papacy from St Peter through to John Paul II.

Food The eponymously titled *Diane Seed's Roman Kitchen* concentrates on the seasonal flavours of Rome. *The Food of Italy* by Waverley Root is an acknowledged classic and will prepare the tastebuds for what awaits the traveller in Italy. Marcella Hazan is arguably Italy's most famous cook and any of her cookbooks will provide useful information about the history of the various regional cuisines.

Fiction Many contemporary authors regularly use ancient Rome as a backdrop for their stories. Robert Graves' classics *I, Claudius* and *Claudius the God* were brilliantly dramatised by the BBC with Derek Jacobi in the title role; try also novels by Allan Massie. Steven Saylor and Lindsey Davis both set detective novels in ancient Rome; Salyor's books are set in the dying Republic, and Davis' series revolves around

Marcus Didius Falco, best described as a Philip Marlowe of imperial Rome.

Morris West has written a trilogy of Vatican novels: *Shoes of the Fisherman*, *Lazarus*, and *Eminence*; and Peter Robb's *M*, a 'faction' biography of Caravaggio, is highly evocative of 16th and 17th century Rome.

Living in Rome *Living, Studying and Working in Italy* by Travis Neighbor and Monica Larner is an invaluable guide through Italian bureaucracy, for those planning to spend an extended period in Rome. Although the book was written for a US audience, most of the information is applicable to visitors from other non-EU countries. *Getting it Right in Italy: A Manual for the 1990s* by William Ward aims to provide accessible, useful information about Italy, while also providing a reasonable social profile of the people. It is, though, increasingly out od date and should be used with caution.

NEWSPAPERS & MAGAZINES
Italian-Language

Roma C'é is a weekly listings booklet which is published every Thursday (L2000). There is a small section in English towards the end. *Wanted in Rome* (L1500) is a fortnightly English-language listings magazine directed towards the foreign residents of Rome. It contains informative articles about Italian politics and bureaucracy, city news, history, plus arts and entertainment listings and reviews. It also has hundreds of classified ads useful for those seeking accommodation or jobs.

Italian newspapers, available from all newspaper stands, can be frustrating, even for fluent Italian readers. Don't expect the Italian press to give you a balanced view of current events as most newspapers reflect the political or business interests of those who control them. The articles tend to be long-winded and the point, if indeed there is one, is usually buried in the final paragraphs. The domestic politics section, which normally occupies the first four or five pages of the newspaper, is difficult to follow even for the most dedicated reader and if you miss an instalment it's almost impossible to catch up on events.

Il Messaggero is the most popular broadsheet in Rome. It is especially good for news about Rome itself and the Vatican and has a weekly listings supplement, *Metro*. *Corriere della Sera*, which is based in Milan, is the country's leading daily and has the best foreign news pages and the most comprehensive and comprehensible political coverage. *L'Unità*, once the voice of the political left, now wobbles somewhere in the centre of the spectrum. Its cultural pages are always a good read.

The tabloid format *La Repubblica*, also a Rome-based paper, usually has great photos but it also has a reputation for sloppy reporting. Its *Trovaroma* supplement on Thursday provides entertainment listings. The conservative *L'Osservatore Romano* is published daily in Italian (with weekly editions in English and other foreign languages) and is the official voice of il Vaticano. There are several other daily papers. Most Italian daily newspapers cost L1500 (or L2000 if a supplement is included).

Other Languages

The *Herald Tribune* (L3000) is available from Monday to Saturday. It has a daily four-page supplement on Italian news. *The European* (L5000) is a weekly newspaper published on Friday.

British daily papers, including *The Guardian* (L3500), *The Times* (L4500), the *Daily Telegraph* (L5500), *The Independent* (L4500) and the *Financial Times* (L3400) as well as various tabloids, are sent from London. They are available from newspaper stands towards lunchtime on the day of publication. British Sunday papers are usually available in Rome on the following Monday.

US newspapers such as *USA Today* (L2800), *The Wall Street Journal* European edition (L3300) and *The New York Times* (L11,000) are also available. The major German, French, Spanish dailies and some

Scandinavian papers can also be found easily. If you can't find any foreign papers try one of the larger central newspaper stands in Via del Corso, Largo Argentina, Piazza Navona, Via Veneto or at Stazione Termini.

News magazines such as *Time* (L5800), *Newsweek* (L6000) and *The Economist* (L8000) are available weekly.

RADIO & TV
Radio

You can pick up the BBC World Service on medium wave at 648 kHz, short wave at 6195 kHz, 9410 kHz, 12095 kHz, 15575 kHz, and on long wave at 198 kHz, depending on where you are and the time of day. Voice of America (VOA) can usually be found on short wave at 15205 kHz. Vatican Radio (1530 AM, 93.3 FM and 105 FM) broadcasts the news in English at 7 am, 8.30 am, 6.15 pm and 9.50 pm. The reports usually include a run-down on what the pope is up to on any particular day. Pick up a pamphlet at the Vatican information office.

There are three state-owned stations: RAI-1 (1332 AM or 89.7 FM), RAI-2 (846 AM or 91.7 FM) and RAI-3 (93.7 FM). They combine classical and light music with news broadcasts and discussion programs. RAI-2 broadcasts news in English every day from 1 to 5 am at three minutes past the hour.

Commercial radio stations are a better bet if you're after contemporary music. Popular stations are: Radio Centro Suono (101.3 FM); the Naples-based Radio Kiss Kiss (97.25 FM); and Radio Città Futura (97.7 FM) which broadcasts a listing of the day's events in Rome at 10 am daily.

TV

Italian television is so bad that it is compelling. There is an inordinate number of quiz shows and variety programs with troupes of scantily-clad women prancing and thrusting across the set. The home-bred soap operas are so bad that it's sometimes embarrassing to watch, but they attract a huge following. So, too, do the many imported soaps, mainly from the USA, all of which are dubbed into Italian. Current release films transfer to the small screen relatively quickly in Italy, but again, they are always dubbed. The state-run channels are RAI 1, RAI 2 and RAI 3. The main commercial stations are Canale 5, Italia 1, Rete 4 and Telemontecarlo (TMC).

CNN is broadcast nightly on TMC from around 1 am. On Channel 41, known as Autovox, the American PBS McNeill Lehrer News Hour is broadcast nightly at around 8 pm. There is also a French-language TV channel, Antenne 2, which can sometimes be received on Channel 10. Most of Rome's mid to top-range hotels, as well as many bars and restaurants, have satellite TV and can receive BBC World, Sky Channel, CNN and NBC Superchannel.

VIDEO SYSTEMS

Italy uses the PAL video system (the same as in Australia and throughout Europe, except in France). This system is not compatible with NTSC (used in North America, Japan and Latin America) or Secam (used in France and other Francophone countries). However, modern video players are often multi-system and can read all three.

PHOTOGRAPHY & VIDEO
Film & Equipment

A roll of 36 exposure 100 ASA Kodak film costs around L10,000. It costs between L12,000-18,000 to have 36 exposures developed and L8,000-12,000 for 24 exposures. A roll of 36 slides costs L6,000 to L15,000 and around L8,000-12,000 to develope.

There are numerous outlets which sell and process films but beware of poor quality processing. A roll of film is called a *pellicola* but you will be understood if you ask for 'film'. One-hour photo developing is still quite unusual in Rome. It's more likely that you'll get your photos back within a few hours or the next day. Slides (*diapositive*) will take several days to be processed. Don't rely on your photos being

ready exactly when you were told they would be. If you've got a train or plane to catch, and the photos are important, it might be safer to wait and get them done at your next port of call. Photo processing outlets are open normal shop hours, although some close on Saturday afternoon.

Photokina, Via dei Pettinari 4 (Map: Around Piazza Navona), near Ponte Sisto, has its own processing equipment and can usually develop photos within an hour or slides within a few days. Leon Foto, Via del Banco di Santo Spirito 28 (Map 5), just off Corso Vittorio Emanuele, also offers one hour service. Professional photographers use Fotoservice in Prati, Via Marcantonio Colonna (Map 3) just by the Lepanto Metro station on the corner of Viale Giulio Cesare. They can develop slides in three hours. There are several photo processing outlets in the city centre near the Pantheon.

Tapes for video cameras are often available at the same outlets or can be found at stores selling electrical goods.

TIME

Italy operates on a 24-hour clock which will take some getting used to for travellers accustomed to the 12-hour system. Daylight-saving time starts on the last Sunday in March, when clocks are put forward one hour. Clocks are put back an hour on the last Sunday in October. Ensure that when telephoning home you also make allowances for daylight saving in your own country.

Italy is in a single time zone. Countries such as France, Germany, and Spain are in the same zone. Greece, and Israel are one hour ahead, the UK one hour behind. When it's noon in Rome, it's 3 am in San Francisco, 6 am in New York, 11 am in London, 7 pm in Perth, 9 pm in Sydney and 11 pm in Auckland.

ELECTRICITY
Voltages & Cycles

The electric current in Italy is 220V, 50Hz, but make a point of checking with the hotel management because some places, especially those in older buildings, may still use 125V.

Plugs & Sockets
Power points have two or three holes and do not have their own switches, while plugs have two or three round pins. Some power points have larger holes than others. Italian homes are usually full of plug adaptors to cope with this anomaly.

Make sure you bring international plug adaptors for your appliances. It is a good idea to buy these *before* leaving home as they are virtually impossible to get in Italy. If you do forget, there is always the option of taking your appliance to an electrical store and having them replace the foreign plug with an Italian one. Travellers from North America need a voltage converter (although many of the more expensive hotels have provision for 110 V appliances such as electric razors).

WEIGHTS & MEASURES
Italy uses the metric system. Basic terms for weight include *un etto* (100g) and *un chilo* (1kg). Travellers from the USA will have to cope with the change from pounds to kilograms, miles to kilometres and gallons to litres. A standard conversion table can be found at the back of this book.

Note that Italians indicate decimals with commas and thousands with points.

LAUNDRY
Coin laundrettes, where you can do your own washing, were once a rarity in Rome, but fortunately for the traveller are becoming more common. There are several self-service laundrettes in the streets northeast of Stazione Termini. Bolle Blu has two outlets, at Via Palestro 59-61 (Map 6) and Via Milazzo 20b (Map 6), which are open every day from 8 am to 10 pm. A 6.5kg load costs L6000 to wash and L6000 to dry. Oblo Service (Map 6, Via Vicenza 50) is open every day from 9 am to 9pm. An 8kg load costs L6000 to wash and L6000 to dry.

Onda Blu is a chain of laundrettes operating throughout Italy. There are several branches in Rome, all of which are open daily from 8 am to 10 pm. There are laundrettes at Via Lamarmora 10 (Map 6, between Stazione Termini and Piazza Vittorio Emanuele II), Via Vespasiano 50 (Map 5, off Piazza del Risorgimento in Prati), and at Via Amedeo VIII 70b in the San Giovanni area.

Dry-cleaning *(lavasecco)* charges range from around L6000 for a shirt to L12,000 for a jacket. Be careful, though – the quality can be unreliable.

TOILETS
Public toilets are not exactly widespread in Rome. A recent report estimated that there were less than 40 of them in the whole of the city. Most people use the toilets in bars and cafés – although you might need to buy a coffee first!

LEFT LUGGAGE
There are left luggage services at Stazione Termini opposite the end of platforms 1 and 22. They are open from 5.20 am to 12.20 am daily. The daily rate is L1500 per item. There are left luggage facilities in almost every train station throughout Italy, most of which are open seven days a week.

At Fiumicino airport there is a left luggage facility open 24 hours in the international arrivals area on the ground floor. It costs L4100 per item per day. For luggage over 160cm long, you pay an extra L4100 per day. Make sure you have your passport handy, as a photocopy will be made when you leave your luggage.

HEALTH
You are unlikely to have any serious health problems in Rome – except maybe a little indigestion from overeating the delicious food, or blisters on your feet from too much walking. The water in Rome is perfectly safe to drink, although it has a relatively high calcium content, and many Romans prefer to drink bottled water (see under Drinks in Places to Eat chapter).

Air pollution can be a problem, particularly in summer. If you suffer from asthma or other respiratory problems, consider bringing a face mask. There are periodic pollution alerts when it is best to stay indoors; keep yourself informed through your hotel proprietor or a tourist office. Another problem in summer is the severe heat and humidity, which can be debilitating. Pace yourself, wear a hat, apply sunscreen and make sure you drink plenty of water. Use insect repellent to keep mosquitoes and other biting insects at bay.

Condoms can be bought from pharmacies and some tobacconists and supermarkets.

The public health system is administered by local centres generally known as Unità Sanitaria Locale (USL), usually listed under 'A' for Azienda USL. Under these headings you'll find long lists of offices – look for Poliambulatorio (polyclinic) and the telephone number for Accetazione Sanitaria. You need to call this number to make an appointment – there is no point in just rolling up. Opening hours vary widely, with the minimum generally being about 8 am to 12.30 pm Monday to Friday. Some open for a couple of hours in the afternoon and on Saturday morning too.

Medical Cover
Under a new law, all foreigners have the same right as Italians to emergency or essential medical treatment, including ongoing treatment, in a public hospital or clinic.

In addition various countries have longstanding reciprocal agreements with Italy, which won't effect the treatment you receive in a public hospital, but might make the paperwork easier. Citizens of EU countries should have an E111 form (enquire at your national health service before leaving home). Australia also has a reciprocal arrangement with Italy which covers emergency treatment. Medicare in Australia publishes a brochure with the details, and it is advisable to carry your Medicare card.

Private hospitals and clinics throughout the country generally provide excellent services but are expensive for those without medical or travel insurance (see Travel Insurance earlier in this chapter). That said, certain treatments, tests or referrals to specialists in public hospitals may also have to be paid for and in such cases can be equally costly.

Your embassy in Rome can recommend where to go for medical treatment and should be able to refer you to doctors who speak your language. However, if you have a specific health complaint, it would be wise to obtain the necessary information and referrals for treatment before leaving home. In the USA, the International Association for Medical Assistance to Travellers 417 Center Street, Lewiston, NY 14092 (IAMAT, ☎ 716-754 4883, fax 519-836 3412), a nonprofit organisation based in New York, can provide a list of English-speaking doctors in Rome who have been trained in the USA, the UK or Canada.

Hospitals and Clinics
The quality of medical treatment in public hospitals in Rome is well below the standards of many other major Western European cities, but not so much due to a lack in professional expertise – Italy's doctors are highly regarded on an international level, particularly in the area of research – but more because hospital administration is appalling, the facilities and equipment are outdated, the services are oversubscribed and the standard of nursing care is low. In recent years there have been serious hygiene scares, and some of Rome's main hospitals were threatened with closure.

If you need an ambulance cal ☎ 113 or ☎ 06 55 10. For emergency treatment, go straight to the casualty (pronto soccorso) section of a public hospital (ospedale), where you'll also receive emergency dental treatment. You are likely to find doctors who speak English, or a volunteer translator service. The main public hospitals (listed in the telephone directory under Ospedale) are:

Policlinico Umberto I (Map 6, ☎ 06 499 71, Via del Policlinico 155) near Stazione Termini
Ospedale San Giacomo (Map 5, ☎ 06 362 61, Via Canova 29) off Via del Corso near Piazza del Popolo

Ospedale Santo Spirito (☎ 06 683 51, Lungo-
tevere in Sassia 1); this hospital is partially
closed until 2000
Ospedale Bambino Gesù (Map 5, ☎ 06 68 59 23
51, Piazza Sant'Onofrio) on the Gianicolo
(Janiculum hill); Rome's paediatric hospital
Ospedale San Giovanni (Map 8, ☎ 06 770 51, Via
Amba Aradam 8) near Piazza San Giovanni in
Laterano
Ospedale Fatebenefratelli (Map: Around Piazza
Navona, ☎ 06 683 71, Piazza Fatebenefratelli,
Isola Tiberina)
Ospedale San Gallicano (Map 7, ☎ 06 588 23 90,
Via San Gallicano) in Trastevere; skin prob-
lems and venereal diseases
Ospedale Nuova Regina Margherita (Map 7, ☎ 06
581 06 58, Via Morosini 30) in Trastevere
Ospedale San Camillo (Map: Greater Rome, ☎ 06
587 01, Circonvallazione Gianicolense 87)
which has a free clinic providing information
about abortion
Ospedale Villa San Pietro Fatebenefratelli (☎ 06
335 81, Via Cassia 600) some distance from
the city centre
Policlinico A Gemelli (☎ 06 301 51, Largo
Agostino Gemelli 8) some distance from the
city centre
Ospedale Sant'Eugenio (☎ 06 590 41, Piazzale
dell'Umanesimo 10) in EUR

Private Hospitals Rome has several international private hospitals. You should use
their services only if you have health insurance and have consulted your insurance
company. The American Hospital (☎ 06 225
51, Via E Longoni 69) is a long way east of
the city centre off Via Collatina. The European Hospital (☎ 06 65 97 59, Via Portuense
696) is a fair distance south-west of the centre.

Guardia Medica The Guardia Medica are
private associations of doctors who can
make house calls (or visits to hotels) at any
hour of the day or night. They are listed in
the telephone directory under *Guardia
Medica*. This is not a free service and
calling out a doctor for a general medical
problem will cost from L120,000. If you
need a specialist or have a more complicated problem it costs from L150,000. Most
travel insurance policies will cover you for
these consultations.

Bear in mind that if the problem is very
serious you will be sent to casualty anyway,

so you might do better to avoid the wait
and head for the nearest hospital yourself.
Guardia Medica SPRIM (☎ 06 58 20 40
06) has English speaking doctors. Other associations include Guardia Medica Circelli
(☎ 06 785 84 70) and Associazione Profes-
sionale Medica (☎ 06 884 11 81).

Pharmacies

Pharmacies or chemists *(farmacie)* are
usually open Monday to Saturday from 9
am to 1 pm and from 4 to 7.30 pm. They
open on Sunday, at night and for emergen-
cies on a rotation basis. Night pharmacies
are listed in the daily newspapers (usually at
the back near the cinema listings). When a
pharmacy is closed, it is required by law to
post on the door a list of others open nearby.
There is a 24 hour pharmacy at Piazza dei
Cinquecento 51, just outside Stazione
Termini (Map 6, ☎ 06 488 00 19). Within
the station a pharmacy opens daily from
7.30 am to 10 pm (closed in August). For
information on the 24-hour drugstores, see
the Shopping chapter later in this book.

The Farmacia del Vaticano (Map 5, ☎ 06
69 88 34 22), just inside the Porta Sant'
Anna, sells certain drugs that are not available in Italian pharmacies, and will also fill
prescriptions from some other countries,
which Italian pharmacies cannot do (though
it apparently doesn't stock Viagra).

If you take a regular medication, make
sure you bring an adequate supply. Also
make sure you note the drug's generic name
(rather than the brand name) in case you
need a prescription written in Italy.

Opticians

If you lose or break your glasses, you will
be able to have them replaced within a few
days by an optician *(ottico)* as long as you
have your prescription. The Italians are
specialists in making glasses frames and
you'll probably find a good range of frames
at reasonable prices.

HIV/AIDS

The national AIDS hotline is ☎ 1678 61061.
The city council has information on-line at

www.comune.roma.it/comune/ospiti/aids. For HIV/AIDS treatment, contact the Clinica Dermosifilpatica at Ospedale Spallanzani (Map: Greater Rome, ☎ 06 58 23 76 39, Via Portuense 332). The Circolo Mario Mieli di Cultura Omosessuale (☎ 06 54 13 985; see Gay & Lesbian Travellers later in this chapter) runs a free AIDS testing centre every Thursday from 3 to 4 pm at Ospedale San Giovanni (entrance at Via di San Giovanni in Laterano 155). For information call the Circolo Mario Mieli.

Women's Health

Each USL (Unità Sanitaria Locale) area has its own Family Planning Centre (Consultorio Familiare) where you can go for advice on gynaecological problems, contraceptives, pregnancy tests and information about abortion; these are listed under each USL office in the telephone book, otherwise ask at the USL office.

There is a gynaecological/family-planning clinic, known by its acronym AIED (Map 4, ☎ 06 884 06 61, at Via Salaria 58) where foreign women can seek medical advice and assistance. It is open 9 am to 7 pm Monday to Friday. English-speaking doctors work there twice a week so phone for appointments.

Pharmacies can provide creams and pessaries for common fungal infections (candida). Cystitis is known as cistiti; you can buy capsules called Pipram over the counter.

WOMEN TRAVELLERS

Rome is not a dangerous city for women, but women travelling alone will often find themselves plagued by unwanted attention from men. This attention usually involves catcalls, hisses and whistles and, as such, is more annoying than anything else. Lone women will also find it difficult to remain alone – you will have Italian men harassing you as you walk along the street, drink a coffee in a bar or try to read a book in a park. Usually the best response is to ignore them, but if that doesn't work, politely tell them that you are waiting for your husband (marito) or boyfriend (fidanzato) and, if necessary, walk away.

Avoid becoming aggressive as this almost always results in an unpleasant confrontation. If all else fails, approach the nearest member of the police or carabinieri.

Basically, most of the attention falls into the nuisance/harassment category. However, women on their own should use their common sense. Avoid walking alone in deserted and dark streets and look for hotels which are centrally located and within easy walking distance of places where you can eat at night. Areas best avoided are mentioned in the Places to Stay chapter.

Rome is fundamentally a very safe city, especially compared with other European capitals (see the 'Safe City' boxed text). The city centre is well lit, and there is always lots of activity late into the night. However, foreigners in general and women on their own in particular are regarded as prime targets for bag-snatchers, who rush past on a motorino and grab your handbag in a split second. Be alert, use a backpack if you can (it's harder to pull off) or keep one hand on your bag, and be very careful about walking in deserted streets at night.

Watch out for men with wandering hands on crowded buses. The No 64 bus, which travels from Stazione Termini to il Vaticano, is notorious for overattentive males who take advantage of the fact that many passengers on the route are tourists and that the bus is generally packed. If someone starts fondling your backside, or rubbing up against you, make a huge fuss. A loud che schifo! (how disgusting!) will usually do the trick. The locals will sympathise with you and the culprit will almost certainly make a hasty exit at the next stop.

Hitching is not recommended for solo women in the city or elsewhere.

Recommended reading is the Handbook for Women Travellers by M. & G. Moss.

GAY & LESBIAN TRAVELLERS

Homosexuality is legal in Italy and well tolerated in Rome. The legal age of consent is 16. Five years ago the gay capitals of

A Safe City

Italian cities, Rome among them, have a bad reputation for crime which is not always deserved. According to a recent report by the Lazio regional authorities, Rome is one of the safest cities in Europe as far as personal security is concerned.

The report compared crime statistics in Rome, Milan, Berlin, Hamburg, London and Paris. Rome was the safest city as far as rape and assault were concerned, and compared favourably with regard to burglary and bag snatching.

Berlin had the highest rate of violent assault (325 attacks for every 100,000 inhabitants) followed by Paris (254 per 100,000) and Hamburg (172 per 100,000). In Rome there were only 22 assaults for every 100,000 inhabitants. London had the highest incidence of rape (25 for every 100,000 inhabitants) followed by Paris and Berlin. Rome, at the bottom of the list, recorded the figure of 3.1 rapes for every 100,000 inhabitants. London also had the highest level of household burglaries, while Milan was top of the list for bag snatching.

However, Rome had the highest incidence of car theft. In the period 1996-97, 38,956 cars were reported stolen, or 1171 for every 100,000 inhabitants, three times the frequency of Paris or Berlin.

Italy were Milano and Bologna, but Rome is now giving both cities some strong competition. Previously a subculture that operated behind closed doors, Rome's gay scene is now a lot more open and there are numerous bars and clubs, with new venues opening all the time.

On a political level, Italy is still a long way behind most western countries in making gay rights a major issue. During his first term in office, Rome's left-wing mayor, Francesco Rutelli, had a brief courtship with the gay community, appointing an adviser on gay rights and issues, and even leading part of the Gay Pride march in 1994. However, as he climbs the political ladder Rutelli is letting go of his more 'radical' agenda and aligning himself with the Vatican establishment (which periodically launches anti-gay diatribe – Pope John Paul II once referred to homosexual men and women as 'morally corrupt') and more 'traditional' family values. It will be interesting to see what happens in 2000 when Rome hosts World Pride bang in the middle of the Roman Catholic Jubilee year.

In recent years in Rome there has been a spate of murders of middle-aged and older men who happened to be gay. The jury is out as to whether they were murdered because of their sexuality, but it is fair to say that the sexual link is strong. As in all places, you should exercise caution and judgement as to who you leave a bar or club with and where you go.

The lesbian scene is less active than the gay scene and there is not yet any permanent lesbian nightclub, although there are various associations which organise events and some places have exclusively lesbian nights.

Rome has several gay bars and discos and there is even a gay beach (see Gay & Lesbian Venues in the Entertainment chapter). These can be tracked down through local gay organisations. Details are provided in gay publications such as *Babilonia*, a national monthly magazine, and *Guida Gay Italia*, published annually. *Time Out Roma* which is published weekly and available from newsstands (L2,000) also has an extensive listing (in Italian) of gay and lesbian associations, bars and clubs, as does *Guide* a non-profit magazine for gays and lesbians published monthly and available at the various gay and lesbian organisations and bookshops (L4000). *Guide* can also be read on-line at www.gay-italia.com/guide.

Organisations

In Rome the main cultural and political organisation is the Circolo Mario Mieli di

Cultura Omosessuale, Via Corinto 5 (☎ 06 54 13 985, fax 06 54 13 971, mario.mieli@ agora.stm.it) off Via Ostiense near the Basilica di San Paolo, which organises debates, cultural events and social functions. It also runs a free AIDS/HIV testing and care centre (see the Health section earlier in this chapter). Mario Mieli is one of the organisers of Rome Pride which takes place every year in June. It is also one of the chief organisers of World Pride which will take place in Rome from 1 to 8 July in 2000. The program for both events (as well as other information) can be found online at www.mariomieli.it. Mario Mieli also publishes a free monthly magazine *AUT* (predominantly in Italian) available from gay bookshops and organisations.

Arci-Gay Caravaggio (Map 4, ☎ 06 855 55 22, Via Lariana 8) is the Rome branch of AGAL, the national organisation for gay men. It runs a telephone help-line and provides legal assistance and psychological counselling as well as social functions.

The national organisation for lesbians is Co-ordinamento Lesbiche Italiano (CLI), also known as the Buon Pastore Centre (Map 5, ☎ 06 686 42 01) on the corner of Via San Francesco di Sales and Via della Lungara 19 in Trastevere. The weekly political meetings of the Centro Femminista Separatista are held here, as well as conferences and literary evenings. There is also a women-only restaurant, Le Sorellastre.

Arci-Lesbica Roma (☎ 06 41 60 92 40, Via dei Monti di Pietralata 16) near Stazione Tiburtina metro, is the Rome branch of the national lesbian organisation. It runs a helpline and organises regular get-togethers and special events. Information on-line is available from www.women.it/~arciles/roma.

Libreria Babele (Map 5, ☎ 06 68 76 628, Via dei Banchi Vecchi 116), parallel to Corso Vittorio Emanuele near the Tevere, is the only exclusively gay and lesbian bookshop in Rome and has a well-stocked English section. The staff are extremely friendly and helpful and it's a good first stop for information about Rome's gay scene, especially as the offices of some of the other organisations are a bit out of the way. Forthcoming gay and lesbian events are listed on the shop's noticeboard. It is open Monday to Saturday from 10 am to 7.30 pm.

The Libreria delle Donne: Al Tempo Ritrovato (Map 7, ☎ 06 581 77 24, Via dei Fienaroli 31d) in Trastevere, is a women's bookshop with a well-stocked lesbian section, including lots of material in English. The shop's noticeboard is full of information and events.

Zipper Travel Association (Map 6, ☎ 06 488 27 30, Via Castelfidardo 18) north-east of Stazione Termini specialises in customised travel for gays and lesbians.

DISABLED TRAVELLERS

Rome is not an easy city for disabled travellers, who will almost certainly need to depend on other people more than they would in their home countries. Getting around can be a problem for the wheelchair bound. Even a short journey can become a major expedition if cobblestoned streets have to be negotiated and in some areas of the historic centre and Trastevere, for example, there are simply no footpaths. Although many buildings have lifts, they are not always wide enough to accommodate a wheelchair.

Public transport is improving. New wheelchair-accessible buses have been introduced on several busy routes by Rome's bus and tram company ATAC, although if the bus is very crowded it will be difficult to get on. Rome's newer trams are generally accessible. On the Metro system, only the more recent stations at the end of the lines have lifts. Bus No 590 follows the route of Metro Linea A and is specially equipped for disabled passengers and wheelchairs.

Some taxis are equipped to carry passengers in wheelchairs. It is advisable to book a taxi by phone, rather than heading for a taxi rank or trying to hail one on the street. Inform the operator that you need a taxi for a wheelchair *(sedia a rotelle)*. See the Getting Around chapter for details of public transport information and taxi company numbers.

Airline companies should be able to arrange assistance at airports if you notify them in advance of your needs. If you are travelling by train from Stazione Termini to Fiumicino airport or elsewhere, call ☎ 06 488 17 26 in advance to arrange for assistance.

Many of the city's main museums have been overhauled in recent years so things are looking better now for disabled travellers than ever before. Tourists in wheelchairs will find access ramps, special toilets and spacious lifts in the Musei Vaticani, the Galleria Borghese, the Galleria Nazionale d'Arte Moderna, the Palazzo delle Esposizioni and Palazzo Massimo. The Musei Capitolini, currently under restoration, should also feature facilities for the disabled when renovations are completed in 2000.

Organisations

The best point of reference for disabled travellers is Consorzio Cooperative Integrate (COIN) which can provide information about services for the disabled in Rome (including transport and museum access). It operates a telephone help line ☎ 06 23 26 75 04 or 06 23 26 75 05 from 9 am to 1 pm, Monday to Friday. Information is also available on-line from www.coinsociale.it, or contact COIN at coinsociale@coinsociale.it or coin@turismosociali.it.

COIN publishes a multilingual guide, *Roma Accessibile*, which lists the facilities available at museums, department stores, theatres and metro stations. At the time of writing a new guide was being compiled, which should be published by mid-1999. The guide will be available from public offices and by mail order; some tourist offices might have copies. Call the COIN help line for information about availability.

Tourist information offices in Rome can provide some information about museum access and transport for disabled travellers. The Italian State Tourist Office in your country may be able to provide advice on tour operators which organise holidays for the disabled. It may also carry a small brochure, *Services for Disabled People*, published by the Italian railways, which details facilities at stations and on trains.

The Italian travel agency, CIT, can advise on hotels with special facilities, such as ramps etc. It can also request that wheelchair ramps be provided on arrival of your train if you book travel through CIT. See under Tourist Offices earlier in this chapter and under Travel Agents in the Getting Around chapter.

The UK-based Royal Association for Disability & Rehabilitation (RADAR) publishes a useful guide called *Holidays & Travel Abroad: A Guide for Disabled People*, which provides a good overview of facilities available to disabled travellers throughout Europe. Contact RADAR (☎ 0171-250 3222) 250 City Rd, London EC1V 8AS.

SENIOR TRAVELLERS

Senior citizens are entitled to discounts on public transport. The minimum qualifying age is generally 60 years. Admission to most museums in Rome is free for the over-60s. It is always important to ask. You should also seek information in your own country on travel packages and discounts for senior travellers, through senior citizens' organisations and travel agents. Consider booking accommodation in advance to avoid inconvenience.

ROME FOR CHILDREN

Sightseeing in Rome will wear out adults – so imagine how the kids feel! If the weather isn't too hot, children of all ages should appreciate a wander through the Foro Romano and up to the Palatino. Also take them to visit the port city, Ostia Antica. Another interesting, if not tiring, experience is the climb to the top of the dome of Basilica di San Pietro for a spectacular view of the city. There is a Luna Park at EUR, as well as a couple of museums which older children might find interesting (see Things to See and Do chapter). Another museum which might amuse the kids is the Museo Nazionale delle Paste Alimentari (Pasta Museum), Piazza

Scanderberg 117, (between Fontana di Trevi and Palazzo del Quirinale). The well-organised museum traces the history of the nation's favourite dish and has old-fashioned pasta-making machinery on display. A portable CD player provides the commentary. The museum is open every day from 9.30 am to 5.30 pm. Admission is L12,000.

During the Christmas period Piazza Navona is transformed into a festive market place, with stalls selling puppets, figures for nativity scenes and Christmas stockings. Most churches set up nativity scenes, many of them elaborate arrangements which will fascinate kids and adults alike. The most elaborate is an 18th century Neapolitan presepio at the Basilica di SS Cosma e Damiano.

If you can spare the money, take the family on a tour of Rome by horse and cart. You'll pay through the nose at around L180,000 for what the driver determines is the 'full tour' of the city. Make sure you agree on a price and itinerary before you get in the cart – even though prices are supposedly regulated, horror stories abound about trusting tourists who forgot to ask the price!

Fortunately the city has plenty of parks. Take a break for a picnic lunch and an afternoon in the Villa Borghese. Near the Porta Pinciana there are bicycles for rent, as well as pony rides, mini-train rides and a merry-go-round. Roller-blading exhibitions often take place on weekends and are fun to watch. In the Villa Celimontana, on the western slopes of the Celio (entrance from Piazza della Navicella), is a lovely public park and a children's playground.

The Gianicolo hill, between the Basilica di San Pietro and Trastevere, with its panoramic view of Rome, is a good place to take the kids if they need a break. At the top of the hill, just off Piazza Garibaldi there is a permanent merry-go-round and pony rides, and on Sunday a puppet show is often held. In the piazza there is a small bar. Catch bus No 41 from Via della Conciliazione in front of San Pietro to reach Piazza Garibaldi, or walk up the steps from Via Mameli in Trastevere.

Bus No 41 (from the end of Corso Vittorio Emanuele where it meets the Lungotevere) will also take you within easy walking distance of the nearby Villa Doria Pamphili, the largest park in Rome and a lovely quiet spot for a walk and a picnic. Ask for directions to the lake inside the park, which is home to a large population of ducks, a few herons and some strange little rodents known as *nutrie*. A short distance from the southern end of the lake is a children's playground.

Villa Sciarra in Monteverde Vecchio is a bit of an uphill hike from Trastevere (from Piazza San Cosimato take Via Roma Libera and Via Dandolo), but the kids will love it. There's a permanent fun fair (for which you have to pay), lots of shady trees, water fountains and sprinklers (to cool off in during summer).

Italians love children and they will be made a fuss of wherever they go. It is not unusual to see Italian children out with their families even very late at night. Most restaurants can provide high chairs *(seggioloni)*. You can usually ask for a child's portion *(mezzo porzione)*, and most fussy eaters can be tempted by a delicious pizza.

All city transport is free for children under 1m tall. Most museums, galleries and archaeological sites are free for under-18s. At some, children are entitled to discounts.

Chemists sell baby formula in powder or liquid form as well as sterilising solutions such as Milton. Disposable nappies are widely available at supermarkets, chemists (where they are more expensive) and sometimes in larger *cartolerie* (stationery suppliers). A pack of around 30 disposable nappies (diapers) costs around L18,000. Fresh cow's milk is sold in cartons in bars (look for a 'Latteria' sign) and in supermarkets. If it is essential that you have milk you should carry an emergency carton of UHT milk, since bars usually close at 8 or 9 pm.

Many car-rental firms rent out children's safety seats; however, it is strongly advised that you book them in advance.

Information about current events for children can be found in *Roma C'è* (see Children's Corner in the English section) and in *Trovaroma*, the Thursday supplement to *La Repubblica*, under Città dei Ragazzi. For more general information on how to keep the kids amused while travelling, see Lonely Planet's *Travel with Children* by Maureen Wheeler.

LIBRARIES

There are over 700 libraries in Rome. Some have important historical collections with books dating from the 15th century. Entry is sometimes restricted to members of the library (where an annual fee is paid) or to readers with an appropriate letter or presentation stating their area of research. Each of the city's districts or *circoscrizioni* has at least one local library; these are listed under Comune di Roma in the telephone directory.

The main public library is the Biblioteca Nazionale Centrale Vittorio Emanuele II (Map 6, ☎ 06 49 89), Viale Castro Pretorio 105. It is the national repository of books published in Italy, and also has periodicals, newspapers, official acts, drawings, engravings and photographs. It is open Monday to Friday from 8.30 am to 7 pm, and on Saturday from 8.30 am to 1.30 pm. Readers will need an identity document in order to get a day pass.

The Biblioteca Apostolica Vaticana (Map 5, ☎ 06 69 82; fax 06 69 88 47 95), Cortile Belvedere, Porta Sant'Anna, Città del Vaticano, has one of the world's richest collections of illuminated manuscripts and early printed books. However, only serious scholars will be given permission to consult its treasures. Potential readers should apply in writing stating their area of research.

The library at Palazzo Venezia, the Biblioteca di Archeologia e Storia dell'Arte (Map 6, ☎ 06 678 30 34), Piazza Venezia 3, will be of use to archaeology and art history students. The Biblioteca Casanatense (Map 6, ☎ 06 679 89 88), Via di Sant'Ignazio 52, in the heart of the city centre, has a specialist collection of manuscripts and rare books on Rome, religion, philosophy, theatre and music. It is open Monday, Wednesday and Saturday from 8.30 am to 1.30 pm and on Tuesday, Thursday and Friday from 8.30 to 7 pm.

If it's fiction in English that you are after, try the Santa Susanna Lending Library (Map 6, ☎ 06 482 75 10), Via XX Settembre 15 (1st floor) which is usually open Tuesday and Thursday from 10 am to 1 pm, Wednesday 3 to 6 pm, Friday 1 to 4 pm and Saturday and Sunday 10 am to 12.30 pm. You'll have to pay a modest annual fee but you can then borrow all the books you want.

The Biblioteca Centrale per Ragazzi (Map: Around Piazza Navona, ☎ 686 51 16) is a children's library not far from Campo de' Fiori in Via San Paolo alla Regola 16 which lends books and videos to members.

UNIVERSITIES

Rome has three state universities, La Sapienza, Tor Vergata and Roma Tre. The latter two are in outlying areas of the city and student life tends to centre around the San Lorenzo area close to La Sapienza. There is also a private Italian university LUISS (Libera Università Internazionale degli Studi Sociali). There are also about 20 pontifical universities run by different religious orders.

There are a number of international universities in Rome. Tuition fees and course requirements vary from one institution to another. The American University of Rome (Map 7, ☎ 06 58 33 09 19; fax 06 58 33 09 92), Via Pietro Roselli 4 offers degree programs in international business, international relations and liberal arts. The European School of Economics (Map 6, ☎ 06 678 05 03; fax 06 678 02 93), Largo del Nazareno 15 has degree programs in international business (including MBAs). John Cabot University (Map 5, ☎ 68 19 12 21; jcu@johncabot.edu; www.johncabot.edu) is located in Trastevere at Via della Lungara 233, and offers courses in business administration, international affairs, political science and art history. St John's University (Map 5, ☎ 63 69 37; info@stjohns.edu), Via Santa Maria Mediatrice 24 (near il Vaticano) offers MBA degrees and MA programs in government and politics.

There are also a number of schools and study abroad programs affiliated with US universities. For information on US universities with exchange programs in Italy, check out www.studyabroad.com.

CULTURAL CENTRES

In addition to the many museums, galleries and theatres, there is a large number of foreign cultural academies and institutes in Rome, where artists, writers, performing artists and academics come from their home countries to spend several months in Rome, creating, researching and absorbing Italian history and culture. The academies organise exhibitions, poetry readings, drama and dance performances, lectures and conferences. Both *Time Out Roma* and *Wanted in Rome* carry regular listings of the events and they are sometimes listed in *Roma C'è*.

DANGERS & ANNOYANCES
Theft

Pickpockets and bag-snatchers are particularly active in Rome. The best way to avoid being robbed is to wear a money belt under your clothing. You should keep all important items, such as money, passport, other papers and tickets, in your money belt at all times. If you are carrying a bag or camera, ensure that you wear the strap across your body and have the bag on the side away from the road to deter snatch thieves who often operate from motorcycles and scooters. Since the aim of young motorcycle bandits is often fun rather than gain you are just as likely to find yourself relieved of your sunglasses – or worse, of an earring.

You should also watch out for groups of dishevelled-looking women and children. They generally work in groups of four or five and carry paper or cardboard which they use to distract your attention while they swarm around and rifle through your pockets and bag. Never underestimate their skill – they are lightning fast and very adept. Their favourite haunts are in and near major train stations, at tourist sights (such as the Colosseum), and in shopping areas. If you notice that you have been targeted by a group, either take evasive action, such as crossing the street, or shout *va via!* (go away!) in a loud, angry voice.

Pickpockets often hang out on crowded buses (the No 64 bus, which runs from Stazione Termini to il Vaticano, is notorious) and in crowded areas such as markets. There is only one way to deter pickpockets: simply *do not* carry any money or valuables in your pockets, and be very careful about your bags.

Be careful even in hotels and don't leave valuables lying around your room. Parked cars are also prime targets for thieves, particularly those with foreign number plates or rental company stickers. Try removing the stickers, or cover them and leave a local newspaper on the seat to make it look like a local car.

Never leave valuables in your car – in fact, try not to leave anything in the car if you can help it and certainly not overnight. It is a good idea to pay extra to leave your car in supervised car parks, although there is no guarantee it will be completely safe. Throughout Italy, particularly in the south, service stations along the autostradas are favourite haunts of thieves who can clean out your car in the time it takes to have a cup of coffee. If possible, park the car where you can keep an eye on it.

When driving in cities you also need to beware of snatch thieves when you pull up at traffic lights. Keep the doors locked and, if you have the windows open, ensure that there is nothing valuable on the dashboard or on the back seats.

Horror tales abound about women being dragged to the ground by thieves trying to snatch their bags, of people losing wallets, watches and cameras on crowded buses or in a flurry of newspaper-waving children. These things really do happen! Certainly even the most cautious travellers are still prey to expert thieves, but there is no need to be paranoid. By taking a few basic precautions, you can greatly lessen the risk of being robbed.

Unfortunately, some Italians practise a more insidious form of theft: short-changing. Numerous travellers have reported losing money in this way. If you are new to the Italian currency, take the time to acquaint yourself with the denominations. When paying for goods, or tickets, or a meal, or whatever, keep an eye on the bills you hand over and then count your change carefully. One popular dodge goes something like this: you hand over L50,000 for a newspaper which costs L2800; you are handed change for L10,000 and, while the person who sold you the paper hesitates, you hurry off without counting it. If you'd stayed for another five seconds, the rest of the change probably would have been handed over without your needing to say anything.

In case of theft or loss, always report the incident to the police within 24 hours and ask for a statement, otherwise your travel insurance company won't pay out.

In case of emergency, you can contact the police throughout Italy on ☎ 113.

Traffic & Pedestrians

Roman traffic can at best be described as chaotic, at worst downright dangerous, for the unprepared tourist. Many drivers, particularly motorcyclists and scooter riders, do not stop at red lights. Drivers are not keen to stop for pedestrians, even at pedestrian crossings, and are more likely to swerve. Romans simply step off the footpath and walk through the (swerving) traffic with determination – it is a practice which seems to work, so if you feel uncertain about crossing a busy road, wait for the next Italian. Better still, if you see a priest or nun in the vicinity, stick to them like glue, as even the craziest driver tends to slow down for them. If you wait for the traffic to stop, you'll be there all day. Roads which appear to be for one-way traffic sometimes have special lanes for buses travelling in the opposite direction – always look both ways before stepping onto the road.

Pollution

Italy has a poor record when it comes to environmental concerns. Few Italians would think twice about dropping litter in the streets, illegally dumping household refuse in the country or driving a car or motorcycle with a faulty or nonexistent muffler.

Tourists will be affected in a variety of ways by the surprising disregard Italians have for their country, which is of considerable natural and artistic beauty. Noise and air pollution are problems in the major cities, caused mainly by heavy traffic. A headache after a day of sightseeing in Rome is likely to be caused by breathing carbon monoxide and lead, rather than simple tiredness. While most traffic is banned from the historic centre, there are still more than enough cars, buses and motorcycles in and around the inner city to pollute the air.

Particularly in summer, there are periodic pollution alerts. The elderly, children and people with respiratory problems are warned to stay indoors. If you fit into one of these categories, keep yourself informed through the tourist office or your hotel proprietor.

When booking a hotel room it is a good idea to ask if it is quiet – although this might mean you will have to decide between a view and sleep.

One of the most annoying things about Rome is that the footpaths are littered with dog droppings – so be careful where you plant your feet.

The beaches near Rome – Ostia, Fregene and Anzio – are generally heavily polluted by industrial waste, sewage and oil spills from the Mediterranean's considerable sea traffic. The farther south you go, towards Terracina, Gaeta and Sperlonga, the cleaner the beaches are. Even better beaches can be found in Sardegna, Sicilia and the less populated areas of the south.

Roman-Style Service

It requires a lot of patience to deal with the Roman concept of service. What for Italians is simply a way of life can be horrifying for the foreigner – like the bank clerk who wanders off to have a cigarette just as it is your turn (after a one-hour wait) to be served, or the postal worker who has far more important work to do at a desk than to sell stamps to customers. Anyone in a uniform or behind a counter (including police officers, waiters and shop assistants) is likely to regard you with imperious contempt. Long queues are the norm in banks, post offices and any government offices.

It pays to remain calm and patient. Customers who become aggressive, demanding and angry stand virtually no chance of getting what they want.

LEGAL MATTERS

For many Italians, finding ways to get around the law (any law) is a way of life. They are likely to react with surprise, if not annoyance, if you point out that they might be breaking a law. Few people pay attention to speed limits, most motorcyclists and many drivers don't stop at red lights – and certainly not at pedestrian crossings. No-one bats an eyelid about littering or dogs pooping in the middle of the footpath – even though many municipal governments have introduced laws against these things. But these are minor transgressions when measured up against the country's organised crime, the extraordinary levels of tax evasion and corruption in government and business.

The average tourist will probably have a brush with the law only after being robbed by a bag-snatcher or pickpocket.

Drugs

Italy has introduced new drug laws which are lenient on drug users and heavy on pushers. If you're caught with drugs which the police determine are for your own personal use, you'll be let off with a warning – and, of course, the drugs will be confiscated. If, instead, it is determined that you intend to sell the drugs in your possession, you could find yourself in prison. It's up to the discretion of the police to determine whether or not you're a pusher, since the law is not specific about quantities. The sensible option is to avoid illicit drugs altogether.

Drink Driving

The legal blood alcohol level is 0.08% and breath tests are now in use. Drink driving is not a major problem in Italy where heavy alcohol consumption is frowned upon. See Road Rules in the Getting Around chapter for more information.

Police

If you run into trouble in Italy, you're likely to end up dealing with either *la polizia* (police) or the *carabinieri* (military police). The police are a civil force and take their orders from the Ministry of the Interior, while the carabinieri fall under the Ministry of Defence. There is a considerable duplication of their roles, despite a 1981 reform of the police forces which was intended to merge the two. Both forces are responsible for public order and security which means that you can call either in the event of a robbery, violent attack etc.

The carabinieri wear a dark-blue uniform with a red stripe and drive dark-blue cars with a red stripe. They are well trained and tend to be helpful. You are most likely to be pulled over by the carabinieri rather than the police when you are speeding etc. Their police station is called a *caserma*.

The police wear powder-blue pants with a fuchsia stripe and a navy-blue jacket and drive light blue cars with a white stripe, with 'polizia' written on the side. Tourists who want to report thefts, and people wanting to get a residence permit, will have to deal with them. The police headquarters is called the *questura*. It is located at Via San Vitale 15 (Map 6, ☎ 46 86). The Ufficio Stranieri (Foreigners' Bureau, Map 6, ☎ 46 86 29 87) is around the corner at Via Genova 2. It is open 24 hours a day and thefts can be reported here. You need to go here if you want to apply for a *permesso di soggiorno*. For immediate police attendance, call ☎ 112 or 113.

The local police station is called the *commissariato*. Most areas of Rome have either a commissariato or a carabinieri caserma, sometimes both. Shopkeepers or newsstand proprietors should be able to point you in the direction of the nearest one.

Other varieties of police in Italy include the *vigili urbani*, basically traffic police, whom you will have to deal with if you get a parking ticket, or if your car is towed away; and the *Guardia di Finanza*, who are responsible for fighting tax evasion and drug smuggling. It's a long shot, but you could be stopped by them if you leave a shop without a receipt for your purchase.

Your Rights

Italy still has some anti-terrorism laws on its books which could make life very difficult if you happen to be detained by the police. You can be held for 48 hours without a magistrate being informed and you can be interrogated without the presence of a lawyer. It is difficult to obtain bail and you can be held legally for up to three years without being brought to trial. These same laws require that all foreigners must report to the police within eight days of arriving in the country, even if you are here only for a holiday (see Visas & Documents).

BUSINESS HOURS

Generally shops are open Monday to Friday from around 9 am to 1 pm and 3.30 to 7.30 pm (or 4 to 8 pm). In some cities, grocery shops might not reopen until 5 pm and, during the warmer months, they could stay open until 9 pm. Most food shops close on Thursday afternoon. Some will also close on Saturday afternoon. Shops, department stores and supermarkets tend to be closed on Monday morning. Department stores, such as Coin and Rinascente, and most larger supermarkets now have continuous opening hours, from 9 am to 7.30 pm Monday to Saturday. Some even open from 9 am to 1 pm (or longer) on Sunday. Great revolutions were expected of Italy's shopping hours after a government bill to liberalise shop opening hours was passed in 1998. However, at the time of writing the only noticeable changes were that some shops, generally those in central or touristy areas of the city, open on Sunday.

Banks tend to open Monday to Friday from 8.30 am to 1.30 pm and 2.45 to 4.30 pm, although hours can vary. Some banks in the centre of Rome are also open on Saturday morning. It is always possible to find an exchange office open in major tourist areas.

For post office hours see Postal Rates under the Post & Communications section.

For pharmacy hours see Pharmacies under the Health section.

Bars (in the Italian sense, ie coffee and sandwich places) and cafés generally open from 7.30 am to 8 pm, although some stay open after 8 pm and turn into pub-style drinking and meeting places. Discos and clubs might open around 10 pm, but often there'll be no-one there until around midnight. Restaurants open from midday to 3 pm and 7.30 to 11 pm (later in summer). Restaurants and bars are required to close for one day each week, which varies between establishments.

Museum and gallery opening hours vary, although there is a trend towards continuous opening hours from 9.30 am to 7 pm. Most of Rome's museums close on Monday.

PUBLIC HOLIDAYS

Most Romans take their annual holidays in August, deserting the city for the cooler seaside or mountains. This means that many businesses and shops close for at least a part of the month, particularly during the week around Ferragosto (Feast of the Assumption) on 15 August. The city is left to the tourists, who may be frustrated that many restaurants and clothing and grocery shops are closed until early September.

National public holidays include the following: Epiphany (6 January); Easter Monday (March/April); Liberation Day (25 April); Labour Day (1 May); Feast of the Assumption (15 August); All Saints' Day (1 November); Feast of the Immaculate Conception (8 December); Christmas Day (25 December); and the Feast of Santo Stefano (26 December). Rome also has its own public holiday to celebrate the Feast of Saints Peter and Paul, its patron saints, on 29 June.

SPECIAL EVENTS

Italy's calendar bursts with cultural events ranging from colourful traditional celebrations with a religious and/or historical flavour, through to festivals of the performing arts, including opera, music and theatre.

Summer is definitely the best time to visit Rome if you want to catch the best of the festivals, where opera, dance and music (classical, jazz, contemporary or ethnic) share the spotlight. However, the Romaeuropa festival (dance, theatre and opera) is now a feature of the autumn calendar, the Rome opera season runs from December until June and classical and contemporary music are lively all year round. See the Entertainment chapter for further details.

If you wish to time your visit with a particular festival, contact the Italian State Tourist office in your country or write to ENIT in Rome (see the Tourist Offices Abroad section) for dates. ENIT publishes an annual booklet, *An Italian Year*, which lists most festivals, music, opera and ballet seasons, as well as art and film festivals.

DOING BUSINESS

Milano, not Rome, is Italy's business centre. The stock exchange is based there, as are the Italian headquarters of many multinational companies including Fiat, Proctor and Gamble, Blockbuster Video, Del Monte, Hewlett Packard and IBM. However, in the provinces around Rome there are significant manufacturing facilities in a range of sectors, including domestic appliances, pharmaceuticals, steel, electronic components, clothing and footwear.

If you are dealing with multinationals you will probably find that most people you come into contact with speak a certain amount of English. However, this is by no means assured in smaller businesses where fluency, or at least competence in Italian is an enormous advantage.

Useful Contacts Abroad

The trade office of the Italian Embassy in your home country can probably provide

---

Business Etiquette

Italians are extremely polite, especially in the business world. If you speak Italian, always use the formal mode of address, *lei* rather than the familiar *tu*. If your contact reverts to the familiar form, only then should you do it too. See the Language Chapter at the back of this book for further details.

Use correct titles if you know them. Anyone with a university degree is referred to as *Dottore* (doctor), a lawyer is *Avvocato* and an engineer, *Ingeniere*. If in doubt, ask.

Be flexible and don't expect your appointments to run like clockwork. Romans are very relaxed about timekeeping. It is not unusual for a meeting scheduled for 11 am to start at 11.30 or even midday. But it works both ways – if you're running a little late, don't work yourself into a lather.

Make sure you reconfirm any appointment you make, especially if there's more than a few days between the last contact and the meeting. Italians are notorious for not turning up to appointments (both business and social) if there is no prior reconfirmation.

Never mix business with food. If a meeting is scheduled over lunch, make sure you don't bring up the deal or negotiations until the meal is finished. In Italy it's important to pay full attention to the food, *then* get down to business.

Don't plan any business in Rome for late July or for the month of August when the whole country goes on holiday and it's difficult, if not impossible, to get anything done. It's too hot anyway and you'll have more fun (and possibly make better business contacts) at the beach.

initial information and help you establish contacts.

In the USA, the Italy-America Chamber of Commerce (IACC) has branches in Atlanta, Boston, Chicago, Houston, Los Angeles, Miami, New York, Philadelphia and Pittsburgh. It publishes an annual directory of Italian companies that do business in the USA and US companies that do business in Italy. The New York office (☎ 212-459 0044; fax 212-459 0090; www.italian-chamber.com) is at 730 Fifth Avenue, Suite 600, New York, NY 10019.

The Italian Trade Commission (☎ 212-980 1500; fax 212-758 1050) is at 499 Park Avenue, New York, NY 10022 and also has offices in Atlanta, LA and Chicago.

Useful Contacts in Italy

The trade office of your embassy can provide tips and contacts. The *English Yellow Pages*, a telephone directory of English-speaking professionals, commercial activities and organisations in Rome (as well as Firenze, Bologna and Milano) might be of use. It is available in English-language bookshops.

The Istituto Nazionale per il Commercio Estero (ICE) is the main foreign trade commission in Italy. Its offices are at Via Liszt 21, 00144 Roma (☎ 06 59 921; fax 06 59 92 68 99).

The British Chamber of Commerce in Italy (BCCI) has a national office in Milano (☎ 02 877798, Via Camperio 9, 10123 Milano, bcci@bbs.infosquare.it, www.mondoweb.it/bcci) and a regional representative in Rome (☎ 06 69 95 61, fax 06 69 95 66 00, BCCI Lazio chapter, Via Due Macelli 66, 00187 Roma).

The American Chamber of Commerce in Italy is based in Milano (Via Cantú 1, 20123 Milano, ☎ 02 8690661, fax 02 8057737) and has a Rome branch (☎ 06 51 86 11, fax 06 51 86 12 86, c/o AT&T, Via C. Colombo 153, 00147 Roma).

Office Services

A GSM mobile phone and a good laptop computer will probably be all you need to do business in Rome. However, some of the better hotels in the city have business centres or secretarial assistance for guests.

There are companies that provide you with a postal address and someone to take messages, at a fee. Most companies have multi-lingual secretaries and some provide translators and interpreters. Executive Services Business Centres (☎ 06 85 23 72 50, fax 06 85 35 01 87, execrom@executive network.it, www.executivenetwork.it, Via Savoia 78) can provide meeting rooms with video conferencing facilities, company addresses, voice mailboxes, translators and interpreters and other services.

Other companies are listed in the *Pagine Gialle* (Yellow Pages) under 'Uffici arredati e servizi'. You can also try the *English Yellow Pages* under 'Secretarial Services'.

Translators/Interpreters

These are listed in the *Pagine Gialle* under 'Traduzioni servizio'.

Couriers

There are several motorcycle courier companies in Rome which are known as 'ponies'. Two of the largest are Speedy Boys (☎ 06 398 88) and Presto (☎ 06 398 90).

WORK

It is illegal for non-EU citizens to work in Italy without a work permit, but trying to obtain one can be time consuming. EU citizens are allowed to work in Italy, but they still need to obtain a carta di soggiorno from the main questura. See the Visas & Documents section for more information about these permits. New immigration laws require foreign workers to be 'legalised' through their employers, which can apply even to cleaners and babysitters. The employers then pay pension and health insurance contributions. This doesn't mean that 'black' work can't still be found.

Jobs are advertised in *Porta Portese* (published on Tuesday and Friday) and in *Wanted in Rome*. You could also look in *Il Messaggero* and *The Herald Tribune* for job ads, and on the bulletin boards of the English-language bookshops (see Shopping chapter).

A very useful guide is *Living, Studying, and Working in Italy* by Travis Neighbor and Monica Larner.

Working Holiday

The best options, once you're in the country, are trying to find work in a bar, nightclub or restaurant during the tourist season. Babysitting is a good possibility. You may be able to pick up a summer job accompanying a family on their annual beach holiday – you could look in magazines such as *Wanted in Rome*, or even place an advertisement. Another option is au pair work, organised before you come to Italy. A useful guide is *The Au Pair and Nanny's Guide to Working Abroad* by S. Griffith & S. Legg (Vacation Work, paperback). By the same publisher is *Work Your Way Around the World* by Susan Griffith.

Teaching English

The easiest source of work for foreigners is teaching English, but even with full qualifications an American, Australian, Canadian or New Zealander might find it difficult to secure a permanent position. Most of the larger, more reputable schools will hire only people with work permits, but their attitude can become more flexible if demand for teachers is high and they come across someone with good qualifications. The more professional schools will require a TEFL (Teaching English as a Foreign Language) certificate. It is advisable to apply for work early in the year, in order to be considered for positions available in October (language school years correspond roughly to the Italian school year which is late September to the end of June).

There are numerous schools which hire people without work permits or qualifications, but the pay is usually low (around L15,000 an hour). It is more lucrative to advertise your services and pick up private

students (although rates vary wildly, ranging from as low as L15,000 to up to L50,000 an hour). The average rate is around L30,000. Although you can get away with absolutely no qualifications or experience, it might be a good idea to bring along a few English grammar books (including exercises) to help you at least appear professional.

Most people get started by placing advertisements in shop windows and on university notice boards, or in a local publication, such as *Wanted in Rome* or *Porta Portese* both of which are available at newspaper stands.

International Organisations and Embassies

Several international organisations are based in Rome, including the Food and Agriculture Organization of the United Nations and the UN World Food Program. However, unless you've got very specific skills, they are hard to get into. Foreign embassies sometimes require administrative or domestic staff and prefer to employ their own nationals.

Street Performers

Busking is common in Italy although, theoretically, buskers require a municipal permit. Italians tend not to stop and gather around street performers, but they are usually quite generous.

Other Work

There are plenty of markets in Rome where you can set up a stall and sell your wares, although you may need to pay a fee. Selling goods on the street is also illegal unless you have a municipal permit and it is quite common to see municipal police moving people along. Another option is to head for beach resorts in summer, particularly if you have handcrafts or jewellery you want to sell.

Getting There & Away

If you live outside Europe, flying is the easiest way to get to Rome. Competition between the airlines means you should be able to pick up a reasonably priced fare, even if you are coming from as far away as Australia. If you live in Europe, chances are you'll be going to Rome overland, but don't ignore the flight option, as you can often find enticing deals from major European hubs.

AIR

Rome's main airport is Leonardo da Vinci, commonly referred to as Fiumicino, after the town nearby (Map: Around Rome). Rome's second (and much smaller) airport, Ciampino, is used for charter flights and smaller airlines (Map: Around Rome).

Italy's national airline is Alitalia, but many international airlines (including most European ones) also serve Italy. Many of Alitalia's intercontinental flights, including those to and from Australia and South America, as well as intercontinental flights by other carriers, now operate out of Malpensa 2000 airport in Milano, connecting with domestic services to Rome.

Departure Tax

The departure tax payable when you leave Italy by air is factored into your airline ticket.

Other Parts of Italy

Regular domestic flights connect Rome to all major Italian airports. The majority of these are operated by Alitalia and its subsidiary airlines. Other domestic airlines include: Air One (Map 6, ☎ 06 47 87 61, Via Sardegna 14) for flights between Rome, Milano, Torino, Bologna, Napoli, Bari, Reggio Calabria, Crotone; and Meridiana (Map 6, ☎ 06 47 80 41, Via Barberini 29) for flights to Milano, Catania, Verona and Sardegna.

The USA

The North Atlantic is the world's busiest long-haul air corridor and the flight options are bewildering. Several airlines fly direct to Rome. These include Alitalia, TWA, Continental and Delta. United flies to Milano Malpensa. However, if your trip will not be confined to Italy, consult your travel agent on whether cheaper flights are available to other European cities.

The *New York Times*, the *LA Times*, the *Chicago Tribune* and the *San Francisco Examiner* produce weekly travel sections in which you'll find any number of travel agents' ads. Council Travel and STA Travel have offices in major cities nationwide. The magazine *Travel Unlimited* (PO Box 1058, Allston, MA 02134) publishes details of cheap air fares.

Standard fares on commercial airlines are expensive and probably best avoided. However, travelling on a normal scheduled flight can be more secure and reliable, particularly for older travellers and families, who might prefer to avoid the potential inconveniences of the budget alternatives.

Discount and rock-bottom options from the USA include charter flights, stand-by and courier flights. Stand-by fares are often sold at 60% of the normal price for one-way tickets. Airhitch (☎ 212-864 2000; airhitch@netcom.com), 2641 Broadway, New York, NY 10025, specialises in flights from the USA to Europe but you cannot be sure of exactly which trans-Atlantic route you will be offered. All you can do is specify which part of the USA you want to fly to/from (ie. west coast or east coast) and your ideal European destination. Airhitch has several other offices in the USA, including Los Angeles (☎ 310-726 5000), as well as others in London, Paris, Amsterdam, Prague, Madrid and Bonn. You can contact the Rome representative on ☎ 06 77 20 86 55.

Courier flights are those on which you accompany a freight parcel to its destination. A New York-Rome return on a courier flight can cost about US$300 to US$400 in the low season (more expensive from the US west coast). Generally, courier flights require that you return within a specified period (sometimes within one or two weeks, but often up to one month). You will need to travel light, as luggage is usually restricted to what you can carry on to the plane (the parcel or freight you carry comes out of your luggage allowance), and you may have to be a US resident and apply for an interview before they will take you on. Most flights depart from New York.

A good source of information on courier flights is Now Voyager (☎ 212-431 1616), Suite 307, 74 Varrick St, New York, NY 10013. This company specialises in courier flights, but you have to pay an annual membership fee (around US$50), which entitles you to take as many courier flights as you like. Phone after 6 pm to listen to a recorded message detailing all available flights and prices. The Denver-based Air Courier Association (☎ 303-278 8810) also does this kind of thing. You join the association which is used by international air freight companies to provide the escorts.

Prices drop as the departure date approaches. It is also possible to organise the flights directly through the courier companies. Look in your Yellow Pages under Courier Services.

Charter flights tend to be significantly cheaper than scheduled flights. Reliable travel agents specialising in charter flights, as well as budget travel for students, include STA and Council Travel, both of which have offices in major cities. Reputable agencies specialising in cheap fares include:

STA
  48 East 11th St, New York, NY 10003 (☎ 212-477 7166)
  914 Westwood Blvd, Los Angeles, CA 90024 (☎ 213-824 1574)
  166 Geary St, Suite 702, San Francisco, CA 94108 (☎ 415-391 8407)
Council Travel
  148 West 4th St, New York, NY 10011 (☎ 212-254 2525)
  205 East 42nd St, New York, NY 10017 (☎ 212-661 1450)
  1093 Broxton Ave, Los Angeles, CA 90024 (☎ 213-208 3551)
  Suite 407, 312 Sutter St, San Francisco, CA 94108 (☎ 415 423473)

Another potential source of information and flights are the travel forums open to Internet users, and assorted computer information and communication services. They are a step further down the travellers' superhighway from TV teletext services – another source of flights and fares.

Low season return airfares from Rome to New York were around L800,000 to L900,000 at the time of writing, and L1,200,000 to Los Angeles. Low season open return tickets from New York to Rome or Milano go for as little as US$500.

If you can't find a particularly cheap flight, it is always worth considering getting a cheap trans-Atlantic hop to London and prowling around the bucketshops there. See UK & Ireland later in this section and make some calculations.

Canada

Both Alitalia and Air Canada have direct flights to Rome and Milano from Toronto and Montreal. Low season return fares from Rome to Toronto start from around L900,000. Travel CUTS, which specialises in discount fares for students, has offices in all major cities. Otherwise scan the budget travel agents' ads in the *Globe & Mail*, the *Toronto Star* and the *Vancouver Sun*. See the previous section for information on courier flights. For courier flights originating in Canada, contact FB on Board Courier Services (☎ 514-633 0740 in Toronto or Montreal, or ☎ 604-338 1366 in Vancouver). Airhitch (see the USA section) has stand-by fares to/from Toronto, Montreal and Vancouver.

The UK

London is one of the best centres in the world for discounted air tickets. For the latest fares, check out the travel page ads of the Sunday newspapers, *Time Out*, *TNT*, and *Exchange & Mart*. All are available from most London newsstands. Another good source of information on cheap fares is the magazine *Business Traveller*. Those with access to Teletext on television will find a host of travel agents advertising. As in North America, the Internet is another possible source of information.

Most British travel agents are registered with ABTA (Association of British Travel Agents). If you have paid for your flight with an ABTA-registered agent who then goes bust, ABTA will guarantee a refund or an alternative. Unregistered bucket shops are riskier but sometimes cheaper.

One of the more reliable, but not necessarily cheapest agencies is STA (☎ 0171-361 6161 for European flights). It has several offices in London, as well as branches on many university campuses and in cities such as Bristol, Cambridge, Leeds, Manchester and Oxford. The main London branches are:

86 Old Brompton Rd, London SW7 3LH
117 Euston Rd, London NW1 2SX
38 Store St, London WC1E 7BZ
Priory House, 6 Wrights Lane, London W8 6TA
11 Goodge St, London, W1

A similar operation is Trailfinders. Its short haul booking centre is at 215 Kensington High St (☎ 0171-937 5400 for European flights). Other offices are at 42-50 Earls Court Rd, London W8 (☎ 0171-938 3366) and 194 Kensington High St, London W8 (☎ 0171-938 3232). The latter offers an inoculation service and a research library for customers. It also has agencies in Bristol, Birmingham, Glasgow and Manchester.

Campus Travel is in much the same league and has the following branches in London:

52 Grosvenor Gardens, London SW1W 0AG (☎ 0171-730 3402 for European flights, ☎ 0171-730 8111 world-wide flights)
YHA Adventure Shop, 174 Kensington High St, London W8 7RG (☎ 0171-938 2188)
YHA Adventure Shop, 14 Southampton St, London (☎ 0171-836 3343)

The two flagship airlines linking the UK and Rome are British Airways (☎ 0171-434 4700; 24 hour line (local rate) ☎ 0345-222111), 156 Regent St, London W1, and Alitalia (☎ 0171-602 7111), 27 Piccadilly, London W1. They operate regular direct flights (usually several a day) to Rome, Milano, Venezia, Firenze, Torino, Napoli and Pisa, as well other cities, including Palermo, during the summer. The regular published fares for both airlines tend to be the same. The fare differences between destinations tend not to be great, but the main cities are cheapest. Normal fares on a scheduled British Airways flight from London to Rome are UK£256 one way and UK£512 return. However, Apex and other special fares are a better option and can cost considerably less. At the time of writing British Airways standard return Apex fare from London to Rome was UK£199 in high season. Low season fares are significantly cheaper.

In recent years, several smaller, low-cost airlines have been offering great deals for scheduled flights to Rome. On these airlines passengers are not always issued with a ticket but given a booking reference/itinerary instead, which is transferred directly into a boarding pass at the check-in, and no food or drinks are served on the flight. At the time of writing, GO (☎ 01279-666 333), a British Airways subsidiary operating out of Stansted, had return flights to Ciampino from UK£100. GO also flies to Milano. Prices for flights from Rome are similar to fares from Britain, allowing for the exchange rate (from L300,000 return at time of writing). GO is contactable in Rome toll free ☎ 147 88 77 66 or see its website (www.go-fly.com).

In 1998 Debonair (☎ 01541-500300), which operates out of Luton, ran a massive promotion offering flights to Rome for as little as UK£39 return. Such great deals aren't available from Italy, but the prices are still good: around L300,000 return. In Rome contact ☎ 06 65 00 21 62.

Virgin Express (☎ 0800-891199 or 0171-744 0004) flies from Heathrow, Gatwick and Stansted to Brussels with a connection to Rome. The fares are competitive if you've got the extra time to spare and don't mind changing planes. In Rome contact ☎ 167 097 097.

The Irish airline RyanAir offers charter flights to Ciampino from Dublin. Ask a travel agent for details. You cannot purchase RyanAir flights to Ireland from Italy.

Italy Sky Shuttle (☎ 0181-748 1333), 227 Shepherd's Bush Rd, London W6 7AS, specialises in charter flights to 22 destinations in Italy from London, Birmingham, Manchester, Glasgow and Edinburgh. Fly/drive deals are also available. Italy Sky Shuttle also has offices in Rome (☎ 06 474 65 41, c/o a travel agency called Summerland, Via Sistina 143), from where you can buy tickets for charter flights to Britain. If you're booking a charter flight, remember to check what time of the day or night you'll be flying; many charter flights arrive very late at night. Transport into the city centre from either Fiumicino or Ciampino can be difficult after about 11 pm (see the Getting Around chapter).

Another specialist in flights and holidays to Italy is Skybus Italia (☎ 0171-373 6055), 24A Earl's Court Gardens, London SW5 0TA.

It is well worth shopping around. Major airlines sometimes discount flights to fill seats. You needn't necessarily fly from London, as many good deals are as easily available from other major centres in the UK.

Flying as a courier (see also the USA section), might be a possibility – you'll have to go through the Yellow Pages to find companies that do this.

If you're coming from Ireland, it might be worth comparing what is available direct and from London – getting across to London first may save you some money.

Continental Europe

Air travel between Rome and other places in Continental Europe is worth considering if you are pushed for time. Short hops can be expensive, but good deals are available from some major hubs.

Several airlines offer cut-rate fares on legs of international flights between European cities. These are usually cheap, but often involve flying at night or early in the morning. Days on which you can fly are restricted. Ask a travel agent for advice.

France Voyages et Découvertes (☎ 01-42 61 00 01), 21 rue Cambon, is a good place to start hunting down the best airfares in Paris. There are plenty of regular flights between Paris and Rome. From Rome the CTS agency has high season return fares for students or those under 26 starting from L410,000.

Germany In Munich, a great source of travel information and equipment is the Därr Travel Shop (☎ 089-28 20 32) at Theresienstrasse 66. In Berlin, Kilroy Travel ARTU Reisen (☎ 030-310 00 40), at Hardenbergstrasse 9, near Berlin Zoo (with five branches around the city) is a good travel agent. In Frankfurt a/M, you might try SRID Reisen (☎ 069-70 30 35), Bergerstrasse 118. High season return flights between Rome and Berlin can cost from about L365,000.

Greece Shop around the travel agents in the backstreets of Athens between Syntagma Square and Omonia Square.

Netherlands Amsterdam is a popular departure point. Some of the best fares are offered by the student travel agency NBBS Reiswinkels (☎ 020-620 5071); its fares are comparable to those of London bucket shops. NBBS Reiswinkels has branches in Brussels (Belgium) as well.

Spain In Madrid one of the most reliable budget travel agents is Viajes Zeppelin (☎ 547 79 03; fax 542 65 46) Plaza de Santo Domingo 2. Virgin Express offer cheap flights from Rome to Barcelona and Madrid sometimes for as little as L149,000 return. In Rome contact ☎ 167 097 097.

Africa

Italy being an unlikely place to look for cheap tickets, it's an even less likely source of budget air tickets to Africa. Tunisia is the most popular North African destination for Italians, so you might dig up something for Tunis; typically, return tickets from Rome to Tunis cost upwards of L285,000.

Australia

STA Travel and Flight Centres International are major dealers in cheap airfares, but your local travel agent often has heavily discounted fares. Scan the ads in the Saturday travel sections of the Melbourne *Age* and the *Sydney Morning Herald*.

Qantas and Alitalia are joined by a host of other European and Asian airlines flying between Australia and Rome. Many of the European airlines throw in a return flight to another European city so, for instance, BA will fly you return to London with a London-Rome-London flight included in the price.

Discounted return fares on mainstream airlines through reputable agents can be surprisingly cheap. Low season fares average around A$1800 return but can go as low as A$1400 with airlines such as Garuda. High season fares range from A$1700 with Garuda to A$2600 with Qantas.

Qantas flies from Melbourne and Sydney to Rome three times a week. Alitalia flies from Milano to Sydney and Melbourne three times a week, with domestic connections to Rome. Flights from Perth are generally a few hundred dollars cheaper.

The following are some addresses for agencies offering good value fares:

STA Travel
   224 Faraday Street, Carlton, Vic 3053 (☎ 03-9347 6911)
   1st Floor, 732 Harris Street, Ultimo, NSW 2007 (☎ 02-212 1255)
   Hackett Hall, University of Western Australia, Crawley, WA 6009 (☎ 09-380 3779; freecall ☎ 1800-637 444)
Flight Centres International
   Bourke Street Flight Centre, 19 Bourke Street, Melbourne, Vic 3000 (☎ 03-9650 2899)
   Martin Place Flight Centre, Shop 5, State Bank Centre, 52 Martin Place, Sydney, NSW 2000 (☎ 02-9235 0166)
   City Flight Centre, 25 Cinema City Arcade, Perth, WA 6000 (☎ 09-325 9222)
CIT
   263 Clarence St, Sydney, NSW 2000 (☎ 02-9267 1255)
   227 Collins St, Melbourne, Vic 3000 (☎ 03-9650 5510)
   Level 9 QV1 Building, 250 St Georges Terrace, Perth, WA 6000 (☎ 09-322 1096)

New Zealand

STA Travel and Flight Centres International are popular travel agents in New Zealand. The cheapest fares to Europe are routed through the USA, and a round-the-world (RTW) ticket may be cheaper than a return. Otherwise, you can fly from Auckland to pick up a connecting flight in Melbourne or Sydney. Air New Zealand can fly you to Bangkok to connect with a Thai Airways flight to Rome, to Singapore to connect with a Singapore Airlines flight, or to Hong Kong to connect with a Cathay Pacific flight. Garuda flies from Auckland to Rome via Jakarta.

Useful addresses include:

Flight Centres International
   Auckland Flight Centre, Shop 3A, National Bank Towers, 205-225 Queen St, Auckland (☎ 09-309 6171)
STA Travel & International Travellers Centre
   10 High St, Auckland (☎ 09-309 0458)
Campus Travel
   Gate 1, Knighton Rd, Waikato University, Hamilton (☎ 07-838 4242)

Asia

Bangkok is probably the best Asian capital to trawl for bucket shops with cheap flights to Rome.

Airline Offices

All the airlines have counters in the departure hall at Fiumicino. Many of the head offices are now based near the airport, although most have ticket offices in the area around Via Veneto and Via Barberini, north of Stazione Termini. They include:

Alitalia
   Via Bissolati 20 (☎ 06 6 56 42)
Air France
   Via Sardegna 40 (☎ 06 48 79 11)
Air New Zealand
   Via Bissolati 54 (☎ 06 488 07 61)
British Airways
   Via Bissolati 54 (☎ 06 52 49 15 12)
Canadian Airlines
   Via C. Veneziani 58 (☎ 06 6557117, Fiumicino ticket office ☎ 06 65010190).
Cathay Pacific
   Via Barberini 3 (☎ 06 482 09 30)

Lufthansa
Via di San Basilio 41 (☎ 06 46601)
Qantas
Via Bissolati 54 (☎ 06 42 01 23 12)
Singapore Airlines
Via Barberini 11 (☎ 06 47 85 53 60)
TWA
Via Barberini 67 (☎ 06 4 72 11)

BUS
Other Parts of Italy

Lazio COTRAL buses, which service the Lazio region, depart from numerous points throughout the city, depending on their destinations. The company is based at Via Ostiense 131 (call ☎ 167 431 784 for information) and is linked with Rome's public transport system, which means that day tickets are available which are valid for city and regional buses, trams, the Metro, and other train lines.

Buses for Palestrina and Tivoli depart from Ponte Mammolo Metro station on Linea B (also stopping at Rebbibia); buses for Bolsena, Saturnia, Toscana and Viterbo depart from Saxa Rubra, on the Ferrovia Roma Nord train line; buses for the Castelli Romani depart from Anagnina, the last stop on the Metro Linea A; buses for the beaches south of Rome depart from the EUR-Fermi station on the Metro Linea B; for Bracciano, Cerveteri and Tarquinia take a bus from the Lepanto stop on Metro Linea A. Also see under individual destinations in the Excursions chapter later in this book.

Other Regions The main station for Intercity buses is in Piazzale Tiburtina, in front of Stazione Tiburtina. Catch the Metropolitana Linea B from Termini to Tiburtina. Buses run by various companies go to cities throughout Italy. For more detailed information about which companies go to which destinations, go to Stazione Tiburtina, or the Eurojet agency in Piazza della Repubblica 54 (where you can buy tickets for some bus lines). Enjoy Rome or the APT office can also help (see Tourist Offices in Facts for the Visitor chapter).

Some useful bus lines include:

ARPA, SIRA, Di Fonzo, Di Febo & Capuani
Services to Abruzzo, including L'Aquila, Pescasseroli and Pescara
Information at Piazzale Tiburtina
Bonelli
Services to Emilia-Romagna, including Ravenna and Rimini
Information at Piazzale Tiburtina
Lazzi
Services to other European cities and the Alps
Via Tagliamento 27r (☎ 06 884 08 40)
Lirosi
Services to Calabria
Information at Eurojet (☎ 06 474 28 01)
Marozzi
Services to Bari and Brindisi, Sorrento, the Amalfi coast and Pompeii
Information at Eurojet (☎ 06 474 28 01)
SAIS & Segesta
Services to Sicilia
Information at Piazza della Repubblica or Piazzale Tiburtina (☎ 06 481 96 76)
Sena
Services to Siena
Information at Eurojet (☎ 06 474 28 01)
SULGA
Services to Perugia and Assisi, as well as to Fiumicino airport
Information at Eurojet (☎ 06 474 28 01 or ☎ 075-500 96 41)

Europe

Eurolines, in conjunction with local bus companies across Europe, is the main international carrier. Representatives in Rome are: Lazzi Express (☎ 06 884 08 40), Via Tagliamento 27/r; and Agenzia Elios (☎ 06 44 23 39 28), Circonvallazione Nomentana 574, on the Stazione Tiburtina side. The prices quoted below are for high season. There is a 10% reduction for people aged under 26 or over 60. Children of four to 11 years of age pay 50% of the full fare; those under three years old travel free if they are not occupying a seat.

Bear in mind that a discounted airfare might work out cheaper than the long bus trip allowing for food and drink bought en route.

UK Eurolines (☎ 0990-143219) runs buses twice a week from Victoria Coach Station for Milano (23½ hours), Rome (36 hours) and other destinations. Up to four services a week run in summer. Other destinations include Torino, Genova, Firenze, Rimini and Ancona. The lowest youth/under-26 fares from London to Rome are UK£85/129 for single/return. The full adult fares are UK£91/137. The single biggest disadvantage of the bus is that you can't get off along the way. Fares rise in the peak summer season.

Eurolines also offers good-value explorer tickets which are valid up to six months and allow travel between a number of major European cities.

Austria Eurolines' main office in Vienna is at Autobusbahnhof Wien-Mitte, Schalter 2 (Window 2), Hauptstrasse 1b (☎ 01-712 04 53). SITA (see Germany) has a weekly service from Vienna to Padova with connections for Rome and other destinations in Italy. SITA tickets can be bought in Vienna at Fangokur Reisen, Wipplingerstrasse 12 (☎ 533 1360).

France Eurolines has offices in several French cities. In Paris they are at 28 Ave du Général de Gaulle (☎ 01-49 72 51 51). One-way/return adult fares to Paris from Rome cost L180,000/290,000 in high season. Fares to Nice from Rome are L95,000/109,000.

Germany Eurolines and associated companies have stations at major cities across Germany, including Hamburg, Frankfurt and Munich. For the latter, head for Deutsche Touring GmbH, Amulfstrasse 3 (Stamberger Bahnhof, ☎ 089-545 87 00). Otherwise, SITA has buses from Frankfurt, Munich or Hamburg to Padova, where you can pick up a connection for Rome. In Frankfurt, SITA is at Am Römerhof 17 (☎ 069-790 3240).

Netherlands Eurolines is at Rokin 10 in Amsterdam (☎ 020-627 51 51). The adult one-way/return fare from Rome to Amsterdam is L230,000/367,000.

Spain Eurolines and associated companies have representatives across the country, including the Estación Sur de Autobuses (☎ 91-528 11 05), Calle de las Canarias 17,

in Madrid and the Estación Autobuses de Sants (☎ 93-490 40 00), Calle del Viriato s/n, Barcelona. There are at least two weekly services between Rome and Madrid, with stops en route. Fares vary, but from Rome to Madrid can cost adults L232,000/418,000 one way/return. Rome-Barcelona costs L180,000/324,000.

TRAIN
Almost all trains arrive at and depart from Stazione Termini. There are regular connections to other European countries, to all the major cities in Italy and to many smaller towns. There are eight other train stations scattered throughout Rome. Some northbound trains depart from or stop at Stazione Ostiense and Stazione Trastevere.

For train information, ring ☎ 800 88 80 88 from 7 am to 9 pm (in Italian only) or go to the information office at the train station, where English is spoken. Timetables can be bought at most newspaper stands in and around Termini and are particularly useful if you are making multiple train journeys.

Remember to validate your train ticket in the yellow machines on the station platforms. If you don't, you may be forced to pay a fine on the train.

Other Parts of Italy
Travelling by train in Italy is simple, cheap and generally efficient. The Ferrovie dello Stato (FS, www.fs-on-line.com/eng/index.html) is the partially privatised state train system and there are several private train services throughout the country. There are several types of trains:

Regionale (R)
    usually stops at all stations and can be very slow
interRegionale (iR)
    runs between the regions
Intercity (IC) and *Eurocity* (EC)
    services only the major cities

The fast train service between major Italian and European cities is called *Eurostar Italia* and has both 1st and 2nd class.

There are 1st and 2nd classes on all Italian trains, with a 1st class ticket costing a bit less than double the price of 2nd class. On the Eurostar trains, 2nd class is much like 1st class on other trains.

It is recommended that you book train tickets for long trips, particularly if you're travelling on weekends or during holiday periods, otherwise you could find yourself standing in the corridor for the entire journey. Reservations are obligatory for the Eurostar. You can get timetable information and make train bookings at most travel agents in Rome, including CTS, or you can simply buy your ticket on arrival at the station. There are special booking offices for the Eurostar at the relevant train stations. If you are doing a reasonable amount of travelling, it is worth buying a train timetable. There are several available, including the official FS timetables, which are available at newspaper stands in or near train stations for around L5000.

There are left-luggage facilities at all train stations. They are often open 24 hours but, if not, they usually close only for a couple of hours after midnight. They open seven days a week and charge from L1500 per day for each piece of luggage.

Costs To travel on the Intercity and Euro-City trains, you are required to pay a *supplemento*, an additional charge determined by the distance you are travelling. For instance, on the Intercity train between Rome and Firenze you will pay an extra L15,000. On the Eurostar, it is obligatory to make a booking, since they don't carry standing room passengers. The cost of the ticket includes the supplement and booking fee. The one-way fare from Rome to Firenze on the Eurostar is L51,000 in 2nd class and L78,500 in 1st class. The difference in price between the Eurostar (1½ hours) and the cheaper Intercity (around two hours) is only L12,500. For the extra money you get a faster, much more comfortable service, with soem nuts or biscuits thrown in. The Eurostar always takes priority over other trains, so there's less risk of long delays in the middle of nowhere.

Always check whether the train you are about to catch is an Intercity, and pay the supplement before you get on, otherwise you will pay extra on the train. On overnight trips within Italy it can be worth paying extra for a *cuccetta* – a sleeping berth (commonly known as a couchette) which costs an extra L30,500 (for a four-bed compartment) and L21,500 (for a six-bed compartment). It is possible to take your bicycle in the baggage compartment on some trains (L10,000).

Some price examples for one-way train fares (including supplements) are: Rome-Firenze L74,000 (1st class) and L38,500 (2nd class); Milano L68,000 (2nd class); Venezia L68,000 (2nd class); and Napoli L28,500 (2nd class). Return fares are double the one-way fare.

Italian Rail Passes It is not worth buying a Eurail or Inter-Rail pass if you are going to travel only in Italy, since train fares are reasonably cheap. The FS offers its own discount passes for travel within the country.

These include the Carta Verde for young people aged from 12 to 26 years. It costs L40,000, is valid for one year and entitles you to a 20% discount on all train travel, but you'll need to do a fair bit of travelling to get your money's worth. Children aged between four and 12 years are automatically entitled to a 50% discount, and those under four years travel free.

The Carta d'Argento entitles people aged 60 years and over to a 20% discount on 1st and 2nd class travel for one year. It also costs L40,000.

You can buy a *biglietto chilometrico* (kilometric ticket), which is valid for two months and allows you to cover 3000km, with a maximum of 20 trips. It costs L206,000 (2nd class) and you must pay the supplement if you catch an Intercity train. Its main attraction is that it can be used by up to five people, either singly or together.

Two other useful passes are the Italy Railcard and Italy Flexi Rail. With both

STEFANO CAVEDONI

SALLY WEBB

Arco di Constantino with the Colosseo nearby

A Field of Flowers in the Campo de' Fiori

STEFANO CAVEDONI

The Temple of Hercules keeps its traditional circular form

An international newspaper spread

How hot do you like your *arrabbiata*?

Bar Sacchetti, Piazza San Cosmiato

passes, prices include supplements for travel on Intercity trains but not for Eurostar trains. You should have your passport for identification when purchasing either pass. Italy Railcard is valid for eight, 15, 21 or 30 days and is available in 1st or 2nd class. An eight-day pass costs L438,000 in 1st class or L292,000 in 2nd class. A 21-day pass costs L635,000/423,000 1st/2nd class. Italy Flexi Rail is valid for four, eight or 12 days for travel within one month. A four-day pass costs L356,000/237,000 1st/2nd class. A 12-day pass costs L641,000/427,000 1st/2nd class.

Europe

Train travel is a convenient and simple means of travelling from most parts of Europe to Italy. It is certainly a popular way of getting around for backpackers and other young travellers, and even the more well-heeled travellers will find European trains a comfortable and reliable way to reach their destination.

If you plan to travel extensively by train in Europe it might be worth getting hold of the *Thomas Cook European Timetable*, which gives a complete listing of train schedules and indicates where supplements apply or where reservations are necessary. It is updated monthly and is available from Thomas Cook offices and agents in Italy and worldwide. The European Railways and Timetables website, mercurio.iet.unipi .it/misc/timetabl.html, is also helpful. In Rome it is also available at the Anglo-American Bookshop, Via delle Vite 102 (Map 6, near Piazza di Spagna).

EuroCity (EC) trains run from major destinations throughout Europe – including Paris, Geneva, Zürich, Frankfurt, Vienna and Barcelona – direct to major Italian cities. On overnight hauls you can book a *cuccetta* (known outside Italy as a *couchette* or sleeping berth) for around L40,000 (four-bed) or L26,000 (six-bed) for most international trains. In 1st class there are four bunks per cabin and in 2nd class there are six bunks. Sleepers are more expensive, but also much more comfortable.

It is always advisable to book a seat on EuroCity trains, or for any long-distance train travel to/from Italy. Trains are often extremely overcrowded, particularly in summer, and you could find yourself standing in the passageway for the whole trip!

When crossing international borders on overnight trips, train conductors will usually collect your passport before you go to sleep and hand it back the following morning.

Some of the main international services include transport for private cars – an option worth examining to save wear and tear on your vehicle before it arrives in Italy.

UK Travelling from the UK, you have a choice of train tickets covering the channel crossing by ferry, the faster Seacat, or the Eurostar train through the Channel Tunnel, which speeds up the initial part of the journey. Several routes are also available, via Paris and southern France or swinging from Belgium down through Germany and Switzerland.

The cheapest standard return fares from Rome to London at the time of writing were L550,000 (for students) or L582,000.

Austria Regular trains on two lines connect Italy with main cities in Austria.

France & Spain Standard return, 2nd class fares from Rome to Paris cost from L279,000 (students) to L340,000. Fares through France to Barcelona cost from L289,000 (students) to L319,000. The luxury high speed Artesia service using the French TGV and Italian ETR-460 trains connects Paris with Milano and Torino – at a price.

Slovenia Two lines connect Italy with Slovenia.

Switzerland The fast Eurostar ETR470 Cisalpino trains run at speeds of up to 200km/h from Milano to major Swiss destinations. Return fares from Rome to Geneva cost from L212,000 to L218,000.

CAR & MOTORCYCLE

The main road connecting Rome to the north and south of Italy is the Autostrada del Sole, which extends from Milano to Reggio di Calabria. On the outskirts of the city it connects with the Grande Raccordo Anulare, the ring road encircling Rome. From here, there are several exits into the city.

If you are approaching from the north, take the Via Salaria, Via Nomentana or Via Flaminia exits. From the south, Via Appia Nuova, Via Cristoforo Colombo and Via del Mare (which connects Rome to the Lido di Ostia) all provide reasonably direct routes into the city. The Grande Raccordo Anulare and all arterial roads in Rome are clogged with traffic on weekday evenings from about 5 to 7.30 pm, and on Sunday evening, particularly in summer, all approaches to Rome are subject to traffic jams as Romans return home after weekends away.

The A12 connects the city to Civitavecchia and then along the coast to Genova (it also connects the city to Fiumicino airport). Signs from the centre of Rome to the autostrada can be vague and confusing, so invest in a good road map. It is best to stick to the arterial roads to reach the Grande Raccordo Anulare and then exit at the appropriate point.

The main roads out of Rome basically follow the same routes as the ancient consular roads. The seven most important are:

Via Aurelia (SS1)
  starts at il Vaticano and leaves the city to the north-east, following the Tyrrhenian coast to Pisa, Genova and France
Via Cassia (SS2)
  starts at the Ponte Milvio and heads north-west to Viterbo, Siena and Firenze
Via Flaminia (SS3)
  starts at the Ponte Milvio, and goes north-west to Terni, Foligno and over the Appennini into Le Marche, ending on the Adriatic coast at Fano
Via Salaria (SS4)
  heads north from near Porta Pia in central Rome to Rieti and into Le Marche, and ends at Porto d'Ascoli on the Adriatic coast
Via Tiburtina (SS5)
  links Rome with Tivoli and Pescara, on the coast of Abruzzo

Via Casilina (SS6)
  heads south-east to Anagni and into Campania, terminating at Capua near Napoli
Via Appia Nuova (SS7)
  the most famous of the consular roads, it heads south along the coast of Lazio into Campania, and then goes inland across the Appennini into Basilicata, through Potenza and Matera to Taranto in Puglia and on to Brindisi.

Documents

Proof of ownership or registration of a private vehicle should always be carried when driving in Italy. Third party insurance is a minimum requirement throughout Europe, and it is compulsory to have a Green Card, an internationally recognised proof of insurance, which can be obtained from your insurer.

A European breakdown assistance policy such as the AA Five Star Service or the RAC Eurocover Motoring Assistance, is a good investment. The Automobile Club Italiano (ACI) no longer offers free roadside assistance to tourists. Residents of the UK and Germany should be able to organise assistance abroad through their home-country organisations, which entitles them to use ACI's emergency assistance number ☎ 116 for a small fee. Without it, you'll pay a minimum fee of L160,000 if you call ☎ 116. ACI has offices at Via Marsala 8, Rome (☎ 06 499 81); and Corso Venezia 43, Milano (☎ 02 774 51).

Every vehicle travelling across an international border should display a nationality plate of its country of registration. In the UK, further information can be obtained from the RAC (☎ 0181-686 0088 or 0345-331133) or the AA (☎ 01256-20123).

Road Rules

In Italy, as throughout Continental Europe, people drive on the right side of the road and overtake on the left. Unless otherwise indicated, you must give way to cars coming from the right.

A warning triangle (to be used in the event of a breakdown) is compulsory throughout Europe. Recommended accessories are a first-aid kit, a spare bulb kit and a fire extinguisher. It is compulsory to wear seat belts if fitted to the car (front seat belts on all cars, rear seat belts on cars produced after 26 April 1990). If caught without seat belts, you will be required to pay a L58,000 on-the-spot fine, although this doesn't seem to deter Italians, many of whom wear them only on the autostradas.

Tolls apply on most of the main autostradas. You pick up a ticket as you enter and pay as you exit (the amount depends on the distance travelled).

Random breath tests now take place in Italy. If you're involved in an accident while under the influence of alcohol, the penalties can be severe. The limit on blood-alcohol content is 0.08%.

Speed limits, unless otherwise indicated by local signs, are: on autostradas 130km/h for cars of 1100cc or more, 110km/h for smaller cars and for motorcycles under 350cc; on all main, non-urban highways 110km/h; on secondary, non-urban highways 90km/h; and in built-up areas 50km/h. Speeding fines follow EU standards and are L59,000 for up to 10km/h over the limit, L235,000 for up to 40km/h, and L587,000 for more than 40km/h. Driving through a red light costs L117,000.

See Documents, Facts for the Visitor chapter for driving licence requirements.

You don't need a licence to ride a moped under 50cc, but you should be aged 14 years or over, and a helmet is compulsory up to age 18; you may not carry passengers or use the autostradas. The speed limit for a moped is 40km/h. To ride a motorcycle or scooter up to 125cc, you must be at least 16 years old and have a licence (a car licence will do). Helmets are compulsory for everyone riding a motorcycle of more than 50cc engine capacity, although this is a law that Italians choose to ignore.

For motorcycles over 125cc you need a motorcycle licence. Crash helmets are compulsory in Italy. You will be able to enter restricted traffic areas in Italian cities without any problems and Italian traffic police generally turn a blind eye to motorcycles parked on footpaths. There is no lights-on requirement for motorcycles during the day.

See the Getting Around chapter for information about renting cars, motorbikes and mopeds.

Fuel

The cost of leaded petrol in Italy is very high, at around L1900 per litre (slightly less for unleaded petrol). Leaded petrol is *benzina*, unleaded petrol is *benzina senza piombo* and diesel is *gasolio*. If you are driving a car which uses LPG (liquid petroleum gas), you will need to buy a special guide to service stations which have *gasauto* or GPL. By law these must be located in non-residential areas and are usually in the country or on city outskirts, although you'll find plenty on the autostradas. GPL costs around L900 per litre.

BICYCLE

Cycling is a favourite national sport in Italy but there are surprisingly few dedicated bike paths, so most of the time you'll be sharing the tarmac with traffic. Local tourist offices have information about trails in their area.

Bikes can be taken very cheaply on trains (L10,000), although only some trains will actually carry them. Fast trains (IC, EC etc) will generally not accommodate bikes and they must be sent as registered luggage. This can take a few days and will probably mean that your bike won't be on the same train that you travel on. It might be an idea to send your bike in advance, if possible. Check with the FS or a travel agent for more information.

Bikes can usually be transported on aeroplanes for a low fee, or even for free. Ask your airline or travel agent for details.

For information on hiring bikes and bike tours, see the Getting Around chapter.

HITCHING

Hitching is never safe in any country, and we don't recommend it. Travellers who decide to hitchhike should understand they are taking a small, but potentially serious, risk. People who do choose to hitchhike will be safer if they travel in pairs and let someone know where they are planning to go. Women travelling alone should be extremely cautious about hitching anywhere in Italy. It is illegal to hitchhike on Italy's autostradas, but quite acceptable to stand near the entrance to the toll booths. You could also approach drivers at petrol stations and truck stops.

To head north on the A1, take bus No 319 from Stazione Termini, get off at Piazza Vescovio and then take bus No 135 to Via Salaria. To go south to Napoli on the A2, take the Metropolitana to Anagnina and wait in Via Tuscolana.

It is sometimes possible to arrange lifts in advance – ask around at youth hostels. The International Lift Centre in Firenze (☎ 055 28 06 26) as well as Enjoy Rome (see Tourist Offices, Facts for the Visitor chapter) may be able to help. Dedicated hitchhikers might also like to get hold of Simon Calder's *Europe – a Manual for Hitchhikers*.

BOAT

The nearest port to Rome is at Civitavecchia (Map: Lazio), from where ferries depart for Sardegna. Regular trains run from Stazione Termini to Civitavecchia (1½ hours). Services are run by Tirrenia and the FS. Ticket prices vary according to the time of year and are at their most expensive during summer. Travel agencies in Rome will be able to provide information on fares and bookings.

ORGANISED TOURS

There are many options for organised travel to Rome. The Italian Tourist Office can sometimes provide a list of tour operators noting what each specialises in. Offices of CIT (see Tourist Offices in the Facts for the Visitor chapter) abroad can also help. It is always worth shopping around for value, but such tours rarely come cheap. Tours can save you hassles, but they do rob you of independence.

The major airlines often offer short city break packages, which include air fares, accommodation and transfers, but leave you free to do your sightseeing independently. These deals are usually advertised in the travel sections of the national newspapers. Travel agencies or organisations specialising in these include Italia Tours Ltd (☎ 0171-371 1114), 205 Holland Park Ave, London W11 4XBT and Kirker Travel Ltd (☎ 0171-231 3333), 3 New Concordia Wharf, Mill St, London SE1 2BB. Prices vary depending on the time of year you travel (always cheaper in the low season) and the type of accommodation you choose.

TRAVEL AGENTS

Really cheap airfares are hard to come by in Rome where bucket shops don't exist. However, there are a few agencies specialising in youth and budget travel. Bear in mind that the majority of these do not accept payment by credit card. Always check first to avoid being caught without cash.

Most travel agencies in Rome are honest and solvent, but a few rogues will take your money and disappear, only to reopen elsewhere a month or two later under a new name. If you feel suspicious about a firm, don't give them all the money at once – leave a deposit of 10 to 20% and pay the balance when you get the ticket. If they insist on cash in advance, go somewhere else. Once you have the ticket, ring the airline to confirm that you are actually booked on the flight. Always use a travel agent registered with IATA, the international travel agents' association. Although this doesn't mean you can't be ripped off, it does mean that you will have some form of recourse if you are.

CTS (Centro Turistico Studentesco) (Map 5, ☎ 06 687 26 72), Corso Vittorio Emauele II 297, is Italy's official student travel service and offers discounted air, rail and bus tickets to students and travellers under 30 years old. CTS also issues ISIC international student identity cards. It is open from 9.30 am to 1 pm and 3.30 to 7pm Monday to Friday, and from 9.30 am to 1 pm on Saturday. There are other branches at Via Genova 16 (Map 6; ☎ 06

467 92 71) and near La Sapienza university, at Via degli Ausoni 5 (Map 6; ☎ 06 445 01 41). Note that to take advantage of CTS fares if you are not a student, you have to have a CTS card, which costs L45,000 and is valid for a year.

Elsy Viaggi, Via di Torre Argentina 80 (Map: Around Piazza Navona, ☎ 06 68 80 13 72) has some of the cheapest fares around for flights to other European cities as well as good deals on long-haul flights, but it doesn't accept credit cards. It is open from 9 am to 1 pm and 3.30 to 6.30 pm Monday to Friday, and from 9 am to 1 pm on Saturday.

CIT (Compagnia Italiana Turismo) offers a full range of travel services, although not necessarily especially cheap fares. There are several CIT offices in Rome. The most central are Via Barberini 86 (Map 6, ☎ 06 47 86 41, fax 47 86 42 00), and Piazza della Repubblica 65 (Map 6, ☎ 06 481 88 06). There is also a branch at Stazione Termini.

Nouvelles Frontières (Map 5, ☎ 06 322 24 63, Via A. Brunetti 25), off Via del Corso near Piazza del Popolo is another popular travel agency catering for the youth and budget travel markets.

Transalpino, Piazza Esquilino 8a, (Map 6, ☎ 06 487 08 70) offers discounts on European train tickets. It is open from 8 am to 9 pm Monday to Saturday, and from 9 am to 8 pm on Sunday. There is also a branch at Stazione Termini.

WARNING

The information in this chapter is particularly vulnerable to change: prices for international travel are volatile, routes are introduced and cancelled, schedules change, special deals come and go, and rules and visa requirements are amended.

Airlines and governments seem to take a perverse pleasure in making price structures and regulations as complicated as possible. You should check directly with the airline or a travel agent to make sure you understand how a fare (and the ticket you might buy) works. In addition, the travel industry is highly competitive and there are many lurks and perks.

The upshot of this is that you should get opinions, quotes and advice from as many airlines and travel agents as possible before you part with your hard-earned cash. the travel details given in this chapter should only be regarded as pointers and are not a substitute for your own careful up-to-date research.

GETTING THERE & AWAY

Getting Around

TO/FROM THE AIRPORTS
Fiumicino

Rome's main airport, Leonardo da Vinci (Fiumicino), is about 30km south-west of the city centre (Map: Around Rome). The direct Fiumicino-Stazione Termini train (follow the signs to the train station from the airport arrivals hall) costs L15,000. The train arrives at and leaves from platform No 22 at Termini and takes about 30 minutes. Tickets can be bought from vending machines at Fiumicino and Termini, or from the Alitalia office at platform 22, or at the airport. The first direct train leaves the airport for Termini at 7.37 am, then runs hourly (half-hourly at certain times of the day) from 8.07 am until 10.07 pm. From Termini to the airport, trains start at 6.50 am and run hourly and half-hourly until 9.20 pm.

Another train from Fiumicino stops at Trastevere, Ostiense and Tiburtina stations (L7000). From the airport, trains run about every 20 minutes from 6.27 am to 11.27 am and from Ostiense from 5.19 am until 10.49 am. You should allow more time on Sundays and public holidays when there is a reduced service. This train does not stop at Termini.

Tickets for both trains can be bought from vending machines in the main airport arrivals hall. Make sure you have some small notes as these machines rarely have much change. Tickets can also be bought from the ticket office, tobacconist or vending machines in the railway stations. The Alitalia office at platform 22 at Termini also sells them.

From midnight to 5 am an hourly bus runs from Stazione Tiburtina (accessible by bus No 42N from Piazza dei Cinquecento in front of Termini) to the airport. The same bus departs for the city from outside the arrivals hall. Tickets cost L7000. Don't hang around Tiburtina at night when it's not safe.

Fiumicino airport is connected to the city by an autostrada. Follow the signs for Roma out of the complex and exit from the autostrada at EUR. From there, you'll need to ask directions to reach Via Cristoforo Colombo, which will take you directly into the centre.

Taxis leave from outside the arrivals hall. They are expensive: a taxi to the centre of Rome will cost around L70,000 (including a special airport surcharge of L15,000).

Ciampino

Ciampino airport (Map: Around Rome), about 15km south-east of the city, is primarily a military airbase. Most charter flights operate out of Ciampino, but it is becoming popular with discount airlines. Ciampino is connected to Rome by the Via Appia Nuova. Public transport to the city centre is inefficient; if you arrive late or very early, you have little option other than to catch a taxi, which will cost around L60,000. Ask fellow passengers if they want to share a cab.

Blue COTRAL buses (running between 5.45 am and 10.30 pm, running about every 60 to 90 minutes) will take you to the Anagnina Metro station, from where you can catch the Linea A to Stazione Termini. Buses for Ciampino leave from Anagnina every hour or so from 6.10 am to 11 pm. Combined bus-metro tickets (L1500) can be bought from an automatic machine in the arrivals hall or from the newsstand in the departures building. At the time of writing, some airlines, including GO and Debonair, were providing a bus service for passengers on their flights from Ciampino to Piazza Santa Maria Maggiore and back out to the airport for around L20,000. Check with your airline for details.

BUS & TRAM

ATAC is the city bus and tram company, and many of the main buses terminate in Piazza dei Cinquecento at Stazione Termini (Map 6). At the information booth in the centre of the piazza you can obtain a map which outlines the bus routes. The Lozzi map of Rome provides a good enough guide to these bus routes.

Another central point for the main bus routes is Largo di Torre Argentina, near Piazza Navona (Map: Around Piazza Navona). Buses generally run from about 6 am to midnight, with limited services throughout the night on some routes. ATAC's routes seem to be in a constant state of evolution, so if you're planning on using the buses and trams a lot, pick up a free transport map from the information kiosk at Termini or from any tourist information booth.

Travel on Rome's buses, trams, subway and suburban railways is now part of the same system and the same Metrebus tickets are valid for all modes of transport. Single tickets cost L1500 for 75 minutes. Children up to 1m tall travel free. Daily tickets cost L6000, weekly tickets L24,000 and monthly tickets L50,000.

Tickets must be purchased *before* you get on the bus or train and then validated in the machine as you enter. On the subway tickets must be validated as you go through the electronic barriers before you descend to the platform. If changing from bus to metro, the ticket should be validated a second time. The minimum fine for travelling without a validated ticket is L100,000 (but it can be as much as L500,000) and inspectors are growing tired of the same old explanations from tourists that they 'didn't know'. Tickets can be obtained in Piazza dei Cinquecento, at tobacconists, at newspaper stands and from vending machines at main bus stops.

Information about all public transport services can be obtained from ☎ 167-431 784 (from 9 am to 1pm and from 2 to 5 pm).

Useful routes include:

No 8 (tram)
    Largo di Torre Argentina to Trastevere, Stazione Trastevere and Monteverde Nuovo
No 46
    Piazza Venezia to San Pietro and the Via Aurelia

No 64
    Stazione Termini to San Pietro
No 27
    Stazione Termini to the Colosseo, Circo Massimo and the Aventino
No 36
    Stazione Termini along Via Nomentana (for foreign embassies)
No 116 (small electric bus)
    Via Giulia through the city centre to Villa Borghese park
No 175
    Piazzale Partigiani car park at Stazione Ostiense to Stazione Termini
No 218
    Piazza San Giovanni in Laterano to the Via Appia Antica and the Catacombs
No 910
    Stazione Termini to the Villa Borghese
No 590
    follows the route of Metro Line A and has special facilities for disabled passengers

TRAIN

In addition to the underground Metropolitana, Rome has an overground rail network. The rail network is useful only if you are heading out of town to the Castelli Romani, the beaches at Lido di Ostia or the ruins at Ostia Antica (see the Excursions chapter).

One train line, FM1, which runs from Orte and other towns well north of Rome to Fiumicino airport (see the To/From Airports section earlier in this chapter). This train stops in Rome at Stazione Tiburtina, Stazione Tuscolana, Stazione Ostiense and Stazione Trastevere and in the Rome metropolitan area; normal Metrebus tickets can be used. However, if you want to take this train to Fiumicino airport, you have to buy a different ticket which costs L7000 one way.

METROPOLITANA

The Metropolitana (Metro) has two lines, Linea A and Linea B. Both pass through Stazione Termini. The Metro operates from 5.30 am to 11.30 pm (one hour later on Saturday) and trains run approximately every 5 minutes. However, until the end of 1999 Linea A will be closing at 10 pm to allow for major works on the tracks, ventilation and fire safety systems. Useful Metro stations include:

Stations	Linea	Attractions
Spagna	Linea A	Piazza di Spagna
Flaminio	Linea A	Villa Borghese
Ottaviano	Linea A	Il Vaticano
Colosseo	Linea B	Colosseo
Circo Massimo	Linea B	Circo Massimo, Aventino, il Celio, Terme di Caracalla
Piramide	Linea B	Stazione Ostiense, trains to the airport and Lido di Ostia

A new station on Linea A, Musei Vaticani, is expected to open in late 1999 and will give direct access to the Musei Vaticani.

On Sundays you can take your bike on the Metro Linea B and the connecting Lido di Ostia train. You'll have to stamp two tickets – one for you and one for the bike – before you get on the train (front carriage only).

CAR & MOTORCYCLE

Negotiating Roman traffic by car is difficult enough, but you may be taking your life in your hands if you ride a motorcycle or moped in the city. The rule in Rome is to look straight ahead to watch the vehicles in front, and hope that the vehicles behind are watching you!

Most of the historic centre of Rome is closed to normal traffic, although tourists are permitted to drive to their hotels. Traffic police control the entrances to the centre and should let you through if you have a car full of luggage and mention the name of your hotel. The hotel management should provide a pass which allows you to park in the centre (check this when you book). Traffic police are getting very tough on illegally parked cars. At best you'll get a heavy fine (around L200,000), at worst a wheel clamp or your car towed away. In the event that your car goes missing after it was parked illegally, always check first with the traffic police (☎ 06 676 91). You will have to pay about L180,000 to get it back, plus a hefty fine.

A pay parking system has been introduced around the periphery of Rome's city centre. Spaces are denoted by a blue line in most areas including the Lungotevere (the roads beside the Tevere river) and near Termini (Map 6). You'll need small change to get tickets from vending machines, otherwise scratch tickets are available from tobacconists. Parking costs L2000 per hour.

The major parking area closest to the centre is at the Villa Borghese (Map 4); entry is from Piazzale Brasile at the top of Via Veneto. There is also a supervised car park at Stazione Termini. Other car parks are at Piazzale dei Partigiani, just outside Stazione Ostiense (Map 8; you can then take the metro into central Rome from nearby Piramide metro station) and at Stazione Tiburtina, from where you can also catch the metro into the centre.

Car Rental

There's no point renting a car to tour the city but it could be useful if you are travelling to destinations outside Rome. It is cheaper to arrange car rental before leaving your own country, for instance through some sort of fly/drive deal. Most major firms, including Hertz, Avis and Budget, will arrange this, and you simply pick up the vehicle at a nominated point upon arrival or on a specified day.

You will need to be aged 21 years or over (23 years or above for some companies) and possess a valid driving licence to rent a car in Italy. You will find the deal far easier to organise if you have a credit card. No matter where you rent, make sure you understand what is included in the price (unlimited kilometres, tax, insurance, collision damage waiver etc) and what your liabilities are. In some cases you are liable for penalties of between L500,000 and L1,000,000 if the car is stolen.

At the time of writing, Avis offered a special weekend rate for unlimited kilometres which compared well with rates offered by other firms: L285,000 for a Fiat Uno or Renault Clio, or L320,500 for a Fiat Brava, from Friday 9 am to Monday 9 am. Maggiore Budget offered a weekend deal of L147,000 for a Renault Clio, with a limit of 300km. If you pick up or drop off the car at an airport there is a 12% surcharge. The same car for five to seven days, with a limit of 1400km, costs L497,000.

The major rental companies are:

Avis
    central booking (☎ 06 419 99)
    Ciampino airport (☎ 06 79 34 01 95)
    Fiumicino airport (☎ 06 65 01 06 78)
    Stazione Termini (☎ 06 481 43 73)
Dollaroexpress
    (toll-free ☎ 1678 86 51 10)
Europcar
    central booking (☎ 06 52 08 11)
    Fiumicino airport (☎ 06 65 01 08 79)
    Stazione Termini (☎ 06 488 28 54)
Maggiore Budget
    central booking (☎ 1478 670 67)
    Fiumicino airport (☎ 06 65 01 06 78)
    Stazione Termini (☎ 06 488 00 49)

Motorcycle & Moped Rental

Motorcycles, scooters and mopeds can be rented from Happy Rent (Map 6, ☎ 06 481 81 85, Via Farini 3) off Via Cavour between Stazione Termini and Piazza Esquilino. Motorcycle (600cc) rental costs L160,000 per day and scooters and mopeds (50cc to 125cc) cost from L50,000 to L140,000 per day. Happy Rent also rents cars and minivans (baby seats are available) but prices are higher than the major car rental companies. All major credit cards are accepted.

Another option is Bici e Baci (Map 6, ☎ 06 482 84 43, Via del Viminale 5) near Piazza della Repubblica. Scooter rental starts at L40,000 per day. All major credit cards are accepted.

At Stazione Termini, on the north-eastern side of the bus terminus at Piazza dei Cinquecento, is Treno e Scooter (Map 6, ☎ 06 48 90 58 23), an organisation that rents mopeds and scooters. A 50cc moped costs L35,000 for four hours, L55,000 for a day and L230,000 for a week. A 125cc scooter costs L70,000 for four hours, L100,000 a day or L400,000 a week. The organisation operates in conjunction with the railways and if you show a train ticket, you are entitled to a 10% discount on the first day's rental. Chains, locks, helmet and goggles are included, and the organisation will also provide assistance if you break down during office hours. A cash or credit card deposit is required. It is open daily from 8.30 am to 7.30 pm.

See also the Bicycle section below.

TAXI

Taxis are on radio call 24 hours a day in Roma. Cooperativa Radio Taxi Romana (☎ 06 3570) and La Capitale (☎ 06 4994) are two of the many operators. Other numbers to call are ☎ 06 6645 and ☎ 06 5551. Major taxi ranks are at the airports and Stazione Termini and also at Largo Argentina in the historical centre.

If possible, pick up a taxi from a taxi rank as, strictly speaking, taxis are not allowed to be hailed in the street. There are surcharges for luggage, night service, public holidays and travel to and from the airports. The taxi flagfall is L4500 (for the first 3km), then L1200 per km. There is a L5000 supplement from 10 pm to 7 am and L2000 from 7 am to 10 pm on Sunday and public holidays. You'll also be charged L2000 for each large bag or suitcase. If you telephone for a taxi, the driver will turn on the meter immediately and you will pay the cost of travel from wherever the driver was when the call was received.

BICYCLE

If you ignore the fact that Rome was built on seven hills and that most Roman drivers are crazy, cycling is a good way to cover a lot of ground quickly. There are some bicycle paths, along the Tevere river to the north and south of the city centre, but it's you against the traffic in most areas. The Comune di Roma is planning to create more bike paths but, as with many city council projects, their realisation is a slow process. Via dei Fori Imperiali is closed to traffic on Sunday and you can cycle virtually all the way to the Appia Antica from Piazza Venezia on traffic free roads.

Uneven cobblestones are the most common hazard for cyclists, followed by potholes and very slippery roads when it rains. See also the Rome Walks chapter.

Bicycle Rental

Happy Rent (Map 6, ☎ 06 481 81 85)., Via Farini 3, off Via Cavour between Stazione Termini and Piazza Esquilino, rents bicycles for L5000 per hour, L30,000 for a 24 hour period, L70,000 for 3 days and L120,000 for a week. Bici e Baci (☎ 06 482 84 43), Via del Viminale 5 (Map 6, near Piazza della Repubblica) has bicycles from L15,000 per day.

Treno e Scooter (Map 6, ☎ 06 48 90 58 23) on the north-eastern side of the bus terminus outside Stazione Termini, rents bicycles for L4000 an hour, L10,000 a day or L35,000 a week. Mountain bike can be hired for L7000 an hour, L18,000 a day and L54,000 a week. The organisation, which is open every day from 8.30 am to 7.30 pm, operates in conjunction with the railways and various environmental groups. If you show a train ticket, you get a 30% discount on the first day's rental. Chains and locks are included in the price. A cash or credit card deposit is required.

Cicli Collati (Map: Around Piazza Navona, ☎ 06 68 80 10 84), Via del Pellegrino 80-82, near Campo de' Fiori rents bikes by the hour (L5000), half day (L10,000) and day (L15,000). Discounts are given for longer-term rentals. Baby seats and children's bikes are also available.

Bicycles are also usually available for rent in Piazza del Popolo and at the Villa Borghese.

WALKING

The historic centre of Rome is relatively small, and quite manageable on foot. Walking is a great way to see the city, as around every corner there's another beautiful piazza or building or fountain to appreciate. Make sure you wear comfortable shoes. See the Rome Walks chapter for detailed routes.

ORGANISED TOURS
Bus Tours

ATAC operates a special air-conditioned tourist bus, No 110, which leaves from the bus terminus in front of Stazione Termini daily at 2, 3, 5 and 6 pm. Commentary is provided on board in English, Italian and several other languages. The tour takes

three hours and the bus stops at Piazza del Popolo, Piazza San Pietro, Piazza del Campidoglio, Circo Massimo and the Colosseo. Tickets cost L15,000 and are available from the ATAC information booth on stand C at the terminus. For information call ☎ 06 46 95 22 52 or ☎ 06 46 95 22 56.

Stop'n'Go City Tours run by CSR (Consorzio Sightseeing Roma, Map 6, ☎ 06 321 70 54, Piazza del Cinquecento 60) has 9 city tours daily (hourly from 9.30 am to 5.30 pm) with 14 stops en route. Tours depart from Stazione Termini and cost L20,000.

Green Line Tours (Map 6, ☎ 06 482 74 80, Via Farini 5a) near Piazza Esquilino, operates two city tours – a religious tour and a panoramic tour – with recorded commentary in ten languages. There are four religious tours each day and eight panoramic tours. Each tour costs L30,000 (the ticket is valid for 24 hours) and you can hop on and off where and when you want.

Ciao Roma (Map 6, ☎ 06 474 37 95, Via Cavour 113) organises similar classic and religious tours with recorded commentary in ten languages. Each tour costs L30,000. Ciao Roma also has a short river cruise which can be taken together with the classical bus tour.

Walking & Cycling Tours

Enjoy Rome organises walking tours of the major sights for groups of 15 to 20 people most days of the week. The tour lasts three hours and tickets cost L25,000 (people aged under 26) and L30,000 (over 26). Enjoy Rome also organises bicycle tours, which last 3½ hours. Tickets (L30,000) include bike and helmet rental. See Tourist Offices in the Facts for the Visitor chapter.

Scala Reale (☎ 06 44 70 08 98, Via Varese 52), run by an American-Italian couple, organises archaeological walks in small groups with knowledgeable guides. Walks on other themes can be arranged. Bike and scooter tours can also be organised.

Things to See & Do

It doesn't matter how much time you've got to spend in Rome, it won't be enough. The popular saying *'Roma non basta una vita'* (Rome, a lifetime isn't enough) couldn't be more accurate. It is a city on so many levels that even long-term residents have yet to see it all. And it is constantly changing, as new excavations unearth yet more ancient treasures. There will always be more to see. Just make sure you throw a coin in the Fontana di Trevi so you'll be guaranteed to return to Rome.

Be flexible with your sightseeing, as unpredictability is a fact of life in Rome. It's not unusual to find that churches, museums or archaeological sites on your well planned itinerary are closed when you get there. This could be due to any number of factors from ongoing excavations to lack of personnel. Relax, have a cappuccino or a gelato, and head for the next ancient wonder or Baroque architectural extravagance on your list.

Most churches are open daily from around 7 am until midday, and then re-open in the afternoon from around 3.30 or 4 pm to 6 or 6.30 pm. Opening hours that vary drastically have been listed. In some of the larger churches you may be able to wander around during Mass without disturbing worshippers, particularly if the service is being held in one of the side chapels.

Museum entry is generally free for those aged under 18, or over 60, and there are discounts for those with a valid student card. The prices given in this chapter are for full adult admission.

PIAZZA DEL CAMPIDOGLIO (MAP 6)

Designed by Michelangelo in 1538 and located on the Campidoglio (Capitoline hill), this piazza is bordered by three palaces: the **Palazzo dei Conservatori** on the south side, the **Palazzo dei Senatori** at the rear, and the **Palazzo del Museo Capitolino** (also known as the Palazzo Nuovo)

HIGHLIGHTS & LOWLIGHTS

Highlights

- Basilica di San Pietro
- Cappella Sistina and Musei Vaticani
- Colosseo
- Foro Romano and Palatino
- Piazza del Campidoglio
- Museo e Galleria Borghese
- Palazzo Altemps & Palazzo Massimo
- Caffè, pasta, pizza and gelato
- Summer festivals
- Ostia Antica
- Villa Adriana

Lowlights

- Roman drivers
- Roman shop assistants
- Pollution
- Traffic
- Stazione Termini at night
- Restaurant-to-restaurant vendors of roses and cigarette lighters
- Tour groups
- The No 64 bus

---

on the north side. The palace façades were also designed by Michelangelo, and all three have been recently restored.

This hill, now the seat of the city's municipal government, was the centre of the government of ancient Rome, and where Nelson hoisted the British flag in 1799 before he prevented Napoleon from entering the city. The Palazzo dei Senatori is open to the public from 9am to 4pm on Sunday. Admission is free, but you need to bring some identification. It's also possible to climb the tower, the **Torre Campanaria**, on the last Sunday of the month (also free), but you need to book in advance. Visit the commune's website at www.comune.roma .it/gabinetto.

For the greatest visual impact, approach the piazza from Piazza d'Aracoeli and ascend the *cordonata*, a stepped ramp also designed by Michelangelo. It is guarded at the bottom by two ancient Egyptian granite lions and at the top by two mammoth statues of Castor and Pollux, which were found in the nearby ghetto area in the 16th century.

The bronze equestrian statue of Marcus Aurelius in the centre of the piazza is a copy. The original, which dates from the 2nd century AD, was badly damaged by pollution, weather and pigeon droppings and was removed in 1981. It has been restored and is now housed in the Palazzo Nuovo.

At the bottom of the Campidoglio, next to the staircase leading up to Santa Maria in Aracoeli, are the ruins of a Roman apartment block or *insula*. Only the upper storeys are visible; three lower levels are buried below current street level. Buildings of this type was used to house the urban poor, who lived in cramped and squalid conditions.

Musei Capitolini

The **Musei Capitolini** (Capitoline Museums) is the collective name for the two museums on the Campidoglio: the Palazzo del Museo Capitolino and the Palazzo dei Conservatori (comprising the Sale dei Conservatori, the Museo Nuovo, the Braccio Nuovo and the Pinacoteca) opposite. Together they form one of the most impressive collections of ancient sculpture in the world. It is also the world's oldest public collection and museum, and was started in 1471 when Pope Sixtus IV

A Case of Mistaken Identity

The original equestrian statue of Marcus Aurelius is one of only a handful of ancient bronzes not to have been melted down. This statue survived because it had been incorrectly identified as Constantine, the first Christian emperor, an opinion which was maintained for centuries.

Marcus Aurelius was emperor from 161 to 180 AD and is remembered as both a warrior and a philosopher. He spent almost 10 years of his reign on the Danube fighting the local tribes which threatened the border; his victories are commemorated on his Column.

This statue represents him in the act of addressing his people and simultaneously mounting a horse whose right foot, now hanging loose, originally rested on the head of a defeated barbarian. The statue was originally gold plated, traces of which are still visible on the emperor's face and coat and on the horse's head and back.

A curious legend has it that when the gold plating is restored, an owl's hoot will sound from the tuft of hair between the horse's ears, announcing the Last Judgement.

Since the Renaissance, the statue has been used as a model for equestrian monuments. Paul III ordered it to be brought to the Campidoglio from Piazza di San Giovanni in Laterano in 1538. He replaced it in San Giovanni with the 31m obelisk of Tutmosis III which had been found at the Circo Massimo.

The statue on display in the piazza is a very good modern copy, executed using a computer. Having recently undergone 10 years of restoration, the original was put on display behind glass in the safety of the Palazzo Nuovo. During the restoration works on the Musei Capitolini, expected to continue until at least the end of 1999, it is not possible to see the original statue.

donated the first group of bronze sculptures to the city. Subsequent popes followed suit as the city expanded and more and more ancient statues were unearthed.

At the time of writing, both wings of the Musei Capitolini were undergoing major renovations and were closed to the public, with the exception of a few of the rooms in the Palazzo dei Conservatori and the Pinacoteca (picture gallery). Many of the sculptures from the Palazzo dei Conservatori, including pieces which have rarely or never been on display before, have been temporarily transferred to a former thermoelectric plant south of the city centre in Via Ostiense. See 'Musei Capitolioni at Centrale Montemartini' later in this chapter.

The most famous piece in the **Palazzo dei Conservatori** is the *Lupa Capitolina* (Capitoline Wolf), an Etruscan bronze statue from the 6th century BC. The figures of Romulus and Remus were added by Antonio Pollaiolo around 1509. It stands in the Sala della Lupa on the 1st floor. Also of interest in this wing is the *Spinario*, a delicate bronze statue of a boy taking a thorn from his foot, dating from the 1st century BC. (The rooms containing these pieces were still open to the public at the time of writing.)

The inner court of the ground floor of the Palazzo dei Conservatori contains the fascinating remains of a colossal statue of Constantine – the head, a hand and a foot – which were once part of a 12m high acrolith (a composition made of marble and cloth held together by a frame) originally in the apse of the Basilica di Massenzio in the Foro Romano. It depicted the seated emperor with his index finger raised to symbolise the direct contact with God that enabled him to govern with divine inspiration. In the portico on the far side of the courtyard there is a huge Trajanic statue representing Rome. It stands between two grey marble statues of captive barbarian kings (2nd century AD) and another marble head from a colossal statue of Constantine's son and successor, Constans II.

The wall on the left displays high reliefs representing the provinces under Roman dominion, taken from the inner sanctuary in Hadrian's Temple. Above them is an inscription from a triumphal arch which once stood in Via Lata, commemorating Claudius' conquest of Britain in 43 AD.

Unfortunately, the courtyard was inaccessible at the time of writing and was expected to reopen to the public at the end of 1999.

The **Pinacoteca** on the 2nd floor contains fine works and is well worth a visit if the sculpture hasn't worn you out. Artists from the Venetian school, including Giovanni Bellini, Paolo Veronese, Titian and Tintoretto are represented in Sala II. Sala III contains works by Guido Reni, Federico Zucchari, Salvator Rosa, Van Dyck and Rubens. There are also works by Domenichino, Guido Reni, Poussin, the Carracci (in Sala IX), Pietro da Cortona and others. Highlights include Caravaggio's sensual *San Giovanni Battista* in his fully-fledged realist style (in Sala V) and Guercino's immense *Santa Petronilla*, formerly in the Basilica di San Pietro (in Sala VII).

The **Palazzo del Museo Capitolino**, on the other side of the piazza, is the permanent home of several important works, including the impressive *Galata morente* (Dying Gaul), a Roman copy of an original Greek work of the 3rd century BC, a *Satiro in riposo* (Satyr Resting), the *Satiro ridente* (a red marble laughing satyr holding a bunch of grapes – the Marble Faun of Nathaniel Hawthorne's novel) and the beautiful and sensual *Venere Capitolina* (Capitoline Venus), a Roman copy of a 3rd century BC Greek original, in a small chamber of its own. There are also busts and full-length statues of Roman emperors and other famous people of the day as well as the *Sala dei Filosofi* (Hall of the Philosophers) lined with busts of philosophers, poets and politicians, among them Sophocles, Euripides, Homer, Epicuros and Cicero. This wing of the museum was completely closed to the public at the time of writing.

The parts of the museum which are still accessible are open Tuesday to Saturday from 9 am to 7 pm and Sunday from 9 am to 1 pm. Admission has been reduced to L5000 during the restoration period.

Chiesa di Santa Maria in Aracoeli

The **Chiesa di Santa Maria in Aracoeli** is between the Piazza del Campidoglio and Monumento Vittorio Emanuele II at the highest point of the hill. It is accessible either by a long flight of steps from the Piazza d'Aracoeli, or from behind the Palazzo del Museo Capitolino.

The austere brick church is built on the site where legend says the Tiburtine Sybil told Augustus of the coming birth of Christ and dates from before the 7th century. In the 10th century it belonged to Benedictine monks and in the 13th century it was rebuilt in the Romanesque style by the Franciscans but the façade was never completed. The church features frescoes by Pinturicchio painted in the 1480s in the first chapel of the south aisle. It is noted for a statue of the baby Jesus said to have been carved from the wood of an olive tree from the garden of Gethsemane. The statue was stolen in 1994 and a replica is on display. The ceiling is decorated with naval motifs which commemorate the Battle of Lepanto.

PIAZZA VENEZIA (MAP 6)

The piazza is overshadowed by one of Italy's more unusual monuments, dedicated to the Italian king Victor Emmanuel II. Often mockingly referred to by Italians as the *macchina da scrivere* (typewriter), the monument was built to commemorate Italian unification. It incorporates the **Altare della Patria** (Altar of the Fatherland) and the tomb of the unknown soldier. Considered out of harmony with its surroundings, the monument has prompted many calls for its demolition. The **Museo del Risorgimento** (☎ 06 678 06 64) is located beneath the Altare della Patria, and hosts temporary exhibitions. The entrance is from Via di San Pietro in Carcere.

On the west side of the piazza is the **Palazzo Venezia**, the first great Renaissance palace in Rome, which was partially built with materials quarried from the Colosseo. It was built for the Venetian cardinal Pietro Barbo, who later became Pope Paul II. It was begun in 1455 and had bits added onto it until the 16th century. Mussolini used it as his official residence and made some of his famous speeches from the balcony. Major art exhibitions are held here and part of the building houses the Museo del Palazzo di Venezia.

Actually part of the Palazzo Venezia, but facing onto Piazza San Marco, the **Basilica di San Marco** was founded in the 4th century in honour of St Mark the Evangelist. After undergoing several major transformations over the centuries, the church has a Renaissance façade, a Romanesque bell tower and a largely Baroque interior. The main attraction is the 9th-century mosaic in the apse, which depicts Christ with saints and Pope Gregory IV.

Museo del Palazzo di Venezia

The rooms of the former Appartamento Cybo in Palazzo Venezia house the Museo del Palazzo di Venezia which has an interesting collection of paintings and decorative arts.

The painted coffered ceilings of the Appartamento Cybo are particularly note-worthy. The first room as you enter has medieval altarpieces and panel paintings. Paolo Veneziano's 14th century *Coro di angeli* depicting a group of haloed angels with musical instruments stands out, as does a triptych by Jacopo da Montagnana and Pisanello's *Testa di donna*, a fresco fragment of a woman's head with delicately worked hair.

Amongst the paintings by artists of the 14th and 15th century Tuscan school are two beautiful reliquaries by the so-called Master of Santa Chiara da Montefalco (decorated with delicate images of the Madonna and saints) and a splendid, well preserved triptych *Madonna col Bambino, Santa Lucia e Santa Caterina d'Alessandria* by Giovanni Antonio da Pesaro, with the Crucifixion and the Annunciation depicted in the upper panels. Also of note is the two-sided altarpiece of *La Madonna della Misericordia*, with Sts John the Baptist and Sebastian on the reverse.

Notable late 15th century Tuscan works include a remnant of Benozzo Gozzoli's fresco of *Il Redentore*, a beautiful *Natività* (Nativity) from the workshop of Filippo Lippi and a small oblong panel in vibrantly rich colours of the *Matirio di Santa Caterina d'Alessandria* showing the moment when the saint gets her head chopped off.

Other highlights of the painting collection are Guercino's canvas of *San Pietro*, Carlo Maratta's *Cleopatra* which clothes the Egyptian queen in 17th century fashion, and Orazio Borgianni's late 16th century *Cristo Deposto* (The Deposition), a prostrate Christ viewed from his feet, which recalls Mantegna's famous foreshortened image of *Cristo morto* in the Pinacoteca di Brera in Milano. One room is devoted exclusively to 18th and 19th century pastels.

The decorative arts collection contains jewellery, tapestries, silver, ivories, ceramics, hundreds of 15th to 17th century bronze figurines spread over several rooms and carved wooden wedding chests as well as a collection of arms and armour.

The entrance to the museum (☎ 06 679 88 65) is at Via del Plebiscito 118. It is open from 9 am to 2 pm, Tuesday to Saturday, and from 9 am to 1 pm on Sunday. Tickets cost L8000.

FORI IMPERIALI (MAP 6)

Linking Piazza Venezia with the Colosseo is the Via dei Fori Imperiali, an unfortunate project of Mussolini's which saw many 16th century buildings destroyed and part of the Velia hill levelled. The road was opened in 1933 after only superficial excavations and studies had been undertaken. It has been proposed that the road should be closed between Via Cavour and Piazza Venezia in order to create one huge archaeological park. At present, traffic is limited and the entire stretch from the Colosseo to Piazza Venezia becomes a pedestrian zone on most Sundays.

Archaeological excavations are continuing on both sides of Via dei Fori Imperiali in the five forums known collectively as the Fori Imperiali: the Foro di Traiano, Foro d'Augusto, Foro di Cesare, Foro di Nerva and Foro di Vespasiano, which are partially or almost completely covered by Mussolini's thoroughfare.

Foro di Traiano

Designed by Apollodorus of Damascus for Trajan and constructed at the beginning of the 2nd century AD, the Foro di Traiano (Trajan's Forum) was the last of the forums. It was a vast complex, measuring 300m by 185m, extending from what is now Piazza Venezia, and comprised a basilica for the judiciary, two libraries – one Greek and one Latin – a temple, a triumphal arch, and the **Colonna di Traiano** (Trajan's Column). Restored in the late 1980s, the column was erected to mark the victories of Trajan over the Dacians, who lived in what is now Romania. After it was built, Trajan's ashes were interred in a golden urn placed on a marble slab at the base of the column. The urn, along with the ashes, disappeared during one of the barbarian sacks of Rome.

The column is decorated with a spiral series of reliefs depicting the battles between the Roman and Dacian armies, which are regarded as among the finest examples of ancient Roman sculpture. A golden statue of Trajan once topped the column, but it was lost during the Middle Ages and replaced with a statue of St Peter. Apart from the column, all that remains of the grand imperial forum are some of the pillars which once formed part of the Basilica Ulpia, the largest basilica built in ancient Rome.

In comparison, the **Mercati di Traiano** (Trajan's Markets) are well preserved. Also designed by Apollodorus, the markets were constructed on three levels, comprising six floors of shops and offices in a semicircle. This was the ancient equivalent of a modern multi-level shopping centre, selling everything from wine and oil to fresh fruit, vegetables and flowers to imported silks and spices. You can get an idea of their grandeur from the high vaulted roofs. It's worth paying the admission fee if only to reach the high levels of the market, from where there are spectacular views across to the Foro Romano.

The tall red brick tower above the market buildings, the **Torre delle Milizie**, was built in the 13th century for defensive purposes.

Next to Trajan's forum and markets are the scant remains of the **Foro d'Augusto** (Forum of Augustus) vowed by Augustus in 42 BC, but not completed and dedicated until 40 years later. Three columns of a temple dedicated to Mars the Avenger are still standing and others have been reconstructed from fragments, but over half the original area is now covered by Via dei Fori Imperiali. The 30m-high wall behind the Foro d'Augusto was built to protect the area from the fires which frequently swept through the area known as the Suburra.

The markets and forum (☎ 06 679 00 48) are open from 9 am to 7 pm, Tuesday to Sunday, from April to October, and from 9 am to 4.30 pm the rest of the year. They are closed on Monday. Admission is L3750, and includes the Foro di Augusto. The entrance to the markets is at Via IV Novembre 94.

There is a delightful walkway beneath the loggia of the 12th century **Casa dei Cavalieri di Rodi** (ancient seat of the Knights of St John of Jerusalem), which is between the forums of Trajan and Augustus and accessible from either Via dei Fori Imperiali or Piazza del Grillo. The building itself, which contains a beautiful chapel, is open only by appointment.

Next to the Foro di Augusto is the **Foro di Nerva**, much of which is covered by Via dei Fori Imperiali. Part of a temple dedicated to Minerva still remains on the site. The temple was still standing in the 17th century when Pope Paul V had it pulled down to provide marble for the Fontana Paolina on the Gianicolo. The Foro di Nerva connected the Foro di Augusto to the **Foro di Vespasiano**, also known as the Forum of Peace, which was built by Vespasian in 70 AD. A large hall was converted in the 6th

century into a church, Santi Cosma e Damiano (see Chiesa di SS Cosma e Damiano later in this chapter.

Across the Via dei Fori Imperiali is the **Foro di Cesare** (Caesar's forum), which was built by Julius Caesar at the foot of the Campidoglio. It is not open to the public but can be viewed from Via dei Fori Imperiali. Caesar claimed the goddess Venus in his family tree, and his forum included a temple to her as Venus Genetrix – Venus the Ancestor. All that remains today are three columns on a platform. Trajan made various additions to the forum, including the Basilica Argentaria, an important financial exchange, some shops and a heated public lavatory.

Following Via di San Pietro in Carcere you come to the ancient **Carcere Mamertino** (Mamertine Prison), where condemned prisoners were garrotted. St Peter is believed to have been held here prior to his trial and to have created a miraculous stream of water to baptise his jailers and his fellow prisoners. The site was later consecrated and is now the Chiesa di San Pietro in Carcere.

FORO ROMANO & PALATINO (MAPS 6 & 8)
Foro Romano

The commercial, political and religious centre of ancient Rome, the Foro Romano (Roman Forum) stands in a valley between the Capitoline and Palatine hills. Originally marshland, the area was drained during the early Republican era and became a centre for political rallies, public ceremonies and Senate meetings. The forum was constructed over 900 years, with later emperors erecting buildings next to those from the Republican era. Its importance declined along with the Roman Empire after the 4th century AD, and the temples, monuments and buildings constructed by successive emperors, consuls and senators fell into ruin, eventually leading to the site being used as pasture land. In the Middle Ages the area was known as the Campo Vaccino (literally, cow field), an interesting

FORO ROMANO & PALATINO

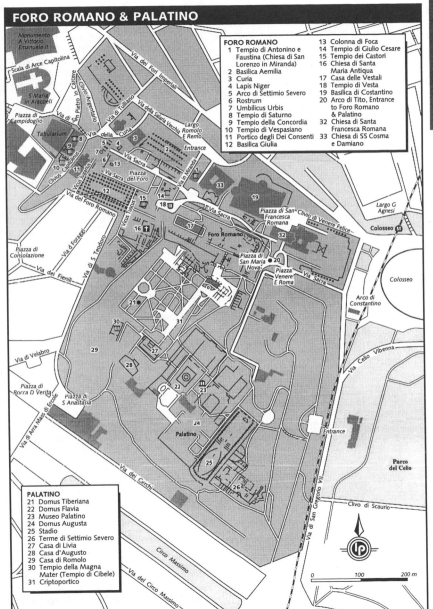

FORO ROMANO
1 Tempio di Antonino e Faustina (Chiesa di San Lorenzo in Miranda)
2 Basilica Aemilia
3 Curia
4 Lapis Niger
5 Arco di Settimio Severo
6 Rostrum
7 Umbilicus Urbis
8 Tempio di Saturno
9 Tempio della Concordia
10 Tempio di Vespasiano
11 Portico degli Dei Consenti
12 Basilica Giulia

13 Colonna di Foca
14 Tempio di Giulio Cesare
15 Tempio dei Castori
16 Chiesa di Santa Maria Antiqua
17 Casa delle Vestali
18 Tempio di Vesta
19 Basilica di Costantino
20 Arco di Tito, Entrance to Foro Romano & Palatino
32 Chiesa di Santa Francesca Romana
33 Chiesa di SS Cosma e Damiano

PALATINO
21 Domus Tiberiana
22 Domus Flavia
23 Museo Palatino
24 Domus Augusta
25 Stadio
26 Terme di Settimio Severo
27 Casa di Livia
28 Casa d'Augusto
29 Casa di Romolo
30 Tempio della Magna Mater (Tempio di Cibele)
31 Criptoportico

example of history repeating itself, since the valley in which the forum stood was used as pasture land in the earliest days of the city's development.

During medieval times the area was extensively plundered for its stone and precious marbles. Many temples and buildings had been converted to other uses and other monuments lay half revealed. Ironically, the physical destruction of ancient Rome can be blamed not on the invading barbarians or natural disasters such as earthquake, but on the Romans themselves. Over the centuries, in the name of progress, the Romans dismantled the ancient city brick by brick and marble block by marble block in order to build their own palaces, churches and monuments.

With renewed appreciation of all things classical of the Renaissance, the forum provided inspiration for artists and architects. The area was systematically excavated in the 18th and 19th centuries, and excavations are continuing. You can watch archaeological teams at work in several locations.

You can enter the forum from Via dei Fori Imperiali and from Piazza di Santa Maria Nova near the Arco di Tito. It is open Monday to Saturday from 9 am to 6 pm (to 4 pm in winter) and from 9 am to 2 pm on Sunday. Admission to the forum is free. At the time of writing there were guided tours in English every day at 10.45 am (cost L6000).

As you enter the forum, to your left is the **Tempio di Antonino e Faustina**, erected by the Senate in 141 AD and dedicated to the Empress Faustina and later, after his death, to Antoninus Pius. It was transformed into the Chiesa di San Lorenzo in Miranda in the 8th century. To your right is the **Basilica Aemilia**, built in 179 BC. The building was 100m long and its façade was a two-storey portico lined with shops. Destroyed and rebuilt several times, the basilica was almost completely demolished during the Renaissance, when it was plundered for its precious marbles.

The **Via Sacra**, which traverses the forum from north-west to south-east, runs in front of the basilica. Continuing along Via Sacra in the direction of the Campidoglio, you will reach the **Curia**, just after the Basilica Aemilia on the right. Once the meeting place of the Roman Senate, it was rebuilt successively by Julius Caesar, Augustus, Domitian and, after a fire in the 3rd century AD by Diocletian. It was converted into a church in the Middle Ages. The church was dismantled and the Curia restored in the 1930s to the form it had under Diocletian. The bronze doors are copies – the Roman originals were moved by Borromini to San Giovanni in Laterano.

In front of the Curia is the **Lapis Niger**, a large piece of black marble which covered a sacred area. According to legend, the tomb of Romulus was beneath it. Down a short flight of stairs (rarely open to the public), under the Lapis Niger, is the oldest known Latin inscription, dating from the 6th century BC.

The **Arco di Settimio Severo** (Arch of Septimius Severus) is considered one of Italy's major triumphal arches. According to the inscription on both sides of the arch, it was erected in 203 AD in honour of the emperor Septimius Severus and his sons, Caracalla and Geta. After Caracalla murdered his brother, the inscription was altered so that the words *optimis fortissimisque principibus* were inscribed over Geta's name. If you look closely at the fourth line of the inscription, you can see the original lettering. A project to renovate the arch left it exactly half cleaned in 1988 when the money ran out, and at the time of writing it was still half covered by scaffolding.

To the south is the **Rostrum**, used in ancient times by public speakers and once decorated with the rams of captured ships. A circular base stone, the **Umbilicus Urbis** (the Navel of the World), beside the arch marks the symbolic centre of ancient Rome.

South along the Via Sacra lies the **Tempio di Saturno** (Temple of Saturn), inaugurated in 497 BC and one of the most important temples in Ancient Rome. It was used as the city's treasury and during

Caesar's rule contained 13 tonnes of gold, 114 tonnes of silver and 30 million *sestertii* in coined silver. Eight granite columns are all that remain. Behind the temple and backing onto the Campidoglio are (roughly from north to south) the ruins of the **Tempio della Concordia** (Temple of Concord), the three remaining columns of the **Tempio di Vespasiano** (Temple of Vespasian) and the **Portico degli Dei Consenti**, of which 12 columns remain (five are restorations). The remains of the **Basilica Giulia**, which was the seat of civil justice, are just across from Basilica Aemilia, at what is known as Piazza del Foro. The piazza was the site of the original forum, which served as the main meeting place during the Republican era.

The **Colonna di Foca** (Column of Phocus), which stands in the piazza and dates from 608 AD, was the last monument erected in the forum. It honoured the Byzantine emperor Phocus who donated the Pantheon to the church. At the south-eastern end of the piazza is the **Tempio di Giulio Cesare** (Temple of Julius Caesar), which was erected by Augustus in 29 BC on the site where Caesar's body was burned and Mark Antony delivered his famous speech. Back towards the Palatino is the **Tempio dei Castori** (Temple of Castor & Pollux), built in 489 BC to mark the defeat of the Etruscan Tarquins and in honour of the Heavenly Twins, or Dioscuri, who miraculously appeared to deliver the news of an important victory. Three elegant Corinthian columns from the temple, which served at times as a banking hall and also housed the city's weights and measures office, survive today. The temple was restored during the 1980s.

In the area south-east of the temple is the **Chiesa di Santa Maria Antiqua**, the oldest Christian church in the forum. Inside the church are some early Christian frescoes. This area, including the church, has been closed to the public since 1992.

Back on the Via Sacra is the **Casa delle Vestali** (House of the Vestal Virgins), home of the virgins who tended the sacred flame in the adjoining **Tempio di Vesta**. The six virgin priestesses, aged between six and 10 years, were selected from patrician families. They had to serve in the temple for 30 years and during this time they were bound by a vow of chastity. The Tempio di Vesta was a circular building surrounded by columns. The sacred flame burnt in the inner chamber, known as the *cella*, and was regarded as the hearth fire of Rome itself. Any priestess who allowed it to go out was beaten. A Vestal accused on breaking her vows of chastity was entombed alive on the reasoning that if she were innocent, then Vesta herself would rescue her. The man involved was taken outside the city walls and clubbed to death.

The next major monument is the vast **Basilica di Costantino**, also known as the Basilica di Massenzio. Maxentius initiated work on the basilica and it was finished in 315 AD by Constantine. Its impressive design provided inspiration for Renaissance architects, possibly including Michelangelo, who is said to have studied its construction when he was designing the dome for San Pietro. The basilica was the largest building in the forum, covering an area of approximately 100m by 65m, and was used for business and the administration of justice. The three massive barrel-vaulted aisles which remain today were used as law courts. One of the basilica's original columns now stands in Piazza Santa Maria Maggiore. A colossal statue of Constantine was unearthed at the site in 1487. Pieces of this statue are on display in the courtyard of the Palazzo dei Conservatori in the Musei Capitolini (see the Campidoglio section earlier in this chapter).

The **Arco di Tito** (Arch of Titus), at the Colosseo end of the forum, was built in 81 AD in honour of the victories of the future emperor Titus against the Jewish rebels in Jerusalem. Titus is represented with Victory personified on one of the reliefs on the inside of the arch; the spoils of Jerusalem are paraded in a triumphal procession on the other. Along with that of Constantine, this arch was incorporated into the Frangipani fortress in the Middle Ages.

Palatino (Map 6)

The **Palatino** (Palatine hill) was the mythical founding place of Rome, and where the remains of Iron Age huts have been discovered. You reach the Palatino from the forum by following the Clivio Palatino to the right from the Arco di Tito. There is another entrance in Via di San Gregorio. It is open Monday to Saturday from 9 am to 6 pm (to 4 pm in winter) and from 9 am to 2 pm on Sunday. Admission is L12,000 and includes entry to the Museo Palatino.

Favoured by its situation above the Tevere and its exposure to sea breezes, the Palatino was the most desirable spot for wealthy Romans to build their homes during the Republican era. It later became the realm of the emperors. Augustus was born on the Palatino and lived there throughout his life, although his residences were modest compared to those of subsequent rulers. This was extended first into the Domus Tiberiana, and further grand complexes were added by subsequent emperors, including Caligula and Domitian – inspiring, in fact, the very word 'palace'.

The Palatino becamean important centre in Roman life and remained so into the early Middle Ages. Representatives of the Byzantine emperors lived on the Palatino in the 7th century, as did some popes.

Like those of the forum, the temples and palaces of the Palatino fell into ruin and in the Middle Ages a few churches, monasteries and castles were built over the remains. During the Renaissance, members of wealthy families established their gardens on the hill, notably Cardinal Alessandro Farnese, who had elaborate gardens laid out over the ruins of the Domus Tiberiana.

The largest part of the Palatino as it appears today is covered by ruins of a vast complex built for the emperor Domitian, which served as the main imperial palace for 300 years. This was an ambitious project to create an official imperial palace, the Domus Flavia, the emperor's private residence, the Domus Augusta, and a stadium. The complex was designed by the architect, Rabirius, who levelled a crest of land, the Palatium, on the steep eastern side of the Palatino, and filled in the depression between it and the next crest, the Germalus, demolishing or burying many Republican era houses in the process. Some of these buried buildings have since been unearthed, and excavations are continuing. The two connecting palaces were built in characteristically Roman style with a series of rooms leading off a *peristilio* (peristyle or garden courtyard).

Domitian was terrified of being assassinated and had the peristyle of the **Domus Flavia** lined with shiny marble slabs so that, from whichever room he was in, he could see who was approaching. (He ended up being murdered in his bedroom, possibly with the connivance of his wife.) There were three large halls to the north, the central one of which was the emperor's throne room, and a large banqueting hall or triclinium *(triclinio imperiale)* to the south, which was paved in coloured marbles that can still be seen. The triclinium looked out onto an oval fountain whose remains are clearly visible. The Domus Flavia was constructed over earlier edifices. One of these, which can sometimes be visited (ask at the Palatino entrance), is the **Casa dei Grifi** (House of the Griffins), so called because of a stucco relief of two griffins in one of the rooms. It is the oldest building on the Palatino and dates from the late 2nd or 1st century BC. It was excavated in the 18th century.

To the east of the Domus Flavia is the **Domus Augustana**, which was built on two levels, with two peristyles on the upper level and one on the lower floor. You can't get down to the lower level, but from above you can see the basin of a fountain and beyond it rooms which were paved with coloured marble. The Domus Augustana had an elaborate two storey colonnaded façade to the south overlooking Circo Massimo (from where you get the best clearest indication of the grand scale of the complex).

The **Museo Palatino**, formerly known as the Antiquario Palatino, houses artworks and artefacts found on the Palatino. A former convent located between the Domus Flavia and the Domus Augustana, the museum was established in the 1860s. For the past century, the most important of the excavated pieces from the Palatino were kept in the Museo Nazionale Romano. Some objects remain in the Museo Nazionale Romano collection (including the stuccoes from the Palatino criptoportico), but many were transferred to the restored Museo Palatino in 1998. Admission is with the same ticket as for the Palatino. Note that the Museo closes one hour earlier than the Palatino itself.

The ground floor illustrates the history of the hill from its origins to the Republican age. In Sale I, II and III there are pots, eating and cooking utensils from the Palaeolithic Age to the Bronze Age as well as models of how the Iron Age huts and tombs might have appeared. Sala IV contains artefacts from the Archaic and the Republican Ages (6th to 1st centuries BC) including an altar to an unknown pagan god and ceramic masks.

On the 1st floor, in Sala V, are artefacts from the Augustan period (29 BC to 14 AD) including reliefs and black marble statues from the Tempio di Apollo which was located next to the Casa di Augusto. Sala VI contains objects pertaining to Nero's reign (54 to 68 AD), including remnants of decorative frescoes. Sale VII and VIII contain sculpted heads and busts dating from the 1st to the 4th century AD and Sala IX contains statuary that decorated the various imperial palaces on the Palatino.

Continuing east beyond the Domus Augustana you find the **Stadio** (stadium) probably used by the emperors for private games and events. An oval recess in the eastern wall is thought to have served as the emperor's private viewing area. Next to the stadio are the scant remains the baths built by Septimius Severus, the **Terme di Settimio Severo**. Considerable engineering skill was required to build this complex on

an extension of the southernmost point of the Palatino. It was supported by enormous arched substructures, best seen from Circo Massimo.

Among the best preserved buildings on the Palatino is the so-called **Casa di Livia** west of the Domus Flavia. It is well below current ground level and is reached by steps down to a mosaic-covered courtyard. Livia was the wife of Augustus; she owned this house and also in a larger villa at Prima Porta to the north of Rome (see section on Palazzo Massimo alle Terme later in this chapter). The Casa di Livia contains a forecourt or *atrium*, leading onto what were once reception rooms. The walls of the house were decorated with frescoes – of mythological scenes, landscapes, and fruits and flowers – some of which can still be seen, although they have been detached from the walls in order to preserve them. In front of the Casa di Livia is the **Casa d' Augusto**, the actual residence of Augustus – the two constructions were most likely part of the same complex. The Casa d'Augusto is still being excavated and is closed to the public but can sometimes be visited by appointment; ask at the entrance to the Palatino. Several rooms have frescoes which are very well-preserved and ofconsiderable interest.

Next to the Casa d'Augusto is the so-called **Casa di Romolo** (House of Romulus) where, it is thought, Romulus and Remus were brought up after their discovery by the shepherd Faustulus. Excavations carried out in the 1940s revealed evidence of supports for wattle and daub huts dating from the 9th century BC. The **Tempio della Magna Mater** is just north of the huts. Also known as the Tempio di Cibele (the Temple of Cybele), it was built in 204 BC to house a black stone connected with the Asiatic goddess of fertility, Cybele.

North of the Casa di Livia is the **Criptoportico** or cryptoporticus, a 128m tunnel, built by Nero to connect his Domus Aurea (see section later in this chapter) with the imperial palaces on the Palatino. The tunnel had windows on one side which

Gladiators

Gladiatorial combat originated as part of Etruscan funerary rites as a form of human sacrifice. By the 1st century BC, gladiatorial games had far outstripped this ritual context; Caesar exhibited 320 pairs of gladiators in 65 BC, Augustus and Trajan each showed 5000 pairs of gladiators on different occasions.

Gladiators were prisoners of war, slaves sold to gladiatorial schools, or volunteers. They were differently equipped, some with heavy swords and shields and others almost naked, armed with a net and a trident. Pairings were made to match a heavily armed gladiator against a lightly armed one.

Bouts were not necessarily to the death. A defeated gladiator could appeal to the crowd and the presiding magistrate who could signal that he had fought well and deserved to be spared. Thumbs down, however, meant death, which the defeated man was expected to face with quiet courage.

Although gambling was technically illegal in Rome, vast sums were wagered on gladiatorial combats. Successful gladiators were popular heroes and lived to enjoy a comfortable retirement, with some running their own training schools.

As with the other blood sports held in Rome, gladiatorial games were more than just particularly gruesome entertainment. This state-run public spectacle was a demonstration of empire through the display of exotic beasts and prisoners of war and, in the people's judgement of the defeated, allowed them to share in the Roman State's authority over life and death.

---

provided light and ventilation. Elaborate stucco decorations once lined part of the crypto-porticus but these have been replaced by copies and the originals moved to the Museo Nazionale Romano. A second tunnel was later added to link it with the Domus Flavia.

The area west of the cryptoporticus was once the **Domus Tiberiana**, Tiberius's palace, which Gaius Caligula extended further north towards the forum.

The area containing the former imperial palaces is today the site of the **Orti Farne-**siani. Cardinal Alessandro Farnese, a grandson of Pope Paul III, bought the ruins of Tiberius's palace in the mid-16th century. He had the ruins filled in and asked the acclaimed and fashionable architect Vignola to design a garden for him. One of Europe's earliest botanical gardens, the garden contained a number of plant species which had never before been planted in Italy. The garden originally extended from the forum up various terraced levels connected with steps. There are various paths, rose gardens and shady parasol pines and it's a great place for a picnic. Twin pavilions stand at the northern point of the garden, from where the view over the forum and the rest of the city is breathtaking.

Basilica di SS Cosma e Damiano & Chiesa di Santa Francesca Romana

East towards the Colosseo along Via dei Fori Imperiali, past the entrance to the Foro Romano, is the 6th century **Basilica di SS Cosma e Damiano** dedicated to the brothers Sts Cosmas and Damian who were doctors with miraculous powers of healing.

The church once incorporated a large hall which formed part of the Foro di Vespasiano, also known as the Forum Pacis (Forum of Peace). In the apse are 6th century mosaics, among the most beautiful in Rome, which were restored in 1989. The central figure of Christ against a deep blue background is flanked by Sts Peter and Paul (in white robes) who are presenting Sts Cosmas and Damian to him. On the far left is St Felix, holding up a model of the church, and on the right is St Theodore. Below this scene is a frieze of the lamb of God (representing Christ) and his flock of 12 lambs (representing the Apostles). These mosaics were copied in several Roman churches, especially in the 9th century. Make sure you have plenty of spare change as this is the meanest mosaic lighting system in Rome – L500 gives you only the briefest of glimpses of these stunning mosaics.

In a room off the 17th century cloisters is a vast Neapolitan *presepio* (nativity scene), dating from the 18th century. Children in particular will love this wonderful model which places the birth of Jesus amongst Neapolitan folk going about their daily business. Among the finely crafted wooden and terracotta figures are animals, a chestnut vendor, a fruit seller, grape harvester, a soldier and an innkeeper. It can be viewed (a donation of L1000 is requested) from 9.30 am to 12.30 pm and from 3 to 6.30 pm.

Past the Basilica di Costantino there is a small stairway leading to the **Chiesa di Santa Francesca Romana**. Built in the 9th

century over an earlier oratory, the church (also known as Santa Maria Nova) incorporates part of the Tempio di Venere e Roma (Temple of Venus and Rome). It has a lovely Romanesque bell tower.

There is a 12th century mosaic in the apse of the Madonna and child and saints, as well as a 7th century painting of the Madonna and child above the high altar. During restoration works in 1949, another painting of the Madonna and child was discovered beneath the 7th-century work. Dating from the early 5th century and probably taken from the Chiesa di Santa Maria Antiqua in the Foro Romano, this precious painting is now in the sacristy which you can enter if the sacristan is around.

Francesca Romana is the patron saint of motorists; on 9 March (her feast day) drivers park their vehicles as close as possible to the church to be blessed. Her skeleton, wrapped in a white diaphanous cloth, holding a book and wearing rather modern looking black leather slippers, is in a chapel under the altar (steps lead down from both sides).

Colosseo (Map 8)

Construction of the Colosseo (Colosseum) was started by Vespasian in 72 AD in the grounds of Nero's private Domus Aurea. Originally known as the Flavian Amphitheatre, after the family name of Vespasian, it was inaugurated by his son Titus in 80 AD. The massive structure could seat more than 50,000 (the 4th century figure of 87,000 is disputed), and the bloody gladiator combat and wild beast shows held there (see the Gladiators boxed text). The splendid games held at the inauguration of the Colosseo lasted for 100 days and nights, during which some 5000 animals were slaughtered. Trajan once held games which lasted for 117 days, during which some 9000 gladiators fought to the death.

With the fall of the Empire, the Colosseo was abandoned and gradually became overgrown. Exotic plants grew there for centuries; seeds had inadvertently been transported from Africa and Asia with the wild beasts that appeared in the arena (including crocodiles, bears, lions, tigers, elephants, rhinos, hippos, camels and giraffes). In the Middle Ages the Colosseo became a fortress, occupied by two of the city's warrior families: the Frangipani and the Annibaldi. Its reputation as a symbol of Rome, the Eternal City, also dates to the Middle Ages, with Bede writing that 'while the Colosseo stands, Rome shall stand, but when the Colosseo falls, Rome shall fall – and when Rome falls, the world will end'.

Damaged several times by earthquake, it was later used as a quarry for travertine and marble for the Palazzo Venezia and other buildings. Pollution and the vibrations caused by traffic and the Metro have also taken their toll. Restoration works have periodically been carried out, the latest starting in 1992. Partly financed by the Banca di Roma, the project was initially expected to take 10 years but at the time of writing it had been at a standstill for several years. Current estimates have a restored Colosseo being unveiled by 2004.

Opening hours in winter are daily from 9 am to 4 pm and until 6 pm in summer. Admission is L10,000.

Arco di Costantino (Map 8)

On the western side of the Colosseo is the triumphal arch built to honour Constantine following his victory over Maxentius at the battle of the Milvian Bridge (near the present-day Zona Olimpica, north-west of the Villa Borghese) in 312 AD.

However, the arch was not built completely from scratch. Its decorative reliefs are an assemblage of pieces taken from earlier structures, probably to speed up construction in order to celebrate Constantine's triumph. The lower stonework dates from Domitian's reign (81-96 AD), and the eight large medallions depicting hunting scenes are Hadrianic (117-138 AD). Four enormous reliefs, on the inside of the central archway and on the sides of the arch, depict Trajan's battle against the Dacians. These were removed from the Foro di Traiano, are

believed to be by the same sculptor who carved Trajan's column.

Incorporated into the Frangipani fortress, the arch was 'liberated' in 1804. Major restoration was completed in 1987.

Walk back towards Via dei Fori Imperiali and turn left into the Via Sacra, towards the Arco di Tito and one of the Foro Romano exits. Just before the gate, head uphill to the left for another panoramic view of the forum.

ESQUILINO (MAPS 6 & 8)

The Esquilino (Esquiline hill) is the largest and highest of Rome's seven hills. It stretches from the Colosseo to Stazione Termini, encompassing Via Cavour (a major traffic artery between Stazione Termini and Via dei Fori Imperiali), the Basilica di Santa Maria Maggiore, the market square of Piazza Vittorio Emanuele II and the Parco del Colle Oppio. The Esquilino originally had four summits. In ancient times the lower slope of the western summit, the Suburra, was occupied by crowded slums while the area between Via Cavour and the Colle Oppio was a fashionable residential district for wealthier citizens. Pompey lived here, as did the famous patron of the arts, Maecenas, and Vergil is said to have had a house in the area. Much of the hill was covered with vineyards and gardens, many of which remained until the late 19th century, when they were dug up to make way for grandiose apartment blocks.

Today, the Esquilino is the most multi-racial area of Rome, home to thousands of immigrants. It is also popular with young artists enticed by low rents and spacious lofts.

Rione Monti (Map 6)

The western side of the Esquilino is known as Rione Monti (or simply Monti) and includes some of Rome's most famous smaller churches. Th elate 3th century **Chiesa di Santa Pudenziana**, is in the characteristic Via Urbana just off Piazza dell'Esquilino. It is dedicated to Pudentiana, the daughter of a Roman senator who is said to have given hospitality to St Peter in his home, the site of which is now occupied by the church. Most of the façade was added in the 19th century although elements from the earlier buildings, such as the delicately carved frieze and medallions dating from the 11th century, were retained. The Romanesque arched windows and the bell tower date from the 12th century.

The interior is noted for its magnificent apse mosaic. An enthroned Christ is flanked by two female figures who are crowning St Peter and St Paul; on either side of them are the apostles as Roman senators dressed in togas. Dating from 390 AD, this is the oldest mosaic of its kind in Rome. You can only see 10 out of the original 12 apostles; the two outer figures were cut off in a 16th century restoration which also sliced off the bottom of the mosaic amputating the legs of the outer apostles. (See also boxed text 'Hidden Treasures' in the Facts about Rome chapter.)

The **Chiesa di Santa Prassede**, Via Santa Prassede 9a, was built in the 9th century by Pope Paschal I on the site of a 2nd century oratory. It is almost hidden, hemmed in by medieval buildings and you enter through a side door. The church is dedicated to Praxedes, the sister of Pudentiana. In 1969 the sainthoods of both Pudenziana and Prassede were declared invalid although the churches have kept their names. Paschal I had mosaic artists brought from Byzantium (later Constantinople) to decorate his church, and the results are breathtaking.

The naturalism evident in earlier mosaics from the late classical period has been replaced with a marked Christian symbolism. On the first triumphal arch angels guard the door to the New Jerusalem. On the underside of both arches are beautifully worked garlands of lilies and foliage. The apse mosaics are slightly blocked from view by the baroque baldicchino. Climb up the red marble steps for a better view if you need to. Christ is flanked by St Peter, St Pudentiana and St Zeno (on the right) and St Paul, St Praxedes and Paschal on the left. All the figures have golden halos except for the figure of Paschal, whose head is shadowed

by a green square or nimbus, indicating that he was still alive at the time the mosaic was done (but expected to be on a fast track to sainthood). Below are the Lamb of God and the faithful flock.

The small **Cappella di San Zenone** in the south aisle was built by Paschal as a mausoleum for his mother. The mosaics on the outside show distinctive Roman faces representing the Virgin and Child, Prassede, Pudenziana and other saints (inner group) and Christ and the Apostles. Enter the chapel and you feel likepart of the mosaic. It is unlikely that you will get much closer to mosaic decoration anywhere in Rome, and you can really appreciate the skill of the artists. A small mosaic in the altar niche depicts the Virgin and Child with Saints Praxedes and Pudentiana; in the vault is Christ with four angels; on the inside of the doorway are St Peter and St Paul supporting the throne; and on the left, facing the altar are Sts Praxedes, Pudentiana and Agnes. The fragment of marble in the glass case on the right is thought to be a piece of the column to which Christ was tied when he was scourged.

If you can tear your eyes away from the mosaics, have a look at other features of the church, such as the trompe l'oeil frescoes in the nave, which are the work of various artists and were completed in the 16th century. The architrave of the nave is made up of ancient Roman fragments, some with inscriptions. The floor is paved in coloured marble. A large round porphyry disc surrounded by an inscription in the nave near the main door marks the spot where Prassede is thought to have hidden the bones of Christian martyrs. (See also the 'Hidden Treasures' boxed text.)

Following Via San Martino ai Monti, you come to the **Chiesa di San Martino ai Monti**, a Carmelite church originally constructed in the 4th century and subsequently rebuilt in the 6th century, in the 9th century, and then completely transformed by Filippo Gagliardi in the 1650s. The 24 Corinthian columns in the nave are all that remain of the 6th century building. Of note are Gagliardi's frescoes of the Basilica di San Giovanni in

Laterano before it was rebuilt in the mid 17th century by Borromini, and the Basilica di San Pietro before it assumed its present appearance in the 16th century by the hands of Bramante, Raphael, Michelangelo, Maderno and others. There are also frescoes by Gaspard Dughet of the Roman Campagna, the countryside surrounding Rome.

The characteristic Via Panisperna, which connects Santa Maria Maggiore to the Fori Imperiali, still gives a clear indication of the topography of the Esquilino. At the western end is **Villa Aldobrandini**, built for the Duke of Urbino in the 16th century. It was subsequently acquired byClement VIII, the Aldobrandini pope, who gave it to his nephews. Now owned by the state, the villa houses an international law library. The extensive formal gardens, which have splendid views over the city, can be reached through a gate at Via Mazzarino 11.

Basilica di Santa Maria Maggiore (Map 6)

One of Rome's four patriarchal basilicas (the others are San Pietro, San Giovanni in Laterano and San Paolo Fuori Le Mura), Santa Maria Maggiore was built on a summit of the Esquilino in the 5th century, during Pope Sixtus III's era. According to legend, in 352 Pope Liberius had a dream in which he was instructed by the Virgin Mary to build a church in the exact place where he found snow. When, on the following morning (5 August), snow fell on the Esquilino, he obeyed. The original church was called Santa Maria della Neve. Each year on 5 August there is a service in the basilica during which white flower petals are released from the ceiling to commemorate the miracle.

Its main façade was added in the 18th century, preserving the 13th century **mosaics** of the earlier façade. These are beautifully illuminated at night. The interior is Baroque and the bell tower Romanesque.

The basilican form of the vast interior, a nave and two aisles, remains intact and the most notable feature is the cycle of **mosaics** dating from the 5th century which decorate the triumphal arch and nave, some of which are so high up that they are difficult to see

(a pair of binoculars or a telephoto lens would be useful). They are the most important mosaics of this period in Rome and depict biblical scenes, in particular events in the lives of Abraham, Jacob and Isaac (to the left), and Moses and Joshua (to the right). Scenes from the life of Christ decorate the triumphal arch. The central image in the apse, signed by Jacopo Torriti, dates from the 13th century and represents the Coronation of the Virgin. The Virgin is seated on the same throne as Christ, and it is thought that the artist was influenced by the mosaics of the same scene in the Chiesa di Santa Maria in Trastevere. Further scenes of the Life of the Virgin are below. At the time of writing the mosaics and Giuliano da Sangallo's coffered ceiling (gilded with the first gold transported from America by Columbus) were completely covered for restoration, due for completion in late 1999.

The **baldacchino** over the high altar is elaborately decorated with gilt cherubs. The altar itself is a porphyry sarcophagus which is said to contain the relics of St Matthew and other martyrs. Steps lead down to the Confessio where a reliquary preserves a fragment of the Baby Jesus' crib. Note the Cosmati pavement of the nave and aisles, dating from the 12th century. The sumptuously decorated **Cappella Sistina**, last on the right, was built by Domenico Fontana in the 16th century and contains the tombs of popes Sixtus V and Pius V. Opposite is the **Cappella Borghese** (or Cappella Paolina), also full of elaborate decoration, erected in the 17th century by Pope Paul V. The *Madonna and Child* above the altar, surrounded by lapis lazuli and agate is believed to date from the 12th to the 13th century.

Piazza Vittorio Emanuele (Map 6)

This piazza is south-east of Santa Maria Maggiore. From Monday to Saturday it is the scene of Rome's largest and most boisterous food market. It is the most multi-ethnic of the city's markets and the place to come for exotic spices or African and Asian foodstuffs. There are also Indian and Chinese food shops in the vicinity. It is a popular area for pickpockets, so watch your wallet or handbag. Within the square are the ruins of the **Trofei di Mario**, once a fountain at the end of an aqueduct. The square itself hosts ethnic food and cultural festivals throughout the year and an outdoor film festival in the summer (see Entertainment chapter).

In the north corner of the piazza is the **Chiesa di Sant'Eusebio**, which was founded in the 4th century and rebuilt twice in the 18th. On 17 January each year worshippers are of the four-legged variety for the annual blessing of the animals, on the saint's day of their protector, St Anthony Abbot. The 1997 blessing was recieved by dogs, cats, and even horses. The church is open only at 6.30 and 6.30 pm.

Colle Oppio (Map 6)

The **Parco del Colle Oppio**, now a haunt of homeless people and drug users, was once the site of part of Nero's fabled **Domus Aurea** (Golden House). Nero had the palace built after the fire of 64 AD. It was a vast complex of buildings covering an area of some 50 hectares, stretching from the Colle Oppio to the Celio and the Palatino. The gardens, which contained a lake and game animals, occupied the valley where the Colosseo now stands.

After Nero's death in 68 AD, his successors were quick to destroy the complex, which had occupied a major part of ancient Rome's centre. Vespasian drained the lake to build the Colosseo, Domitian demolished the buildings on the Palatino and Trajan built his baths, the **Terme di Traiano**, over the buildings on the Colle Oppio. During the Renaissance, artists descended into the ruins of the wing of the Domus Aurea on the Colle Oppio to study its architectural features and the rich paintings which adorned its walls.

Archaeologists believe that the Colle Oppio is the richest area in Rome for frescoes and works of art, but its excavation has been limited for many years due to lack of funding. In 1998, archaeologists working in an area underneath the ruins of the Terme di Traiano (Trajan's Baths) discovered a large wall painting of a city, yet to be identified,

in the cryptoporticus or service passage. The fresco is believed to have adorned an arch or a monumental doorway in a garden pavilion in the grounds of the Domus Aurea. It is the most important archaeological discovery in Rome in recent years. Once the excavations are completed, the site will be opened to the public.

Little remains of the **Terme di Tito** in the south-west corner of the Colle Oppio. Maecenas earlier occupied a villa on the site.

San Pietro in Vincoli (Map 6)

From the Colle Oppio, follow the Via Terme di Tito and turn left into Via del Monte to reach the **Basilica di San Pietro in Vincoli**, built in the 5th century by the Empress Eudoxia, wife of Valentinian III, to house the chains of St Peter. Legend has it that when a second part of the chains was returned to Roma from Constantinople, the two pieces miraculously joined together.

While the presence of the chains makes the church an important place of pilgrimage, the church offers another great treasure – Michelangelo's unfinished tomb of Pope Julius II, with his powerful *Moses* and unfinished statues of *Leah* and *Rachel* on either side. These were being restored at the time of writing. Michelangelo was frustrated for many years by his inability to find time to complete work on the tomb. In the end, Pope Julius was buried in the Basilica di San Pietro without the great tomb he had envisioned and the unfinished sculptures which were to have adorned it are in the Louvre and the Galleria dell'Accademia in Firenze. A flight of steps through a low arch leads down from the church to Via Cavour.

San Clemente (Map 8)

At the base of the Colle Oppio near the Colosseo, is the **Basilica di San Clemente** in Via San Giovanni in Laterano (across Via Labicana). Dedicated to one of the earliest popes, the church defines how history in Rome exists on many levels. The 12th century church at current street level was built over a 4th century church which was, in turn, built over a 1st century Roman house containing a late 2nd century AD temple to the god Mithras (an eastern deity especially popular with soldiers). Further, it is believed that Republican foundations lie beneath the house.

It is possible to visit the first three levels. You enter the church through a side door. If the main door at the eastern end of the church is open go through it into the courtyard outside and then come back into the church the way it was designed to be entered. The mosaic decoration is even more stunning and effective.

In the medieval church, note the Schola Cantorum, a marble choir screen dating from the 6th century which was originally in the older church below. It is decorated with panels of white and coloured marbles and the early Christian symbols of the fish, the dove and the vine. The high marble pulpit on the left, together with the beautiful Paschal candlestick decorated with Cosmati mosaics, was added when the new church was built. High pulpits, common in medieval churches, were probably designed so that the priest could read from illuminated manuscripts in the form of scrolls and, as he read, the congregation could see the pictures. The floor is paved with intricate patterns of coloured marbles.

The stunning mosaics in the apse, dating from the 12th century, are the highlight of the church. On the triumphal arch are Christ and the symbols of the four Evangelists. In the apse itself is depicted the Triumph of the Cross, with 12 doves symbolising the apostles. Figures around the cross include the Madonna and St John, as well as St John the Baptist and other saints encircled by a vine growing from the foot of the cross. There are also beautifully detailed animals and acanthus leaves. The gold background of the mosaics are typical of the later Byzantine style. However, it is thought that the designs were partially based on mosaics in the earlier church and that some of the mosaic tiles were actually salvaged from it. The early Renaissance frescoes by Masolino da Panicale in the Cappella di Santa Caterina depict scenes from the life of St Catherine of Alexandria.

You have to buy a ticket to descend to the lower levels of the church. Take some time to study the plans of the various levels to orient yourself and follow the suggested route. Not much remains of the 4th century church, which was virtually destroyed by Norman invaders in 1084, although some 11th century Romanesque frescoes illustrating the life of St Clement can be seen at the eastern end. In a left aisle is a *piscina* or deep pit, discovered by archaeologists in 1967, which was probably used as a font or fountain. Other fresco cycles are faded or damaged beyond repair.

Descending another level, you arrive at the 1st century Roman house and the temple of Mithras. At the eastern end is a catacomb with 16 wall tombs dating from the 5th or 6th century. The temple, probably one the *triclinium* or banquet room of the house, is situated directly under the apse of the 4th century church, and dates from the late 2nd century or early 3rd century. It contains an altar with a sculpted relief of Mithras slaying the bull. Don't be afraid if you hear the sound of running water in the deepest level of the church. Behind an iron door at the western end of the excavations is a drain that joins up with the Cloaca Maxima, the main water drain of ancient Rome, near the Colosseo.

From San Clemente turning right into Via dei Quercei you reach the **Chiesa dei Santi Quattro Coronati**, a fortified medieval convent. The four crowned saints to whom the is dedicated were four Christian sculptors killed for refusing to make a statue of a pagan god. The squat bell tower dates from the 9th century. To note are extremely well preserved 13th century frescoes of St Sylvester and Constantine in the **Cappella di San Silvestro**. There is also a pretty cloister and garden off the north aisle (ring the bell for admission) built in the early 13th century.

SAN GIOVANNI (MAPS 6 & 8)
Basilica di San Giovanni in Laterano (Map 8)

This was the first Christian basilica constructed in Rome – founded by Constantine in the 4th century – and it remains one of the most important in the Christian world. It is Rome's cathedral and the pope's seat as Bishop of Rome. It has been destroyed by fire twice and rebuilt several times. In 1425 Martin V had the floor inlaid with stone and mosaic looted from other derelict Roman churches.

Borromini was commissioned to transform its interior into the Baroque style in the mid-17th century. The eastern façade, which is the basilica's main entrance, faces on to Piazza di Porta San Giovanni. The bronze main doors were moved here by Borromini from the Curia in the Foro Romano. The portico, built by Alessandro Galilei in 1736, is surmounted by colossal statues representing Christ with Saints John the Baptist and John the Evangelist and the 12 apostles. The Gothic baldacchino over the papal altar dates from the 14th century and contains many relics, including the heads of Saints Peter and Paul and part of St Peter's wooden altar table. The frescoes in the transepts depict the conversion of Constantine. The apse was rebuilt in the 19th century. The mosaics that we see today are copies of the originals which were destroyed during the rebuilding. One of the nicest architectural features of the basilica is Borromini's treatment of the various funerary monuments in the aisles; he surrounded them with sculptural frames and placed his trademark oval window above each one.

Fortunately the beautiful 13th century cloister escaped the fires which ravaged the rest of the basilica. Built by the Vassalletto family in Cosmati style, the cloister has columns which were once completely covered with inlaid marble mosaics. The damage done by time and pollution is sadly evident and few of the wonderful twisted columns have any mosaic decoration left, but a major restoration is imminent. The central court is off limits so you can't get a really good look at the architrave above the columns which is also highly decorated. The outer walls of the cloister are lined with inscriptions, sarcophagi and various sculptures. Of note on the south side is the inscription of a Papal Bull of Sixtus IV and, on the west side, four small columns supporting a marble slab, which Christians in the Middle Ages regarded as representing the height of Christ. The cloister is open from 9 am to 5 pm (6 pm in summer) and costs L4000.

A second entrance into the basilica is through the northern façade, which faces on to Piazza San Giovanni in Laterano. The two-tiered portico, built by Domenico Fontana in 1586, was damaged by a bomb attack in 1993 and has recently been restored. Leaving the church by this door and crossing the piazza you come to the domed **baptistry** which was also built by Constantine, but has been remodelled several times. Sixtus III gave it its present octagonal shape which became the model for many baptistries throughout the Christian world. A green basalt font is in the centre of the baptistry, beneath the dome decorated with modern copies of frescoes by Andrea Sacchi. The outer walls are decorated by 17th century frescoes. It is surrounded by several chapels with magnificent mosaic decorations.

The **Cappella di Santa Rufina** is decorated with a stunning 5th century mosaic of vines and foliage against a deep blue background while the **Capella di San Giovanni Evangelista** has a mosaic in the vault of the lamb of God surrounded by birds and flowers. The **Capella di San Venanzio** was added by Pope John IV in the 7th century. It has extremely well preserved mosaics; in the apse are Christ with angels and the Madonna and saints, and on the triumphal arch are Christian martyrs. Right at the top are views of Jerusalem and Bethlehem. The baptistry is open from 9 am to 1 pm and from 4 to 6 pm Monday to Thursday and from 9 am to 1 pm on Friday and Saturday.

The **Palazzo Laterano**, which adjoins the basilica, was the papal residence until the pope moved to Avignon in the 14th century. It was largely destroyed by fire in 1308 and most of what remained was demolished in the 16th century. The present building houses the Rome Vicariate and offices of the diocese of Rome.

The building on the eastern side of Piazza di Porta San Giovanni is all that remains of the original Palazzo Laterano and contains the **Scala Santa** and the **Sancta Sanctorum**. The Scala Santa (Holy Staircase) is said to be from the palace of Pontius Pilate in Jerusalem where Christ himself had trod; people are allowed to climb it only on their knees. To protect them the 28 marble steps are covered with wooden boards. Colourful frescoes by a group of unknown Roman artists from the late 13th century cover the ceiling and walls above the stairs.

The Scala Santa and two other staircases lead to the Sancta Sanctorum. This was the popes' private chapel. The name, meaning 'the holy of holies', refers to the numerous relics that were once housed in the chapel but which have now been moved to il Vaticano. The silver panelled altarpiece, originally a painting of Christ said to have been done by St Luke and an angel, has been restored and repainted so many times that it bears no resemblance to how it once was. The vaulted ceiling above it is covered with 13th century mosaics. The Cosmati marblework on the floor is particularly fine. The lower walls are panelled with sheets of marble. Above are 13th century frescoes (by the same group of artists who frescoed the stairwells) of the Apostles and saints separated by swirling Gothic columns and, higher still, frescoes clearly illustrating the various ways that martyrs met their deaths.

The Sancta Sanctorum is open from 10.30 to 11.30 am and 3 to 4 pm on Tuesday, Thursday and Saturday. Admission is L5000. The Scala Santa (☎ 06 70 49 46 19) is open from 6.15 am to noon and from 3.30 to 6.45 pm from April to September and from 6.15 am to noon and from 3 to 6.15 pm from October to March. The rest of the

building has been occupied by a Passionist convent since 1953; the crypt below now houses an active visual and performing arts space, **Sala 1** (entrance in Piazza Porta di San Giovanni) which is open Tuesday to Saturday from 5 to 8 pm.

Santa Croce in Gerusalemme (Map 8)

Following Viale Carlo Felice east from Piazza di Porta di San Giovanni, you reach the church of **Santa Croce in Gerusalemme** in the piazza of the same name. The church is thought to have been founded in 320 AD by St Helena, Constantine's mother, who brought Christian relics, including a piece of the cross on which Christ was crucified, to Rome from Jerusalem. The church was rebuilt in 1144 by Lucius II who added a bell tower. Benedict XIV made major alterations to the church in 1744, adding the façade and oval vestibule. The frescoes in the apse date from the 15th century and represent the legends of the Cross. The relics are housed in a chapel at the end of the north aisle.

Next to the church are the columns and bricked up arches of the 3rd century BC **Anfiteatro Castrense**, once part of an imperial palace on the site. The small amphitheatre was used for games and baiting animals. North of the church are former military barracks which house two military museums and the **Museo Nazionale degli Strumenti Musicali** (Map: Greater Rome) which has a unique collection of musical instruments dating from Roman times to the 19th century and including instruments from Asia, Africa and the Americas. The museum (☎ 06 701 47 96) is open Tuesday to Saturday from 9 am to 1.30 pm and admission is L4000.

Via Eleniana leads north from Santa Croce to the **Porta Maggiore** (Map 6), also known as the Porta Prenestina, a gateway to ancient Rome built by Claudius in 52 AD. The main southbound road, Via Prenestina and Via Labicana, passed beneath the gateway and ruts made by carriage wheels can still be seen in the basalt flagstones under the arches. The arch supported two aqueducts – the Acqua Claudia and the Acqua Aniene Nuova – one on top of the other. It was later incorporated into the Aurelian Walls of the city.

Just outside the gate is a rather pretentious travertine monument, the **Sepolcro di M Virgilio Eurisace** (map 6), commonly known as the Baker's Tomb, built around 30 BC by the widow of the baker Vergilius Eurysaces in memory of her husband. The tomb is decorated with reliefs depicting the industrious baker at work, and the monument itself is in the shape of an enormous bread oven.

CELIO TO PORTA SAN SEBASTIANO (MAP 8)
Celio

The Celio (Caelian hill) is accessible either from Via di San Gregorio or, from the other side, from Via della Navicella. The **Villa Celimontana** is a large public park on top of the hill, perfect for a quiet picnic (as long as it isn't overrun by wedding parties having photographs taken – common on Saturday). There is also a children's playground. The Renaissance villa, which originally belonged to the noble family, now houses the Italian Geographical Society.

The 4th century **Chiesa di SS Giovanni e Paolo**, in the piazza of the same name on Via di San Paolo della Croce (which runs off Via della Navicella), is dedicated to two Romans, Sts John and Paul. They had served Constantine II and were beheaded by his anti-Christian successor, Julian, for refusing to serve in his court. The church was built over their houses. A beautiful 13th century fresco of Christ with the Apostles is in a small room by the altar. It is usually locked but you can ask the sacristan to let you in. The arches in the piazza are the remains of 3rd century Roman shops.

Walk downhill along the Clivio di Scauro, an atmospheric road dating from the 1st century BC. A road to the left leads up to the 8th century **Chiesa di San Gregorio Magno** was built in honour of Pope Gregory I (the Great) on the site where he

dispatched St Augustine to convert the people of Britain to Christianity. The church was remodelled in the Baroque style in the 17th century. The atrium, designed by Giovanni Battista Soria, contains tombs of prominent Englishmen including Sir Edward Carne, an envoy of Henry VIII and Mary I, who was sent to Rome several times. One of his missions was to obtain a papal annulment of the king's marriage to Catherine of Aragon. He died in 1561.

The interior of the church was transformed into the Baroque style in the 18th century by Francesco Ferrari. The Cappella di San Gregorio, at the end of the right aisle, contains a 1st century BC marble throne. A gate to the left of the church leads to three small chapels among cypress trees. On the right, the Cappella di Santa Silvia (dedicated to Gregory the Great's mother) contains a fresco of angels by Guido Reni. The central chapel, the Cappella di Sant'Andrea contains a painting by Domenichino of the flagellation of St Andrew and Guido Reni's depiction of St Andrew on the way to his martyrdom. The fresco on the inside of the entrance is by Giovanni Lanfranco and depicts Sts Silvia and Gregory. The altarpiece, by Pomarancio, depicts Madonna with Sts Andrew and Gregory. The third chapel is dedicated to Santa Barbara, and along with a statue of St Gregory, contains frescoes illustrating St Augustine's mission. The chapels are open Tuesday to Sunday from 9.30 am to 12.30 pm.

Chiesa di Santo Stefano Rotondo

This fascinating round church is on Via di S Stefano Rotondo, just across Via della Navicella from the Villa Celimontana. Inside are two rings of antique granite and marble columns. The circular wall is lined with frescoes depicting the various ways in which saints were martyred. The vivid scenes are quite grotesque and you might not make it through all 34 of them. Watch out for a little priest pointing to your shoes – he is worried you will dirty the polished wooden floor. At the time of writing, the church resembled a building site, as excavations beneath it were carried out and parts of the wooden floor had been pulled up.

The church is open from 9 am to 1 pm and from 1.50 to 4.20 pm Tuesday to Saturday, and from 1.50 to 4.20 pm on Monday. In summer it is also open on the second Sunday of each month, from 9 am to noon.

Terme di Caracalla

South of the Celio is the Via delle Terme di Caracalla accessible by bus Nos 160 and 628 from Piazza Venezia. The big white building on the corner of Piazza di Porta Capena, houses the **Food and Agriculture Organization of the United Nations** in front of which is the Axum obelisk taken from Ethiopia by Mussolini as war booty. At the time of writing it was covered in scaffolding as experts ascertained whether it could be taken apart and returned to Ethiopia. Next to the FOA is the Parco di Porta Capena which now contains a modern athletics stadium.

In Piazza Santa Balbina (off Viale Guido Baccelli which runs through the park), is the **Chiesa di Santa Balbina**, one of the oldest churches in Rome, which dates from the 4th century. To note is the fine Cosmati tomb of Stefanus de Surdis which dates from the early 14th century. The church was extensively restored in the 1930s when 1st century AD Roman mosaics found in other parts of the city were installed there.

Santa Balbina overlooks the magnificent ruins of the **Terme di Caracalla** (Baths of Caracalla). Begun by Antonius Caracalla and inaugurated in 217 AD, the baths were used until the 6th century AD. They are the best preserved of the imperial Roman baths in the city. Covering 10 hectares, Caracalla's Baths could hold 1600 people and had shops, gardens, libraries and gym facilities. Men and women bathed at different times of the day and the process was convoluted. Excavations of the baths in the 16th and 17th centuries unearthed important sculptures and statues from the site which found their way into the Farnese family collection.

Two enormous basins now serve as twin fountains in Piazza Farnese.

From the 1930s until 1993 the Terme di Caracalla were an atmospheric venue for opera performances in summer. In recent years these have been banned to prevent further damage to the ruins. The baths are open Tuesday to Saturday from 9 am to 6 pm in summer, and from 9 am to 3 pm in winter, and on Sunday and Monday from 9 am to 1 pm. Admission is L8000.

Porta San Sebastiano

Via di Porta San Sebastiano runs from Piazzale Numa Pompilio in front of the Terme di Caracalla to the beginning of the Via Appia Antica (see 'Appia Antica and the Catacombs' later in this chapter). Behind the high stone walls are luxurious private villas and gardens, and on the eastern side, a small public park. At the end of the road is the **Porta San Sebastiano**, the largest and best preserved gateway in the Mura Aureliane, the walls which surrounds the city.

It is now a museum, the **Museo delle Mura**, which documents the history of the wall surrounding the city built by Aurelian (270-275) for defensive purposes and continued by his successor Probus (276-282). The perimeter of the wall measures around 19km with 18 gates and 381 towers and all seven of Rome's hills were incorporated within it. Maxentius (306-312) subsequently doubled its height. Most of the Mura Aureliane survive today. (See Geography in the Facts about Rome chapter and the Rome Walks chapter.) The museum contains prints, drawings and models, and visitors can walk along the ramparts for about 400m. It is open Tuesday to Sunday from 9 am to 7 pm. Admission costs L3750.

Circo Massimo

The **Circo Massimo** (Circus Maximus) lies between the Palatino and the Aventino in a valley once known as the Vallis Murcia. There is not much to see here: only a few ruins remain of what was once a chariot racetrack, about 600m long and 90m wide,

nterior decorating for an empress – frescoe from the House of Livia

Bernini's angels lead the way across the Tevere to the Castel Sant'Angelo

Mythical two-stroke engine, Gallerai delle Carte Geografiche, Musei Vaticani

Which way to the butcher's?

High fashion at high prices

On a fine afternoon, it's worth the extra cost to sit down in a caffè.

decorated with statues and columns and surrounded by wooden stands which held more than 200,000 spectators. Races were run anti-clockwise around the track, the greatest excitement coming when the chariots had to negotiate the tight turns at each end.

The history of the circus goes back a long way. A brick structure was built to substitute earlier wooden structures in the 2nd century BC. In 46 BC Julius Caesar had battles recreated here, using prisoners of war and method acting. Augustus erected the obelisk of Ramses II in 10 BC, which now stands at the centre of Piazza del Popolo. The great fire of 64 AD that destroyed much of the city is thought to have started in the Circo Massimo's wooden stands. The circus was rebuilt by Trajan in about 100 AD; by this time it could hold 250,000 spectators. It was later expanded by Caracalla and restored by Constantine, who decorated it with a second obelisk, that of Tutmosis III, which now stands in Piazza San Giovanni in Laterano.

The Circo Massimo remained in use until 549 AD. Excavations of the ruins continue at the eastern end. It's now a popular place for jogging and walking dogs.

AVENTINO (MAPS 7 & 8)

South of the Circo Massimo is the Aventino (Aventine hill), best reached from Via di Circo Massimo by either Via di Valle Murcia or Clivo dei Pubblici to Via di Santa Sabina. (It is also easily accessible by bus No 27 from Stazione Termini and the Colosseo, or on the Metro Linea B, disembarking at the Circo Massimo station). Along the way, you will pass the **Roseto Comunale**, a beautiful public rose garden, best seen obviously when the roses are in bloom in May and June, and the pretty, walled **Parco Savello**, planted with orange trees. There is a stunning view of Rome from the park.

Next to the park is the **Basilica di Santa Sabina** (Map 7), founded by Peter of Illyria in 422 AD, one of the most important and beautiful early Christian basilicas in Rome. The church was added to in the 9th century and again in 1216, just before it was given by Honorius III to the newly founded Dominican order. Of particular note is the 5th century door carved from cypress wood, to the far left as you stand under the 15th century portico facing the church. The door features 18 carved wooden panels depicting biblical scenes. The crucifixion scene is one of the oldest in existence but it is interesting to note that Christ's cross is not shown.

The three naves in the solemn interior are separated by 24 Corinthian columns made (strangely enough for the period) specifically for the occasion. They are the first example in Rome of columns after the Ravenna model, supporting arches rather than architraves. Above and to the sides of the arches there is a red and green frieze in *opus sectile* (5th and 6th century). Light streams in to the interior of the church from high nave windows added in the 9th century. Also dating from the 9th century are the carved choir, the pulpit and the bishop's throne.

In the centre of the nave is a mosaic tombstone of Muñoz de Zamora, one of the first leaders of the Dominicans. Only a small amount of the mosaic decoration that once covered the walls still remains. The fresco in the apse was painted in the 19th century. The 13th century cloister was recently restored and can be visited with permission of the sacristan. The basilica is open daily from 6.30 am to 12.45 pm and 3.30 to 7 pm.

Farther south along Via Santa Sabina is the Piazza Cavalieri di Malta and the **Priorato di Malta** (Map 7), the headquarters of the Order of the Knights of Malta. The order was founded in the 12th century in Rhodes and later in Malta, to assist pilgrims en route to the Holy Land. The villa is the residence of the Grand Master of the Knights of Malta and served as the Order's embassies to Italy and il Vaticano. It is surrounded by a beautiful garden with laurel hedges and palm trees.

Piranesi redesigned the **Chiesa di Santa Maria del Priorato** (Map 7) in 1765. Entering it is like walking into a Piranesi drawing; it is loaded with architectural details and elaborate stucco work. The complex is rarely open to the public. Should you be passing on a day when it is, a visit is a must. If it's closed, look through the keyhole in the central door of the entrance for a surprising view through a tunnel of trees to the dome of San Pietro framed in the distance. Piranesi also designed Piazza Cavalieri di Malta which is decorated with mini obelisks and coats of arms.

On the other side of the hill is the **Chiesa di Santa Prisca** (Map 8) in Piazza Santa Prisca dating from the 4th century AD. The church was built on top of a Mithraic shrine which the Christians all but destroyed. This was extensively excavated in the 1950s and damaged wall paintings, showing the seven stages of initiation into the Mithraic cult, have been restored although it is not open to the public. The church is open every day from 8 am to noon and 4.30 to 7.30 pm.

Across Viale Aventina in Via di San Saba is the picturesque **Chiesa di San Saba** (Map 8) which dates from the 10th century although it has been substantially rebuilt. Cosmati marble work from the 13th century decorates the main door and floor. The portico contains a number of sculptural and an intricately carved Roman sarcophagus. Above the portico is a loggia which was added in the 16th century. The church is open daily from 7 am to noon and from 4 to 6.30 pm.

Piazza Bocca della Verità (Map 8)

Between the Aventino and the Tevere is the recently refurbished **Chiesa di Santa Maria in Cosmedin** in Piazza Bocca della Verità, regarded as one of the finest medieval churches in Rome. Two earlier structures that stood on the site – an arcaded colonnade that was part of an Imperial era market inspector's office and walls from a 7th century Christian welfare centre – were incorporated into the church built by Pope Hadrian I in the 8th century. The church was further enlarged in the 12th century when the seven-storey bell tower and medieval portico were added. The church's interior, including the beautiful floor, the high altar

and the schola cantorum or choir, was heavily decorated with Cosmati inlaid coloured marble. There are 12th century frescoes in the aisles, inside the arches of the nave and scant remains high up on the nave walls. An 8th century mosaic fragment is preserved in the souvenir shop.

Under the portico is the famous **Bocca della Verità** (Mouth of Truth), a large disk in the shape of a mask which probably once served as the cover of an ancient drain. Legend says that if you put your right hand into the mouth while telling a lie, it will snap shut. The church is open from 10 am to 1 pm and from 3 to 5 pm, although the portico is open from 9 am to 6 pm.

Opposite Santa Maria in Cosmedin are two tiny Roman temples dating from the Republican era both of which have been recently restored: the round **Tempio di Ercole Vincitore** and the **Tempio di Portunus**. The temples were consecrated as churches in the Middle Ages. They stand in an area once known as the Forum Boarium (cattle market) which existed even before the Foro Romano. The Forum Boarium later became an important commercial centre and had its own port on the Tevere. To its north are the ruins of the **Casa dei Crescenzi**, a former tower fortress transformed into a mansion in the 11th century by the powerful Crescenzi family. It is one of the few medieval Roman houses to have survived.

Off Piazza della Bocca della Verità, towards the Palatino in Via del Velabro, is the **Arco di Giano** (Arch of Janus), a four-sided Roman arch which once covered a crossroads. In ancient times, cattle dealers used it to shelter from sun and rain. Beyond the arch, on the northern side of the street is the medieval **Chiesa di San Giorgio in Velabro**. The church's portico which dates from the 7th century has been rebuilt after it was completely destroyed by a Mafia bomb attack in 1993. The convent beside the church was also damaged and has been restored.

Turning left into Via di San Teodoro, you reach the circular **Chiesa di San Teodoro** which nestles at the foot of the Palatino. A church was built on this site in the 6th century on the ruins of warehouses that stood between the Foro Romano and the Tevere. The present church dates from the mid-15th century and was built by Pope Nicholas V, but the breathtaking mosaic in the apse has survived from an earlier building. The church was restored in 1704 by Carlo Fontana working under the commission of Pope Clement XI. Fontana designed the double stairway which leads down from street level to a courtyard, in the centre of which is an altar from a pagan temple. The church has inconsistent opening hours. You might be lucky to find it open between about 9 am and 1 pm and from 3.30 to 6 pm. Otherwise it is open for Mass on Sunday at 10.30 am.

Fascist era buildings line Via Petroselli, the road from Piazza Bocca della Verità to Teatro Marcello. These house municipal offices including the Anagrafe, or public records office. To the right, Vico Jugario leads up to Piazza della Consolazione at the top of which is the **Chiesa di Santa Maria della Consolazione** which has 16th century frescoes by Taddeo Zuccari. On the corner of Via Petroselli and Via del Foro Olitorio is the **Chiesa di San Nicola in Carcere**. It was built in the 11th century and remodelled in 1599 by Giacomo della Porta. The church was built on the site of the Republican era vegetable and oil market, and marble columns from temples that once stood there were used in the church's façade and interior.

Continuing along Via del Teatro di Marcello, you come to the **Teatro di Marcello**, (Theatre of Marcellus), planned by Julius Caesar and built around 13 BC by Augustus. See Walk 2 in the Rome Walks chapter.

Ghetto
(Map: Around Piazza Navona)

Via del Portico d'Ottavia is the centre of what remains of the Jewish Ghetto. In the 16th century Pope Paul IV ordered the confinement of Jewish people in this area, marking the beginning of a period of intolerance which continued into the 20th century. See Walk 2 in the Rome Walks chapter.

The tightly packed buildings on the northern side of the street incorporate the remains of old Roman and medieval buildings. The house at No 1 (on the corner of Piazza Costaguti) dates from 1468 and the façade is decorated with pieces of ancient Roman sculpture including a fragment from an ancient sarcophagus. At street level, in a tiny unmarked shop, an all-female bakery produces traditional Jewish breads, pastries and cakes.

Heading through Piazza delle Cinque Scole, you see the rear of the imposing **Palazzo Cenci**, the biggest palazzo in the area. In Via dell'Arco dei Cenci you can see the main façade which is decorated by elaborate stucco work around small balconies. The palazzo belonged to the family of the ill-fated Beatrice Cenci, who was abused by her tyrannical father; she eventually killed him and was subsequently beheaded. Shelley based his tragedy *The Cenci* on the family and a portrait of her by Guido Reni is one of the most famous works in the Galleria Nazionale d'Arte Antica at Palazzo Barberini.

In the nearby Piazza Mattei is the **Fontana delle Tartarughe** (Fountain of the Tortoises), one of the most delightful of all Rome's fountains, created in 1585 by Taddeo Landini based on a design by Giacomo della Porta.

At the end of Via del Portico d'Ottavia is the majestic **Portico d'Ottavia**. The portico was erected in 146 BC and then rebuilt by Augustus in 23 BC. The original builder was called Octavius, and Augustus kept the name since it coincided nicely with that of his sister, Octavia. The few remaining columns and fragmented pediment are a small part of the original complex, which was an enormous square colonnade of about 300 columns, which enclosed two temples and a library.

In 755 AD the portico was remodelled to incorporate **Sant'Angelo in Pescheria**. A medieval fish market established in the portico was operational until the end of the 19th century (see the Rome Walks chapter).

Anti-Semitism in Rome

There is a certain irony in the fact that Europe's longest surviving Jewish community – there have been Jews in Rome for over 2000 years – can be found in the heart of the city that is the centre of the Christian world.

The Jews of ancient Rome, former slaves and prisoners of war who became traders and merchants, had originally settled in Trastevere, where they had good access to the Tevere for cargo transportation.

However, by the 13th century, they had started to move across the river into the area which later became the ghetto. During medieval times Rome's Jewry enjoyed a degree of security. The popes, impressed by their medical and financial skills, brought the Jews under their direct jurisdiction, protecting them from violence and even allowing them to build a synagogue. But security came at a price. The first documented tax on Roman Jews since the *fiscus judaicus* of ancient Rome dates from 1310.

In 1555, in the midst of the Counter-Reformation, the anti-semitic Pope Paul IV decreed that Christians and Jews should be segregated. Walls were built around the area of highest concentration of Jews, curfews were enforced, the inhabitants were forced to wear distinctive clothing and attend sermons for their conversion. Their livelihood was limited to the trade in used clothing and money lending (regarded as a mortal sin for Christians).

These restrictions remained in force until the unification of Italy in 1870, by which time conditions for the 7000 inhabitants of the Ghetto were desperately cramped and squalid. The new government immediately tore down the walls and rebuilt large sections of the area, notably the area between Via del Portico d'Ottavia and the Tevere.

Rome's Jews suffered more persecution under the Fascist regime and during WWII. When the Germans occupied the city in September 1943, they demanded 50kg of gold from the Jewish community, to be produced in 36 hours. After an appeal to which both Jews and Gentiles responded the target was reached, but the ransom did not guarantee security. During the nine-month Nazi occupation, 2091 Jews were deported. Of these, only 15 survived.

Continuing along Via del Portico d' Ottavia to the river, you come to the 19th century **synagogue** which also houses the **Museo della Comunità Ebraica**, a museum of Roman Jewish history. The building is under constant armed guard after a bomb exploded there in 1983, killing a small child. The museum is open from 9.30 am to 4.30 pm, Monday to Thursday, 9.30 am to 1.30 pm on Friday and 9.30 am to noon on Sunday. Tickets cost L8000 and include a visit to the synagogue. Opposite the synagogue, on the other corner of Via del Portico d'Ottavia, is the little **Chiesa di San Gregorio**, one of the places where ghetto Jews were forced to attend Mass. An inscription above the door in Hebrew and Latin reproaches the Jews for not converting to Christianity.

Isola Tiberina (Maps 5 & 7)

The Isola Tiberina (Tiber Island) is the only island in the Tevere and lies between the Ghetto and Trastevere. From the Ghetto, you cross the **Ponte Fabricio** (Map 5) which was built in 62 BC and is Rome's oldest standing bridge.

Reputedly the world's smallest inhabited island, it is only 300m long and 80m wide. According to some ancient writers the island was formed by the grain stores thrown into the river after the expulsion of the Tarquins from the city. Another version states that a Greek ship ran aground at this spot and was later surrounded by a travertine wall. In its shape, the island still resembles a ship but it is in fact made of volcanic rock. The island has been associated with healing since the 3rd century BC when the Romans adopted Aesculapius, the Greek god of healing, as their own and erected a temple to him on the island. Today it is the site of the Ospedale Fatebenefratelli.

The recently restored **Chiesa di San Bartolomeo** (Map 7) was built in the 10th century on the ruins of the Roman temple. It has a Romanesque bell tower and a marble well-head, believed to have been built over the same spring which provided healing waters for the temple. The church has suffered damage from floods several times. Floating mills were a feature of the Tevere near the Isola Tiberina (and upstream to the Ponte Sisto) from the 6th to the 19th centuries.

The **Ponte Cestio** (Map 7) built in 46 BC, connects the island to Trastevere. It was rebuilt in the late 19th century. The remains of a bridge to the south of the island are part of the **Ponte Rotto** (Broken Bridge), which was ancient Rome's first stone bridge. Most of the bridge was swept away in a terrible flood in 1598.

TRASTEVERE (MAPS 5 & 7)

The settlement at Trastevere was, in early times, separate from Rome. Although it was soon swallowed by the growing city, this sense of separation continued during medieval times when the area, on the other side of the river – the name Trastevere comes from *trans Tiberim* meaning 'across the Tevere' – developed its own identity. Trastevere residents have always regarded themselves as *noantri* or 'we others'. It is said that even today many of the old people of Trastevere rarely cross the river to the city. In recent years it has become a fashionable place to live and is always very busy on weekends and during summer, when tourists and Romans alike flock here to eat in the many trattorie or to drink at the numerous bars.

Santa Cecilia in Trastevere (Map 7)

The **Basilica di Santa Cecilia in Trastevere** in Piazza di Santa Cecilia was built in the 9th century by Paschal I over the house of St Cecilia where she was martyred in 230. Cecilia was the Christian wife of Valerian,

a Roman patrician. Despite her marriage, she maintained her vow of chastity, and her husband was so impressed by her faith that he too converted. Valerian was martyred for this act; Cecilia was arrested while burying his body and was subsequently martyred herself. Her murderers at first tried to scald her to death by locking her in the caldarium of the baths in her own house. She emerged unscathed and was then beheaded, but the executioner did such a bad job that she took three days to die. Legend has it that she sang as she was dying, and for this reason she became the patron saint of music and musicians.

An 18th century façade leads into a pretty courtyard and then to the portico, decorated with colourful 12th century mosaic medallions, and Baroque façade of the church itself. The impressive mosaic in the apse was executed in 870 and features Christ giving a blessing. To his right are saints Peter, Valerian (husband of St Cecilia) and Cecilia. To his left are Saints Paul, Agatha and Paschal. The holy cities are depicted underneath. The baldacchino over the main altar was carved by Arnolfo di Cambio, and the statue of St Cecilia in front of the altar is by Stefano Maderno. This finely carved statue depicts with considerable compassion the body of the saint as she was found when her tomb was opened in 1599.

In the right-hand nave the **Cappella del Caldarium** marks the spot where the saint was allegedly tortured with steam for three days before being martyred. There are two works by Guido Reni here.

Of great interest are the excavations of Roman houses, one of which was perhaps the house of St Cecilia, underneath the church. These ruins of ancient houses are accessible from the room at the end of the left aisle, as you enter the church. Admission is L2000. Note the large room with deep basins in the floor, which is thought to have been a tannery, the remains of black and white mosaic paving and the elaborate crypt which was decorated in the 19th century in Byzantine style.

There is a magnificent 13th century fresco of the Last Supper by Pietro Cavallini in the nun's choir, entered through the convent. The fresco used to be the inside façade of the old church. It was boarded up for many years and only rediscovered around 1900, hence its excellent state of preservation and amazingly rich colours and clear details. The fresco can be seen only on Tuesday and Thursday from 10 to 11.30 am and on Sunday from around 11.15 am (after Mass) to 11.45. Admission is L2000. The church itself is open daily from 10 to 11.45 am and from 4 to 5.30 pm.

Nearby, in the pretty Piazza in Piscinula is the medieval **Chiesa di San Benedetto**. The church has a roofed bell tower, Cosmati paving and a fine 13th century fresco depicting St Benedict. On Viale Trastevere, the busy traffic thoroughfare that dissects Trastevere, at Piazza Sonnino is the **Chiesa di San Crisogono** with a Romanesque bell tower dating from the 12th century and a portico which was added in the 17th century. The columns are ancient as are some of the marble fragments in the mosaic floor. A fine mosaic in the apse representing the Madonna and Child flanked by St James and St Chrysogonus is by Pietro Cavallini and his pupils. Beneath the present building (you enter through the sacristy) are the remains of an early Christian church dating from 5th century which was itself built on the site of a *titulus*, a private house used for secret Christian worship.

Santa Maria in Trastevere (Maps 5 &7)

Via della Lungaretta connects Piazza Sonnino to the lovely **Piazza Santa Maria in Trastevere** (Map 7), the heart of Trastevere and a popular neighbourhood meeting place. It's worth paying extra for a cappuccino or an aperitvo to sit down at one of the bars in the piazza. You'll enjoy not only a great view but also the passing people traffic. The fountain in the centre of the piazza is of Roman origin and was restored by Carlo Fontana in 1692. An ancient legend says that on the day that Christ was born a miraculous fountain of pure oil sprang from the ground in this area and flowed for a whole day down to the Tevere.

Via della Fonte d'Olio, a small street leading off the northern side of the piazza, commemorates this event.

The **Basilica di Santa Maria in Trastevere** (Map 7) is believed to be the oldest place of worship dedicated to the Virgin in Rome. Although the first basilica was built on this site in the 4th century AD, the present structure was built in the 12th century and features a Romanesque façade, with a stunning 12th century mosaic of the Virgin feeding the baby Jesus flanked by 10 women holding lamps. Two tiny figures kneeling at the Virgin's feet were probably donors to the church. At the top of the Romanesque bell tower whose bells ring every 15 minutes is a small mosaic of the Virgin. The portico, embedded with fragments of ancient and medieval sculpture, inscriptions and sarcophagi, was added by Carlo Fontana in 1702.

The impressive interior features 21 ancient Roman columns with Ionian and Corinthian capitals. The 17th century wooden ceiling was designed by Domenichino who painted the central panel depicting the Assumption of the Virgin. The mosaics in the apse and on the triumphal arch date from the 12th century and are absolutely stunning. At the top of the triumphal arch are the symbols and names of the four Evangelists. On either side are Isaiah and Jeremiah, each with an image of a caged bird representing Christ imprisoned by the sins of humankind. At the top of the apse are the signs of the zodiac, beneath which is a splendid mosaic against a gold background of the Christ and the Virgin enthroned. They are flanked by various saints and, on the far left, Pope Innocent II holding a model of the church. Note the richly patterned and detailed robes of the Virgin. Below this are a series of six 13th century mosaics by Pietro Cavallini illustrating the Life of the Virgin.

On the right of the altar is a beautiful Cosmati Paschal candlestick placed, it is said, on the exact spot of the miraculous fountain of oil. The small chapel on the left of the altar, the Cappella Altemps, is decorated with 16th century frescoes and stuccoes. A Byzantine painting of the Madonna and angels dating from the 8th century or earlier, was once the altarpiece and is now substituted by a photograph. The badly deteriorated original is displayed in a room to the left. The church is open every day from 7 am to noon and from 3 to 7 pm.

Heading west from Piazza Santa Maria you come to Piazza Sant'Egidio. The 17th century building on the eastern side of the piazza, formerly a Carmelite convent, today houses the **Museo del Folklore e dei Poeti Romaneschi** (Map 7). The exhibits here include paintings, drawings, prints and waxwork tableaux depicting daily life and customs in 18th and 19th century Rome, as well as material relating to Roman poets such as Gioacchino Belli and Carlo Alberto Salustri (better known as Trilussa), both of whom are commemorated in neighbourhood piazzas. The museum even houses a reconstruction of Trilussa's studio.

At the time of writing the museum had been closed for restoration for several years; it should re-open in 2000. Piazza Sant'Egidio leads on to the pretty Via della Scala and Piazza della Scala. The church of Santa Maria della Scala, recently restored, dates from the 16th century. Next to it is the historic Farmacia di Santa Maria della Scala, which is still run by monks from the adjacent monastery. If it's open, go in and have a look.

Passing through the city walls at Porta Settimiano, you reach the long, straight Via della Lungara, built by Pope Julius II to connect the area of the Borgo (near il Vaticano) to Trastevere. **Palazzo Corsini** (Map 5), the large white building originally dating from the 15th century but rebuilt in the 18th century for Cardinal Neri Maria Corsini, a nephew of Pope Clement XII. The building had a series of illustrious occupants. Queen Christina of Sweden, who had fled her native country after becoming a Catholic, died there in 1689, and Napoleon's mother Letizia took up residency there in 1800. Cardinal Corsini's valuable art collection was acquired by the state in 1883 and now forms part of the **Galleria Nazionale d'Arte Antica**. The rest of the collection is in Palazzo Barberini.

The galleries are decorated with *trompe l'oeil* frescoes. Highlights of the collection (of mainly 16th and 17th century works) are Van Dyck's superb *Madonna della Paglia* in Room 1 and Murillo's *Madonna and Child* in Room 2. The same subject painted by Girolamo Siciolante de Sermoneta demonstrates the difference between a good and a bad artist. Sermoneta's baby is overly flushed and muscular and appears to be choking on its mother's milk.

The paintings of the Bologna school in Room 7 stand out, including Guido Reni's richly coloured and expressive *St Jerome* and melancholy *Salome*, Giovanni Lanfranco's very beautiful *St Peter healing St Agatha* and a haunting *Ecce Homo* by Guercino.

The museum (☎ 06 68 80 23 23, enter at Via della Lungara 10) is open 9 am to 7 pm, Tuesday to Friday, 9 am to 2 pm Saturday and 9 am to 1 pm on Sunday. Admission costs L8000.

The gardens of the Palazzo Corsini subsequently became the **Orto Botanico** (Map 5), Rome's botanical garden, which has some of the rarest plants in Europe. Highlights include the Mediterranean succulents, an avenue of palms, a collection of cactus plants and a rock garden of mountain flowers from the Apennines and other ranges in Europe and Africa. It is open from 9 am to 6 pm, Monday to Saturday. Tickets cost L4000.

Opposite Palazzo Corsini is the Renaissance **Villa Farnesina** (Map 5), built by Baldassarre Peruzzi between 1508 and 1511 for the Sienese banker Agostino Chigi as his suburban residence. Chigi was a patron of Raphael, who devised the decorative scheme of the frescoes and painted the superb *Galatea* in the Loggia della Galatea. The rest of the work was carried out by Raphael's pupils, including Giulio Romano, Giovanni da Udine and Francesco Penni, and also by Peruzzi and Sebastiano del Piombo. Gaspard Dughet added various frescoes in the 17th century. The villa (☎ 06 6838831 or 68801767) is open 9 am to 1 pm, Monday to Saturday. Admission is L6000.

The building also houses the **Gabinetto Nazionale delle Stampe** (national print collection) part of the Istituto Nazionale per la Grafica, which can be consulted by scholars (☎ 06 69 98 01 for information).

Returning to the Porta Settimiano, Via di Santa Dorotea to the left leads to Piazza Trilussa and **Ponte Sisto** (Map 5), a footbridge over the river which connects Trastevere to Via Giulia and the Campo de' Fiori area. The bridge was built during the pontificate of Sixtus IV (1471-1484) to replace the ancient Pons Janiculensis.

AROUND CAMPO DE' FIORI
Via Giulia (Maps 5 & Around Piazza Navona)

This street, running parallel to the Tevere river, was designed by Donato Bramante for Pope Julius II who wanted a new approach road to San Pietro. It is lined with Renaissance palaces, antique shops and art galleries.

At its southern end near Ponte Sisto, is the **Fontana del Mascherone** (Map: Around Piazza Navona), a baroque fountain made by combining two ancient pieces of sculpture – a grotesque mask and a stone basin. Just beyond it, spanning the road, is the **Arco Farnese** (Map: Around Piazza Navona) from which ivy tendrils hang like stalactites. Built to a design by Michelangelo, the arch was intended to be part of a bridge across the Tevere connecting the Palazzo Farnese and its gardens with the Villa Farnesina on the opposite side of the river. Note the two giant falcon heads which glare at each other across the doorway of the **Palazzo Falconieri** (Map: Around Piazza Navona, Via Giulia 1) which houses the Hungarian Academy. Borromini had a hand in the enlargement and decoration of the building.

Off to the left, in Via di Sant'Eligio is the 16th century **Chiesa di Sant'Eligio degli Orefici** (Map 5), the goldsmiths' church, which was designed by Raphael. Further along on the right is **Palazzo Ricci** (Map 5),

famous for the 16th century frescoes on its façade. Beyond the ruined church of San Filippo Neri are the **Carceri Nuove** (Map 5), built in 1655 and used as a prison until the 19th century when they were replaced by Regina Coeli prison on the other side of the Tevere.

The **Museo Criminologico** (crime museum, Map 5) in the adjacent building is devoted to crime and punishment throughout the ages. The displays cover instruments of torture and execution, including guillotines which were used by the Papal States until 1860. The museum (☎ 06 68 30 02 34), Via del Gonfalone 29 is open on Tuesday from 9 am to 1 pm and from 2.30 to 6.30 pm, on Wednesday, Friday and Saturday from 9 am to 1 pm and on Thursday from 2.30 to 6.30 pm. Admission is L4000.

There are several massive Renaissance palaces with elaborate façade decoration at the northern end of Via Giulia. This area is sometimes known as the Quartiere Fiorentino because of the Florentine colony that at one time inhabited the area. Many Florentine artists and architects contributed to the construction and decoration of the **Chiesa di San Giovanni Battista dei Fiorentini** (Map 5). Jacopo Sansovino won a competition for its design. The construction of the church took over a century, Sansovino's design being continued by Antonio Sangallo the younger and Giacomo della Porta. Carlo Maderno completed the elongated cupola (a Roman landmark) in 1614. Of note inside are the sculptures on the high altar by Antonio Raggi representing the baptism of Christ. The altar is by Borromini, who is buried in the church.

Palazzo Spada
(Map: Around Piazza Navona)

South of Campo de' Fiori in Piazza Capodiferro, this 16th century palace has an elaborately decorated façade. It was restored by Francesco Borromini a century later, after Cardinal Bernardino Spada had acquired the palace. The building now houses the Italian Council of State (or Supreme Court) and the **Galleria Spada**.

It used to be possible to sneak past the guards to get a look at the delightful courtyard and its elaborate stucco decoration, and you could ask the porter to show you Borromini's trompe l'oeil perspective in a lower courtyard. This appears to be a long colonnade stretching out to a large statue at the end; on closer inspection the colonnade is only a quarter of the length it seems, and the statue much smaller than it first appears. But the gallery administrators have wised up, and the perspective can be seen only if you buy a ticket to the Galleria Spada.

The private collection of the Spada family was acquired by the state in 1926 and has works by Titian, Andrea del Sarto, Guido Reni, Guercino, Rubens and Caravaggio. Entrance to the museum is from Vicolo del Polverone 15b. The museum is open Tuesday to Saturday from 9 am to 7 pm and Sunday to 1 pm, (L10,000).

Piazza Farnese
(Map: Around Piazza Navona)

Piazza Farnese is one of Rome's most elegant squares. It is dominated by the enormous **Palazzo Farnese**, a magnificent Renaissance building, which was started in 1514 by Antonio da Sangallo, continued by Michelangelo and completed by Giacomo della Porta. Built for Cardinal Alessandro Farnese (later Pope Paul III), it is now the French Embassy. The palazzo (which is very rarely open to the public) is famous for its magnificent frescoes by Annibale and Agostino Caracci. The twin fountains in the piazza were enormous granite baths taken from the Terme di Caracalla.

Campo de' Fiori
(Map: Around Piazza Navona)

This is a lively piazza where a flower and vegetable market is held every morning except Sunday. Now lined with bars and trattorie, the piazza was once a flowery meadow before it became a place of execution during the Inquisition. Giordano Bruno was burned at the stake for heresy in the piazza in 1600 and his statue now stands at its centre. (See the History section in the Facts about Rome chapter.)

Many of the streets near Campo de' Fiori are named after the artisans who traditionally occupied them, for example Via dei Cappellari (hatters), Via dei Baullari (trunk makers) and Via dei Chiavari (key makers). Via dei Giubonnari (jacket makers) runs off the southern corner of the piazza and leads to the **Chiesa di San Carlo ai Catinari** built in the 17th century. The church and beautiful dome were designed by Rosato Rasati. Inside, there are altarpieces by Pietro da Cortona and Giovanni Lanfranco among others. It is open from 7.30 am to noon and from 4.30 to 7 pm.

The northern corner of Campo de' Fiori leads to Piazza della Cancelleria which is dominated by the **Palazzo della Cancelleria**, a Renaissance palace built in the late 15th century for Cardinal Raffaello Riario. At one time it housed the Papal Chancellery and it is still used by il Vaticano. It is thought that Bramante designed the double loggia in the magnificent interior courtyard. Recent excavations beneath the palazzo have revealed ruins of one of the most important early Christian churches in Rome, the Basilica di San Lorenzo in Damaso, which was finally demolished in the 15th century to make way for a new church (of the same name) and the palazzo into which it is incorporated.

Heading towards Piazza Navona, on the corner of Via dei Baullari and Corso Vittorio Emanuele II, is a small palazzo known as the Piccolo Farnesina, built for a French clergyman, Thomas Le Roy, in 1523. It is now home to the **Museo Barracco**, one of the city's most charming museums. Senator Giovanni Barracco presented his exquisite collection of Greek, Roman, Assyrian and Egyptian sculpture and artefacts to the city in 1902. Underneath the museum are remains of what is said to be a Roman fish shop, complete with counter and a water trough (ask for access). Fresco fragments found there are displayed on the ground floor. The museum is open from 9 am to 7 pm, Tuesday to Saturday, and from 9 am to 1 pm on Sunday. Admission is L3750.

Opposite the Museo Barracco is the Palazzo Braschi which houses the **Museo di Roma** (☎ 06 687 58 80), founded in 1930 to illustrate the history and life of Rome from the Middle Ages to the present. Many of the exhibits, which include paintings, statues and architectural decorations, came from buildings that have since been demolished. The museum has been closed for several years, but it is scheduled to reopen in 2000.

Heading in an easterly direction along Corso Vittorio Emanuele II you come to the late 16th century **Chiesa di Sant'Andrea della Valle**. The elaborate façade was completed in the 17th century and is in high baroque style. The church's dome is the highest in Rome after that of the Basilica di San Pietro and was designed by Carlo Maderno. Frescoes by Giovanni Lanfranco and Domenichino decorate the inside of the dome. Domenichino also did the frescoes around the apse and altar. The competition between the artists was fierce, especially when they were working at the same time, and legend has it that Domenichino once even took a saw to Lanfranco's scaffold. The church is open from 7.30 to noon and from 4.30 to 7.30 pm.

AROUND PIAZZA NAVONA

Piazza Navona
(Map: Around Piazza Navona)

Lined with Baroque palaces, this vast and beautiful piazza was laid out on the ruins of a stadium built by Domitian in 86 AD, ruins of which can still be seen at the northern end of the piazza. The stadium had seating for around 30,000 spectators. Originally called the *Circus Agonalis* (circus of the Agonalia), it became known in the Middle Ages as the Campus Agonis, which in time became 'n'agona' and eventually 'navona'. The arena was used for festivals and sporting events, including jousts, until the late 15th century, when it was paved over and transformed into a market place and public square. The ruins of the stadium can be

visited by appointment only (see the boxed text 'Open Only on Request'.)

Piazza Navona is a popular gathering place for Romans and tourists alike. Take time to relax on one of the stone benches and watch the artists who gather in the piazza to do their work, have your *tarocchi* (tarot cards) read, or pay top prices to enjoy a drink at one of the outdoor cafés, such as Tre Scalini. The piazza is best avoided from early December until 6 January when a gaudy market and mini funfair take over.

There are three fountains, the central one being Bernini's masterpiece, the **Fontana dei Quattro Fiumi** (Fountain of the Four Rivers) depicting the Nile, Ganges, Danube and the Rio Plata. The fountain took four years to build and was completed in 1651; funds to build the fountain were raised by an unpopular tax on bread. Bernini designed the figures, but the actual carving was done by assistants. The obelisk once stood in the Circo di Massenzio on the Via Appia Antica.

The **Fontana del Moro** at the southern end of piazza was designed by Giacomo della Porta in 1576. Bernini altered the fountain in the mid-17th century when he designed the central figure of the Moor holding a dolphin. The surrounding tritons are 19th century copies. The fountain at the northern end of the piazza dates from the 19th century and has a central figure of Neptune fighting with a sea monster, surrounded by sea nymphs.

In the centre of the piazza facing the Fontana dei Quattro Fiumi is the **Chiesa di Sant'Agnese in Agone**, its façade designed by Bernini's bitter rival, Borromini. The tradition is that the statues of Bernini's Fontana dei Fiumi are shielding their eyes in disgust from the sight of Borromini's church, but the truth is that Bernini completed the fountain two years before his contemporary started work on the façade and in fact the figure is shielding its face to indicate that the source of the river at that time had been undiscovered.

The largest building in the piazza is the elegant **Palazzo Pamphili** built between

Open only on Request

Several archaeological sites in Rome are open to the public only on request. To gain entry to a closed site, you should send a letter or fax well in advance of your trip to: Ufficio Monumenti Antichi e Scavi del Comune di Roma, Ripartizione X, Via del Portico d'Ottavia 29, 00186 Roma (fax 06 689 21 15 or 06 67 10 31 18).

You should state the dates of your stay in Rome, the monuments you want to see and how many people are in the party. Letters and faxes can be written in English. The office will then write back to you (probably in Italian) with possible dates and times. A further confirmation from you might also be required. Once organised and booked, the accompanied visit costs L3750 per person.

One confusing thing to note is that there are three different archaeological authorities: at Comune or city level (Ripartizione X), regional level and national level, and that there are further divisions in each of these authorities. Even the people who work in these offices don't always know who is responsible for what.

The Ripartazione X governs 21 archaeological areas in Rome, of which eight are described in this chapter: Monte Testaccio, Area Sacra di Largo Argentina, Circo Massimo, Colombario di Pomponio Hylas in Via Latina, Insula Ara Coeli (Roman apartment block at the foot of the Campidoglio), Mausoleo di Augusto, Stadio di Domiziano (Piazza Navona) and the Teatro di Marcello. These sites can be visited on request as outlined above.

If you don't manage to organise a special visit in advance of your trip, all is not lost. At the time of writing it had been suggested that several of the 21 areas for which Ripartizione X is responsible should be opened up on a permanent basis, but no firm decision had been reached. The archaeological authorities also organise group visits to some sites. These are expected to increase in number and frequency during the year 2000. Tourist information booths can provide information.

1644 and 1650 by Girolamo Rainaldi and Borromini for Giovanni Battista Pamphilj when he became Pope Innocent X. It was later occupied by his domineering sister-in-law, Olimpia Maidalchini, who like other members of the pope's family received enormous riches and favours during his pontificate. It is now the Brazilian Embassy.

At the southern end of Piazza Navona is the small **Piazza di Pasquino**. The statue, an ancient Roman torso which was much admired by Bernini, was placed in the square in 1501. This became known as a 'talking statue' to which people attached witty or caustic criticisms of the people who ruled the city. A prosperous tailor in the area, Pasquino, was credited with having inaugurated this form of public satire, and the messages left on the statue (and other similar statues around the city) became known as *pasquinade*.

Via del Governo Vecchio (Maps 5 & Around Piazza Navona)

The narrow **Via del Governo Vecchio** (Map: Around Piazza Navona) was once part of the papal thoroughfare from the Palazzo Laterano in San Giovanni to San Pietro. It takes its name from the 15th century Palazzo del Governo Vecchio (also known as the Palazzo Nardini) at No 39, which was the seat of the papal government in the 17th and 18th centuries. Bramante is thought to have lived in the palazzo opposite (No 123). Former workshops that lined the street have been converted into shops selling second-hand goods such as leather jackets, old linens and lace, watches and clocks and antique furniture. See the Shopping chapter.

Via della Chiesa Nuova, to the left off Via del Governo Vecchio, leads to the **Chiesa Nuova** (Map: Around Piazza Navona). Formerly known as Santa Maria in Vallicella, it was given to San Filippo Neri by Pope Gregory XIII in 1575 in recognition of the work he and his order did in reviving the spiritual life of the city and caring for the sick, homeless and mentally disturbed. San Filippo had the church rebuilt, and it was decorated after his death.

The interior is elaborately gilded throughout. Pietro da Cortona was responsible for the decoration of the vault, apse and dome, there are paintings by Rubens over the high altar, and there is a beautiful painting in the north transept by Federico Barocci of the Presentation of the Virgin in the Temple. San Filippo is buried beneath the altar in a chapel to the left of the apse. Next to the church is an **oratory**, mainly by Borromini, which was completed in 1652. San Filippo was responsible for the invention of the oratory as a form of spiritual celebration through music.

Behind the Chiesa Nuova is the **Torre dell'Orologio** (Map 5) a clock tower built by Borromini to decorate one corner of the convent attached to the church. Piazza dell' Orologio takes its name from the clock tower. Via dei Banchi Nuovi continues towards the Tevere. The early 16th century **Palazzo del Banco di Santo Spirito** (Map 5) at the end of the street was designed by Antonio Sangallo the Younger and was the mint of papal Rome. The façade of the building resembles a Roman triumphal arch and the two statues crowning it represent Charity and Thrift.

Via dei Coronari runs from Via del Banco di Santo Spirito back towards Piazza Navona. It follows the course of an ancient Roman road which ran in a straight line from the area of Piazza Colonna to the Tevere and was a popular thoroughfare for pilgrims. The rosary bead sellers *(coronari)* that once lined the street have been replaced by antiques shops, but many of the original buildings remain. The **Chiesa di San Salvatore in Lauro** (Map: Around Piazza Navona) in the pretty piazza of the same name, dates from the 16th century and has an altarpiece by Pietro da Cortona. At the eastern end, Vicolo del Montevecchio (off to the right)

leads to Piazza Montevecchio and Piazza della Pace.

The **Chiesa di Santa Maria della Pace** (Map: Around Piazza Navona) was built for Pope Sixtus IV in the early 1480s. The façade and semi-circular portico of the church was added in the 17th century by Pietro da Cortona for Pope Alexander VII. Inside, the church has an octagonal dome. The first chapel on the south side contains frescoes by Raphael representing the Sibyls having the future revealed to them by angels. These were painted for the banker Agostino Chigi in 1514. The first chapel on the northern side is decorated with frescoes by Baldassare Peruzzi who also did the *Presentation in the Temple* to the right of the high altar. Next to the church is a beautiful **chiostro** (cloister) added by Bramante in 1504 which is regarded as one of the architect's finest works in Rome. Bramante employed classical rules of proportion in this two-storey arcade, creating a monumental feeling in a relatively small space.

Palazzo Altemps
(Map: Around Piazza Navona)

Palazzo Altemps, in Piazza Sant'Apollinare, at the north end of Piazza Navona, was begun around 1477 for Girolamo Riario and was altered by subsequent owner Cardinal Francesco Soderini between 1511 and 1523. It was completed in the late 16th century by the Milanese Cardinal Marco Sittico Altemps and his heirs. Antonio da Sangallo the Elder, Baldassarre Peruzzi and Martino Longhi all had a hand in its design. For centuries the palace housed the notable Altemps family collection of antiquities as well as an extensive library. It was acquired by the Italian state in 1982 and underwent a careful and lengthy restoration, before opening in 1997 as the new home of part of the **Museo Nazionale Romano** collection.

The Egyptian collection from the Museo Nazionale Romano is housed here together with the Mattei collection, formerly at Villa Celimontana (once the Mattei family estate), and 16 remaining works from the Altemps collection. However, the prestigious

Colossal head of Juno, Palazzo Altemps

Algardi and Filippo Buzzi – to repair and 'enhance' the works he had acquired. They didn't think twice before replacing a missing limb with one that had been found elsewhere or sculpting a new, 17th century head to stick on top of a headless torso. Throughout the museum, instructive labels illustrate which parts of the statue are original and which are Baroque additions. One of the most interesting things about Palazzo Altemps is that the sculptures are displayed in a way that is very similar to common 16th century exhibition criteria, so you get a good idea of how a Renaissance palazzo and collection would have looked.

Most of the rooms are named after the pieces in them. A large hall off the courtyard, the Salone delle Erme, contains six double-faced herms and twin 1st century AD statues of Apollo playing the lyre. Next to it, the Sala dell'Atena contains an ancient statue of Athena with a serpent which was restored by Antonio Algardi in the 17th century. In the south loggia by the entrance are several delicately carved sarcophagi reliefs. The most beautiful of these depicts a ritual foot bathing and is probably the work of a 2nd century AD Greek sculptor.

Baroque frescoes throughout the building not only provide a decorative backdrop for the ancient sculpture but are fascinating exhibits themselves. The walls of the Sala delle Prospettive Dipinte (on the 1st floor) are decorated with landscapes and hunting scenes seen through trompe l'oeil windows. These frescoes were painted in the 16th century for Cardinal Altemps. The Sala della Piattaia, once the main reception room of the palazzo, has a magnificent 15th century fresco by Melozzo da Forlì of a cupboard displaying gifts received by Girolamo Riario and Caterina Sforza on the occasion of their wedding.

One of Bernini's 'touch-ups', the *Ares Ludovisi*, a Roman copy of an original Greek work, can be seen in this room. Bernini added a pointing foot and carved a demon on the hilt of Ares' sword and changed the face of the small cupid at his feet. Another Bernini 'enhancement' is in the Sala con Obelischi (so called because of

Ludovisi Boncompagni collection forms the main body of the exhibits. Cardinal Ludovico Ludovisi was a nephew of Pope Gregory XV and a ravenous collector of the ancient sculpture which was being unearthed and sold off on an almost daily basis in the building boom of Counter-Reformation Rome. He took advantage of his wealth and position to build up one of the most extensive and celebrated private collections of all time. It was displayed in the gardens of his palazzo in the present-day Via Veneto area, among follies, mazes, orchards and formal gardens, and for two centuries attracted civilised travellers from all over Europe.

Most of the statuary that was dug up was damaged in some way. Ludovico Ludovisi employed the leading sculptors of his day – including Gian Lorenzo Bernini, Alessandro the obelisks painted on the window frames), where in a sculptural group of a satyr and nymph; both figures have heads which belonged to other statues.

The Sala della storie di Mosè, decorated with a wall frieze depicting the 10 plagues of Egypt and the Exodus (about half of which remains) contains the *Trono Ludovisi*, one of the prize pieces in the Ludovisi collection. The carved marble throne was discovered at the end of the 19th century in the grounds of the Villa Ludovisi. Most scholars believe that the Trono Ludovisi came from one of the Greek colonies in Italy and was produced in the 5th or 6th century BC, although its precise dating and authenticity is still a subject of debate. The throne shares the room with two colossal heads, one of which is the goddess Juno and dates from around 600 BC.

A series of portrait busts is displayed in the painted loggia on the 1st floor. The loggia is decorated with trompe l'oeil windows, floral arbours, vines, decorative vases, cherubs, exotic animals and exotic fruits. It was commissioned by Cardinal Altemps around 1595 and has been superbly restored. The small fountain at the end, decorated with mosaics, marble sculptures and stucco decoration, was completed in 1594.

Two of the highlights of the museum are in the Sala del Camino, named after the monumental fireplace built for Cardinal Altemps. A giant sarcophagus with intricately carved marble graphically depicting a Roman battle scene is breathtaking. The image reads in three levels: at the top are the victors, in the middle the fighters and at the bottom the vanquished. The expression and movement extracted from a huge lump of stone is astonishing. Equally impressive is the sculptural group *Galata suicida* depicting a Gaul killing himself and a dead woman at his feet. This is a marble copy commissioned by Julius Caesar of a Pergamon bronze. You are spared little of the detail; blood spurts out of his flesh as the Gaul knifes himself to death. The small chapel, entered from the Sala del Camino, was added to in the 17th century and is

covered in elaborate gilt stucco and richly coloured marble decoration.

The entrance to Palazzo Altemps (☎ 06 689 70 91) is at Piazza Sant'Apollinare 44. It is open from 9 am to 7 pm, Tuesday to Saturday, from 9 am to 2 pm Sunday (opening hours are usually extended in summer). Admission is L10,000.

Corso del Rinascimento (Map: Around Piazza Navona)

Piazza delle Cinque Lune, at the north end of Piazza Navona, leads to **Chiesa di Sant' Agostino**. The plain white façade is one of the earliest of the Renaissance. The church, built in the 15th century and renovated in the 18th, is dedicated to St Augustine. It contains two great artworks. A fresco of Isaiah on the third column in the nave was painted by Raphael in 1512. The powerful figure shows the influence of Michelangelo, with whom Raphael was in close contact when both artists were working in il Vaticano. A marvellous painting by Caravaggio, the *Madonna dei Pellegrini* (also known as the *Madonna di Loreto*) hangs in the first chapel on the left aisle and is considered one of his best works. See the boxed text 'On the Caravaggio Trail'.

Until 1935 the **Palazzo della Sapienza** housed Rome's university, La Sapienza, which was founded by Pope Boniface VIII in 1303. Giacomo della Porta designed the Renaissance façade. The building now houses the state archives. Borromini designed a library in the palazzo as well as its courtyard which has porticoes on three sides. The fourth side is occupied by the tiny **Chiesa di Sant'Ivo alla Sapienza**, a masterpiece of Baroque architecture and considered to be one of Borromini's most original creations. The walls alternate between being convex and concave, and the bell tower is crowned by a distinctive twisted spiral.

The 16th century **Palazzo Madama** was originally the Rome residence of the Medici family. It was enlarged in the 17th century when the Baroque façade was added together with the decorative frieze of cherubs and bunches of fruit. The building is named after 'Madama' Margaret of Parma, the illegitimate daughter of Charles V, who lived here from 1559 to 1567. It has been the seat of the Senate, the upper house of the Italian parliament, since 1871. Unless you're a politician, the only way to get into Palazzo Madama is on a guided tour. These take place on the first Saturday of each month at regular intervals from 10 am to 6 pm. Admission is free. Call ☎ 06 670 61 or 06 67 06 22 25 for information.

Via del Salvatore leads to Piazza San Luigi dei Francesi. The **Chiesa di San Luigi dei Francesi** dates from the 16th century and is the French national church in Rome. Giacomo della Porta designed the façade and the interior has elaborate marble decoration. There are tombs of eminent French citizens – artists, cardinals and soldiers – who spent time in Rome, including a monument to Claude Lorrain. Frescoes by Domenichino illustrating the life of St Cecilia decorate the second chapel, although these are in a poor state of repair. St Cecilia is also depicted in the altarpiece by Guido Reni, which is in fact a copy of a work by Raphael. Most people visit the church to see the paintings by Caravaggio illustrating the life of St Matthew in the fifth chapel on the left. These have been recently restored and show Caravaggio's distinctive realism and highly dramatic use of light. See the 'On the Caravaggio trail' boxed text.

Pantheon
(Map: Around Piazza Navona)

This is the best preserved building of ancient Rome. The original temple was built by Marcus Agrippa, top general and son-in-law of Augustus, in 27 BC and dedicated to all the gods. It was rebuilt by Domitian after it burned down in 80 AD, and was rebuilt again after being struck by lightning. Although the temple was rebuilt by Hadrian around 120 AD, Agrippa's name remained inscribed over the entrance, leading historians to believe it was the orig-

inal building until excavations in the 1800s revealed traces of the earlier temple.

After being abandoned under the first Christian emperors, the temple was given to the church by the Byzantine emperor Phocus in 608 AD and dedicated to the Madonna and all martyrs. (A column was erected in honour of Phocus in the Foro Romano to mark the occasion.) Over the centuries the temple has been consistently plundered and damaged. The gilded bronze roof tiles were removed by an emperor of the Eastern empire and, in the 17th century, the Barberini pope, Urban VIII, had the bronze ceiling of the portico melted down to make the baldacchino (canopy) over the main altar of San Pietro and 80 cannons for Castel Sant'Angelo.

The height and diameter of the building's interior both measure 43.3m and the extraordinary dome is considered the most important achievement of ancient Roman architecture.

The Italian kings Victor Emmanuel II and Umberto I, and the artist Raphael are buried here. The Pantheon is in the Piazza della Rotonda and is open from 9 am to 6.30 pm Monday to Saturday and from 9 am to 1 pm Sunday and holidays. Admission is free.

Chiesa di Santa Maria Sopra Minerva (Map: Around Piazza Navona)

The **Chiesa di Santa Maria Sopra Minerva** in Piazza della Minerva, just east of the Pantheon, was built on the site of an ancient temple of Minerva (Athena). This 13th century Dominican church is one of the few ancient churches in Rome to have been built in the Gothic style. It contains a number of important art treasures dating from the 13th to the 17th centuries.

There are magnificent frescoes dating from the 15th century by Filippino Lippi (the son of Filippo Lippo) in the Cappella Carafa, the last chapel in the south transept), depicting events in the life of St Thomas Aquinas. The central *Annunciation* also shows St Thomas Aquinas presenting Cardinal Olivieri Carafa to the Virgin. To the

On the Caravaggio Trail

Michelangelo Merisi da Caravaggio (1573-1610) arrived in Rome around 1590. Much of the information that scholars have gathered about Caravaggio's time in Rome has been gleaned from police records. Trouble with the law was a fact of daily life for the artist.

He had a reputation for wandering around the streets of the historic centre, from Campo de' Fiori to the Pantheon, brandishing (and sometimes using) a long sword. One of his girl-friends was a prostitute who worked in Piazza Navona and he was arrested on several occasions, once for launching a tray laden with artichokes at a waiter in a restaurant and another time for throwing rocks at the windows of his former landlady's house.

He was, however, fortunate to meet a number of influential churchmen who recognised his artistic genius, provided him with lodgings and introduced him to important dealers and collectors.

He fled Rome in 1606 after a ball game in Campo de' Fiori during which he killed his opponent, and spent four years on the run in Napoli, Malta and Sicilia. He died in Porto Ercole in Toscana at the age of 36.

Rome has more masterpieces by Caravaggio than any other city in the world. They are spread between museums, churches and private collections.

Caravaggio's paintings were controversial. His innovative and dramatic use of lighting influenced generations of subsequent artists. He used peasants, beggars and prostitutes as his models which gave the Madonnas and saints of his paintings a realism that was not always well received. On several occasions he had to repaint commissions for churches because the subjects were deemed to be too lifelike: saints would *not* have had such dirty feet.

Several of these rejected works were snapped up by intuitive private collectors. One of these collectors, Cardinal Scipione Borghese, is said to have used his influence in the Church (he was a nephew of Pope Paul V) to dissuade several churches and religious confraternities which had commissioned works from Caravaggio to reject the completed paintings for being too 'realistic'. Caravaggio would then be constrained to produce a more acceptable version of the same subject, and Scipione was able to buy the offending work, soon to be considered a masterpiece, at a bargain price.

left of the high altar is Michelangelo's statue of *Christ bearing the Cross*. Michelangelo completed the figure of Christ around 1520 but the bronze drapery was added later. An altarpiece of the *Madonna and Child* in the second chapel in the north transept is attributed to Fra Angelico, the Dominican friar and painter, who is also buried in the church. The body of St Catherine of Siena, minus her head (which is in the Chiesa di San Domenico in Siena) lies under the high altar. The tombs of two Medici popes, Leo X and Clement VII, are in the apse. The church was heavily restored in the Gothic style in the 19th century, when the rose windows were added and the vault painted with overly vibrant colours. It is open daily from 7 am to 7 pm.

In the piazza in front of the church is a delightful Bernini statue of an elephant supporting an Egyptian obelisk, known as the **Elefantino**. The monument was unveiled in 1667, the result of many consultations between Bernini and Pope Alexander VII, whose reign it was intended to glorify. Alexander VII composed the inscription on its base, which states that 'You who see here the figures of wise Egypt carved on a column carried by an elephant, the strongest of animals, understand it is the proof of a robust mind to sustain solid wisdom.'

Largo Argentina
(Map: Around Piazza Navona)

The four Republican temples of the **Area Sacra di Largo Argentina** get lost amongst

On the Caravaggio Trail

Two interesting early works which lack the theatrical illumination and realistic figures of his mature style, a *Riposo nella fuga in Egitto* (Rest during the Flight into Egypt) and *Mary Magdalene*, are in the Galleria Doria Pamphili. The Galleria Borghese contains six paintings including the *Ragazzo con canestro di frutta* (Boy with a Basket of Fruit) the *Bacchino malato* (Sick Bacchus) and the famous *Madonna dei Palafrenieri*, commissioned for a chapel in San Pietro but rejected for being too realistic and snapped up by Cardinal Scipione Borghese for his Casino Borghese instead.

The dramatic *Davide con la testa di Golia* (David with Goliath's head) and *San Giovanni Battista* showing a young St John the Baptist, were apparently given by the artist to Scipione in exchange for clemency from Pope Paul V for the murder he committed in 1606. Another *St John the Baptist* is in the Pinacoteca of the Musei Capitolini. The Galleria Nazionale d'Arte Antica at Palazzo Barberini has a striking *Narcissus* and a gruesome *Guiditta e Oloferne* (Judith and Holofernes). Caravaggio's *Deposizione* (Descent from the Cross) is in the Pinacoteca of the Musei Vaticani.

Caravaggio's first great religious works were the three canvases of the life of St Matthew in the Chiesa di San Luigi dei Francesi. The artist had obtained the commission through the influence of the powerful Cardinal Francesco del Monte. The first version of *San Matteo e l'Angelo* (St Matthew with the Angel), the central canvas in the chapel, was rejected because the saint was depicted as a tired old man with dirty feet.

The *Madonna dei Pellegrini* in the Chiesa di Sant'Agostino is regarded as one of Caravaggio's most beautiful works. A superbly serene Madonna is surrounded by scruffy and filthy pilgrims. Two masterpieces are in the Chiesa di Santa Maria del Popolo. The *Conversione di San Paolo* (Conversion of St Paul) is a bravura composition dominated by the rear end of a horse, below which the saint is sprawled. The *Crocifissione di San Pietro* (Crucifixion of St Peter) depicts the moment when St Peter is tied upside down on the cross and uses dramatic foreshortening of figures.

---

the heavy traffic circulating around the square. The ruins were discovered during construction work in the 1920s. The Area Sacra can be visited by appointment only (see the 'Open only on Request' boxed text). However, you can get a good look at it from outside. The ruins are now home to hundreds of stray cats cared for by the volunteers at the cat sanctuary at the south end.

Chiesa del Gesù and Sant'Ignazio (Maps 5 & 6)

The **Chiesa del Gesù** (Map: Around Piazza Navona) in the piazza of the same name was the first Jesuit church in Rome. The Jesuits were founded in 1540 by the Spanish soldier Ignatius Loyola who had joined the Church after being wounded. He came to Rome in 1537 and three years later founded the Society of Jesus (the Jesuits). The order trained missionaries and teachers and sent them all over the world to convert both civilised and uncivilised peoples

Construction of the church began in 1568 and it was consecrated in 1584. The interior was designed by Vignola and the façade by Giacomo della Porta. The high point of Counter Reformation Baroque architecture, the Gesù was extremely important to the subsequent design of churches in Rome and throughout the Catholic world. The church's interior is elaborate, following the Jesuits' intention to attract worshippers with splendour and spectacle. It was financed by

Alessandro Farnese, who was subsequently regarded as being the owner of the three most beautiful things in Rome – his family palazzo, his daughter and the church of the Gesù. The church is open every day from 6 am to 12.30 pm and from 4 to 7.15 pm. At the time of writing much of the interior was under restoration.

The extraordinary fresco on the vault, depicting the *Triumph of the Name of Jesus*, is by Giovanni Battista Gaulli (known as Il Baciccia). The wonderfully foreshortened figures appear to tumble from the vault onto the coffered ceiling. Baciccia was also responsible for the frescoes inside the cupola and designed the church's stucco decoration. St Ignatius is buried in the Cappella di Sant'Ignazio in the north transept in an opulent marble and bronze tomb with columns encrusted with lapis lazuli. The tomb, which doubles as an altar, was made by Andrea del Pozzo and other artists and is topped by a group of the *Trinity* with a terrestrial globe which is in fact the largest single piece of lapis lazuli in the world. The marble sculpture to the right of the tomb represents *Religion Triumphing over Heresy*, which just about sums up what the Jesuits were all about. To the right of the church are rooms where St Ignatius lived from 1544 until his death in 1556 which have been restored and display paintings and memorabilia, including a masterful trompe l'oeil perspective by Andrea del Pozzo. They can be visited from 4 to 6 pm, Monday to Saturday, and from 10 am to noon on Sunday.

A Jesuit College, the **Collegio Romano** (Map 6), was built in 1585 under orders from Pope Gregory XIII. Many future popes studied there, including Urban VIII, Innocent X, Clement IX, Clement X, Innocent XII, Clement XI, Innocent XIII and Clement XII. Dominating the north side of Piazza del Collegio Romano (take Via del Gesù north from the Chiesa del Gesù and turn right into Via del Piè di Marmo), the building is now used partly by the national heritage ministry.

The **Chiesa di Sant'Ignazio di Loyola**, another Jesuit church, occupies the northeastern corner of the Collegio Romano building (take Via di Sant'Ignazio from Piazza del Collegio Romano) and rivals the Gesù for opulence and splendour. The church was commissioned by Cardinal Ludovico Ludovisi and built by the Jesuit mathematician and architect Orazio Grassi. The sumptuous interior is covered with paintings, stucco, coloured marble and gilt. Paintings in the nave show the Jesuit fathers doing their missionary work and a masterpiece by Andrea del Pozzo showing the *Triumph of St Ignatius*. A highlight of the Baroque interior is the trompe l'oeil ceiling perspective by Jesuit artist Andrea del Pozzo. His ingenious decorative scheme makes the walls appear to extend beyond their limits, and an illusionary dome painted on canvas covers the area where the real thing should have been. A small yellow spot on the floor of the nave indicates the best vantage point.

Piazza Sant'Ignazio (Map: Around Piazza Navona) in front of the church, has been described as delightfully frivolous. The theatrical piazza was designed by Filippo Raguzzini in the early 18th century. The picturesque and elegant buildings opposite the church are wasted as a police station.

Via del Corso (Maps 5 & Around Piazza Navona)

Via del Corso, known also as *Il Corso*, is a straight street over 1km in length which connects Piazza Venezia to Piazza del Popolo. The name comes from the fact that in the 15th century from the Carnival races that were transferred there from Piazza Navona and Testaccio by Pope Paul II in 1466. These continued until the late 19th century.

Palazzo Doria Pamphili (Map 6)

The **Palazzo Doria Pamphili** takes up an entire block at the southern end of Via del Corso, bordered by Via del Plebiscito, Via della Gatta and Piazza del Collegio Romano. It has been the residence of the

Doria Pamphili family, Roman nobles, since the 17th century.

The **Galleria Doria Pamphili** (the entrance is at Piazza del Collegio Romano 2) contains the family's private art collection, which was started by the Pamphili pope, Innocent X. It is dazzling even by Roman standards. The elaborate picture galleries, decorated with frescoed ceilings, gilding and mirrors, had a major facelift in 1996. The walls are crammed with paintings from floor to ceiling, hung exactly as they were in the 18th century. The most famous work in the collection is the Velasquez portrait of Innocent X, in its own room at one corner of the picture galleries. There is also a wonderfully expressive bust of Innocent X by Bernini. Four newer rooms house paintings by Hans Memling, Raphael, Titian, Tintoretto and two early works by Caravaggio (see boxed text 'On the Caravaggio Trail' in this chapter). There is also a collection of sculpture.

The gallery (☎ 06 679 73 23) is open daily except Thursday, from 10 am to 5 pm. Admission is L13,000. Guided tours of the private apartments take place between 10.30 am and 12.30 pm and cost L5000.

Piazza Colonna (Maps 5 & 6)

This piazza gets its name from the **Colonna Antonina** or Column of Marcus Aurelius in its centre. The column was inspired by Trajan's Column which is almost a century older. It was erected after death of Marcus Aurelius in 180 AD to commemorate his victories over the barbarian tribes of the Danube. It is 30m high and made of 28 drums of marble. The carved reliefs on the lower part of the column represent the war of 169-173 AD against the Germanic tribes; those on the upper part commemorate the war against the Sarmatians in 174-176 AD. In 1589 a statue of the Marcus Aurelius that originally crowned the column was replaced by a bronze figure of St Paul. The column is a pain in the neck (literally) for tourists who want to appreciate the intricate reliefs. An easier option is to study the casts of the reliefs in the Museo della Civiltà

Romana in EUR (see EUR section later in this chapter).

Palazzo Chigi (Map 6) on the north side of the piazza is the official residence of the prime minister. The building was started in the 16th century by Matteo di Castello and finished in the 17th century by Felice della Greca.

South of Piazza Colonna in Piazza della Pietra is the **Tempio di Adriano** (Map: Around Piazza Navona), which dates from 145 AD and is one of the most complete relics of antiquity in Rome. However, it is often overlooked since the colonnade of 11 columns, each 15m high, was converted in the 17th century into the former stock exchange building.

To the west of Piazza Colonna is Piazza di Montecitorio and the **Palazzo di Montecitorio** (Map: Around Piazza Navona), which has been the seat of the Chamber of Deputies, the lower house of the Italian parliament, since 1871. Its rear façade is on Piazza del Parlamento. The original palazzo was built for the Ludovisi family in 1650 by Gian Lorenzo Bernini. It was enlarged by Carlo Fontana at the end of the 17th century and given a larger façade with steps leading up to the entrance by Art Nouveau architect Ernesto Basile in 1918. A new look piazza was unveiled in 1998 which returned to Bernini's original plan of a gently sloping ramp up to the entrance of the building articulated by three radiating semicircles.

The obelisk in the centre of the piazza was brought to Rome from Heliopolis in Egypt by Augustus to celebrate his victory in 30 BC over Cleopatra VII and her ally Mark Antony. It was originally set up in the area known as Campus Martius and served as part of a huge sundial;. It was excavated from an area north of the piazza and erected on its present site in 1792. Free guided tours of Palazzo di Montecitorio take place on the first Sunday of each month at regular intervals from 10 am to 5 pm (call ☎ 06 676 01 or 06 6760 45 65 for information).

Farther north along Via del Corso is **Piazza San Lorenzo in Lucina** (Map 5)

transformed thanks to a recent facelift into an elegant pedestrian area. The **Chiesa di San Lorenzo in Lucina** dates from at least the 5th century but was rebuilt in the 12th century. Six ancient Ionic columns support a long portico, and the church has a pretty Romanesque bell tower. The simple façade hides an elaborate interior totally overhauled in the 17th century, when numerous side chapels were added. Guido Reni's *Crucifixion* is positioned above the main altar, and there is a fine portrait bust by Bernini in the stucco Cappella Fonseca, the fourth chapel on the south side. The French painter Nicholas Poussin is buried in the church.

Piazza Augusto Imperatore (Map 5)

The **Mausoleo di Augusto** in the Piazza Augusto Imperatore was once one of the most imposing monuments in ancient Rome. Today it looks like an unkempt mound of earth overgrown with weeds and covered with litter, although the city council has long-term plans to turn the mausoleum and piazza into an important urban space. Built in 28 BC, the mausoleum was the tomb of Augustus and his descendants. Nerva was the last to be interred there, in 98 AD. It served as a fortress in the Middle Ages, and was later used as a vineyard, a private garden and a travertine supply for new buildings. The mausoleum was excavated and restored in the 1920s, not long before the fascist-era buildings went up on three sides of the surrounding piazza.

Ara Pacis (Map 5)

The fourth side of Piazza Augusto Imperatore is occupied by the **Ara Pacis Augustae** (Altar of Augustan Peace) which was inaugurated in 13 BC to commemorate the peace which Augustus had established both at home and abroad. The actual altar is enclosed by a marble wall decorated with reliefs – historical scenes on the north and south friezes and mythological scenes at the east and west. It is one of the most important works in the history of ancient Roman sculpture, and represents the point at which Roman art emerged as a distinct entity.

The Ara Pacis was originally located in the Campus Martius, under a palazzo at the corner of Via del Corso and Via di Lucina (near Piazza del Parlamento). Parts of the altar were unearthed during excavations in the 16th, 17th and 18th centuries and the sculpted reliefs were acquired by the Medici, il Vaticano and even the Louvre. Large-scale excavations were carried out in 1903 and again in 1937 when the remaining part of the altar was extracted. The altar was placed in its present site in 1938 under Mussolini's orders and a fascist style pavilion hastily erected around it. Some of the missing carvings were returned to Rome and others replaced by facsimiles made from casts of the originals. The inscription on the outer wall of the current Ara Pacis display is the text of the *Res Gestae* (Things Achieved), Augustus' official account of his reign. This was originally inscribed on two bronze pillars set outside his mausoleum.

Tellus, the Earth Goddess, from the east frieze of the Ara Pacis Augustae

At the time of writing, plans were being finalised for a new museum pavilion to be built around the altar. Designed by the American architect Richard Meier, it will be the first modern building to be constructed in Rome's city centre for decades. The Ara Pacis is open from 9 am to 5 pm, Tuesday to Saturday and 9 am to 1 pm, Sunday. Admission is L4000.

Johann Wolfgang von Goethe lived in an apartment at Via del Corso 18 between 1786 and 1788. This was transformed into a museum, the **Casa di Goethe** (☎ 06 32 65 04 12) in 1997, which contains some interesting drawings and etchings by Goethe as well as documents relating to his Italian sojourn. It is open every day except Tuesday from 10 am to 6 pm. Admission is L5000.

Piazza del Popolo (Maps 3, 5 & 6)

This vast piazza was laid out in the early 16th century at the point of convergence of the three roads – Via di Ripetta, Via del Corso and Via del Babuino – which form a trident at what was the main entrance to the city from the north. The piazza has been recently and magnificently restored, and is now one of the finest of Rome's traffic-free pedestrian areas.

The two Baroque churches that divide the three roads are **Santa Maria dei Miracoli** (Map 5) bordering Via di Ripetta, and **Santa Maria in Montesanto** (Map 5) often referred to as the twin churches. The porticoes and domes of the two churches are almost identical, but on closer inspection the bell towers, lanterns on top of the domes and apse windows are quite different.

The piazza was redesigned in the neoclassical style by Giuseppe Valadier in the early 19th century. In the piazza's centre is an obelisk brought by Augustus from Heliopolis, in ancient Greece, and moved to the piazza from the Circo Massimo in the mid-16th century. To the east is a ramp leading up to the **Pincio** (Map 6), which affords a stunning view of the city.

The **Chiesa di Santa Maria del Popolo**
(Map 3) next to the Porta del Popolo at the northern end of the piazza, was originally a chapel built in 1099 on the site where Nero was buried. It was enlarged in the 13th century and rebuilt during the early Renaissance. In the 17th century the interior was renovated by Bernini.

The Cappella Chigi (the second chapel in the north aisle after you enter the church) was designed by Raphael for the famous banker Agostino Chigi. Raphael died, thus leaving the chapel unfinished. It was completed more than 100 years later by Bernini, and contains a mosaic of a kneeling skeleton, representing death. The apse was designed by Bramante and contains the tombs of Cardinal Ascanio Sforza and Cardinal Girolamo Basso della Rovere, both signed by the Florentine sculptor Andrea Sansovino.

The frescoes in the vault are by Bernardino Pinturicchio. They were painted in 1508-09 and represent classical and biblical scenes. Pinturicchio also painted the lunette frescoes and the *Adoration* above the altar in the Della Rovere chapel (the first chapel in the south aisle after you enter the church). In the first chapel to the left of the high altar are two paintings by Caravaggio, the *Conversion of St Paul* and the *Crucifixion of St Peter*, and an altarpiece, *The Assumption* by Annibale Carracci. (See the 'On the Caravaggio Trail' boxed text.)

Piazza di Spagna & Scalinata della Trinità dei Monti (Map 6)

The piazza, church and famous Scalinata Spagna (Spanish Steps) have long provided a gathering place for foreigners. Built with a legacy from the French in 1725, but named after the Spanish Embassy to the Holy See (which is still located in the piazza), the steps lead to the French church, **Trinità dei Monti**. In the 18th century the most beautiful women and men of Italy gathered here, waiting to be chosen as an artist's model.

In May each year the steps are decorated with pink azaleas. If you can't manage the steps there's a lift to the top outside the

Piazza di Spagna metro station. It might look like the perfect spot for a picnic, but don't get too enthusiastic. Theoretically you are not allowed to eat whilst sitting on the steps. The municipal police who patrol the area can be quite strict, and transgressors can be fined. It's all aimed at keeping the steps clean after a major restoration in 1995-96, but the police would do better to catch the vandals who are defacing Rome's monuments with graffiti.

To the right as you face the steps is the house where John Keats died in 1821, now the **Keats-Shelley Memorial House**, a small museum crammed with memorabilia of Keats, Percy Bysshe Shelley, Mary Shelley, Lord Byron and other Romantics. It is open from 9 am to 1 pm and 2.30 to 5.30 pm, Monday to Friday. Admission is L5000. In the piazza is the boat-shaped fountain called the **Barcaccia**, believed to be by Pietro Bernini, father of the famous Gian Lorenzo.

The Viale della Trinità dei Monti at the top of the steps leads to the Pincio. Half way along the road on the right is the **Villa Medici**, perhaps Rome's best piece of real estate with undoubtedly one of the city's best views. The palazzo was built for Cardinal Ricci da Montepulciano in 1540. Ferdinando dei Medici bought it in 1576 and it remained his family's property until Napoleon acquired it in 1801, when the French Academy was transferred here. The academy was founded in 1666 to provide talented French artists, writers and musicians – *Prix de Rome* winners – an opportunity to study and absorb the enormous classical heritage that Rome offered.

A good way to get inside the building is by seeing one of the regular art exhibitions that are held there. Guided tours of the villa's spectacular gardens (cost L6000) take place at 10.30 and 11.30 am on Saturday and Sunday from March to late May and from September to late October. From June to August in 1999 and 2000 you can visit the gardens by buying a ticket for the academy's annual sculpture exhibition. Contact the French Academy (☎ 06 676 11) for opening hours.

The **Pincio** (Map 6) was laid out by Giuseppe Valadier in the early 19th century. An elegant park with avenues of shady trees, it gets its name from the Pinci family who owned it in the 4th century. It is a popular spot for a weekend *passeggiata* and has a wonderful view of Rome over to San Pietro. The Pincio joins Villa Borghese park.

Via Condotti and shopping streets (Maps 5 & 6)

One of Rome's most elegant shopping streets, **Via Condotti**, runs off Piazza di Spagna towards Via del Corso. The famous **Caffè Greco** (Map 6) is at No 86, where artists, musicians and the literati used to meet, including Goethe, Keats, Byron and Wagner. Other elegant shopping streets in the area include Via Frattina, Via della Croce and Via della Carozza. See also Shopping chapter. Another exclusive shopping street is **Via del Babuino** which runs off Piazza di Spagna towards Piazza del Popolo. The pretty **Via Margutta** (parallel to Via del Babuino) is lined with contemporary art galleries and a few antiques shops. The Italian film director Federico Fellini lived in Via Margutta for many years.

Heading back towards Via del Corso you come to Piazza San Silvestro, where there is a busy bus terminus and the main post office. The **Chiesa di San Silvestro in Capite** (Map 6) was given to the English Roman Catholics by Leo XIII in 1890. The original church was built in the 7th century on the site of a Roman building. The current church has a Romanesque bell tower and some interesting 17th century frescoes. The **Chiesa di Santa Maria in Via** (Map 6) across Via del Tritone, has a display of nativity scenes or *presepi* at Christmas.

Via Veneto and Piazza Barberini (Map 6)

The area around Via Vittorio Veneto was once an estate belonging to Julius Caesar. It subsequently was occupied by the Roman historian Sallust and, in the 17th century, by

Cardinal Ludovico Ludovisi who housed his celebrated collection of ancient sculpture in the grounds of his palazzo there. Via Veneto was Rome's hot spot in the 1960s, where film stars could be seen at the expensive sidewalk cafés. The atmosphere of Fellini's Rome is long dead, and the street is little more than a thoroughfare for traffic to and from the centre. It is lined with five-star hotels, bank headquarters, insurance company offices and a few upmarket boutiques. The US embassy in the late 19th century Palazzo Margherita takes up a sizeable chunk of the street. You can still pay through the nose for a meal or a coffee in one of the glass-enclosed restaurants but you'll get a better *Dolce Vita* feel in the Piazza del Popolo or Piazza Navona.

The **Chiesa di Santa Maria della Concezione** is an austere 17th century church, but the Capuchin cemetery beneath (access is on the right of the church steps) features a bizarre display of the bones of some 4000 monks, used between 1528 and 1870 to decorate the walls of a series of underground chapels. The monks who guard the cemetery are a grumpy and greedy lot so make sure you've got a few L1000 notes handy for the 'compulsory' donation.

In the centre of **Piazza Barberini**, at the southern end of Via Veneto, is the spectacular **Fontana del Tritone** (Fountain of the Triton), created by Bernini in 1643 for Pope Urban VIII, patriarch of the Barberini family. It features a Triton (with an enviable washboard stomach) blowing a stream of water from a conch shell. He is seated in a large scallop shell which is supported by four dolphins. The fountain suffers from its traffic-ridden position – it was once the focal point of the Baroque piazza in front of the Barberini family palazzo – and has been restored many times, most recently in 1998.

In the north-west corner of the piazza is another Bernini fountain, the **Fontana delle Api** (Fountain of the Bees), also created for the Barberini family. Their crest, which features three bees, can be seen on many buildings throughout Rome.

Palazzo Barberini (Map 6)

Palazzo Barberini was built for Pope Urban VIII between 1625 and 1633. Carlo Maderno's original design was embellished by both Bernini and Borromini. Bernini was responsible for the monumental staircase on the left (looking at the main façade). Borromini added the elegant oval staircase on the right and the windows of the upper storey. A master of artificial perspective, he created windows that from a distance seem to be the same size as those on the floor below, but are in fact significantly smaller, in keeping with the interior plan. The palazzo houses part of the **Galleria Nazionale d'Arte Antica**, the other part being in Palazzo Corsini in Trastevere. Large parts of the building have been used as an officers' mess for decades, and at the time of writing the first steps had been taken in the re-acquisition of the whole building for the museum.

A highlight of the museum is the ceiling fresco of the *Gran Salone* on the 1st floor of the palazzo, entitled the *Trionfo della Divina Provvidenza* (Triumph of Divine Providence), painted by Pietro da Cortona to glorify Urban VIII's pontificate and the Barberini family. The collection is arranged chronologically and is particularly strong in 16th and 17th century paintings. There are works by Guido Reni, Bronzino and Guercino. Raphael's *La Fornarina* is widely believed to be a portrait of his mistress, a baker's daughter, although some scholars suggest that it was in fact a portrait of a courtesan and not by Raphael at all. An ethereal *Annunziazione* by Filippo Lippi stands out, as does Andrea del Sarto's *Sacra Famiglia*.

Two paintings by Bernini, a portrait of Urban VIII and *Davide con la testa di Golia* depicting David with the head of Goliath, show that his skill lay in sculpture and architecture rather than painting. There are two paintings by Caravaggio, *Judith e Holfernes*, a gruesome masterpiece of theatrical lighting, and *Narcissus*. A recent addition to the collection is Jacopo Zucchi's *Il Bagno di Betsabea* (Bethsheba's Bath) dating from the late 1580s which was lost after WWII, found in Paris, bought by an American museum and returned to Italy in 1998.

The gallery is open from 9 am to 7 pm, Tuesday to Saturday, and from 9 am to 1 pm on Sunday. Admission is from Via Barberini 18 and costs L8000.

QUIRINALE (MAP 6)

The Quirinale (Quirinal hill) is the highest of Rome's seven hills. At its summit is the **Palazzo del Quirinale**, in the piazza of the same name, the official residence of the president of the republic. Built and added to from 1574 to the early 18th century, the palace was the summer residence of the popes from 1592 until 1870, when it became the royal palace of the kings of Italy.

Several leading architects worked on the building, including Domenico Fontana, who designed the main façade; Carlo Maderno who designed the chapel; and Bernini, who was responsible for the long wing that runs the length of Via del Quirinale. The obelisk in the centre of the piazza was moved here from the Mausoleo di Augusto in 1786. It is flanked by large statues of the Dioscuri, Castor and Pollux, which are Imperial Roman copies of 5th century BC Greek originals.

The palace is open to the public on the second and fourth Sunday of the month, from 8.30 am to 12.30 pm. Arrive early, since it is usually not possible to join the queue after about 11 am. Call ☎ 06 46 99 25 68 for information. Admission is L10,000.

Along Via del Quirinale are two excellent examples of Baroque architecture: the churches of **Sant'Andrea al Quirinale**, designed by Bernini, and **San Carlo alle Quattro Fontane**, designed by Borromini. The Chiesa di Sant'Andrea is considered one of Bernini's masterpieces. He designed it with an elliptical floor plan, and with a series of chapels opening on to the central area. The interior is decorated with polychrome marble, stucco and gilding. Note the cherubs which decorate the lantern of the dome. The Chiesa di San Carlo was the first church designed by Borromini in Rome

and was completed in 1641. It is one of his best known buildings and the first project he completed on his own. The small cloister, also designed by Borromini, was restored in 1996. The church stands at the intersection known as **Quattro Fontane**, after the late 16th-century fountains at its four corners which represent Fidelity, Strength, the Aniene river and the Tevere. From the intersection you can see Porta Pia and the obelisks of the Quirinale, Trinità dei Monti and the Esquilino.

Via XX Settembre continues in a north-easterly direction to Largo di Santa Susanna and the smaller Piazza San Bernardo, on the south side of which is the **Chiesa di San Bernardo alla Terme**. The church was built in the late 16th century into the ruins of a circular tower that had been part of the Terme di Diocleziano. Not dissimilar to the Pantheon, the church has a dome with a small oculus at the top to illuminate the interior. On the western side of the intersection is the **Chiesa di Santa Susanna** the Catholic church of the American community in Rome. Dating from the 4th century, the church was rebuilt several times. The impressive façade was added by Carlo Maderno in 1603 and is considered his masterpiece.

Maderno also designed the **Chiesa di Santa Maria della Vittoria** on the north side of the intersection, although the façade was by Giovanni Battista Soria. The interior boasts colourful marble decoration in the baroque style. The second chapel on the left as you enter the church contains an altarpiece by Domenichino, *La Madonna che porge il Bambino a San Francesco*, depicting the Madonna showing the baby Jesus to St Francis. In the Cappella Cornaro (the fourth chapel on the right) there are two works by Bernini. The spectacular sculptural group above the altar, known as *Santa Teresa trafitta dall'amor di Dio* (The Ecstasy of St Theresa), presents a smiling angel pointing an arrow at the heart of St Teresa, who is obviously enjoying the experience. Below is a gilded bronze relief of the Last Supper. The late 19th century fresco in the apse commemorates the victory of a Catholic army over Protestant forces in Prague in 1620.

On the corner of Via XX Settembre and Via Vittorio Emanuele Orlando, the **Fontana della Acqua Felice** is also known as the Moses Fountain because of the huge figure of Moses in its central niche. It was designed by Domenico Fontana and completed in 1586 to mark the terminus of the Acqua Felice aqueduct, which carried clean water to this part of the city for the first time. The water may still be relatively clean, but the statues, which are suffering bady from pollution caused by the passing traffic, are filthy.

Piazza della Repubblica (Map 6)

Formerly known as Piazza Esedra, Piazza della Repubblica follows the line of the exedra of the adjacent Terme di Diocleziano. The fountain in its centre, the **Fontana delle Naiadi**, was erected at the turn of the century and has been recently restored. It was designed by Mario Rutelli and features a central figure of Glaucus wrestling with a fish, surrounded by four naiads or water nymphs. When the fountain is shooting the right way the nymphs really do look like they are frolicking in the water. The scantily clad figures caused a furore when they were first put in place. The models for the curvaceous nymphs were two sisters, well known musical stars of their day. It is said that in their old age the sisters visited the fountain daily and that once a year the sculptor would travel from his native Sicily to take them out to dinner.

Terme di Diocleziano and Museo Nazionale Romano (Map 6)

Started by Diocletian, these baths were completed in the early 4th century. The complex of baths, libraries, concert halls and gardens was the largest in ancient Rome, covering about 13 hectares and with a capacity of 3000 people. The *caldarium* (hot room) extended into what is now Piazza della Repubblica. After the aqueduct which fed

the baths was destroyed by invaders in about 536 AD, the complex fell into disrepair. However, large sections of the baths were incorporated into the Chiesa di Santa Maria degli Angeli, which faces Piazza della Repubblica, and the Museo Nazionale Romano, facing Piazza dei Cinquecento.

At the time of writing most of the baths complex – including the Museo Nazionale Romano – was closed for restoration. An ambitious project aims to reconnect all the remaining parts of the complex by pulling up part of Via Cernaia which covered some of the ruins. No date has yet been given for the reopening of the baths or the Museo Nazionale Romano.

Some of the sculptures from the Terme di Diocleziano (as well as pieces found at other Imperial baths in Rome) are on permanent display in the **Aula Ottagona**, a domed octagonal hall which was a main hall in the baths. Roman foundations can be seen through a glass panel in the floor. It is open from 9 am to 7 pm, Tuesday to Sunday. Admission is from Via Romita and is free of charge.

The **Basilica di Santa Maria degli Angeli** was designed by Michelangelo and incorporates what was the great central hall and *tepidarium* (lukewarm room) of the original baths. During the following centuries his work was drastically changed and little evidence of his design, apart from the great vaulted ceiling, remains. An interesting feature of the church is a double meridian in the transept, one tracing the polar star and the other telling the precise time of the sun's zenith, visible at midday (solar time). The church is open from 7.30 am to 12.30 pm and 4 to 6.30 pm. Through the sacristy is an entrance to a stairway leading to the upper terraces of the ruins. A plaque near the stairway records the traditional belief that the baths were built by thousands of Christian slaves.

The **Museo Nazionale Romano** opened in 1889 and incorporated several halls of the ancient baths. The huge cloister was for many years attributed to Michelangelo but this is unlikely as it was built in 1565, a year after his death. In the centre is a 17th century fountain surrounded by cypress trees, one of which dates from the same period. There are also huge statues of animals' heads, which it is thought came from the Foro di Traiano. The courtyard at the front of the museum (facing Piazza dei Cinquecento) is littered with so many fragments of ancient monuments and statues that it looks like a junkyard. Part of the valuable collection of ancient art, which includes Roman wall paintings and Greek and Roman sculpture, is now housed in the Palazzo Massimo alle Terme (diagonally across Piazza dei Cinquecento) and at Palazzo Altemps (near Piazza Navona).

Palazzo Massimo alle Terme (Map 6)

Palazzo Massimo, the new home of part of the **Museo Nazionale Romano** collection, boasts some of the best examples of Roman art in the city. It took 16 years and L68 billion for the 19th century building, a former Jesuit college, to be transformed into a museum. It is one of Rome's best – light-filled and spacious and blissfully air-conditioned in summer. The ground floor opened in 1995, and the rest of the building in June 1998.

The ground and 1st floors are devoted to sculpture and statuary dating from the end of the Republican age (2nd to 1st centuries BC) to the late Imperial era (4th century AD). Some original 5th century BC Greek sculptures are dotted amongst the numerous Roman copies of Greek originals and the portraits of emperors and their families and of eminent citizens.

One of the first pieces you see as you enter is *Minerva*, a huge polychrome statue of the goddess made of alabaster, white marble and black basalt. The face is a modern plaster cast taken from another statue of Minerva. The statue, possibly inspired by early Greek artists working on the Italian peninsula, was found at the bottom of the Aventino, and probably formed part of a temple to Minerva on the hill.

A light and spacious courtyard is surrounded by three long galleries containing portrait busts, off which are rooms arranged thematically. The first two contain funerary reliefs, portrait busts and statues of emperors, statesmen and their families. These were commissioned works, and represented the ruling classes as they wanted to be depicted. Realism had little to do with these statues; they were idealised images and self-glorification was the order of the day.

An anonymous Republican general (in Sala I) depicted in heroic nudity, semi draped with his armour next to him, shows evidence of Greek sculpting techniques and dates from the 1st century BC. A full length portrait of Augustus (in Sala V) depicts him as Pontifex Maximus (Chief Priest), his head covered with a fold of his toga. A portrait head of Augustus' wife, Livia, with her distinctive braided hairdo is one of many images of the emperor's wife which had a strong influence on private portraiture of the period.

Terracottas, reconstructed from fragments, found in the area of the Domus Tiberiana on the Palatino in the 1980s are on display in Sala VI. Sala VII contains a superb original Greek sculpture, dating from the 5th century BC, of a young woman trying to extract an arrow from her back. The statue, along with other Greek originals, found in the Horti Sallustiani (now the Via Veneto area), which belonged to Julius Caesar, was later the estate of the Roman historian Sallust and which in the 17th century was where Ludovico Ludovisi housed his magnificent collection of ancient statuary which is also now part of the Museo Nazionale Romano (see Palazzo Altemps earlier in this chapter).

Sculptures from the time of the Flavian emperors (late 1st to 4th century AD) demonstrate various iconographic trends in official Roman art. Among the highlights (Sala V) are pieces that come from Nero's residence at Anzio (two full length statues) and a wonderfully naturalistic image of a voluptuous *Afrodite* crouching down, a Roman copy of a Greek original from the Villa Adriana at Tivoli.

The badly damaged *Apollo del Tevere* in Sala VI shows what too long in polluted water can do to marble; this piece was discovered in the banks of the Tevere during the embankment process in the late 19th century. In the same room are the *Discobolus Lancellotti* and the *Discobolus di Castelporziano*, two marble statues of a discus thrower copied from one of the most famous of all Greek bronzes.

The highlight of Palazzo Massimo is the collection of Roman paintings and mosaics, displayed on the 2nd floor. Many of these rare pieces have been out of public view for decades and have undergone extensive restoration. Thoughtfully installed in their new home, these examples of Roman interior decoration positively sparkle.

Among the most beautiful are the frescoes (in Sala II) from the Villa Livia, a house which belonged to the wife of Augustus. The villa, located on the Via Flaminia north of Rome, was excavated in the 19th century. The frescoes were removed from the villa in 1951 and transferred to the Museo Nazionale Romano. The room in which they were originally painted was half underground and covered by a barrel vault decorated with stuccoes and reliefs (unfortunately only a small part of this vault decoration has survived and is too delicate to exhibit). It was probably a summer *triclinium*, a large living and dining area protected from the heat, and has been recreated in Palazzo Massimo in a specially constructed gallery space. The frescoes, which surround you totally, depict an illusionary garden, with all the plants in full bloom, regardless of the season. There are tall cypresses, pines and oak trees, shrubs and bushes of oleander, myrtle and laurel, and fruit trees abundant with ripe pomegranates and quinces. The style is datable to between 20 and 10 BC.

Frescoes from the Villa Farnesina, a Roman villa in the Trastevere area, are on display in Galleria II and Sale III, IV and V. The villa was discovered and excavated in the 19th century during the embankment of the Tevere. Dating from around 20 BC, these frescoes are among the most important examples of Roman painting that survive. It is thought that the villa belonged

to an important figure close to Augustus' circle. The substantial fragments illustrate clearly the style and taste of the period. There is a great variety of decoration which in most cases was related to the function of the room: landscapes, narrative friezes that have an almost Egyptian appearance, illusionary architectural elements such as columns, cornices and vases (known as the scenes.

The museum also boasts a stunning collection of inlaid marbles and mosaics, including (in Sala VII) the surviving wall mosaics from a nymphaeum at Nero's villa in Anzio. In the basement is an extensive display of ancient and medieval coins, including a collection donated to the state by King Vittorio Emanuele II.

At the time of writing, the Palazzo Massimo is open from 9 am to 7 pm, Tuesday to Saturday, am to 2 pm Sunday. Opening hours are usually extended (to 10 pm) in the summer. Admission is L12,000.

Via Nazionale (Map 6)

Via Nazionale is a busy shopping street and traffic thoroughfare connecting Piazza della Repubblica to the Quirinale and Piazza Venezia. To the left (heading towards Piazza Venezia) off Via Torino in Piazza Beniamino Gigli, is Rome's opera house, the **Teatro dell'Opera**. The Fascist-era exterior hides a richly decorated 19th century interior of plush red velvet seats, gilded stucco and a glittering chandelier in the centre of the auditorium.

On the corner of Via Napoli is the American Episcopal church of **St Paul's within-the-Walls**, famous for its magnificent Pre-Raphaelite mosaics designed by Edward Burne-Jones which were completed in 1907.

It is difficult to miss the **Palazzo delle Esposizioni**, a massive white edifice with triumphal arch and grand Corinthian columns. Rome's purpose-built exhibition centre was designed by Pio Piacentini and opened its doors in 1882. The building has had a chequered history. Apart from serving its original brief, it once housed the Communist Party and was used as a mess for allied servicemen. It also served as a polling station and as a public lavatory.

After years of restoration it was re-launched in 1990, and is today a vibrant multi-media centre. There is a changing program of art exhibitions, live performances and cinema, with many films screened in their original language. There's also an excellent book and gift shop and a café. It is open every day except Tuesday from 10 am to 9 pm.

Piazza Santi Apostoli and Palazzo Colonna (Map 6)

The long, thin **Piazza dei Santi Apostoli** runs off Via Cesare Battisti, east of Piazza Venezia. It is a popular place for political demonstrations. The **Museo delle Cere**, a rather tacky museum of waxworks, is at No 67 (on the corner of Via Cesare Battisti). It is open daily from 9 am to 8 pm and admission costs L6000.

The **Palazzo Colonna** spans one side of the piazza. It was begun in the 15th century for Pope Martin V (who lived here from 1424 until his death in 1431) although most of the building dates from the 18th century. It is still occupied by members of the Colonna family. The private gardens behind the palazzo, on the site of a 3rd century AD Temple of Serapis rise in terraces up to the grounds of the Palazzo del Quirinale.

The **Chiesa dei Santi Apostoli** is wedged into the front of the palazzo. Originally built in the 6th century and dedicated to the Apostles James and Philip (whose relics are in the crypt), the church was enlarged in the 15th and 16th centuries and then rebuilt in the early 18th century by Carlo and Francesco Fontana who were responsible for the baroque interior. The unusual façade with Renaissance arches dates from the early 16th century. The church contains the tomb of Pope Clement XIV by Antonio Canova.

The façade of the building opposite the church, **Palazzo Odelscalchi**, was designed by Bernini in 1664. At the end of the piazza is the baroque **Palazzo Muti** which was given to James Stuart, the Old Pretender, in 1719 by Pope Clement XI.

Galleria Colonna (Map 6)

The entrance to the Galleria Colonna is at Via della Pilotta 17, a pretty street spanned by four arches which connect the Palazzo Colonna to its gardens. The gallery contains one of the most important private collections in Rome which is arranged in magnificent baroque galleries.The vestibule, at the top of the stairs, leads into the Sala della Colonna Bellica lined with fine portraits of Colonna family members and others. In the centre of the room is a carved *colonna* (column) of red marble dating from the 16th century. Steps lead down to the lavishly gilded Salone – don't trip over the cannon ball which became lodged there during the 1849 siege of Rome.

The magnificent ceiling paintings are by Giovanni Coli and Filippo Gherardi and represent the life of Marcantonio Colonna who commanded the papal forces at the Battle of Lepanto. These are among the most vibrant ceiling decorations in Rome. The paintings on the walls are somewhat overpowered but include a notable *San Giovanni Battista* by Salvator Rosa, Guido Reni's *San Francesco d'Assisi con gli angeli* (St Francis with the angels) and *San Paolo eremita* (St Paul the Hermit) by Guercino. The Sala degli Scrigni (Room of the Desks) contains classical landscapes by Gaspard Dughet and other artists, ceiling frescoes by Sebastiano Ricci depicting the Battle of Lepanto, and two ornate cabinets. One is made of ebony with inlaid carved ivory bas-reliefs reproducing works by Raphael and Michelangelo (the central panel is his *Giudizio Universale* from the Cappella Sistina).

The adjacent room is named after the *Apoteosi di Martino V* by Benedetto Luti which decorates its ceiling and contains Annibale Carracci's delightful *Mangi fagiuoli* (Bean Eater), which is an amusing departure from more serious religious and historical subjects. In the Sala del Trono beyond it a chair is kept ready (turned to the wall) in case of a papal visit. The gallery (☎ 06 679 43 62) is open on Saturday from 9 am to 1 pm (closed all of August). Admission is L10,000.

Fontana di Trevi (Map 6)

This high-Baroque fountain is one of the city's most famous monuments. Completely dominating a tiny piazza, it was designed by Nicola Salvi in 1732. His theatrical design incorporates the façade of the adjacent Palazzo Poli. Water for the fountain is supplied by one of Rome's earliest aqueducts. Work to clean the fountain and its water supply was completed in 1991, but the effects of pollution have already dulled the brilliant white of the clean marble.

The famous custom is to throw a coin into the fountain (over your shoulder while facing away) to ensure you return to Rome. For a second coin you can make a wish. The terraces around the fountain are always packed with tourists throwing coins and, on average, L230 million is recovered from the basin each year. Italian currency goes into city council coffers and the foreign coins are given to the Red Cross. The name Trevi is thought to come from *tre vie*, referring to the three roads which converged at the fountain.

OUTSIDE THE WALLS

If you've got the time, there are a number of sights further afield that are well worth visiting. While the centre of the city was filled with monumental temples, baths and arenas, most of the populace actually lived in the outskirts, both inside and outside the walls. Fearful of persecution, the early Christians met in private houses and many of these houses, known as *tituli*, later became the first churches in Rome. The pagan cemeteries and Christian catacombs were also established outside the city walls, and several churches were later built on top of the burial place of a venerated martyr or saint. Most of these locations are easily reached by metro, bus or tram. (See Getting Around chapter for information about Rome's public transport system.)

Villa Borghese (Map 4)

This beautiful park, just north-east of the Piazza del Popolo, was once the estate of Cardinal Scipione Borghese. Taking papal nepotism to its extremes, when Camillo Borghese became Pope Paul V in 1605, he granted his nephew Scipione the title of cardinal and gave him a sizeable chunk of Rome, just outside the Aurelian Walls. There, between 1605 and 1614, Scipione built his *casino* (mansion) to house his enormous collection of paintings and sculpture (now the Museo e Galleria Borghese) and had the grounds laid out by leading landscape designers such as Jacob More from Edinburgh.

The main entrance is from Piazzale Flaminio, although it is also accessible through the park at the top of the Pincio hill, from Porta Pinciana at the top of Via Veneto, from Via Mercadante on the northeast side and from Viale delle Belle Arti on the north side. Take a picnic to the park if the tourist trip starts to wear you down and certainly take the kids there for a break.

The park is divided into different areas by avenues of trees, hedged walks, planted flower beds, gravel paths and named roads. The pretty, English-style **Giardino del Lago** in the centre of the park was laid out in the late 18th century. Equestrian events are held in May in **Piazza di Siena**, an amphitheatre built around 1792. The park is dotted with sculptures of various periods, although many of these are not the real thing. The city authorities have been systematically removing the originals for several years and replacing them with resin copies. The originals will eventually be put on display in a museum in the park, possibly in the so-called **Casina di Raffaello**, built in the late 18th century, when it is restored.

The small **Museo Canonica** (☎ 06 884 22 79, Viale Pietro Canonica 2) houses the collection, private apartment and studio of the sculptor and musician Pietro Canonica who died in 1959. The building, which formerly belonged to the Borghese family, was acquired by the city and given to Canonica in 1927. It is open from 9 am to 6.45 pm, Tuesday to Saturday and 9 am to 1 pm Sunday and public holidays. Admission is L3750.

The **Giardino Zoologico** (zoo), now known as the **Bioparco**, is at the north of the park in Viale del Giardino Zoologico (☎ 06 321 65 64). For many years the zoo suffered from an appalling reputation. It was managed inefficiently and the animals were poorly housed. A new program is currently under way to improve the cages and facilities. There are currently 1200 animals on the 17-hectare site; this number is likely to be reduced, but the conditions for the remaining animals will be improved. Exotic animals are gradually being phased out and sent to other zoos and ultimately the park will have only animals compatible with the ecosystem and climate of central Italy and animals from the Mediterranean area which are in danger of extinction.

There are better ways to spend L10,000 (L7000 for children aged five to 12, free for children under five) but kids might enjoy it, especially as a children's zoo will be established in 1999. It is open from 9.30 am to 5 pm daily.

Museo e Galleria Borghese Hailed as the 'queen of all private collections', the Galleria e Museo Borghese is one of the most spectacular displays of art in Rome. Cardinal Scipione Borghese was the most passionate and knowledgeable art collector of his day. He had a keen appreciation for the antique but also patronised his contemporaries including the Caracci, Caravaggio and Gian Lorenzo Bernini. He stopped at nothing to add to his treasures; he had the fashionable painter Cavaliere d'Arpino flung into jail in order to confiscate his canvases, and had Domenichino arrested, to force him to surrender his painting of *The Hunt of Diana*.

Scipione's house, the Casino Borghese, surrounded by formal gardens and parkland, was a private treasure chest where he entertained lavishly. The collection and the building in which it was housed attracted illustrious visitors through the centuries, and both were augmented by the cardinal's heirs. In the late 18th century Scipione's descendant, Prince Marcantonio Borghese, had the casino redecorated in a neo-classic style with elaborate gilding, faux-marble

finishes and trompe l'oeuil frescoes which is how it appears today. The mannerist nude figures and cheeky cherubs surrounded by ornate garlands of golden acanthus leaves are at times over the top. However, not all of the original art collection remains. Much of the antique statuary was carted off to the Louvre under the orders of Napoleon, whose sister Paolina was married to Marcantonio's son Camillo. Other pieces were sold off over time.

The entire collection and the mansion were acquired by the Italian state in 1902, but it was badly neglected. Structural problems in the building became evident in the 1940s. In 1983 part of a ceiling fresco by Giovanni Lanfranco in one of the 1st floor rooms crashed to the ground. In 1984 the gallery had to be shut down. After 13 years of restoration, it re-opened in summer 1997.

The Museo Borghese (the ground floor rooms) contains some important classical statuary. In the Salone are intricate floor mosaics of fighting gladiators dating from the 4th century AD and a *Satiro combattente* (Fighting Satyr) from the 2nd century AD (restored by Bernini). High on the wall opposite the entrance is a gravity-defying bas-relief, *Marco Curzio a cavallo*, of a horse and rider falling into the void of the room, which was created by Pietro Bernini (Gian Lorenzo Bernini's father) by combining ancient fragments and modern pieces. Throughout the ground floor rooms there are full length representations and busts of Roman gods, emperors and public figures. In Sala V, a 1st century AD *Ermafrodito* (Sleeping Hermaphrodite), a Roman copy of a Greek original, faces a wall so you can't see the evidence. She/he lies on a rather comfortable looking bed carved by Bernini.

A daring sculpture by Antonio Canova of Paolina Bonaparte Borghese as a reclining *Venere Vincitrice* (Sala I) is one of the most famous works in the collection. Her diaphanous drapery leaves little to the imagination and in its day the statue was considered outrageous and provocative. Paolina Borghese had quite a reputation, and tales abounded of her grand habits, her many lovers and her sometimes shocking behaviour. When asked how she could have posed almost naked she apparently replied: 'Oh, there was a stove in the studio.'

Bernini's spectacular carvings – flamboyant depictions of pagan myths – are the stars of the ground floor Museo. Cardinal Scipione Borghese was one of Bernini's earliest patrons. The sculptor's precocious talent is evident in works such as *Il Ratto di Proserpina* (The Rape of Proserpine) in Sala IV, where Pluto's hand presses into Proserpine's solid marble thigh and in his *Davide* (Sala II), grim-faced and muscular, thought to be a self-portrait and done around 1624. In Sala III, Bernini's stunning, swirling *Apollo e Dafne* depicts the exact moment when the nymph is transformed into a laurel tree, her fingers becoming leaves, her toes turning into tree roots, while Apollo watches helplessly.

Other pieces by Bernini include, in Sala VI, an early work *Enea e Anchise* (Aeneas and Anchises) where the sculptor is still somewhat afraid of his medium and his carving hasn't quite reached its full potential for depicting movement, and *La Verità* (Truth) a rather strange later work done between 1645 and 1652, monumental in character but showing little of the mastery evident in the other magnificent pieces here and in other parts of Rome.

In Sala VIII, a 2nd century AD *Satiro danzante* (Dancing Satyr), a Roman copy of an earlier Greek work, is surrounded by six paintings by Caravaggio. The luscious *Ragazzo con canestro di frutta* (Boy with a basket of fruit) and the *Bacco malato* (Sick Bacchus), a self-portrait by Caravaggio painted when he was suffering from malaria, are early works completed between 1593 and 1595, not long after his arrival in Rome. Both include magnificent representations of still life. The *Madonna dei Palafrenieri*, also known as the Madonna of the Serpent, was commissioned in 1605 by the Confraternity of the Palafrenieri (footmen) for their chapel in the Basilica San Pietro. This is one of Caravaggio's masterpieces and to our eyes it is a wonderfully naturalistic work, but its

uninhibited realism was incompatible with early 17th century ecclesiastical sensibilities and, rejected by the Palafrenieri, Scipione snapped it up. The other works depict *San Girolamo*, *San Giovanni Battista* (a young St John the Baptist), and *Davide con la testa di Golia*, a dramatic image where Goliath's severed head is said to be a self-portrait. (See the 'On the Caravaggio Trail' boxed text.)

The paintings in the Galleria Borghese on the 1st floor, representing the flowering of the Tuscan, Venetian, Umbrian and northern European schools, are testimony to Scipione's connoisseur's eye. In Sala IX are Raphael's *La Deposizione di Cristo* (Descent from the Cross) dated 1507 and his earlier portraits *Ritratto d'uomo* (1502) and *Dama con liocorno*, a beautiful woman holding a mythological animal, painted in 1506. In the same room are the superb *Adorazione del Bambino* by Fra Bartolomeo and Perugino's *Madonna col Bambino*. Correggio's rather erotic *Danae* – perhaps an early version of soft porn – is in Sala X. In Sala XX it is interesting to compare Titian's early masterpiece *Amor sacro e Amor profano* (Sacred and Profane Love) with his much later and less powerful *Venere che benda Amore*. There are also masterworks by Giovanni Bellini, Giorgione, Veronese, Botticelli, Guercino, Domenichino, Antonello da Messina, Rubens and Cranach, to name but a few.

The museum is at Piazzale Museo Borghese in the Villa Borghese park (☎ 06 328 10, fax 06 32 65 13 29). The opening hours vary according to season (always call to check) and booking is compulsory. Don't just turn up as you won't get in. At the time of writing winter hours were from 9 am to 7 pm, Tuesday to Saturday with admission (for a maximum of two hours) at 9 am, 11 am, 1, 3 and 5 pm. On Sunday and holidays admission is at 9 am and 11 am. In summer the gallery is usually open from 9 am to 10 pm, with admission hourly. Admission is L12,000, which includes the compulsory booking fee. The museum is equipped for disabled visitors and there's a bar/caffè which serves snacks and light meals.

Galleria Nazionale d'Arte Moderna (Map 4)

The Galleria Nazionale d'Arte Moderna, the national collection of modern art, is just outside Villa Borghese park, at Viale delle Belle Arti 131 (☎ 06 32 29 81). Cesare Bazzini's *Belle Epoque* palace is one of the few remaining buildings erected for the Rome international exhibition in 1911. The museum has been extensively renovated recently. Original features such as decorative friezes and columns have been restored and long-closed wings have been opened up.

The collection covers the 19th and 20th centuries, mostly Italian artists. There is a representative holding of academic history painting (some of it very good, some of it overly sentimental) and works by the *macchiaioli*, who produced an Italian version of pointillism using thousands of dots of pure colour to build up the picture, and by the Italian symbolists. The 20th century collection includes work by De Chirico, Carrà, Casorati, Marini and Fontana as well as exponents of futurism (Boccioni, Severini, Balla), *Arte Povera* (Burri, Colla, Manzoni, Pascali) and the *Transavanguardia* (Enzo Cucchi, Francesco Clemente and Mimmo Paladino among others). The modern foreign art includes work by Degas, Cézanne, Kandinsky, Duchamp, Mondrian, Henry Moore and Cy Twombly.

The wing to the left of the entrance has been transformed into a sculpture gallery. Dynamic white marbles, such as Canova's majestic *Ercole* (Hercules), contrast dramatically against walls painted in rich, solid colours. The museum is open from 9 am to 8 pm Tuesday to Sunday. Hours of opening on Sunday and public holidays are sometimes reduced in the summer. Admission is L8000. There is an excellent bar/restaurant with a lovely outdoor terrace.

The museum can be reached by tram No 225 from Piazzale Flaminio or tram No 19 from Piazza del Risorgimento, both of which travel along Viale delle Belle Arti. Current opening hours are from 9 am to 7 pm Tuesday to Sunday, though these are likely to be extended in summer.

Museo Nazionale Etrusco di Villa Giulia (Map 3)

The delightful Villa Giulia (at the top end of the Villa Borghese in the Piazzale di Villa Giulia) was built in the mid-16th century for Pope Julius III. Vignola, Vasari, Bartolomeo Ammannati and Michelangelo all had a hand in its design. The pope's summer residence, it was made up of numerous courtyards, shady loggias covered in decorative frescoes and an elaborate sunken nymphaeum which was much copied in later 16th century villas. In the summer the garden hosts classical music concerts by the Accademia di Santa Cecilia orchestra.

Since 1889 Villa Giulia has been home to the national collection of Etruscan treasures, many found in tombs at sites throughout Lazio. If you plan to visit Etruscan sites near Rome (see Excursions chapter) a visit to the museum before setting out will give you a good understanding of Etruscan culture.

The museum contains thousands of exhibits, ranging from domestic objects and cooking utensils to terracotta vases and amphoras to the remains of a horse drawn chariot. There is an instructive reconstruction of an Etruscan tomb (in the basement of the left wing as you enter), divided into male and female areas and complete with burial objects and armchairs sculpted into the rock. Among the most fascinating exhibits are the personal items, such as safety pins and hairclips, and the small bronze figurines. Have a look at the jewellery and you'll see that design hasn't progressed all that far since.

Of particular note is the polychrome terracotta statue of *Apollo* and other pieces found at Veio, dating from the late 6th century or early 5th century BC. Another highlight is the *Sarcofago degli Sposi* (Sarcophagus of the Married Couple) in Room 9, presumably made for a husband and wife, from a tomb at Cerveteri. This piece is finely sculpted and demonstrates the heights of creativity and skill that the Etruscan artists could reach. It has been restored several times, most recently in 1998 when a cleaner in the museum knocked one of the wife's arms off.

The *Sora Margherita* restaurant doesn't need a sign outside.

Antipasto in the raw

STEFANO CAVEDONI

Keeping the kids amused

SALLY WEBB

Home away from home in the Piazza Farnese

TERESA GAUDIO

Keeping the pigeon population happy

QUENTIN FRAYNE

Tell Caesar there's a knife grinder in the piazza!

Considering the richness of the collection, it is a shame that many of the rooms (particularly those on the left of the entrance) still have the appearance of a poorly maintained provincial museum, with the exhibits crowded together and poorly labelled. However, things are looking up. The ground and 1st floor rooms to the right of the entrance have recently been renovated and the objects are now well displayed with leaflets in both Italian and English guiding the visitor through each room.

The museum (☎ 06 320 19 51, Piazzale di Villa Giulia 9) is open from 9 am to 7 pm, Tuesday to Saturday, and from 9 am to 2 pm on Sunday. Admission is L8000. It can be reached by tram No 225 from Piazzale Flaminio or tram No 19 from Piazza del Risorgimento both of which travel along Viale delle Belle Arti to Piazzale di Villa Giulia.

Gianicolo and Villa Doria Pamphili (Maps 5 & 7)

The Gianicolo (Janiculum hill) rises behind Trastevere and stretches to the Basilica di San Pietro. In 1849 it was the scene of one of the fiercest battles in the struggle for Italian unity, when a makeshift but brave army commanded by Giuseppe Garibaldi defended Rome against French troops sent to restore papal rule. Garibaldi is commemorated by a monument erected at the peak of the hill.

His Brazilian-born wife, Anita, is also commemorated on the Gianicolo with an equestrian **monument** (Map 5) by Mario Rutelli (about 200m away, towards the Basilica di San Pietro) completed in 1932. The statue was presented to the city of Rome by the Brazilian government and shows Anita Garibaldi mounted on a rearing horse, cradling a baby in her left arm and brandishing a pistol in her right. High relief sculptures depicting Anita Garibaldi's heroic activities during her husband's campaign are at the base of the monument.

On a clear day the panoramic view of Rome from **Piazza Garibaldi** (Map 5) is breathtaking. This is a good place to take the kids if they need a break. Just off Piazza Garibaldi,there is a permanent merry-go-round and pony rides, and a puppet show on most Sundays. In the piazza there is a small bar. Take bus No 870 from Via Paola at the end of Corso Vittorio Emanuele where it meets the Lungotevere, or walk up the steps from Via Mameli in Trastevere.

About five minutes walk from Piazza Garibaldi, following the uphill fork of the Passeggiate del Gianicolo past the Porta di San Pancrazio, you reach Rome's largest park, **Villa Doria Pamphili** (Map 7). An enormous private estate – its perimeter measures 9km – Villa Doria Pamphili was laid out around 1650 by Alessandro Algardi for Prince Camillo Pamphili, a nephew of Innocent X. At its centre is the superb Casino del Belrespiro, also designed by Algardi, surrounded by manicured formal gardens and citrus trees. The casino was acquired by the state in the late 1950s, and is now used for official government functions.

The surrounding grounds were acquired by the city authorities between 1965 and 1971 and turned into a public park. It is open every day from sunrise to sunset and is a lovely quiet spot for a walk or a picnic. Even at its most crowded on weekend afternoons in spring and autumn, you can still find a secluded spot beside a Baroque fountain or beneath parasol pines. The park can also be reached by bus No 870 (from Via Paola at the end of Corso Vittorio Emanuele where it meets the Lungotevere).

Heading downhill from Piazza Garibaldi, you pass the **Fontana dell'Acqua Paola** (Map 7) opposite a terrace with a magnificent panorama of the city. The fountain was built in 1612 for Pope Paul V using marble pillaged from the Foro Romano. Four of the fountain's six pink stone columns came from the façade of the old Basilica di San Pietro. The large granite basin was designed by Carlo Fontana in 1690.

Further downhill along Via Garibaldi is the **Chiesa di San Pietro in Montorio** (Map 7) and in a courtyard next to it, Bramante's circular **Tempietto**, built on a site wrongly assumed to be the place of St Peter's crucifixion (he was actually crucified in the circus that once occupied the site of the Basilica di San Pietro). The tempietto, which has just been restored, was built in 1502 and is a Renaissance masterpiece of classical proportion and elegance. See also Walks section later in this chapter.

Via Salaria (Map 4)

This road heads north from the city centre. One of the oldest Roman roads, used to transport salt *(sale)*, it is now a busy residential and shopping district. Not far out of the city centre, after the intersection with Viale Regina Margherita, is an architecturally interesting area known as **Coppedè**. The streets in this small pocket of an otherwise unexceptional residential zone are lined with villas and palazzi built just after WWI in an extravagant Art Nouveau style. The best examples are in Via Dora and Piazza Mincio, one block east of Viale Regina Margherita. Bus No 56 from Trastevere, Piazza Venezia and Piazza Barberini and bus No 319 from Stazione Termini run along Via Tagliamento, parallel to Via Salaria.

The walls of **Villa Ada** park border much of the Via Salaria. The villa was once the private residence of Vittorio Emanuele III but it is now the Egyptian embassy. The villa's grounds are now a huge public park with sloping lawns, shady areas, lakes and ponds. It's great for a picnic year round and in summer hosts a festival of world music.

The **Catacombe di Priscilla**, originally part of the estate of the patrician Acilii family in the 1st century AD, were greatly expanded in the 3rd and 4th centuries and became a popular 'society' burial ground – with appropriate upmarket decoration, quite a lot of which has survived. Several popes were buried in the catacombs between 309 and 555. A funerary chapel known as the Cappella Greca is thought to have been part of the criptoportico from the Acilii villa. It retains good stucco decoration and well-preserved late 3rd century frescoes of biblical scenes. At Via Salaria 430 (☎ 06 86 20 62

72), the catacombs are open from 8.30 am to noon and from 2.30 to 5 pm, Tuesday to Sunday. Admission is L8000.

Via Nomentana (Maps 4 & 6)

Bus Nos 36 and 317 from Stazione Termini and Bus No 60 from Trastevere, Piazza Venezia and Piazza Barberini take you to Porta Pia and the tree-lined Via Nomentana which heads north east out of the city. **Porta Pia** (Map 6), built beside the ruins of the ancient Porta Nomentana, was Michelangelo's last architectural work, commissioned by Pius IV in 1561. It was near Porta Pia that the Italian troops entered Rome on 20 September 1870 and brought to an end the temporal power of the popes. The ugly modern building just inside the city walls is the British Embassy. Opposite it is the Villa Paolina, the residence of Napoleon's sister Paolina Bonaparte from 1816 to 1824, and now the French embassy to the Holy See.

About 1km from Porta Pia on the right (heading away from the city) is **Villa Torlonia** park (Map 4), once a splendid estate belonging to the noble Torlonia family. There are several buildings in the park, including a large 'neo-classical' villa built by Giuseppe Valadier in 1806, which Mussolini used as his private residence in the 1930s. The villa was occupied by Allied troops after WWII, then abandoned. In 1978 the estate was expropriated by the city council as a public park. A program is under way to bring the park back to its former glory.

One of the most interesting buildings in the park is the **Casina delle Civette** (Map 4) The house was built between 1840 and 1930 and is an eclectic combination of a Swiss cottage, a turreted Gothic castle and an Arts and Crafts farmhouse with Art Nouveau decoration. It was already in an advanced state of abandon when it was gutted by a fire in 1991. It was reopened as a museum in 1997 after a lengthy and detailed restoration. The museum is dedicated to stained glass and contains the house's original windows, including work done between 1908 and 1930 by leading Italian decorative artists including Duilio Cambelotti, as well as new leadlights based on early 20th century designs. There are also over 100 designs and sketches for stained glass, decorative tiles, elaborate parquetry floors and boiseries. The museum (☎ 06 44 25 00 72) is open Tuesday to Sunday from 9 am to 7 pm (April to September) and from 9 am to 5 pm (October to March). Admission is L5000.

Sant'Agnese Fuori le Mura and Santa Costanza Further along Via Nomentana, at No 349, is the **Basilica di Sant'Agnese Fuori le Mura** one of a group of early Christian buildings rebuilt and restored in the 15th, 16th and 19th centuries. The church is named after St Agnes, who was buried here in 304. According to tradition, having rejected the advances of one of Diocletian's courtiers, the 13-year-old Agnes was exposed naked in the Stadium of Domitian. Miraculously, her hair grew to preserve her modesty. She was then burnt at the stake but was untouched by the flames. Eventually, she was beheaded. Her relics are preserved beneath the high altar.

A beautiful apse mosaic dating from the 7th century shows St Agnes, dressed in a purple robe with a golden stole, flanked by two popes. The church is open from 9 am to noon and from 4 to 6 pm. On Sunday it is open only in the afternoon and on Monday only in the morning. The Catacombe di Sant'Agnese date from the 3rd century and contain many Christian inscriptions. The entrance is from the left aisle of the basilica; the catacombes keep the with the same opening hours as the church. Admission is L8000.

In the same complex, across the convent courtyard, is the **Mausoleo di Santa Costanza**, also known as the **Chiesa di Santa Costanza**. It was built in the 4th century as a mausoleum for Constantine's daughters Constantia and Helena, and later converted into a baptistry. The pretty circular building has a dome supported by 12 pairs of granite columns. The ambulatory that runs outside of the arches has a barrel vaulted ceiling covered with beautiful 4th century mosaics of fruit, flowers, vines and animals as well as geometric designs. There were once mosaics in the dome – said to be even more astounding than those in the ambulatory – but were destroyed by Paul V in 1622. The original porphyry sarcophagi of Constantia and Helena were moved to il Vaticano in 1790 and are on display in the Musei Vaticani. Santa Costanza is open the same hours as Sant'Agnese.

San Lorenzo
(Map: Greater Rome)

Just outside the city walls, San Lorenzo is home of Rome's La Sapienza university and a popular area for student life. It is easily reached by public transport (bus No 71 from Piazza San Silvestro or No 492 from Piazza Cavour, Piazza Venezia, Piazza Barberini and Stazione Termini or tram No 19 or No 30).

The **Basilica di San Lorenzo Fuori le Mura** in the heart of the area, is one of Rome's seven pilgrimage churches and is dedicated to the martyred St Lawrence. One of the most revered of early Christian martyrs, he had been burnt at the stake under the orders of Valerian in 258 AD. The original structure was erected by Constantine in the 4th century over St Lawrence's burial place but it was rebuilt in the 6th century by Pope Pelagius II. The church was subsequently altered several times between the 8th and 13th centuries; these works included the incorporation of a nearby 5th century church and knocking the two buildings into one. The nave, portico and much of the decoration date from the 13th century.

Of note are a restored 6th century mosaic inside the triumphal arch of Christ with saints and Pelagius offering a model of his church to Christ, the 12th century Cosmati mosaic on the floor, the medieval frescoes of the life and martyrdom of St Lawrence in the portico, the 13th century pulpits and the bishop's throne. The remains of Saints Lawrence and Stephen are in the church crypt beneath the high altar. A pretty barrel-vaulted cloister contains inscriptions and sarcophagi and leads to the Catacombe di Santa Ciriaca where St Lawrence was initially buried (ask the sacristan for admission). The church is open from 8.30 am to noon and from 4 to 6.30 pm.

The **Cimitero di Campo Verano**, to the right of the basilica is the city's largest cemetery. It was designed in the early 19th century by Giuseppe Valadier. From the 1830s to the 1980s virtually all Catholics who died in Rome (with the exception of popes, cardinals and royalty) were buried here, although the main cemetery and crematorium is now located north of Rome at Prima Porta. Campo Verano gets particularly crowded with people and flowers on *I Morti* (All Souls' Day), 2 November, when thousands of Romans flock to visit their dear departed.

Via Appia Antica
(Map: Greater Rome)

Known to ancient Romans as the *regina viarum* (queen of roads), the Via Appia Antica (Appian Way) extends from the Porta San Sebastiano, near the Terme di Caracalla, to Brindisi on the coast of Puglia. It was started around 312 BC by the censor Appius Claudius Caecus, but did not connect with Brindisi until around 190 BC. The first section of the road, which extended 90km to Terracina, was considered revolutionary in its day because it was almost perfectly straight – perhaps the world's first autostrada.

Every Sunday, a long section of the Via Appia Antica becomes a no-car zone. You can walk or ride a bike from the Porta di San Sebastiano for several kilometres.

Monuments along the road near Rome include the catacombs and Roman tombs. The **Chiesa di Domine Quo Vadis** is built at the point where St Peter had a vision of Christ as he was escaping the Neronian persecution. Noticing that he was going towards the city, Peter asked 'Domine, quo vadis?' – 'Lord, where are you going?'. When Jesus replied that he was going to Rome to be crucified again, Peter took the hint and returned to the city, where he was arrested and martyred.

Circo di Massenzio This circus, built around 309 AD by Maxentius, is better preserved than the Circo Massimo. In front of

the circus is the **Tomba di Romolo** (Tomb of Romulus), built by the same emperor for his son, and next to both are the ruins of the imperial residence. The circus is open only on from 11-11.30 am and 3-3.30 on Saturday and Sunday. Admission is L10,000; phone ☎ 320 39 98 for information.

Tomba di Cecilia Metella Farther along Via Appia is this famous tomb of Caecilia Metella, who's father-in-law was the fabulously wealthy Marcus Crassus – which shows. The tomb was incorporated into the castle of the Caetani family in the early 14th century. It is open Tuesday to Saturday from 9 am to 6 pm in summer (to 4 pm in winter and to 1 pm on Sunday and Monday. Admission is free.

Not far past the tomb is a section of the actual ancient road, excavated in the mid-19th century. It is very picturesque, lined with fragments of ancient tombs. Although it is in an area where the rich have built their villas, the road is in a bad state, littered with rubbish and the ruins vandalised. It is advisable not to wander there alone after dark.

To get to Via Appia Antica, catch bus No 218 from Piazza San Giovanni in Laterano. For more detailed information about these and other monuments on the Via Appia Antica, see the Rome Walks chapter.

Catacombe

There are several catacombs along and near Via Appia – kilometres of tunnels carved out of the soft tufa rock, which were the meeting and burial places of early Christians in Rome from the 1st to the early 5th centuries. People were buried wrapped in simple white sheets, and usually placed in rectangular niches carved into the tunnel walls, which were closed with marble or terracotta slabs.

The catacombs can be visited only with a guide. The visit is limited to specially-adapted areas, with exhaustive multi-lingual commentaries. In winter the catacombs operate a system of rotating closure agreed mutually each year, so that one catacomb always remains open (San Sebastiano closes from mid-November to mid-December roughly and San Callisto closes in or around February). The same applies to weekly closure. (See the Rome Walks chapter).

To get to the area of the catacombs catch bus No 218 from Piazza San Giovanni in Laterano (at the Basilica di San Giovanni in Laterano) or Metro Linea A from Stazione Termini to the Colli Albani train station and then bus No 660 to the Via Appia Antica.

Catacombe di San Callisto These catacombs at Via Appia Antica 110 are the largest and most famous and contain the tomb of the martyred St Cecilia (although her body was moved to the Basilica di Santa Cecilia in Trastevere). Founded at the end of the 2nd century on private land, these catacombs became the official cemetery of the newly established Roman church. Fifty martyrs from the time of persecution and 16 of the first popes, themselves mostly martyrs, are buried here. The catacombs are named after Pope Calixtus I, who was killed in Trastevere in 222 while saying Mass. He had been responsible for the catacombs for 20 years. They cover an area of 15 hectares and 20km of tunnels have been explored to date. Archaeologists have found the sepulchres of some 500,000 people, as well as Greek and Latin inscriptions and frescoes.

The catacombs (☎ 06 51 30 15 80, s.cali sto@catacombe.roma.it) are open from 8.30 am to noon and 2.30 to 5.30 pm (5 pm in winter) every day except Wednesday. Admission is with a guide only and costs L8000. The catacombs are closed each year from late January to late February.

Basilica & Catacombe di San Sebastiano The basilica was built in the 4th century over the catacombs, which were used as a safe haven for the remains of saints Peter and Paul during the reign of the Vespasian, who repressed and persecuted the Christians. Originally know as the *Memoria Apostolorum* (Memory of the

Apostles), the basilica was dedicated to St Sebastian, after he was martyred and buried in the late 3rd century.

Preserved in the Capella delle Reliquie, in the right-hand nave of the basilica, is one of the arrows used to kill the saint and the column to which he was tied.

The Catacombe di San Sebastiano were the first catacombs to be so called, the name deriving from the Greek *kata* (near), and *kymbas* (cavity), because they were located near a cave. Subsequently, this term was extended to all the other underground burial grounds. Over the centuries this catacomb was one of only three to remain open and receive pilgrims. For this reason the first of its three levels is now almost completely destroyed. The public can see the 2nd floor, including areas with frescoes, stucco-work and epigraphs. There are also three perfectly preserved mausoleums and a plastered wall with hundreds of invocations to the Apostles Peter and Paul, engraved by worshippers in the 3rd and 4th centuries.

Admission to the catacombs is with a guide only. The church and catacombs, at Via Appia Antica 136 (☎ 06 788 70 35), just past the main entrance to the Catacombs of San Callisto, are open every day except Sunday from 8.30 am to midday and from 2.30 to 5.30 pm (5 pm in winter). Admission is L8000. The catacombs are closed each year from mid November to mid December.

Catacombe di San Domitilla Among the largest and oldest catacombs in Rome, they were established on the private burial ground of Flavia Domitilla, a niece of Domitian. They contain Christian wall paintings and the underground Chiesa di SS Nereus e Achilleus. The catacombs (☎ 06 511 03 42) are situated in Via delle Sette Chiese 283 (take bus No 218) and are open every day except Tuesday from 8.30 am to noon and from 2.30 to 5 pm. Admission is L8000. These catacombs close from late December to late January.

Mausoleo delle Fosse Ardeatine (Map: Greater Rome)

If you walk back to Via Ardeatine and turn right to reach the **Mausoleo delle Fosse Ardeatine,** you will come to the site of one of the worst Nazi atrocities committed in Italy during WWII.

After a brigade of Roman urban partisans blew up 32 German military police in Via Rasella, the Germans took 335 random prisoners (including 75 Jews) to the Ardeatine Caves and shot them. The Germans used mines to explode sections of the caves and thus bury the bodies. After the war, the bodies were exhumed, identified and reburied in a mass grave at the site, now marked by a huge concrete slab and sculptures.

The massacre continues to anger and distress Italians. The German SS commander, Erich Priebke, who has admitted to killing at least two of the victims himself, was tried and convicted in 1996, but will probably serve most of his sentence under house arrest.

The Mausoleo delle Fosse Ardeatine (☎ 06 513 67 42) are open from 8.15 am to 5.45 pm from Monday to Saturday and from 8.45 to 5.15 pm on Sunday and public holidays. Admission is free.

Porta San Paolo, Testaccio and Via Ostiense (Maps 7 & 8)

Porta San Paolo, one of the ancient city gates, is situated south of the Aventino. Via Ostiense runs south from here towards Ostia, once Rome's main commercial sea port (see Excursions chapter). The area is known as Piramide (Map 8), after the pyramid monument, 27m high, inside which Gaius Cestius, a plebeian tribune, was buried in 12 BC. The pyramid was incorporated into the Aurelian walls in the 3rd century AD.

Behind it is the **Cimitero acattolico per gli stranieri** (Protestant cemetery, Map 7)), the final resting place of numerous distinguished foreigners, including John Keats, who died in Rome in 1821. It is a shady and pleasant place for a peaceful wander. Percy Bysshe Shelley certainly thought so – 'It might make one in love with death to think that one should be buried in so sweet a place,' he wrote. His heart was brought to Rome and buried there after his death in 1822. The cemetery (entrance at Via Caio Cestio 5, off Via Nicola Zabaglia) is open Tuesday to Sunday from 9 am to 6 pm (to 5 pm from October to March).

Situated south west of the Aventino between Via Marmorata and the Tevere, **Testaccio** (Map 7) was the river port of ancient Rome from the 2nd century BC to the 3rd century AD. Supplies of wine, oil and grain were transported from Roman colonies to the city via Ostia and the Tevere. The containers for these goods – huge terracotta amphorae and other pots – were then dumped. At first the pots were tossed into the river; when the Tevere became almost unnavigable as a consequence, the pots were smashed to pieces and stacked methodically in a pile which over time grew into a large hill, the Monte Testaccio.

The word Testaccio comes from the Latin *testae*, meaning potsherds. In the Middle Ages the area was the scene of jousts and particularly vicious Carnival games, when pigs, bulls and other animals were packed into carts and sent flying down the 45m hill. Those that survived were slaughtered anyway and eaten.

Most of the area is now occupied by low cost housing that went up at the end of the 19th century to house workers for the new capital city. Although it is off the regular sightseeing trail, Testaccio is a good place to visit if you want to try the most Roman of Roman culinary specialties – offal (see Places to Eat chapter). There is an excellent morning market from Monday to Saturday selling fruit, vegetable, herbs, flowers and (rather incongruously) cheap shoes.

The area around Monte Testaccio and the former slaughterhouse (which is now an active social centre) is also becoming increasingly popular for nightlife (see Entertainment chapter) with some bars and clubs occupying caves carved out of the artificial hill and the neatly stacked amphora pieces clearly visible. If you want to get into or onto Monte Testaccio, contact the Sovrintendenza Archeologica di Roma (see the boxed text 'Open only on Request').

Musei Capitolini at Centrale Montemartini (Map: Greater Rome)

About 500m outside the city walls, heading along Via Ostiense away from the centre, are (on the left) the **Mercati Generali**, Rome's wholesale food markets. Plans are afoot to move the markets to a new site on the periphery of the city. The present buildings will be used for Rome's third university, Roma Tre.

Beyond the Mercati, on the right, at No 106, is a former power station, **Centrale Montemartini** which in 1997 became the temporary home of many pieces of ancient sculpture from the Musei Capitolini, parts of which, at the time of writing, were closed for major renovation. The Centrale Montemartini is open from 10 am to 6 pm Tuesday to Friday and from 10 am to 7 pm on Saturday and Sunday. Admission is L12,000. Take Bus Nos 23 or 702 from Piramide Metro station (Linea B).

The juxtaposition of early 20th century industrial machinery and delicately carved marble that is around 2000 years older is unusual, but surprisingly effective. The move has given the Musei Capitolini curators an opportunity to research the collection, to display sculptures and mosaics which have been hidden for decades in Capitoline storage vaults, and to exhibit together connected pieces (for example sculptures which came from the same monument) which have previously been displayed separately. When the collection returns to the Musei Capitolini in 2000, the new exhibition philosophy will be maintained. Most of the exhibits came to light during excavations in Rome in the late 19th century, when there was large-scale building and development of the new national capital.

On the ground floor beyond the entrance is the Sala Colonne where the oldest pieces in the collection – sculpture and ceramics dating from the 7th century BC – are displayed. These include Etruscan and Greek pieces as well as discoveries from a necropolis on the Esquilino.

Metal stairs lead up to the Sala Macchina, painted a garish blue, where antiquities dating from the late Republican period to the height of the Empire share the exhibition space with two mammoth 7500 HP diesel engines. Of note are several Roman copies of original Greek works, including a number of statues of *Athena* (grouped together), a black basalt statue of *Orantes* (recently identified as being a portrait of Agrippina, the niece of Claudius), and heads of divinities and statues from the pediment of the Tempio di Apollo Soianus, a temple that once stood near the Teatro di Marcello. These statues depict a battle between Greeks and Amazons and were originally coloured. There are also sculptures found on the Campidoglio, in the Area Sacra di Largo Argentina and near the Teatro di Pompeo (in the Campo de' Fiori area).

The Sala Caldaia, painted a rather sickly hospital green, has the highlights of the collection set against the backdrop of a giant furnace. Many pieces were excavated from imperial and patrician villas and gardens and represent the taste of the emperors and nobility. The magnificent floor mosaic of hunting scenes has rarely been exhibited before. It was found during excavations near the Porta Maggiore. Two of the most beautiful pieces are statues of young girls, the *Fanciulla seduta* sitting with her elbow resting on her knee, and *Musa Polimnia* standing, leaning on a pedestal and gazing dreamily into the distance. At the far end of the room, flanked by two attendants and against the backdrop of a giant furnace, is the milky white *Venus Esquilina* from the 1st century BC discovered on the Esquilino in 1874.

Basilica di San Paolo Fuori le Mura (Map: Greater Rome)

The **Basilica di San Paolo Fuori le Mura** is in Via Ostiense, about 3km from Porta San

Paolo and some distance from the city centre (take Metro Linea B to San Paolo). The original church was built in the 4th century AD by Constantine over the burial place of St Paul and, until the construction of the present-day Basilica di San Pietro, was the largest church in the world. The church was destroyed by fire in 1823 and the present structure was erected in its place.

The triumphal arch was part of the former church; its 5th century mosaics of Christ with angels, Saints Peter and Paul and symbols of the Evangelists have been heavily restored. On the other side of the arch are mosaics by Pietro Cavallini. The mosaics in the apse were done by Venetian artists and show the figures of Christ with St Peter, St Andrew, St Paul and St Luke. The 13th century marble canopy over the high altar was designed by Arnolfo di Cambio together with another artist, possibly Pietro Cavallini. The paintings between the windows of the nave show the life of St Paul. Below are mosaic portraits of all the popes from St Peter to John Paul II.

The beautiful **cloisters** of the adjacent Benedictine abbey survived the fire. These are a masterpiece of Cosmati mosaic work and, along with the cloisters at the Basilica di San Giovanni in Laterano, are generally considered to be the most beautiful example of their kind in Rome. The octagonal and spiral columns supporting the elaborate arcade are arranged in pairs and are inlaid with colourful mosaics. The sacristy contains other objects from the old church, including four frescoe portraits of past popes.

EUR

This acronym, which stands for Esposizione Universale di Roma, has become the name of a peripheral suburb of Rome, interesting for its many examples of Fascist architecture, including the **Palazzo della Civiltà del Lavoro** (Palace of the Workers), a square building with arched windows known as the Square Colosseum. Mussolini ordered the construction of the satellite city about 5km south of Rome for an inter-

national exhibition to have been held in 1942. Work was suspended with the outbreak of war and the exhibition was never held; however, many buildings were completed during the 1950s.

The **Museo della Civiltà Romana** (☎ 06 592 61 35, Piazza G Agnelli) reconstructs the development of Rome with the use of models. There's a particularly good model of the centre of Ancient Rome, and plaster casts of the reliefs on the Colonna Antonia (Column of Marcus Aurelius). It's open Tuesday to Saturday from 9 am to 7 pm and Sunday to 1.30 pm. Admission is L5000.

Also of interest is the **Museo Nazionale Preistorico Etnografico Luigi Pigorini** (☎ 06 54 95 21) on the corner of Piazza Marconi and Viale Lincoln. Its Museo Preistorico covers the development of civilisation in the region, while its ethnographical collection includes exhibits from around the world. The museum is open from 9 am to 2 pm, Tuesday to Saturday, and from 9 am to 1 pm on Sunday. Admission is L8000.

On the other side of the enormous Piazza Marconi (at No 8) is the **Museo delle Arti e Tradizioni Popolari** (☎ 06 592 61 48). Its collection illustrates traditional Italian culture through history and includes agricultural and artisan tools, popular arts and crafts, clothing, furniture, musical instruments and jewellery. It is open from 9 am to 2 pm, Tuesday to Saturday, and from 9 am to 1 pm on Sunday. Admission is L4000.

EUR is accessible on the Metro Linea B.

IL VATICANO (MAP 5)

After unification, the Papal States of central Italy became part of the new Kingdom of Italy, causing a considerable rift between the church and state. In 1929, Mussolini signed the Lateran Treaty with Pius XI, giving the pope full sovereignty over what is now the Città del Vaticano (Vatican City).

The city has its own postal service, currency, newspaper, radio station and train station (now used only for freight). It also has its own army of Swiss Guards, responsible for the pope's personal security. The corps was established in 1506 by

The Pope's Army

The Swiss Guards are the pope's private bodyguard. Despite the colourful uniform which makes them look like they have just stepped out of a television period drama, all Swiss Guards are highly trained soldiers.

The selection process for potential recruits is rigid; they are hand-picked for their total precision, total loyalty and total dedication. Not only must these men be in excellent physical condition, but they must also be Swiss-born, practising Catholics, of impeccable moral standing and they must have completed their national military service in Switzerland.

The full complement of Swiss Guards is 100, although in recent years il Vaticano has had problems filling its quota, and few of them tend to make a career out of being one of the pope's guardian angels. The soldiers are paid very low wages; they cannot live outside il Vaticano and therefore if they want to marry, they might have to wait years before suitable accommodation is available.

The soldiers do a lot more than guard the entrances to and perimeters of il Vaticano. A typical day might include martial arts practice or weapons training (all guards are skilled in using their traditional 15th century pike) as well as more conventional modern weapons, or sessions on anti-terrorism tactics. The soldiers always accompany the pope when he makes public appearances – a Swiss Guard was at John Paul II's side during the assassination attempt in Piazza San Pietro in 1981 – and two (plain-clothes) guards travel with him whenever he goes abroad.

Recently, questions have been asked as to whether the Swiss Guards provide the right sort of security for today's world. In May 1998, a young recruit, Cedric Tornay, entered the private apartment of the newly-appointed head of the Swiss Guards, Colonel Estermann, and shot and killed Colonel Estermann and his wife before turning the gun on himself. It was hastily explained that the crime as a 'moment of madness' of an insane young man, triggered by professional disappointment (Tornay had been cautioned for breaking rules earlier in 1998 and was also refused a decoration) and possibly due to a mind addled by drug abuse.

However, questions such as whether he was on or off duty at the time, why he was wandering around Il Vaticano armed, how he had access to the commander's apartments, and why he killed Mrs Estermann have remained unanswered. Torney's mother has consistently rejected the finding of murder suicide, claiming an official cover-up. Doubts have also been expressed about whether Torney's fatal gunshot wounds could have been self-inflicted. One lurid suggestions in the local press is that Torney and Estermann were homosexual lovers.

Many people now wonder whether more modern security arrangements should now take the Swiss Guards' place.

Julius II to defend the Papal States against invading armies. The guards still wear the traditional eye-catching red, yellow and blue uniform (not, as legend would have it, designed by Michelangelo) and brandish unwieldy 15th century pikes, but they are in fact highly trained soldiers. The guards are at the pope's side whenever he appears in public and accompany him on all overseas trips.

Information & Services

The Ufficio Informazioni Pellegrini e Turisti (tourist office) is in Piazza San Pietro to the left of the basilica (☎ 06 69 88 44 66 or 06 69 88 48 66, fax 06 69 88 51 00). It is open Monday to Saturday from 8.30 am to 7 pm and has general information about San Pietro and il Vaticano.

Il Vaticano post office, said to provide a faster and more reliable service than the normal Italian postal system, is a few doors from the tourist office (there is another outlet on the other side of the piazza and one in the Musei Vaticani). Letters can be posted in blue Vatican post boxes only if they carry Vatican stamps.

The only way you can get in to see the **Giardini del Vaticano** (Vatican Gardens) is on a guided tour which can be booked at the tourist office. The gardens contain fortifications, grottoes, monuments and fountains dating from the 9th century to the present day, as well as a heliport and manicured gardens in various styles tended by 30 full-time gardeners. There's a formal Italian area, a flower-filled French garden and a naturalistic English wood. There is even a kitchen garden which provides produce for the pontifical household, although tour groups don't get close enough to check out the papal tomatoes. The tours take place on Monday, Tuesday, Thursday, Friday and Saturday from March to October but are less frequent at other times of the year. Tickets cost L18,000. Bookings can be made by telephone on the numbers given for the Ufficio Informazioni Pellegrini e Turisti above, but you need to pay for your ticket several days before the tour. It's advisable to book well in advance.

Papal Audiences

The pope usually gives a public audience every Wednesday at 11 am in the Aula delle Udienze Pontificie (Papal Audience Hall). For permission to attend, go to the Prefettura della Casa Pontifica (☎ 69 88 30 17), through the bronze doors under the colonnade to the right of San Pietro as you face the church. The office is open from 9 am to 1 pm and you can apply on the Tuesday before the audience (or, at a push, on the morning of the audience). You can also apply in writing to the Prefettura della Casa Pontifica, 00120 Città del Vaticano or fax 06 69 88 58 63.

You should specify the date you'd like to attend and the number of tickets required. If you have a hotel in Rome, the office will forward the tickets there. Individuals shouldn't have too much trouble obtaining a ticket at short notice.

The pope also occasionally celebrates Mass at the basilica and information can be obtained at the same office. You will be required to leave your passport with the Swiss Guards at the bronze doors. People wanting to attend a normal Mass at San Pietro can ask for the times of daily Masses at the tourist office in the piazza.

Piazza San Pietro

Bernini's piazza is considered a masterpiece. Laid out in the 17th century as a place for the Christians of the world to gather, the immense piazza is bounded by two semicircular colonnades, each of which is made up of four rows of Doric columns. These are topped with 140 statues of saints by Bernini's pupils and followers. In the centre of the piazza is an obelisk brought to Rome by Gaius Caligula from Heliopolis in Egypt.

When you stand on the dark paving stones between the obelisk and either of the fountains, the colonnade on that side appears to have only one row of columns. On Sunday the pope makes his regular address and recites the Angelus at noon from the building to the right of the piazza. His office is on the top floor, the second window from the right. At Christmas, a huge nativity scene is erected in the centre of the square.

Basilica di San Pietro

In the same area where the church (St Peter's Basilica) now stands, there was once the Circo Vaticano, built by Nero. It was probably in this stadium that St Peter and other Christians were martyred between 64 and 67 AD. The body of the saint was buried in an anonymous grave next to the wall of the circus, and his fellow Christians built a humble 'red wall' to mark the site. In 160 AD the stadium was abandoned and a small monument erected on the grave. In 315, Constantine ordered construction of a basilica on the site of the apostle's tomb. This first Basilica di San Pietro was consecrated in 326.

After more than 1000 years, the church was in a poor state of repair and, in the mid-15th century, Pope Nicholas V put architects, including Alberti, to work on its reconstruction. But it was not until 1506, when Pope Julius II employed Donato Bramante, that serious work began. Bramante designed a new basilica on a Greek cross plan, with a central dome and four smaller domes. He oversaw the demolition of much of the old basilica and attracted great criticism for the unnecessary destruction of many of its precious works of art – including Byzantine mosaics and frescoes by artists including Giotto.

It took more than 150 years to complete the basilica, involving the contributions of Bramante, Raphael, Antonio da Sangallo, Michelangelo, Giacomo della Porta and Carlo Maderno. It is generally held that San Pietro owes most to Michelangelo, who took over the project in 1547 at the age of 72 and was responsible for the design of the dome. He died before the church was completed.

The façade and portico were designed by Carlo Maderno, who took over the project

---

Nero Rules, OK?

Although Nero was in Anzio when the great fire of Rome broke out in 64 AD, the rumour quickly spread that he was responsible. One tale was that he callously used the burning city as a backdrop for a recital on the fall of Troy; even worse was the rumour that he had actually started the fire. The pleasure with which he used a large amount of the ruined city for his new palace, the Domus Aurea (Golden House), hardly helped calm popular feeling.

Unnerved, Nero looked for scapegoats, and he chose the early Christian community, for whom the rest of the population had little understanding and no sympathy. Some were thrown to the wild animals in the circus, and others, in perverse retribution for arson, were burned alive as human torches.

The crucifixion of St Peter

Sts Peter and Paul are said to have been martyred during this period. Peter was crucified (upside down at his own request so as not to imitate the death of Jesus too closely) near Nero's racetrack in il Vaticano, and Paul, a Roman citizen, was given the privilege of decapitation.

Michelangelo in Rome

Michelangelo Buonarotti was born in Caprese near Arrezzo in Toscana in 1475, the son of a Tuscan magistrate. He was moody and solitary figure, easily offended and irritated. The true Renaissance man, he was a supremely talented architect and painter, but he regarded himself as a sculptor above all else.

It was as a sculptor that Michelangelo achieved his early recognition. One of his greatest early carvings is the *Pietà* in the Basilica di San Pietro which he completed when he was 25.

Michelangelo came to work in Rome for Pope Julius II who wanted a grand marble tomb for himself which would surpass any funerary monument that had ever been built. Michelangelo was dispatched to the marble quarries of Carrara in northern Toscana (which still provide stone for sculptors today) and spent eight months selecting and excavating suitable marble blocks which, when brought to Rome, repeatedly filled half of Piazza San Pietro.

Although the tomb preoccupied Michelangelo throughout his working life, it was never completed and Julius II lies in an unadorned grave in San Pietro. The original design included 40 statues. The famous figure of Moses as well as statues of Leah and Rachel are in the Chiesa di San Pietro in Vincoli. Two of the slaves are now in the Louvre and several famous unfinished slaves are in the Accademia in Firenze.

Despite claiming to be a reluctant painter, Michelangelo's single greatest artistic achievement, one of the most awe-inspiring acts of individual creativity in the history of the visual arts, is the ceiling of the Cappella Sistina, painted between 1508 and 1512.

Michelangelo never wanted the commission (also from Julius II) and the project was problematic from the outset. First the artist rejected the scaffolding that Bramante had built for him; then he considered his assistants so incompetent that he dismissed them all, scraped off their work, and ended up painting the entire ceiling single handedly. The artist was pushed to his physical and emotional limits, and was continually harassed by the pope and his court, who wanted the job finished.

Michelangelo returned to Rome aged 59 at the request of Pope Clement VII to paint the *Giudizio Universale* (Last Judgement) on the altar wall of the Cappella Sistina. Once again he accepted the commission against his will, preferring to continue sculpting figures for Julius II's tomb which he did secretly while he prepared the Last Judgement cartoons.

On Clement VII's death, his successor Paul III was determined to have Michelangelo working exclusively for him and have the Cappella Sistina completed; in 1535 he appointed Michelangelo as chief architect, sculptor and painter to il Vaticano, and the artist started

after Michelangelo's death. He was also instructed to lengthen the nave towards the piazza, effectively altering Bramante's original Greek cross plan to a Latin cross. At the time of writing the façade was completely covered for restoration work to clean the travertine marble and repair damage caused by age and pollution. The scaffolding should be down before the end of 1999. The basilica is open from 7 am to 7 pm from April to September and from 7 am to 6 pm from October to March.

The cavernous interior, decorated by Bernini and Giacomo della Porta, can hold up to 60,000 people. It contains treasures including Michelangelo's superb **Pietà**, at the beginning of the right aisle, sculpted when he was only 25 years old and the only work to carry his signature (on the sash across the breast of the Madonna). It is now protected by bulletproof glass after having been attacked in 1972 by a hammer-wielding, mentally disturbed vandal.

The red porphyry disk just inside the main door marks the spot where Charlemagne and

Michelangelo in Rome

The *Pietà*

working on the Last Judgement, which was unveiled in 1541 and claimed by some as surpassing not only the other masters who had decorated the chapel walls but also his own ceiling frescoes.

Paul III then commissioned Michelangelo to create a new central square for the city on the Campidoglio and to design a suitable grand approach to it. The work was not finished until the middle of the 17th century, but successive architects closely followed the original plans.

Michelangelo's design for the upper storey of the Palazzo Farnese was also realised posthumously when Giacomo della Porta completed the building, and his design for the city gateway at Porta Pia was finished a year after his death.

The artist spent his last years working – unhappily – on the Basilica di San Pietro; he felt that it was penance from God. He disapproved of the plans that had been drawn up by Antonio da Sangallo the Younger before his death, claiming that they deprived the basilica of light, and argued with Sangallo's assistants who wanted to retain their master's designs. Instead Michelangelo created the magnificent light-filled dome based on Brunelleschi's design for the Duomo cupola in Firenze, and a stately façade.

In his old age he was said to work with the same strength and concentration as he had as a younger man. He continued to direct the work until his death on 18 February 1564. He was buried in the Chiesa dei Santi Apostoli although his remains were later moved to Firenze. The dome and façade of San Pietro were completed to his designs by Vignola, Giacomo della Porta and Carlo Fontana.

---

later Holy Roman Emperors were crowned by the pope. Bronze plates in the marble floor indicate the respective sizes of the 14 next largest churches in the world.

Bernini's Baroque **baldacchino** (canopy) stands 29m high in the centre of the church and is an extraordinary work of art. The bronze used to make it was taken from the roof of the Pantheon. The high altar, which only the pope can serve at, stands over the site of St Peter's grave.

Michelangelo's **dome**, a majestic architectural masterpiece, soars 119m above the high altar. Its balconies are decorated with reliefs depicting the so-called Reliquie Maggiori (major relics) – the lance of St Longinus, which he used to pierce Christ's side; the cloth of St Veronica, which bears a miraculous portrait of Christ; and a piece of the True Cross, collected by St Helena, the mother of Constantine. Entry to the dome is to the right as you climb the stairs to the atrium of the basilica. Access to the roof of the church is by elevator (admission L6000) or stairs (admission L5000). From there, ascend the stairs to the base of the dome for a view down into the basilica. From here, a narrow staircase leads eventually to the top of the dome and San Pietro's lantern, from where you have an unequalled view of Rome. It is well worth the effort, but bear in mind it is a long and tiring climb and not to be recommended for those who suffer from vertigo or claustrophobia. You can climb the dome from 8 am to one hour before the basilica closes.

To the right as you face the high altar is a famous bronze statue of St Peter, believed to be a 13th century work by Arnolfo di Cambio. The statue's right foot has been worn down by the kisses and touch of pilgrims. It's dressed in papal robes on the Feast Day of Sts Peter and Paul, 29 June.

The entrance to the **Sacre Grotte Vaticane** (Vatican Grottoes) the resting place of numerous popes, is next to the pier of St Longinus (one of four piers supporting the arches at the base of Michelangelo's cupola) to the right as you approach the papal altar. The tombs of many early popes were moved here from the old Basilica di San Pietro, and recent popes, including John XXIII, Paul VI and John Paul I, are buried here. The grottoes are open daily from 8 am to 6 pm (April to September) and 8 am to 5 pm (September to March). Ask the attendant if the entrance seems to have moved.

The excavations beneath San Pietro, which began in 1940, have uncovered part of the original church, an early Christian cemetery and Roman tombs. Archaeologists believe they have also found the tomb of St Peter; the site of the empty tomb is marked by a shrine and a wall plastered with red. Nearby is another wall, scrawled with the graffiti of pilgrims; in 1942 the bones of an elderly, strongly built man were found in a box placed in a niche behind this wall. In 1976, after many years of forensic examination, Paul VI declared the bones to be those of St Peter. John Paul II had some of the relics transferred to his hospital room when he was recovering from the 1981 assassination attempt. The bones were then returned to the tomb and are kept in hermetically sealed perspex cases designed by NASA.

The excavations can be visited only by appointment, which can be made either in writing or in person at the Ufficio Scavi (☎ 06 69 88 53 18, fax 06 69 88 55 18), in Piazza Braschi. Address your letter to Ufficio Scavi, 00120 Città del Vaticano, Roma, and stipulate the date you'd like to visit. The office will then contact you to confirm the time and date. You need to book at least one week ahead. The office is open Monday to Saturday from 8 am to 5 pm. Small groups are taken most days between 9 am and noon and 2 to 5 pm. It costs L10,000 to visit the excavations with a guide.

Dress regulations are stringently enforced at San Pietro. It is forbidden to enter the church in shorts (men included), or wearing a short skirt, or with bare shoulders.

Musei Vaticani

From the Piazza di San Pietro, follow the wall of il Vaticano north to the museums' entrance. A regular bus service from outside the Arco delle Campane (to the left of the basilica just near the information office) to the museums had been suspended at the time of writing, due to construction and restoration work for the Jubilee. It should be reinstated in 1999 or 2000 – ask at the information office.

The museums contain an incredible collection of art and treasures accumulated by the popes, and you will need several hours to see the most important areas and museums. One visit is probably not enough to appreciate the full value of the collections and it's worth trying to make at least two visits if you have the time. There are four 'one-way' itineraries which have been mapped out with the aim of simplifying visits and containing the huge number of visitors. It is basically compulsory that you follow the itineraries (which vary in duration from 1½ to 5 hours), but you can make some deviations if you want.

Another point to note is that the Cappella Sistina comes towards the end of a full visit. If you want to spend most of your time in the chapel, or you want to get there early to avoid the crowds, it is possible to walk straight there and then walk back to the Quattro Cancelli to pick up one of the itineraries. Most tour groups (and there are many!) head straight to the chapel and it is almost always very crowded. It is also important to note that, while the museums don't officially close until 1.45 pm, the guards at the Cappella Sistina often refuse to let people in well before then. Of great assistance, and well worth the L16,000 investment, is the *Guide to the Vatican Museums and City*, on sale at the Musei. You can also hire CD audio guides which provide a commentary for what you are seeing.

The museums are well equipped for disabled visitors; there are four suggested itineraries, several lifts and specially fitted toilets. Ask for a brochure at the ticket window or information desk or call in advance ☎ 06 69 88 38 60. Wheelchairs can be reserved. Parents with young children can take pushchairs into the museums.

The Musei Vaticani are open Monday to Saturday from 8.45 am to 1.45 pm with last admission at 12.45 pm. From mid-March to the end of October, they are open Monday to Friday from 8.45 am to 4.45 pm (last admission 3.45 pm) and on Saturday from 8.45 to 1.45 pm (last admission 12.45 pm). Admission is L15,000. The museums are closed on Sunday and holidays, but open on the last Sunday of every month from 9 am to 1.45 pm (free admission, but queues are always very long).

The buildings that house the Musei Vaticani are known collectively as the Palazzo Apostolico. Most of the palazzi that now house the collection were originally built for Renaissance popes. After he returned from Avignon in 1378, Gregory XI took up permanent residence in il Vaticano in a fortified palazzo erected around 1208 for Innocent III. Nicholas V expanded the building and added the Cortile dei Pappagalli, and Sixtus IV had the Cappella Sistina built in 1473.

The Belvedere was added under Innocent VIII in the late 15th century. Julius II situated his impressive collection of classical sculpture in the Belvedere and had Donato Bramante design a new entrance to the palace which included a spiral staircase up which horses could be ridden. Under Julius II, Bramante also created the Cortile del Belvedere when he joined the Belvedere to Nicholas V's palace and the Cappella Sistina with long corridors. The courtyard was subsequently sliced into three smaller sections with the additions of the Biblioteca Apostolica and the Braccio Nuovo. The northern courtyard, the Cortile della Pigna, is named after the colossal bronze fir cone dating from the 1st or 2nd century placed there in 1608 by Paul V. As part of the conversion of the Belvedere into a museum in the late 18th century, a monumental staircase (by Michelangelo Simonetti) was added as well as a new entrance, the Atrio dei Quattro Cancelli. New buildings were added in 1932 and 1970.

At the time of writing a new entrance to the museums was being built which is expected to be completed by late 1999. It will comprise a reception area on four levels with a winding ramp leading up to the Atrio dei Quattro Cancelli, from where the various itineraries depart. New facilities will include a meeting point, information desks, currency exchange booths, cloakroom, bathrooms, medical officers and a caffè/restaurant.

The buildings to the west of the Quattro Cancelli are the most recent and house the Museo Gregoriano Profano, the Museo Pio-Cristiano, the Pinacoteca, the Museo Missionario-Etnologico and a carriage museum. These galleries are the last on the longer itineraries and are probably the ones to miss if you run out of time and energy.

Museo Gregoriano Profano This museum houses Classical antiquities and was started by Gregory XVI in 1844. Exhibits include original Greek sculpture dating from the 5th and 4th centuries BC and Roman sculpture from 1st to 3rd centuries AD.

Museo Pio-Cristiano The Museo Pio-Cristiano contains early Christian antiquities, including inscriptions and sculpture from catacombs and early Christian basilicas and sarcophagi decorated with carved reliefs of biblical scenes. The collection was founded by Pius IX in 1854. Both these collections were formerly kept in the Palazzo Laterano; they were moved toil Vaticano in 1970.

Pinacoteca The popes' picture gallery was founded by Pius XI and houses a magnificent collection of paintings dating from the 11th to the 19th century. Napoleon carted off many of the pictures in 1797 but they were returned to Rome in 1815. They are hung in chronological order and include works by Fra Angelico, Filippo Lippi, Benozzo Gozzoli, Federico Barocci, Guido Reni, Guercino, Nicholas Poussin, Van Dyck and Pietro da Cortona.

There are several works by Raphael, who has a room to himself, including the *Madonna di Foligno*, originally kept in the church of Santa Maria in Aracoeli, and the magnificent *La Trasfigurazione* (Transfiguration) completed just before he died in 1520. Other highlights of the collection include Giotto's *Polittico Stefaneschi* (Stefaneschi triptych) which was originally an altarpiece in the Sacristry of San Pietro, Giovanni Bellini's *Pietà*, Leonardo's unfinished *San Gerolamo* and Caravaggio's *Deposizione*.

Museo Missionario-Etnologico This museum contains ethnological and anthropological material from Africa, the Americas, Asia, Australasia, and the Middle East, some of which was gathered during missionary expeditions.

Museo Gregoriano Egizio The Egyptian museum is on the lower floor of the Belvedere, on the east side of the Quattro Cancelli. It was founded by Pope Gregory XVI in 1839 and contains many pieces taken from Egypt in Roman times. The collection is small, but there are some fascinating exhibits. The rooms were decorated in the 19th century in Egyptian style and have decorative details such as cornice friezes with inscriptions in hieroglyphics, and midnight-blue ceilings peppered with gold stars. They were restored and rearranged in 1989.

Of particular note in Room I is the **Trono di Rameses II**, part of a statue of the seated king. Room II contains painted wooden sarcophagi dating from around 1000 BC, whose colours are unbelievably fresh and rich. There are two mummies, one of which is totally bandaged. The other has its blackened hands and feet exposed, and you can see the henna-treated hair and a hole where the mummy's left eye should have been; the eye was probably removed so that the brain could be extracted before mummification. There are also two carved marble sarcophagi from the 6th century BC. Room III has Roman sculptures in Egyptian style which were used as decoration at the Villa Adriana in Tivoli (see Excursions chapter). Of note in Room IV is the black marble statue representing the Nile.

Museo Chiaramonti From the Egyptian Museum, a short flight of stairs leads down to a long corridor which runs the length of the Cortile della Pigna. It contains hundreds of marble statues of gods, sculptures of playful cherubs and busts of Roman patricians. It's a great way to get an idea of fashionable Roman hairstyles. Near the end of the Museo Chiaramonti, off to the right is the **Braccio Nuovo** (New Wing). It contains important works, including a famous statue of Augustus, and a statue depicting the Nile as a reclining god with 16 babies playing on him, which are supposed to represent the number of cubits the Nile rose when in flood.

Visible through a gate at the end of the Museo Chiaramonti is the **Galleria Lapidaria** which is open only to scholars on request. It contains over 3000 Christian and Roman inscriptions, mounted into the walls of the gallery. The Christian inscriptions are on the right side and the Classical ones on the left.

Museo Pio-Clementino The Museo Pio-Clementino is in the Belvedere and accessible through the Egyptian Museum or from the Cortile della Pigna. Entering through the square vestibule, you come to the Gabinetto dell'Apoxyomenos which contains a 1st century AD Roman statue found in Trastevere in 1849. The statue depicts an athlete towelling himself off and is actually a copy of a bronze original thought to date from around 320 BC.

In the elegant **Cortile Ottagono** (Octagonal Courtyard), which forms part of the gallery, are several important ancient statues, bas-reliefs and sarcophagi. To the left as you enter, in a niche in the corner, is the famous *Apollo Belvedere*, a 2nd century Roman copy in marble of a 4th century BC Greek bronze, considered one of the great masterpieces of classical sculpture. Also on the left is an impressive statue of a river god (Tigris). Beyond it is another notable piece, the *Laocoön*, depicting a Trojan priest of Apollo and his two sons in mortal struggle with two sea serpents. When discovered in 1506 on the Esquilino (Michelangelo was said to have been present), the sculpture was recognised from descriptions by the Roman encyclopaedist Pliny the Elder and purchased by Pope Julius II.

Back inside the Belvedere is the **Sala degli Animali**, filled with sculptures of all sorts of creatures. The floors of both sides of the gallery contain magnificent mosaics dating from the 4th century AD. Don't miss the delightful crab (made from rare green porphyry stone) at the far end of the room on the right. Facing it, mounted on the wall, is a charming mosaic showing a cat (which has caught a chicken) with ducks and fruit. There are also two small mosaic landscapes which came from the Villa Adriana. Beyond the Sala degli Animali are the Galleria delle Statue, with several important classical pieces, the Sala delle Buste, which contains portrait busts of important Roman emperors and political figures, and the Gabinetto delle Maschere, which is named after the floor mosaics of theatrical masks; there are several interesting pieces in this room including two statues of Venus and a group representing the three Graces.

In the **Sala delle Muse** (Room of the Muses) is the *Torso Belvedere*, a Greek sculpture of the 1st century BC, which was found in the Campo de' Fiori during the time of Pope Julius II and was much admired by Michelangelo and other Renaissance artists. The next room, the round **Sala Rotonda**, built by Michelangelo Simonetti in 1780, was inspired by the Pantheon. It contains a number of colossal statues including the gilded bronze figure of *Ercole* (Hercules). The ancient mosaic on the floor, featuring sea monsters and battles between Greeks and centaurs, is quite exquisite. The enormous basin in the centre of the room was found at the site of Nero's Domus Aurea and is made out of a single piece of red porphyry stone.

In the **Sala a Croce Greca** (Greek Cross Room) are the porphyry sarcophagi of Constantine's daughter, Constantia, and his mother, St Helena. These were originally in the Mausoleo di Santa Constanza in Via Nomentana.

Museo Gregoriano Etrusco On the upper level of the Belvedere off the Simonetti staircase is the Museo Gregoriano Etrusco (Etruscan Museum) which contains artefacts from Etruscan tombs of southern Etruria. Of particular interest are those in Room II from the Regolini-Galassi tomb, discovered in 1836 south of Cerveteri. Those buried in the tomb included a princess, and among the finds on display are gold jewellery, and a funeral carriage with a bronze bed and funeral couch, dating from the 7th century BC. The Etruscan rooms were refurbished and expanded in 1996. The exhibits are arranged by subject matter so it is easy to compare pieces.

The **Sala dei Bronzi** has the *Marte di Todi* (Mars of Todi), a full-length bronze statue of a warrior dating from the 4th century BC, as well as bronze figurines, statuettes of young boys, armour, hand mirrors and candelabras. Beyond it, the **Sala delle Pietre** displays sarcophagi and statues in volcanic stone such as tufa and peperino which were favoured by the Etruscans as they were soft and easy to carve, then hardened over time. The **Sala degli Ori** is devoted to beautifully displayed Etruscan jewellery.

The **Sala delle Terracotte** displays terracotta pieces, including some wonderfully expressive portrait heads. Don't miss the bust of an elderly woman. The Etruscan Museum also incorporates a collection of Greek vases and Roman antiquities, a highlight of which is a vase signed by the Greek artist Exekias dating from around 530 BC which is decorated with an image of Achilles and Ajax playing draughts. Magnificent views of Rome can be had from the last room at the end of the wing. From here you can also get a glimpse down the full drop of Bramante's spiral staircase which was designed so that horses could be ridden up it. The stairway was built for Julius II inside a square tower which was at one time the entrance to the Belvedere.

Galleria dei Candelabri The Galleria dei Candelabri (Gallery of the Candelabras) was originally an open loggia and is packed with classical sculpture including several elegantly carved marble candelabras which give the room its name. In the middle section of the long gallery note the fragments of Roman frescoes and the vividly coloured still-life mosaics. Further on is a charming sculpture of a boy strangling a goose, and opposite it a flute player.

Galleria degli Arazzi You have to walk through the Galleria degli Arazzi (Tapestry Gallery) to get to the Cappella Sistina, and it is worth a brief look. The tapestries on the left (opposite the windows) date from the 16th century. They were designed by students of Raphael and woven in the Brussels workshop of Pieter van Aeist. Note the intricate details of flowers and foliage in the penultimate tapestry showing Christ appearing to Mary Magdalen. The tapestries on the right date from the 17th century and were woven by the Barberini workshop.

Galleria delle Carte Geografiche Covered from one end to another with fascinating topographical maps, the Galleria delle Carte Geografiche (Map Gallery) also merits more than a cursory glance from the hoards of people heading single-mindedly to the Cappella Sistina. The 40 topographical maps were painted between 1580 and 1583 for Pope Gregory XIII based on cartoons by Ignazio Danti, one of the leading cartographers of his day. The ceiling frescoes, representing the lives of saints and the history of the church, are related geographically to the maps below them.

Next to the Map Gallery is the **Appartamento di San Pio V**, containing some interesting Flemish tapestries, and the **Sala Sobieski**, named after the enormous 19th century canvas on its north wall (depicting the victory of the Polish King John III Sobieski over the Turks in 1683). These rooms lead into the magnificent Stanze di Raffaello.

Stanze di Raffaello The 'Raphael Rooms' were the private apartments of Pope Julius II. Raphael painted the Stanza della Segnatura and the Stanza d'Eliodoro, while the Stanza dell'Incendio was painted by his students to his designs and the ceiling was painted by his master, Perugino.

The far room, the **Sala di Costantino**, was decorated by Raphael's students with some of the works based on his designs. Off this room is the Sala dei Chiaroscuri and the Cappella di Niccolo V. The **Sala dei Chiaroscuri** was decorated in 16th century and used for ceremonial purposes. Raphael designed the ceiling which, along with the chiaroscuro figures on the walls, was executed by his students. A small door leads to the tiny **Cappella di Niccolo V** which was Pope Nicholas V's private chapel. The superb frescoes were done by Fra Angelico around 1450 and depict the lives of St Stephen (upper cycle) and St Lawrence (lower level).

Back in the Stanze di Raffaello you enter the **Stanza d'Eliodoro**. Raphael's masterpiece, *Cacciata d'Eliodoro* (Expulsion of

Heliodorus from the Temple), on the main wall (to the right as you enter from the Sala dei Chiaroscuri), depicts Julius' military victory over foreign powers. To the left is *Mass of Bolsena*, showing Julius II paying homage to the relic of a 13th century miracle at Orvieto. Next is *Leone X ferma l'invasione di Attila* (Leo X Repulsing Attila), by Raphael and his school, and on the fourth wall is *Liberazione di San Pietro* (Liberation of St Peter), which depicts St Peter being freed from prison, but is actually an allusion to Pope Leo's imprisonment after the battle of Ravenna (also the metaphorical subject of the Attila fresco).

In the **Stanza della Segnatura** is another masterpiece by Raphael and perhaps his best known work: *La Scuola d'Atene* (The School of Athens), featuring philosophers and scholars gathered around Plato and Aristotle. The lone figure in front of the steps is believed to be a portrait of Michelangelo, who was painting the Cappella Sistina at the time. The figure of Plato (pointing to the sky) is said to be a portrait of Leonardo da Vinci. In the lower right, the figure of Euclide (bent over and drawing with a compass) is Bramante. Raphael included a self portrait at the lower right of the fresco (second figure from right). Opposite is *La Disputa del Sacramento* (Dispute over the Holy Sacrament), also by Raphael.

From Raphael's rooms, go down the stairs to the **Appartamento Borgia**, but only to see the ceiling in the first room, decorated with frescoes by Bernardino Pinturicchio. The Vaticano collection of modern religious art was installed in the Borgia apartments in 1973, but it really isn't worth visiting.

Cappella Sistina

The private papal chapel, completed in 1484 for Pope Sixtus IV, the Cappella Sistina (Sistine Chapel) is used for some papal functions and for the conclave which elects the popes. But the chapel is best known for one of the most famous works of art in the world: Michelangelo's wonderful frescoes of the *Genesis* (Creation) on the

Musical Spoilsports

Gregorio Allegri (1582-1652) is best know for his setting of the *Miserere*, which is still sung in the Cappella Sistina each year during Holy Week.

Ironically, the stratospheric treble line which rises so thrillingly above the plainsong chant is part of the ornamentation which individual singers would have added, and therefore not written by Allegri at all.

Legend has it that the manuscript was kept under lock and key until the 14-year-old Mozart wrote out the jealously guarded piece from memory after one hearing. Musicologists with no romantic sense have pointed out that this would have been possible for anybody with perfect pitch and a good memory, and an absolute pushover for someone of Mozart's prodigious talents.

barrel-vaulted ceiling, and the *Giudizio Universale* (Last Judgment) on the end wall. Both have been restored; the ceiling was unveiled after a 10-year restoration project in 1990 and work on the Last Judgment was completed in 1994, and the rich, vibrant colours used by Michelangelo have been brought back to the surface.

Michelangelo was commissioned by Pope Julius II to paint the ceiling and although very reluctant to take on the job (he never considered himself a painter), he started work on it in 1508. The complex and grand composition which Michelangelo devised to cover the 800 sq m of ceiling took him four years to complete. He worked on scaffolding which the restorers believe was inserted into holes under the windows. The restorers also learned much about the way in which the artist worked and how his painting skill developed as he progressed through the great project.

Vasari records Michelangelo's suffering and frustration, as well as his problems with an impatient Pope Julius and the fact that he

Waiting for the White Smoke

Despite his failing health, John Paul II looks like he will see in the Jubilee Year 2000, for which he has been planning for almost a decade. However, in recent years, there has been significant speculation about his possible successor, with bookmakers offering odds on possible future incumbents, and the world's media poised to descend on Rome for the Conclave of cardinals which elects a new pope.

The Conclave will be made up a maximum of 120 cardinals, none of whom may be over 80. They will be locked up in uncomfortable conditions inside il Vaticano, with no communication to the outside world, until a new pope is chosen through a series of secret ballots.

What are the requirements for the Roman Catholic Church's top job? There is a list of unwritten prerequisites. The candidate needs to be well known in the Curia, the papal court and government of the Roman Catholic Church. He must have a reputation as a theologian and must have written prominent Vatican documents. He must also have worked in one of the Church's international organisations. In addition, the candidate must be in good health (to avoid a repeat of John Paul I's month-long papacy); he should be neither too young (there's a feeling that John Paul II's 20-year papacy has been too long) nor too old; and he must be media-friendly and capable of projecting a charismatic image. On top of all that, candidates must never appear actually to be campaigning for the job.

Almost all the current cardinals were appointed by John Paul II, and thus he has ensured the continuation of his own legacy. Although the election of a new pope frees the Church to change its course, the new pope cannot actively contradict the teaching of his predecessor, so even if a more liberal pope is appointed, contradictory proclamations will be curtailed.

Ill health has ruled out a number of former front runners, including the Brazilian Cardinal

did the work almost entirely alone, after dismissing in disgust the Florentine masters he had gathered to help him.

Twenty-four years later Michelangelo was commissioned by Clement VII to paint the Last Judgment (the pope died shortly afterwards and the work was executed under Paul III). Two frescoes by Perugino were destroyed to make way for the new painting, which caused great controversy in its day. Criticism of its dramatic, swirling mass of predominantly naked bodies was summarily dismissed by Michelangelo, who depicted one of his greatest critics, Paul III's master of ceremonies, as Minos with

donkey's ears. As with the Creation, the Last Judgment was blackened by candle smoke and incense, but it was also damaged by poor restorations and by the addition of clothes to cover some of the nude figures. One of Michelangelo's students, Daniele da Volterra, was commissioned by Pius IV to do the cover-up job.

Looking towards the Last Judgement, the scenes down the middle of the ceiling represent nine scenes from the book of Genesis: the Division of Day from Night; Creation of the Sun, Moon and Planets; Creation of the heavens; Separation of land from sea; Creation of Adam; Creation of

Waiting for the White Smoke

Lucas Moreira Neves, who suffers from diabetes, and the Belgian Godfried Daneels, Archbishop of Brussels, who had a heart attack in late 1997.

One possible contender is the charismatic and clever Nigerian Cardinal Francis Arinze, a popular figure who has been in charge of the Church's ecumenical relations, with Islam in particular, since 1985. Just as John Paul II has dealt with Communism during his papacy, perhaps Arinze will be the one to be able to handle the Church's relations with other religions into the next century. But is the Catholic world ready for a black African pope? Arinze would not be the first – that honour was taken by Gelasius I who reigned from 492 to 496 – but the excitement and media attention that greeted the first mention of him as a possible candidate in the early 1990s has probably not worked in his favour.

The charismatic Archbishop of Milano, Carlo Maria Martini, a brilliant linguist and preacher, famous for his pastoral work, would be a popular choice, but he has several things against him. He has been branded as a liberal (relative to John Paul II's hard-line conservatism), he is prepared to be critical of the Church, and believes in consultation and debate, which the Curia shuns. Secondly, he is a Jesuit; and not only has there never been a Jesuit pope, but there has never even been a Jesuit cardinal who was seriously considered as a candidate.

Several of the most recently elected cardinals (who gained their red hats early in 1998) may also be in the running. These include the Archbishop of Vienna, Christoph Schönborn (who at 53 is possibly a bit young), another Eastern European, Miloslav Vlk, from Prague, Dionigi Tettamanzi from Genova, and Francis George of Chicago.

After so long with a foreigner at the helm of the Church, and given that the pope is also Bishop of Rome, it is not unreasonable to assume that an Italian will be given the job. In this case the scale could tip in favour of Vatican insiders, the Secretary of State Cardinal Angelo Sodano, whose friendship with General Augusto Pinochet when he served as Nuncio in Chile stands against him, or Cardinal Achille Silvestrini, Prefect of the Congregation of Oriental Churches. Silvestrini is well regarded and has pushed the role of the Oriental Churches as a bridge to the East, but his age (he will be 76 in October 1999) is not in his favour.

Only one thing is sure. When Pope John Paul II dies and a group of men in red hats get together to elect his successor, the reverberations will be felt around the world, and Rome once again will be the focus of the world's attention.

Eve; Temptation and Expulsion of Adam and Eve from the garden of Eden; Noah's sacrifice; the Flood; the Drunkenness of Noah. These main scenes are framed by the *Ignudi*, athletic male nudes. Next to them, on the lower curved part of the vault, separated by *trompe l'oeuil* cornices, are large figures of Hebrew Prophets and androgynous pagan Sibyls. In the lunettes over the windows are the ancestors of Christ.

The walls of the chapel were painted by famous Renaissance artists including Botticelli, Domenico Ghirlandaio, Pinturicchio and Luca Signorelli. Even if you find it hard to drag your attention away from Michelangelo's frescoes, take time to appreciate these paintings, which were executed in the late 15th century and depict events in the life of Moses (to the left looking at the *Last Judgment)* and Christ (to the right). However, the first parts of each cycle, the Finding of Moses and the Birth of Christ, were the Perugino frescoes destroyed to make way for the Last Judgement.

The second fresco on the right depicting the *Tentazione di Cristo* (Temptations of Christ) and the *Purificazione del lebbroso* (Cleansing of the Leper) by Botticelli is particularly beautiful. Note the typical Botticelli maiden in diaphanous dress in the foreground. In the fifth fresco on the left which depicts the Punishment of the Rebels), Botticelli uses the Arco di Costantino as a backdrop for the action and includes a self-portrait (the figure in black behind Moses on the far right). Ghirlandaio's *Vocazione di Pietro e Andrea* (Calling of Peter and Andrew), the third fresco on the right, includes among the crowd of onlookers portraits of prominent contemporary figures. Perugino's *Consegna delle Chiavi* (Christ Giving the Keys to St Peter), the fifth fresco on the right, also includes a self-portrait (the fifth figure from the right).

Returning to the Quattro Cancelli area, you pass through the splendid frescoed halls of the **Biblioteca Apostolica Vaticana** (the Vatican library) which was founded by Nicholas V in 1450. The library contains over 1.5 million volumes including illuminated manuscripts, early printed books, prints and drawings, and coins. Selected items from the collection are displayed in the **Salone Sistino**, which has particularly beautiful frescoes on the ceiling and walls. If you haven't run out of time, take a moment to stop and look.

Castel Sant'Angelo

Originally the mausoleum of Hadrian, this building was converted into a fortress for the popes in the 6th century AD. It was named Castel Sant'Angelo by Pope Gregory the Great in 590 AD, after he saw a vision of an angel above the structure heralding the end of a plague in Rome. The fortress was linked to the Vatican palaces in 1277 by a wall and passageway, used often by the popes to escape to the fortress in times of threat. During the 16th century sacking of Rome by Emperor Charles V, hundreds of people lived in the fortress for months.

The Castel Sant'Angelo is open Tuesday to Sunday from 9 am to 8 pm (admission up to 7 pm). Admission is L8000.

Hadrian built the **Ponte Sant'Angelo** across the Tevere in 136 AD to provide an approach to his mausoleum. It collapsed in 1450 and was subsequently rebuilt, incorporating parts of the ancient bridge. In the 17th century, Bernini and his pupils sculpted the figures of angels which now line the pedestrian-only bridge.

The area between il Vaticano and the Tevere is known as the Borgo. Not much is left of the medieval (and earlier) buildings, as Mussolini had the area virtually razed to the ground to make way for Via della Conciliazione.

ACTIVITIES

Walking and cycling are great ways to get around Rome. See the Rome Walks and Getting Around chapters.

Swimming

If you're in Rome during the hot summer months, chances are you'll want to cool off before long. If you can't be bothered making the trek out to the beaches on the Lazio coast (see Excursions chapter) there are a few public swimming pools you could try.

Generally they are well outside the city centre and can be difficult to reach on public transport (indications are given). Admission is usually around L8000 to L15,000 with a L10,000 annual membership fee payable on the first visit.

Bear in mind that these pools usually close for part of August (some close for the whole month) and opening hours and days vary. Some pools also require a doctor's certificate before you are allowed to swim. Call first to check.

Via Manduria 21 (☎ 06 259 23 80) off Via Prenestina east of the city. Take tram No 14 from Via Turati near Stazione Termini. Get off just after it turns right into Via Togliatti, then follow Via Ascoli Satriano and Via Conversano to Via Manduria.

Viale dei Consoli (☎ 06 76 90 06 27) off Via Tuscolana south-east of the city. Take Metro Linea A to Numidio Quadrato then follow Via San Curione to Viale dei Consoli.

Via Bravetta (☎ 06 66 16 09 85) beyond Villa Doria Pamphili park. Take Bus No 98 from Via Paola at the end of Corso Vittorio Emanuele II.

There are also several privately run pools, which are a little more accessible, including pools run by upmarket hotels where you can swim and lounge – at a price.

Piscina delle Rose (☎ 06 592 67 17), Viale America 20, EUR. Take Metro Linea B to EUR Palasport. Open 9 am to 7 pm daily, June to September. L18,000 full day, L13,000 half day.

Sporting Club Villa Pamphili, (☎ 06 66 15 85 55) Via della Nocetta 107

Cavalieri Hilton Hotel (☎ 06 350 91), Via Cadlolo 101, Monte Mario. Open 9 am to 7 pm, May to September. L70,000 Monday to Friday, L85,000 weekends (children under 18 are half price). Take bus No 907 or No 991 from Piazza del Risorgimento to Piazzale Medaglie D'Oro.

Hotel Parco dei Principi (☎ 06 85 44 21), Via G Frescobaldi 5, (on the north side of Villa Borghese). Open 10 am to 6 pm daily, May to September. L50,000 Monday to Friday, L70,000 weekends (20% discount for children). Take bus No 3 or No 910 from Stazione Termini or No 52 from Piazza San Silvestro.

Holiday Inn St Peter's (☎ 06 66 42), Via Aurelia Antica 415 (beyond Villa Pamphili park). The pool is open from May to September. L40,000 Monday to Friday, L50,000 weekends. Take bus No 98 or No 881 from Via Paola at the end of Corso Vittorio Emanuele II.

Jogging

Good places to jog include Circo Massimo, Villa Borghese, Villa Ada and Villa Doria Pamphili. See relevant sections earlier in this chapter.

Horse Riding

The prices at the exclusive Il Galoppatoio club in Villa Borghese (Map 4, ☎ 06 322 67 97, Via del Galoppatoio 25) make horse riding an expensive exercise. You pay for a minimum of 10 lessons (L300,000) plus an annual registration fee of L400,000 and about L40,000 insurance.

COURSES
Language Courses

Centro Linguisitico Italiano Dante Alighieri (Map: Greater Rome, ☎ 06 44 23 14 00, fax 06 44 23 10 07, clidar@tin.it, www.clidante.it) at Piazza Bologna 1, runs courses throughout the year. Four-week courses (four hours per day) cost L950,000 with books an extra L36,000. Groups are kept to a maximum of 12 students.

Berlitz (Map: Around Piazza Navona, ☎ 06 683 40 00 or 06 68 80 69 51, www .berlitz.com), Via di Torre Argentina 21 (and two other locations), has four-week intensive courses for L660,000.

Centro Studi Flaminio (Map 3, ☎ 06 361 09 03 or 06 361 08 96), Via Flaminia 21, 50m from Flaminia Metro station (Linea A), has intensive (two hours per day) and extensive (four hours per week) courses, for a total of 32 hours for each of four levels. Courses cost L360,000.

Italiaidea (Map: Around Piazza Navona, ☎ 06 68 30 76 20, fax 06 689 29 97) is located near Campo de' Fiori at Piazza della Cancelleria 85 and has four-week intensive courses of three hours per day which cost L750,000 (plus L30,000 enrolment fee).

Istituto Italiano (Map 6, ☎ 06 70 45 21 38, fax 06 70 08 51 22, istital@uni.net, www.istitutoitaliano.com) in Via Machiavelli 33 (near Piazza Vittorio) has four-week intensive courses of either three hours per day (L760,000) or 4½ hours per day (L1,020,000). A L100,000 enrolment fee applies and covers books and other teaching materials. There are seven levels and a minimum of three and a maximum of 12 students in each group.

In the same area is Torre di Babele Centro di Lingua e Cultura Italiana (Map 6, ☎ 06 700 84 34, fax 06 70 49 71 50, info@torredibabele.it) at Via Bixio 74. Intensive courses of four hours per day run for two-week blocks and cost L530,000. There is also a L50,000 enrolment fee which covers books and cultural excursions.

Cooking Courses

Well known cookery writer Diane Seed, author of *The Top One Hundred Pasta Sauces* and *Diane Seed's Roman Kitchen*, runs rather expensive cooking courses four or five times a year from her kitchen in the Doria Pamphili palace. Week-long courses cost around L1,250,000. For information call ☎ 06 679 71 09 or fax 06 679 71 03.

Rome Walks

Rome is so densely packed with important monuments that it is easy to feel overwhelmed and confused by the juxtaposition of art and architecture from so many different periods in the city's long history. You might, for instance, find yourself looking at a church built in the Middle Ages, which incorporates the precious marbles and columns of a Roman temple which once stood on the site. The same church might have been rebuilt several times and could be a mix of architectural styles, from Romanesque to Baroque.

As you dash around the city, taking in the obligatory sights such as the Colosseo, the Foro Romano and il Vaticano (certainly more than enough to keep you very busy for a few days), you can too easily overlook the rich architectural and artistic heritage of the city, which is visible in almost every narrow alleyway and piazza in the form of palaces, fountains, churches and more.

The three walks outlined in this chapter are designed to help you discover this heritage *con calma* (roughly translated as calmly taking your time). The time needed to complete the following itineraries is not stated, because this depends on the number of stops you make en route and your individual pace. Each route can take up to a full day, or if you want to enjoy them at a really relaxed pace, you can extend them over two days. The itineraries, especially Walk 3 on the Via Appia Antica, can also be done by bicycle (for information regarding bicycle hire see Getting Around chapter).

The first walk starts on the Gianicolo from where you have a glorious panorama of the city centre, takes you though the medieval neighbourhood of Trastevere and across the Tevere to the beautiful Aventino.

The second walk concentrates on Ghetto area, takes you up to the Campidoglio, the traditional seat of Roman government and ends with a spectacular view of the Foro Romano.

The third walk is the longest in terms of distance, starting near the Terme di Caracalla and taking you along the Via Appia Antica, the most famous of the ancient Roman consular roads.

WALK 1: PIAZZALE GARIBALDI TO PIAZZALE UGO LA MALFA

This is an easy route that crosses the southwestern confines of the historic centre of Rome, taking in parks and gardens, breathtaking panoramas and significant Romanesque churches, with centuries-old mosaics. It takes you from the fortified bastions of the Gianicolo, the hill that dominates the centre of Rome, through the lively streets of Trastevere and up to the Giardino degli Aranci on the Aventino hill. It ends at a very panoramic point, from where you have a view across the remains of the Circo Massimo to the Palatino, the hill that was once home to the Roman emperors.

City bus No 870 runs up to Piazzale Garibaldi from the terminus in Via Paola at the north-west end of Corso Vittorio Emanuele II, near Ponte Principe Amedeo Savoia Aosta.

In **Piazzale Garibaldi**, which sits like a terrace on top of the 17th century bastions of the Gianicolo (82m above sea level) the bronze equestrian statue of General Garibaldi faces the city of Rome, turning its back on Michelangelo's huge dome of the Basilica di San Pietro as a reminder that the battles fought by the general against the papacy and the Bourbon rulers of Naples led to the unification of Italy in 1870.

From here there is a marvellous panorama and it is interesting to see how many monuments you can identify. (There is an even better panorama – the best in Rome – if you walk about 200m north, just past the elegant Villa Lante, built in 1518 by Giulio Romano on the remains of the Roman villa of Marziale.) You have a view extending from Castel Sant'Angelo to the Villa Borghese park behind the pale façade of the Villa Medici with its two symmetrical turrets to

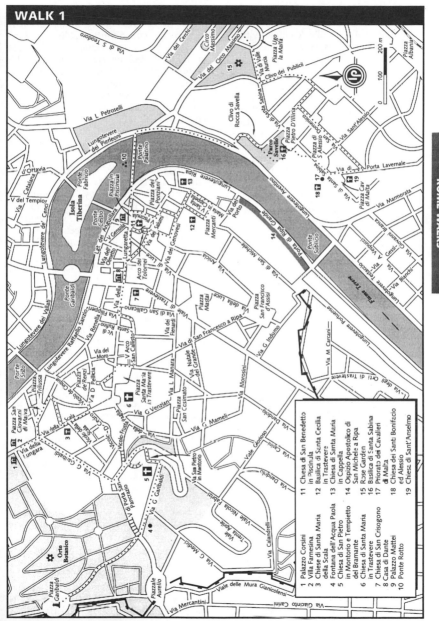

WALK 1

1   Palazzo Corsini
2   Villa Farnesina
3   Chiese di Santa Maria della Scala
4   Fontana dell'Acqua Paola
5   Chiesa di San Pietro in Montorio e Tempietto del Bramante
6   Chiesa di Santa Maria in Trastevere
7   Chiesa di San Crisogono
8   Casa di Dante
9   Palazzo Mattei
10 Ponte Rotto
11 Chiesa di San Benedetto in Piscinula
12 Basilica di Santa Cecilia in Trastevere
13 Chiesa di Santa Maria in Cappella
14 Ospizio Apostolico di San Michele a Ripa
15 Rose Garden
16 Basilica di Santa Sabina
17 Priorato dei Cavalieri di Malta
18 Chiesa dei Santi Bonifacio ed Alessio
19 Chiesa di Sant'Anselmo

the left (north-east), and across to the majestic Roman remains of the Palatino and the leafy outline of the Colle Aventino with its churches and gardens on the right (south-east).

On a clear day, the domes, palaces and campanili of Baroque Rome stand out against the backdrop of the foothills of the Apennines, terminating to the south-east among the outlines of the volcanic Colli Albani. Every day at midday in the square beneath the terrace of Piazzale Garibaldi a troop of gunners notifies the city that it is lunch-time with a round of canon fire.

To your right as you are looking out over the panorama, the so-called *passeggiata del Gianicolo* (Gianicolo walk) divides in two. Take the path to the left, which descends between tall trees, and pass the 17th century Villa Aurelia (now part of the American Academy in Rome) on your right to emerge onto the semi-circular piazza in front of the **Fontana dell'Acqua Paola**, from where there is another famed view of Rome. The fountain is known locally as the *Fontanone del Gianicolo* (big fountain of the Janiculum) because of its monumental form, inspired by the triumphal arches of ancient Rome. The spot is often frequented by Roman newly-weds in fairy-tale outfits and their photographers in search of appropriate backdrops for their snaps. The fountain was built by order of Pope Paul V in 1608 to showcase the workings of the newly-restored aqueduct originally built by the emperor Trajan.

Go down Via Garibaldi until you reach the nearby church of **San Pietro in Montorio**, built in the 9th century on the spot thought to have been the site where St Peter was crucified upside down. The current structure dates from the end of the 15th century, when Ferdinand II of Aragon ordered it to be rebuilt. To the right of the elegant Renaissance façade with its Gothic rose window, a door leads into the modest cloister of the adjoining convent and the famous **Tempietto di Bramante**, built in 1508-1512 and used as a model by numerous architects in the early 16th century (at

the time of writing the Tempietto di Bramante was closed for restoration but it is expected to reopen for the Jubilee). Behind the Tempietto di Bramante, a double flight of stairs, added by Bernini in the 17th century, leads to the crypt where an opening in the floor is all that remains of the place where St Peter was thought to have been martyred. A gate to the left of the door as you leave the cloister leads to Via San Pietro in Montorio, a flight of steps, lined with the stations of the cross, which cuts down to Via Garibaldi.

Turn left and follow Via Garibaldi downhill to reach the intersection with Via della Lungara, commissioned by Pope Julius II at the beginning of the 16th century to link Trastevere with the Vatican. Go through the **Porta Settimiana**, a 16th century reconstruction of an ancient gate in the Roman Mura Aureliane, adorned with Ghibelline battlements, and you come to the elegant Via Corsini on the left.

The road runs alongside the 18th century Palazzo Corsini to Rome's **Orto Botanico** (Botanical Gardens), founded in the 19th century in the former gardens of the palace. The gardens are noted for their collections of orchids and tropical species and are an ideal place for a rest. (Open Monday to Saturday from 9.30 am to 5.30 pm. Admission is L4000.)

Back on Via della Lungara, walk the length of **Palazzo Corsini**, which is now a museum housing paintings dating from the 14th to 18th centuries, including work by Caravaggio, Tiziano, Guido Reni, Fra Angelico, Rubens and Poussin. Opposite is the **Villa Farnesina**. Built in the early 16th century, it is one of the first examples of a single-standing residence surrounded by gardens and features the *Galatea* fresco by Raphael in the Loggia della Galatea (see Things to See & Do).

Retrace your steps back through the Porta Settimiano and turn left into Via Santa Dorotea to reach the heart of characteristic Trastevere. From the small Piazza San Giovanni della Malva, with a church of the same name, turn right into Via Benedetta.

Note the two-storey 15th century house at No 20/21, with arched windows typical of the period. Shortly afterwards, turn right into the narrow Vicolo del Bologna (the street sign is a few metres from the corner), to reach a tiny triangular square with a drinking fountain.

From here, take the right-hand fork of Vicolo del Bologna (the left-hand fork has the same name) and you'll soon reach the 17th century church and adjacent Carmelite monastery of **Santa Maria della Scala**. On the second floor of the monastery the monks have left a perfectly-preserved *speziaria* (pharmacy) dating from the 18th century. Groups of 10 or more can ask to see the pharmacy with an appointment (L5000 optional donation suggested). For bookings contact Dr Piccioni on ☎ 06 440 42 37. These monks are renowned for having commissioned and then rejected Caravaggio's *Il transito della Vergine*, now in the Louvre.

Turn left into Via della Scala and after about 50m turn left again into Vicolo del Cinque. Straight away you come to a five-road junction. Take Via della Pelliccia in front of you on the right, and follow it until you get to the large Piazza de' Renzi, now used as a car park. Here, on the left at No 20 there is a small medieval house and two restaurants, including Augusto, which is famous for its informal style, Roman-style food and budget prices (see Places to Eat). Back in Via della Pelliccia, turn left immediately into Vicolo del Piede, and when this bends to the right turn left into Via Fonte dell'Olio.

Follow a tight s-bend in the road and you'll soon catch sight of a beautiful fountain designed by Carlo Fontana in the 17th century. The fountain stands in the centre of the **Piazza Santa Maria in Trastevere**, the heart of this lively neighbourhood and one of Rome's most picturesque piazzas. Dominating the piazza is the basilica of the same name, thought to have been the first church in Rome to be officially dedicated to the Virgin Mary. Tradition has it that the church was established by Pope Calixtus in the early third century and subsequently rebuilt by Julius I in 337 AD on the spot where in 38 BC oil had miraculously gushed out of the earth (hence the name Via Fonte dell' Olio). The current church dates back to 1138 when it was rebuilt by Innocent II using second-hand building material. For instance, the irregular columns and capitals in the central nave come from the Terme di Caracalla (see Things to See & Do).

From Piazza Santa Maria in Trastevere, turn right to reach Piazza San Calisto and turn left into Via dell'Arco di San Calisto, passing under an arch. Don't miss the tiny medieval house at No 42. Said to be the smallest house in Rome, it has an external staircase and is decorated with a small, painted figure of the Madonna. At the end of the street, turn left into Piazza Santa Rufina. From here you can see the graceful 12th century Romanesque **belltower** of the Chiesa di SS Rufina e Seconda inside the convent of the same name.

On the far side of the piazza turn right into Via della Lungaretta and follow it to the busy Viale Trastevere. On the right is the **Chiesa di San Crisogono**, a Baroque reconstruction of a medieval church dating from 1123. The medieval church itself stands on top of a 5th century early Christian basilica. The sacristan will take you down to the basilica on request for L3000. The three naves in the Baroque interior are decorated with a beautiful cosmati floor dating from the 13th century and are separated by granite columns taken from ancient Roman ruins. The church is open Monday to Saturday from 7 to 11.30 am and 4 to 7.30 pm. On Sunday and public holidays it opens 8 am to 1 pm and 4 to 7.30 pm.

Cross the road and continue along Via della Lungaretta, past the so-called **Casa di Dante**, a 13th century towered stronghold once belonging to the patrician Anguillara family, and now a centre for Dante studies.

Continuing on, you get to Piazza del Drago. Here you have two options. If you want to wander through some of Trastevere's more characteristic, deserted streets, go to the diagonally-opposite corner of the square and turn left into Vicolo del Buco. Skirt the Romanesque apse of Santa Maria della Luce, built in 1100, cross Via della Luce and walk along Via dei Salumi. Before long you'll reach Via Anicia on the right, with the medieval Arco dei Tolomei on the left.

If you'd prefer not to bother with this detour, continue out of Piazza del Drago along Via della Lungaretta. At No 160 is quite a rare sight: an original 14th century house with Gothic console-arches and an external staircase. Just past the house is Piazza in Piscinula, from where you go up to the right along Via Arco dei Tolomei, under a characteristic medieval arch named after the Sienese family that lived in this area in the 14th century. On the other side of the arch you will find yourself at the junction with Via dei Salumi, from where the earlier mentioned detour emerges.

Follow Via Anicia, and at the next intersection you find yourself in front of the beautiful Romanesque apse of the **Basilica di Santa Cecilia**. Turn left into Via dei Genovesi and shortly after, turn right into Via di Santa Cecilia and the piazza of the same name, from where you can enter the basilica. This church contains numerous artistic treasures and is definitely worth visiting (see Things to See & Do) although you'll need to time your arrival carefully to coincide with its short opening hours.

From here, go into the adjacent Piazza dei Mercanti, and take Via Santa Maria in Cappella to the left. You will soon find a courtyard containing the small, run-down church of **Santa Maria in Cappella**, which has a lovely Romanesque belltower with two orders of mullioned windows, dating from the 12th century. Turn left into Via Jandolo, which becomes Via dei Genovesi and turn right into the narrow Vicolo dell'Atleta, so called because of the discovery here in 1844 of the statue of Apoxyomenos, the *Atleta* (athlete) now in the Museo Pio Clementino in the Musei Vaticani. The medieval building at No 14, with a 13th century loggia, is thought to be the oldest medieval synagogue left in Rome.

Turn left into Via dei Salumi, then right into Via in Piscinula to reach Piazza in Piscinula near the Tevere river. There's a snack bar here, where you can buy water or a gelato. On the side of Piazza in Piscinula closest to river, is **Palazzo Mattei**, a medieval building dating from 1300 and restored in 1926. On the opposite side of the square you can see the smallest belltower in Rome.

The 12th century Romanesque structure contains a bell dating from 1069 AD. It is part of the **Chiesa di San Benedetto in Piscinula**, which contains the cell where St Benedict, the founder of the Benedictine Order, prayed. To visit, ring the doorbell at the convent at No 40. Daily opening times are 9 to 11 am and 4 to 6 pm.

From the piazza go right along Via della Lungaretta until you get to Piazza Castellani. Taking care of the aggressive Roman traffic, cross over to the Ponte Palatino. To your left is the Isola Tiberina and the surviving arch of the so-called **Ponte Rotto** (broken bridge), also known as the **Senatorio**. This is a Renaissance reconstruction of the ancient Pons Aemilius, the first Roman bridge to be built in stone in 182 BC. This reconstruction still bears the traces of Pope Gregory XIII's coat of arms featuring a dragon. It collapsed in 1598 during the most violent of the disastrous floods that plagued Rome before the construction of the river embankments in 1900.

On the opposite side of the river, you can see a large arch dug out of the wall of the embankment, which marks the mouth of the **Cloaca Maxima**, the drainage system begun by the Romans as early as the 6th century BC to drain the valley of the Foro Romano which became an extensive sewerage system as the ancient city developed.

As you cross the bridge, enjoy the view of the city. On the left you can see the square dome of the synagogue and the large dome of the Basilica di San Pietro in the distance. On the right, you can see the leafy heights of the Aventino and the long 17th-18th century façade (334m) of the former **Ospizio Apostolico di San Michele a Ripa** on the Trastevere side of the river. This now houses the Ministero per i Beni Culturali e Ambientali (Ministry for Culture and the Environment).

Once across the bridge, turn right into the busy Lungotevere Aventino and follow the river for about 200m. On the other side of the road, off Via Santa Maria in Cosmedin, just past the traffic lights of Via della Greca, you will notice a flight of steps called Clivo di Rocca Savella, leading up onto the Aventino hill through the walls of a 10th century fortress. The fortress was built by Emperor Alberico II and subsequently inherited by the Savelli family. At the top, a narrow footpath leads to the **Parco Savello**, also known as the Giardino degli Aranci because of its orange trees, where there is a panoramic terrace looking over the Gianicolo and the historic centre. Exiting from the opposite side of the park you will reach the 5th century **Basilica di Santa Sabina**, one of the most important early Christian basilicas in Rome (see Things to See & Do).

Turning right into Via di Santa Sabina, you'll pass another panoramic garden and will come to the **Chiesa dei Santi Bonifacio ed Alessio**, a medieval church rebuilt on numerous occasions and almost completely restored in 1750. It still has a lovely Romanesque campanile and a cosmati door dating from 1200. The church is open daily from 8.30 am to 12.30 pm and 3.30 to 6.30 pm from April to October. From November to March it closes at 5 pm.

At the end of Via di Santa Sabina is the **Piazza dei Cavalieri di Malta**, designed by Piranesi, famous for his etchings of Rome, in 1734 for the Order of the Knights of Malta. Join the line of people queuing to peer through the keyhole in the door that leads to the splendid gardens (accessible only on special occasions) of the **Priorato di Malta**, the headquarters of the order.

From the piazza, take Via di Porta Lavernale, passing the **Chiesa di Sant'Anselmo**, a 20th century church in Romanesque-Lombard style, to reach the Piazza Sant'Anselmo. Here, turn left into Via di San Domenico and follow it until you get to the

nearby Piazza Giunone Regina. Go past the three arches of a sober building dating from the Fascist period, turn right into Via Sant'Alberto Magno and you come to Largo Arrigo VII. Turn left out of Largo Arrigo on the far side, passing beneath the pine trees in the gardens, and descend to the left along Clivo dei Publici. Turn right into Via di Valle Murcia, which passes through the city **rose garden**, open to the public in May and June when the flowers are in bloom. The walk finishes in Piazzale Ugo La Malfa, site of a monument to Giuseppe Mazzini, another father of Italian unity.

Walk across the busy Via del Circo Massimo to admire the view of the ruins on the Palatino, site of the ancient Imperial residence. What looks like an oval park between you and the Palatino is actually the remains of the **Circo Massimo**, where up to 250,000 spectators could watch chariot races and other spectacles (see Things to See & Do).

At the end of the route, turn right out of Piazzale Ugo La Malfa and follow the road downhill to reach the Circo Massimo stop on the Metropolitana Linea B. From here you can take the subway to Stazione Termini. Otherwise, a number of buses serve Piazzale Ugo La Malfa, including bus No 81 going to the Colosseo and San Giovanni in Laterano. On the other side of Circo Massimo on Via dei Cerchi the same bus goes towards Piazza Venezia and Piazza Navona, the Mausoleo di Augusto and il Vaticano.

WALK 2: LARGO DI TORRE ARGENTINA TO THE PIAZZA DEL CAMPIDOGLIO

This is a short route through the heart of Rome, an area dense with important monuments, where Renaissance buildings and the impressive ruins of classical antiquity coexist. It explores the courtyards of patrician palaces and the narrow streets of one of the city's more characteristic areas. You end up at Michelangelo's beautiful Piazza del Campidoglio and nearby there is a breathtaking view over the Foro Romano.

Teatro di Marcello

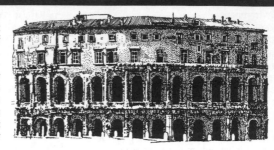

This theatre was originally planned by Julius Caesar, but was unfinished at the time of his assassination in 44 BC. Augustus inherited the project and named it after Marcellus, his nephew who had died prematurely in 23 BC. Although the theatre was in use by 17 BC, it was not formally dedicated until 13 or 11 BC.

Capable of holding over 20,000 people, seated according to social status, the Teatro di Marcello was the most important of Rome's three ancient theatres.

The theatre was restored on many occasions following fires and earthquakes, until it finally fell into disuse and became a quarry for building material. In 365 the theatre was partially demolished and the stone used to restore the nearby Ponte Cestio.

The Perleone family converted it into a fortress during the 11th and 12th centuries, and in the 16th century Baldassarre Peruzzi converted the fortress into a luxurious palace for the Savelli, preserving the original form of the theatre. In 1712 the palace was inherited by the Orsini who partly restored the theatre.

The original building was partially restored in 1926. Open air concerts are held at Teatro Marcello nightly in summer. The theatre and the ruins at its base can be visited only be request from the Sovrintendenza Archeologica del Comune di Roma.

It is easy to get to Largo di Torre Argentina since it is very well-served by public transport, including buses from Piazza Venezia and Stazione Termini (Nos H, 64, 640), from the Vaticano (Nos 64, 62), from San Giovanni in Laterano and the Colosseo (No 87) and from Via del Corso and Via Veneto (No 56). The No 8 tram from Trastevere-Casaletto terminates in Largo di Torre Argentina.

Start on the south side of the large and noisy Largo di Torre Argentina and archaeological zone, at the corner Via delle Botteghe Oscure and Via Florida. Cross Piazza della Enciclopedia Italiana, skirting the elegant **Palazzo Mattei di Paganica**, built in 1541 and which now houses the Istituto per l'Enciclopedia Italiana. This is one of five palaces built by the patrician Mattei family in the area, causing it to be renamed *L'isola dei Mattei* (Mattei Island) in the mid-16th century.

If you cross Piazza Paganica and follow Via Paganica you come to the charming **Piazza Mattei** with its elegant **Fontana delle Tartarughe**, designed by Giacomo della Porta. The bronzes, executed by Taddeo Landini, were added between 1581 and 1584. Legend has it that the fountain was built in a single night for the Duke of Mattei, who owned the surrounding palaces. The duke had apparently just lost all his money and consequently his fiancée, and wanted to prove to her father that he was still capable of great things. In the piazza at No 10 is the 16th century **Palazzo Costaguti** and at Nos 17-19 **Palazzo di Giacomo Mattei**. The building on the right has a beautiful 15th century courtyard with a staircase and an open gallery.

Go to the left along Via dei Funari and enter the **Palazzo Mattei di Giove** at No 3. Built by Carlo Maderno in 1598, today it houses the Centro Italiano di Studi Americani (the Italian Centre for American Studies); sections are open to the public. The palazzo, which is adorned with numerous pieces of ancient Roman sculpture, bas-reliefs and stuccoes, is a good example of the taste of the noble classes for all things classical, which flowered along with humanism during the Renaissance. The courtyards contain ancient Roman bas-reliefs set into the walls, and busts and statues from what remains of the Mattei collection, once one of the most valuable collections of Roman antiquities. The monumental staircase decorated with classical stucco and ancient sculptures leads to a library. There is a loggia, from where you get a better view of the decorative scheme.

The balustrade is decorated with 16th century busts of numerous emperors.

In the library, there is large hall, with ceiling frescoes and interesting Renaissance floor with the family coat of arms at its centre. The palace's entrance area is open to the public from Monday to Saturday. The library is open Monday to Thursday from 10 am to 6 pm and on Friday from 10 am to 2 pm.

From Piazza Mattei take Via della Reginella, where there are workshops of local artisans. The street passes through the heart of the old Jewish ghetto area (see the boxed text 'Anti-Semitism in Rome') around Via del Portico d'Ottavia. A short detour to the right brings you to the curious **Casa di Lorenzo Manilio** at Via del Portico d'Ottavia 1. The building was constructed in 1468, or, according to the Latin inscription on its façade, 2221 years after the traditional founding of Rome in 753 BC

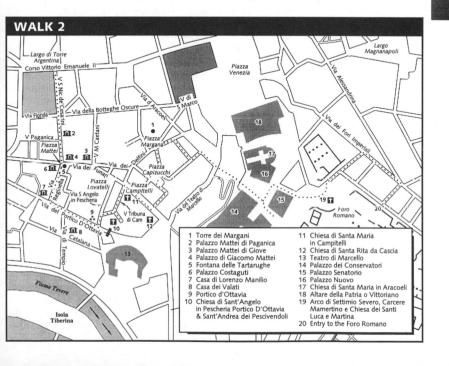

WALK 2

1   Torre dei Margani
2   Palazzo Mattei di Paganica
3   Palazzo Mattei di Giove
4   Palazzo di Giacomo Mattei
5   Fontana delle Tartarughe
6   Palazzo Costaguti
7   Casa di Lorenzo Manilio
8   Casa dei Valati
9   Portico d'Ottavia
10 Chiesa di Sant'Angelo
    in Pescheria Portico D'Ottavia
    & Sant'Andrea dei Pescivendoli
11 Chiesa di Santa Maria
    in Campitelli
12 Chiesa di Santa Rita da Cascia
13 Teatro di Marcello
14 Palazzo dei Conservatori
15 Palazzo Senatorio
16 Palazzo Nuovo
17 Chiesa di Santa Maria in Aracoeli
18 Altare della Patria o Vittoriano
19 Arco di Settimio Severo, Carcere
    Mamertino e Chiesa dei Santi
    Luca e Martina
20 Entry to the Foro Romano

(AB URB CON MMCCXXII). Another Latin inscription on the doors on the ground floor tells us the owner's name: LAUR MANLIUS. There is also an inscription in Greek and fragments of Roman sculpture set into the wall, including a relief depicting a lion killing a fallow-deer, a Greek stela with two dogs and a funereal relief with four busts.

Go back to the junction with Via della Reginella and follow Via del Portico d'Ottavia. Go past the **Case dei Fabi** with their beautiful 16th century windows and the 13th century **Torre dei Grassi**, until you reach the remains of an entrance to the **Portico d'Ottavia** (see Things to See & Do). Once a vast rectangular portico measuring 132m by 119m, it enclosed temples dedicated to Juno and Jupiter; the latter was the first temple in Rome to be built entirely of marble. It also contained a Latin and a Greek library, and numerous magnificent statues and works of art.

By the Middle Ages the Roman structure had already been sacked for its marble and been pulled down. The city fish market was established here and two columns were removed from the original entrance. They were replaced by the large brick arch leading to the **Chiesa di Sant'Angelo in Pescheria**, which has the surviving colonnade of the portico incorporated into its façade. Recent excavations have uncovered the remains of a small fishmonger's stand, complete with a bench for displaying the wares, clam shells and a stone basin in which the fish were washed.

On one of the brick pillars outside the church a stone plaque states that the fish sellers had to give city officials the head *usque ad primas pinnas inclusive* (up to and including the first fin) of any fish longer than the plaque itself. Fish heads and, particularly those of the sturgeon still living in the Tevere at the time, were prized particularly for soup.

To the right of the portico you will notice the stucco façade of the 17th century oratory of **Sant'Andrea dei Pescivendoli**

(1689) and, behind it at No 29 the 14th century **Casa dei Valati**, which now houses the X Circoscrizione of the Comune di Roma, which oversees the city's cultural patrimony. Unusually for this area, the building stands in isolation, since the surrounding buildings were demolished in 1927 during the restoration of the Teatro di Marcello at the rear. Wander along the narrow pedestrian street to the left of the portico to get a feeling for the traditional atmosphere of the Ghetto.

The narrow passage opens onto the deserted Via Sant'Angelo in Pescheria. From here head along Via Tribuna di Campitelli, go around the back of the church and then bear right until you come to a dead end. From this isolated spot you get a view of the arches of the **Teatro di Marcello**. Only twelve of the original 41 arches, which are made of large travertine blocks, remain. You can also see the three marble columns with Corinthian capitals and beams of the Tempio di Apollo Sosiano, dedicated in 431 BC and rebuilt in 34 BC.

Retrace your steps out of the dead end street, and take Via della Tribuna Campitelli to the right. On the corner, at No 23 there is a house incorporating a medieval portico with granite columns and Ionian capitals. After a short walk you'll come to **Piazza Campitelli**. On the west and north-eastern sides of the piazza stand a row of fine palaces belonging to five noble families: the Gaetani-Lovatelli family at Via Tribuna Campitelli 16, the Patrizi-Clementi family at Via Cavaletti 2 (16th century), the Cavaletti family at Piazza Campitelli 1 (16th century), the Albertoni family (early 17th century) and the Capizucchi family (late 16th century).

On the other side of the piazza, the **Chiesa di Santa Maria in Campitelli** was built by Carlo Rainaldi and is a masterpiece of late Baroque style. The elegant travertine façade has been recently cleaned. The church was built in 1662 in honour of the Virgin Mary, who was believed to have halted the plague of 1656. Inside, on the

Not everybody's impressed by the colossus of Octavian.

LAUREN SUNSTEIN

The ancient and the modern converge at Montemartini.

LAUREN SUNSTEIN

Piazza Cosmiato market, Trastevere

Cola di Rienzo in front of the Campidoglio

A Capricorn in the Palazzo Altemps

main altar there is an image of the miraculous Madonna in silver leaf and enamel.

To the left of the church there is a pretty fountain designed in 1589 by Giacomo della Porta. The 17th century façade of the building at No 6, was designed by the architect Flaminio Ponzio and once adorned his house in Via dei Fori Imperiali. It was rebuilt here after the house was demolished in 1933 when the area was cleared to make way for the Via dei Fori Imperiali From the internal courtyard of the building next door there is a view of the archaeological area around the Teatro di Marcello against the backdrop of a medieval house.

Slightly further on in Via Montanara is the **Chiesa di Santa Rita da Cascia**, now deconsecrated. It was built by Carlo Fontana in 1665 at the foot of the nearby Scalinata dell'Aracoeli and rebuilt on this spot in 1940 to allow for an urban revamp. Via Montanara brings you out onto Via de Teatro di Marcello, from where you have another good view of the Teatro Marcello crowned by Palazzo Orsini. Turn back and take Via Capizucchi to the right. This takes you through deserted narrow streets into Piazza Capizucchi, and then to the left into Piazza Margana with the **Torre dei Margani**. Together with the surrounding buildings, the tower looks like a fortified medieval residence. Set n the wall is an ancient column with an Ionic capital. In the door next to it are large pieces of cornice from buildings of the late Empire.

Turn right into Via di Tor Margana and then right again into the darkness of Vicolo Margana. Go under an arch and you will emerge into Via Tribuna di Tor de' Specchi. Here at No 3 there is another medieval tower. Turn left to reach the chaotic Piazza d'Aracoeli, from where you have a splendid 180° view extending from the Palazzo Venezia to the Campidoglio. Turn right and go past the 16th century façade of Palazzo Pecci-Blunt at No 3 and the 17th century Palazzo Massimo di Rignano. This brings you to the **Cordonata di Michelangelo**, the monumental flight of steps designed by Michelangelo which lead up to the **Campidoglio**. If you are making this tour by bicycle, a road to the right of the stairway leads up to the square (closed to ordinary traffic).

The flight of steps is guarded at the bottom by two Egyptian basalt lions (turned into fountains in 1588), and almost touches the older staircase on the left, which leads up to the **Chiesa di Santa Maria in Aracoeli**, also accessible from the Campidoglio. Climb the stairs, noting the shift in perspective as you approach on the colossal mounted Dioscuri, Castor and Pollux, at the top. These statues date from the late Empire and were found in a temple complex dedicated to them near Monte dei Cenci. On the same balustrade in a symmetrical arrangement are the **Trofei di Mario** representing barbarian weapons which date back to the reign of Domitian and statues of Constantine and his son Constans, found at the Terme di Costantino. There are also two mile stones taken from the Via Appia Antica, which bear inscriptions of Nerva and Vespasian.

Once at the top of the stairs, the piazza, designed by Michelangelo, will take you breath away. It is bordered by the **Palazzo dei Conservatori** on the south side, the **Palazzo dei Senatori** at the rear, and the **Palazzo del Museo Capitolino** (also known as the Palazzo Nuovo) on the north side and in its centre stands a very good copy of an original bronze equestrian statue of Marcus Aurelius (see Things to See & Do).

Walk towards the **Palazzo Senatorio** at the far end of the piazza, the official seat of Rome's mayor. In front of the palace's double staircase is a fountain displaying a marble and porphyry statue of a sitting **Minerva** which dates from the time of Domitian. On either side are colossal statues of the Tevere on the right and the Nile on the left. Martino Longhi il Vecchio's belltower replaced an old medieval tower in 1578. This had been part of the fortress built by the Corsi family on top of the remains of the **Tabularium**, the state archive of ancient Rome built in 78 BC and turned into a salt deposit and prison in the early Middle Ages. Incorporated into the rear of the building, the monumental façade of the Tabularium, with 11 large supports in tufa blocks, formed an imposing architectural backdrop to the Foro Romano.

Take the road going downhill to the right of the Palazzo Senatorio. This takes you past the impressive entrance of the Tabularium and brings you to a crowded terrace overlooking the ancient Foro Romano and the Colosseo against the backdrop of the city and the Colli Albani – definitely one of the best views in Rome.

The route ends here. However if you want to visit the **Foro Romano** (admission is free), go back to the Piazza del Campidoglio and descend to the left of Palazzo Senatorio. Via di San Pietro in Carcere begins here. Note the column bearing a reproduction of the famous *lupa capitolina* (Capitoline wolf) suckling Romulus and Remus. In front of you is a view of the Foro and **Arco di Settimio Severo**. Steps lead down into the area of the **Carcere Mamertino** where Saint Peter was held captive. You

will pass the Baroque Chiesa dei Santi Luca e Martina before reaching the Via dei Fori Imperiali. Head right to reach the entrance to the Foro Romano.

WALK 3: PIAZZALE NUMA POMPILIO TO THE TOMBA DI CAECILIA METELLA, VIA APPIA ANTICA.

This route begins near the Terme di Caracalla and crosses the Mura Aureliane, the walls of the ancient Roman city, to reach the archaeological area of the Appia Antica, all that remains of the romantic Roman countryside extolled by the German writer Goethe and other famous travellers of the past. It takes you to a handful of interesting churches, the fascinating Museo delle Mura, two of the most famous catacombs, the monumental remains of ancient tombs and the ruins of Roman chariot racing track. From the end of the route you can take the bus back into town.

This long route can easily be cycled. On bicycle you can go beyond the Tomba di Cecilia Metella, which is 5km from the start

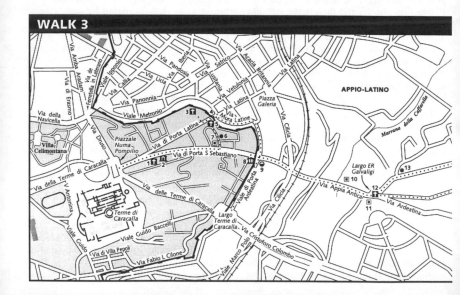

of Via Appia Antica, to reach the intersection with the GRA (Grande Raccordo Anulare) 6km further on.

Piazzale Numa Pompilio is easily reached from Piazza Venezia on bus No 160, or from Stazione Termini and San Giovanni in Laterano on bus No 714. If you want to shorten the walk, catch bus No 218 from San Giovanni in Laterano to Porta San Sebastiano and start your walk there.

At the end of the route, shortly after the Tomba di Cecilia Metella, at the intersection of Via Appia Antica and Via Cecilia Metella (on the No 660 bus route), there is a snack bar with a garden and outside tables (at the rear) which has bicycles for rent at L8000 for an hour, or L6000 per hour for two hours or more.

To head back, you can catch bus No 660 from here to the Colli Albani metro stop on Linea A on Via Appia Nuova. It is also possible to start here and do the walk in reverse: take metro Linea A to the Colli Albani stop and then bus No 660 to the intersection.

The section of Via Appia Antica between Via Cecilia Metella and the GRA is not served by public transport. On Sunday and public holidays Via Appia Antica is closed to traffic and becomes a haven for pedestrians and cyclists from 9.30 am to 7 pm. During these hours it is served by the No 760 shuttle bus from Circo Massimo as far as Via Cecilia Metella. The service doesn't operate during winter. Call the ATAC green number ☎ 167 43 17 84 (English spoken).

To gain access to some of the monuments on this route, you will need to fax a request to the Comune di Roma Ripartizione X, specifying the preferred date and time of your visit. You can then phone the following day to be allocated a visiting time according to the availability of wardens; call ☎ 06 67 10 38 19 (fax 06 68 92 115) in the morning and ask for Geometra Rapaccioni.

From the busy Piazzale Numa Pompilio, near the Terme di Caracalla, go south-east along Via di Porta San Sebastiano. The road begins after a 12th century circular shrine and is often busy, especially during rush hour. Almost immediately, Via di Porta Latina branches off to the left, but you keep

ROME WALKS

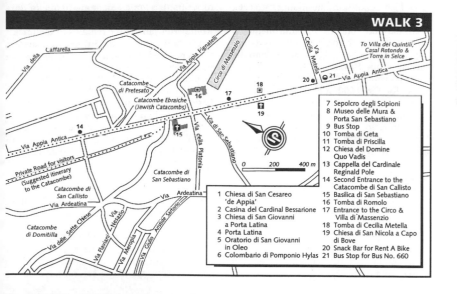

WALK 3

7 Sepolcro degli Scipioni
8 Museo delle Mura & Porta San Sebastiano
9 Bus Stop
10 Tomba di Geta
11 Tomba di Priscilla
12 Chiesa del Domine Quo Vadis
13 Cappella del Cardinale Reginald Pole
14 Second Entrance to the Catacombe di San Callisto
15 Basilica di San Sebastiano
16 Tomba di Romolo
17 Entrance to the Circo & Villa di Massenzio
18 Tomba di Cecilia Metella
19 Chiesa di San Nicola a Capo di Bove
20 Snack Bar for Rent A Bike
21 Bus Stop for Bus No. 660

1 Chiesa di San Cesareo 'de Appia'
2 Casina del Cardinal Bessarione
3 Chiesa di San Giovanni a Porta Latina
4 Porta Latina
5 Oratorio di San Giovanni in Oleo
6 Colombario di Pomponio Hylas

The Catacombs

Recent scholarship suggests that the long-held theory that the catacombs were used as clandestine meeting places by the early Christians hiding from persecution by the Roman authorities rs is totally unfounded.

It seems that the desire for communal burial was the main aim, and that the choice of underground graves was probably influenced by contemporary practices (eg *columbaria*), and also by practical and economic concerns. Catacombs were often established in areas where there were existing quarries or underground passages: the soft volcanic earth of the Roman countryside enabled the Christians to dig to a depth of 20m or so. They maximised on the land donated by wealthy members of the Christian community by digging on numerous levels, retaining for security purposes only a few entrances.

During the periods of persecution, many martyrs were buried beside the fathers of the Church and the first popes. Many Christians wanted to be buried in the same place as the martyrs and consequently a trade in tomb real estate developed, becoming increasingly unethical until Gregory I issued a decree in 597 abolishing the sale of graves. However, Christians had already started to abandon the catacombs as early as in 313, when Constantine issued the Milan decree of religious tolerance.

to Via di Porta San Sebastiano. Here on the right you will find the **Chiesa di San Cesareo 'de Appia'** or 'in palatio' (to visit ring at the iron gate at No 4). The ancient church was built in the 8th century on top of a Roman building and was rebuilt in the early 17th century in late Mannerist style. The interior was decorated by Cavalier D'Arpino and contains splendid medieval marble pieces with coloured mosaics dating from the 13th century. These come from the transept of the Basilica di San Giovanni in Laterano which had been restored in preparation for the 1600 Jubilee. In the crypt corresponding to the level of the Roman building, there is still a splendid black-and-white mosaic floor with marine scenes dating from the 2nd century (not visitable at the time of writing).

To the right of the church is the **Casina del Cardinal Bessarione** (accessible only on request to the Comune di Roma Ripartizione X). This is a delightful example of a 15th century rural residence. On the side facing the road you can see the Guelph-cross windows typical of the period. The other side is graced with a beautiful frescoed loggia looking out onto a garden visible from the gate.

Via di Porta San Sebastiano is lined with houses and gardens that evoke the long-gone atmosphere of 18th century suburban Rome. Just under 1km along the road, to the left at No 9 is the entrance to the **Sepolcro degli Scipioni** (under restoration at the time of writing), a tomb belonging to one of the most important families in Republican Rome. You can see the remains of the brick house built here in the 3rd century, many times restored. The door next to it takes you up a flight of stairs and into the **Parco degli Scipioni**, created in 1929 to embellish the burial ground, that also includes the **Colombario di Pomponio Hylas**, a tomb dating from the early Imperial period and featuring mosaics and a ceiling painted with leaf motifs. (The tomb is accessible only on request from the Comune di Roma Ripartizione X).

On the far side of the park exit onto Via di Porta Latina. Turn left and on your right there is a road leading to the delightful medieval **Chiesa di San Giovanni a Porta Latina**. The church was built by Celestine III in the 12th century, although an earlier church was founded on the site in the 5th century. An interesting cycle of 12th century paintings in the central nave, now

The Catacombs

Increasingly, Christians opted to bury their dead near the churches and basilicas that were being built, often above pagan temples. This became common practice under Theodosius, who made Christianity the state religion in 394. The catacombs became sanctuaries for remembering the martyrs buried there.

In about 800 the increasingly frequent incursions by invaders necessitated the removal of the saintly bodies of the martyrs and the first popes to the basilicas inside the city walls. The catacombs were thus left abandoned and eventually many were forgotten and filled up with earth. In the Middle Ages only three catacombs were known about, and those of San Sebastiano were the most frequented as a place of pilgrimage, since they had earlier been the burial place of Saints Peter and Paul.

The Catacombe di Santa Priscilla on Via Salaria were discovered by chance at the end of the 16th century, following the collapse of a tufa quarry. From that time on, groups of curious aristocrats began to lower themselves into the dark underground passages on a regular basis, often risking losing themselves permanently in the underground labyrinths. From the mid-19th century onwards passionate scholars of Christian archaeology began a program of scientific research and more than 30 catacombs in the Rome area have been uncovered.

sadly faded, depicts Old and New Testament scenes. In the presbytery, there are the symbols of the Evangelists and the 24 elders of the Apocalypse dating from the same period. Outside, the beautiful porticoed façade stands in the shade of an ancient cedar tree which provides a balance to the handsome three-ordered Romanesque campanile. An ancient well bearing 9th century inscriptions adds the final touch to the picture. The church (☎ 06 77 20 98 98) is open from 8 am to 12.30 pm and from 3 to 6 pm..

Once back on Via di Porta Latina, go back past the entrance to the park to reach the oratory of **San Giovanni in Oleo**, founded in the 5th century on the site where the saint was said to have been immersed in a cauldron of boiling oil without being harmed. After this miraculous event, he was pardoned and exiled to the Greek island of Patmos. The octagonal building was restored by Borromini in the 17th century.

Just past the oratory is the **Porta Latina** and the mighty Mura Aureliane (see Geography in Facts about Rome). Unlike other *porte* (entrances) in the walls, this one retains much of its original 3rd century appearance.

Turn right into Viale delle Mura Latine and follow the wall's perimeter. You will soon reach **Porta San Sebastiano** on Via Appia Antica. This is the largest and the most majestic entrance in the walls and houses the very interesting **Museo delle Mura**. The museum visit includes the panoramic view of Via Appia Antica from one of the towers and a walk along the battlements as far as Porta Ardeatina and Sangallo's 16th century bastions. The museum (☎ 06 70 47 52 84), Via di Porta San Sebastiano 18, is open year-round Tuesday to Sunday from 9 am to 7 pm, admission is L3750 or L2500 for EU students and free for under 18s and over 60s.

The area inside the museum door is covered by the **Arco di Druso**, a simple arch supporting the Antonius aqueduct, a branch of the Acqua Marcia aqueduct, that passed overhead at this point on its way to the Terme di Caracalla. It was built on a monumental scale to celebrate the importance of Via Appia, an important line of communication with Naples and the port of Brindisi in Apulia, the main departure point for the East. In medieval times the arch was used as an outer door to protect a fortified internal courtyard.

Outside the walls, the Via Appia Antica, used as a short-cut by rush-hour traffic, technically begins with the first milestone set into the wall on the right, just after the No 218 bus stop coming from San Giovanni in Laterano. The road is narrow and slopes downwards and there is no pavement. However, if you make it past the modern bridge that passes over an ancient cemetery, the road widens and levels out.

Just past a restaurant on your right, you can see to the left the remains of the **Tomba di Geta**, and above them a 16th century house. One hundred metres further on is the **Tomba di Priscilla**, which is hidden from view by the restaurant at No 68, but you can see it from a gate near the intersection a bit further on, or from the car park behind the restaurant. The tomb was used by the Caetani family in the 13th century as the base for a military tower. The tomb was under restoration at the time of writing.

At the intersection where Via Ardeatina goes off to the right, there is a large sign to a private road for visitors to the **Catacombe di San Callisto**. The road is open from 8 am to 6.30 pm, or 5.30 pm in winter, daily except Wednesday. It is much better to take this route than to brave the fast-moving traffic on Via Appia Antica, where there is no footpath. It is pleasant to walk this peaceful 2km route on a ridge between fields dotted with tombs and old country residences. About halfway along is the entrance to the Catacombe di San Callisto and the route ends at another gate next to the **Catacombe di San Sebastiano** (See the Things to See & Do chapter).

Back on Via Appia Antica, you can see the **Chiesa del Domine Quo Vadis?**. The church stands on the spot where Jesus appeared to St Peter who was fleeing Rome to escape the Neronian persecution (see Things to See & Do). The church houses a stone said to bear Jesus' footprints, although it is more likely to be an offering of thanksgiving made by an ancient traveller having escaped from danger.

If for some reason you choose not to follow the private road and continue along the busy Via Appia Antica, you will note a run-down 16th century **chapel** with a circular base leaning against a country house at the corner of Via della Caffarella. The chapel was built as an offering by Cardinal Reginald Pole, who had come to Rome after having refused to participate in the Protestant reform in his native England. The chapel stands on the site where in 1539 the cardinal escaped death at the hands of Henry VIII's hired assassins.

As you continue, you will pass another entrance to the Catacombe di San Callisto and then, after the intersection with Via Appia Pignatelli on the left, you will come to the **Jewish catacombs** of Vigna Rondanini (accessible only with permission from the synagogue in Rome.) Note that there is no sign indicating the catacombs from the road.

After passing the third and final entrance to the Catacombe di San Callisto you'll reach the **Basilica & Catacombe di San Sebastiano**, built in the 4th century on the spot where the bodies of the Apostles Peter and Paul were buried, before being transferred to the respective basilicas built in their honour (see Things to See & Do).

Not much further along Via Appia Antica, you'll reach the archaeological area of **Villa di Massenzio** on the left. The area encompasses the **Mausoleo di Romolo**, the **Circo di Massenzio** and the remains of Maxentius' imperial palace. Maxentius was emperor from 306 to 312 AD, when he was challenged and killed by the first Christian emperor, Constantine, in the battle of Ponte Milvio. The palace, situated on high ground overlooking the circus, has not yet been completely excavated, and the ruins are covered in vegetation. The mausoleum, undergoing restoration at the time of writing, was built by the emperor for his young son Romulus. It stands on a circular base measuring 33m in diameter. It was crowned with a large dome and had a rectangular portico similar to the Pantheon. The lower part of the mausoleum comprises a large circular area with niches, supported in the centre by a large pillar measuring 7.5m in diameter. It was incorporated into a 19th century country residence. The monument was surrounded on all sides by an imposing portico measuring 107m by 121m, in part still visible.

In almost perfect condition, the circus is the most interesting part of the complex, and you can enjoy a pleasant walk along the 513m that make up its length. Entrance to the circus is through two towers on the curved side (west). Here you will also find traces of the 12 stalls (*carceres*) for the two- and four-horse chariots. It is interesting to note that this side is positioned at a slight oblique angle to allow all the quadrigae to cover an identical distance before reaching the beginning of the low wall in the centre. The wall, 1000 Roman feet or 296m in length, consisted of a channel formed by a series of basins. These contained sculptures and tabernacles on columns displaying the seven eggs and the seven dolphins that represented the seven laps that had to be completed to cover a distance of three Roman miles, approximately 4440m. The centre was dominated by the obelisk of Domitian, brought here from Campo Marzio and later removed to Bernini's fountain in Piazza Navona on the order of Pope Innocent X in 1650.

The spectators would have been able to watch the race from the steps that rested on sloping vaults, now largely collapsed. The disintegration of the structure has, however, revealed a curious but effective method of engineering typical of the time: the insertion of amphorae into the brickwork to lighten the structure. However, it seems that the circus did not reach completion before the owner Maxentius died, and scholars think it unlikely that it ever actually saw a chariot race.

The ruins of the Villa Massenzio archaeological zone (☎ 06 78 01 324) are open daily except Monday from 9 am to 5 pm from October to March and from 9 am to 7 pm from April to September. Admission is L3750 (EU students L2500).

A bit further along is the imposing **Tomba di Cecilia Metella**. The mausoleum was built, as stated on the inscription, for Caecilia Metella, daughter of Quintus Metellus Creticus, and wife of Crassus. Cylindrical in shape and 11m high and roughly 30m in diameter, the mausoleum encloses an interesting burial chamber, now roofless. The walls are made of travertine and decorated with a lovely sculpted frieze featuring Gaelic shields, ox skulls and festoons. The Ghibelline battlements were added in the Middle Ages. Because of its location, the mausoleum was turned into a keep for the 14th century castle built by the Caetani astride the road to extract money, rather like a modern motorway toll booth. The inside is being restored (with the work due to finish at the end of 1999), and only limited sections are accessible. It is open every day from 9 am to 4 pm in winter, to 7 pm in summer, and to 1 pm on Saturday, Sunday and public holidays.

On the other side of the road the roofless **Chiesa di San Nicola a Capo di Bove** is a rare example of Gothic architecture in Rome. The church of 'Saint Nicola at the Bull's Head' gets its unusual name from the carved bulls' skulls (*bucrania*) which decorate the Tomba di Caecilia Metella situated immediately opposite the church.

If you have walked this far, you will probably want to take the bus back into the city. If you choose to continue, ideally by bicycle, you will encounter more inspiring ruins and an increasingly Felliniesque atmosphere as, moving away from the area frequented by tourists, the road begins to turn into an innocuous, but unsettling backdrop for prostitutes plying their trade in cars parked behind tombs and in nearby woods.

Via Appia Antica continues in an unbroken line of tombs and ruined monuments. The vast ruins of **Villa dei Quintili** (undergoing restoration at the time of writing) are on the left after Via di Tor Carbone. The villa was built with a central heating system, a private aqueduct and a hippodrome. Not far from here is the unusual **Casal Rotondo**, a large circular tomb (approximately 35m in diameter) dating from the time of Augustus and now the basement of an old farm house.

On the left, after Via di Torricola you will find the characteristic **Torre in Selce**, built during the 12th century above an ancient

ROME WALKS

tomb. Over many years these monuments were largely ignored and fell into serious decay. Fortunately, extensive restoration work is now underway as part of a plan to restore the entire area of the **Parco Archeologico dell'Appia Antica**. In the section that was cut off by the Grande Raccordo Anulare, roughly 10km from the start of the road, work is underway to build an underpass that should help to restore the queen of roads, which has been the main road of communication with the east for so long.

Places to Stay

Rome has a vast number of pensioni and hotels, but it is always best to book. While summer is the peak period, tourists and pilgrims flock to Rome year-round. If you haven't already booked, go to the tourist office at Stazione Termini or Fiumicino airport, the main APT office or Enjoy Rome (see Tourist Offices in Facts for the Visitor chapter). A hotel booking service is available free of charge for new arrivals in Rome. Called HR Hotel Reservations, the service is offered by a consortium of Rome hotel owners and has booths at Fiumicino airport in the International Arrivals Hall, at Stazione Termini opposite Platform 10, and on the Autostrada del Sole at the Tevere Ovest service station. The service operates daily from 7 am to 10 pm; phone ☎ 06 699 10 00. It will also make bookings at hotels in other major Italian cities.

Avoid the people at the train station who claim to be tourism officials and offer to find you a room. They usually lead you to pretty seedy accommodation for which you end up paying more than the official rate. The Associazione Cattolica Internazionale al Servizio della Giovane (also known as Protezione della Giovane), downstairs at Stazione Termini, is usually open from 9 am to 1 pm and 2 to 8 pm, and offers young women accommodation. If the office is closed, try contacting the head office (☎ 06 488 00 56) at Via Urbana 158, which runs parallel to Via Cavour, off Piazza Esquilino.

Most of the budget pensioni and larger hotels which cater for tour groups are located near Stazione Termini. The area south-west (to the left as you leave the station) can be noisy and unpleasant. It teems with pickpockets and snatch thieves and women may find it unsafe at night. To the north-east you can find accommodation in quieter and somewhat safer streets in a more pleasant residential area. However, the historic centre of Rome is far more appealing and the area around il Vaticano is

much less chaotic; both of these areas are only a short bus or Metro ride away.

You will often find three or four budget pensioni in the same building, although many are small establishments of 12 rooms or less which fill up quickly in summer. The sheer number of budget hotels in the area should, however, ensure that you find a room.

Most hotels will accept bookings in advance, although some demand a deposit for the first night.

Although Rome does not have a low season as such, the majority of hotels offer significant discounts in July and August and from November to March (excluding the Christmas/New Year period). A lot of mid-range and top end hotels also offer special deals for families and discounts for extended stays – so be sure to enquire. There is a terrible lack of on-site parking facilities in the city centre, but your hotel should be able to direct you to a private garage. All hotels listed here accept credit cards and travellers cheques unless otherwise indicated.

PLACES TO STAY – BUDGET
Camping

All of Rome's camping grounds are a fair distance from the centre. *Seven Hills* (☎ 06 30 31 08 26, Via Cassia 1216), charges L9500 per person, per day. It costs L8000 per tent and L10,000 per person, and an extra L5000 if you have a car. It is open from 15 March to 30 October. It's a bit of a hike from Termini: catch the Metro Linea A to Ottaviano, walk to Piazza del Risorgimento and take bus No 907 (ask the driver where to get off). From Via Cassia it is a 1km walk to the camping ground.

A good option is *Village Camping Flaminio* (☎ 06 333 26 04, Via Flaminia 821) which is about 15 minutes from the city centre by public transport. It costs L13,000 per person and L12,400 for a site. Tents, caravans and bungalows are available for rent. From Stazione Termini catch bus No

910 to Piazza Mancini, then bus No 200 to the camping ground. At night, catch bus No 24N from Piazzale Flaminio (just north of Piazza del Popolo).

Hostels

The HI *Ostello Foro Italico* (☎ *06 323 62 67)* is at Viale delle Olimpiadi 61. Take Metro Linea A to Ottaviano, then bus No 32 to Foro Italico. It has a bar, restaurant and garden and is open all year. It is closed from 9.30 am to midday. Breakfast and showers are included in the price, which is L24,000 per night. A meal costs L14,000.

The Italian youth hostels association, Associazione Italiana Alberghi per la Gioventù *(Map 6, ☎ 06 487 11 52, Via Cavour 44)* has information about all youth hostels in Italy, and will assist with bookings to stay at universities during summer. You can also join HI here.

A good option for women travellers is the *YWCA (Map 6, ☎ 06 488 04 60, fax 06 487 10 28, Via Cesare Balbo 4)*, near Piazza dell'Esquilino and Santa Maria Maggiore. This is the place for early risers with a serious sightseeing agenda, but is probably best avoided by night-owls as there's a midnight curfew. Singles cost L60,000 (or L80,000 with bathroom), doubles cost L50,000 per person (L60,000 with bathroom) and triples and quads cost L40,000 per person. Breakfast is included. Payment is by cash only. Take Via Cavour from Termini station and turn right into Via A. Depretis at Piazza dell' Esquilino. Via Cesare Balbo is the second street on the right.

Student Accommodation

People planning to study in Italy can usually organise accommodation through the school or university they will be attending. Options include a room with an Italian family, or a share arrangement with other students in an independent apartment. Some Italian universities operate a *casa dello studente*, which houses Italian students throughout the school year and lets out rooms to others during the summer break (July to the end of September).

It can be very difficult to organise a room in one of these institutions. The best idea is to go through your own university, or contact the Italian university directly.

Religious Institutions

There are a number of religious institutions in Rome which offer accommodation including several near Stazione Termini and il Vaticano. To stay in one, you usually apply to the nearest Catholic archdiocese in your home town, although some institutions (including most listed here) will consider independent requests. In view of the millions of Catholic pilgrims expected in Rome in the lead up to and during the Jubilee year in 2000, anyone wishing to use religious accommodation is advised to make their enquires and bookings well in advance.

Bear in mind that all religious institutions have strict curfews, and the accommodation, while clean, is of the basic, no-frills variety. Breakfast is included for all prices listed below and almost all rooms include private bathrooms unless stated otherwise. All of the following are on Map 5 unless otherwise stated.

The *Domus Aurelia delle Suore Orsoline* (☎ *06 63 67 84, fax 06 39 37 64 80, Via Aurelia 218)* about 1km from the Basilica di San Pietro has singles/doubles for L70,000/ 110,000. Triples are L140,000. From Stazione Termini catch bus No 64 to Largo Argentina, then No 46 to Via Aurelia. Get off the bus after it has done a steep ascent and made a sharp left turn.

The *Padri Trinitari* (☎ *06 638 38 88, Piazza Santa Maria alle Fornaci)* very close to the Basilica di San Pietro, has singles/ doubles for L75,000/130,000 and triples for L160,000.

The *Suore Teatine* (☎ *06 637 40 84; fax 06 39 37 90 50, Salita Monte del Gallo 25)*, off Via Gregorio VII, offer beds with breakfast for L65,000 in a single room or L53,000 per person in a double.

Nearby, the English-speaking *Franciscan Sisters of the Atonement* (☎ *06 63 07 82; fax 06 638 61 49, Via Monte del Gallo 105)* offer beds for L60,000 a single or L50,000 per person in double rooms.

The **Suore Dorotee** (☎ 06 68 80 33 49, fax 06 68 80 33 11, Via del Gianicolo 4/a) is located in the green and leafy area off a steep winding road that leads up from the Lungotevere to the top of the Gianicolo hill. Rooms are L85,000 per person.

Villa Bassi (Map 7, ☎ 06 581 53 29, Via Giacinto Carini 24) is at the top of the Gianicolo hill in the Monteverde area, very close to both Trastevere and Il Vaticano. Take bus No 75 from Stazione Termini. Clean, simple singles/doubles are L60,000/ 80,000, L110,000 for a triple and L130,000 a quad. The rooms do have bathrooms and breakfast is not included.

As far as location is concerned you cannot do better than the convent of the **Suore di Santa Brigida** (Map: Around Piazza Navona, ☎ 06 68 89 25 96, fax 06 68 21 91 26, brigida@mclink.it, Piazza Farnese 96) which is run by a Swedish order of nuns. The entrance is actually at Via Monserrato 54. The sisters offer beds for L145,000 (single) and L125,000 per person in double rooms which is on the pricier side for religious accommodation.

Bed & Breakfast

Bed & breakfast is a relatively new concept in Rome. However, it is taking off in light of the impending influx of pilgrims for the Jubilee year for whom there is just not enough existing budget accommodation. Lists of private B&B operators can be obtained from the APT. They are also listed in the magazine *Wanted in Rome* (see under Newspapers and Magazines in Facts for the Visitor chapter).

The bonus of B&B accommodation is that Italian houses are invariably spotlessly clean. The drawback is that you are staying in someone's home, and will probably be expected to operate within the family's timetable. Keys are not always provided. A hotel or pensione would be more suitable for those who expect to be coming in late at night or may be making a lot of noise.

Most of the accommodation is fairly central but when making the booking (which should be done well in advance of your stay)

make sure you understand fully the location of the accommodation that is being proposed, to avoid finding yourself in an outer suburb with limited public transport.

Bed & Breakfast Italia (☎ 06 687 86 18, fax 06 687 86 19, md4095@mclink.it, Corso Vittorio Emanuele II 282) is one of several B&B networks. It offers accommodation in three different price categories. Rooms with shared bathrooms cost L50,000 a single, L95,000 a double and L130,000 a triple; rooms with private bathroom cost L70,000/ 130,000/150,000; luxurious rooms with private bathroom cost L85,000/160,000/ 190,000.

Pensioni & Hotels

Rome has a wide range of pensioni and hotels in this price range, although real budget establishments are becoming more and more difficult to find. Prices have risen considerably in Rome in recent years, and not always with a corresponding upgrade in services and facilities.

Traditionally, a pensione was more personal and smaller than a hotel, often occupying one or two floors in a building housing other, similar establishments. However, the distinction is becoming blurred, particularly as pensioni get caught up in the rush to upgrade in preparation for the Jubilee.

Unless otherwise stated, the prices quoted for hotels in this section are for rooms without a shower or bath, and do not include breakfast (although this is often available for an extra charge).

North-East of Termini (Map 6) To reach the pensioni in this area, head to the right as you leave the train platforms, onto Via Marsala, which runs alongside the station.

Off Via Vicenza, **Pensione Giamaica** (☎ 06 445 19 63; fax 06 445 19 63; md0991 @mclink.it, Via Magenta 13) is fairly basic with frightful decor but it has well priced singles/doubles for L50,000/ 78,000 including breakfast. The communal bathrooms are clean and each room has its own basin. Some of the rooms look onto a dark and grimy internal courtyard; try to get one looking onto the street or out the back of the building instead. There's no curfew and the owners will provide front door keys for those planning to come in late.

In the same building on the 3rd floor is *Hotel New York* (☎ *06 446 04 56, fax 06 499 07 14)*, which has singles/doubles for L80,000/L120,000 (L110,000/L195,000 with bathroom). Triple rooms with bathroom cost L200,000, quads L260,000 and rooms for five L300,000. The management changed recently and renovations are still being carried out. See if you can get one of the better rooms that has already been spruced up.

Fawlty Towers (☎ *06 445 03 74, fax 06 445 03 74, Via Magenta 39)*, offers hostel-style accommodation and is without doubt one of the best budget options in Rome. A bed in a four-person dorm is L30,000 (or L35,000 in a three-bed dorm), single rooms are L60,000 (L75,000 with bathroom) and doubles are from L85,000 (L110,000 with bathroom). Run by the people at Enjoy Rome (see under Tourist Offices in Facts for the Visitor chapter), it offers lots of information about Rome. Added bonuses are the sunny terrace, satellite TV, communal fridge and microwave. Fawlty Towers only accepts advance bookings for the private (non-dorm) rooms. To reserve a dorm bed, you have to call in (either in person or by phone) at 9 pm the night before you wish to stay there, and they'll hold the bed until around 10 the following morning. It's also a good place to go if you've arrived in Rome late at night and the accommodation agencies are closed, as the staff can usually recommend a pensione with vacancies.

Nearby in Via Palestro are several reasonably priced pensioni. *Pensione Restivo* (☎ *06 446 21 72, Via Palestro 55)* is the quintessential old-fashioned Italian pensione experience. It is run by the friendly and helpful Signor Restivo (a former *carabiniere* officer) and his elderly mother. Former guests have been known to send gifts and thank-you letters to the owners, which are proudly displayed. The place is spotlessly clean and has large

singles/doubles for L70,000/L110,000 and triples for L125,000. Breakfast is not included but Signor Restivo usually offers guests a cup of coffee before they set off for the day. Bookings are taken only in the morning and there is a midnight curfew.

On the ground floor of the same building is *Hotel Cervia* (☎ *06 49 10 57, fax 06 49 10 56)*. The rooms in this 19th century building have high vaulted ceilings and seem enormous. They are also very reasonably priced. Singles are L55,000, doubles L90,000, triples L105,000 and quads L120,000. Rooms with bathrooms are also available: doubles cost L130,000 and triples L150,000.

Pensione Ventura (☎ *06 445 19 51)* is on the ground floor at Via Palestro 88, near the corner of Via Castro Pretorio. Double rooms, all with bathrooms, are well priced at L80,000 to L120,000. There are no single rooms; single occupancy of a double room costs L80,000. Despite renovations a few years ago, the place still seems fairly run down and, being on street level, it is very noisy, especially for the rooms that look out onto the busy road. Breakfast is included, and there is a coffee machine and cold drinks dispenser for general use.

Around the corner, on the other side of Viale Castro Pretorio, is *Pensione Ester* (☎ *06 495 71 23, Viale Castro Pretorio 25)*. Walk through the entrance into a tree-filled, shady courtyard, and take the stairs on the right to the 2nd floor. This family-run pensione is clean and there's no extra charge for use of the bathrooms. Doubles are L75,000 and triples L105,000, but these rates drop for stays of 10 days or more. Breakfast is not included and there's a 1 am curfew.

In the same building on the 1st floor is *Pensione Enrica* (☎ *06 445 37 42)*, where doubles (no twins) with bathroom cost L100,000, breakfast not included. This place is very popular with the families and friends of cadets at the nearby police academy, and more Italians than tourists stay here. However, the quirky owner speaks basic English, German and French and is very helpful.

North-West of Termini (Map 6) The family-run *Pensione Lachea* (☎ 06 495 72 56, fax 06 445 46 65, Via San Martino della Battaglia) has large singles/doubles for L65,000/95,000 and doubles with shower for L110,000. Dorm beds cost L45,000.

In the same building and under the same helpful management is the newly restructured *Hotel Dolomiti* (☎/fax as above). Prices are reasonable given the three-star rating; singles cost L100,000 and doubles/triples start at L150,000/210,000 respectively, including breakfast in the delightful marble-panelled bar-breakfast area. The rooms are elegant and airy and all have private bathroom. Facilities include minibar, TV, telephone, air-conditioning, double glazing, safe and hairdryer. Booking is recommended.

Downstairs is *Tre Stelle* (☎ 06 446 30 95, fax 06-44 68 29) with singles/doubles for L60,000/90,000 (L90,000/130,000 with bath and air-conditioning) and triples for L140,000, breakfast excluded.

Albergo Sandra (☎ 06 445 26 12, fax 06 446 08 46, Via Villafranca 10),between Via Vicenza and Via San Martino della Battaglia, is a medium-sized pensione run by a house-proud Italian *mamma* and her English-speaking son. The rooms are clean and pleasant and singles/doubles cost in the region of L80,000/140,000. Prices go down by up to L30,000 for stays of more than three nights.

Albergo Mari 2 (☎ 06 474 03 71, fax 06 44 70 33 11, Via Calatafimi 38) is a quirky, family-run establishment offering generous hospitality at reasonable prices. Singles/doubles are L60,000/120,000 (L80,000/150,000 with shower). The accommodation itself is nothing to rave about and there is a notable lack of communal space; but these shortcomings are made up for by the reception you'll receive from the larger-than-life owner and her staff. Safe left-luggage facilities are available.

In the same street, *Papa Germano* (☎ 06 48 69 19, Via Calatafimi 14a) is a popular budget choice. Prices start at L50,000/70,000, and doubles with a bath cost

L100,000, including hairdryer. The English and French speaking management nurture a friendly family atmosphere; and judging by the enthusiastic comments in the visitor's book their efforts are not in vain. Free city maps are available and there are guide books available on loan. The hotel also takes bookings for city tours and trips out of town (pick-up from reception).

Nearby is the more expensive *Hotel Floridia* (☎ 06 481 40 89, ☎ 06 488 43 39, fax 06 444 13 77, Via Montebello 45). Singles/doubles are L110,000/160,000 and triples/quads are 180,000/200,000, including breakfast, although prices fall by 20% out of season. The elegant entrance area on the ground floor gives a false impression of quality; the rooms themselves are small and basic, but all have telephone and private bath.

Hotel Ascot (☎ 06 474 16 75, Via Montebello 22), has quiet old-fashioned singles/doubles with bathroom for L80,000/110,000. Ask for No 24 which still has its original parquet floor. The hotel itself is fine – as long as you're not concerned about the porn cinemas and sex shops in the area.

Hotel Castelfidardo (☎ 06 446 46 38, fax 06 494 13 78, Via Castelfidardo 31), off Piazza dell'Indipendenza, is one of Rome's better one-star pensioni. It has clean and pleasant singles/doubles for L60,000/85,000, and triples for L95,000; a double/triple with private bathroom costs L110,000/125,000. The English-speaking staff are friendly and helpful.

On the other side of Via XX Settembre, 10 minutes from Stazione Termini, is the newly refurbished *Hotel Ercoli* (☎/fax 06 474 54 54, 06 474 40 63, Via Collina 48). Singles/doubles seem expensive at L115,000/160,000, but the price reflects the facilities on offer (private bath, TV, telephone and hairdryer) and includes breakfast in the sunny breakfast room.

Downstairs in the same building is the welcoming *Pensione Tizi* (☎ 06 482 01 28, ☎/fax 06 474 32 66, Via Collina 48), also recently refurbished. The light and spacious rooms are a bargain at L55,000/80,000

(L100,000 with bath) and there are reasonable discounts out of season and for stays of more than five days. Payment is in cash only.

There is paid street parking in the area, as well as reasonably priced garage parking facilities, so ask at your hotel.

South-West of Termini (Map 6) This area is decidedly seedier than the other side of the station, but prices remain the same. Upon leaving Stazione Termini follow Via Gioberti to Via G Amendola, which becomes Via Filippo Turati. This street and the parallel Via Principe Amedeo harbour a concentration of budget pensioni and you shouldn't have any trouble finding a room. The area improves as you head away from the train station and towards the Colosseo and Foro Romano. All items are on Map 6 unless otherwise stated.

A good choice is the recently renovated *Hotel Kennedy* (☎ 06 446 53 73, fax 06 446 54 17, Via F Turati 62), a large establishment with spacious and comfortable rooms with private bath, satellite TV and air-conditioning. Prices are not cheap (singles cost around L110,000 and doubles around L180,000) but they are somewhat justified by the quality of the accommodation. The hotel offers considerable discounts during the low season (November through March). Prices include breakfast (a generous buffet-style spread with no fewer than four types of cereal). Other facilities include a bar (open all day), three communal areas with TV and a left-luggage area.

The newly restructured *Pensione Everest* (☎ 06 488 16 29, Via Cavour 47), on the main street running south-west from the piazza in front of Termini, is expensive given the facilities it offers. Singles/doubles are L140,000/220,000 (L80,000/130,000 out of season). Street parking is available in front of the nearby Basilica di Santa Maria Maggiore.

Hotel Sandy (☎ 06 488 45 85, fax 06 445 07 34, Via Cavour 136), closer to the Foro Romano, is probably the closest thing in

Rome to a backpackers' crash pad. Go through the discreet entrance and the hotel is on the 5th floor (no lift). Beds are in dorms for between three and five people (eight in summer) and cost L25,000 per person or L20,000 out of season. There are metal lockers but no keys and the hotel lacks adequate bathroom facilities – so be prepared to queue. Reservations are not accepted and payment is in cash only.

Hotel Il Castello (Map 8, ☎ 06 77 20 40 36, fax 06 70 49 00 68, Via Vittorio Amedeo II 9), is well-located between Piazza Vittorio Emanuele and the Basilica di San Giovanni and close to the Manzoni Metro stop, south of Termini. It is a good budget choice (and no prizes for guessing where it gets its name). Singles/doubles are L70,000/120,000 and beds in dorms are L25,000 per person. Doubles/triples with bath are L120,000/150,000. Prices fall by up to 20% from November through March. The rooms and communal bathrooms are clean and pleasant and the friendly English-speaking staff provide a limited bar service in the entrance area (although at L2000 for a cappuccino it's better to go to a bar). Free parking is available in nearby streets.

Off Via Nazionale is the excellent *Hotel Elide* (☎ 06 488 39 77 or 06 474 13 67, fax 06 48 90 43 18, Via Firenze 50). Comfortable doubles are L130,000 (L150,000 with bath) and prices drop by around L50,000 from December to March. Prices include breakfast, either in the small breakfast room or in the bar opposite. Ask for room No 18, which has an elaborate, gilded ceiling.

Hotel Galatea (☎ 06 474 30 70, Via Genova 24), on the other side of Via Nazionale, is through the grand entrance of an old palace. Its beautifully furnished singles/doubles are a bargain at L70,000/89,000. A triple costs around L165,000; and rooms with private bathroom cost an additional L10,000 to L45,000. The hotel does a lot of business with school groups so don't be surprised if the place is overrun with kids. The staff boast no fewer than six European languages.

City Centre (Map: Around Piazza Navona) Really economical hotels in Rome's historical centre basically don't exist. But in the areas around Piazza di Spagna, Piazza Navona, the Pantheon and Campo de' Fiori, you do have the convenience and pleasure of staying right in the centre of historic Rome. The easiest way to get to Piazza di Spagna is on the Metro Linea A to Spagna. To get to Piazza Navona and the Pantheon area, take bus No 64 from Piazza dei Cinquecento, in front of Stazione Termini, to Largo di Torre Argentina and walk. The following are all on the Around Piazza Navona map unless otherwise stated.

One of the most centrally located hotels in this area is the recently renovated *Pensione Primavera* (☎ 06 68 80 31 09, fax 06 686 92 65, Piazza San Pantaleo 3), on Corso Vittorio Emanuele II (good for transport), just south of Piazza Navona. Go through the magnificent entrance and reception is on the 1st floor. Singles/doubles are expensive at L125,000/L170,000 but triples are a better deal at L60,000 per person. Prices include breakfast and there is a 10% discount from November through March (excluding the Christmas/New Year period). The rooms are clean and comfortable and all have private bathroom, air-conditioning and double glazing to keep out the traffic noise. The management has plans to install satellite TV throughout the establishment. Booking is recommended (you need to pay a deposit to the amount of one night's stay). Credit cards are not accepted.

Albergo Abruzzi (☎ 06 679 20 21, Piazza della Rotonda 69), has the advantage of its position in front of the Pantheon, but the rooms can be very noisy until late at night when the piazza is finally deserted. Basic singles/doubles are L93,000/130,000. Credit cards are not accepted.

Pensione Mimosa (☎ 06 68 80 17 53, Via Santa Chiara 61), off Piazza della Minerva, has singles for L85,000 and doubles/triples for L60,000 per person (plus L15,000 for a private bathroom). Meals are available for L25,000 a head for three courses (special

diets are catered for on request). The consumption of alcohol is not allowed in the hotel, and smoking is permitted only in the entrance area and dining room. The English-speaking owner and her son are helpful and friendly and provide free city maps and other information. Payment is in cash only.

Albergo della Lunetta (☎ 06 686 10 80 or 06 687 76 30, ☎ 06 687 76 59, fax 06 689 20 28, Piazza del Paradiso 68), east of Campo de' Fiori, has singles/doubles for L70,000/110,000 (L90,000/150,000 including shower). Triples start from L145,000. There is a television in the ground-floor lounge area and parking is sometimes available in the Piazza in front of the hotel (although you'll need to obtain a permit from the hotel).

Hotel Pomezia (☎ /fax 06 686 13 71, Via dei Chiavari 12) has basic doubles for L130,000 and singles/doubles with private bathroom for L130,000/180,000, including breakfast in the sterile breakfast room. There is a negotiable discount of up to 60% in the low season and all the rooms have fans. There is also a television room and a small bar.

Pensione Fiorella (Map 5, ☎ 06 361 05 97, Via del Babuino 196) is in an area that is good for shopping. It has basic accommodation at reasonable prices. Singles/ doubles are L65,000/105,000 including breakfast. Smoking is not allowed on the premises and there is a 1 am curfew. Payment is in cash only.

Right in the heart of the ancient city is *Casa Kolbe* (Map 8, ☎ 06 67 94 974, fax 06 69 94 15 50, Via San Teodoro 44). Located in an ex-Franciscan convent, it takes its name from a Polish monk who lived there before his death during WWII in Auschwitz. The 64 spacious rooms are reasonable at L130,000 for a double and L165,000/L180,000 for a triple/quad. Meals are available for an additional cost in the huge refectory-style restaurant. The hotel looks onto the Foro Romano on one side and opens onto a large sheltered garden on the other, accessible through an equally large bar-lounge and TV room.

Near Il Vaticano (Map 5) Although there aren't many bargains in this area, it is comparatively quiet and still close to the main sights. Bookings are an absolute necessity because rooms are often filled with people attending conferences etc at il Vaticano, and the entire area is likely to be booked out for the entire Jubilee year.

The simplest way to reach the area is on the Metro Linea A to Ottaviano. Turn left into Via Ottaviano, and Via Germanico is a short walk away. Otherwise, take bus No 64 from Stazione Termini to the Basilica di San Pietro and walk away from the basilica, north along Via di Porta Angelica, which becomes Via Ottaviano after the Piazza del Risorgimento – about a 5 minute walk.

By far the best budget hotel in the area is the friendly and informal *Pensione Ottaviano* (☎ 06 39 73 81 38 or 06 39 73 72 53, gi.costantini@agora.stm.it, Via Ottaviano 6), near Piazza del Risorgimento and the musei Vaticani. It has dorm beds for L30,000 per person (L20,000 out of season) and doubles/triples for L70,000/90,000. The rooms all have a fridge and metal lockers. The reception area provides the social hub with tables and chairs, colourful murals, satellite TV and a microwave. The staff speak English and email access is available after 9 pm.

Hotel Giuggioli (☎ 06 324 21 13, Via Germanico 198), in one of the more pleasant residential areas of Rome, is very small, but a delight. A double costs L110,000, or L130,000 with bathroom. Rooms are well furnished. Parking is available in the street below.

In the same building, *Hotel Lady* (☎ 06 324 21 12, fax 06 324 34 46), on the 4th floor, is a quiet, old-fashioned pensione with pleasant rooms for L100,000 a single (L130,000 with bathroom) and L120,000 for a double (L150,000 with bathroom). Triples cost L180,000 (no bathroom) and there is a small discount on prices out of season. Ask for room No 4 or 6, both of which still have the original beamed ceiling. The eccentric owner and his wife do

not speak English, but their eager conversation will give you lots of practice in Italian. *Pensione Nautilus* (☎ 06 324 21 18), on the 2nd floor of the same building, has clean and simple doubles/triples for L110,000/140,000. Rooms with bathroom are an extra L30,000. There is a small lounge-TV area. Payment is in cash only.

Pensione San Michele (☎ 06 324 33 33, Via Attilio Regolo 19), off Via Cola di Rienzo, and *Pensione Valparaiso (Map 3, ☎ 06 321 31 84, Viale Giulio Cesare 47)*, near the Lepanto metro stop, are run by the same management and offer almost identical facilities at the same reasonable prices. To get to Pensione San Michele go through the entrance into the internal courtyard and up the short flight of steps on the right. The pensione is on the 3rd floor. The rooms are simple, but sunny and cost L60,000 for a single and L90,000 for a double. Pensione San Michele has one triple room available for L120,000. Payment is in cash only.

Trastevere (Map 7) Trastevere has surprisingly few hotels or pensione. The one budget choice is *Carmel* (☎ 06 580 99 21, Via Mameli 11) which has singles/doubles for L80,000/100,000 with bathroom. There is a shady roof terrace which can be used by guests.

PLACES TO STAY – MID-RANGE

All rooms in this section have private bathroom unless otherwise stated.

North-East of Termini (Map 6)

If you can get past the grouchy doorman-cum-receptionist guarding the rather grand looking mirrored and wood-panelled entrance of *Hotel Rimini* (☎ 06 446 19 91, Via Marghera 17), you'll find clean, renovated rooms (all with TV) with singles/doubles for L120,000/190,000 including breakfast. Triples are L250,000 and quads L280,000.

Via Palestro is a good street for mid-range hotels. The three-star *Hotel Adventure* (☎ 06 446 90 26, fax 06 446 00 84, hoteladventure@mbox.netway.it) is at No 88. It has been decorated by someone with a particular predilection for pastel pink, fake stucco and reproduction antiques, and there are more chandeliers in the reception area than you'd find in a lighting showroom. However, it's spotlessly clean and is very safe, with video cameras and security doors monitoring those who enter and exit each floor. Doubles are L180,000 to L240,000 (single occupancy L170,000), triples are L300,000 and quads L450,000 (one huge room on the top floor has its own private terrace). All rooms have air conditioning and TV. The rooms looking onto the internal courtyard are quieter than those facing onto the street.

Also at No 88, on the 1st and 2nd floors, is the two-star *Hotel Gabriella* (☎ 06 445 01 20, fax 06 446 14 41, gabriel@micanet .it). It's an unassuming place, family-run and friendly. Singles/ doubles cost L130,000/160,000, but discounts are available for longer stays. The hotel has been redecorated fairly recently and all rooms now have air-conditioning but you'll be charged L20,000 a day if you want to use it.

At Via Palestro 49, there are three good mid-range hotels. *Hotel Continentale* (☎ 06 445 03 82, fax 06 445 26 29) is on the ground floor on the right. All the rooms are very clean if a little drab. Some rooms have been renovated (try to get one of these). Singles are L75,000, doubles L140,000, triples L180,000 and quads L200,000. The owners and staff are friendly and speak several languages, including English.

Hotel Positano (☎ 06 49 03 60, fax 06 446 91 01, hotposit@tin.it) is right next door to the Continentale. It is a family-run hotel which is particularly good for families, as they do not charge for children under six years of age. There is a limited number of doubles/triples without bathroom for L110,000/L130,000. The rest of the rooms have bathrooms and all mod cons (air conditioning, TV, telephone, safe, minibar and hairdryer) and cost L150,000 a single, L180,000 a double, L220,000 a triple and L240,000 a quad.

Also at Via Palestro 49 (on the left-hand side of the entrance, 1st floor) is another

family-run establishment, *Hotel Romae* (☎ 06 446 35 54, fax 06 446 39 14, htlromae @flashnet.it). All rooms have minibar, satellite TV and an electronic safe, but despite these mod-cons it still seems fairly basic and you can do better in the price range. Singles range from L130,000 to L150,000, doubles from L180,000 to L200,000. Extra beds (L30,000 each) can be added to some rooms, and a family room (a double bed plus two singles) costs L240,000.

North-West of Termini (Map 6)

North-west of the train station, in Via Firenze, off Via Nazionale, there are a couple of good-value hotels. *Hotel Seiler* (☎ 06 488 02 04, fax 06 488 06 88) at No 48 has a friendly, helpful management and clean and comfortable singles/doubles for L160,000/220,000 and triples for L260,000. There are also family rooms for five people (more if necessary) for between L40,000 and L60,000 per person – ask for room No 405, known as *la camera degli angeletti* (room of the angels), for its ceiling fresco dating from 1885.

Hotel Oceania (☎ 06 482 46 96 or 06 482 08 52, fax 06 488 55 86, hoceania@tin.it) at No 38 is an ideal family hotel – although it is on the expensive side. Large singles/ doubles are L190,000/245,000, and triples/ family rooms cost between L310,000 and L410,000. There is a 5% discount for stays in excess of four days. This hotel stands out for the unbeatable hospitality offered by the delightful owner, Armando, and his son, Stefano.

Hotel Caravaggio (☎ 06 48 59 15, or 06 487 09 29, fax 06 474 73 63, carvagio @mbox.vol.it, Via Palermo 73/75), just off Via Nazionale and a 10 minute walk from Stazione Termini, is a pleasant three star hotel offering singles/doubles/triples for L210,000/320,000/432,000 and discounts of up to 40% out of season. The reception and breakfast/bar areas are at No 75 and the rooms are next door at No 73, although there are plans to build a connecting corridor in the near future. The rooms are small, but beautifully furnished, and all have at least one antique piece; No 16 is worth mentioning for its 19th century mosaic floor. Room services include TV, minibar and air-conditioning, and the hotel has a jacuzzi.

South-West of Termini (Map 6)

A short distance from the train station is *Hotel Igea* (☎ 06 446 69 11 or 06 446 69 13, fax 06 446 69 11, igea@venere.it, Via Principe Amedeo 97). It has singles/doubles for L140,000/200,000 and triples for L210,000, breakfast not included. The rooms are simple, but all have satellite TV, double glazed windows and air-conditioning.

Hotel Dina (☎ 06 474 06 94 or 06 481 88 85, fax 06 48 90 36 14, Via Principe Amedeo 62), is clean and the management is extremely friendly. Singles/doubles are reasonable at L90,000/160,000 (L65,000/100,000 without bath), not including breakfast. There is a 10% discount on stays in excess of three nights. The hotel has two rooms equipped for disabled people, with open showers and hand rails – unusual for hotels in this price range. Access to the hotel (1st floor) is a bit more problematic, but the lift should be wide enough to take most wheelchairs.

At No 47 is *Hotel Sweet Home* (☎ 06 488 09 54). Singles are L100,000 (L80,000 without bath) and doubles are L150,000, not including breakfast. Triples are also available. The rooms vary in size and comfort; ask for one facing away from the street as these are larger and quieter.

In the same building on the 4th floor is *Albergo Onella* (☎ 06 488 52 57, fax 06 488 19 38, Via Principe Amedeo 47). Rooms are pricey at L180,000/280,000, given the lack of space. Out of season rates drop dramatically. Triples cost L310,000.

The stylish *Hotel Contila* (☎ 06 446 68 87 or 06 446 68 75, fax 06 446 69 04, contila@tin.it, Via Principe Amedeo 81), is more reasonable. Singles cost L150,000 (L90,000 out of season) and doubles cost L200,000 (L100,000 out of season), and triples start at L150,000. There is also a

20% discount for children aged under 14. The rooms are spotless and have satellite TV and independent air-conditioning.

Hotel Palladium Palace (☎ 06 446 69 18, fax 06 446 69 37, nox@iol.it, Via Gioberti 36), is an expensive choice at L280,000 for a single and L360,000/510,000 for a double/triple. The hotel has been stylishly refurbished and the rooms are large and comfortable but the feel of the place is somewhat impersonal – except for the cosy pastel-coloured basement breakfast room. Services include TV room, bar and a roof garden with sauna. There are also four rooms for disabled people, one on each floor.

Hotel d'Este (☎ 06 446 56 07, fax 06 446 56 01, d.este@italyhotel.com, Via Carlo Alberto 4b) is a stone's throw from the Basilica di Santa Maria Maggiore and is one of the better medium-range hotels in the area. It has beautifully furnished rooms and a pleasant roof garden, and there is also a bar, restaurant and laundry/dry cleaning service. Singles/doubles cost up to L260,000/380,000 and triples are L420,000, although prices vary considerably according to the season and are negotiable by phone – so it is wise to ring first. The hotel organises tour guides.

City Centre

Albergo del Sole (Map: Around Piazza Navona, ☎ 06 687 94 46, ☎ 06 68 80 68 73, fax 06 689 37 87, alb.sole@flashnet.it, Via del Biscione 76), very close to Campo de' Fiori, dates from 1462 and is claimed by some to be the oldest hotel in Rome. It has large, comfortable rooms with attractive antique furniture and prices are reasonable. Singles/doubles are L120,000/180,000 (L95,000/140,000 without bath), excluding breakfast. There is lots of communal space, including a TV room, an internal patio and a roof terrace, open to guests until 11 pm. The hotel provides garage facilities at L40,000 per day. Credit cards are not accepted.

Hotel Campo de' Fiori (Map: Around Piazza Navona, ☎ 06 68 80 68 65, Via del Biscione 6) is a peculiar establishment in a six-storey building (no lift) just off Campo de' Fiori. You need go no further than the entrance to appreciate the character of the place; the narrow corridor is lined with mirrors and columns to create an unsettling kaleidoscopic *trompe l'oeil* effect. The 27 rooms (all doubles) are uniquely furnished (in every sense of the word) and cost L210,000 (including shower and toilet) or L170,000 (shower only), and L150,000 (no bathroom). Discounts are negotiable out of season. The hotel has a panoramic roof terrace. It also has nine mini-apartments in the area, which can sleep up to five people. They cost from L200,000 to L250,000 per day.

Near Piazza di Spagna is *Hotel Pensione Suisse (Map 6, ☎ 06 678 36 49, fax 06 678 12 58, Via Gregoriana 56)*. It has good-quality singles/doubles for L140,000/200,000 (L115,000/150,000 without bath), and triples for L265,000. Prices include room-service breakfast. There is an attractive, old-fashioned sitting room with TV and a safe is available at reception. The hotel requires that 50% of payment is in cash.

Closer to Piazza del Popolo is *Hotel Margutta (Map 5, ☎ 06 322 36 74, fax 06 320 03 95, Via Laurina 34)*, between Via del Corso and Via del Babuino. The rooms (all doubles) are small and dark, but very clean, and cost L175,000. Some of the ground floor rooms have wheelchair access.

Hotel Forte (Map 6, ☎ 06 320 76 25, or 06 320 04 08, fax 06 320 27 07, Via Margutta 61) is ideally located on a charming street lined with shops selling antiques and oriental carpets. The rooms are comfortable and quiet and prices are reasonable. Singles/doubles are L130,000/200,000 and triples/quads are L250,000/280,000. Out of season prices fall by up to L60,000 per room.

Hotel Pensione Merano (Map 6, ☎ 06 482 17 96, or 06 482 18 08, fax 06 482 18 10, Via Vittorio Veneto 155) is a quaint old place with dark, heavy furniture. It is surprisingly cheap given the upmarket location. Singles/doubles (all with twin beds) are L125,000/175,000 and triples are L230,000, and there is a discount of up to L30,000 out of season. The rooms are carpeted and have double glazing to keep out the roar of traffic on the busy Via Veneto, but they are not air-conditioned and so get hot in summer.

The recently restructured *Hotel Julia (Map 6, ☎ 06 488 16 37, tel 06 487 34 13, fax 06 481 70 44, hotel.julia@rpilo.it, Via Rasella 29)*, off Via delle Quattro Fontane near Piazza Barberini, offers simple comfort in a tranquil environment. Singles (with shower) cost L170,000 and doubles (with bath) cost L270,000 and all rooms have satellite TV, independent air-conditioning, hairdryer and safe facilities.

Villa Borghese (Map 4)

The comfortable and friendly *Hotel Villa Borghese (☎ 06 85 30 09 19 or 06 841 34 18, fax 06 841 41 00, Via Pinciana 31)* is in an attractive Liberty-style building notable for being the birthplace and home of the famous 20th century Roman writer Alberto Moravia. Homely singles/doubles/triples are L215,000/275,000/335,000 and there is a suite for L360,000. Room services include satellite TV, minibar and independent air-conditioning. Small discounts are available from November through March. The hotel has a small lounge area on the ground floor and an attractive terrace that doubles as a breakfast area in summer. There is no lift.

Coppedè (Map 4)

Hotel Coppedè (☎/fax 06 854 95 35, Via Chiana 88), in the largely residential Via Salaria area north-east of Termini, is a bit out of the way, but it is perfectly adequate for travellers looking for a base from which to explore the city. It has one single for L160,000 and doubles/triples for L250,000/300,000, including room-service breakfast. There is no communal lounge/TV area but the 11 rooms are large and fully furnished.

Near Il Vaticano (Map 5)

Just outside the Vatican wall, off Via de' Corridori is *Hotel Bramante (☎ 06 68 80 64 26, fax 06 687 98 81, bramante@excalhq.it, Vicolo delle Palline 24)*. It offers reasonable accommodation in a 16th century building designed and lived in by the Swiss architect, Domenico Fontana, until he was expelled from Rome by Pope Sixtus V. Singles/ doubles are L132,000/ 176,000 with shower. Without bathroom, they cost L97,000/ 132,000. The hotel has only one TV in the downstairs lounge, but there are plans to place televisions in all the rooms. There is no lift, but there are only two floors.

Hotel Prati (☎ *06 687 53 57, fax 06 68 80 69 38, prati@italyhotel.com, Via Crescenzio 89)*, has small singles/doubles for L120,000/180,000 and triples for L240,000. A small discount is available in July and August and from November to February. Singles/doubles without bathroom are L90,000/120,000. The hotel is on four floors and there is no lift.

Hotel Adriatic (☎ *06 68 80 80 80, fax 06 689 35 52, adriatic@ats.it, Via Vitelleschi 25)*, on the continuation of Via Porcari, off Piazza del Risorgimento, this has singles/ doubles for L140,000/180,000 and triples/ quads for L240,000/300,000, excluding breakfast and offers a discount of up to L30,000 in winter. The rooms are basic, but comfortable and there is a large terrace.

At Via Cola di Rienzo 243, there are two good-quality hotels, both excellent value considering their location. The recently re-structured *Hotel Joli* (☎/*fax 06 324 18 54)* is on the 6th floor. It has large, pleasant rooms and is ideal for families. Singles/ doubles are L80,000/120,000 and triples/ quads are L160,000/200,000. The spacious breakfast room doubles as a TV lounge and a private television is available on request at an additional cost of L10,000 a night. Book well in advance.

Hotel Florida (☎ *06 324 18 72, fax 06 324 18 57)*, on the 2nd floor, is small and quiet and has singles/doubles for around L120,000/ 160,000 (L70,000/105,000 without bath) and triples/quads for around L200,000/230,000, breakfast not included. Discounts are available out of season and if you pay in cash. The rooms are attractively furnished and have ceiling fans; independent air-conditioning costs an additional L30,000 a night. There is a bar service from 8.30 am to 8 pm. The hotel doesn't have its own garage, but guarantees space in a nearby garage for L25,000 a day.

Hotel Ticino (☎/*fax 06 324 32 51, Via dei Gracchi 161)* is a small establishment with clean and spacious rooms and a friendly management. Singles cost L125,000 and doubles start at L180,000, and discounts are negotiable out of season. The hotel also has three family rooms which cost from L238,000.

Hotel Amalia (☎ *06 39 72 33 54, fax 06 39 72 33 65, Via Germanico 66)*, on the corner of Via Ottaviano, is a stone's throw from Il Vaticano. Singles/doubles are L150,000/220,000 and triples are L300,000, including breakfast and private bathroom with shower. The rooms are light and spacious and all have a fridge, double glazing and a safe. There is no air-conditioning, but fans are provided.

Trastevere (Map 7)

Hotel Manara (☎ *06 581 47 13, fax 06 588 10 16, Via Luciano Manara 24a-25)*. This pensione used to be a well-located dive but following a major renovation in 1998 it is now one of the area's, if not the city's, best deals, with three-star quality at excellent prices. All spotlessly clean rooms have bathrooms (with hair-dryers) and TV, and most of them look out over the market square of Piazza San Cosimato. Singles/doubles are L100,000/130,000, triples L150,000 and quadruples L170,000. There are only nine rooms so book early.

The *Hotel Cisterna* (☎ *06 581 72 12, Via della Cisterna 7-9)*, off Via San Francesco a Ripa, is another mid-range option. It is located in a quiet, pretty street around the corner from the busy Piazza Santa Maria in Trastevere, and close to all the best restaurants, cafés and night spots in the area. The rooms are unexceptional but comfortable and clean. Some of the rooms are much larger and airier than others. Singles/ doubles L120,000/160,000 and triples are L215,000.

PLACES TO STAY – TOP END

There is no shortage of expensive hotels in Rome, but many, particularly those near Stazione Termini, are geared towards large tour groups and, while certainly offering all the usual conveniences, they tend to be a bit anonymous. The following three and four-star hotels have been selected on the basis of their individual charm, as well as value for money and location. All rooms are with bathroom, telephone and TV.

Where two prices have been quoted for a double room the first is for use of a double as a single and the second is for a standard double. Breakfast is generally included in the given price, but it is wise to check.

Aventino (Map 7)

The *Aventino – Sant'Anselmo Hotels* (☎ 06 574 51 74, fax 06 578 36 04, Piazza di Sant'Anselmo 2) are four separate turn of the century villas run by one company. They are situated in a predominantly residential area, but still only a stone's throw from the historic centre (to the north) and the restaurants of Testaccio (to the south). The Aventino provides two-star accommodation; singles/doubles cost L150,000/230,000, triples are L250,000 and quads L260,000. The other villas are in the three-star category; singles/doubles cost L190,000/ 290,000, triples are L340,000 and quads L360,000. All prices include breakfast.

These hotels are the perfect place if you prefer quieter surroundings or if you have a car as street parking is fairly easy to find. There are pleasant gardens and courtyards where you have your breakfast or a drink.

Near Stazione Termini (Map 6)

All of the following are located on Map 6 unless otherwise stated.

Hotel Venezia (☎ 06 445 71 01, fax 06 495 76 87, Via Varese 18), on the corner of Via Marghera, is beautifully furnished in antique style. Singles/doubles cost L174,000/242,000 and triples L320,000. Prices drop in the low season. The multilingual staff are charming.

At *Hotel Montecarlo* (☎ 06 446 00 00, fax 06 446 00 06, info@hotelmontecarlo.it, Via Palestro 17a) singles/doubles cost L170,000/250,000, triples L347,000 and quads L444,000. It also offers generous discounts on rooms in the low season.

Hotel Piemonte (☎ 06 445 22 40, fax 06 445 16 49, Via Vicenza 34), has very pleasant singles/doubles for up to L200,000/ 280,000. The rooms have all been renovated, there's double glazing throughout, and the bathrooms are particularly nice.

Termini to Foro Romano/Colosseo (Map 6)

On the other side of the Stazione Termini near the Basilica di Santa Maria Maggiore is *Hotel Giada* (☎ 06 488 58 63, fax 06 482 03 44, Via Principe Amedeo 9), which has good quality rooms for reasonable prices, although the atmosphere is impersonal. Singles/doubles are L190,000/230,000 and triples/quads are L290,000/310,000, and prices fall out of season and in August. All rooms have showers. Guide books are available for purchase from reception and there is a bar service on request.

Just behind the Fori Imperiali, in the area once known as the *Suburra* are two superb hotels. The *Hotel Forum* (☎ 06 679 24 46, fax 678 64 79, forum@venere.it, Via Tor de' Conti 25), is in an ex-convent and has very comfortable singles/doubles for L360,000/ 520,000 (L270,000/390,000 out of season). Triples are L630,000. The hotel's best assets are its delightful roof garden and restaurant, from which there are panoramic views of the Foro Romano and Palatino. The hotel is often full, so book well in advance.

The nearby *Hotel Nerva* (☎ 06 678 18 35, fax 06 69 92 22 04, Via Tor de'Conti), is a cosy establishment offering comfortable singles/doubles for L250,000/360,000, including breakfast. Considerable discounts are available out of season and if you pay in cash. There are also two rooms (a single and a double) outfitted with facilities for disabled people.

Two minutes east of the Colosseo is *Hotel Celio* (Map 8, ☎ 06 70 49 53 33, fax

06 709 63 77, Via dei Santi Quattro 35c). Singles/doubles are L295,000/350,000 and triples are L390,000. The 20 rooms are a bit cramped, but the lack of space is made up for by the extensive additional services offered by the hotel, including photocopying and fax facilities, car rental, an extensive film library, video recorders (for rent) and a laundry/dry cleaning service. The hotel is also due to be expanded in the near future.

Closer to Stazione Termini, between the Rome Opera and the Terme di Diocleziano off Piazza della Repubblica, is *Hotel Columbia* (✆ *06 474 42 89, fax 06 474 02 09, info@hotelcolumbia.com, Via del Viminale 15)*. Singles are L181,000 and doubles are L223,000/246,000, including breakfast on the roof terrace, and there is a small discount on prices out of season. Rooms are large and bright and business travellers will be interested to know that rooms also have modem plugs.

On Via Nazionale is the elegant *Hotel Artemide* (✆ *06 48 99 11, fax 06 48 99 17 00, Via Nazionale 22)*. Comfortable singles/ doubles start at L350,000/490,000, and additional beds cost L100,000, or L60,000 for children (cots for infants are available free of charge). A full breakfast is included. There is one twin room with facilities for disabled people. Hotel/room services include a restaurant-bar, roof terrace, mini bar with free mineral water and soft drinks, and free daily newspaper.

City Centre

Several of Rome's better hotels are located near Piazza di Spagna. The *Gregoriana* (Map 6, ✆ *06 679 79 88, fax 06 678 42 58, Via Gregoriana 18)*, has long been an institution for the fashionable set: Naomi Campbell and Claudia Schiffer have both stayed here. Its rooms are not numbered, but are instead adorned with letters by the 1930s French fashion illustrator Erté. Singles start at L220,000 and doubles cost L360,000/380,000, including room-service breakfast. Prices are negotiable out of

season. The hotel provides a laundry service. Credit cards are not accepted.

Dubbing itself 'Your Home in Rome', the friendly and informal *Hotel Scalinata di Spagna* (Map 6, ✆ *06 679 30 06, fax 06 69 94 05 98, Piazza Trinità dei Monti 17)* is superbly located at the top of the Spanish Steps and has newly-refurbished, comfortable singles/doubles for L380,000/450,000 and triples for L550,000. Breakfast can be eaten on the panoramic roof terrace. Room No 18 has a private terrace and connects with an adjoining room to make a family suite costing L850,000. Cot facilities are available. The hotel is very popular, so book well in advance.

The luxurious *Hassler Villa Medici* (Map 6, ✆ *06 69 93 40, fax 06 678 99 91, hasslerroma@mclink.it, Trinitá dei Monti 6)*, is a long-standing symbol of Roman hospitality and can claim among its guests the Royal families of Sweden, Greece and England, President Kennedy and Elizabeth Taylor. However, luxury doesn't come cheap: singles cost from L480,000 to L515,000 and doubles cost from L695,000 to L1,030,000, not including breakfast. The hotel offers honeymoon packages and special weekend and 'romance' packages at certain times of the year. Hotel facilities include a beauty salon, an in-room massage service and free bicycles for touring the historic centre. The hotel's rooftop restaurant was Rome's first panoramic restaurant.

To the west of Piazza di Spagna is the delightful *Hotel Carriage* (Map 6, ✆ *06 699 01 24, fax 06 678 82 79, Via delle Carozze 36)*, a smallish establishment offering simple comfort in a quiet setting. Singles/ doubles are L270,000/370,000 and triples are L460,000. There is also a suite for four people, costing L580,000 and two of the rooms have private rooftop patios.

Hotel Sistina (Map 6, ✆ *06 474 41 76, fax 06 481 88 67, Via Sistina 136)*, between Piazza di Spagna and Piazza Barberini, has singles/doubles for L260,000/ 370,000 and triples for L440,000, including breakfast on the roof terrace in summer. The rooms are spacious and light and windows are double glazed to keep out the street noise.

Behind Piazza di Spagna, near Via Veneto is **Hotel Eden** (Map 6, ☎ 06 47 81 21, fax 06 482 15 84, Via Ludovisi 49), one of Rome's top luxury hotels. Built as a hotel in 1889, it closed in 1992 for refurbishment and was reopened by Baroness Thatcher in 1994. Prices are high, but this does not seem to put people off, so book well in advance. Standard singles/doubles start at L590,000/850,000 (not including breakfast or IVA), and deluxe rooms cost considerably more. The hotel has a panoramic roof-top restaurant and bar, where you might like to have Sunday brunch, as well as piano bar with live music in the evenings.

Hotel Locarno (Map 5, ☎ 06 361 08 41, fax 06 321 52 49, locarno@venere.it, Via della Penna 22), near Piazza del Popolo, is a friendly alternative to some of the more impersonal top-end hotels. Singles are L235,000 and doubles are L360,000/ 390,000, including breakfast, served in the garden or on the roof terrace during the summer for a small additional fee. The hotel offers a 10% discount in August. Facilities include modem plugs in the rooms, an attractive Art Deco lounge-bar and free use of bicycles. There is one room equipped for disabled people.

The **Fontana Hotel** (Map 6, ☎ 06 678 61 13, fax 06 679 10 56, Piazza di Trevi 96), is appealing because of its location – opposite the Trevi fountain. The establishment, an ex-17th century convent, is good value given its location and some rooms have a view of the fountain. Singles/doubles start at L280,000/L330,000 (you pay more for a view of the fountain) and triples/quads are L430,000/500,000. Prices are lower out of season. Unfortunately, the rooms are quite noisy, since there is usually a large crowd gathered around the fountain.

One of Rome's top hotels is the **Minerva** (Map: Around Piazza Navona, ☎ 06 69 94 18 88, fax 679 41 65, minerva@pronet.it, Piazza della Minerva 69). This deluxe hotel belongs to the Crowne Plaza chain and offers extensive facilities in absolute

comfort – as you'd expect given the price. Singles are L500,000 and doubles are L550,000/750,000, and suites start at L1,150,000, not including breakfast. The hotel is located in a 17th century palace redesigned in post-modern style by Paolo Portoghesi in the late 1980s. Services include a ground floor restaurant and lobby bar and a fitness room on the 1st floor. The hotel also has no smoking rooms and there is one room for disabled people. Cheques are not accepted.

The elegant **Hotel Senato** (Map: Around Piazza Navona, ☎ 06 678 43 43, fax 06 69 94 02 97, Piazza della Rotonda 73) faces onto the Pantheon, and is surprisingly quiet, considering its position. Singles/doubles start at L250,000/345,000, but special offers are available at specific times of the year so check. Hotel facilities include a laundry service, and the attractive ground floor bar is open from 5 pm.

Albergo Teatro di Pompeo (Map: Around Piazza Navona, ☎ 06 687 28 12, fax 06 68 80 55 31, Largo del Pallaro 8), just off Campo de' Fiori, has plenty of old world charm — in fact parts of the hotel go back as far as the Roman Republic. It has quiet, comfortable doubles starting at L310,000 and guests have breakfast in the remains of Pompey's Theatre (55 BC). Services include private safe facilities and radio. The hotel also takes bookings for guided tours of the city (pick-up at reception).

North of Piazza Navona, in a quiet street lined with craft shops and jewellers, is the very pleasant **Hotel Portoghesi** (Map: Around Piazza Navona, ☎ 06 686 42 31, fax 06 687 69 76, portoghesi@venere.it, Via dei Portoghesi 1). Singles are L210,000 (L190,000 in August and from January to March) and doubles are L290,000. The hotel also has suites, including one with terrace, from L310,000. Extra beds cost L50,000 and prices include breakfast on the roof terrace. The hotel does not accept American Express or Diners Club cards.

Around the corner in Largo Febo, between Piazza Navona and the Tevere, is the ivy-clad **Hotel Raphael** (Map: Around

Piazza Navona, ☎ *06 68 28 31, fax 06 687 89 93, info@raphaelhotel.com, Largo Febo 2),* by far one of the most congenial establishments in Rome, and ideally located for exploring the city centre on foot. In the reception area is a display of antiques and a valuable collection of ceramics by Pablo Picasso. Prices range from L335,000 to L395,000 for a single room and from L495,000 to L590,000 for a double (from L615,000 to L715,000 for a deluxe double) depending on the time of year. The hotel offers special weekend rates for a minimum of two nights stay (subject to availability). The hotel has two restaurants, including one on the roof terrace, which has a stunning view of the city centre. The hotel also has a fitness room and a sauna and there are three rooms equipped for disabled people.

Near Il Vaticano (Map 5)

Hotel Columbus (☎ *06 686 54 35, fax 06 686 48 74, Via della Conciliazione 33)* is in a magnificent 15th century palace in front of Basilica of San Pietro. Quiet and surprisingly homely given its history and proportions, it is a Renaissance curiosity with its splendid halls, frescoes by Pinturicchio and heavy wooden furnishings. Its attractive internal courtyard doubles as a free car park. It has singles/doubles for L300,000/400,000. Hotel services include a roof terrace, bar and an in-house laundry service, and there is a delightful restaurant in the old refectory of the palace, offering Italian and international cuisine.

The small and cosy *Hotel Sant'Anna* (☎ *06 68 80 16 02, fax 06 68 30 87 17, santanna@travel.it, Borgo Pio 133),* on the other side of Via della Conciliazione, is virtually in the shadow of the Basilica. It has high quality accommodation at reasonable prices. Light and spacious singles/doubles are L230,000/300,000, and there is a discount of up to L80,000 out of season. There are also two rooms equipped for disabled people. Booking is recommended.

Further away from the Vatican, between the Lepanto and Flaminio metro stops, is the recently opened *Hotel Mellini* (☎ *06*

Doss Down with the Romantics

If you fancy staying in the building where the poet John Keats died, contact the Landmark Trust in the UK. Established as a charity in 1965, the trust restores and conserves a host of architectural marvels in the UK, as well several in Italy including the 3rd floor apartment where Keats died in Piazza di Spagna, Rome.

The trust also administers the Casa Guidi in Firenze where the poet Robert Browning lived and the Villa Saraceno, near Vicenza, an early Palladio commission. For any further information, contact The Landmark Trust (☎ 0628-825 925), Shottesbrooke Maidenhead, Berkshire SL6 3SW, UK.

32 47 41, fax 06 32 47 78 01, htl.dei.mellini @flashnet.it, Via Muzio Clementi 81). The rooms are large and comfortable and there are excellent facilities for disabled people, including an external lift for access from the street. Singles/doubles are L340,000/ 420,000 and a suite is L540,000. Hotel services include a roof terrace overlooking the Palazzo della Giustizia and a snack bar serving light meals. The 6th floor is reserved for non-smokers.

RENTAL ACCOMMODATION

Apartments near the centre of Rome are expensive and you can expect to pay a minimum of L1,500,000 a month for a studio apartment or a small one-bedroom place. On top of the rent there are bills for electricity (which is quite expensive in Italy) and gas. There is usually also a building maintenance charge *condominio,* of between L50,000 and L300,000 depending on the size and location of the apartment.

A room in a shared apartment will cost at least L600,000 a month, plus bills. You will usually be asked to pay a deposit equivalent to one or two months' rent and the first month in advance.

Several of the English-language bookshops in Rome have noticeboards where people looking for accommodation or offering a room on a short or long-term basis place their messages. Try the Economy Book and Video Center (Map 6), Via Torino 136 (near Via Nazionale) or The Corner Bookshop (Map: Around Piazza Navona), Via del Moro 48 in Trastevere, between Piazza Santa Maria in Trastevere and Piazza Trilussa.

Another good way to find a shared apartment is to buy *Wanted in Rome* (published fortnightly on Wednesday) or *Porta Portese* (published twice weekly on Tuesday and Friday) at newspaper stands. Bear in mind that many shared apartments in Rome have a communal kitchen and bathroom but no common living space. What was once the living room is often converted into an additional bedroom to keep costs down.

There are many estate agencies specialising in short-term rentals in Rome, which charge a fee for their services. You will also be asked for a hefty deposit. They are listed in the telephone directory under *Agenzie immobiliari*. English-speaking agencies are also listed in *Wanted in Rome*.

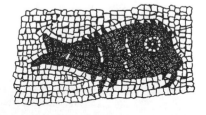

Places to Eat

FOOD
Eating is one of life's great pleasures for Romans. Be adventurous and don't ever be intimidated by eccentric waiters or indecipherable menus and you will find yourself agreeing with the locals, who believe that nowhere in the world is the food as good as in Italy.

Roman Cuisine
The roots of Roman food are in the diet of the poor and offal has always been an important ingredient. Historically, the ordinary folk ate the *quinto quarto* (fifth quarter) of the animal, which was all that was left after the rich had taken their pickings. Offal eaters shouldn't miss the opportunity to try *coda* (oxtail) or *trippa* (tripe) here, where they are done best. If you can stomach it, try the pasta *pajata*, made with the entrails of very young veal, considered a delicacy since they contain the mother's congealed milk.

Deep frying, which has its origins in Jewish cooking, is another important feature of Roman cuisine. Deep-fried fillets of *baccalà* (salted cod), *fiori di zucca* (zucchini flowers) stuffed with mozzarella and anchovies, and *carciofi alla giudia* (artichokes) are a must on any Roman gastronomic itinerary, whether they be eaten as a fast-food snack, as a prelude to a pizza or as a course in themselves.

In recent years fish has become an important fixture on the menus of Rome's better eateries. More often than not it is grilled whole and then filleted by the waiter at the table. It is, however, more expensive than any other main course. A word of warning for fish eaters: only order it on Tuesday or Friday, when the markets have it fresh, unless you are eating at one of the top restaurants.

Antipasto dishes in Rome are particularly good and many restaurants allow you to make your own mixed selection from a buffet. See the Pasta boxed text for typically Roman pasta dishes.

Roman meat dishes to look out for are *saltimbocca alla Romana*, a thin fillet of veal topped with a slice of *prosciutto crudo* (cured ham), white wine and sage, and *abbacchio al forno*, spring lamb roasted with rosemary and garlic – an Easter favourite.

Try these vegetable dishes: *carciofi alla Romana*, artichokes stuffed with mint or parsley and garlic; a salad of curly *puntarelle* (Catalonian chicory) tossed in a garlic, olive oil and anchovy dressing; and, in spring, freshly shelled *fave* (broad beans) served with a slice of pecorino Romano.

The city's neighbourhoods have their own specialties. Testaccio, home of the former slaughterhouse which is now used as a social centre and live music venue (the Entertainment chapter), is still known as *the* place to go for the authentic Roman dining experience. See the Food Glossary in the Language chapter later in this book

Where to Eat
Eateries are divided into several categories. A *tavola calda* (literally 'hot table') usually offers cheap, pre-prepared meat, pasta and vegetable dishes in a self-service style. A *rosticceria* usually offers cooked meats, but often has a larger selection of takeaway food. A *pizzeria* will of course serve pizza, but usually also a full menu including antipasto, pasta, meat and vegetable dishes. An *enoteca* is a wine shop which also serves wine by the glass (or bottle); light snacks, such as cheeses or cold meats, are usually also available. An *osteria* is likely to be either a wine bar offering a small selection of dishes, or a small *trattoria*. A trattoria is a cheaper version of a *ristorante* (restaurant), which in turn has a wider selection of dishes and a higher standard of service. The problem is that many of the establishments that are in fact restaurants call themselves trattorie and vice versa for reasons best known to themselves. It is best to check the menu, usually posted by the door, for prices.

Pasta al Dente

Cooking good pasta according to the Italian way is no mean feat. First, the pasta has to be of the highest quality and second it has to be cooked for precisely the correct length of time, so that it is *al dente* – firm. Italians almost salt the boiling water before adding the pasta and they never throw in *(buttare)* the pasta until everyone is present. Don't complain if your pasta takes a while to arrive in a restaurant – you'll need to wait the 10 to 12 minutes it takes to cook.

Italian pasta is infinitely varied. It comes in a dazzling variety of shapes and sizes, ranging from *spaghetti* and *linguini* to tube pasta such as *penne* and *rigatoni*, or it can be shell-shaped *(conchiglie)*, bow-shaped *(farfalle*, which means butterflies), corkscrew-shaped *(fusilli)* and many other shapes.

Packet, or dried pasta, is made with high quality durum wheat and water. On the other hand, fresh egg pasta *(pasta all'uovo*, or *fatto a mano)* is made with eggs and flour and is used to make stuffed pasta such as tortellini and ravioli, or cut into strips called tagliatelle (thinner strips are also called *taglionini* or *tagliarini)*. Egg pasta is usually served with richer, creamier sauces than those which usually accompany dried pasta and are most likely to be tomato based.

Pasta sauces traditionally vary quite dramatically between the north and south of the country. Traditional Roman pasta dishes include *spaghetti carbonara* (with egg yolk, cheese and *pancetta* or cured bacon) and *all'amatriciana* (with a sauce of tomato, pancetta and a touch of chilli). *Penne all'arrabbiata* (literally 'angry' pasta) has a sauce of tomato and chilli.

Another favourite Roman pasta dish is *spaghetti al cacio e pepe*, a deceptively simple dish of piping hot pasta topped by freshly grated *pecorino Romano*, ground black pepper and a dash of good olive oil. It appears on many Roman menus, traditionally in the more humble *osterie* and *trattorie*, although in recent years there has been a fashion in more up-market eateries for this and other dishes of the *cucina povera* school. Spaghetti *alla gricia* is similar but with the addition of pancetta. It comes from the town of Griciano in northern Lazio.

Although pasta with seafood sauces hails from the south of Italy, many Roman restaurants serve delicious spaghetti *alle vongole* (with clams) – best on Tuesday or Friday when the seafood is guaranteed to be really fresh.

In many Roman restaurants, Thursday is *gnocchi* day. The traditional Roman recipe uses semolina flour and the gnocchi – usually served with a tomato or meat *ragù* – are quite heavy.

Non-squemish eaters might want to try pasta *pajata*, made with the intestines of a very young veal calf. If you want something really hearty and warming try *pasta e lenticchie* (pasta with lentils) but be prepared for the post-meal anaesthetic effect!

Freshly grated cheese is the magic ingredient for most pasta (although don't try adding it to a seafood sauce unless you want really strange looks and comments). Parmesan *(parmigiano)* is the most widely used, particularly in the north. Look for the name 'Parmigiano Reggiano' on the rind to ensure you're getting the genuine article because there is also the similar, but lower-quality, *grana padano*. In and around Rome (and also in Sardegna) there is a tendency to use the sharp and slightly salty sheep's milk *pecorino*.

Gnocchi   Tortellini   Fusilli   Ravioli   Farfalle   Rigatoni

Don't judge the quality of a ristorante or trattoria by its appearance. You are likely to eat your most memorable meal at a place with plastic tablecloths in a tiny back street, a dingy *piazza* or on a back road in the country.

And don't panic if you find yourself in a trattoria which has no printed menu: they are often the ones which offer the best and most authentic food and have menus which change daily to accommodate the availability of fresh produce. Just hope that the waiter will patiently explain the dishes and cost.

Numerous restaurants offer tourist menus, with an average price of L20,000 to L30,000 (usually not including drinks). Generally the food is of a reasonable standard, but choices will be limited and you can usually get away with paying less if you want only pasta, salad and wine.

After lunch and dinner, head for the nearest *gelateria* (ice-cream parlour) to round off the meal with some excellent *gelati*, followed by a *digestivo* (after-dinner liqueur) at a bar.

For a light lunch, or a snack, most bars serve *tramezzini* (sandwiches) and *panini* (rolls), and there are numerous outlets where you can buy pizza by the slice (*a taglio*). Another option is to go to one of the many *alimentari* and ask them to make a panino with the filling (usually cold meats and cheeses) of your choice. At a *pasticceria* you can buy pastries, cakes and biscuits.

Fast food is becoming increasingly popular in Rome. There are McDonald's outlets throughout the city as well as numerous other chain restaurants and US-style hamburger joints.

Costs

Most eating establishments have a cover charge, usually around L2000 to L3000 per person, and a service charge of 10% to 15% which is included in the total. There is no obligation to tip on top of this, but most people leave a small tip of L2000 to L5000, unless the service has been particularly bad. Make sure you check the bill *(il conto)* closely, especially in restaurants in touristy areas, as items that were never ordered sometimes mysteriously appear on the bill, or the bill can be added up 'incorrectly'.

When you pay your bill you should be given a detailed receipt *(ricevuta fiscale)*. Hang onto it. Technically, if you leave the restaurant without it and are stopped by the *guardia di finanza* (finance police), you could be fined up to two million lire.

Never assume that credit cards or travellers cheques are accepted. Budget eateries rarely accept anything other than cash, and even some of the mid-range and top-end places accept only cash or debit cards issued by Italian banks. If you want to pay by credit card, check first.

Eating Customs

Italians rarely eat a sit-down *colazione* (breakfast). They tend to drink a cappuccino, usually *tiepido* (warm), and eat a *cornetto* (croissant) or other type of pastry while standing at a bar.

Pranzo (lunch) is traditionally the main meal of the day and many shops and businesses close for three to four hours every afternoon to accommodate the meal and siesta which is supposed to follow.

A full meal will consist of *antipasto*, which can vary from *bruschetta*, a type of garlic bread with various toppings, to fried vegetables, or *prosciutto e melone* (cured ham wrapped around melon). Next comes the *primo piatto* – a pasta or risotto, followed by the *secondo piatto* of meat or fish. Italians often then eat an *insalata* (salad) or *contorno* (vegetable side dish) and round off the meal with fruit (occasionally with a sweet) and *caffè*, often at a bar on the way back to work.

The evening meal *(cena)* was traditionally a simpler affair, but habits are changing because of the inconvenience of travelling home for lunch every day.

Vegetarian

Vegetarians will have no problems eating in Rome. While there are only a few restaurants devoted to them, vegetables are a staple of the Italian diet. Most eating establishments serve a good selection of antipasti, *contorni* (vegetable side dishes prepared in a variety of ways) and salads. Most traditional Roman pasta dishes are suitable for vegetarians. Other dishes to look out for are: *pasta e fagioli*, a thick soup made with borlotti beans and pasta; *pasta al pesto*, with basil, parmesan, pine nuts and olive oil; and *orecchiette ai brocoletti*, ear-shaped pasta with a broccoli sauce, often quite spicy. Risotto is usually a good choice, although sometimes it is made with a meat or chicken stock.

Self-Catering

If you have access to cooking facilities, it is best to buy fresh fruit and vegetables at open markets, and prosciutto, salami, cheese and wine at *alimentari* or *salumerie*, which are a cross between grocery stores and delicatessens. Fresh bread is available at a *forno* or *panetteria* (bakeries which sell bread, pastries and sometimes groceries) and usually at alimentari. *Latterie* sell milk, yoghurt and cheese. Some bars also sell milk and dairy products. See the Self-Catering section later in this chapter.

DRINKS
Nonalcoholic Drinks

Coffee The first-time visitor to Rome is likely to be confused by the many ways in which the locals consume their caffeine.

Tea Italians don't drink a lot of tea *(tè)* and generally only do so in the late afternoon, when they might take a cup with a few *pasticcini* (small cakes). You can order tea in bars, although it will usually arrive in the form of a cup of warm water extracted from the espresso machine (with a strange smell and sometimes a slightly rotten taste) with an accompanying tea bag. If this doesn't suit your taste, ask for the water *molto caldo* or *bollente* (boiling).

Quality packaged teas, such as Twinings tea bags and leaves, as well as packaged herbal teas, such as chamomile, are often sold in supermarkets, alimentari and some bars. You can find a wide range of herbal teas in a herbalist's shop *(erboristeria)*, which sometimes also stocks health foods.

Caffè Society

An *espresso* is a small amount of very strong black coffee. You can ask for a *doppio espresso*, which means double the amount, or a *caffè lungo* (although this can sometimes mean a slightly diluted espresso). If you want a long black coffee (as in a weaker, watered-down version), ask for a *caffè Americano*.

A *corretto* is an espresso with a dash of grappa or some other spirit and a *macchiato* is espresso with a small amount of milk – on the other hand, *latte macchiato* is milk with a spot of coffee. *Caffè freddo* is a long glass of cold black coffee.

Then, of course, there is the *cappuccino*, coffee with hot, frothy milk; if you want it without the froth, ask for a *caffè latte* or a cappuccino *senza schiuma*. Italians tend to drink cappuccino only with breakfast and during the morning. They never drink it after meals or in the evening and, if you order one after dinner, don't be surprised if the waiter asks you two or three times, just to make sure that they heard correctly.

You will also find it difficult to convince bartenders to make your cappuccino hot rather than lukewarm. Ask for it *molto caldo* and wait for the same 'tut-tut' response that you attracted when you ordered a cappuccino after dinner.

Granita *Granita* is a drink made of crushed ice with fresh lemon or other fruit juices, or with coffee topped with fresh whipped cream. A slightly different kind of ice drink, and uniquely Roman, is *grattacheccha*, ice grated off a huge block and flavoured with syrups or juices. There used to be grattachecche kiosks all over Rome, but there are now only a few left (two in Testaccio and one on the Trastevere side of the Isola Tiberina).

Water Rome's water is among the cleanest in Italy and you can drink the water from any of the ubiquitous street fountains. Most of these run continuously and have a small hole in the spout to facilitate drinking; just hold your finger over the bottom of the spout and a jet of water will emerge higher up. The water is icy cold year round, which is especially refreshing in summer.

The water does contain relatively high levels of calcium, and many Romans prefer to drink bottled mineral water *(acqua minerale)*. This is either sparkling *(frizzante* or *gasata)* or still *(naturale)* and you will be asked in restaurants and bars which you prefer. If you want a glass of tap water, ask for *acqua dal rubinetto*, although simply asking for *acqua semplice* will also suffice.

Alcoholic Drinks

Beer The main local labels are Peroni, Dreher, Nastro Azzuro and Moretti, all very drinkable and cheaper than the imported varieties. If you want a local beer, ask for a *birra nazionale*, which will be either in a bottle or on tap. Italy also imports beers from throughout Europe and the rest of the world.

All the main German beers are, for instance, available in bottles or cans; English beers and Guinness are often found *alla spina* (on tap) in *birrerie* (bars specialising in beer), and Australians might be pleased to know that you can even find a Foster's and a Castlemaine XXXX. There has lately been a proliferation of pubs which specialise in international beers. See Pubs & Bars in the Entertainment chapter.

Wine & Spirits Wine *(vino)* is an essential accompaniment to any meal, and *digestivi* are a popular way to end one. Italians are very proud of their wines and find it hard to believe that anyone else could produce wines as good as theirs. Many Italians drink alcohol only with meals and the foreign custom of going out for a drink is still considered unusual although, in some parts of Italy, it is common to see men starting their day with a grappa for breakfast and continuing to consume strong drinks throughout the day.

Wine is reasonably priced and you will rarely pay more than L15,000 for a good bottle of wine, although prices can be up to more than L30,000 for really good quality. There are three main classifications of wine which will be marked on the label: DOCG *(denominazione d'origine controllata e garantita)*, DOC *(denominazione di origine controllata)* and *vino da tavola* (table wine). A DOC wine is produced subject to certain specifications, although the label does not certify quality. DOCG is subject to the same requirements as normal DOC but it is also tested by government inspectors. Table wines can vary considerably in quality, some are very good and others best avoided.

Although some excellent wines are produced in Italy, most trattorie stock only a limited selection of bottled wines and generally only cheaper varieties. Most people tend to order the house wine *(vino della casa* or *vino sfuso)* or the local wine *(vino locale)* when they got out to dinner.

The styles of wine vary throughout the country. While many wine buffs would argue that Rome and the Lazio region is the poor relation as far as Italian wine production is concerned, some good white wines are produced in the Castelli Romani area (south-east of the city), notably Frascati Superiore. You can taste local and not-so-local wine in many of Rome's *enoteche*. See Wine Bars in the Entertainment chapter.

Before dinner, Italians might drink a Campari and soda, or a fruit cocktail, usually pre-prepared and often without alcohol *(analcolico)*. After dinner try a shot of *grappa*, a very strong clear grape spirit, or an *amaro*, a dark liqueur prepared from herbs. If you prefer a sweeter liqueur, try an almond-flavoured *amaretto*, a sweet aniseed *sambucca* or, in the hotter months, a chilled *limoncello*.

PLACES TO EAT

Rome offers a pretty good range of eating places: there are some excellent places offering typical Roman fare to suit a range of budgets, as well as some good, but usually fairly expensive, restaurants offering international cuisines such as Indian, Chinese, Vietnamese and Japanese. The best areas to look for good trattorie are Trastevere and between Piazza Navona and the Tevere.

During summer these areas are lively and atmospheric and most establishments have outside tables. Restaurants usually open for lunch from 12.30 to 3 pm, but many are not keen to take orders after 2 pm. In the evening, restaurants open from about 8 pm, although in tourist areas they will often open earlier. If you want to be sure of finding a table (especially if you want one outside), either drop into the restaurant during the day and make a booking, or arrive before 8.30 pm. Many restaurants close for some or part of August.

Always remember to check the menu posted outside for prices, cover and service charges. Expect to pay around L20,000 per person in a pizzeria, L30,000 at a simple trattoria, up to L50,000 at a mid-range restaurant and around L100,000 or more at Rome's top eating places. These prices are for a three-course meal and wine. Eating only a pasta and salad and drinking the house wine at a trattoria can keep the bill down. If you order meat or fish you will push up the bill substantially.

Good options for cheap, quick meals are the hundreds of bars around the city, where sandwiches cost L2500 to L5000 taken at the bar (al banco), or at takeaway pizzerie, where a slice of freshly cooked pizza, sold by weight, can cost as little as L2500. Bakeries, numerous in the Campo de' Fiori area, are another good choice for a cheap snack. Try a piece of *pizza bianca*, a flat bread resembling focaccia, which costs from around L1500 a slice. See the Light Meals section for details.

Generally, the restaurants near Stazione Termini are to be avoided if you want to pay reasonable prices for good-quality food. The side streets around Piazza Navona and Campo de' Fiori harbour many good-quality, low-priced trattorie and pizzerie, and the areas of San Lorenzo (to the east of Termini, near the university) and Testaccio (south of the city centre near the Piramide

di Cestio mausoleum) are popular eating districts with the locals. Trastevere might be among the most expensive places to live in Rome but it offers an excellent selection of rustic-style eating places hidden in tiny piazzas, and pizzerie where it doesn't cost the earth to sit at a table on the street.

Bear in mind that pizzerie are usually open only in the evenings, and that many restaurants, especially the cheaper pizzerie, osterie and trattorie, don't accept credit cards.

Where prices are quoted for full meals, this refers to a three-course meal (antipasto or primo, secondo with wine).

City Centre

Budget Roman and regional Italian cooking can be enjoyed in the heart of the fashionable shopping area at **Otello alla Concordia** (Map 6, ☎ 06 679 11 78, Via della Croce 81). It has an attractive courtyard which is used as a winter garden in the colder months and is well priced. There's a three-course tourist menu including wine for L36,000, but the restaurant also offers single meat dishes served with vegetables (unusual for Italian restaurants) that are a filling meal in themselves for L15,000 to L20,000. It is popular with journalists, writers and proprietors of the nearby antiques shops. Try the exceptionally good *spaghetti all'Otello* which is a secret recipe. It is closed on Sunday. **Da Edy** (☎ 06 36 00 17 38, Vicolo del Babuino 4) is another good bet in an area not known for good value. You can expect a meal to cost around L40,000. The menu changes according to what's in season; the house speciality, *spaghetti al cartoccio* (pasta with seafood), comes wrapped up in a silver-foil parcel. It is closed on Sunday.

For a bargain pizza, try **Pizzeria Il Leoncino** (Map 5, ☎ 06 687 63 06, Via del Leoncino 28) across Via del Corso from Via Condotti. You can eat and drink for around L15,000 to L20,000; it's closed on Wednesday. Off Via del Campo Marzio near Piazza del Parlamento is **Da Gino** (Map: Around Piazza Navona, ☎ 06 687 34 34, Vicolo Rosini 4), a trattoria of the old school with old-fashioned prices. It's always full and popular with politicians and journalists, especially at lunchtime. Try the home-made fettuccine cooked with peas and *guanciale* (bacon made from the pig's cheek) or the *coniglio al vino bianco* (rabbit cooked in white wine). It is closed on Sunday. Don't mind the old family retainer who slumps over a table at the entrance. He's not dead, just asleep.

There are several good budget spots in the Piazza Navona area. *Cul de Sac (Map: Around Piazza Navona,* ☎ *06 68 80 10 94, Piazza Pasquino 73)*, just off the southern end of Piazza Navona, is actually a wine bar but also serves hearty soups and pasta, pâté and dips and a large selection of cheeses and cured meats. Prices are at the higher end of the budget range (L30,000 to L40,000 a head). The long, narrow room, panelled in wood and lined with bottles of wine, is cosy in winter, but there are also outdoor tables in summer. Credit cards are not accepted.

Next door, *Insalata Ricca (Map: Around Piazza Navona,* ☎ *06 68 30 78 81, Piazza Pasquino 72)* serves pasta and meal-in-themselves salads. It's good value (a meal will cost around L20,000) and has become so popular with young Romans that new branches are popping up all over the city. There is another one nearby at Largo dei Chiavari 85 *(Map: Around Piazza Navona,* ☎ *06 85 68 80 36)*, on the other side of Corso Vittorio Emanuele II. Both have tables outdoors and are open every day.

Via del Governo Vecchio is home to countless second-hand clothing stores and two of Rome's most popular budget dining spots. *Pizzeria da Baffetto (Map: Around Piazza Navona,* ☎ *06 686 16 17, Via del Governo Vecchio 11)* is a Roman institution and is open every day. Its large pizzas would feed an army and deserve their reputation as among the best (and best value) in Rome. Expect to join a queue if you arrive after 9 pm and don't be surprised if you end up sharing a table. Pizzas are around L8000 to L12,000, a litre of wine costs L8000 and the cover charge is L1500. Farther along the

street at No 18 is a tiny, nameless *osteria (Map: Around Piazza Navona, no* ☎*)* run by Antonio Bassetti, where you can eat an excellent meal for around L20,000 to L30,000. The consistently good food and low prices make it one of the best-value eating places in Rome. There is no written menu, but don't be nervous: even when very busy, the owner/waiter will try to explain (in Italian) the dishes. It is closed on Sunday.

Following Via del Corallo from Via del Governo Vecchio, you reach the Piazza del Fico, full of character. At No 29 is *Trattoria Pizzeria da Francesco (Map: Around Piazza Navona,* ☎ *06 686 40 09)*, which has decent pasta from L8000 to L12,000 and a good selection of antipasto and vegetables. Pizzas range in price from around L9000 to L14,000, beer is L6000 and wine L10,000. It is open for lunch and dinner every day except Tuesday, when it is open only for dinner. Almost next door, *Pizzeria Corallo (Map: Around Piazza Navona,* ☎ *06 68 30 77 03, Via del Corallo 10)* has good pizzas and is open late. A meal will cost around L25,000.

Across Corso Vittorio Emanuele II is *Trattoria Polese (Map 5,* ☎ *06 686 17 09, Piazza Sforza Cesarini 40)*, where you can eat outside beneath a huge fig tree. It's better value for a pizza (L8000 to L12,000) than a full meal (around L35,000) but it's a good bet if you don't have time to waste wandering off the main thoroughfare. It is closed on Tuesday. At Via dei Banchi Vecchi 140/a, is the charming *Albistrò (Map 5,* ☎ *06 686 52 74)*. It's the place to go if you want something other than Roman cuisine, as the strictly seasonal menu has an international flavour (one of the owners is Swiss). Prices are at the higher end of the budget range (around L40,000 for three courses) but it is a delightful place with good service and excellent wines at reasonable prices. It is closed on Wednesday and booking is essential on weekends.

Hostaria Giulio (Map 5, ☎ *06 68 80 64 66, Via della Barchetta 19)*, in a tiny street between Via Monserrato and Via Giulia, is another good-value family-run establishment serving traditional fare. The building

LAUREN SUNSTEIN

Back view of Mario's Triumph, Campidoglio

STEFANO CAVEDONI

Guarding the President on the Quirinale

LAUREN SUNSTEIN

Bernini's Elefantino making a long-distance trunk call

Equestrian statue of Marcus Aurelius

Night view, Altare della Patria

Fontana delle Tartarughe, Piazza Mattei

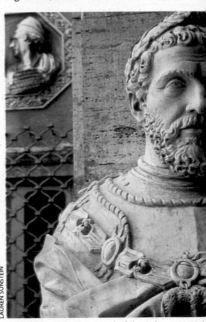

A glimpse of the courtyard of the Palazzo Mattei

dates from the 16th century, the dining room has a vaulted ceiling and it's decorated cheerfully, with plenty of tables outdoors in summer. It is closed on Sunday.

Pizzeria Montecarlo (Map: Around Piazza Navona, ☎ 06 686 18 77, Vicolo Savelli 12), off Via del Pellegrino, is a very traditional pizzeria, with paper sheets for tablecloths. The pizzas are good and a meal with wine or beer will cost around L16,000. It's open every day. On Piazza della Cancelleria, between Piazza Navona and Campo de' Fiori, is *Grappolo d'Oro (Map: Around Piazza Navona, ☎ 06 686 41 18)*, which serves excellent-quality, traditional Roman food for around L30,000 for a full meal. It is closed on Sunday. Opposite, at No 72, is *Ditirambo (Map: Around Piazza Navona, ☎ 06 687 16 26)*, where a meal will cost around L40,000. The wood beamed rooms and wooden floors give the place a rustic feel and the bread and pasta are home-made. It is closed Monday lunchtime.

There are several restaurants on Campo de' Fiori, although some establishments trade off their picturesque setting and serve mediocre food at inflated prices. *Hosteria Romanesca (Map: Around Piazza Navona, ☎ 06 686 40 24)* is not one of them and is usually a good bet. It is tiny, so arrive early in winter, when there are no outdoor tables. Pasta courses cost L10,000 to L12,000 and a full meal will set you back by around L35,000. It is closed on Monday.

Da Sergio (Map: Around Piazza Navona, ☎ 06 686 42 93, Via delle Grotte 27), off Via dei Giubbonari near Campo de' Fiori, serves decent pizzas for under L10,000 and enormous helpings of traditional Roman pastas as well as good meat and fish dishes. Pictures of the various items on the menu decorate the walls, both inside and out. It's got a great atmosphere and has tables outside in summer. It is closed on Sunday.

The main item on the menu at *Dar Filettaro a Santa Barbara*, which is also known as *Filetti di Baccalà (Map: Around Piazza Navona, ☎ 06 686 40 18, Largo dei Librari 88)*, off Via dei Giubbonari is deep-fried salted cod. The fish fillets, which literally melt in the mouth, are presented wrapped in paper, and you eat them with your fingers rather than with a knife and fork. Various antipasto dishes, salads (including a Roman favourite of puntarelle with an anchovy and garlic dressing) and desserts are also available. You can satisfy moderate hunger and thirst for around L10,000 to L15,000. It is closed on Sunday.

On the other side of Via Arenula is one of Rome's best and most popular lunch spots (open Monday to Saturday), *Benito (Map: Around Piazza Navona, ☎ 06 686 15 08, Via dei Falegnami 14)*. There's a daily choice of two pasta dishes and a range of meats and vegetables. A plate of pasta and a salad will set you back L11,000. *Sora Margherita (Map: Around Piazza Navona, ☎ 06 686 40 02, Piazza delle Cinque Scole 30)*, in the heart of the old ghetto, is open only for lunch from Monday to Friday. It is so well known and popular with the locals that there isn't even a sign over the door. Don't let the formica table tops put you off: you're here for the food – traditional Roman and Jewish fare – and the bargain prices. Get here early to avoid a queue (especially on Thursday if you want the fresh gnocchi).

Also in the Jewish quarter is *Al Pompiere (Map: Around Piazza Navona, ☎ 06 686 83 77, Via Santa Maria de' Calderari 38)*, a huge first-floor dining room with frescoed ceilings. Its prices are reasonable and the food is great. Try the *carciofi alla giudia* and keep some room for a slice of ricotta and sour plum tart supplied by the Jewish bakery around the corner. It is closed on Sunday.

Mid-Range *Osteria Margutta (Map 6, ☎ 06 323 10 25, Via Margutta 82)* off Via del Babuino near Piazza di Spagna has a good selection of vegetable antipasto dishes and pasta with tasty sauces such as broccoli and sausage. It is closed on Sunday. Off Piazza di Spagna, the very popular *Mario (Map 6, ☎ 06 678 38 18, Via delle Vite 55)* offers Tuscan food – fabulous bean soup, grilled meat and game – for around L65,000 a full meal but the service can be dreadful. It's closed on Sunday.

Al 34 (Map 6, ☎ 06 679 50 91, Via Mario de' Fiori 34) combines Roman cooking with regional dishes from throughout Italy. It is consistently good and very popular so booking is essential. It is closed on Monday. A full meal will cost around L55,000. Try the rigatoni with pajata if you can stomach it, or the spaghetti with zucchini if you can't. For those with a really large appetite, a *menu degustazione* (gourmand's menu) is also available. The well known *Dal Bolognese (Map 5, ☎ 06 361 14 26, Piazza del Popolo 1-2)* is in a prime position to attract tourists, but maintains high culinary standards and reasonable prices. Expect to part with around L75,000 for a full meal. You must book if you want an outside table in summer. It is closed on Monday.

'Gusto (Map 5, ☎ 06 322 62 73, Piazza Augusto Imperatore 9), opposite the Mausoleo di Augusto, is a trendy new arrival on the gastronomic scene and brings a touch of New York to Rome. It's a huge place, with exposed brick walls and a converted warehouse feel. A new concept in Roman dining, it offers several possibilities for eating: substantial bar snacks, a pizzeria serving Neapolitan-type pizzas (with a thicker crust), or a more formal restaurant on the first floor. What you spend depends on which area you choose to eat in. Bar snacks cost from L10,000 to L20,000. A pizza with a bruschetta and drinks will cost around L35,000, and meals in the restaurant from L50,000. There's also a bookshop-cookshop, a wine shop and a cigar room. The eating-bar areas are closed on Monday.

Near the Fontana di Trevi, in a little street which runs between Via dei Crociferi and Via delle Muratte, is *Al Moro (Map 6, ☎ 06 678 34 95, Vicolo delle Bollette 13)*. A good-quality, traditional Roman meal will come to around L70,000. It is closed on Sunday. *Tullio (Map 6, ☎ 06 475 85 64, Via San Nicola da Tolentino 26)*, which runs off Piazza Barberini, is one of the best restaurants in Rome specialising in Tuscan cuisine. The food is excellent (you'll pay around L70,000 for a meal), the place is usually packed and the service fast and ef-

ficient. It is closed on Sunday. Also near Piazza Barberini is *Colline Emiliane (Map 6, ☎ 06 481 75 38, Via degli Avignonesi 22)*, a recently redecorated trattoria which serves superb Emilia-Romagnan food. Try the home-made pasta stuffed with pumpkin and the *vitello* (veal) with mashed potatoes – both are delicious. It is closed on Friday. A meal will set you back around L50,000.

Osteria dell'Ingegno (Map: Around Piazza Navona, ☎ 06 678 06 62, Piazza della Pietra 45), near Piazza Colonna, is new on the dining scene in Roman terms and the designer décor gives the place a modern feel. The cuisine is central Italian with an international twist. The ravioli stuffed with chestnuts is unusual but delicious and meat dishes tend to be in robust or rich sauces. There's also a good selection of salads and an excellent wine cellar to choose from. Pasta dishes start at L14,000 and a full meal will set you back around L45,000. It is closed on Sunday.

Il Bacaro (Map: Around Piazza Navona, ☎ 06 686 41 10, Via degli Spagnoli 27), around the corner from the Pantheon, is a tiny restaurant where miracles are performed in a minute kitchen. The pasta and risotto dishes are imaginative and delicious and they do great things with beef and veal. It's got an excellent (and well-deserved) reputation, and as there are only a handful of tables inside and a couple in the street in summer, booking is essential. It is closed on Sunday. A meal with wine will cost L50,000 to L60,000. *La Campana (Map: Around Piazza Navona, ☎ 06 686 78 20, Vicolo della Campana 18)*, at the top end of Via della Scrofa, is believed to be Rome's oldest restaurant. Its distinctive Roman ambience and food, without the usual noise and confusion, make it an eternal favourite. It is closed on Monday. A full meal will cost around L65,000.

Il Cardinale – GB (Map 5, ☎ 06 686 93 36, Via delle Carceri 6), between Via dei Banchi Vecchi and Via Giulia, is another well-known restaurant with superb Roman food and an elegant rustic feel. A full meal should come to under L80,000. *Pierluigi*

(Map 5, ☎ 06 686 13 02), on Piazza de' Ricci, just off Via Monserrato, used to be one of Rome's best mid-range restaurants, with consistently good food and set on a picturesque piazza. The food (Italian from all regions) is still good and the location delightful, but in recent years the prices have increased (you'll pay around L60,000 for a meal) and the service has become haphazard. The restaurant is closed on Monday.

La Carbonara (Map: Around Piazza Navona, ☎ 06 68 64 783) takes up virtually one side of Campo de' Fiori. It is a consistently good restaurant, serving traditional Roman fare at honest prices. As the name might suggest, it is known for its *spaghetti alla carbonara*. Expect to pay around L60,000 for a full meal. It is closed on Tuesday.

Da Giggetto (Map: Around Piazza Navona, ☎ 06 686 11 06, Via del Portico di Ottavia) is a local institution and has been serving Roman Jewish cooking for years (the deep-fried artichokes are especially good). The location – in the heart of the ghetto, right next to the ancient Portico d'Ottavia – can't be beaten, especially if you get a table on the footpath. A meal will cost under L50,000. It is closed on Monday. *Piperno (Map: Around Piazza Navona, ☎ 06 68 80 66 29, Via Monte de' Cenci 9)* does similar food but is more famous and more expensive (L80,000 for a meal). Piperno has made deep frying an art form; the house special is a mixed platter of deep-fried fillets of baccalá, stuffed zucchini flowers, vegetables and mozzarella cheese. Offal eaters will be well satisfied. It is closed on Sunday evening and Monday.

The terrace of *Vecchia Roma (Map: Around Piazza Navona, ☎ 06 686 46 04, Piazza Campitelli 18)* is one of the prettiest in Rome and it's an extremely pleasant spot to pass a few hours. The pan-Italian menu is extensive and changes seasonally. In summer there are imaginative salads, in winter lots of dishes based on polenta, year-round good pasta and risotto. Expect to part with around L85,000. It is closed on Wednesday.

On the nearby Piazza Margana, *La Taverna degli Amici (Map: Around Piazza Navona, ☎ 06 69 92 06 37)* also has a delightful terrace covered with shady market umbrellas. It is extremely popular with Romans who work in the area (especially politicians from the nearby Democratici di Sinistra headquarters) and at lunchtime the service can be very slow. The menu is extensive and offers a wide choice of antipasto, pasta and risotto dishes and main courses of meat and fish. Pasta dishes start at L15,000. A full meal will set you back around L50,000, but expect to pay up to L70,000 if it includes a meat or fish. It is closed on Monday.

Another restaurant with a fabulous terrace but also very nice in winter is *St Teodoro (Map 8, ☎ 06 678 09 33, Piazza dei Fienili 49-50)*, which is tucked away in a quiet area between Teatro di Marcello and the Foro Romano. The extensive menu combines favourite Roman dishes with regional cuisine (the rich cooking of Emilia Romagna features) and a strong emphasis on fish. Pasta dishes with seafood are especially good (the pasta is freshly made each day by the owner's mother). Try the *tonarelli St Teodoro*, which is incredibly light pasta with a sauce of juicy prawns, zucchini and cherry tomatoes. There's an interesting selection of wines from all over Italy in addition to good house wine. A full meal will cost around L60,000. It is open daily.

Top End You cannot find a more perfect setting for a restaurant than that of *Camponeschi (Map: Around Piazza Navona, ☎ 06 687 49 27)* on the beautiful (and delightfully car free) Piazza Farnese. It is a favourite with politicians, diplomats and the glitterati, all of whom are happy to pay between L100,000 and L130,000 for a meal here. It is closed on Sunday and open only for dinner. *Il Convivio (☎ 06 686 94 32, Via dell'Orso 44)*, between Piazza Navona and the Tevere, is an elegant restaurant, noted for its *cucina creativa* (the Italian version of *nouvelle cuisine*) and professional service. A full meal will set you back around L100,000.

La Rosetta *(Map: Around Piazza Navona, ☎ 06 686 10 02, Via della Rosetta 8-9)*, near the Pantheon, is without doubt the best seafood restaurant in Rome. The menu features innovative combinations of flavours and ingredients and the owner-chef is regarded as one of the best in Italy. But reputations come at a price: expect to part with at least L130,000 for a memorable meal here. It is closed on Sunday and booking is essential. Nearby is another excellent fish and seafood restaurant, **Quinzi e Gabriele** *(Map: Around Piazza Navona, ☎ 06 687 93 89, Via delle Coppelle 6)*, which is frequented by well-heeled Romans as well as some of the city's top chefs on their nights off. A meal costs around L130,000 and it is closed on Sunday.

The terrace of **L'Angoletto** *(Map: Around Piazza Navona, ☎ 06 686 80 19)* spills out onto the picturesque Piazza Rondanini. This traditional restaurant has a faithful clientele and trades off its long-standing reputation for good food rather than creativity or innovation. The *spaghetti alla vongole* (with clams, olive oil, garlic and chilli) is delicious. Expect to pay around L60,000 for a meal. It is closed on Sunday.

El Toulà *(Map 5, ☎ 06 687 34 98, Via della Lupa 29)* is one of Rome's most prestigious restaurants, which is reflected in the prices – more than L130,000 for a full meal. The menu features dishes from the Veneto region in the north of Italy. It is closed Saturday lunch and Sunday. **Andrea** *(Map 6, ☎ 06 482 18 91, Via Sardegna 24-28)*, close to Via Vittorio Veneto, is one of the most popular top restaurants and often full of business-suited executive types. A full meal will be in the range of L80,000 to L100,000.

Il Vaticano (Maps 3 & 5)

Budget Most establishments around San Pietro and il Vaticano are geared towards tourists and can be extremely overpriced for fairly mediocre food. If you head north from il Vaticano or north-east towards the Tevere, you'll find better-value options.

Osteria dell'Angelo *(Map 3, ☎ 06 38 92 18, Via G Bettolo 24)* is in the Trionfale area north of il Vaticano – walk along Via Leone IV from Piazza del Risorgimento. A hearty Roman meal can be had for around L30,000. **Pizzeria Giacomelli** *(Map 3, ☎ 06 38 35 11, Via Emilia Faà di Bruno 25)* is off Via della Giuliana past Largo Trionfale. The pizzas are good, big and cheap. **Il Tempio della Pizza** *(Map 5, ☎ 06 321 69 63, Viale Giulio Cesare 91)* is open late and has reasonably-priced, good-quality food.

Between Piazza Mazzini and the Tevere is **Cacio e Pepe** *(Map 3, ☎ 06 321 72 68, Via Avezzana 11)*, a tiny place with a handful of tables. It is not much more than a hole in the wall but the food is fabulous. You would be pushed to find better home-made pasta or better value for money in the entire city. Enormous helpings of pasta cost L7000. The *spaghetti carbonara* and namesake, *spaghetti al cacio e pepe*, are delicious, as is the *melanzane parmigiana*, eggplant with tomato and cheese. In the summer the tables spill out onto the street, and even in winter hungry Romans will sit outside, wrapped in overcoats and scarves, rather than have to wait for a table indoors.

Mid-Range *Da Cesare (Map 5, ☎ 06 686 12 27, Via Crescenzio 13)*, closed Sunday evening and Monday, is just off Piazza Cavour and is a reliable option in an area not renowned for its eating establishments. It is a traditional place with a clubby feel and is especially popular in the autumn and winter, when the menu offers game, truffles, porcini mushrooms and wonderful soups made from lentils, chick peas, borlotti and cannellini beans. Expect to part with around L60,000 to L70,000 for a full meal.

Diagonally opposite, on the corner of Piazza Cavour and Via Tacito, is **Il Simposio** *(Map 5, ☎ 06 32 13 210)*, a wine bar which is part of the Enoteca Costantini, one of Rome's best-known winesellers. Open every day, the restaurant has gained a reputation of its own and people now go there as much for the food as for the wine. On offer each day is a selection of hot dishes, plus cured meats, smoked salmon, cheeses and desserts. A meal will cost around L55,000.

Trastevere & Testaccio (Map 7)

In Trastevere's maze of tiny streets there are any number of pizzerie and cheap trattorie. There are also plenty of upmarket restaurants. The area is beautiful at night and most establishments have outside tables. It is also very popular, so arrive before 9 pm unless you want to queue for a table. Testaccio, a traditional working class area, is off the beaten tourist track but very popular with young Romans as the place to go for a good, cheap meal. All the following items are on Map 7 unless otherwise stated.

Budget *Osteria Der Belli (☎ 06 580 37 82, Piazza Sant'Apollonia 9-11)* just off Piazza Santa Maria in Trastevere is a reliable trattoria with a great antipasto selection and large helpings of pasta. The main courses are nothing special (don't order the fish unless it's Tuesday or Friday, as it is unlikely to be fresh). It is closed on Monday. A decent meal will cost around L30,000. They also do good pizzas. *Mario's (Map: Around Piazza Navona, ☎ 06 580 38 09, Via del Moro 53)* near Piazza Trilussa is a local favourite for its cheap pasta (around L10,000) but you can find better quality elsewhere. It is closed on Monday.

Da Augusto (Map: Around Piazza Navona, ☎ 06 580 37 98, Piazza de' Renzi 15) is another great spot for a cheap meal and the atmosphere is great. Rickety tables spill out onto the piazza in summer. Try the home-made fettuccine. If you arrive early there is also a good selection of vegetables. A meal with wine will cost around L20,000. It is closed on Sunday and every so often closes on other days of the week as well.

Just across the piazza at No 31a is *Casetta di Trastevere (☎ 06 580 01 58)*. Huge servings of pasta are L9000. The antipasto is also very good. It is closed on Monday. Another very cheap family-run place, hidden behind an anonymous frosted-glass door, a few paces from the square on Via della Pelliccia is *Da Corrado (no ☎)*, where you can choose from two or three pastas and two or three meat dishes daily. You'll pay under L25,000. This is a traditional workers' canteen with no frills and is a favourite haunt of Trastevere's shopkeepers, especially at lunchtime. It is closed on Sunday and throughout August.

Farther along Via della Pelliccia, at No 47-53, is *Da Otello in Trastevere (☎ 06 589 68 48)*. A hearty meal will cost around L30,000 but you could almost get away with just a large helping of the excellent antipasto (L9000), which you serve yourself from a huge buffet. It is closed on Monday.

Da Gildo (Map 5, ☎ 06 580 07 33, Via della Scala 31) is a pizzeria-trattoria with a range of pizzas and good-quality food. A full meal will cost around L25,000. It is closed on Wednesday. Nearby is *Da Lucia (☎ 06 580 36 01, Vicolo del Mattinato 2)*, which has excellent antipasto and pasta as well as Roman specialities such as *pollo con peperoni* (chicken with peppers) and *trippa all romana* (tripe). In summer it has outside tables where you sit beneath the neighbours' washing, but it's very atmospheric all year. A full meal will cost around L35,000. It is closed on Monday.

Da Giovanni (Map 5, ☎ 06 686 15 14, Via della Lungara 41) is a good 10 minute walk from the centre of Trastevere towards il Vaticano. It is a popular eating place and you will probably have to wait for a table. The food is very good, especially the home-made pasta and the pizzas, and the prices are excellent. It is closed on Sunday.

Pizzeria San Calisto (☎ 06 581 82 56) on Piazza San Calisto has outdoor tables and serves enormous pizzas that fall off your plate (L10,000 to L14,000). It is closed on Monday. For a Neapolitan-style pizza with a thicker base, try *Pizzeria da Vittorio (☎ 06 580 03 53, Via di San Cosimato 14)* between Piazza San Calisto and Piazza San Cosimato. You'll have to wait for an outside table if you arrive after 9 pm, but the atmosphere is great. There are all the regular pizzas plus a few house specials such as the *Vittorio* (fresh tomato,

PLACES TO EAT

basil, mozzarella and parmesan) and the *Imperiale* (fresh tomatoes, lettuce, cured ham and olives). A bruschetta, pizza and wine will cost around L20,000. It is closed on Monday.

Pizzeria Ivo (☎ 06 581 70 82, Via San Francesco a Ripa 158) has outdoor tables on a busy street, but the pizzas could be bigger for the price (from L9000). The bruschetta is an excellent start to the meal. The house wine comes in bottles and is not a bargain at L8000. It is closed on Tuesday. *Pizzeria Popi-Popi* (☎ 06 589 51 67, Via delle Fratte di Trastevere 45) is very popular among young people, who flock to its outside tables in summer. Inside it's huge so you shouldn't have to wait too long for a table. The pizzas are good and cheap. It's closed on Thursday.

Panattoni (☎ 06 580 09 19, Viale di Trastevere 53) is also known as *L'Obitorio* (the morgue) on account of its cold hard marble tables. Open late and always crowded, it is one of the more popular pizzerie in Trastevere. You can eat there for around L15,000. It is closed on Wednesday and during August.

In Testaccio on the other side of the Tevere there are several good budget restaurants. You won't find a noisier, more popular pizzeria in Rome than *Pizzeria Remo* (☎ 06 574 62 70, Piazza Santa Maria Liberatrice 44). Its popularity is not surprising: it's a lively place and the pizzas are, arguably, the best in Rome. They are huge but have a very thin crust. You make your order by ticking your choices on a sheet of paper given to you by the waiter. A meal will cost around L16,000. Expect to queue if you arrive after 8.30 pm. It is closed on Sunday.

Augustarello (☎ 06 574 65 85, Via G Branca 98), off the piazza, specialises in offal dishes. Pasta dishes are L11,000, secondi are L13,000 to L15,000 and vegetables and salads are L11,000. It is closed on Sunday. *Trattoria da Bucatino* (☎ 06 574 68 86, Via Luca della Robbia 84) is a popular Testaccio eating place, with pasta from L10,000 to L12,000, second courses for L12,000 and pizzas from L8500 to

L12,000. It also serves traditional Roman fare and has excellent deserts. It is closed on Monday and all credit cards are accepted.

Da Felice (☎ 06 574 68 00, Via Mastro Giorgio 29) is a local institution and is especially popular at lunchtime with shoppers and stallholders at the nearby Testaccio market. Ask nicely for a table as the proprietor will only let you sit down if he likes the look of you; he keeps reserved signs on all the tables to cover his tracks! If you're one of the privileged few, you'll enjoy true Roman fare, great pasta and lots of meat and offal, all for a bargain price. It is closed on Sunday.

Opposite the former slaughterhouse is *Saperi e Sapori* (☎ 574 31 67, Via di Monte Testaccio 34b), an excellent pizzeria with tables outdoors. Pizzas cost from L7000 to L12,000, bruschetta is L3000 and a medium beer is L6000. It is closed on Monday.

Mid-Range Trastevere has dozens of good mid-range restaurants. Just wander the streets and you'll find something that appeals.

Paris (☎ 06 581 53 78, Piazza San Calisto 7) is the best place outside the ghetto proper to sample true Roman-Jewish cuisine. The menu never changes, but the ingredients are always the freshest available. The delicate *fritto misto con baccalá* (deep-fried vegetables with salt cod) is memorable, as are simpler dishes such as the *pasta e ceci* (a thick chick pea soup in which the pasta is cooked) and fresh gilled fish. It's as popular with tourists as it is with Romans, but it's at the higher end of mid-range. You'll part with around L80,000 for a full meal. It is closed Sunday evening and Monday.

Nearby is the appropriately named *Ripa 12* (☎ 06 580 90 93, Via San Francesco a Ripa 12), a Calabrian family restaurant serving original pasta, fish and seafood dishes. It is credited by some with having invented *carpaccio di spigola* (very fine slices of raw sea bass). There are some tables on the street but, unless you want your fish smoked by traffic fumes, you'll do better sitting inside. It is closed on Sunday.

La Tana di Noantri (☎ 06 580 64 04, *Via Paglia 1*), between Piazza Santa Maria in Trastevere and Piazza Sant'Egidio, has an extensive menu and is a good place to take children, who can tuck into a pizza (from L8000) while their parents enjoy more sophisticated fare. The helpings are not enormous so you'll probably want three or four courses, for which you'll pay around L50,000. The antipasto and meat and fish dishes are particularly good and there's the usual range of pastas. In the warmer months tables are set up under huge umbrellas in the small courtyard opposite the restaurant, tucked into the side of the church of Santa Maria in Trastevere. It's an excellent spot to watch the passing parade of human (rather than vehicular) traffic. It is closed on Tuesday.

Fricandò (☎ 06 581 47 38, *Vicolo del Leopardo 39/a*) is hidden in the backstreets of Trastevere. In summer you'll eat outside beneath the neighbours' washing, and probably feel that you're part of their conversations and arguments as well. The menu would appeal to both offal lovers and vegetarians; meat courses and Roman specialities (such as tripe and oxtail) are balanced by delicate savoury tarts and a host of different pastas. A full meal will cost around L55,000; it's closed on Tuesday.

In Testaccio, *Cecchino dal 1887* (☎ 06 574 63 18, *Via di Monte Testaccio 30*) is a local institution and serves superb Roman food – which means, of course, lots of offal. It constantly features in articles about dining in Rome and was selected in 1994 as one of the best restaurants in Italy by the international newspaper the *Herald Tribune*. A meal will cost around L75,000. It is closed on Monday.

Top End If it's fish you want and you're in Trastevere, *Alberto Ciarla* (☎ 06 581 86 68, *Piazza San Cosimato 40*) is the obvious choice. This restaurant has been doing great things with fish and seafood for decades although unfortunately the décor hasn't been updated for the same period of time. Its signature dishes are a Roman speciality of baccalà with tomato sauce, dried currants

and pinenuts, and 'dry-fried' seafood lightly coated in semolina and fried in olive oil. Expect to pay around L90,000 to L100,000 for a full meal with wine. There are a handful of tables outside in summer. It is open only in the evening and closed on Sunday.

San Lorenzo to Foro Romano (Map 6)

Budget As Rome's university district, eating places in San Lorenzo are influenced by the student population. One of the more popular places, *Pizzeria l'Economia* (*Via Tiburtina 44*) serves local fare and good pizzas at prices students can afford.

Formula 1 (*Map 6*, s another good-value pizzeria, where you'll pay around L15,000 for bruschetta, pizza and wine. It is closed on Sunday. *Le Maschere* (*Map 6*, ☎ 06 445 38 05, *Via degli Umbri 8*) charges the same sort of prices and both are popular with students.

If you have no option but to eat near Stazione Termini, try to avoid the tourist traps offering overpriced full menus. There are many tavole calde in the area, particularly to the west of the train station, which offer panini and pre-prepared dishes for reasonable prices. There is a self-service place in the station complex, *La Piazza*, where you can eat good food at reasonable prices.

There are a few good-value restaurants in the area. *Da Gemma alla Lupa* (*Map 6*, ☎ 06 49 12 30, *Via Marghera 39*), northeast of the station, is a simple trattoria with prices to match: a full meal will cost under L30,000. *Trattoria da Bruno* (*Via Varese 29*) has good food at reasonable prices: around L8000 for a pasta and up to L14,000 for a second course. Home-made gnocchi are served on Thursday. *Hostaria Angelo* (*Via Principe Amedeo 104*) is a traditional trattoria with reasonable prices.

Alle Carrette (☎ 06 679 27 70, *Vicolo delle Carrette 14*) is a decent pizzeria off Via Cavour near the Foro Romano, well placed to rest weary legs after a hard day's sightseeing. A pizza and wine will come to around L15,000-L20,000.

Da Ricci (☎ 06 488 11 07, *Via Genova 32*), off Via Nazionale, is reputed to be

Rome's oldest pizzeria. It started up as a wine shop in 1905 and has been run by the same family ever since. The pizzas turned out here have a slightly thicker crust than the normal Roman variety, but some say this is the best pizza in town. There are also good salads and home-made desserts.

Between Piazza Vittorio Emanuele and the Basilica di San Giovanni in Laterano is *Galilei (Map 8, ☎ 06 731 56 42, Via Galilei 12)*, a good, cheap pizzeria. Towards the Colosseo is *Hostaria di Nerone (☎ 06 474 52 07, Via delle Terme di Tito 96)*. This place has always been popular with tourists, but is slowly gaining a reputation as being one of Rome's only gay restaurants. There are tables outside in the summer and the food is good. Try the *fettuccine Nerone*. An antipasto, pasta and salad will cost about L30,000.

Also near the Colosseo is *Trattoria Colosseo (Map 8, ☎ 06 700 16 84, Via Capo d'Africa 26)*, which offers reasonable food at reasonable prices. It is also a pizzeria and has outside tables.

Mid-Range *Il Dito e la Luna (☎ 06 494 07 26, Via dei Sabelli 49-51)*, in the San Lorenzo district, is a cut above your ordinary trattoria and serves a Sicilian inspired menu. There are interesting dishes such as fresh anchovies marinated in orange juice, a savoury tart made with onions and melted Parmesan, *caponata* (a sort of Sicilian ratatouille) or fish cooked in a potato crust. A meal will set you back around L50,000. It is closed on Sunday.

One of San Lorenzo's more famous trattorie is *Pommidoro (Map: Greater Rome, ☎ 06 445 26 92, Piazza dei Sanniti 44)*, which is popular with artists and intellectuals. Specialties are grilled meats and, in winter, game. An excellent meal will cost around L40,000. It is closed on Sunday. You'll understand how *Tram Tram (Map: Greater Rome, ☎ 06 49 04 16, Via dei Reti 44)* got its name when you hear the trams rumbling past, but don't mind them, as this is a great San Lorenzo haunt. The menu has a southern Italian slant and is moderately priced. It's a good place for vegetarians as

the menu includes several main course veggie dishes. It is closed on Monday.

Gastone (☎ 06 47 82 47 80, Via Parma 11a) off Via Nazionale had just opened at the time of writing. It is a huge place with tables in several rooms and serves interesting dishes which marry Italian tradition with 'international' innovation. It is staffed by enthusiastic bilingual staff. Expect to part with around L50,000 for a meal.

Just off Via Cavour in the tiny Via dell' Angeletto is *Osteria Gli Angeletti, (☎ 06 474 33 74)*, an excellent little restaurant. It has outside tables on the characteristic Piazza Madonna dei Monti, the heart of the Rione Monti. While the service can get a bit slow when they're busy, the food is good. You'll pay L10,000 to L14,000 for a pasta and around L16,000 for a main course. It is open every day but closes in December.

La Tana del Grillo (Map 6, ☎ 06 70 45 35 17, Via Alfieri 4-8), on the corner of Via Merulana, a few streets north of Piazza San Giovanni in Laterano, offers typical cuisine from Ferrara in northern Emilia Romagna. The menu features meat and regional cheeses and pasta such as *cappellacci di zucca*, pouches filled with pumpkin that look vaguely like a floppy hat. There is also the usual Roman fare. A full meal will cost from L40,000 to L50,000. It is closed Sunday and Monday lunchtime.

The restaurants and bars on the street opposite the Colosseo are overpriced and best avoided, but if you wander east into the grid of streets behind you'll find a number of options. One of the best is *Pasqualino (Map 8, ☎ 06 700 45 76, Via dei Santi Quattro 66)*, a real neighbourhood trattoria frequented by locals. It serves reliable food at honest prices. The pasta with seafood in a creamy tomato sauce is excellent and the fish is usually excellent. It is closed on Monday.

Top End Your tastebuds are in for a treat at *Agata e Romeo (☎ 06 446 61 15, Via Carlo Alberto 45)* near Santa Maria Maggiore. The intimate and elegant restaurant serves innovative Roman and southern Italian dishes using only the freshest ingredients, expertly prepared. The deserts are memorable, especially the legendary *mille foglie*. Antipasti cost L28,000, primi L25,000, main courses L35,000 and deserts L15,000.

Ethnic Restaurants

Restaurants serving international cuisine are not common anywhere in Italy, but Rome has a better choice than any other city. A good area for foreign restaurants and food shops is around Piazza Vittorio Emanuele II near Stazione Termini.

Chinese food is very popular, but the food is often heavily salted and can leave a lot to be desired. *Golden Crown (Map 6, ☎ 06 678 98 31, Via in Arcione 85)*, between Via del Tritone and the Palazzo del Quirinale, is a good choice. A meal will cost up to L40,000.

For an excellent Japanese meal, head for *Sogo Asahi (Map 6, ☎ 06 678 60 93, Via di Propaganda 22)* near Piazza di Spagna. It is expensive, however, at around L70,000 a head. There's a sushi bar, for which you have to book. It is usually open during August.

Suria Mahal (Map: Around Piazza Navona, ☎ 06 589 45 54) on Piazza Trilussa is an Indian restaurant with a delightful garden terrace right next to the fountain on Piazza Trilussa in Trastevere. A delicious meal will cost around L45,000. On the other side of Trastevere, near the Basilica di Santa Cecila, is *India House (Map 7, ☎ 06 581 85 08, Via di Santa Cecilia 8)*. It has good-value set menus for around L25,000, but the food is average.

Thien Kim (Map: Around Piazza Navona, ☎ 68 30 78 32, Via Giulia 201) does an Italian take on Vietnamese cooking, but it's all pretty tasty. A meal will cost around L35,000 to L45,000. It is closed on Sunday.

If Egyptian food is more your style, try *Shawerma (Map 8, ☎ 06 700 81 01, Via Ostilia 24)* near the Colosseo, which serves great couscous. Expect to pay up to L35,000 for a full meal. It is closed on Monday.

Tex-Mex food can be found at *Oliphant (☎ 06 686 14 16)*, on the corner of Via della Scrofa and Via delle Coppelle. If all you really want is a Big Mac, you'll find McDonald's outlets on Piazza della Repubblica

(with outside tables), Piazza di Spagna, Piazza della Rotonda (with a view of the Pantheon that many a chic eatery would kill for) and Viale di Trastevere (between Piazza Sonnino and Piazza Mastai). At *Marconi (Map 6, Via di Santa Prassede 9)*, opposite Santa Maria Maggiore, you can munch on fish and chips, baked beans and other assorted stodgy English dishes.

Vegetarian

All trattorie serve a good selection of vegetable dishes, but there are other options for vegetarians in Rome. *Centro Macrobiotico Italiano (Map 6, ☎ 06 679 25 09, Via della Vite 14)* is a vegetarian restaurant which also serves fresh fish in the evenings. It charges an annual membership fee (L8000, which reduces as the year goes by), but tourists can usually eat there and pay only a small surcharge. Dishes start at L10,000. At *Margutta Vegetariano (Map 5, ☎ 06 678 60 33, Via Margutta 19)*, which is on the street running parallel to Via del Babuino, the décor and prices are upmarket and a meal will cost no less than L40,000. It is open every day of the week. If you want a designer vegetarian picnic, this is the place to call. They are happy to cater for parties and picnics – at a price.

Il Canestro (Map 7, ☎ 06 574 62 87, Via Luca della Robbia 47) in Testaccio is another good option for vegetarians. A full meal will cost around L35,000. It is also a health food shop and is closed on Sunday.

Caffès

Remember that prices skyrocket in caffès as soon as you sit down, particularly in major tourist haunts such as near Piazza di Spagna, Piazza Navona or the Pantheon, where a cappuccino at a table can cost as much as L10,000. The same cappuccino taken at the bar will cost around L1600. The narrow streets and tiny piazzas in the area between Piazza Navona and the Tevere offer a number of popular caffès and bars.

Those seeking the best coffee in Rome should head towards the Pantheon (Map:

PLACES TO EAT

Around Piazza Navona) for two of the best bars: *Tazza d'Oro*, just off Piazza della Rotonda on Via degli Orfani, and *Bar Sant' Eustachio* on Piazza Sant'Eustachio. The latter makes *gran caffè*, a wonderful, almost bubbly, coffee made by beating the first drops of espresso and several teaspoons of sugar into a frothy paste, then adding the coffee on top.

Fashionable (and expensive) places to drink coffee or tea are the *Caffè Greco (Map 6, Via dei Condotti 86)* near Piazza di Spagna, and *Babington's Tea Rooms (Map 6, ☎ 06 678 60 27, Piazza di Spagna 23)*, where you'll pay through the nose for English-style tea and cakes. In summer tables are set up on the piazza.

Caffè Rosati on Piazza del Popolo (Map 5) has always been popular but has recently become an especially pleasant spot to catch some afternoon sun and sip a coffee since the 'people's piazza' became fully pedestrianised.

Caffè Farnese (Map: Around Piazza Navona), on one corner of the lovely Piazza Farnese, is a great spot for people watching, especially on Saturday morning when the Campo de' Fiori market is at its busiest. At *Caffè Marzio (Map 7)*, on Piazza Santa Maria in Trastevere, you will pay L5000 for a cappuccino if you sit down outside, but it's worth it as this is one of Rome's most beautiful and atmospheric piazzas.

You won't find a panoramic view or a sun-filled piazza at *Bar Vezio* on Via dei Delfini in the ghetto area (Map: Around Piazza Navona), but you should find some old *compagni* without much effort. Vezio's bar, also known as the *bar comunista* (communist bar), is a local institution and the neighbourhood watering hole for the nearby Democratici di Sinistra party headquarters. If you start talking politics with the owner, Vezio Bagazzini (who is as much a local legend as the bar itself), expect to be there for quite some time. It's a veritable archive of Italian communist memorabilia; Stalin competes with Che Guevera for space on the walls and there's even Fidel Castro's visiting card.

See also Pubs & Bars in the Entertainment chapter.

Light Meals

Paladini (Via del Governo Vecchio 29) might look like a run-down alimentari but it makes mouthwatering pizza bianca on the premises, filled with whatever you want, for L3000 to L5000. Try the prosciutto and fig – an unusual combination but delicious. Mineral water is supplied free of charge. On Via di Ripetta (which runs off Piazza del Popolo, parallel to Via del Corso) there are several bars and take-aways with good fare. *Caffè Sogo (Map 5, Via di Ripetta 242)* has Japanese snacks, as well as coffee etc. Next door is a tiny Japanese grocery.

Paneformaggio (Map 5, Via di Ripetta 7) and *M & M Volpetti (Map: Around Piazza Navona, Via della Scrofa 31)*, near Piazza Navona, are upmarket sandwich bars-rosticcerie where you can buy gourmet lunch snacks for above-average prices. Closer to Termini is *Il Golasone (Map 6)* on Via Venezia, off Via Nazionale, a sandwich bar and tavola calda where you can sit down without paying extra. Another option is *Dagnino (Map 6)* in the Galleria Esedra, off Via VE Orlando.

Among the more famous sandwich outlets in Rome is *Frontoni (Map 7)* in Viale di Trastevere, on the corner of Via San Francesco a Ripa, opposite Piazza Mastai. It makes its panini with both pizza bianca and bread and you can choose from an enormous range of fillings. Sandwiches are sold by weight and a generously filled one will cost around L6000. It also has excellent pizza by the slice. Another great place in Trastevere for a sandwich is the *forno* (Map: Around Piazza Navona) on Via del Moro (opposite the Corner Bookshop). Piping hot pizza bianca is filled with virtually anything you want and there's also great pizza by the slice.

It is worth making a special trip to Testaccio to eat lunch at *Volpetti Più (Map 7, Via A Volta 8)*. It is a tavola calda, so you don't pay extra to sit down. The pizza by the slice is extraordinarily good and there are plenty of pasta, vegetable and meat dishes.

Takeaway pizza is very popular in Rome and there are numerous outlets all over the city. Usually you can judge the quality of the pizza simply by taking a look. Some good places are *Pizza Rustica* (Map: Around Piazza Navona) in Campo de' Fiori, *Pizza a Taglio* (*Map: Around Piazza Navona, Via Baullari*), between Campo de' Fiori and Corso Vittorio Emanuele II, and *Pizza a Taglio* (Map 6) on Via delle Muratte, just off Piazza di Trevi. Near Piazza di Spagna is *Fior Fiore* (*Via della Croce 18*). *Zì Fenizia* (*Map: Around Piazza Navona, Via Santa Maria del Pianto 64*) in the Ghetto is better known as the kosher pizzeria and is closed on Jewish holidays. There's no cheese on this kosher variety, but you don't miss it. The toppings are not the usual fare and this is pizza a taglio *par excellence*.

Gelati

Rome's three most famous gelaterie are in the heart of the city centre between the Pantheon and Piazza Colonna. *Gelateria Giolitti* (*Map: Around Piazza Navona, Via degli Uffici del Vicario 40*) has long been a Roman institution. It was once the meeting place of the local art crowd and writers. Today it remains famous for its fantastic gelati. Around the corner, *Gelateria della Palma* (*Map: Around Piazza Navona, Via della Maddalena 20*) has a huge selection of flavours and some say the gelati is better than at Giolitti. *Fiocco di Neve* (*Map: Around Piazza Navona, Via del Pantheon 51*) is also good. All three establishments also have cakes and pastries, but none of them are overly generous with their servings. A small cone with three flavours costs around L3000.

You'll get much better value for your money at *La Fontana della Salute* (*Map 7, Via Cardinal Marmaggi 2-6*) in Trastevere. It has arguably the best gelati in Rome and the servings are generous. Another good spot in Trastevere for gelato is *Bar San Calisto* (Map 7) on the piazza of the same name. The common consensus among

Rome's ice cream cognoscenti is that this is the best chocolate gelato in the city.

If you're in Testaccio, make sure you stop at *Il gelato di Antonio* on the corner of Piazza Santa Maria Liberatrice and Via Mastro Giorgio (Map 7). It's the area's best.

An atmospheric spot for a good gelati is *Il Ristoro della Salute* on the Piazza del Colosseo (Map 8). Buy a cone or a *frullato* (fruit drink) and wander across the road to the Colosseo.

Bread & Pastries

Antonini (*Map 3, Via Sabotino 21-29*), near Piazza Mazzini in Prati, is one of Rome's best pasticcerie. *Ruschena* (*Map 5, Lungotevere Mellini 1*), also in the Prati area near Piazza Cavour, has excellent cakes, biscuits and pastries.

Bella Napoli (*Map: Around Piazza Navona, Corso Vittorio Emanuele 246*) is a Neapolitan bar-pasticceria. The *sfogliatelle*, light pastries filled with ricotta, are delicious. The owners set up a lovely Neapolitan *presepio* at Christmas.

There's no shortage of good pasticcerie in Trastevere. *Valzani* (*Via del Moro 37*) in Trastevere is one of them and displays its mouthwatering chocolate cakes in the window. A local favourite with shoppers and stallholders at Piazza San Cosimato market is *Sacchetti* (*Map 7, Piazza San Cosimato 61*). Ignore the grumpy proprietors: these cakes are something special. Just around the corner is *Pasticceria Trastevere* (*Map 7, Via Natale del Grande 49-50*), where delightful staff sell you delicious cakes and biscuits.

Bernasconi (*Map: Around Piazza Navona, Piazza B Cairoli 16*) has a tempting selection of cakes and great pastries. *La Dolceroma* (*Map: Around Piazza Navona, Via del Portico d'Ottavia 20*), between the Teatro di Marcello and Via Arenula, specialises in Austrian cakes and pastries. It also has American treats like cheesecake, brownies and chocolate-chip cookies. On the same street at No 2 is the kosher bakery *Il Forno del Ghetto*, a very popular outlet for traditional Jewish cakes and pastries run by an all-female team. You will need to look for the street number as there is no sign. People come from all parts of Rome for the ricotta and damson tart. Buy a slice and you'll know why.

Near Stazione Termini is *Panella l'Arte del Pane (Map 6, Largo Leopardi 2-10)* on Via Merulana, with a big variety of pastries and breads.

SELF-CATERING

Hundreds of small outlets in the centre of Rome sell cheese, prosciutto, salami, bread and groceries. There is also a growing number of supermarkets in Rome's suburbs. One of the easiest to get to from the centre is the *Standa* (Map 7) on Viale Trastevere. The following are some of Rome's better-known gastronomic establishments.

Alimentari

Gino Placidi (Map: Around Piazza Navona, Via della Maddalena 48), near the Pantheon, is one of central Rome's best alimentari. *Ruggeri (Campo de' Fiori 1)* has a good range of cheeses and meats. *Billo Bottarga (Map: Around Piazza Navona, Via di Sant'Ambrogio 20)*, near Piazza Mattei, specialises in kosher food and is famous for its *bottarga* (tuna or mullet roe).

Castroni (Map 5, Via Cola di Rienzo 196), in Prati near il Vaticano, has a wide selection of gourmet foods, packaged and fresh, including international foods (desperate Aussies will find Vegemite here, albeit at a huge mark-up). It also has an outlet at Via delle Quattro Fontane 38, off Via Nazionale.

Volpetti (Map 7, Via Marmorata 47) in Testaccio has high-quality cheeses and meats and is always packed with shoppers.

Markets

Rome is famous for its open markets, where you can buy fresh fruit and vegetables as well as cheese, meat and fish (on Tuesday and Friday). There are street markets in every part of the city and they are open daily (except Sunday) from about 7.30 or 8 am to 1.30 or 2 pm.

The lively daily market in *Campo de' Fiori* (Map: Arond Piazza Navonais cer-

tainly the most picturesque, but also the most expensive. Prices seem to rise if the shopper has a foreign accent. Trastevere locals shop at the excellent *Piazza San Cosimato* market (Map 7), adjacent to one of the best food shopping streets in Rome, Via Natale del Grande. Just north of the Vatican, there is a good market at *Via Andrea Doria* (Map 5), near Largo Trionfale. The *Ponte Milvio* market, north of the city centre, caters for well-heeled shoppers.

The market at *Piazza Vittorio Emanuele* (Map 6) near Stazione Termini is Rome's biggest and goes all the way around the piazza. It is one of the cheapest markets in Rome and the place to find exotic ingredients, as it is in the most multi-racial area of the city. It is colourful but not the most salubrious of places – watch your handbag.

Testaccio's market on *Piazza Testaccio* (Map 7), on the other side of the Aventino from the Circo Massimo, is the most Roman of all the city's markets. It is noted for its excellent quality and good prices. The huge wholesale food markets, the *Mercati Generali* on Via Ostiense, some distance from the city centre, are open Monday to Saturday from 10 am to around 1 pm.

Health Food

Buying muesli, soy milk and the like can be expensive in Italy. The following outlets have a good range of products, including organic fruit and vegetables at relatively reasonable prices.

L'Albero del Pane (Map: Around Piazza Navona, Via Santa Maria del Pianto 19), in the Jewish quarter, has a wide range of health foods, both packaged and fresh. It has an outlet for organic fruit and vegetables at Via dei Baullari 112, just off Campo de' Fiori. *Emporium Naturae (Map 3, Viale Angelico 2)* is a well-stocked health-food supermarket; take Metro Linea A to Ottaviano. *Il Canestro (Map 7, Via Luca della Robbia 47)*, in Testaccio near the market, also has a large selection of health food, as well as fresh fruit and vegetables and take-away food. There is a vegetarian restaurant attached to it.

Entertainment

Roma C'è is published every Thursday and is the most comprehensive entertainment guide. There's a small section in English. It costs L2000 and is available from newsstands. Two other guides, both published on Thursday, are *Metro*, a supplement to *Il Messaggero*, and *Trovaroma*, which comes with *La Repubblica*. Both newspapers also publish daily listings of cinema, theatre and concerts.

Wanted in Rome is a fortnightly magazine in English that contains listings and reviews of the most important festivals, exhibitions, dance, classical music, opera and cinema. It also has details on bars, pubs etc. It's available from all central newsstands and at some international bookshops (see the Bookshops section of the Shopping chapter). *Time Out Rome* is published weekly in Italian. It's available at all newsstands and costs L2000.

OPERA

A night at the opera is an unforgettable experience. The functional fascist-era exterior of the Teatro dell'Opera di Roma does not prepare you for the elegance and rich decoration of the 19th century interior which is all red velvet and gold leaf paint.

Rome's opera doesn't compare favourably with Milan's La Scala or Naples' San Carlo and has suffered from lack of consistent artistic direction and poor management. At the time of writing two new appointments had been made – Sergio Sablish as director, and Giuseppe Sinopoli, one of Italy's most talented conductors as artistic consultant – and great improvements are expected.

The opera season at the *Teatro dell'Opera* (Map 6, ☎ 06 48 16 02 55, numero verde ☎ 16 701 66 65, fax 06 488 17 55, Piazza Beniamino Gigli) starts in December and continues until June. Tickets are expensive: the cheapest upper balcony seats (not recommended for vertigo sufferers) start at L32,000 and prices go up to L170,000. First-night performances cost more.

In summer, opera is performed outdoors, traditionally on a specially erected stage at the Terme di Caracalla. However, in recent years, due to the heritage authorities' concern for the ancient ruins and in an attempt to attract a wider audience, performances have been moved to the Stadio Olimpico, where tickets start at L20,000.

Many of the summer festivals include opera performances in their programmes. Check magazines for current events.

THEATRE

English language theatre is presented periodically by the International Theatre at *Teatro Agora (Map 5, ☎ 06 687 41 67, Via della Penitenza 33)* in Trastevere. French and Spanish productions are also staged there. Off Night Repertory Theater is an international company that performs contemporary one acts in English every Monday at *Teatro dell'Orologio (Map 5, ☎ 06 68 30 87 35, Via dei Filippini 17a)*. On other nights there's fringe theatre and works by contemporary Italian playwrights. Other theatres occasionally perform plays in English. Check *Wanted in Rome* or *Roma C'é* etc for details.

If you understand Italian there's a wealth of theatre to enjoy, although Italian theatre is often more melodramatic than dramatic. There are over 80 theatres in the city, many of them worth visiting as much for the architecture and decoration as for the production itself. The ones listed here are merely a selection.

Teatro Argentina, (Map: Around Piazza Navona, ☎ 06 68 80 46 01, Largo di Torre Argentina 52). State funded theatre, official home of the Teatro di Roma, stages major theatre productions and some dance performances.

Teatro Quirino, (Map 6, ☎ 06 679 45 85, Via Minghetti 1). Classical Italian works such as *Commedia dell'Arte*.

Teatro Sistina, (Map 6, ☎ 06 482 68 41, Via Sistina 129). Musicals.

A New Auditorium for a New Millennium

Rome has been in need of a new music auditorium ever since Mussolini dismantled a concert hall in Piazza Augusto Imperatore in 1936. A massive project costing over L250 billion should ensure that the city gets it in 2000.

The new auditorium complex is situated north of the city in a former wasteland that had been declared totally devoid of interest. Three scarab-shaped concert halls of varying sizes plus modern facilities such as car parking and restaurants have been designed by Italy's leading contemporary architect Renzo Piano.

Although it is, strictly speaking a city project and not part of the Jubilee construction works, the auditorium will probably be one of the few new buildings actually completed by 2000.

However, there were moments when it was feared the project might never be realised. Just as the site was being cleared in order to lay the foundations of the new concert halls, a machine burrowing 4m below current ground level hit Roman remains.

And not just any old Roman remains: as excavations were hurriedly carried out it was discovered that the (quite well preserved) ruins were of a Roman villa that had been used as a farmhouse. It dates from the early to middle Republic, between the 5th and 2nd centuries BC, a period from which very little architecture survives. As a working farm – possibly a vineyard – it is also important to the history of Roman agriculture.

What this illustrates is the ongoing polemic between the need to build modern facilities for a modern city and the necessity of preserving Rome's extraordinary cultural patrimony. Thankfully, in this instance, the two were able to be combined successfully, although not without much hand-wringing and significant delays.

Teatro Valle, (Map: Around Piazza Navona, ☎ 06 68 80 37 94, Via del Teatro Valle 23a). Modern English-language works translated into Italian.

Teatro Vascello, (Map 7, ☎ 06 588 10 21, Via Carini 72, Monteverde). Fringe theatre, dance, workshops.

In summer, various theatre productions are performed outdoors. Classical Greek and Latin works and 18th century Italian comedies are performed from July to September each year in the ancient *Anfiteatro della Quercia del Tasso* (☎ 06 575 08 27) on the Gianicolo. There are also afternoon performances for children. Some theatre productions in the annual Romaeuropa festival are performed outdoors. Check magazines or the daily press for details.

DANCE

There's an active dance scene in Rome and many of the world's best companies tour Italy although quality home-grown companies are few and far between. The Accademia Filar-monica Romana includes several dance events in its annual music program at *Teatro Olimpico* (☎ 06 323 49 36, Piazza Gentile da Fabriano 17) north of Piazza del Popolo, ranging from classical ballet to ethnic dance and avant-garde performances.

The *Teatro dell'Opera* (Map 6, ☎ 06 48 16 02 55, fax 06 488 17 55, Piazza Beniamino Gigli) includes a few classical ballets in its season. These productions are worth seeing only if there are important guest stars as the opera's *corps de ballet* has been in a sorry state for many years. The cheapest seats cost L21,000 (L29,000 for a first night) and go up to L87,000.

CLASSICAL MUSIC

During the winter months, the *Accademia di Santa Cecilia (Map 5, ☎ 06 68 80 10 44, Via della Conciliazione 4)* holds its international chamber music season in its 'temporary' home in the Auditorio Pio (see the boxed text 'A New Auditorium For a New Millennium' above). World class international performers join the highly regarded Santa Cecilia orchestra directed by Myung-Whun Chung. Short festivals dedicated to a single composer are a feature of the autumn calendar. In June the orchestra and its guest stars move to the beautiful gardens of the Renaissance Villa Giulia (Map 3) for its summer concert series.

The *Accademia Filarmonica* holds its season at the *Teatro Olimpico (☎ 06 323 48 90, Piazza Gentile da Fabriano 17)*. The academy was founded in 1821 and its members have included Rossini, Donizetti and Verdi. The program features mainly chamber music, with some contemporary concerts and multi-media events.

From October to May, the *Istituzione Universitaria dei Concerti (Map 6, ☎ 06 361 00 52, Piazzale Aldo Moro)* has recitals and chamber music concerts in the Aula Magna of La Sapienza university. *Teatro Ghione (Map 5, ☎ 06 637 22 94, Via delle Fornaci 37)*, near San Pietro, has a varied program of recitals, often featuring major international opera stars.

From June to October, there are concerts in the ruins of the Teatro di Marcello near Piazza Venezia every evening at 9 pm. These are organised by *Concerti al Tempietto (☎ 06 481 48 00, Via di Teatro Marcello 44)*.

The *Associazione Musicale Romana (☎ 06 39 36 63 22, Via dei Banchi Vecchi 61)* organises recitals and concerts throughout the year as well as two prestigious events: an international organ festival in September (in the Basilica di San Giovanni de' Fiorentini) and an international harpsichord festival during spring.

In December and January free concerts of sacred music are held in some of Rome's churches, including the Pantheon (Map: Around Piazza Navona). The programs are generally excellent and not to be missed. Details are published in *Roma C'è* or *Trovaroma*.

ROCK

International artists don't always include Rome on their tour schedule, as there is no specialist music venue and the organisation and promotion of events is often haphazard. When top acts do come to Rome, they tend to be part of one of the summer festivals.

If you are into Italian performers, there's plenty of choice. Rock concerts are held throughout the year and are advertised on posters plastered around the city. Concerts by major performers are usually held at the *Palazzo dello Sport* in EUR or *Stadio Flaminia*, both a good distance from the city centre. For information and bookings, see local listings publications or contact the Orbis agency (☎ 06 482 74 03) in Piazza Esquilino 37 near Stazione Termini.

There are plenty of smaller live music venues, the scene is active and there's something for everyone most nights of the week. See the Nightclubs & Music Venues section in this chapter.

JAZZ

Rome's leading jazz and blues club is *Alexanderplatz (Map 5, ☎ 06 39 74 21 71, Via Ostia 9)* off Via Leone IV near il Vaticano. Top international (especially American) musicians and well known Italian artists feature on the program nightly (except Sunday) from October to June. You can also get light meals. In July and August the club moves to the grounds of the Renaissance *Villa Celimontana (Map 8)* on the Celio hill for *Jazz and Image at Villa Celimontana*, one of Rome's most popular summer festivals. The daily papers and listings magazines carry the program.

Big Mama (Map 7, ☎ 06 581 25 51, Vicolo San Francesco a Ripa 18) in Trastevere has branded itself as the 'home of the blues'. *Four XXXX (Map 7, ☎ 06 575 72 96, Via Galvani 29)* in Testaccio has live jazz every evening.

Folkstudio (☎ 06 48 71 06 30, Via Frangipane 42) near Via Cavour is a Roman music scene institution, and provides a stage for jazz, folk and world music as well as young artists just starting out.

The *Roma Jazz Festival* takes place annually in October and November and attracts top international names. All the listings magazines carry details.

In the summer true jazz aficionados head to *Umbria Jazz* in Perugia, which hosts some of the best international and Italian acts. Umbria Jazz has now expanded and holds a winter edition in Orvieto and an Easter edition (featuring gospel and soul music) in Terni. For information contact ☎ 075-573 24 32.

CINEMA

There are more than 80 cinemas in Rome, some of them multi-screen. Most foreign films are dubbed into Italian; those shown in the original language with Italian subtitles are indicated in listings by *versione originale* or 'VO' after the title.

Films are screened daily in English at the *Pasquino (Map 7, ☎ 06 580 36 22, Piazza Sant'Egidio)*, just off Piazza Santa Maria in Trastevere, and at the *Quirinetta (Map 6, ☎ 06 679 00 12, Via Minghetti 4)* off Via del Corso. On Monday you can see films in their original language at *Alcazar (Map 7, ☎ 06 588 00 99, Via Merry del Val 14)* off Viale Trastevere. The *Nuovo Sacher (Map 7, ☎ 06 581 81 16, Largo Ascianghi 1)* between the Porta Portese area and Trastevere, shows films in their original language on Monday and Tuesday. Tickets cost between L8000 and L12,000. Afternoon and early evening screenings are often cheaper.

A popular form of entertainment in the hot Roman summer is outdoor cinema. *Isola del Cinema* is an international film festival that takes place on the Isola Tiberina (Map 5). The program often features recent 'art' films. *Massenzio* is one of Rome's most popular summer festivals. Several films, both current release and old favourites, are shown each night on a huge screen in the Parco del Celio opposite the Colosseo. *Sotto le Stelle di San Lorenzo* is an outdoor film festival held in the gardens of Villa Mercede in Via Tiburtina in the San Lorenzo district. For *Notti di Cinema a Piazza Vittorio* a huge screen is erected in the multicultural Piazza Vittorio Emanuele II (Map 6) near

Stazione Termini. The *Drive In* at Casal Palocco, south east of the city centre, is the biggest one in Europe and was resurrected a couple of years ago. It shows recent box office hits throughout the summer. Check one of the listings magazines or daily press for programs, ticket prices and starting times.

DISCOS/CLUBS

Roman discos are expensive. Expect to pay up to L40,000 to get in, which may or may not include one drink. Hot spots include: *Alien (Map 4, ☎ 06 841 22 12, Via Velletri 13)* which is decked out like a science fiction film set and has dancers on raised platforms; *Piper (☎ 06 841 44 59, Via Tagliamento 9)* which plays house and underground music as well as 70s disco and on Sunday night is transformed into a 'Salsa Club'; and *Gilda (Map 6, ☎ 06 678 48 38, Via Mario de'Fiori 97)* near Piazza di Spagna, whose plush interior attracts an older, wealthier crowd.

In summer many of the city discos relocate to Rome's beaches (mainly to Fregene and Ostia) for open air dancing.

NIGHTCLUBS & MUSIC VENUES

Entry to most nightclubs costs between L10,000 and L20,000. In some cases the entrance cost takes the form of a *tessera* (membership card) that allows cheaper or free entry on subsequent visits.

One of the most popular places in the centre that hosts the hippest Italian and some foreign bands is *Locale (Map: Around Piazza Navona, ☎ 06 687 90 75, Via del Fico 3)*, off Via del Governo Vecchio. On Friday and Saturday nights expect to queue. Also in the centre near Piazza Navona and equally popular among young foreigners and Italians is *The Groove (Map: Around Piazza Navona, ☎ 06 687 24 27, Vicolo Savelli 10)* that has a reputation for having Rome's trendiest DJs.

Testaccio (Map 7) is alive with nightclubs, most on Via di Monte Testaccio. One of the more interesting and popular places is *Radio Londra (☎ 06 575 00 44)* at No

65b, an old air raid shelter, which has live music four nights a week. Other places include: *Akab* (☎ *06 574 44 85*) at No 69, which launched acid-jazz in Rome and now hosts international musicians most nights; *Caruso Caffè* (☎ *06 574 50 19*) at No 36, which has live Brazilian and Caribbean music; and *Caffè Latino* (☎ *06 574 40 20*) at No 96, which has live Latin American music each night, followed by a disco.

In the same area is *Villaggio Globale* (☎ *06 573 00 39, Lungotevere Testaccio*) in the former slaughterhouse (accessible from Largo G B Marzi at the Ponte Testaccio), an alternative hang-out for people who really know the meaning of 'angst'. This is one of Rome's several *centri sociali*, a type of squatters' club frequented by ageing hippies, new-age types and people who are still into punk and 'grunge' (see the boxed text below). Common throughout Italy, these places are often associated with extreme left-wing politics, although in Rome they are principally entertainment venues.

From June until September part of Via di Monte Testaccio is transformed into *Testaccio Village*, an outdoor entertainment complex with several dance areas, bars and live music – international acts, Italian performers, rock, pop, jazz, ethnic sound – every night. A weekly ticket for L12,000 allows unlimited entry, although there's an additional charge for some concerts. Check listings magazines and daily press for details.

GAY & LESBIAN VENUES

It's unlikely that you'll find gay and lesbian nightlife in Rome without a bit of research. The fashion for gay and lesbian caffés popular in other parts of Europe has yet to hit Rome, so the scene tends to be nocturnal and can be a bit sleazy. Dark rooms are still a feature of several clubs. Popular cruising spots in Rome are listed in the back of *Guide* magazine but cruising is not recommended for unwary travellers as these places are often frequented by hustlers and

---

Centri Sociali

Italy's independent *centri sociali* (social centres) provide an alternative social life for young people. The entertainment on offer varies from place to place and can include anything from music to theatre to cinema to debates. Entrance is cheap - from L3000 to L10,000 depending on the location and the event. Many centri sociali also run short courses in film making, theatre, music and art. The artists who perform at the centres, as well as the young people who flock to them, belong to an anti-establishment counter-culture and it's not unusual for local bands that cut their teeth on the centri sociali circuit before making it big to return to their launching pad to perform at popular prices.

There are over 30 centri sociali in and around Rome. Most of these are located on the outskirts of the city in disused factories, garages or industrial estates. The biggest and best known centres are Forte Prenestino (☎ 06 21 80 78 55, Via F. Delpino, Centocelle), east of the city centre and Villaggio Globale in Testaccio (Map 7).

Forte Prenestino is an early 20th century fort and has been a social centre for about 12 years. It hosts mainly rock and punk bands. Other centres include Auro e Marco (☎ 06 508 85 65, Viale dei Caduti nella Guerra di Liberazione 286, Spinaceto, EUR), Corto Circuito (Via F Serafini, Cinecittá), Kaos (Via Passino 21, Garbatella), Onda Rossa 32 (Via dei Volsci 32, San Lorenzo) and Garage (Piazza Sonnino, Trastevere).

The left-wing daily newspaper *Il Manifesto* and the weekly *Roma C'é* usually carry listings of events at the various centri sociali. Shops at the Forte Prenestino and Auro e Marco centres also provide information.

rent boys – usually impoverished and desperate illegal immigrants.

Details of Rome's gay bars and clubs are provided in gay publications (see Gay & Lesbian Travellers in the Facts for the Visitor chapter) and through local gay organisations. As clubs come and go and in some places only certain nights are 'gay' it's wise to check the information first.

Gay Bars & Clubs

Admission to clubs usually costs between L10,000 and L20,000, although in some places you get in free but are then obliged to buy a drink. Most venues (bars and clubs) require you to have an annual Arci-Gay membership card. These cost L20,000 and are available from any venue that requests them, or from Arci-Gay itself (see Gay & Lesbian Travellers in the Facts for the Visitor chapter). They are valid throughout Italy for one year from the date of issue.

Many gay bars are springing up in suburban areas, especially on and near Via Casilina but the longer-established locales are centrally located.

Hangar (Map 6, ☎ 06 488 13 97, Via in Selci 69) just off Largo Venosta in the Esquilino area, is run by an American. It is Rome's oldest gay bar and has a varied clientele, both international and Italian, of all age groups but with a significant portion of gym bunnies. Gay videos are shown. Just around the corner, off Piazza San Martino ai Monti is *L'Apeiron* (Map 6, ☎ 06 482 88 20, Via dei Quattro Cantoni 5). Membership of this 'club' costs L5000 a year. You can choose to hang out in one of several distinct lounge and bar areas or in the basement video and dark room. It's friendly and relaxed.

The long established *Max's Bar* (Map 6, ☎ 06 70 20 15 99, Via Achille Grandi 3a) is near Porta Maggiore. An institution in gay Rome, it's an informal place – the ordinary man's bar – with little attitude and great music. It's frequented by young, old and everything in between. Entry costs L15,000.

Edoardo 2 (Map 6, ☎ 06 69 94 24 19, Vicolo Margana 14) just off Piazza Venezia offers amusing decor (it's done up like a medieval castle) and a mixed clientele (mostly dressed in black). There's no dancing, it's just a bar.

L'Alibi (Map 7 ☎ 06 574 34 48, Via di Monte Testaccio 44) opposite the former slaughterhouse in Testaccio has been regarded as Rome's premier gay venue for years but insiders say that it's now attracting an increasingly mixed crowd and that it's in the autumn of its life as the city's top gay disco. There are two levels, each with bar and dance floor and a fabulous roof terrace in summer.

Alpheus (Map 7, ☎ 06 541 39 58, Via del Commercio 271b) off Via Ostiense south of Piramide metro station hosts the *Muccassassina* DJ crew from the Mario Mieli centre for a mixed gay and lesbian disco every Friday night.

Lesbian Clubs

There is no permanent lesbian club in Rome but local organisations will have information about special events (see Gay & Lesbian Travellers in the Facts for the Visitor chapter). On Saturday a predominantly young lesbian crowd heads for the *Joli Coeur* (Map: Greater Rome, ☎ 06 86 21 58 27, Via Sirte 5), near Via Nomentana. It opens at 10 pm.

Alpheus (Map 7, ☎ 06 541 39 58, Via del Commercio 271b) off Via Ostiense south of Piramide metro station hosts the *Muccassassina* mixed gay and lesbian disco every Friday night. Admission costs L18,000. The *Buon Pastore Centre* (Map 5, ☎ 06 686 42 01) on the corner of Via San Francesco di Sales and Via della Lungara in Trastevere has a caffé and a women-only restaurant called Le Sorellastre.

Saunas

There are several gay saunas in central Rome. *Sauna Mediterraneo* (Map 8, ☎ 06 77 20 59 34, Via Villari 3) off Via Merulana in San Giovanni is open every day from 2 to 11 pm. It's noted for its cleanliness and staff speak English, Spanish and Arabic. Admission is L20,000 but you must have an annual Arci-Gay card (which you can purchase here). *Europa Multiclub* (Map 6,

☎ 06 482 36 50, Via Aureliana 40) is open Monday to Thursday from 3 pm to midnight, Friday and Saturday from 2 pm to 6 am, and Sunday from 2 pm to midnight. Admission costs L25,000 with an Arci-Gay card, or L20,000 for students. Friday is party night; entrance costs L20,000 and includes drinks. Both saunas have good facilities. Other gay saunas and mixed saunas that have gay nights are listed in the gay press.

Apollion (☎ 06 482 53 89, *Via Mecenate 59a*) has a Turkish bath, jacuzzi, bar and dark room and attracts an older clientele and a few rent boys. Admission costs L20,000. It's open daily from 2 to 11 pm and until 2 am on Friday and Saturday.

Gay Beach

Il Buco, Rome's gay beach, is located 9km south of Lido di Ostia (the closest seaside resort to Rome and really an outer suburb) on the road to Torvaianica. Don't expect white sand (it's black) or sparkling clear water (it's often heavily polluted) but at Il Buco you can let it all hang out and check out everyone else doing the same.

The beach isn't exclusively gay – it attracts everything from nudists to fully swimming-costumed middle-aged couples – but the dunes behind the beach are a popular daytime cruising ground. To get there take the Lido di Ostia train from Porta San Paolo station (right next to Piramide station on metro Linea B). From there a bus will take you past all the expensive bathing clubs to the *spiaggia libera* (free beach). Ask for directions on the bus.

PUBS & BARS

Pubs are the new big thing in Rome. There are over 400 of them, most styled after traditional English or Irish pubs. There are also places with Australian or American themes. They offer a wide selection of beers and many have Guinness on tap. A favourite haunt of young foreigners, they're also popular with the locals.

In the centre, try *The Drunken Ship* (Map: Around Piazza Navona, Campo de' Fiori 20) or *Trinity College* (Map 6, Via del Collegio Romano 6) off Via del Corso. Both have happy hours and get packed to overflowing on Friday and weekends. Near Largo di Torre Argentina, there's *John Bull Pub* (Map: Around Piazza Navona, Corso Vittorio Emanuele II 107a) and *Mad Jack's* (Map: Around Piazza Navona, Via Arenula 20).

Ned Kelly's (Map: Around Piazza Navona, Via delle Coppelle 13) around the corner from the Pantheon is an Australian-style bar serving Foster's Lager and other brews. Another home-away-from-home for Australians is *Four XXXX* (Map 7, Via Galvani 29) in Testaccio which has (not surprisingly) Castlemaine XXXX beer on tap. *Velabro Club* (Vicolo del Velabro 2) near Circo Massimo, serves Belgian beers and has happy hour from 5 to 9 pm.

In Trastevere, Irish pub fans will find what they want at *Molly Malone* (Map 7, Via dell'Arco di San Calisto 17).

The *Fiddler's Elbow* (Map 6, ☎ 06 487 21 10, Via dell'Olmata 43) near Santa Maria Maggiore, was one of the first Irish pubs to hit Rome and it's still very popular. There are a few pubs near Stazione Termini (Map 6) including: the *Druid's Den*, (Via San Martino ai Monti 28); *Julius Caesar Pub*, (Via Castelfidardo 49), which has over 40 different beers; and *Marconi* (Map 6, Via Santa Prassede 9) serves real pub food of the stodgy English variety, such as fish and chips and baked beans. You can play darts at *The Shamrock* (Map 8, Via Capo d'Africa 26d) near the Colosseo.

If you're after a more traditional Roman ambience, try *Bar del Fico* (Piazza del Fico 26). Open every day until the early hours, it's popular with local actors and artists. Special gas heaters allow you to sit outside even in winter. Take some serious attitude with you to *Bar della Pace* (Map: Around Piazza Navona) in Via della Pace off Via del Governo Vecchio. It's a popular place for the 'in' crowd.

In Trastevere there is the *Bar San Calisto* (Map 7) in the piazza of the same name, with tables outside. This bar is seedy but cheap, and you can sit down without paying extra. A much more comfortable place to drink is

San Michele aveva un Gallo *(Map 7, Via San Francesco a Ripa)*, across Viale Trastevere near the corner of Piazza San Francesco d'Assisi. You can also eat light meals here.

On the other side of Trastevere in Piazza Trilussa, is a tiny hole in the wall, *L'Anomalia* *(Map: Around Piazza Navona, Piazza Trilussa 43)*, which has a large selection of imported beers plus wine and spirits. Nearby, *Stardust Live Jazz Bar* *(Map: Around Piazza Navona, Vicolo dei Renzi 4)* is a cross between a bar and a pub. There's often live jazz music and on Sunday there are bagels and American coffee for brunch.

If you're serious about checking out Rome's pub and bar scene and you can read Italian, get a copy of *Locali a Roma* published by Roma C'é (L9500 from bookshops) which lists over 400 establishments.

WINE BARS

Wine bars, known as *enoteche* or *vini e oli*, are a feature of most Roman neighbourhoods, especially in the older areas of the city. They sell wine, spirits and olive oil and are often frequented by groups of elderly locals enjoying a glass of wine and a chat in much the same manner as they might have a coffee at a bar. In recent years a more sophisticated breed of enoteca has appeared on the scene attracting a different crowd from the regular pub-goers. Many of these offer snacks or light meals in addition to an extensive range of wines that you can taste by the glass *(alla mescita* or *al bicchiere)* or buy by the bottle. Some have live music and some run courses in Italian regional wines.

The *Vineria* in Campo de' Fiori *(Map: Around Piazza Navona, ☎ 06 68 80 32 68)*, also known as *Da Giorgio*, has a wide selection of wine and beers and was once the gathering place of the Roman literati. Today it is less glamorous but is still a good place to drink (although cheap only if you stand at the bar) and has some light snacks. Off one end of Campo de' Fiori, in Via dei Balestrari is *L'Angolo Divino* *(Map: Around Piazza Navona, ☎ 06 686 44 13)*, a charming place with wooden beams and terracotta floors. For many years it was a simple vini e oli

outlet but now serves a variety of interesting dishes, including at least one hot dish each day and an excellent selection of cheeses to compliment its changing selection of a dozen wines by the glass. The owner is well informed and happy to share his knowledge. Themed wine-tasting evenings are held throughout the year.

The *Bevitoria Navona* *(Map: Around Piazza Navona, ☎ 06 68 80 10 22, Piazza Navona 72)*, charges reasonable prices (around L2500 for a glass of average wine and up to L10,000 for better quality wine – although expect to pay higher prices to sit outside). In winter mulled wine is available. Ask the owner to take you down to the cellar to see some remains of Domitian's stadium, on top of which Piazza Navona was built.

Cul de Sac *(Map: Around Piazza Navona, ☎ 06 68 80 10 94, Piazza Pasquino 73)*, just off Piazza Navona at the start of Via del Governo Vecchio, is a popular wine bar, with tables outside, that also serves excellent food. *Enoteca Piccolo* *(Map: Around Piazza Navona, ☎ 06 68 80 17 46)*, further along Via del Governo Vecchio at No 75, has a good selection of Italian wines and also serves snacks. Across Corso Vittorio Emanuele II at Via dei Banchi Vecchi 14 is *Il Goccetto* *(Map 5, ☎ 06 68 64 268)* one of Rome's more serious wine bars with a huge selection of wines (well-priced) from all over the world. There's usually a choice of up to 20 wines by the glass, and plates of cheese or salami are available to soak up what you're tasting. The proprietors are friendly, welcoming and informative. Most of the customers are regulars who live nearby and drop in for a drink after work.

Trimani *(Map 6, ☎ 06 44 69 661, Via Cernaia 37)*, near Stazione Termini, is Rome's biggest enoteca that also serves excellent soups, pasta and *torta rustica* (quiche). Trimani has a vast selection of Italian regional wines and regularly hosts wine tasting courses. The popular *Cavour 313* *(Map 6, ☎ 06 678 54 96, Via Cavour 313)* is always full of people. You can choose from over 500 bottles, many of which are by the glass, and there are hot and cold snacks to keep you going.

Antica Enoteca (Map 5, ☎ 06 679 08 96, Via della Croce 76b) is a local institution in the Piazza di Spagna area, and has always been popular with the shopkeepers and shoppers. There are tables outside in summer, and the inside is wood-panelled. Wines by the glass range from L4000 to L10,000. There's a cold buffet at the impressive polished wood and brass counter and a good selection of wines. There's also a restaurant at the back if you need something more substantial.

Towards il Vaticano, on the corner of Piazza Cavour and Via Tacito is *Il Simposio di Piero Costantini (Map 5, ☎ 06 321 15 02)*. In-the-know Romans now frequent this enoteca for the food as much as the wines; if you can't afford either (it is on the pricey side) it's worth going just to see the vine and grape motif decoration that covers the place. Another cheaper option, although less central, is the tiny *Tastevin (Map 3, ☎ 06 320 80 56, Via Ciro Menotti 16)*. The list features around 120 wines, with a weekly selection of a dozen wines that you can taste by the glass (L3000-7000). The food is good too. You can nibble on cheeses and salamis or tuck into a daily hot dish or a choice of salads. Save space for a slice of *torta caprese*, a delicious almond and chocolate cake. It's closed for Saturday lunch, all day Sunday and Monday evening.

In Trastevere, *Ferrara (Map Around Piazza Navona, ☎ 06 580 3769, Via del Moro 1a)* has an exhaustive list of regional Italian wines and great food (the hearty winter soups and desserts are especially good). There's no messing around here – the wine list is actually two encyclopedic volumes – one for reds and one for whites. You'll probably have to book to get a table. Nearby, at *Il Cantiniere di Santa Dorotea (Map 5, ☎ 06 581 90 25, Via di Santa Dorotea 9)*, there's a lengthy selection of wine by the glass (or beer if you prefer) and a good value menu. The vaulted ceilings and exposed bricks give the place a cellar feel. The tables outside are inviting in summer although there's a lot of passing traffic.

SPECTATOR SPORTS
Football

Il calcio excites Italian souls more than politics, religion, good food and dressing up all put together. Football (soccer) is one of the great forces in Italian life, so if you can get to one of the big games you'll be in for a treat. Spirits run wild and at times overflow, although Italian crowds have not yet plumbed the depths reached by the worst of the UK's football hooligans.

Eighteen teams tough out the Italian football honours in Serie A (the top division). Serie B teams consist of a further 20 teams, while another 90 teams dispute the medals at Serie C level, itself split up into several more manageable sub-competitions.

Predicably enough, Serie A is dominated by an elite group of *squadre* (teams) that generally take honours. Among the championship teams, well known to football fans beyond Italy too, are Juventus (based in Torino) that won its 25th league title in 1998, Inter Milano, AC Milan and Parma.

Both local teams, AS Roma and Lazio, play in Serie A. The teams share the Stadio Olimpico at Foro Italico, north of the city centre and play all their home matches there.

Lazio was the first Italian team to be quoted on the stock exchange. Its president is Sergio Cragnotti, head of an international food processing conglomerate that owns (among other things) Del Monte (tinned fruits, fruit juices etc.) and Rome's main dairy. It's regarded as the billion dollar club and has spent huge sums buying leading international players such as the Spaniard De la Pena and the Chilean Salas. Despite such star players, it's not regarded as a really cohesive team and has not won a league championship since 1974. Lazio fans are traditionally from provincial towns outside Rome although the team is now very popular with the wealthier middle classes.

Roma's supporters, known as *romanisti*, are traditionally from the working-class left, from Rome's Jewish community and from Trastevere and Testaccio. The team has an innovative coach and plays an attacking game that is entertaining to watch. Star players include the Brazilian defenders Cafu and Aldair as well as the promising young Italian Francesco Totti. In the 1980s and early 1990s Roma was the stronger of the two local clubs and is still regarded as a better all-round team but at the time of writing Lazio was doing better in the national championships.

There is great rivalry between the teams which sometimes spills over into other facets of life. For example, when the Lazio president (and central dairy owner) spent a record sum to secure the services of star Italian striker Cristian Vieri in August 1998 and the same week announced an increase in the price of milk, romanisti all over the city boycotted their morning *cappuccino* in protest!

Whatever the form or place on the ladder of the various teams, some local derbies make for particularly hot clashes – for instance when AC Milan and rivals Inter come face to face, or when Roma takes on Lazio. Both are traditionally sell-out excuses for a little sporting lunacy – with *tifosi* (fans) even more vociferous than usual. At the Stadio Olimpico, true Roma fans flock to the Curva Sud (southern stand) while Lazio supporters sit in the Curva Nord. Tickets for games start at around L30,000 and can rise to L120,000. They are best purchased from the Stadio Olimpico box office (☎ 06 323 73 33) or from authorised ticketing agencies such as Orbis (☎ 06 482 74 03), Piazza Esquilino 37.

Basketball

Basketball is the second most popular spectator sport in Rome. The arrival of several star players from the United States and from the former Yugoslavia has spiced up the Italian league. The season runs over the winter months and matches are played at the Palazzetto dello Sport in EUR.

Tennis

The Italian International Tennis Championships take place each May on the clay courts at the Foro Italico. The championships attract the world's best male and female players. Tickets can be bought at the Foro Italico each day of the tournament, except for the final days, which are sold out weeks in advance. Call ☎ 06 321 90 64 for information.

Athletics

The Golden Gala athletics meet takes place in June at the Stadio Olimpico. It's organised by the Federazione Italiana di Atletica Leggera. Call ☎ 06 365 81 for information.

Equestrian

The annual Piazza di Siena show jumping competition is held in May in Villa Borghese. Tourist information offices can provide details on how to obtain tickets.

Rome Marathon

The Rome Marathon, that starts and finishes at the Colosseo and passes most of the city's major monuments, takes place in late March. If you think you're up to 42km on cobblestones, you should register well in advance with Italia Marathon Club, ☎ 06 406 50 64 or 06 445 66 26.

Cycling

Cycling is especially popular in provincial areas. Second only to the Tour de France, the Giro d'Italia is *the* event on the summer cycling calendar. Little wonder, since Italy has a long record of producing world-class riders.

The race was first held in 1909 and has been staged every year since, interrupted predicably enough by the two world wars. Initially a mostly Italian affair, it's perhaps not surprising that the 1909 winner, Luigi Ganna, was followed by a long succession of Italian victors. Only in 1950 did a non-Italian finally break the home side's long winning streak, when the Swiss Hugo Koblet took the finishing line honours. In total, the Giro has been won by non-Italians 24 times, and by Italian riders 55 times. This event is one of the few things in life that are free: if you want to watch, find out when the race is passing a location convenient to you and wait for the cycliststo pass – it's as simple as that.

Shopping

Don't feel bad if you find that Rome's shop windows are competing with its monuments for your attention. Just make sure there is plenty of time in your itinerary for shopping. You'll find all of the big designer names in Rome and even if your budget doesn't allow for an Armani suit, a Prada bag or a pair of Gucci loafers, you can still have fun trying them on.

If you confine your expeditions to the main shopping districts, you'll find a concentration of clothing and accessories shops that, apart from the designer outlets, sell fairly tacky stuff at inflated prices. By exploring the side streets and seeking the more out-of-the-way shopping areas you will uncover a side of Rome often hidden from its residents. In this chapter we have tried to cover the main places to shop and things to buy, as well as the more off-beat side to shopping in Rome.

There are several shopping districts in and near Rome's historical centre, many based around particular streets. The area between Piazza di Spagna and Via del Corso (Maps: Around Piazza Navona, 5 & 6), including Via Condotti, Via Frattina, Via delle Vite and Via Borgognona harbours most of the main designer shops for clothing, shoes, leather goods and other accessories, with a fair sprinkling of more affordable shops.

Via Nazionale, Via del Corso and Via dei Giubbonari are good streets for more affordable clothing shops, but quality can be lacking. Second-hand clothes can be found along Via del Governo Vecchio, a winding, cobblestone street that runs from a small piazza just off Piazza Navona towards the river. If you're looking for antiques or an unusual gift, try Via dei Coronari or Via del Babuino.

Across the river, near il Vaticano (Map 5) is an extensive shopping area. The most interesting street here is Via Cola di Rienzo, where you'll find a good selection of clothing and shoe shops, as well as some

excellent fine food outlets. Trastevere (Map 7), just across the river from the historical centre, offers lots of interesting little boutiques and knick-knack shops tucked away in narrow medieval streets and lanes.

Rome has been slower than some of the northern Italian cities to adopt the trend towards department stores, malls and supermarkets. There is only one department store actually in the historical centre, Rinascente, on the corner of Via del Tritone and Via del Corso, but it's hardly a Harrods or Macy's. All of the large shopping malls are quite a distance from the city centre and a couple are listed in this chapter.

If you can time your visit to coincide with the sales, you'll pick up some marvellous bargains. Although, if you're shopping for clothes or shoes you might have difficulty finding your size within a few days of the start of the sales. Winter sales run from early January to mid-February and the summer sales run from July to early September. Shops usually open from 9.30 am to 1 pm and 3.30 to 7.30 pm (in winter) or 4 to 8 pm (summer), although a small boutique might not open until 10 am and afternoon hours might be shortened. There is a trend towards continuous opening hours from 9.30 am to 7.30 pm but usually only larger shops and department stores have these hours.

Most shops will accept credit cards and many will accept travellers cheques or foreign cash. See the Facts about Rome chapter for information on exemption from value-added tax, known in Italy as IVA. It's also important to remember that you are required by Italian law to ask for a *ricevuta* (receipt) for your purchases.

ANTIQUES

The main areas to find the best antique shops are around Via Giulia, Via dei Coronari and Via del Babuino. Even if you're just window shopping, it is fascinating to browse – particularly along Via dei Coronari. Most shops specialise in particular periods. The shops mentioned in this section are located throughout the city centre and have been selected for both their peculiarity and more affordable prices.

Lilia Leoni (Map 5, ☎ 06 678 32 10), Via Belsiana 86, has unusual objects and furniture. For example, you'll find collectable Murano drinking glasses and Art Nouveau (known as Liberty in Italy) garden furniture, as well as pieces dating from the early 1900s to the 1950s. Alinari (Map 6, ☎ 06 679 29 23), Via Alibert 16/a, sells photography books and photographic prints (mostly of Rome views) reproduced from the archives of the work of the Alinari brothers. The archives contain more than a million glass plate negatives of photographs taken by these famous Italian photographers in the late 19th century.

Animalier e Oltre (Map 5, ☎ 06 320 82 82), Via Margutta 47, stocks original bric-a-brac and a huge selection of animal-shaped antiques. Here you'll find exquisitely made porcelain dogs, animal-shaped salt and pepper sets and bedside lamps.

Antichità Tanca (Map: Around Piazza Navona, ☎ 06 687 52 72), Salita de' Crescenzi 12, near the Pantheon, has a fascinating atmosphere. In addition to a wide range of antique prints, it has an excellent selection of bronze, silver and china ware, as well as crystal, jewellery and paintings dating from the 18th century to the turn of the 20th century. Nardecchia (Map: Around Piazza Navona, ☎ 06 686 93 18), Piazza Navona 25, is a Roman landmark – although it is perhaps not quite as famous as Bernini's Fontana dei Fiumi just outside. It sells antique prints, including 18th century engravings of views of Rome by Giovanni Battista Piranesi, which usually sell for a minimum of L3,000,000. The shop also stocks more inexpensive 19th century views of Rome.

Not far from Campo de' Fiori is Comics Bazar (Map 5, ☎ 06 688 02 923), at Via dei Banchi Vecchi 127-128, a veritable warehouse of antiques, crammed with objects, lamps and furniture dating from the late 19th century to the 1940s, including a large selection of Viennese furniture by Thonet. Lumieres (Map: Around Piazza Navona, ☎ 06 580 36 14), at Vicolo del Cinque 48, a lane in the heart of Trastevere, has a large collection of lamps, from Art Nouveau and Art Deco to the 1950s.

BOOKSHOPS
English-Language

The Corner Bookshop (Map: Around Piazza Navona, ☎ 06 583 69 42), Via del Moro 48, Trastevere, has an excellent range of English-language books and travel guides (including the Lonely Planet series) and is run by a helpful Australian woman, Claire Hammond. The Anglo-American Bookshop (Map 6, ☎ 06 678 96 57), Via della Vite 27, off Piazza di Spagna, has an excellent range of literature, travel guides (including Lonely Planet) and reference books and is the Thomas Cook agent for Italy.

The Lion Bookshop (Map 5, ☎ 06 326 54 007), has moved to Via dei Greci 33/36. It stocks a good range of books and magazines. Feltrinelli International, (Map 6) Via VE Orlando 84, just off Piazza della Repubblica, has an extensive range of books for adults and children in English, Spanish, French, German and Portuguese, plus lots of guidebooks for Rome, Italy, and the rest of the world (Lonely Planet guides included). See also Feltrinelli in Largo Argentina (Map: Around Piazza Navona). The Economy Book & Video Center, (Map 6) Via Torino 136, has a good selection of books, as well as second-hand paperbacks.

Italian-Language

Bibli (Map 7, ☎ 06 588 40 97), Via dei Fienaroli 28, near Piazza Santa Maria in Trastevere, is a bookshop cum Internet café, as well as an occasional concert venue. Open daily until midnight, it's a great place to meet for a chat. See Internet Cafés in the Facts for the Visitor chapter for more information.

Near Piazza della Repubblica, at Via Nazionale 254/255, is Mel Bookstore (Map 6, ☎ 06 488 54 05), a combination bookshop, music store and coffee shop on three levels. It has a wide selection of literature, fiction, reference books, dictionaries, school books, travel guides and a range of half-price books. It also has some books in English and French. The store is open on Sunday.

Feltrinelli (Map: Around Piazza Navona, ☎ 06 688 032 48), Largo di Torre Argentina 5/a, is a well-organised bookshop with a wide range of books on art, photography, cinema and history, as well as an extensive selection of Italian literature and travel guides. The store is open on Sunday. Other Feltrinelli bookshops are at Via del Babuino 39 and Via VE Orlando 84, beside Feltrinelli International.

For something different, there is Franco Maria Ricci (Map 6, ☎ 06 679 34 66), Via Borgognona 4/d, a small bookshop tucked in between the high fashion boutiques, that sells splendidly produced and illustrated books on art and culture, published by Franco Maria Ricci.

For travellers, Libreria del Viaggiatore (Map: Around Piazza Navona, ☎ 06 688 01 048), Via del Pellegrino 78, is a real find. This intimate bookshop is devoted to travelling and is crammed with travel guides (including Lonely Planets) and travel literature. It also has a huge range of maps for countries, regions, cities etc around the world, as well as hiking maps. Some books are available in English and French.

Other Languages

Herder Buchhandlung (Map: Around Piazza Navona, ☎ 06 679 53 04), Piazza Montecitorio 120, in front of the Italian parliament building, has German-language books. French speakers will find a good selection of literature, fiction, non-fiction, general interest and children's books at La Procure (Map: Around Piazza Navona, ☎ 06 683 07 598), Piazza San Luigi dei Francesi 23. You might like to pop into the church next door to see the paintings by Caravaggio. Libreria Sorgente (Map: Around Piazza Navona, ☎ 06 688 06 950), Piazza Navona 90, has a wide range of books and some videos in Spanish. It also stocks some books

in Portuguese (from Portugal and Brazil). As mentioned under English-language books, Feltrinelli International stocks books in a number of languages.

CLOTHING
Designer Wear

Did anyone say 'recession'? For those with a mission, get ready to join a queue to buy that Prada backpack! Most of the designer clothing stores are located in the area around Piazza di Spagna, including all of the big names. Prices are eye-popping but there are some more affordable names, such as MaxMara at Via Frattina 28 (Map 6, ☎ 06 679 36 38), Via Condotti 17 and Via Nazionale 28; Max & Co (Map 5, ☎ 06 678 79 46), Via Condotti 46; and Benetton (Map 6, ☎ 06 699 24 010), Via Cesare Battisti 129 and several other locations throughout the centre.

Cenci (Map: Around Piazza Navona, ☎ 06 699 06 81), Via Campo Marzio 1/7, stocks a big selection of all the top Italian and international labels for men, women and children and is a good bet if you prefer classic fashions on the conservative side. Etro (Map 6, ☎ 06 678 82 57), Via del Babuino 102, uses fine fabrics to create exclusive, ethnic-style clothing and accessories.

Brioni (Map 6, ☎ 06 485 855), Via Barberini 79/81, is Rome's most elegant tailor. A creator of costumes for James Bond films, Brioni also makes classic ready-to-wear fashions.

Following is a list of the main designer stores (Map 6 unless otherwise stated):

Dolce e Gabbana (☎ 06 679 22 94), Piazza di Spagna 82/83
Emporio Armani (☎ 06 360 02 197, Via del Babuino 140
Fendi (☎ 06 679 76 41), Via Borgognona 36/40
Ferre (☎ 06 679 74 45), Via Borgognona 6
Genny (☎ 06 679 60 74), Piazza di Spagna 27
Gianni Versace (☎ 06 679 50 37), Via Borgognona 24/25, (men)
Gianni Versace (☎ 06 678 05 21), Via Bocca di Leone 26, (women)
Giorgio Armani Boutique (Map 6, ☎ 06 699 14 60), Via Condotti 77
Gucci (☎ 06 678 93 40), Via Condotti 8

Krizia (☎ 679 37 72), Piazza di Spagna 87

Laura Biagiotti (Map 5, ☎ 06 679 12 05), Via Borgognona 43/44

Missoni (☎ 06 679 25 55), Piazza di Spagna 78

Moschino (☎ 06 692 00 415), Via Belsiana 53/57

Prada (☎ 06 679 08 97), Via Condotti 92/95

Roccobarocco (☎ 06 679 79 14), Via Bocca di Leone 65/a

Salvatore Ferragamo (☎ 06 679 15 65), Via Condotti 73/74, (women)

Salvatore Ferragamo (☎ 06 678 11 30), Via Condotti 66, (men)

Trussardi (Map 5, ☎ 06 678 02 80), Via Condotti 49/50

Valentino (☎ 06 678 36 56), Via Condotti 13

Lingerie

You could always head for the nearest Standa to pick up some reliable cotton underpants but for a real splurge try the following outlets. Fogal (Map 6, ☎ 06 678 45 66), Via Condotti 55, is a good choice for fancy lingerie and for a large variety of high-quality and very expensive stockings and socks.

Brighenti (Map 6, ☎ 06 679 14 84), Via Frattina 7/10, is a favourite of Italian actors (the female variety) for its luxurious lingerie. Schostal (Map 5, ☎ 06 679 12 40), Via del Corso 158, has been selling high-quality underwear and lingerie from this elegant shop since 1870. The shop also stocks knitwear and shirts. Tebro (Map: Around Piazza Navona, ☎ 06 687 34 41), Via dei Prefetti 46/54, is well stocked with underwear and nightwear for men, women and children. It also carries bed and table linen, bath towels, and the like.

Second-hand Clothing

Via del Governo Vecchio is the main street for second-hand clothing outlets. However, you'll pick up better bargains at markets such as Porta Portese and Via Sannio (see Markets later in this chapter).

Distanés (Map: Around Piazza Navona, ☎ 06 683 33 63), Via della Chiesa Nuova 17, specialises in remainders, second-hand clothes and accessories from the 1960s and 70s. In spring and autumn, apart from normal shop hours, it also opens from 10.30 pm to midnight. Around the corner at Via

del Governo Vecchio 45, is the trendy Vestiti usati Cinzia. Omero e Cecilia (Map: Around Piazza Navona, ☎ 06 683 35 06), Via del Governo Vecchio 68, specialises in second-hand military wear.

In the area known as the Ghetto is Reginella (Map: Around Piazza Navona, ☎ 687 28 37),Via della Reginella 8/a, that stocks lots of vintage 1970s gear, as well as its own label. Le Gallinelle (Map 6, ☎ 06 488 10 17), Via del Boschetto 76, is a former butcher's shop where the meat hooks now hold up good quality second-hand clothes, as well as interesting clothing created with vintage fabrics.

Children

PréNatal (Map 6, ☎ 06 488 14 03), Via Nazionale 45, is one of a number of children's clothing chain stores in Italy. It has its own range of affordable, good quality clothing for kids up to 11 years, as well as for expecting mothers. It also stocks equipment such as baby carriages, strollers, cradles etc. Check in the Rome phone book for the location of other outlets.

There is a good range of kids' casual wear, as well as a children's hairdresser on the second floor of United Colors of Benetton (Map 6, ☎ 06 699 24 010), at Via Cesare Battisti 129. An added bonus is the view of Piazza Venezia. Among the many other Benetton outlets in Rome is Zerododici di Benetton (Map 5, ☎ 06 688 09 381), at Via Tomacelli 137, which stocks clothing exclusively for children 12 years and under.

Heading up the price ladder is La Cicogna (Map 6, ☎ 06 678 55 07), Via Frattina 138, which sells a selection of fashionable children's clothes by top designers. It also has its own label. If you're looking for something really special, try Sotto una Foglia di Cavolo (Map 5, ☎ 06 360 02 960), Via del Vantaggio 25, a small shop crammed with classic and unusual clothing from Italy, France and the Netherlands for babies and children up to eight years. Leri (Map 6, ☎ 06 678 45 16), Via del Corso 344, also stocks classic and sporty-elegant wear for sophisticated babies and children with lots of cash.

Accessories

For accessories by the top designers, see Designer Wear.

Federico Fellini was a patron of Ottica Spiezia (Map 5, ☎ 06 361 05 93), Via del Babuino 199. This tiny shop, just off Piazza del Popolo, is crammed with stylish, high-quality spectacle frames and sunglasses.

Sermoneta Gloves (Map 6, ☎ 06 679 19 60), Piazza di Spagna 61, is famous for its range of quality leather gloves in every imaginable model and colour. There are two other Sermoneta shops in Piazza di Spagna, one stocking ties and scarves and the other, handbags and luggage. Beny (Map 6, ☎ 06 679 58 69), Via Nazionale 164, stocks designer ties and scarves, including a selection reproducing patterns created in the 1950s by the eclectic Italian designer, Piero Fornasetti. For cheaper ties and scarves go to the Beny shop next door at 162.

Alberta Gloves (Map: Around Piazza Navona, ☎ 06 678 57 53), Corso Vittorio Emanuele II 18/a, has a fascinating selection of handmade gloves, ranging from evening wear to nifty driving gloves. Nearby is Galleria di Orditi e Trame (Map: Around Piazza Navona, ☎ 06 689 33 72), at Via del Teatro Valle 54, where you'll find an interesting, if a bit expensive, range of funky handmade hats, scarves, gloves, bags and clothing – all woven from colourful cotton (credit cards not accepted). Troncarelli (Map: Around Piazza Navona, ☎ 06 687 93 20), Via della Cuccagna 15, just off Piazza Navona, stocks top brand hats for men and women, including bowlers, top hats, panama hats, Borsalino and Florence's straw hats.

SHOES & LEATHER GOODS

For shoes and leather goods by the top fashion designers see Designer Wear in this section.

Mandarina Duck (Map 6, ☎ 06 699 40 320), Via di Propaganda 1, just off Piazza di Spagna, makes popular, trendy handbags wallets and luggage in leather and other materials such as rubber and the latest nylon fabric. Furla (Map 6, ☎ 06 692 00 363), Piazza di Spagna 22, right next to the Spanish Steps is another well-known brand of high quality leather bags and accessories, including wallets, belts, sunglasses, watches and costume jewellery.

Sergio Rossi (Map 6, ☎ 06 678 32 45), has a showroom at Piazza di Spagna 97/100, with glamorous day and evening shoes created by this top Italian designer on display. Fratelli Rossetti (Map 6, ☎ 06 678 26 76), Via Borgognona 5/a, is another outlet for classic, high-quality shoes, bags and leather jackets. Fausto Santini (Map 6, ☎ 06 678 41 14), Via Frattina 120, has more unusual shoes and bags. It has another outlet at Via Cavour 106, near the Basilica of Santa Maria Maggiore, where you can pick up remainders from past collections at half price. There are lots of bargains but it might be hard to find your size.

De Bach (Map 6, ☎ 06 678 33 84), Via del Babuino 123, has stylish women's shoes. One of the better-known Italian shoe makers is Bruno Magli (Map 6, ☎ 488 43 55), at Via Veneto 70/a. Magli also has outlets in Via del Gambero and at Leonardo da Vinci Airport. In the same street at No 149 is Raphael Salato (Map 6, ☎ 06 481 76 41), Via Veneto 149, where you'll find a large selection of Italian and foreign brand shoes, bags and leather clothing, in addition to its own label shoes and leather goods.

Just off Campo de' Fiori is Loco (Map: Around Piazza Navona, ☎ 06 688 08 216), at Via dei Baullari 22, a good spot to look for trendy shoes for men and women. Nearby is Borini (Map: Around Piazza Navona, ☎ 06 687 56 70), Via dei Pettinari 86/87, originally a shoe repair shop, now crowded with girls looking for fancy shoes at affordable prices.

In Prati, close to the Musei Vaticani, is Grandi Firme (Map 5, ☎ 06 397 23 169), Via Germanico 8, an unassuming outlet where you can pick up designer bags, luggage, ties, belts, scarves, umbrellas and shoes at warehouse prices.

JEWELLERY

Bulgari (Map 6, ☎ 06 679 38 76), Via dei Condotti 10, is Italy's most prestigious and

SHOPPING

famous jeweller. If you're just window shopping, you can admire the precious and unique pieces of jewellery displayed as though they were in a museum.

Siragusa (Map 6, ☎ 06 679 70 85), Via delle Carrozze 64, creates exceptionally beautiful and unusual jewellery by setting antique coins and gems set in gold.

Nicla Boncompagni (Map 6, ☎ 06 678 32 39), Via del Babuino 115, has a charming collection of very expensive vintage jewellery dating from the mid-19th century to the 1960s, including pieces by Van Cleef and Cartier and American jewellery of the 1940s and 50s.

Tempi Moderni (Map: Around Piazza Navona, ☎ 06 687 70 07), Via del Governo Vecchio 108, stocks a large selection of vintage costume jewellery dating from 1880 to 1970, with an emphasis on pieces from the Art Nouveau and Art Deco periods. Pieces include 19th century resin brooches, Bakelite from the 1920s and 30s and costume jewellery created by couturiers such as Chanel, Dior and Balenciaga in the 1950s and 60s. Not far from the Colosseo, at Via del Boschetto 148, is Fabio Piccioni (Map 6, ☎ 06 474 16 97), an artisan who recycles old trinkets to create exquisite handcrafted jewellery (credit cards not accepted).

Hausmann & Co watchmakers (Map 5, ☎ 06 687 15 01), Via del Corso 406, founded in 1794, is still making a limited number of its own watches. The shop also stocks a selection of the top international brands of watches.

COSMETICS

The top European brands are widely available in shops called *profumerie* (perfumeries), as well as in department stores. The following outlets have been suggested because they offer something a bit different.

Materozzoli (Map 5, ☎ 06 688 92 686), Piazza San Lorenzo in Lucina 5, is a charming perfume shop that has become a Roman landmark. It stocks a selection of rare perfumes, particularly from France and England, as well as cosmetics and exquisite beauty accessories.

Officina Profumo-Farmaceutica di Santa Maria Novella (Map: Around Piazza Navona, ☎ 06 687 96 08), Corso Rinascimento 47, has various scents and unusual cosmetic products based on the original recipes handed down by the Dominican monks of Santa Maria Novella in Florence. Casamaria (Map: Around Piazza Navona, ☎ 06 683 30 74), Via della Scrofa 71, is roomy and well stocked with the best cosmetic brands at good prices.

HOME WARES

De Sanctis (Map: Around Piazza Navona, ☎ 06 688 06 810), Piazza Navona 82/84, has a good selection of Alessi products (including replacement parts) and other designer kitchenware and tableware. Of particular interest is the selection of Italian ceramics, including the colourful work of the Sicilian ceramicist De Simone.

Budget & Mid-Range

Just around the corner from the Fontana di Trevi is Il Tucano (Map 6, ☎ 06 679 75 47), Piazza dei Crociferi 10, where you can pick up anything from home furnishings to kids' toys to haberdashery. Everything is on display in the shop's windows, then the staff will retrieve your selection from the storeroom (credit cards not accepted, open on Sunday).

Home (Map: Around Piazza Navona, ☎ 06 686 84 50), Largo di Torre Argentina 8, (open on Sunday) is a good place to find bargain-priced home wares, including kitchen utensils, glassware, haberdashery, furniture and rugs. A similar, but more expensive store is Habitat (Map 5, ☎ 06 323 01 36), Via Cola di Rienzo 197.

Leone Limentani (Map: Around Piazza Navona, ☎ 06 688 06 686), in the basement at Via Portico d'Ottavia 47, is a warehouse-style shop with an unbelievable choice of kitchenware and tableware. Here you'll find high-priced fine porcelain and crystal alongside bargain basement items. It also stocks plenty of Alessi (including replacement parts) and a good selection of quality pots and pans.

Stockmarket (Map 5, ☎ 06 686 42 38), at Via dei Banchi Vecchi 51-52, specialises in seconds and end-of-series home wares and furnishings, at very affordable prices.

In the characteristic Rione Monti area is Io Sono un Autarchico (Map 6, ☎ 06 228 66 48), Via del Boschetto 92, a tiny shop packed full of interesting home ware. The shop has a high turnover, so the stock changes continuously.

Designer

One of Rome's premier home wares stores is Spazio Sette (Map: Around Piazza Navona, ☎ 06 688 04 261),Via dei Barbieri 7, just off Largo di Torre Argentina. If you can manage to tear your attention away from the frescoed ceiling at the entrance, you will find three levels of high quality furniture, design home ware, kitchenware and tableware.

Interno Rosso (Map: Around Piazza Navona, ☎ 06 688 08 472), just off Piazza Farnese at Via Monserrato 101, is a quirky little place – more like an art gallery than a shop – that stocks unusual and creatively designed furnishings, pottery and objects.

Alternatively, you might prefer to spend a small fortune on what might best be described as weirdly stylish furnishings by some of Italy and Europe's top avant-garde designers, at Contemporanea (Map 5, ☎ 06 688 04 533), Via dei Banchi Vecchi 143. Unusual and fanciful best describes the furniture at La Corte di Boboli (Map 5, ☎ 06 323 29 86), Via del Corso 75. This shop/workshop opens only in the afternoon (credit cards not accepted). At Tad (Map 5, ☎ 06 360 01 679), Via S. Giacomo 5, you'll find furniture, home wares and textiles in trendy ethnic style.

Xom (☎ 06 320 71 26), Via del Babuino 48, is a showroom of bold design furniture, most of it made from transparent Plexiglas.

Near Piazza di Spagna is C.U.C.I.N.A. (Map 6, ☎ 06 679 12 75), Via del Babuino 118/a, an underground open space special-ising in kitchenware. It has a large selection of stainless steel items. Don't be put off by the store's not-so-helpful staff.

Lighting

There are two shops selling top brands of modern lighting near the Piazza di Spagna. Artemide (Map 5, ☎ 06 360 01 802), is at Via Margutta 107, and Flos (Map 6, ☎ 06 320 76 31), is at Via del Babuino 84/85.

DRUGSTORES

Twenty-four hour convenience stores, known as drugstores, have only recently been introduced in Rome. The city's origi-nal 24-hour store was in Stazione Termini but it now opens only until 11.30 pm. See the Facts for the Visitor chapter for more information on pharmacies in Rome.

Rosatidue (Map 3, ☎ 06 397 41 139), Via Go-lametto 4/A, in Prati near the Piazzale Clodio – open 24 hours, it has a bar/pastry shop, a su-permarket and a McDonald's.

Museum Drugstore Peroni Music Café (☎ 06 559 33 42), Via Portuense 313, open 24 hours, it has a well-stocked supermarket, a newsstand and a pub/caffè.

FOOD & DRINK

Rome has no shortage of *alimentari* (deli-catessens) selling wide selections of Italian cheeses, salami, olives and other gourmet delights. Only a few of the more notable outlets are listed in this section. If you're looking for food of other nationalities, try the Ghetto area (centred around Via di Portico di Ottavia) for shops stocking kosher food and delicious pastries, or the area around Piazza Vittorio Emanuele (Map 6) for Middle Eastern, Asian and African food stores. See the Places to Eat chapter.

Alimentari

Castroni (Map 5, ☎ 06 687 43 83), Via Cola di Rienzo 196/198, in Prati near il Vati-cano, has a wide selection of gourmet foods and food products from around the world (desperate Aussies might find Vegemite here). Credit cards not accepted. Next door is Franchi (Map 5, ☎ 06 687 46 51), a very well-stocked *salumeria* (delicatessen) and takeaway.

Volpetti (Map 7, ☎ 06 574 23 52), Via Marmorata 47, in Testaccio, is famous for its gastronomic specialities, including a large selection of unusual cheeses from throughout Italy. Just around the corner is Volpetti Più, a gourmet *tavola calda* where you can get arguably the best *pizza a taglio* in Rome (see Places to Eat).

Wine

Achilli al Parlamento (Map: Around Piazza Navona, ☎ 06 687 34 46), Via dei Prefetti 15, near the parliament building, is a characteristic Italian *enoteca* (wine shop), where you can buy or sample wines and taste more than 50 different kind of small sandwiches. Buccone (Map 5, ☎ 06 361 21 54), Via di Ripetta 19, near Piazza del Popolo, is another well-stocked wine shop. Go there for a wine tasting or for lunch in the back room.

Health Foods

Buying muesli, soy milk and the like can be expensive in Italy. The following outlets have a good range of products, including organic fruit and vegetables at relatively reasonable prices.

L'Albero del Pane, (Map Via Santa Maria del Pianto 19, in the Jewish quarter, has a wide range of health foods, both packaged and fresh. It has an outlet for organic fruit and vegetables at Via dei Baullari 112, just off Campo de' Fiori. Emporium Naturae, Viale Angelico 2 (take Metro Linea A to Ottaviano), is a well-stocked health-food supermarket. Il Canestro, (Map 7) Via Luca della Robbia 47, in Testaccio near the market, also has a large selection of health food, fresh fruit and vegetables and take-away food.

Markets

One of the best ways to get a feeling for the real Roman way of life is to spend time at one of the city's fresh produce markets, which are treasured reminders of a more traditional way of life. Rome's markets generally have a dazzling array of fresh fruit and vegetables, the usual delicatessen fare and stalls selling clothing, shoes and bric-a-brac. Unfortunately, the large super-markets that are starting to pop up all over the city are bound to have an impact on the viability of the fresh produce markets eventually. Markets usually open from around 6.30 am to 1.30 pm Monday to Saturday.

Among the numerous fresh produce markets around Rome are those held in Campo de' Fiori (Map: Around Piazza Navona; also a flower market), Piazza Testaccio (Map 7; lots of good quality shoes at low prices), and the extensive, colourful market in Piazza Vittorio Emanuele (Map 6), where you'll find lots of exotic foods alongside the usual fare. The covered market of Piazza dell' Unità near il Vaticano, (Map 5; entry also from Via Cola di Rienzo) opens from 8 am to 8 pm Monday to Friday and from 8 am to 2 pm Saturday.

GIFTS

Depending on your point of view, it could be either a good or a bad thing that Romans have begun to embrace the concept of one-stop shopping. Department stores and *centri commerciali* (large shopping centres) are popping up all over the place, although most are on the outskirts of the city.

La Rinascente (Map 6, ☎ 06 679 76 91),Via del Corso at the corner of Largo Chigi – good range of medium-quality clothing and accessories, as well as big name cosmetics. Open on Sunday from 10.30 am to 8 pm. Another store is in Piazza Fiume, (Map 6) also stocking home wares.

UPIM (Map 6, ☎ 06 678 33 36), Via del Tritone 172 – budget store, although the quality of goods can be patchy. Open on Sunday from 10.30 am to 8 pm.

MAS (Map 6, ☎ 06 446 80 78), Via dello Statuto 11 – dirt cheap goods and sometimes you can pick up quality stuff at low prices.

COIN (Map 8, ☎ 06 708 00 91), Piazzale Appio 7 – reasonable quality clothing and accessories, cosmetics and a good range of home wares. Open on Sunday from 10 am to 1 pm and 4 to 8 pm.

Standa (Map 5, ☎ 06 324 32 83), Via Cola di Rienzo 173 – budget store similar to UPIM, also has a supermarket in the same building. Open on Sunday from 9 am to 1.30 pm and 4 to 8 pm.

Auchan (☎ 06 43 20 71), Via Alberto Pollio 50, between Via Tiburtina and Via Prenestina – a centro commerciale with 60 shops and a hypermarket. Open on Sunday from 10 am to 8 pm.

I Granai (☎ 06 519 55 890), Via Mario Rigamonti 100, in EUR – has 130 shops and a hypermarket. Open on Sunday from 10 am to 8 pm.

Cinecittà Due (☎ 06 722 09 10), Via P Togliatti 2 on the corner of Via Tuscolana, near the famous Cinecittà film studios – more than 100 shops, a supermarket and a COIN department store. Open on Sunday 10 am to 8 pm.

MUSIC

Ricordi Media Store (Map 6, ☎ 06 679 80 22), Via Cesare Battisti 120/d is one of Rome's biggest music stores. Open seven days a week, it's well-stocked with music of all sorts and music videos (and films in original language). In the shop next door there's a large selection of classical music, musical instruments, musical scores and music books. Ricordi also has outlets in Via del Corso, Viale Giulio Cesare and Piazza Indipendenza.

Rinascita (☎ 06 699 22 436), Via delle Botteghe Oscure 5, open seven days a week, specialises in world and contemporary music and the latest trends.

Disfunzioni Musicali (Map 6, ☎ 06 446 19 84), Via degli Etruschi 4-14, open seven days a week, is in the heart of Rome's university area. It specialises in alternative, non-commercial music, rare records and bootlegs. There is a second-hand record and CD shop nearby at Via dei Marrucini 1.

L'Allegretto (Map 3, ☎ 06 320 82 24), Via Oslavia 44, is outside the city centre, in Prati, however, it's worth seeking out for an excellent selection of opera and classical music.

TOYS

If the kids need a break from sightseeing, giving them a few hours in a toy shop is not such a bad idea. First choice (although perhaps only for browsing) should be Al Sogno (Map: Around Piazza Navona, ☎ 06 686 41 98), Piazza Navona 53. Its first floor is a wonderland of expensive dolls and stuffed animals of every shape and size.

At the opposite side of the piazza is Bertè (Map: Around Piazza Navona, ☎ 06 687 50 11), very well-stocked with quality toys for children of all ages. Rome's best toy shop is, however, Città del Sole (Map: Around Piazza Navona, ☎ 06 688 03 805), Via della Scrofa 65, that stocks only the best quality educational and creative toys for kids and adults. If you really want to buy up big, head for Toys 'R' Us (☎ 06 726 71 843), Via Orazio Raimondo 21, next to the major shopping centre, La Romanina, just outside Raccordo Annulare (ring road) and quite a distance from the city centre.

DEPARTMENT STORES & SHOPPING CENTRES

If you're looking for something unusual, you are likely to find it at Amati & Amati (Map: Around Piazza Navona, ☎ 06 686 43 19), Via dei Pianellari 21, which stocks unusual imported objects and home wares, small pieces of furniture from Morocco, as well as clothing and accessories.

Stilo Fetti (Map: Around Piazza Navona, ☎ 06 678 96 62), Via degli Orfani 82, near the Pantheon, has a wide selection of antique and new fountain and ballpoint pens, as well as writing desk sets and diaries.

La Chiave (Map: Around Piazza Navona, ☎ 06 683 08 848), Largo delle Stimmate 28, stocks reasonably-priced imported handicrafts, including small furnishings, textiles, rugs and bric-a-brac. If you're looking for something special, try the shop inside the Palazzo delle Esposizioni (Map 6, ☎ 06 482 80 01), one of Rome's main exhibitions spaces. The shop is accessible from the building's side entrance, at Via Milano 9/a, and has a range of unusual design objects, gadgets and home wares. There's also a bookshop, that specialises in art and photography books.

Single (Map 6, ☎ 06 679 07 13), Via Francesco Crispi 47, near Via Sistina, has a good selection of design objects, including unusual watches, Alessi kitchenware and expensive fountain pens. Guaytamelli (Map: Around Piazza Navona, ☎ 06 588 07

04),Via del Moro 59, in Trastevere, is a workshop/retail outlet selling handcrafted compasses, hourglasses, and sundials, based on 16th to 18th century designs.

An excellent place to find special gifts is Pandora (Map 7, ☎ 06 589 56 58), Piazza Santa Maria in Trastevere 6. Here you'll find unusual costume jewellery from around the world, but in particular, gorgeous necklaces made from Murano glass. The shop also sells ceramics, some glassware and scarves.

MARKETS

Rome's biggest and best-known flea market is Porta Portese, held every Sunday until around 1 pm in the area extending south from the Porta Portese, an ancient Roman port on the Tevere river, in the streets parallel to Viale Trastevere. A mish-mash of new and old, the market has all manner of incredible deals – but you'll need to be a hard bargainer. Watch out for pickpockets.

There is a covered market selling new and second-hand clothing and shoes in Via Sannio (Map 8), near Porta San Giovanni and the Basilica di San Giovanni. It opens daily (except Sunday) from 8 am to 1 pm.

The Borghetto Flaminio market, held at Piazza della Marina 32 (Map 3) on Sundays from 10 am to 7 pm (entry L3000; closed in August), is another good flea market where many private individuals (as opposed to professional marketeers) set up stalls. Here you'll find inexpensive antiques, bric-a-brac and second-hand clothes.

The Mercatino di Ponte Milvio is an antique and bric-a-brac market, held on the Lungotevere Capoprati on the first Sunday of the month, from 9 am to sunset (closed in August). It extends along the Tevere river from the Ponte Milvio to the Ponte Duca d'Aosta, every 1st Sunday (sometimes also on Saturday) of the month, from 9 am to sunset (except in August).

Underground, (Map 6) held in an underground car park at Via Francesco Crispi 96, between Via Sistina and Via Veneto, specialises in collectables. It's held on the first weekend of the month, on the Saturday from 3 to 8 pm and the Sunday from 10.30 am to 7.30 pm (closed July and August).

For prints and books, head for the market at Piazza Borghese (Map 5) held daily (except Sunday) from 8 am to sunset.

In Rome, everybody needs to take a breather now and again...

An entrance to the Etruscan afterlife at Cerverteri

The spectacularly endowed Diana of Ephesus

The 'Barberini Mosaic' in Palestrina

Excursions

Rome demands so much of your time and concentration that most tourists forget the city is part of the Lazio region. Declared a region in 1934, the Lazio area (Latium) has, since ancient Roman times, been an extension of Rome.

Through the ages, the rich built their villas in the Lazio countryside and many towns developed as the fiefs of noble Roman families, such as the Orsini, Barberini and Farnese. Even today, Romans build their weekend and holiday homes in the picturesque areas of the region (the pope, for instance, has his summer residence at Castelgandolfo, in the Colli Albani south of Rome) and Romans continue to migrate from their chaotic and polluted city to live in the Lazio countryside. This means the region is relatively well-served by public transport, and tourists can take advantage of this to visit places of interest.

While the region does not abound in major tourist destinations, it does offer some worthwhile day trips from the city. A tour of Etruria, the ancient land of the Etruscans, which extended into northern Lazio, is highly recommended. Visits to the tombs and museums at Cerveteri and Tarquinia provide a fascinating insight into Etruscan civilisation. The ruins of Villa Adriana (Hadrian's villa), near Tivoli, and of the ancient Roman port at Ostia Antica, are both easily accessible from Rome, as is the medieval town of Viterbo to the north.

In summer, tired and overheated tourists can head for the lakes north of Rome, including Bracciano, Bolsena and Vico, which are somewhat preferable to the polluted beaches near the city, or head south of Rome to the relatively clean, sandy beaches of Sabaudia or Sperlonga.

There are some hilltop towns south of Rome which are worth visiting, such as Anagni (and the remarkable frescoes in its Romanesque cathedral), Alatri and those of the Castelli Romani in the hills just past Rome's outskirts.

Rome is also a suitable base for excursions to places outside Lazio. Day trips to major tourist destinations such as Firenze and Napoli or the ancient city of Pompeii are easy by train, and a two-day break in Venezia is not out of the question (take the night train from Rome for optimum time in the city). To the east, the mountains and the Parco Nazionale di Abruzzo, one of the oldest national parks in Italy, provide an ideal escape from the noise and the crowds in an area renowned for its breathtaking scenery and fauna.

When you are making plans bear in mind that in Italy buses and trains stop early in the evenings, and that services are limited on Sunday and public holidays. For up-to-date timetable information telephone COTRAL/Ferrovia dello Stato on the freecall number ☎ 167 43 17 84. If you have your own transport, try to avoid day trips out of Rome on Saturday and Sunday, particularly during summer, when you will find that the whole of Lazio is on the move. On your return on Sunday evening you are likely to find yourself in traffic jams extending for many kilometres, even on the autostrada.

OSTIA ANTICA

Founded by the Romans at the mouth of the river Tevere in the 4th century BC and functioning as Rome's main port for 600 years, Ostia Antica gives a fascinating insight into contemporary life in a working ancient Roman town.

Populated by Roman and foreign merchants, sailors and slaves, it became a strategically important centre of defence and trade, and the ruins of the city provide an interesting contrast to the ruins of the ancient city at Pompeii, which was a resort town for the rich upper classes. The cultural, religious and ethnic diversity of Ostia Antica's inhabitants is attested to in the sanctuaries, temples and shrines dedicated

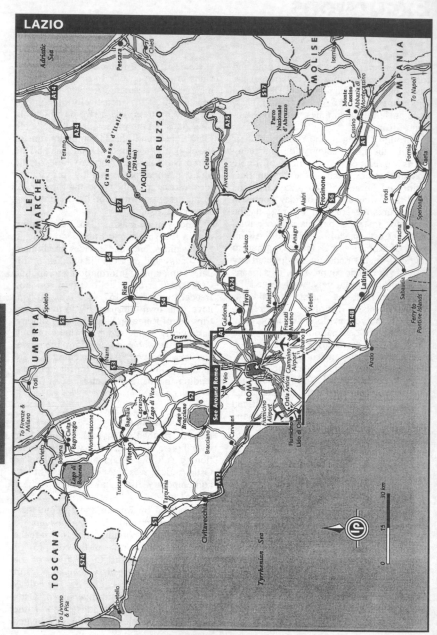

LAZIO

to different deities, and the scope of their activity can be seen in the range of clearly discernible buildings: restaurants, laundries, bakeries, shops, residential properties and meeting places.

Barbarian invasions and the outbreak of malaria led to the city's eventual abandonment and it slowly became buried under river silt, up to 2nd floor level, which explains the excellent state of preservation of the remains. Pope Gregory IV re-established the town in the 9th century. The walls of this *borgo* are still standing, although the town has spread beyond them (See Information & Orientation below). It is interesting to visit the borgo and 15th century castle, which are opposite the entrance to the ruins of the Roman Ostia Antica.

You need to give yourself a good three to five hours to really *do* Ostia Antica. Go early on a sunny weekday to experience the ruins and their leafy park-like setting at their most enchanting. The most important ruins are marked, but it is well worth leaving the beaten track and exploring the ruins at random.

Information about the town and ruins is available at the APT office in Rome (see Tourist Office in Facts About Rome).

Information and Orientation

The entrance to the ruins is a five minute walk from the railway station. Cross the footbridge in front of the station exit and follow the signs. Near the excavations is the medieval fortified borgo of Ostia Antica, dominated by an imposing, moated castle built between 1483 and 1486 for the future Julius II, from whom it takes its name. The castle is open from 9 am to 1 pm Tuesday to Sunday. On Tuesday and Thursday it is also open in the afternoon from 2.30 to 4.30 pm. Only groups of 30 people can enter at a time. To get to the town from the excavations go straight on until you get to a main road. Here turn left and follow the road to the right until you get to the town centre.

For a meal try *Il Monumento* in Piazza Umberto I 18 on the main road into the town (closed Monday). In the same square there is also a bar and an alimentari for picnic provisions if you want to picnic in the ruins (the restored amphitheatre makes an ideal spot). Remember to take your rubbish away with you afterwards. There are no toilet or restaurant facilities inside the archaeological area.

The excavations are open from 9 am Tuesday to Sunday and close at 4 pm from November to February, 5 pm in March, and 6 pm from April to October. The Ostiense archaeological museum inside the site is open from 9 am to 2 pm. Admission to the excavations and museum costs L8000.

Things to See & Do

The ruins are located along the **Decumanus Maximus**, Ostia Antica's main thoroughfare, over 1km long and leading to the sea. Entrance to the city is through the **Porta Romana** to the east, built in the 1st century BC. The **Porta Marina** at the other end of the road marks the exit to the old seafront. Built in squared masonry with two projecting towers, its structure differs from that of the other gates. The area outside the gate bears evidence of use as a cemetery in the first instance, and then later as a residential area during the Empire.

Of particular note in the area around the Porta Romana are the **Terme di Nettuno** (2nd century) on the right just after entering the city. Take a look at the large gymnasium and the black-and-white mosaic depicting Neptune and Amphitrite. Next to the baths is a **Roman theatre**, built by Agrippa during the Augustan era and then enlarged under the Severi. Holding up to 3000 people, it was restored in 1927 and is now used for staging classical performances and concerts. Behind the theatre is **Piazzale delle Corporazioni**, the location of the offices of Ostia's merchant guilds, displaying mosaics depicting their different interests.

Returning to the Decumanus Maximus, you come to Via dei Molini containing a large **bakery** dating from the 2nd century, one of several establishments which produced bread for Ostia and Rome. Every stage of production took place here, from the grinding of the corn in the mills made of volcanic stone to the sale of the finished item over the shop counters at the front. Round the corner in Via di Diana is the perfectly preserved **Casa di Diana**, the ancient Roman answer to the problem of high-density housing, built in the 2nd century when space was at a premium.

The house consists of three floors, accessible through a central courtyard. Opposite is the **Thermopolium**, a sort of bar with sinks for washing dishes, an adjacent kitchen and courtyard seating. Of interest too are the **forum**, built in the 1st century and then partly demolished in the following century to make way for the existing structures. These include the raised **Capitolium**, the **Tempio di Roma e Augusto**, with its statue of Roma Virtrix (Rome the Conqueror), and the **Tempio Rotondo**. Follow the Vico del Pino and Via del Tempio Rotondo to the Cardo Maximus to reach the **Domus Fortuna Annonaria**, the heavily decorated home of one of Ostia's better-off citizens.

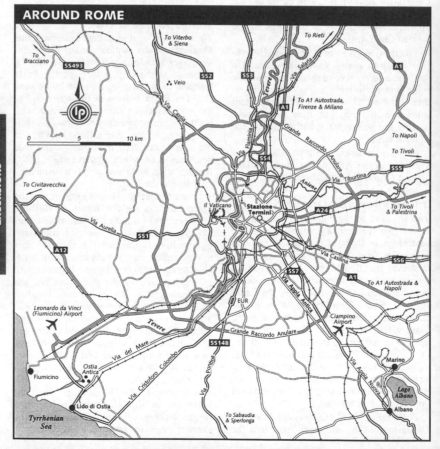

AROUND ROME

Retrace your steps and you get to the Bivio di Castrum and Via della Foce. There is a shrine at the intersection, erected during the Republic to mark the importance of the crossroads within the developing street system. Via della Foce leads to the mouth of the river Tevere and pre-existed the foundation of Ostia. Immediately on the right is the sacred area of the Republican temples, the most important of which is dedicated to Hercules Invictus (Hercules the Unconquered).

Cut through the **Terme dei Sette Sapienti** to reach the Cardo degli Aurighi, and then the continuation of the Decumanus Maximus. On the left towards the Bivio is the **Basilica Cristiana**, built in the late 4th century, and the largest Christian building within the city walls.

The **Ostiense Museum**, housing statues, mosaics and wall paintings found at the site, is at the end of Via dei Dipinti, behind the Casa di Diana.

Getting There & Away

Trains leave Ostiense (Porta San Paolo) approximately every half hour (more frequently at peak times). Take Metropolitana Linea B to Piramide and follow signs for the Ferroviere Roma-Lido. Ostia Antica is seven stops away. The journey takes about 25 minutes and is covered by a standard BIT ticket. Twenty-five kilometres from Rome, the ruins are also an easy ride by car. Take the Via del Mare (SS8), or the parallel Via Ostiense. There is a carpark at the entrance to the site, where you pay a flat fee of L4000.

Around Ostia

The coast at Ostia Lido is only a stone's throw away from the excavations. Take the train from the Ostia Antica station and get off at Lido Centro. From here cross Piazza della Stazione del Lido in front of the station and go straight on until you hit the sea (five minutes). The beach is very crowded in summer and the water isn't terribly clean, so we don't recommend taking a dip there. See The Coast section later in this chapter.

TIVOLI

Tivoli, Roman Tibur, nestles on the lower slopes of the Sabine Hills by the Aniene river, around 30km east of Rome. By the 1st century BC, it had become a holiday resort for Roman aristocrats who were attracted by the town's clean air and its beautiful situation among olive groves overlooking the Roman Campagna, the countryside surrounding Rome that stretches from the Tyrrhenian Sea to the mountains some 50km inland. The poets Catullus and Horace had villas in or near Tivoli, as did Cassius (one of Julius Caesar's assassins) and the emperors Trajan and Hadrian.

During the Middle Ages, Tivoli was frequently overrun by invaders who used the town as a base from which to attack Rome. During the Renaissance the town became once again a summer playground for the moneyed classes and wealthy cardinals.

The town has long been famous for its Travertine marble and the quarries that line the road from Rome testify to the continuing flourishing trade. Easily reached by car or public transport, Tivoli is one of the most popular day trips from Rome. It can get quite crowded in Summer and the traffic on the approaching road can be very heavy.

Orientation & Information

Buses stop in Piazzale Nazioni Uniti, opposite Largo Garibaldi, in the centre of the town, and continue on to the terminus in Piazza Massimo (☎ 0774 33 50 96) near Villa Gregoriana park. The train station is located in Viale Mazzini, to the east of the town on the far side of the Aniene river.

The tourist office, Ufficio di informazione ed accoglienza turistica (IAT, ☎ 0774 31 12 49, Largo Garibaldi), is open Monday to Saturday from 9 am to 3 pm. It provides a useful information leaflet which contains a street map indicating Tivoli's main sites and can supply a list of accommodation options in and around the town.

Things to See & Do

Tivoli is dominated by the **Castello Rocca Pia**, an imposing castle built by Pope Pius

II in the 1460s to remind the inhabitants of who was in charge. The town had a long history of struggles with Rome, once even defeating its neighbour and capturing a pope. The ruins of an ancient Roman amphitheatre, over which the castle was built, can still be seen. After 1870, the Rocca Pia was used as a prison, and currently houses temporary exhibitions.

Most visitors head straight for the **Villa d'Este**, next to the church of Santa Maria Maggiore in Piazza Trento. However, the labyrinthine streets of the rest of the town are definitely worth seeing, either briefly before you go to the Villa d'Este or in a more leisurely fashion if you are staying overnight.

Just north of the Villa d'Este, on the steep and narrow Via del Colle, is the 12th-century Romanesque **Chiesa di San Silvestro**. Some interesting early medieval frescoes representing the legend of Constantine decorate the triumphal arch and the apse.

At the other end of the town, two Roman temples built during the Republican era share the most picturesque location in Tivoli on the edge of a ravine overlooking a deep valley. The circular **Tempio di Vesta**, dating from the 1st century BC, was converted into a church in the Middle Ages. Next to it is the rectangular **Tempio della Sibilla** built in the 2nd century BC. The temples are now incorporated into the gardens of a restaurant. Ask nicely and the proprietors will let you in for a closer look.

A better view of the temples can be had from the wooded park of Villa Gregoriana below (enter from Largo Sant'Angelo). The waterfalls and gardens of Villa Gregoriana were created when Pope Gregory XVI diverted the flow of the Aniene river to put an end to the periodic flooding in the area. There are two main waterfalls – the smaller one at the neck of the gorge was designed by Bernini. Shady paths surrounded by lush vegetation wind down to various viewpoints over the waterfalls. The park also contains the remains of a Roman villa and there's a picnic area where ancient column capitals double as stools.

Villa Gregoriana is open every day from 9 am to one hour before sunset. Admission is L3500.

Villa d'Este There's a sense of faded splendour about the Renaissance pleasure palace created in 1550 by Cardinal Ippolito d'Este, the son of Lucrezia Borgia and grandson of Borgia Pope Alexander VI. Originally a Benedictine convent, the site was transformed by Ippolito d'Este into a sumptuous villa with a breathtaking formal garden full of elaborate fountains and pools.

Some of the remaining Mannerist frescoes in the villa have recently been restored and deserve a quick look, but the residence is totally upstaged by the gardens. These are an almost entirely symmetrical series of terraces, shady pathways and spectacular fountains, powered solely by gravitational force, and include one that once played the organ and another that imitated the call of birds.

Sadly neither of these are functional today, but the visitor can still get a sense of the fantastic creation that the garden once was. There are delightful features such as the long terrace of grotesque heads, all spouting water, and the Rometta fountain (on the far left going down the terraces) which has reproductions of Rome's major buildings. From 1865 to 1886 the villa was home to Franz Liszt and inspired his composition, *Fountains of the Villa d'Este*.

Villa d'Este is open from 9 am to 7.30 pm Tuesday to Sunday between April and September and from 9 am to 5.30 pm between October and March. Admission is L8000.

Villa Adriana Constructed between 118 and 134 AD, Villa Adriana was one of the largest and most sumptuous villas in the Roman empire. It was the country palace of Hadrian and was later used by other emperors. After the fall of the empire, it was plundered by barbarians and Romans alike for building materials. Many of its original decorations were used to embellish the Villa d'Este.

A model near the entrance gives you some idea of the scale of the complex. The site is enormous and you'll need several hours to see it properly.

Hadrian travelled widely and was a keen architect, and parts of the villa were inspired by buildings he had seen around the world. The massive Pecile, through which you enter, was a reproduction of a building in Athens. The Canopo, on the far side of the site, is a copy of the sanctuary of Serapis near Alexandria, with the long canal of water, originally surrounded by Egyptian statues, reproducing the Nile.

Highlights of the excavations include the fishpond (probably used less for keeping fish than for creating decorative reflections and plays of light) encircled by an underground gallery where the emperor took his summer walks, the **Piccole e Grandi Terme** (Small and Large Baths), and Hadrian's private retreat, the **Teatro Marittimo**, a small circular palace on an island in an artificial pool, which could be reached only by a retractable bridge. There are also nymphaeums, temples and barracks and a museum displaying the latest discoveries from ongoing excavations. Archaeologists have found features such as a heated bench with steam pipes under the sand, and a network of subterranean service passages for horses and carts.

Villa Adriana is open daily from 9 am to 5 pm between November and January, to 6 pm in February and October, to 6.30 pm in March and September, to 7 pm in April and to 7.30 pm between May and August. Tickets are sold until one hour before closing and cost L8000.

Local bus No 4 goes to Villa Adriana, leaving Tivoli from Piazza Massimo near Villa Gregoriana park. Otherwise take the COTRAL bus to Rome from the terminus in Piazza Massimo or from the stop outside the tourist office on Largo Garibaldi and get off at the town of Villa Adriana, from where it's an easy 1km walk to the villa itself.

Bagni di Tivoli You can't ignore the smell of the sulphurous waters of **Terme Acque Albule** (☎ 0774 37 10 07) at Bagni di Tivoli, 8km from Tivoli on the Via Tiburtina. Vergil wrote about these springs in the *Aeneid*, and many Romans built their country villas nearby to benefit from the healing waters. Today's visitors to the baths complex (admission L20,000, children L5000) benefit from the same sulphurous springs which fill the four huge swimming pools. A vast array of mud, inhalation and massage treatments is available at extra cost.

To get to Bagni di Tivoli you can take the COTRAL bus to Rome and get off at the town of the same name. Otherwise the tourist office can supply details of local bus routes and timetables.

Places to Stay

Hotel Igea (☎ 0774 33 52 85, Viale Mannelli 2), is central and has spotless and comfortable singles/doubles/triples with bath for L80,000/100,000/130,000. The hotel is above the Caffè Igea on the corner of Viale Arnaldi and Viale Mannelli. The bar in the café doubles as a hotel reception.

Places to Eat

Antica Trattoria del Falcone (☎ 0774 31 23 58) on the medieval Via del Trevio 34, serves good pasta and pizza. A meal with wine will cost you about L25,000. You can eat outside in the courtyard in the warmer months.

Trattoria L'Angolino (☎ 0774 31 20 27, Via della Missione 3), has pizzas for L7000 to L10,000, pasta for between L9000 and L12,000 and meal-in-themselves salads for L10,000.

M31 pub (☎ 0774 33 32 43, Via della Missione 56/58), has excellent sandwiches for L4000, pasta dishes for L6000, beer from L3000 and coffee for L1000. It's also open late and often has live music in the evening.

Close to Villa Adriana, *Villa Esedra* (☎ 0774 53 47 16, Via di Villa Adriana 51), has tasty risottos and home-made pasta dishes. It's on the expensive side though and you'll pay about L30,000 to L35,000 for a full meal.

Getting There & Away

Tivoli is 30km east of Rome. To get there from Rome, take Metro Linea B to Ponte Mammolo. The COTRAL bus to Tivoli leaves from outside Ponte Mammolo station every 10 minutes Monday to Saturday and every 20 minutes on Sunday and holidays. It also stops at the Rebibbia stop at the end of Metro Linea B before taking Via Tiburtina to Tivoli, stopping at the towns of Bagni di Tivoli and Villa Adriana along the way.

Tivoli can also be reached from Rome by train but it's a slow journey on the Avezzano line from Termini or Tiburtina stations. By car take Via Tiburtina SS5 or Roma-L'Aquila autostrada A24.

ETRUSCAN SITES

Lazio has a number of important Etruscan archaeological sites, most within easy reach of Rome by car or public transport. These include Tarquinia, Cerveteri, Veio and Tuscania (four of the main city-states in the Etruscan League).

Predominantly navigators and traders, the Etruscans developed a political and social system to rival the Romans and their great artistic sense found expression in the tomb paintings and artefacts that have been discovered since excavations began in the 18th century. Profoundly influential on the growing culture in nearby Rome, Etruscan culture reached a peak in the 7th and 6th centuries BC. However, surrender of their trade routes to the more powerful Greeks in the 5th century precipitated a long period of decline that culminated in the eventual absorption of the Etruscan culture by the Republic in the 1st century BC.

Most of what is known about Etruscan culture has been gleaned from the archaeological evidence of their tombs and religious sanctuaries. Their belief in life after death gave rise to the practice of burying the deceased with everything that he or she might need in the next life: food and drink, clothes, ornaments and jewellery. These items and the colourful tomb paintings depicting scenes from everyday life, constitute the single most important source of information regarding the Etruscans. Many can now be seen in museums including the Villa Giulia and Il Museo Vaticano. The smaller museums at Tarquinia and Cerveteri are also well worth a visit.

The sheer number of tombs in the area has long supported the illegitimate industry of the *tombaroli* (tomb robbers), who have been plundering the sites for centuries and selling their 'discoveries' on the black market. It is said that, since many tombs are still to be excavated, a good number of tombaroli remain active. Prospective buyers of illicit Etruscan artefacts should, however, beware: another notorious activity of the tombaroli is the manufacture of fake anqituities.

A few days spent touring at least Tarquinia and Cerveteri, combined with visits to their museums and the Villa Giulia should constitute one of your most fascinating experiences in Italy. A useful guidebook to the area, *The Etruscans*, is published by the Istituto Geografico de Agostini and has a map. If you really want to lose yourself in a poetic journey, take along a copy of D.H. Lawrence's *Etruscan Places* (published by Penguin in the compilation *D.H. Lawrence and Italy*).

Tarquinia

Believed to have been founded in the 12th century BC, and home of the Tarquin kings who ruled Rome before the creation of the Republic, Tarquinia was an important economic and political centre of the Etruscan League. The town has a small medieval centre, with a good Etruscan museum, but the major attractions here are the painted tombs of its burial grounds.

Orientation & Information By car or bus you will arrive at the Barriera San Giusto, just outside the main entrance to the town. See Getting There & Away in this section. The APT office (☎ *0766 85 63 84*) is on your left as you walk through the medieval ramparts, at Piazza Cavour 1. It's open from 8 am to 2 pm Monday to

Etruscan Mysteries

Much of the fascination of the Etruscans comes from the fact that so much about this complex civilisation remains unknown. The jury is still out as to whether the Etruscans were native to Italy, or whether they migrated from somewhere in Asia Minor. The Etruscan language is yet to be fully understood. They did, however, leave a wealth of archaeological remains, and also had an enormous influence on Roman culture.

The boundaries of Etruria were the Arno River in the north, the Tevere in the south, and the Mediterranean Sea. Many of the major sites are in Toscana, but some, most notably Tarquinia, Cerveteri, Veio, Viterbo, and Tuscania, are in Lazio. The foundations and some of the elaborately decorated terracotta tiles from the wooden temples survive, but the Etruscan cemeteries hold the main attraction.

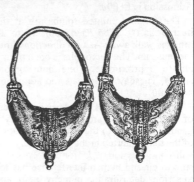

Etruscan earrings from the Cerveteri tombs

The grandest tombs were built to resemble houses, even down to their arrangement in neat 'streets'. The wealthy dead were buried in spectacular portrait sarcophagi, which often depicted women as the apparent social equals of their husbands. The tomb walls were painted with cheerful scenes of the afterlife, which like that of the Egyptians, closely resembled the nicest aspects of this existence – the Etruscans looked forward to a boisterous eternity of parties and hunting. They also packed suitable grave goods for a pleasant afterlife, including distinctive black bucchero tableware, bronze mirrors engraved with mythological scenes, and exquisite gold jewellery.

The Etruscans also excelled in bronzework, surviving examples of which include the Capitoline wolf (originally minus the twins), and the Mars of Todi now in the Musei Vaticani.

The deep-seated ambivalence the Romans felt towards the Etruscans is reflected in their legends. Of the three Etruscan kings who ruled Rome, Servius Tullius is credited with building the first walls and organising the political and military systems, while the last, Tarquinius Superbus (Tarquin the Proud), was expelled from Rome after his son raped a nobleman's wife.

The Romans did adopt many Etruscan civil and religious customs, including the study of the flight of birds and the entrails of sacrificed victims to determine the will of the gods, and the *fasces,* an axe inserted into a bundle of rods which symbolised the State's powers of corporal and capital punishment. A common motif in Roman art, the fasces were also adopted by Mussolini.

Saturday. It is possible to see Tarquinia on a day trip from Rome, but if you want to stay overnight in the medieval town, it is advisable to make a booking.

Things to See The 15th century Palazzo Vitelleschi, located in Piazza Cavour, houses the **Museo Nazionale Tarquiniese** (☎ 0766 85 60 36) containing a significant collection of Etruscan treasures, including reconstructions of the **Tomba del Triclinio** and the **Tomba delle Olimpiadi** with the frescoes removed from the original tombs. There is a beautiful terracotta frieze of winged horses, taken from the temple **Ara della Regina** (see below). Numerous sarcophagi found in the tombs are also on display. The museum is open from 9 am to 7 pm Tuesday to Sunday. Admission is L8000.

The famous painted tombs are at the **necropolis** (☎ *0766 85 63 08*), 15 to 20 minutes walk away. Ask for directions from the museum. The necropolis is open from 9 am to approximately one hour before sunset, Tuesday to Sunday and admission is L8000.

Nearly 6000 tombs have been excavated, of which about 60 are painted, but only a handful are open to the public. Excavation of the tombs started in the 15th century and still continues today. Unfortunately, exposure to air and human interference has led to serious deterioration in many tombs and they are now enclosed and maintained at constant temperatures. The painted tombs can be seen only through glass partitions.

D.H. Lawrence, who studied the tombs before measures were taken to protect them, wrote extensive descriptions of the frescoes he saw, and it is well worth reading his *Etruscan Places* before seeing the tombs of Tarquinia. Entering the famous **Tomba dei Leopardi**, Lawrence noted how, despite the extensive destruction of the tombs through vandalism and neglect, the colours of the wall paintings were still fresh and alive. Equally noteworthy are the **Tomba della Caccia e della Pesca**, the **Tomba del Barone**, and the **Tomba del Guerriero**, depicting scenes of convivial life, hunting and fishing scenes and scenes from mythology.

If you have a car, drive to the remains of the Etruscan acropolis of Tarxuna, on the crest of the Civita hill 5km away, on the Monte Romano road running east. There is little evidence of the ancient city, apart from a few limestone blocks which once formed part of the city walls, since the Etruscans generally used wood to build their temples and houses. However, the foundations of a large temple, the **Ara della Regina**, was discovered on the hill and has been excavated this century.

If you have time, wander through the pleasant medieval town of Tarquinia, for-

merly called Corneto. There are several churches worth a look, including the late 13th century **Chiesa di San Francesco**, in Via Porta Tarquinia, and the beautiful Romanesque **Chiesa di Santa Maria di Castello**, in the citadel at the north-west edge of town.

Places to Stay & Eat There is a camping ground by the sea at Tarquinia Lido, *Tusca Tirrenia* (☎ *0766 86 42 94, Viale delle Neriedi*), 5km from the medieval town, open from May to September/October.

There are no budget options in the old town if you want to stay overnight, and it can be difficult to find a room if you don't book in advance. The *Hotel San Marco* (☎ *0766 84 22 34, Piazza Cavour 10*) is in the medieval section of town, near the museum. It has newly renovated singles/doubles for L65,000/100,000 and half board/full board for L75,000/85,000 per person.

The *Hotel all'Olivo* (☎ *0766 85 73 18, fax 0766 84 07 77, Via Togliatti 13/15*) in the newer part of town is a 10-minute walk downhill from the medieval centre. Singles/doubles cost L70,000/120,000 including breakfast.

Closer to the town centre, but more expensive, is *Hotel Tarconte* (☎ *0766 85 61 41, fax 0766 85 65 85, Via Tuscia 19*). Singles/doubles cost up to L100,000/ 140,000, including breakfast, although prices fall to L60,000/90,000 out of season. Half board/full board costs L125,000/ 150,000 per person.

At Tarquinia Lido *Hotel Miramare* (☎ *0766 86 40 20, Viale dei Tirreni 36*) is a good budget choice. A double room with a bath costs L90,000, excluding breakfast. A room without a bath costs L70,000.

There are few places to eat in Tarquinia, but for a good, cheap meal, go to *Trattoria Arcadia*, Via Mazzini 6. *Cucina Casareccia* is opposite at No 5.

Getting There & Away Buses leave approximately every hour for Tarquinia from outside the Lepanto stop on Metro Linea A, arriving at Tarquinia at the Barriera San

Giusto, a short distance from the tourist office. You can also catch a train from Rome, but Tarquinia's train station is at Tarquinia Lido, approximately 3km from the town centre. You will then need to catch one of the regular local buses to the Barriera San Giusto. Buses leave from the Barriera for Tuscania, near Tarquinia, every few hours.

If you are travelling by car, take the autostrada for Civitavecchia and then the Via Aurelia (SS1). Tarquinia is about 90km north-west of Rome.

Around Tarquinia

Tuscania, 24km from Tarquinia, is worth a visit. The leading Etruscan city after the 4th century BC, it has a good **Museo Archaeologico** (☎ 0761 43 62 09), Via Donna del Riposo. The museum is open from 9 am to 7 pm Tuesday to Sunday and admission is free.

Also worth a visit are the churches of **San Pietro** and **Santa Maria Maggiore**, dating from the 8th century AD with 11th and 12th century additions.

By car, Tuscania is an easy drive from Tarquinia. Otherwise there is a COTRAL bus which leaves Tarquinia from the Barriera San Giusta just off Piazza Cavour.

Cerveteri

Forty-five kilometres north-west of Rome on a spur overlooking the sea, Cerveteri, classical Caere, was founded by the Etruscans in the 8th century BC. It enjoyed a time of great prosperity as one of the most important commercial centres in the Mediterranean from the 7th to the 5th century, before entering into a long period of decline. In 358 BC the city was annexed to Rome and the inhabitants granted Roman citizenship.

This colonisation of the city (as of the other cities in the Etruscan league in the same period) resulted in the absorption of the Etruscan culture into Roman culture and its eventual disappearance. After the fall of the Roman Empire the spread of malaria and repeated Saracen invasions caused further decline. In the 13th century there was a mass exodus from the city to the nearby town of Ceri, further inland; and

Caere became Caere Vetus ('old Caere'), from which its current name derives. The first half of the 19th century saw the first tentative archaeological explorations in the area and in 1911 systematic excavations began in earnest.

The main attractions here are the tombs known as *tumoli*, great mounds of earth with carved stone bases laid out in the form of a town with streets and squares. Reproducing the inside of Etruscan homes with doors, ceilings, chairs, beds and other household objects either illustrated or carved into the rock, they are an important document of Etruscan architecture and daily life. Treasures taken from the tombs can be seen in the Musei del Vaticano, the Museo di Villa Giulia and the Louvre.

Information The Pro Loco tourist office is at Piazza Risorgimento 19 (☎ 06 99551971) in the centre of the medieval town. It is open from 10.30 am to 12.30 pm on Tuesday and from Thursday to Saturday, and from 3.30 to 6 pm on Wednesday.

Things to See & Do The medieval town boasts a 16th century **castello** and a small **museo archeologico** (☎ 06 994 13 54, Piazza S. Maria) containing an interesting display of pottery and sarcophagi dating from the 9th century BC from Cerveteri and the nearby port of Pyrgi. The museum is open from 9 am to 7 pm Tuesday to Sunday, (between November and March you have to ring the bell after 2 pm). Admission is free.

The lovely **Chiesa di Santa Maria Maggiore** is also worth a visit. Behind it, the **Chiesa Vecchia** contains a notable fresco from the school of Antoniazzo Romano and a board painting of the *Madonna and Child* by Lorenzo da Viterbo executed in 1472.

The main necropolis area is **Banditaccia** (☎ 06 9940001), a couple of kilometres from the town centre. If you are in Cerveteri on Saturday or Sunday there is a bus that leaves the medieval town from the main square at 9, 10 and 11 am. The return

EXCURSIONS

bus leaves the necropolis at 10.15 and 11.15 am. Otherwise it is a pleasant 20 minute walk and there are signposts from the main piazza. The necropolis is open from 9 am to 4 pm Tuesday to Sunday (hours are extended to 7 pm in summer), and admission is L8000.

You can roam freely once inside the area, although it is advisable to follow the recommended routes to see the best preserved tombs. Signs detailing the history of the main tombs are in Italian only and you are advised to take a guide book; otherwise the Pro Loco tourist office can supply a good itinerary. There is enough to keep you occupied at the necropolis for half a day at least.

One of the more interesting tombs is the **Tomba dei Rilievi**, dating from the 4th century BC. The tomb belonged to the Mantuna family and is decorated with painted reliefs of cooking implements and other household items. The tomb has been closed to avoid further damage to its paintings but can be viewed through a glass window.

Follow the signs to the **Tomba dei Capitelli** and the **Tomba dei Vasi Greci**. Don't miss the **Tomba degli Scudi e delle Sedie**, outside the main area, accessible only if accompanied by a guarde. It has chairs carved out of the tufa rock and bas-reliefs of shields on the walls.

Getting There & Away Cerveteri is easily accessible from Rome by COTRAL bus from outside the Lepanto stop on Metro Linea A. Buses leave about every half hour and the journey takes 30 minutes. Buy a regional ticket (BIRG) for L8500 covering the return journey by bus or train and public transport in Cerveteri.

Otherwise, catch the train from Termini, Tiburtina, Ostiense or Trastevere and get off at Ladispoli. From here a COTRAL bus will take you the remaining 6km to the town centre. The BIRG covers both stages. By car take either Via Aurelia or the Civitavecchia autostrada (A12) and come off at the Cerceteri-Ladispoli exit. The journey takes approximately 20 minutes.

Around Cerveteri

Ceri is a small medieval town 9km from Cerveteri. It was founded by the inhabitants of Cerveteri to escape the double threat of malaria and attack by the Saracens. There is a small church notable for its frescoes. Ceri is an easy drive from Rome. You can catch a bus there from Cerveteri's main piazza. Timetables are available at the Pro Loco tourist office in Cerveteri.

Veio

Your visit to Etruria should include Veio (Vei), 19km north of Rome. This was the largest of the Etruscan League cities and a major rival to nearby Rome. In 396 BC, after a siege lasting 10 years, Furius Camillus entered the acropolis at Veio through a tunnel and conquered and destroyed it. It became a municipium under Augustus, but eventually declined in importance and was abandoned.

Little evidence remains of the city. However, important finds came to light during excavations of the site in the 18th century, including the famous statue of Apollo, now in the Museo di Villa Giulia in Rome. In Veio, things to see include the foundations of the temple of Apollo, ornamental terracotta pieces and the remains of a swimming pool. There is also the **Tomba Campana**, a frescoed chamber dating from the 7th and 6th centuries BC, and the Ponte Sodo, a tunnel cut out by the Etruscans to create a watercourse.

By car, take the Via Cassia out of Rome and exit at Isola Farnese. Signs will point you towards Veio. Otherwise, take bus No 201 for Olgiata from Piazza Mancini, near Ponte Milvio, to Isola Farnese and ask the bus driver to let you off at the road to Veio (although there is probably not enough to see at Veio to warrant the trouble of taking public transport).

VITERBO

Founded by the Etruscans and later taken over by Rome, Viterbo developed into an important medieval centre and in the 13th century became the residence of the popes, offering a safe house during the violent Church-Empire conflict revolving around Rome.

Papal elections were held in the town's Gothic Palazzo dei Papi, and stories abound about the antics of impatient townspeople anxious for a decision. In 1271, when the college of cardinals failed to elect a new pope after three years of deliberation following the death of Clement IV, the Viterbesi first locked them in a turreted hall of the palazzo, and then removed its roof and put them on a starvation diet. Only then did the cardinals manage to elect Gregory X.

Although badly damaged by bombing during WWII, Viterbo remains Lazio's best preserved medieval town, to the extent that the historical San Pellegrino quarter is frequently used as a movie set. Wandering around the narrow streets you will feel as though you have been transported back in time, or into a scene from Dante's *Divina Commedia*. Located 75km north of Rome, Viterbo is a full day trip from the city.

Apart from its historical appeal, Viterbo is famous for its therapeutic hot springs. One of the best known is the sulphurous Bulicame pool, to which Dante refers in his *Inferno*. It is the pool of boiling blood into which Henry of Cornwall's murderer Guy de Montfort is immersed.

Orientation & Information

The town of Viterbo is neatly divided between the newer section to the north and east and the older part to the south, centring on Piazza San Pellegrino and the network of narrow streets that make up the medieval town. Hotels are in the newer part of Viterbo and you must cross the Piazza del Plebiscito, with its 15th and 16th century palaces, before reaching the old town and the real reason for your visit.

There are train stations north and southeast of the town centre, at the Porta Fiorentina and Porta Romana entrances to the city, just outside the town walls. The station for intercity buses is located somewhat inconveniently at Riello, a few kilometres out of town. To get to the medieval centre, get off at Porta Romana and take Via Giuseppe Garibaldi in front of you. This brings you to Piazza Fontana Grande. From here bear left and then right into Via Cardinale la Fontaine. Go straight on and in a few minutes you will find yourself in the heart of the medieval quarter.

The APT office (☎ 0761 30 47 95) is at Piazza San Carluccio in the medieval quarter. Go through the large iron gate on the south side of the square and the office (in temporary premises) is on your right. Opening hours are from 9 am to 1 pm and 1.30 to 3.30 pm Monday to Friday and from 9 am to 1 pm on Saturday. There is a car park in the piazza.

The main post office is in Via F Ascenzi, just off Piazza del Plebiscito. The Telecom office is at Via Cavour 28, between Piazza del Plebiscito and Piazza Fontana Grande.

Things to See & Do

Piazza del Plebiscito The piazza is enclosed by 15th and 16th century palaces, the most imposing of which is the **Palazzo dei Priori**, or Palazzo Comunale, dating from 1500. The arched entrance leads into a pretty courtyard with an elegant 17th century fountain and a lovely view over the Faul valley. The staircase on the left as you enter the courtyard leads to the elaborately decorated Senate Rooms on the 1st floor, open to visitors during office hours.

Notable are the newly restored 16th century frescoes by Baldassare Croce in the **Sala Reggia** that give a comic representation of the myths and history of Viterbo. Of interest also is the ornate wooden tribunal supporting the figure of Justice in the **Sala Consiglio** and the small pulpit, or *bigonoia*, between the two windows, into which dissenters had to climb to voice their disagreements during council meetings.

Cattedrale di San Lorenzo & the Palazzo dei Papi The black-and-white striped **cathedral** in Piazza San Lorenzo dates from the 12th century with 16th century and post-war revisions, although the interior has just been restored to its original

Romanesque simplicity. The building contains a 15th century marble font and paintings from various epochs, as well as the tomb of John XXI, the only Portuguese pope, killed in 1277 when the floor of his room in the Palazzo dei Papi collapsed.

Also in the piazza is the **Palazzo dei Papi**, built for the popes between 1255 and 1267 with the aim of enticing them away from Rome. The graceful loggia with its double row of fine columns to the right of the steps is in the early Gothic style. The part facing the valley collapsed in the 14th century and you can see the bases of some of the columns. Go up the steps and you come to the hall in which papal conclaves were held, now used frequently for concerts, meetings and exhibitions, including the annual **Mostra dell'Antiquariato** in October/ November. It is open on Saturday from 3 to 6 pm and on Sunday from 9 am to midday and 3 to 6 pm. To enter the palace on a weekday go to the curia (☎ 0761 34 11 24) off the adjacent loggia.

Piazza Santa Maria Nuova From the Palazzo dei Papi, head back to the Piazza della Morte and take Via Cardinale la Fontaine to reach this piazza. The Romanesque church of the same name dates from the 12th century and as such is one of the oldest churches in Viterbo, although it has been largely restored after sustaining bomb damage in WWII.

On the façade, above the door, there is an ancient relief sculpture of Jupiter's head, adding weight to the theory that the church stands on the pre-existing site of an ancient pagan temple. The pulpit on the left was used by St Thomas Aquinas. Follow the side wall to the back of the church and you get to the remains of a small Lombard cloister, always open and well worth a visit.

Piazza del Gesù Located in the piazza of the same name, this church supposedly stands at the geographical centre of the old town. Immortalised by Dante in his *Inferno*, it is the site of the murder of Henry, Duke Cornwall, cousin of Edward I, in 1272. He was killed by Guy and Simon de Montfort to revenge their father's murder. Note the crude sculpture of the lion, the symbol of Viterbo, on the roof. It is a comic alternative to the ornate Gothic lion sculptures that abound throughout the city.

The Medieval Quarter Via San Pellegrino takes you through the medieval quarter into **Piazza San Pellegrino**. The very well-preserved buildings which enclose this tiny piazza are considered the finest group of medieval buildings in Italy.

Other Sights Built in the early 13th century, the **Fontana Grande**, in Piazza Fontana Grande, is the oldest and largest of Viterbo's Gothic fountains.

Back at the entrance to the town is the **Chiesa di San Francesco**, in the piazza of the same name, a Gothic building restored after suffering serious bomb damage in January 1944. The church contains the tombs of two popes, Clement IV (died 1268) and Hadrian V (died 1276). Both tombs are lavishly decorated, notably that of Hadrian, featuring Cosmati work, a mosaic technique used in the 12th and 13th centuries.

There is no shortage of museums in Viterbo. The **Museo della Macchina di Santa Rosa** (☎ 0761 34 51 57), in Via San Pellegrino, documents the history of the local festival that takes place on 3 September of each year, when the *Viterbesi* parade a 30m tower around the town. The museum is open from 10 am to 1 pm and 4 to 7 pm Wednesday to Sunday and admission is free.

The **Museo Civico** (☎ 0761 34 82 75) has reopened after a 10 year restoration project. It is housed in the convent of the Chiesa di Santa Maria della Verità, just outside the Porta della Verità on the north-east side of town. Among the works in the museum are the lovely *Pietà* by Sebastiano del Piombo (1515), along with a Roman sarcophagus which is said to be the tomb of Galiana, a beautiful woman murdered by a Roman aristocrat after she refused his advances. The museum is open from 9 am Tuesday to

Sunday, closing at 6 pm from November to March and at 7 pm from April to October. Admission is L6000.

If you want to shop, go to Corsa Italia, the main commercial area. Stop for a coffee at **Caffè Schenardi** at No 11, built by the important Ghigi family in the 15th century and used as a bank and then as a hotel before being turned into a caffè in 1818. The art deco interior is the setting for frequent art exhibitions. For antiques, carpets and handicrafts try the area around Piazza San Pellegrino.

Places to Stay & Eat

For good-quality budget accommodation try the *Hotel Roma* (☎ *0761 22 72 74*, ☎ *0761 22 64 74, fax 0761 30 55 07, Via della Cava 26*), off Piazza della Rocca, two minutes from the Porta Fiorentina entrance to the city. Singles/doubles are L50,000/ 75,000 (L70,000/105,000 plus bath), and prices include breakfast. Garage facilities cost a mere L8000 a day.

For three-star accommodation try *Hotel Tuscia* (☎ *0761 34 44 00, fax 0761 34 59 76, Via Cairoli 41*), on the right as you walk away from Piazza dei Caduti. Here too prices are reasonable. Singles/doubles are L85,000/140,000 and triples are L165,000, including breakfast. There are also single/double suites for L110,000/160,000 and the hotel offers small discounts in low season. All rooms have TV and shower. Air-conditioning costs an additional L10,000 and garage facilities are available for L12,000.

For a reasonably priced meal go to *All' Archetto* (☎ *0761 32 57 69, Via San Cristoforo*), off Via Cavour. Nestling under a medieval arch in a delightful triangular piazza, it offers a decent selection of dishes in a traditional environment. A full meal costs around L25,000.

Il Richiastro (☎ *0761 22 80 09 Via della Marrocca 18*), serves good, simple fare using local ingredients in a cosy semi-basement setting (there is outside seating in summer). Soups are a specialty and cost L8000, or L14,000 for four. Pasta costs

from L10,000 and a meat course is around L14,000. Try the lentil and mushroom soup, which is based on an ancient Roman recipe. The restaurant is closed from Monday to Wednesday and on Sunday evening and from July to September. Booking is recommended.

If you fancy a pizza, try *Il Ciuffo* (☎ *0761 30 82 37*) in Piazza Capella, just off Piazza San Pellegrino in the heart of the medieval quarter. It is open in the evenings only from 7.30 to 11.30 pm (closed Tuesday).

Getting There & Away

There is no easy way to get to Viterbo. However, your cheapest and quickest bet is to take the COTRAL bus from Saxa Rubra (☎ 06 332 83 33) on the Ferrovia Roma-Nord line. Take Metro A to Flaminio and follow the blue signs to Roma Stazione Nord (Piazzale Flaminio). The 10 minute journey to Saxa Rubra costs L1500 and is covered by the standard BIT ticket. Buses leave Saxa Rubra approximately every half hour and a single costs L6400. The journey to Viterbo takes 1½ hours. The intercity bus station is at Riello, a few kilometres north-west of the town centre. However, buses also stop at the Porta Romana and Porta Fiorentina entrances to the city. If you find yourself at Riello, catch city bus No 11 into Viterbo. The journey takes five minutes and costs L1000.

Trains for Viterbo leave from Termini or Ostiense, but times are irregular and the journey sometimes involves several changes. Ring the freecall number ☎ 167 43 17 84 and select option two for up-to-date information about the train service before you set out.

By car, the easiest way to get to Viterbo is on the Cassia-bis (about 1½ hours drive); alternatively take the Autostrada del Sole (A1) and follow signs from Orte. Enter the old town through the Porta Romana onto Via G Garibaldi and follow the street as it becomes Via Cavour, through Piazza del Plebiscito. There are numerous public car parks scattered

EXCURSIONS

throughout the town, although the best is probably Piazza della Rocca.

AROUND VITERBO

Viterbo's **thermal springs** are within a 10km radius of the town. Used by both the Etruscans and the Romans (who built large bath complexes, of which virtually nothing remains), they were then abandoned, before being restored by the 13th century popes. There are both public and private facilities, used by locals and visitors alike. Travellers wanting to take a cure or relax in the hot sulphur baths will find the privately-owned Terme dei Papi (☎ 0761 35 01) the easiest to reach. Take city bus No 2 from the bus station in Piazza Martiri d'Ungheria, near the APT office.

If you have a car, follow the signs from the Terme dei Papi for the Etruscan **necropoli** at Castel d'Asso 5km away. The ancient tombs are interesting and have recently been restored. Theatrical performances are occasionally staged here in summer.

At Bagnaia, a few kilometres northeast of Viterbo, is the beautiful **Villa Lante** (☎ 0761 28 80 08), a 16th century villa noted for its fine Renaissance gardens. The two, superficially identical, palaces are not open to the public, although you can wander in the large public park for free or pay L4000 for a guided tour of the gardens. Climb to the highest terrace and look down over the gardens as they fall away in front of you. The park is open from 9 am to one hour before sunset Tuesday to Sunday. Guided tours of the gardens leave every half-hour. Unfortunately, picnics are not permitted in the park. From Viterbo, take city bus No 6 from Piazza Caduti.

At Caprarola, south-east of Viterbo, is the splendid **Palazzo Farnese** (☎ 0761 64 60 52). Designed by Vignola, it is one of the most important examples of Mannerist architecture in Italy. You need to wait for an attendant to take you through rooms richly frescoed in the 16th century by artists such as Taddeo and Federico Zuccari. Tours leave every 15 minutes (every 30 minutes on Sunday and public holidays).

The palace is open to the public Tuesday to Sunday from 9 am to 4 pm, and entry is L4000. It is surrounded by gardens and a park that can be visited at 10 and 11 am and 12 and 3 pm (10 am, 12 and 3 pm on Sunday and public holidays). There are seven buses a day that leave from the Riello bus station just outside Viterbo for Caprarola, and the last bus returns from Caprarola at 6.35 pm.

The **Parco dei Mostri** or **Sacro Bosco** (☎ 0761 92 40 29) at Bomarzo, north-east of Viterbo, will be particularly interesting for people with young children. The park, created for the Orsini family in the 1570s as a private pleasure garden, was brought to light and restored by Giovanni Bettini, the owner since 1954. Gigantic and grotesque sculptures are scattered throughout, including an ogre, a giant and a dragon.

Also of interest are the octagonal *tempietto* (little temple) dedicated to Julia Farnese and the crooked house, allegedly built without the use of right angles but really the result of the land subsiding. The park is open from 8 am to sunset and admission is L15,000. To get there from Viterbo, catch the COTRAL bus from the stop near Viale Trento to Bomarzo, then follow the signs to Palazzo Orsini.

Another interesting place near Viterbo is the tiny, hill-top medieval town of **Civita di Bagnoregio**, near its newer Renaissance counterpart, Bagnoregio, (north of Viterbo). In a picturesque area of tufa ravines, Civita is known as the 'dying town' because continuous erosion of its hill has caused the collapse of many buildings. Abandoned by its original residents, who moved to Bagnoregio, most of the buildings in the town were purchased by foreigners and artisans and, in recent years, Civita has been restored and developed into a minor tourist attraction.

Regular COTRAL buses connect Bagnoregio with Viterbo, leaving from the Riello bus station. From the bus stop, ask for directions to Civita, which has been connected to Bagnoregio's outskirts by a pedestrian bridge.

THE LAKES

There are four lakes in northern Lazio: Bracciano, Martignano, Vico and Bolsena. The attraction of water and the natural beauty of the surroundings make them popular recreational spots in summer for hot Romans. For sports lovers they offer a range of activities including sailing and horseriding, and there is a good selection of accommodation and restaurant facilities if you want to stay. On Saturday and Sunday the lakes can be crowded, especially in summer. If it is peace and quiet you are after try to go mid-week.

Lago di Bracciano

Forty kilometres north of Rome, this lake is easily accessible by public transport, and is ideal if you need a break from the noise and confusion of the city. Occupying a series of craters in the volcanic Monti Sabatini range, it measures 31km in circumference and is the eighth largest lake in Italy.

The lake is dominated by the pleasant hilltop town of **Bracciano**. To the northeast is **Trevignano Romano**, a picturesque medieval fishing town with a pretty *lungolago* (waterfront) and a modest beach.

The fortified town of **Anguillara** stands on a basalt promontory on the south-eastern shore overlooking the lake and was a popular location for holiday homes in ancient times. Its name is thought to come from the eels (*anguille*) that populate the lake.

Orientation & Information The APT tourist office in Bracciano is at Via Claudia 58 (☎ 06 998 67 82). It is open daily except Saturday and Sunday from 8 am to 2 pm and on Tuesday and Thursday from 3 to 6 pm. The COTRAL stop for buses to/from Rome and the other towns around the lake is in Piazza Roma near the central Piazza I Maggio, a short distance from the castello.

Things to See & Do The **Castello Orsini-Odelscalchi** (☎ 06 99 80 43 48) in Bracciano is a must for castle-lovers. Built in 1470 by Napoleone Orsini and decorated by Antoniazzo Romano and the Zuccari brothers, it is an excellent example of Renaissance military architecture. The castello is signposted from Piazza I Maggio. In summer it is open from 10 am to 7 pm Tuesday to Friday, from 9 am to 12.30 pm and 3 to 7.30 pm Saturday and from 9 am to 12.40 pm and 3 to 7.40 pm Sunday. In winter it is open from 10 am to 12 pm and 3 to 5 pm Tuesday to Saturday and from 10 am to 12.30 pm and 3 to 5.30 pm Sunday. It is also possible to visit the castle at night. For times, telephone the ticket office on the above number.

In Trevignano Romano there is the **Museo Civico Etrusco-Romano**, on the ground floor of the Palazzo Comunale in Piazza Vittorio Emmanuele III. The museum houses a small but interesting collection of Etruscan and Roman pieces testifying to the ancient history of the area. At the time of writing the collection was being reorganised and the museum (incomplete) was open Saturday and Sunday from 10 am to 1 pm.

Have a look at the **Chiesa di Santa Maria Assunta** on the hill in the heart of the medieval town. To get there go through the arch on the right of the Piazza as you face the Palazzo Comunale. Follow the narrow road for about 500m until you come to a small square on your left. From here take the path leading up to the church (clearly signposted). This parish church has recently been restored and the apse contains frescoes by the school of Raphael. The **Chiesa di San Bernadino** is also interesting. Dedicated to the patron saint of Trevignano, it dates from the second half of the 15th century.

In Trevignano on the second Sunday of the month there is the Fiera dei Sogni (dream fair), a lively market selling local produce and handicrafts. In October and early November the town plays host to a popular series of six classical music concerts. The concerts take place on Sunday at 6 pm in the Sala Convegni at the Banca di Credito Cooperativo in Piazza Vittorio Emmanuele III next to the Palazzo Comune (for information and program details ☎ 06

EXCURSIONS

999 12 02 03 or ☎ 06 998 50 10, or check the *spettacoli* section in the daily papers).

In Anguillara there is an interesting castle with fortified walls measuring 15m at the thickest point. Outside the walls there is the pretty **Chiesa di San Francesco**, dating from the 10th century.

About 5km from Anguillara is the picturesque **Lago di Martignano**, an off-shoot of the Bracciano crater. It has a small beach and pedaloes, sailing boats and canoes for hire. You will need to ask for directions to reach this lake.

Places to Eat In Bracciano try the excellent little trattoria *Da Regina* near the castello. To get there from Piazza I Maggio take Via G Palazzi. Follow the road round to the left and then take Via Sant' Antonio on the right. This brings you to a pretty square (unnamed) and the restaurant is on the left. It has an excellent selection of dishes including *pasta al forno* and fresh fish from the lake. Portions are generous and the prices are unbeatable; a full meal including coffee costs less than L20,000. The restaurant is open for lunch and supper from 7.15 to 9.15 pm (closed Friday). To be sure of a table go early and queue (no reservations).

Trattoria del Castello (☎ 06 99 80 43 39), in the same piazza as the castello, has excellent food and specialises in *funghi porcini* (porcini mushrooms). A full meal will cost around L40,000.

In Trevignano Romano a good bet is *La Tavernetta* (☎ 06 999 90 26, Via Garibaldi 62), a rustic, family-run establishment with lakeside seating in summer and lovely niche paintings executed by a local artist. A full meal costs in the region of L25,000 to L30,000. For excellent home-made ice cream try *Bar Sandro* at Via dell'Arena 16A and enjoy it with the strollers on the promenade or at a shady table by the lake.

You are unlikely to want to stay overnight in Lago di Bracciano. However, if you do the tourist office can supply a list of accommodation options including campsites in the area.

Getting There & Away There are two COTRAL buses that go to Bracciano. The first goes directly to Bracciano from Rome (final destination Manziana). The second takes a slightly longer route, stopping at Anguillara and Trevignano on the way. Both buses leave approximately every hour from the Lepanto stop on Metropolitana Linea A.

You can also get to Bracciano and Anguillara by a combination of train and bus, leaving from Ostiense and changing at Pineto. By car, take Via Braccianense (SS493) to Anguillara and Bracciano, and Via Cassia (SS2) to Trevignano Romano.

Lago di Vico

Legend has it that the horse shoe-shaped Lago di Vico came into being when Hercules, passing through the area in search of Melissa and Amaltea, thrust his club into the ground to prove his identity. When the local inhabitants failed to meet his challenge to extract the weapon, Hercules pulled it out himself, leaving a hole which then filled with water to create the lake. In reality, the lake derives from an ancient volcano.

Today it is part of a sizeable nature reserve (☎ 0761 647444) that includes an area of marshland popular with migrating birds. For this reason the area around the lake is relatively undeveloped and restaurant and accommodation facilities are minimal. However, for lovers of the outdoors the lake offers a range of activities, including canoeing, horseriding and cycling. There is also a campsite, *Natura* (☎ 0761 61 23 47), at the lakeside about 3km from the town of Caprarola. It is open during the summer months and bookings are recommended.

Getting There & Away Lago di Vico is not easily accessible from Rome by public transport. However, the COTRAL bus to Caprarola passes nearby. Catch it from the Saxa Rubra stop on Ferrovia Roma Nord and ask the driver when to get off. If you find yourself in Caprarola, take the local bus to the lake. By car, take Via Cassia for Viterbo and follow signs to Vico.

Lago di Bolsena

Lago di Bolsena, 100km north of Rome, is too far to reach in a day. It is, however, easily accessible if you are staying in nearby Viterbo (see the Viterbo section earlier in this chapter). The elliptical lake is the fifth largest lake in Italy, and like the others in Northern Lazio it is volcanic in origin. It is surrounded by a number of towns, the most important being its namesake, Bolsena.

The town is renowned for the miracle that took place here in 1263, when a bohemian priest who harboured doubts about the doctrine of transubstantiation (the miraculous transformation of the Eucharist into the physical body of Christ) saw blood drip from the host that he was holding. Pope Urban IV founded the festival of Corpus Domini to commemorate the event and it has been celebrated by Raphael in his *Miracle of Bolsena* in the Raphael Stanze in the Musei Vaticani. The townspeople remember the event in June by holding a 3km procession and decorating the town with flowers.

Orientation & Information The Pro Loco tourist office is at Piazza Matteotti 9 (☎ 076179 95 80). The town also has a web site: www.pelagus.it/bolsena/bolsena.html (in English and Italian). Bolsena is a very popular destination in summer.

Things to See & Do Castello Monaldeschi in the medieval quarter has an interesting history. The original structure dates from between the 13th and 16th centuries. However, it was pulled down by the locals in 1815 to prevent it from being taken by Luciano Bonaparte. It has subsequently been rebuilt to a square design with four towers and it now houses the **Museo Territoriale del Lago di Bolsena** (☎ 0761 79 86 30) documenting the geology and archaeology of the area. The museum is open Tuesday to Friday from 9.30 am to 1.30 pm and from 4 to 8 pm in summer and from 10 am to 1 pm in winter. On Saturday and Sunday it is open from 10 am to 1 pm and from 3 to 6 pm.

Also of interest are the 11th century **Basilica di Santa Cristina** and the **catacombs** beneath it. The Basilica houses the remains of Santa Cristina, found in the catacombs in 1070. Tradition says that the young Christian was thrown into the lake tied to a huge stone that miraculously floated her safely to the shore, an event celebrated on 23 July in a theatrical performance staged by Bolsena's young people dressed as Romans. Just before the entrance to the catacombs is the **altare del miracolo**, marking the spot where the miracle of Bolsena occurred. The catacombs are notable because they contain tombs that are still sealed.

Boat trips around the lake and the islands of Martana and Bisentina (tips of the submerged volcanic cone) leave daily from Bolsena. For information and bookings contact Navigazione Alto Lazio (☎ 0761 79 80 33).

If you're touring the area by car, it is worth heading on to **Montefiascone**, a hilltop town dominated by the huge dome of the **duomo**, the third largest in Italy. Also of interest is the Romanesque church of **Sant'Andrea** and, on the town's outskirts on the road to Orvieto, the Romanesque church of **San Flaviano**.

The town is known for its white wine, Est! Est! Est! Local history has it that on his travels a monk wrote 'Est' (it is) to indicate the places where the wine was good. On arriving at Montefiascone he was so overcome by the quality of the wine that he exclaimed 'Est! Est! Est!'.

Places to Stay There are numerous campsites and hotels on or near the lake of Bolsena. Try *Villaggio Camping Lido* (☎ *0761 79 92 58)*, a large campsite 1½km from Bolsena. It has a bar, restaurant and bungalow facilities. *Hotel Eden (☎ 0761 79 90 15, Via Cassia),* by the lake, has singles/doubles for L60,000/90,000 and half board/full board for L80,000/100,000 per person. Parking facilities are available.

Getting There & Away In summer COTRAL operates a direct bus service to Bolsena from the Saxa Rubra stop on Ferrovia Roma-Nord (catch the train from the station in Piazzale Flaminio). Otherwise you need to change at Viterbo. There are regular COTRAL buses to Bolsena from Viterbo, Monday to Saturday, leaving from the bus station at Riello. On Sunday there is only one bus that leaves at 9 am (return 6.05 pm).

By car, take the Via Cassia (SS2) to Viterbo and follow the signs.

CASTELLI ROMANI

Just past the periphery of Rome are the Colli Albani (Alban Hills) and the 13 towns of the Castelli Romani. A summer resort area for wealthy Romans since the days of the Empire, its towns were mainly founded by popes and patrician families. Castel Gandolfo and Frascati are perhaps the best known; the former is the summer residence of the pope and the latter is famous for its crisp white wine. The other towns are Monte Porzio Catone, Montecompatri, Rocca Priora, Colonna, Rocca di Papa, Grottaferrata, Marino, Albano Laziale, Ariccia, Genzano and Nemi.

Frascati

Of the Castelli, Frascati is the closest to Rome and makes a good starting point for a tour of the area.

Orientation & Information If you arrive by train, go out of the station and up the steps in front of you. Immediately you will find yourself in the main Piazzale Marconi. From here it is a short walk left into the old town and the main sights.

If you arrive by car, follow the road into town and park in one of the many pay-to-park car parks. The COTRAL bus drops you in Piazzale Marconi. Buses for the other Castelli also leave from here and there is a timetable posted on the wall of the Palazzo Marconi.

The APT tourist office is at Piazzale Marconi 1 (☎ 06 942 03 31). It is open from 8 am to 2 pm Monday to Saturday. From Tuesday to Friday it is also open from 3.30 to 6.30 pm.

Things to See & Do The 16th century **Villa Aldobrandini**, on the hill overlooking Piazzale Marconi, is one of a number of exquisite villas in the area. Designed by Giacomo della Porta and built by Carlo Maderno in 1598, it contains frescoes by Domenichino. Unfortunately it is now a private residence and is not open to the public. However, with a permit you can wander through the extensive gardens surrounding the villa from 9 am to 1 pm and 3 to 6 pm in summer (to 5 pm in winter) Monday to Friday. Permits are available free from the tourist office in Piazzale Marconi.

Other places of interest include the **Cattedrale di San Pietro Apostolo**, which dominates the piazza of the same name, just off the main square. It was built in the 17th century and then restored to its original form after sustaining serious bomb damage during WWII. Take a look at the lovely carved marble altarpiece depicting Christ giving Peter the keys to the church.

Around the corner in Piazza del Gesù is the 16th century **Chiesa del Gesù**, notable for its magnificent painted architecture, executed by Andrea Pozzo in an attempt to compensate for the modesty of the church itself due to the lack of funding. At the heart of the historical centre are the 15th century **Palazzo Vescovile** and the adjacent **belltower**, dating from 1305.

Places to Stay & Eat It is unlikely that you will stay the night here. However, if you fancy a quiet couple of days away from the city smog try *Hotel Panorama (☎/fax 06 942 18 00, Piazza Carlo Casini 3)*. Prices for a single are a little on the high side at L100,000, excluding breakfast. Doubles are better value at L120,000 and an extra bed costs L35,000. The hotel is small and friendly and has a superb view.

There is no shortage of eateries in Frascati, especially in the historic centre. For a decent meal try *Il Pinnocchio* in Piazza del Mercato. Three courses will cost in the region of L30,000, and there is also a good selection of pizzas starting at L7000. The restaurant is open for lunch and supper (closed Tuesday).

For a snack go to *Il Fornaretto* next door It offers a mouth-watering selection of home-baked bread, pizza, cakes and biscuits, including the famous *ciambelle al vino*, ideally dipped into a glass of chilled local wine. Otherwise, stop at one of the numerous kiosks selling *porchetta* (roast pork).

If you're after Frascati wine, head for any one of the *cantina*, rustic outlets serving simple food and wine on tap. Some also allow you to bring your own food and even your empty bottles to fill and take away.

Around Frascati

Above Frascati is the ancient city of **Tuscolo**, founded in or around the 9th century BC. Imposing and impregnable, it remained independent until 380 BC, when it came under Roman domination. Towards the end of the Republican era, patrician families started to build country residences here, setting a trend that is still going on today. In 1191, it was destroyed and the inhabitants founded the nearby towns of the Castelli.

Today, scant evidence of the city remains. There is a small amphitheatre (reputedly now the site of black masses and satanic rituals), the remains of a villa and a stretch of ancient Roman road leading up to the city. Tuscolo is signposted from Frascati. If you have a car you can drive to the top of the hill. Otherwise it is a short walk through the woods, and you can enjoy the view as you go.

At **Grottaferrata** there is the **Abbazia di Grottaferrata** (☎ 06 945 93 09), in Viale San Nilo, founded in the 11th century and home to a congregation of Greek monks. The abbazia also contains an interesting **museo** containing sculpture, frescoes and icons. It is open from 8.30 am to noon and

4.30 to 6 pm Tuesday to Saturday and from 8.30 to 10 am and 4.30 to 6 pm Sunday (at the time of writing the museum was closed for restoration but it should be open by summer 1999).

Nemi is worth a visit to see the pretty **Lago di Nemi**, in a volcanic crater. In ancient times there was an important sanctuary beside the lake where the goddess Diana was worshipped. Today, very little remains of this massive temple complex, but it is possible to see the niche walls of what was once an arcade portico. New excavations at the site have recently started.

The incongruous-looking building at the edge of the lake, near the ruins of the temple, has an interesting story attached to it. It was built by Mussolini to house two ancient Roman boats (one 73m long, the other 71m), Gaius Cailgula's pleasure craft, which were recovered from the bottom of the lake when it was partly drained in 1927-32. The official story is that retreating German troops burned the ships on June 1, 1944. Locals tell a different story, but you'll have to go there to find out!

There is a delightful trattoria in Nemi, the *Trattoria la Sirena del Lago* (☎ 06 936 80 20), located literally on the edge of a cliff behind the Palazzo Ruspoli and overlooking the lake. Signs will direct you there from the town centre. A simple, but excellent meal will cost L30,000, including wine.

Getting There & Away

It is really best to tour this area by car: you could see most of the more interesting sights on an easy day trip from Rome. Take the Via Tuscolana (SS5) to Grottaferrata and Frascati and the Via Appia (SS7) to Genzano and Nemi. However, most of the towns of the Castelli Romani, including Nemi, are accessible by the regular COTRAL bus from the Anagnina station on Metro Linea A, or from the main square in Frascati if you want to go on from there.

Trains also leave from the Lazio platform at Stazione Termini for Frascati and Castel-Gandolfo/Albano Laziale.

EXCURSIONS

PALESTRINA

The present town stands on the site of an ancient temple erected in the 6th century BC and dedicated to the oracle of Fortuna Primigenia, and rebuilt by Sulla after he conquered the town in 87 BC. However, the history of the settlement dates back as far as the 7th century BC, making it one of the oldest in the region. Originally known as Praeneste, it has attracted people since ancient times because of its altitude and healthy air, and it makes an interesting half-day trip out of the city.

Orientation & Information The Pro Loco tourist office is in Piazza Santa Maria degli Angeli 2 (☎ 06 957 31 76) in the town centre. In theory it is open daily from 10.30 am to midday, but on Sunday and during the winter months it is advisable to telephone first.

Things to See The town of Palestrina is dominated by the massive **Santuario della Fortuna Primigenia**. Built by the ancient Romans on a series of terraces on the slope of Monte Ginestro, the sanctuary was topped by a circular temple with a statue of the goddess Palestrina on the top. The 17th century **Palazzo Colonna Barberini** now stands at this point and houses the **Museo Archeologico Nazionale Prenestino** (☎ 06 953 81 00), open daily from 9 am to around 5 pm (hours are extended in summer).

Extensive restoration has recently carried out on the museum and it now houses an important collection of Roman artefacts. Of particular interest is the spectacular **Barberini mosaic**, also known as the Nile Mosaic, which comes from the most sacred part of the temple (where the cathedral with its Romanesque belfry now stands). It depicts the Nile in flood from Ethiopia to Alexandria and it is fascinating to study the numerous individual scenes. The view from the sanctuary is stupendous and this on its own should warrant a visit to this town.

Apart from its historical and archaeological importance, Palestrina is also renowned for being the birthplace of the 16th century choral composer, Giovanni da Palestrina. Craft-lovers can purchase locally produced beaten copper work in the shape of shells and 'Palestrina point' embroidery.

Getting There & Away Palestrina is accessible from Rome by COTRAL bus from the Anagnina stop on Metro Linea A. Buses leave approximately every half hour and the journey takes one hour. Otherwise it is a straightforward 39km by car on the Via Prenestina (SS155).

ANAGNI & ALATRI

These medieval towns are in an area about 40 minutes south of Rome, known as the Ciociaria. **Anagni**, birthplace of a number of medieval popes, including Innocent III and Gregory IX, is of particular interest for its lovely Lombard-Romanesque cathedral, built in the 11th century. Its pavement was laid by Cosmati marble workers of the Middle Ages. In the crypt is an extraordinary series of vibrant frescoes, painted by three Benedictine monks in diverse periods during the 13th century. Depicting a wide range of subjects, the frescoes are considered a major example of pre-Giotto medieval painting. The frescoes were recently unveiled after a four-year restoration project and certainly deserve a look. The crypt's pavement was also laid by the Cosmati.

Alatri has a couple of interesting churches, including the 13th century **Chiesa di Santa Maria Maggiore** in its main piazza. Its ancient **acropolis** is surrounded by massive 6th century BC walls, built by the town's original inhabitants, the Hernici.

To get to Anagni by bus you have to change at Colle Ferro. COTRAL buses for Colle Ferro leave from the Anagnina stop on the Metropolitana Linea A approximately every half hour. From here take the bus to Anagni. Otherwise take the Frosinone train from Rome's Stazione Termini (leaving approximately every hour) and get off at Anagni-Fiuggi. To get to Alatri, catch the train to Anagni and then take the COTRAL bus to Alatri.

THE COAST

There is no shortage of beaches close to Rome if you feel like a swim, although large crowds and heavy pollution make them rather unattractive destinations.

Ostia

Lido di Ostia is the closest seaside resort for Romans, an easy 30 minute train ride from Ostiense, although its badly polluted waters make it inadvisable to swim there. The town is chaotic and characterless and safety is increasingly a problem. Female travellers need to be particularly careful, especially at night. The Pro Loco office (☎ 06 562 78 92) is inside the railway station in the main hall. Opening times are Monday to Friday from 5 to 7.30 pm.

On either side of Ostia there are long stretches of beach lined with very degraded sand dunes. These beaches include **Fregene**, or **Focene**, a rapidly-expanding seaside resort near Fiumicino airport, but neither is worth writing home about. South of Ostia, there is the sandy beach at **Torvaianica**. If you choose to stop here don't miss the archaeological excavations in the nearby town of **Pratica di Mare**, a short distance inland. The town stands on the site of the ancient town of Lavinium, allegedly founded by Aeneas after his escape from Troy,. You can see 13 archaic altars and a number of tomb sanctuaries. An Iron Age necropolis has also been identified here.

Further south are the port towns of **Anzio** and **Nettuno**. Anzio dates back to the Latium civilisation at the beginning of the first millennium BC. It was then occupied by the Volsci, before becoming a popular resort and port of call in Roman times. Cicero and Augustus both had residences here, and it was the birthplace of Nero, who built the harbour, now an important archaeological site. Statues from the Imperial Villa, also built by Nero, are on display in museums throughout the world.

After the fall of the Roman Empire, Anzio was plundered by the Barbarians and the Saracens, forcing the population to move out and found the nearby city of Nettuno. The town was re-established by Innocent XII in 1700, when he financed the building of the harbour still bearing his name. On 22 April 1944 the allies landed here before going on to liberate Rome from the Germans. The event is commemorated in the colossal American and British war cemeteries that surround the town.

There is an APT tourist office in Anzio at Piazza Pia 19 (☎ 06 984 51 47). If you arrive by train take the road in front of the station and go straight on until you get to the main square. The APT office is next to the church. It is open from 8 am to 2 pm Tuesday to Saturday and also from 3 to 6 pm Tuesday and Thursday. The staff are able to supply a list of accommodation options and restaurants upon request.

Buses to Anzio leave Rome from the EUR-Fermi stop on the Metropolitana Linea B, following the coastal road, or from the Cinecittà stop on the Metropolitana Linea A, passing inland (final destination Nettuno). In both cases the journey takes 1¾ hours and costs around L5000. Otherwise take the regular train from Stazione Termini. The journey takes 1¼ hours and costs L5100. By car take Via Pontina (SS148) going south.

You'll need to go further south to **Sabaudia** and **Sperlonga** to find more attractive spots for a swim.

Sabaudia

Rivalling the Capalbio coast in Tuscany for the cleanliness of its sea, Sabaudia is an up-market resort and a favourite with the Italian intellectual elite in summer. It also has the added attraction of sand dunes (protected by an EU initiative) and the **Parco Nazionale del Circeo**, a wetlands nature reserve along the coast encompassing Monte Circeo, the promontory to the south.

The town itself grew up in the 1930s on former marshland and is an important monument to Fascist architecture with large squares and wide avenues. On the fourth Sunday of the month there is the lively **Mercatino di Archimede** in Piazza del Comune selling antiques, books and handicrafts.

EXCURSIONS

Places to Stay & Eat *Mini Hotel (☎ 0773 51 76 42, Corso Vittorio Emanuele 120)* is a small hotel in the town centre, approximately 1.5km from the sea. Pleasant and spotlessly clean singles/doubles cost L110,000/180,000 (L85,000/110,000) including breakfast. The hotel also offers a half board option, although this involves travelling 5km to Torre Paola, at the foot of Monte Circeo, to the restaurant *Sapporetti*, owned by the same people. The restaurant does a roaring trade and is particularly popular with the artistic elite, who come here to be seen.

You can buy *trecce* (ropes) of fresh mozzarella from the dairy on Via Litoranea running parallel to the coast. It is situated approximately 300m before the first major crossroad as you are coming from Rome.

Getting There and Away Sabaudia is accessible by COTRAL bus from outside the EUR-Fermi stop on Rome's Metropolitana Linea B. Take the bus going to San Felice Circeo and get off at Sabaudia. By car take the Pontina (SS148) from EUR going south.

Sperlonga

The small coastal town of Sperlonga is a good destination for a weekend break and has a pretty beach. The town is divided into two parts, the medieval Sperlonga Alta at the top of the hill and the modern Sperlonga Bassa at sea level.

The main attraction in the area is the **Grotta di Tiberio**, a cave with a circular pool used by the emperor Tiberius. It used to contain sculpture groups celebrating the adventures of Ulysses and his companions, erected for Tiberius between 4 and 26 AD. These were smashed by a group of zealous iconoclastic monks in 511 AD and the pieces were discovered only in 1957. The sculptures have since been restored and are on show in the nearby **museo archaeologico**. Among them is a large group in the style of the *Laocoön*, which is in the Musei Vaticani. The remains of Tiberius' villa are in front of the cave.

In early September the town celebrates the feast of the patron saints Rocco and Leo the Great. There is a religious procession, music and fireworks in the evening. On Saturday, Sperlonga hosts a lively food and second-hand clothes market.

Places to Stay & Eat If you want to stay, try the *Albergo Major (☎ 0771 54 92 44, Via Romita I 4)*. Singles/doubles are L80,000/100,000 including breakfast in low season and L110,000 per person for half board in high season. Private beach facilities are available for a small supplement of L10,000. The hotel is open all year.

For a meal go to *Lido da Rocco (☎ 0771 544 93, Via Spiaggia Angelo 22)*, on the seafront. For something a bit more special try *Agli Archi (☎ 0771 54 300, Via Ottaviano 17)* in the heart of the medieval town. The restaurant specialises in fish and there are a lot of dishes to choose from. A full meal can cost anything between L40,000 and L120,000. The restaurant is open from 10.30 am to 3.30 pm and from 6.30 to midnight (closed Wednesday).

For a snack, try Filippo's *cornetti caldi* (hot croissants) available from *Fiorelli* in Sperlonga Bassa, or from any one of the town's many bars on request. You need to go early though, as they are popular and run out fast.

Getting There & Away To get to Sperlonga from Rome, take the COTRAL bus from the EUR-Fermi stop on the Metropolitana Linea B. Alternatively, catch the train to Napoli (not the Intercity) from Stazione Termini and get off at Fondi-Sperlonga. From here take the COTRAL bus to Sperlonga. In theory the bus timetable coincides with the train. Otherwise you can take a taxi. The return bus leaves from the main piazza at the top of the hill in the centre of Sperlonga Alta.

Sperlonga is 120km from Rome by car. Take Via Pontina (SS148) from EUR going south and follow signs to Terracina. From Terracina it is a short drive on the SS213 to Sperlonga.

Pontine Islands

Foreign tourists are only just beginning to discover this group of small islands between Rome and Napoli. The archipelago comprises two groups of islands: Ponza, Palmarola, Gavi and Zannone to the north, and Ventotene and Santo Stefano to the south. Only two of the islands, Ponza and Ventotene, are inhabited, and their striking natural beauty and efficient services make them popular summer holiday destinations for Italians.

They are especially crowded at weekends, when they fill up with inhabitants from the nearby cities of Napoli and Rome. Prices are not cheap, and budget travellers are best to go out of season when the islands are more affordable.

The history of the islands goes back a long way. Homer refers to Ponza in Book Ten of the *Odyssey*, attesting to the presence of the ancient Greeks, confirmed by the remains of the tombs on the bluff overlooking Chiaia di Luna. In 313 BC, the archipelago came under Roman rule, and later came the building of sumptuous villas for the emperor and his circle. The collapse of the Empire brought about a period of decline on the islands, during which they sustained violent attacks by Saracens and by groups from mainland Italy and the nearby Isole Eolie.

Unfaithful wives, promiscuous daughters and persecuted Christians counted among the large number of people exiled to the islands at this time.

The recent history of the islands begins in 1734, when surrender to the Bourbon ruler Charles III gave rise to a wave of migration to Ponza that was to last the rest of the century. Commerce on the island flourished, at the expense of the natural habitat, largely destroyed in the rush to build and to cultivate. The island of Ponza is ecologically in pretty poor shape. Almost every inch of the hilly island was terraced and used for farming, and now there's a lot of erosion. Bird hunting is virtually an obsession for the locals; migrating birds pass over on their journeys between Europe and Africa. However, all the islands are now under National Park protection.

Orientation & Information Ponza is the largest of the islands and a good base for exploring the archipelago. The port is at Ponza town, the largest settlement on the island. The other main settlement is Le Forna, 8km to the north by road. Both have okay beaches and a good choice of hotels and restaurants. For the most part the coast is steep and the stony beaches are most easily reached by boat (there is an efficient ferry service from the port and a return trip costs approximately L7000). The two major exceptions are Spiaggia di Frontone and Chiaia di Luna, both accessible on foot.

Palmarola is uninhabited but in summer there are facilities for tourists.

Zannone, slightly closer to Ponza, is part of the Parco Nazionale di Circeo and is a sanctuary for migratory birds that pass over on their journeys between Europe and Africa.

Ventotene is where Julia, the daughter of Augustus, and Octavia, the divorced wife of Nero, lived in exile. (Octavia was killed shortly afterwards.)The remains of their villa are to be found near Punta Eolo. Popular with fishing enthusiasts, the island has a very small permanent population and limited accommodation facilities. The use of motor vehicles is not permitted on the island, but the hotels operate a mini bus service to and from the port.

There is a Pro Loco tourist information office on Ponza in the main town (☎ 0771 800 31), Via Molo Musco, near the port. In summer it is open daily from 9 am to 1 pm and 4 to 7.30 pm. In spring and autumn it is open daily from 10 am to noon. In winter the office is open from 10 am to noon on Saturday and Sunday only. On Ventotene for information go to the private travel agency Bemtilem (☎ 0771 853 65).

Things to See & Do On the west coast of Ponza is **Chiaia di Luna**, a spectacular bay so-called because of the effect produced by

EXCURSIONS

the reflection of the 100m-high rock face on the sea. **Monte Guardia** in the south is the highest point on the island and has a breathtaking view. To get there take the path that leads from the road out of Ponza going south. If you carry on past Monte Guardia you get to the ancient **faro** (lighthouse).

Punta Incenso at the other end of the island is another high point and looks over Ventotene and Zannone. **Grotte di Pilato** on the promontory that dominates Ponza town are the remains of an ancient Roman fish farm, located at the foot of a large residence, also in ruins. The complex consists of five pools (four covered), notable for the skill with which they have been cut out of the rock. The ruins and the tunnel that connects Ponza town and Chiaia di Luna are the only Roman remains on the island.

Places to Stay & Eat *Hotel Mari (☎ 0771 801 01, fax 0771 802 39, Corso Pisacane 19)* has singles/doubles for L100,000/ 190,000 in high season (from July through September) and L70,000/120,000 in low season, including breakfast. In the summer months booking is essential. Out of season ring first to check that the hotel is open. Many locals rent out individual rooms to tourists for much less and you'll find them touting at the port; otherwise go to the tourist information office for an authorised list.

The Pontine Islands are renowned for their fish-based cuisine. Lentil soup is also a local speciality. On Ponza try the excellent *Ristorante da Ciro (☎ 0771 80 83 88, Via Calacaparra)*, a kilometre or so past the town of Le Forna. A full meal of fresh seafood costs between L35,000 and L45,000. The restaurant is open all year for lunch and dinner and there is a west-facing terrace with a view of Palmarola.

Getting There & Away The islands are accessible by car ferry or hydrofoil from Anzio, Terracina or Formia. Timetable information is available from most travel agents. During the summer the timetables are also published in the *Cronaca di Roma* section of the national daily newspapers *Il Messaggero* and *Il Tempo*.

Getting Around The use of cars and large motorbikes is forbidden on Ponza during the high season but there is a good local bus service that covers the main points of interest. Otherwise, you can rent a scooter at the port, either at one of the numerous outlets, or from one of the touts who will meet you at the ferry. There is a hydrofoil that runs between Ponza and Ventotene.

The other islands are best visited on an organised day trip (for information go to the port or to the Pro Loco office). Otherwise, hire a boat privately. A small boat carrying six people costs around L100,000 for the day, excluding the cost of petrol.

Language

Many Italians speak some English because they study it at school. Staff at most hotels, pensioni and restaurants usually speak a little English, but you will be better received if you at least attempt to communicate in Italian.

Italian is a Romance language related to French, Spanish, Portuguese and Romanian. The Romance languages belong to the Indo-European group of languages, which include English. Indeed, as English and Italian share common roots in Latin, you will recognise many Italian words.

Visitors to Italy with more than the most fundamental grasp of the language need to be aware that many older Italians still expect to be addressed by the third person formal, ie *lei* instead of *tu*. Also, it is not considered polite to use the greeting *ciao* when addressing strangers, unless they use it first; it's better to say *buongiorno* (or *buonasera*, as the case may be), and *arrivederci* (or the more polite form, *arrivederla*). We have used the formal address for most of the phrases. The informal address appears in square brackets. Italian, like other Romance languages, has masculine and feminine forms. These two forms appear separated by a slash, the feminine form first.

See LP's *Italian Phrasebook* for a comprehensive list of words and phrases.

PRONUNCIATION

Italian is not difficult to pronounce once you learn a few easy rules. Although some of the more clipped vowels, and stress on double letters, require careful practice for English speakers, it is easy enough to make yourself understood.

Vowels

Vowels are generally more clipped than in English:

a	as the second 'a' in 'camera'
e	as in 'day' but a shorter sound
i	as in 'inn'
o	as in 'dot'
u	as in 'cook'

Consonants

The pronunciation of many Italian consonants is similar to that of English. The following sounds depend on certain rules:

c	'k' before 'a', 'o' and 'u'. Like the 'ch' in 'choose' before 'e' and 'i'
ch	hard 'k' sound
g	hard, like the 'g' in 'get' before 'a', 'o' and 'u'. Like the 'j' in 'job' before 'e' and 'i'.
gh	hard, as in 'get'
gli	like the 'lli' in 'million'
gn	like the 'ny' in 'canyon'
h	always silent
r	a rolled 'rrr' sound
sc	like the 'sh' in 'sheep' before 'e' and 'i'. Hard like the 'sch' in 'school' before 'h', 'a', 'o' and 'u'.
z	like the 'ts' in 'lights'. Like the 'ds' in 'beds' when the first letter of a word.

Note that when 'ci', 'gi' and 'sci' are followed by 'a', 'o' or 'u', the 'i' is not pronounced unless there is an accent on it. Therefore, the name 'Giovanni' is pronounced 'joh-*vahn*-nee'.

Double consonants are pronounced as a longer, often more forceful sound than a single consonant.

Stress

Stress often falls on the second-last syllable, as in spa-*ghet*-ti. An accent indicates where the stress falls, as in cit-*tà* (city).

WORDS & PHRASES
Language Problems

Please write it down.	*Può scriverlo, per favore?*

Can you show me (on the map)?	Me lo puo mostrare (sulla carta/ pianta)?
I (don't) understand.	(Non) capisco.
Do you speak English?	Parla [parli] inglese?
Does anyone speak English?	C'è qualcuno che parla inglese?
How do you say ... in Italian?	Come si dice ... in italiano?
What does ... mean?	Che vuole dire ...?

Paperwork

name	nome
nationality	nazionalità
date of birth	data di nascita
place of birth	luogo di nascita
sex (gender)	sesso
passport	passaporto
visa	visto consolare

Greetings & Civilities

Hello.	Buongiorno [ciao]
Goodbye	Arrivederci [ciao]
Yes.	Sì
No	No
Please	Per favore [per piacere]
Thank you	Grazie
That's fine/you're welcome.	Prego
Excuse me	Mi scusi [scusami]
Sorry (forgive me)	Mi scusi/mi perdoni.

Small Talk

What is your name?	Come si chiama? [Come ti chiami?]
My name is ...	Mi chiamo ...
Where are you from?	Di dov'è [di dove sei]?
I am from ...	Sono di ...
How old are you?	Quanti anni ha [hai]?
I am ... years old.	Ho ... anni.
Are you married?	È [sei] sposata/o?
I'm (not) married.	(Non) sono sposata/o.
I (don't) like ...	(Non) mi piace ...
Just a minute.	Un momento.

Getting Around

I want to go to ...	Voglio andare a ...
What time does ... leave/arrive?	A che ora parte/ arriva ...?
the boat	la barca
the (city) bus	l'autobus
the (intercity) bus	il pullman/ il corriere
the train	il treno
the aeroplane	l'aereo
the first	il primo
the last	l'ultimo
one-way ticket	un biglietto di solo andata
return ticket	un biglietto di andata e ritorno
1st class	prima classe
2nd class	seconda classe
platform number...	binario numero...
station	stazione
ticket office	biglietteria
timetable	orario
train station	stazione
The train has been cancelled/delayed	Il treno è soppresso/ in ritardo.
I'd like to rent ...	Vorrei noleggiare ...
a car	una macchina
a bicycle	una bicicletta
a motorcycle	una motocicletta

Useful Signs

APERTO	OPEN
CAMPEGGIO	CAMPING GROUND
CHIUSO	CLOSED
COMPLETO	NO VACANCIES/ FULL
GABINETTO/BAGNI	TOILETS
INFORMAZIONE	INFORMATION
INGRESSO	ENTRANCE
TELEFONO	TELEPHONE
USCITA	EXIT
VIETATO FUMARE	NO SMOKING

Directions

Where is ...?	*Dov'è ...?*
Go straight ahead	*Si va (Vai) sempre diritto*
Turn left	*Gira a sinistra.*
Turn right	*Gira a destra.*
at the next corner	*al prossimo angolo*
at the traffic lights	*al semaforo*
behind	*dietro*
in front of	*davanti*
far (from)	*lontano (di)*
near (to)	*vicino (a)*
opposite	*di fronte a*

Around Town

I'm looking for ...	*Cerco ...*
a bank	*un banco*
the church	*la chiesa*
the city centre	*il centro (città)*
the ... embassy	*l'ambasciata di ...*
my hotel	*il mio albergo*
the market	*il mercato*
the museum	*il museo*
the post office	*la posta*
a public toilet	*un gabinetto/ bagno pubblico*
the telephone centre	*il centro telefonico*
the tourist infomation office	*l'ufficio di turismo/ d'informazione*
I want to exchange some money/ travellers cheques	*Voglio cambiare del denaro/ degli assegni per viaggiatori*
beach	*la spiaggia*
bridge	*il ponte*
castle	*il castello*
cathedral	*il duomo/ la cattedrale*
island	*l'isola*
main square	*la piazza principale*
market	*il mercato*
mosque	*la moschea*
old city	*il centro storico*
palace	*il palazzo*
ruins	*le rovine*
synagogue	*la sinogoga*
square	*la piazza*
tower	*la torre*

Accommodation

I'm looking for a ...	*Cerco un ...*
hotel	*albergo*
guesthouse	*pensione*
youth hostel	*ostello per la gioventù*
Where is a cheap hotel?	*Dov'è un albergo che costa poco?*
What is the address?	*Cos'è l'indirizzo?*
Could you write the address, please?	*Può scrivere l'indirizzo, per favore?*
Do you have any rooms available?	*Ha camere libere/ C'è una camera libera?*
I would like ...	*Vorrei ...*
a bed	*un letto*
a single room	*una camera singola*
a double room	*una camera matrimoniale*
room with two beds	*una camera doppia*
a room with a bathroom	*una camera con bagno*
to share a dorm	*un letto in dormitorio*
How much is it per night/per person?	*Quanto costa per la notte/ciascuno?*
Can I see it?	*Posso vederla?*
Where is the bathroom?	*Dov'è il bagno?*
I am/We are leaving today.	*Parto/Partiamo oggi.*

Shopping

I would like tobuy ...	*Vorrei comprare ...*
How much is it?	*Quanto costa?*
I don't like it.	*Non mi piace.*
Can I look at it?	*Posso dare un' occhiata?*
I'm just looking.	*Sto solo guardando.*
Do you accept credit cards/travellers cheques?	*Accetta carte di credito/assegni per viaggiatori?*
It's cheap.	*Non è cara/o.*
It's too expensive.	*È troppo cara/o.*

more	*più*	13	*tredici*
less	*meno*	14	*quattordici*
smaller	*più piccola/o*	15	*quindici*
bigger	*più grande*	16	*sedici*
		17	*diciassette*

Time & Dates

What time is it?	*Che ora è/ore sono?*	18	*diciotto*
It is 8 o'clock ...	*Sono le otto...*	19	*diciannove*
in the morning	*di mattina*	20	*venti*
in the afternoon	*di pomeriggio*	21	*vent'uno*
in the evening	*di sera*	22	*ventidue*
today	*oggi*	30	*trenta*
tomorrow	*domani*	40	*quaranta*
yesterday	*ieri*	50	*cinquanta*
year	*anno*	60	*sessanta*
		70	*settanta*
Monday	*lunedì*	80	*ottanta*
Tuesday	*martedì*	90	*novanta*
Wednesday	*mercoledì*	100	*cento*
Thursday	*giovedì*	1000	*mille*
Friday	*venerdì*	2000	*due mila*
Saturday	*sabato*	one million	*un milione*
Sunday	*domenica*		

Health

January	*gennaio*	I am ill.	*Mi sento male.*
February	*febbraio*	It hurts here.	*Mi fa male qui.*
March	*marzo*		
April	*aprile*	I'm ...	*Sono ...*
May	*maggio*	diabetic	*diabetica/o*
June	*giugno*	epileptic	*epilettica/o*
July	*luglio*	asthmatic	*asmatica/o*
August	*agosto*		
September	*settembre*	I'm allergic ...	*Sono allergica/o ...*
October	*ottobre*	to antibiotics	*agli antibiotici*
November	*novembre*	to penicillin	*alla penicillina*
December	dicembre		

Numbers

0	*zero*	antiseptic	*antisettico*
1	*uno*	aspirin	*aspirina*
2	*due*	condoms	*preservativi/*
3	*tre*		*profilitachi*
4	*quattro*	contraceptive	*anticoncezionale*
5	*cinque*	diarrhoea	*diarrea*
6	*sei*	medicine	*medicina*
7	*sette*	sunblock cream	*crema/latte solare*
8	*otto*		*(per protezione)*
9	*nove*	tampons	*tamponi*
10	*dieci*		

Emergencies

11	*undici*	Help!	*Aiuto!*
12	*dodici*	Call a doctor!	*Chiama [chiami] un*
			dottore/un medico!

| Call the police! | *Chiama [chiami] la polizia!* |
| Go away! | *Va via!* |

FOOD GLOSSARY

This glossary is intended as a brief guide to some of the basics and by no means covers all of the dishes you are likely to encounter in Rome or the rest of Italy. Names and ingredients of dishes often vary from region to region, and even pizza toppings can change. Most travellers to Italy will already be well acquainted with the various Italian pastas, which include spaghetti, fettucine, penne, rigatoni, gnocchi, lasagne, tortellini and ravioli. The names are the same in Italy and no further definitions are given here.

Useful Words

affumicato	smoked
arrosto	roasted
bollito	boiled
alla brace	cooked over hot coals
al dente	firm (as all good pasta should be)
cameriere/a	waiter/waitress
coltello	knife
il conto	bill/cheque
cotto	cooked
ben cotto	well done (cooked)
crudo	raw
cucchiaio/ cucchiaino	spoon/ teaspoon
forchetta	fork
fritto	fried
alla griglia	grilled
menù	menu
piatto	plate
ristorante	restaurant

Staples

aceto	vinegar
burro	butter
cacio (dialect)	cheese
formaggio	cheese
limone	lemon
marmellata	jam
miele	honey
olio	oil
olive	olives
pane	bread
pane integrale	wholemeal bread
panna	cream
pepe	pepper
peperoncino	chilli
polenta	cooked cornmeal
riso	rice
risotto	rice cooked in wine and stock
sale	salt
uovo/uova	egg/eggs
zucchero	sugar

Meat & Fish

acciughe	anchovies
agnello/abacchio	lamb
aragosta	lobster
baccalà	reconstituted dried cod
bistecca	steak
calamari	squid
cervello	brain (usually lamb's)
coda	oxtail
coniglio	rabbit
cotoletta	cutlet or thin cut of meat, often crumbed and fried
cozze	mussels
dentice	dentex (type of fish)
fegato	liver
gamberi	prawns
granchio	crab
manzo	beef
merluzzo	cod
ostriche	oysters
pesce	fish
pesce spada	swordfish
pollo	chicken
polpo	octopus
salsiccia	sausage
sarde	sardines
sgombro	mackerel
sogliola	sole
spigola	sea bass
tacchino	turkey
tonno	tuna
trippa	tripe
vitello	veal
vongole	clams

Vegetables

arugla	rocket
asparagi	asparagus
carciofi	artichokes
carote	carrots
cicoria	chicory
cipolla	onion
fagiolini	string beans
fava	broad beans
finocchio	fennel
melanzane	eggplant
patate	potatoes
peperoni	peppers (capsicum)
piselli	peas
spinaci	spinach
verza/cavolo	cabbage

Fruit

arance	oranges
fragole	strawberries
banane	bananas
ciliegie	cherries
mele	apples
pere	pears
pesche	peaches
uva	grapes

Soups & Antipasti

brodo	broth/soup
carpaccio	very fine slices of raw beef dressed with oil, capers and shaved parmesan
insalata caprese	salad of sliced tomatoes with mozzarella and basil
insalata di mare	seafood salad, generally crustaceans
minestrina in brodo	pasta in broth
minestrone	vegetable soup
olive ascolane	stuffed, deep-fried olives
prosciutto e melone	cured ham with melon

ripieni	stuffed baked vegetables
stracciatella	chicken soup with egg and grated parmesan

Pasta Sauces

al ragù	meat sauce (bolognese)
arrabbiata	tomato and chilli
carbonara	egg, bacon, parmesan and black pepper
cacio e pepe	pecorino (salty sheep's milk cheese) and black pepper
alla gricia	pecorino, bacon and black pepper
alla matriciana	tomato and bacon
napoletana	tomato and basil
panna	cream and prosciutto, sometimes with peas
pesto	basil, garlic, parmesan and oil, often with pine nuts
vongole	clams, garlic and oil, sometimes with tomato

Pizzas

All pizzas listed have a tomato and sometimes mozzarella base.

capricciosa	olives, prosciutto, mushrooms, artichokes
frutti di mare	seafood
funghi	mushrooms
margherita	oregano
napoletana	anchovies
pugliese	tomato, mozzarella and onions
quattro formaggi	with four types of cheese
quattro stagioni	'four seasons', the same as a capricciosa, but sometimes with egg
verdura	mixed vegetables (usually peppers, zucchini, eggplant, sometimes spinach)

Glossary

aereo – aeroplane
albergo – hotel
alimentari – grocery shop
amaro – bitter herbal digestive liqueur
apse – domes or arched recess at the altar end of a church
arco – arch
autobus – bus
autostrada – freeway (motorway)

bagno – bathroom, also toilet
baldicchino – ornate canopy over the high altar
bancomat – ATM
bar – café
basilica – originally a Roman public building with a colonnaded central nave and an apse at the end; later, a church with these architectural features
benzina – petrol
bibilioteca – library
bicicletta – bicycle
biglietteria – ticket office, box office
binario – train platform

caffè – coffee, also a café
calcio – football (soccer)
cambio – currency exchange bureau
camera – room
campanile – bell tower
cappella – chapel
carabinieri – paramilitary police
Carnival – festival marking the beginning of Lent
carta telefonica – phonecard
caserma – carabinieri station
casino – mansion
catacomb – underground tomb complex, generally early Christian or Jewish
centro sociale (**centri sociali** plural) – social clubs
cena – evening meal
centro commerciale – shopping centre
chiesa – church
Ciampino – Rome's second airport
circus – racetrack

colazione – breakfast
colle – hill
colonna – column
columbarium (**columbaria** plural) – niche tombs which resemble dovecotes, hence the name
commissariato – local police station
comune – municipal government
coperto – cover charge (restaurant)
Cosmati – decorative mosaics composed of geometric patterns; common in the 12-13th centuries
cupola – dome

deposito bagagli – left luggage
digestivo – after-dinner liqueur
Dioscuri – the twins Castor and Pollux
domus – house
drugstore – 24-hour convenience store

enoteca – specialist wine shop
(un) etto – 100g
EUR – Esposizione Universale di Roma, a facist-era cultural complex south of the city centre

farmacia – pharmacy (chemist)
fermo posta – poste restante
ferrovia – train station
Fiumicino – common name of Leonardo da Vinci airport
fontata – fountain
forno – bakery
foro – forum
forum (**fora** plural) – public square
fresco – technique of painting with watercolours onto wet plaster

gabinetto – toilet, WC
gelateria – ice-cream parlour
Ghetto – Jewish quarter

IVA – (Imposta di Valore Aggiunto) value-added tax

largo – lake

289

lavanderia – laundrette
lavaseco – dry-cleaning
libreria – bookshop
mercato – market
Metropolitana (Metro) – suburban underground train system
monte – mountain
motorino – moped
museo (musei plural) – museum
mura – city walls

necropolis – 'city of the dead'; aboveground tomb complex, often Etruscan
numero verde – freecall phone number

oggetti religiosi – holy kitsch
oggetti smarriti – lost property
orto (orti plural) – garden
ospedale – hospital
ostello – hostel
osteria – wine bar, or a small trattoria

pagine gialle – Yellow Pages
palazzo – palace
parco – park
passeggiata – evening stroll
pasta – pasta; cake or pasty; dough
pasticceria (pasticcerie plural) – bakery/cake shop
piazza – square
piazzale – large square
pinacoteca – picture gallery
polizia – police
ponte – bridge
Porta – city gate
posta aerea – airmail
presepio – model Nativity scene
profumeria – perfumery
pronto socorso – first aid; emergency/casualty ward
questura – police headquarters

Risorgimento – late 19th century movement led by Garibaldi and others to create a united, independent Italian state
ristorante – restaurant
rosticceria – restaurant specialising in meat dishes, often take-away

sala – room in a museum or gallery
salumerie – delicatessan
Scalinata di Spagna – Spanish Steps
scavi – excavations
servizio – service charge
stazione – train station
Stazione Termini – Rome's main train station
tabacchi – tobacconists, authorised to sell newspapers, stamps and phonecards
tavola calda – 'hot table', pre-prepared meat, pasta and vegetable selection, often self-service
teatro – theatre
tempio – temple
terme – baths
titulus – a private house used for clandestine Christian worship
torre – tower
trattoria – smaller, less expensive restaurant
treno – train
trompe l'oeil – painting designed to 'deceive the eye'

ufficio postale – post office
ufficio stranieri – foreigners' bureau (police)
via – street or road
vigili urbani – traffic police
villa – townhouse or country house; also the surrounding grounds
vino – wine

LONELY PLANET

Phrasebooks

L onely Planet phrasebooks are packed with essential words and phrases to help travellers communicate with the locals. With colour tabs for quick reference, an extensive vocabulary and use of script, these handy pocket-sized language guides cover day-to-day travel situations.

- handy pocket-sized books
- easy to understand Pronunciation chapter
- clear & comprehensive Grammar chapter
- romanisation alongside script to allow ease of pronunciation
- script throughout so users can point to phrases for every situation
- full of cultural information and tips for the traveller

'...vital for a real DIY spirit and attitude in language learning'
– *Backpacker*

'the phrasebooks have good cultural backgrounders and offer solid advice for challenging situations in remote locations'
– *San Francisco Examiner*

Arabic (Egyptian) • Arabic (Moroccan) • Australian *(Australian English, Aboriginal and Torres Strait languages)* • Baltic States *(Estonian, Latvian, Lithuanian)* • Bengali • Brazilian • Burmese • Cantonese • Central Asia • Central Europe *(Czech, French, German, Hungarian, Italian, Slovak)* • Eastern Europe *(Bulgarian, Czech, Hungarian, Polish, Romanian, Slovak)* • Ethiopian (Amharic) • Fijian • French • German • Greek • Hill Tribes • Hindi/Urdu • Indonesian • Italian • Japanese • Korean • Lao • Latin American Spanish • Malay • Mandarin • Mediterranean Europe *(Albanian, Croatian, Greek, Italian, Macedonian, Maltese, Serbian, Slovene)* • Mongolian • Nepali • Papua New Guinea • Pilipino (Tagalog) • Quechua • Russian • Scandinavian Europe *(Danish, Finnish, Icelandic, Norwegian, Swedish)* • South East Asia *(Burmese, Indonesian, Khmer, Lao, Malay, Tagalog Pilipino, Thai, Vietnamese)* • Spanish (Castilian) *(also includes Catalan, Galician and Basque)* • Sri Lanka • Swahili • Thai • Tibetan • Turkish • Ukrainian • USA *(US English, Vernacular, Native American languages, Hawaiian)* • Vietnamese • Western Europe *(Basque, Catalan, Dutch, French, German, Greek, Irish)*

LONELY PLANET

Lonely Planet On-line
www.lonelyplanet.com *or* AOL keyword: lp

Whether you've just begun planning your next trip, or you're chasing down specific info on currency regulations or visa requirements, check out Lonely Planet On-line for up-to-the minute travel information.

As well as mini guides to more than 250 destinations, you'll find maps, photos, travel news, health and visa updates, travel advisories, and discussion of the ecological and political issues you need to be aware of as you travel. You'll also find timely upgrades to popular guidebooks which you can print out and stick in the back of your book.

There's also an on-line travellers' forum where you can share your experience of life on the road, meet travel companions and ask other travellers for their recommendations and advice.

And of course we have a complete and up-to-date list of all Lonely Planet travel products including travel guides, diving and snorkeling guides, phrasebooks, atlases, travel literature and videos, and a simple on-line ordering facility if you can't find the book you want elsewhere.

Lonely Planet Diving & Snorkeling Guides

Known for indispensible guidebooks to destinations all over the world, Lonely Planet's Pisces Books are the most popular series of diving and snorkeling titles available.

There are three series: **Diving & Snorkeling Guides**, **Shipwreck Diving** series and **Dive Into History**. Full colour throughout, the **Diving & Snorkeling Guides** combine quality photographs with detailed descriptions of the best dive sites for each location, giving divers a glimpse of what they can expect both on land and in water. The **Dive Into History** series is perfect for the adventure diver or armchair traveller. The **Shipwreck Diving** series provides all the details for exploring the most interesting wrecks in the Atlantic and Pacific oceans. The list also includes underwater nature and technical guides.

FREE Lonely Planet Newsletters

We love hearing from you and think you'd like to hear from us.

Planet Talk

Our FREE quarterly printed newsletter is full of tips from travellers and anecdotes from Lonely Planet guidebook authors. Every issue is packed with up-to-date travel news and advice, and includes:

- a postcard from Lonely Planet co-founder Tony Wheeler
- a swag of mail from travellers
- a look at life on the road through the eyes of a Lonely Planet author
- topical health advice
- prizes for the best travel yarn
- news about forthcoming Lonely Planet events
- a complete list of Lonely Planet books and other titles

To join our mailing list, residents of the UK, Europe and Africa can email us at go@lonelyplanet.co.uk; residents of North and South America can email us at info@lonelyplanet.com; the rest of the world can email us at talk2us@lonelyplanet.com.au, or contact any Lonely Planet office.

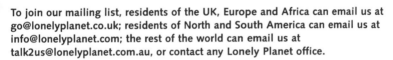

Comet

Our FREE monthly email newsletter brings you all the latest travel news, features, interviews, competitions, destination ideas, travellers' tips & tales, Q&As, raging debates and related links. Find out what's new on the Lonely Planet Web site and which books are about to hit the shelves.

Subscribe from your desktop: www.lonelyplanet.com/comet

LONELY PLANET

Guides by Region

Lonely Planet is known worldwide for publishing practical, reliable and no-nonsense travel information in our guides and on our Web site. The Lonely Planet list covers just about every accessible part of the world. Currently there are nine series: travel guides, shoestring guides, walking guides, city guides, phrasebooks, audio packs, travel atlases, diving and snorkeling guides and travel literature.

AFRICA Africa – the South ● Africa on a shoestring ● Arabic (Egyptian) phrasebook ● Arabic (Moroccan) phrasebook ● Cairo ● Cape Town ● Central Africa ● East Africa ● Egypt ● Egypt travel atlas ● Ethiopian (Amharic) phrasebook ● The Gambia & Senegal ● Kenya ● Kenya travel atlas ● Malawi, Mozambique & Zambia ● Morocco ● North Africa ● South Africa, Lesotho & Swaziland ● South Africa, Lesotho & Swaziland travel atlas ● Swahili phrasebook ● Trekking in East Africa ● Tunisia ● West Africa ● Zimbabwe, Botswana & Namibia ● Zimbabwe, Botswana & Namibia travel atlas
Travel Literature: The Rainbird: A Central African Journey ● Songs to an African Sunset: A Zimbabwean Story ● Mali Blues: Traveling to an African Beat

AUSTRALIA & THE PACIFIC Australia ● Australian phrasebook ● Bushwalking in Australia ● Bushwalking in Papua New Guinea ● Fiji ● Fijian phrasebook ● Islands of Australia's Great Barrier Reef ● Melbourne ● Micronesia ● New Caledonia ● New South Wales & the ACT ● New Zealand ● Northern Territory ● Outback Australia ● Papua New Guinea ● Papua New Guinea (Pidgin) phrasebook ● Queensland ● Rarotonga & the Cook Islands ● Samoa ● Solomon Islands ● South Australia ● Sydney ● Tahiti & French Polynesia ● Tasmania ● Tonga ● Tramping in New Zealand ● Vanuatu ● Victoria ● Western Australia
Travel Literature: Islands in the Clouds ● Sean & David's Long Drive

CENTRAL AMERICA & THE CARIBBEAN Bahamas and Turks & Caicos ● Barcelona ● Bermuda ● Central America on a shoestring ● Costa Rica ● Cuba ● Dominican Republic & Haiti ● Eastern Caribbean ● Guatemala, Belize & Yucatán: La Ruta Maya ● Jamaica ● Mexico ● Mexico City ● Panama
Travel Literature: Green Dreams: Travels in Central America

EUROPE Amsterdam ● Andalucía ● Austria ● Baltic States phrasebook ● Berlin ● Britain ● British phrasebook ● Central Europe ● Central Europe phrasebook ● Croatia ● Czech & Slovak Republics ● Denmark ● Dublin ● Eastern Europe ● Eastern Europe phrasebook ● Edinburgh ● Estonia, Latvia & Lithuania ● Europe ● Finland ● France ● French phrasebook ● Germany ● German phrasebook ● Greece ● Greek phrasebook ● Hungary ● Iceland, Greenland & the Faroe Islands ● Ireland ● Italian phrasebook ● Italy ● Lisbon ● London ● Mediterranean Europe ● Mediterranean Europe phrasebook ● Paris ● Poland ● Portugal ● Portugal travel atlas ● Prague ● Provence & the Côte D'Azur ● Romania & Moldova ● Russia, Ukraine & Belarus ● Russian phrasebook ● Scandinavian & Baltic Europe ● Scandinavian Europe phrasebook ● Scotland ● Slovenia ● Spain ● Spanish phrasebook ● St Petersburg ● Switzerland ● Trekking in Spain ● Ukrainian phrasebook ● Vienna ● Walking in Britain ● Walking in Italy ● Walking in Ireland ● Walking in Switzerland ● Western Europe ● Western Europe phrasebook
Travel Literature: The Olive Grove: Travels in Greece

INDIAN SUBCONTINENT Bangladesh ● Bengali phrasebook ● Bhutan ● Delhi ● Goa ● Hindi/Urdu phrasebook ● India ● India & Bangladesh travel atlas ● Indian Himalaya ● Karakoram Highway ● Nepal ● Nepali phrasebook ● Pakistan ● Rajasthan ● South India ● Sri Lanka ● Sri Lanka phrasebook ● Trekking in the Indian Himalaya ● Trekking in the Karakoram & Hindukush ● Trekking in the Nepal Himalaya
Travel Literature: In Rajasthan ● Shopping for Buddhas

LONELY PLANET

Mail Order

L onely Planet products are distributed worldwide. They are also available by mail order from Lonely Planet, so if you have difficulty finding a title please write to us. North and South American residents should write to 150 Linden St, Oakland, CA 94607, USA; European and African residents should write to 10a Spring Place, London NW5 3BH, UK; and residents of other countries to PO Box 617, Hawthorn, Victoria 3122, Australia.

ISLANDS OF THE INDIAN OCEAN Madagascar & Comoros ● Maldives ● Mauritius, Réunion & Seychelles

MIDDLE EAST & CENTRAL ASIA Arab Gulf States ● Central Asia ● Central Asia phrasebook ● Iran ● Israel & the Palestinian Territories ● Israel & the Palestinian Territories travel atlas ● Istanbul ● Jerusalem ● Jordan & Syria ● Jordan, Syria & Lebanon travel atlas ● Lebanon ● Middle East on a shoestring ● Turkey ● Turkish phrasebook ● Turkey travel atlas ● Yemen
Travel Literature: The Gates of Damascus ● Kingdom of the Film Stars: Journey into Jordan

NORTH AMERICA Alaska ● Backpacking in Alaska ● Baja California ● California & Nevada ● Canada ● Florida ● Hawaii ● Honolulu ● Los Angeles ● Miami ● New England USA ● New Orleans ● New York City ● New York, New Jersey & Pennsylvania ● Pacific Northwest USA ● Rocky Mountain States ● San Francisco ● Seattle ● Southwest USA ● USA ● USA phrasebook ● Vancouver ● Washington, DC & the Capital Region
Travel Literature: Drive Thru America

NORTH-EAST ASIA Beijing ● Cantonese phrasebook ● China ● Hong Kong ● Hong Kong, Macau & Guangzhou ● Japan ● Japanese phrasebook ● Japanese audio pack ● Korea ● Korean phrasebook ● Kyoto ● Mandarin phrasebook ● Mongolia ● Mongolian phrasebook ● North-East Asia on a shoestring ● Seoul ● South-West China ● Taiwan ● Tibet ● Tibetan phrasebook ● Tokyo
Travel Literature: Lost Japan

SOUTH AMERICA Argentina, Uruguay & Paraguay ● Bolivia ● Brazil ● Brazilian phrasebook ● Buenos Aires ● Chile & Easter Island ● Chile & Easter Island travel atlas ● Colombia ● Ecuador & the Galapagos Islands ● Latin American Spanish phrasebook ● Peru ● Quechua phrasebook ● Rio de Janeiro ● South America on a shoestring ● Trekking in the Patagonian Andes ● Venezuela
Travel Literature: Full Circle: A South American Journey

SOUTH-EAST ASIA Bali & Lombok ● Bangkok ● Burmese phrasebook ● Cambodia ● Hill Tribes phrasebook ● Ho Chi Minh City ● Indonesia ● Indonesian phrasebook ● Indonesian audio pack ● Jakarta ● Java ● Laos ● Lao phrasebook ● Laos travel atlas ● Malay phrasebook ● Malaysia, Singapore & Brunei ● Myanmar (Burma) ● Philippines ● Pilipino (Tagalog) phrasebook ● Singapore ● South-East Asia on a shoestring ● South-East Asia phrasebook ● Thailand ● Thailand's Islands & Beaches ● Thailand travel atlas ● Thai phrasebook ● Thai audio pack ● Vietnam ● Vietnamese phrasebook ● Vietnam travel atlas

ALSO AVAILABLE: Antarctica ● Brief Encounters: Stories of Love, Sex & Travel ● Chasing Rickshaws ● Not the Only Planet: Travel Stories from Science Fiction ● Travel with Children ● Traveller's Tales

Index

Text

Bold indicates maps.
Italics indicates boxed text.

Bold indicates maps.
Italics indicates boxed text.

Boxed Text

Etruscan winged horses, Tarquinia

Dedicated to King Victor Emmanuel II, this monument is commonly called the 'typewriter'.

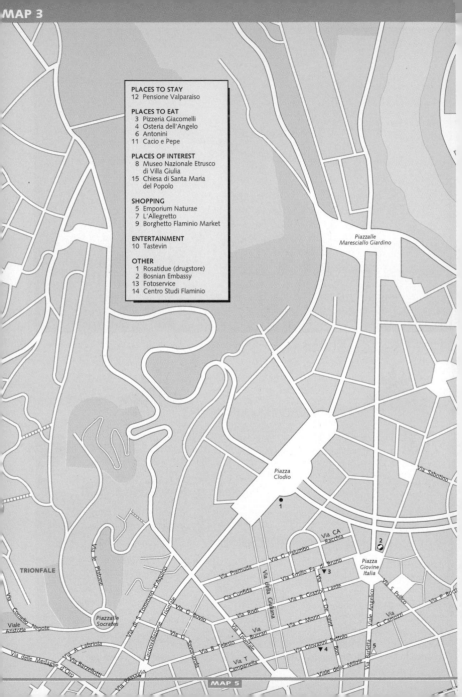

MAP 3

PLACES TO STAY
12 Pensione Valparaiso

PLACES TO EAT
3 Pizzeria Giacomelli
4 Osteria dell'Angelo
6 Antonini
11 Cacio e Pepe

PLACES OF INTEREST
8 Museo Nazionale Etrusco
   di Villa Giulia
15 Chiesa di Santa Maria
   del Popolo

SHOPPING
5 Emporium Naturae
7 L'Allegretto
9 Borghetto Flaminio Market

ENTERTAINMENT
10 Tastevin

OTHER
1 Rosatidue (drugstore)
2 Bosnian Embassy
13 Fotoservice
14 Centro Studi Flaminio

Piazzalle
Maresciallo Giardino

Piazza
Clodio
1

Via CA
Racchia

2

Piazza
Giovine
Italia

TRIONFALE

Via le Pittore

Via Premuda

Via G. Palumbo

Via Cunfida

Via della Giuliana

Via Emilio Fa di Bruno

▼3

Via R Grazioli Lante

Via S. Pellico

Viale Angelico

Via C Camozzi

Via
Via P Bos

Piazzalle
Socrates

Via Cornelio Nepote

Viale
Aristotle

Via delle Medaglie d'Oro

Via A Labriola

Via A Barzellotti

Via Pascaglia

Via Trasimaniane Lingotto

Via G. Govio

Via B refesio

Via Savonarola

Via Rodi

Via Buccari

Via
Infantalia

Via T
Campanella

Via C Morin

Via Giovanni Bettolo

▼4

Via Battietta

Via
Satotino

Viale delle Milizie

5

MAP 5

MAP 3

MAP 4

0   100   200 m

Fiume Tevere

Via A Para

Via M Prestinari

Piazza
Monte
Grappa

Piazzalle D
Belle Arti

Viale di Belle Arti

Viale B Buozzi

Piazzalle
di Villa
Giulia

🏛 8

Viale Giuseppe Mazzini

△ 7

Via Oslavia

Piazza
Mazzini

10

11

Piazza dei
Martiri di
Belfiore

9
△
Piazza
Monte
Grappa

Villa
Borghese

Via N. Ricciotti

Viale Settembrini

Lungotevere delle Armi

Ponte
G Matteotti

Via P
Fortuny

Via Flaminia

Piazza
delle
Cinque
Giornale

Stanislou Mancini

Via P Mamiani

Via Fracassini

Via A Mordini

Via E Ferrari

Via Vigliena

Via Fanfoyo

Via degli Scialoia

Ponte
P Nenni

Via Cesare Beccaria

Lungotevere Arnaldo da Brescia

Via F Casati

Via P Carrara

Via degli Scialoia

14 ●

Piazzale
Flaminio

Viale Washington

Viale delle Milizie

Via Brofferio

Via Lepanto

Via Dandria

Lepanto
M

12   13

Via Giulio Cesare

Via Luisa di Savoia

Flaminio

🛈 15

Piazza
del Popolo

Pincki
Hill

Viale del Muro Torto

MAP 5

MAP 4

0   100   200 m

Piazza
Euclide

Via M
Pelaiolo

Via D V GA
Prima

Via Euclide

1

Piazza
Santiago
del Cile

2

Via M
Michel

Via G. Antonelli

Chellini

Piazza
B Gastaldi

Via F Siacci

Viale dei Parioli

Largo Bellini

Via V Locchi

Viale Romania

Via Panama

Via D. Chiveto

Via D V GA Prima

Viale Bruno Buozzi

Via A
Stoppani

3

Piazza
Cuba

Piazza
Ungheria

Viale Liegi

Viale Bruno Buozzi

Piazzale
G Minzoni

Via di Villa Sacchetti

Via M.

Mercati

4

5

Via U. Aldrovandi

Via G. Rossini

Via Cavalieri

Via G. D'Arezzo

8

Piazza
G Verdi

V. G. Carissimi

9

Via N Porpora

Via G. Palestrina

7

Viale del Giardino   Zoologica

Piazza
Giardino
Zoologico

Via S. Mercadante

Largo N
Spinelli

6

Piazzale
di Daini

Viale dell'Uccelliera

Piazza San
Borghese

Viale dei Due Mascheroni

Via G. Vasamio

Piazza San
Borghese

12

Viale di
Valle Giulia

Viale
G Washington

10

Largo
Aqua Felix

Villa
Borghese

Via Pietro Canonica

Piazza
di Sienna

Piazza le dei
Cavalli Marini

Cavalli Marina

Via del Museo Borghese

Via Pinciana

13

Via Po

Via Salaria

Viale
delle Magnolie

Piazza le
di Canestre

Viale San Paolo de Brasile

Viale Wolfango Goethe

Via Pegana

Via Isonzo

Via Teresa

Via Sesti

Galoppatio

11

MAP 6

Corso d'Italia

MAP 3

MAP 4

PLACES TO STAY
13 Hotel Villa Borghese
18 Hotel CoppedÈ

PLACES OF INTEREST
6 Galleria Nazionale
   d'Arte Moderna
7 Bioparco (Zoo)
10 Museo Canonica
11 Il Galoppatio
   Equestrian Club
12 Museo e Galleria Borghese
16 Catacombe di Priscilla
22 Casina della Civetta

ENTERTAINMENT
15 Alien

OTHER
1 Slovenian Embassy
   & Consulate
2 Swiss Embassy & Consulate
3 Greek Consulate
4 Dutch Embassy & Consulate
5 Israeli Embassy
8 Greek Embassy
9 Austrian Consulate
14 AIED (Family Planning Clinic)
17 Arci-Gay Caravaggio
19 Australian Embassy
   & Consulate
20 New Zealand Consulate
21 Canadian Consulate
23 Canadian Embassy

MAP 5

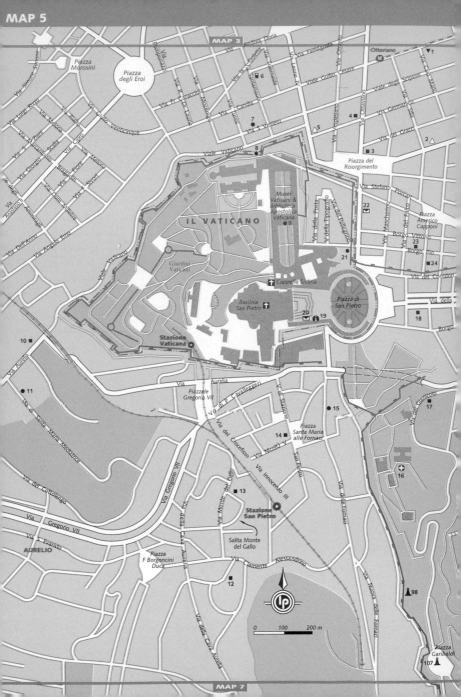

MAP 3

Ottaviano ▼1

Piazza
Morosini

Piazza
degli Eroi

Via A. Colletti

■ 6

Viale Giulio Cesare

Viale degli Scipioni

7
● Via S. Vaalieri

4 ■

Via Germanico

Via dei Gracchi

▲ 2

5 ▲

8 ●

Viale Vaticano

Piazza del
Risorgimento

■ 3

Via Stefano Porzari

IL VATICANO

Musei
Vaticani &
Biblioteca
Apostolica
Vaticana
● 9

22
⊠

Piazza
Americo
Capdoni

Borgo Vittorio

Giardini
Vaticani

23

Borgo Pio

21 ■

■ 24

Via dei Corridori

Cappella Sistina ✝ ●

Basilica
San Pietro ✝

Piazza di
San Pietro

Via della

20 ●
19
ℹ

18 ■

Borgo

10 ■

Stazione
Vaticana

Via Aurelia

Via Aurelia

Piazzale
Gregorio VII

Via di P. P. Cavallegeri

11 ●

Via di Santa Maria Mediatrice

15 ●

17 ▲

Via del Crocefisso

Via Nicolo V

Via S. Pietro

Via Innocenzo III

Piazza
Santa Maria
alle Fornaci

14 ■

16 ✚

Via Gregorio VII

Via del Monte del Gallo

13 ■

Stazione
San Pietro

Via della Fornaci

Via Gregorio VII

Via S. Evaristo

AURELIO

Piazza
F Borgoncini
Duca

Salita Monte
del Gallo

Via Clemente Alessandrino

Via Nuova delle Fornaci

▲ 98

12 ■

LP

0   100   200 m

Piazza
Garibaldi
▲ 107

MAP 7

MAP 5

MAP 3

See Around Piazza Navona Map

MAP 7

The Arco Farnese straddling Via Giulia

Detail of fountain, Piazza Navona

The approach to San Pietro

Bernini's Saint Teresa being transcendental

MAP 5

STEFANO CAVEDONI

MAP 6

MAP 4

MAP 8

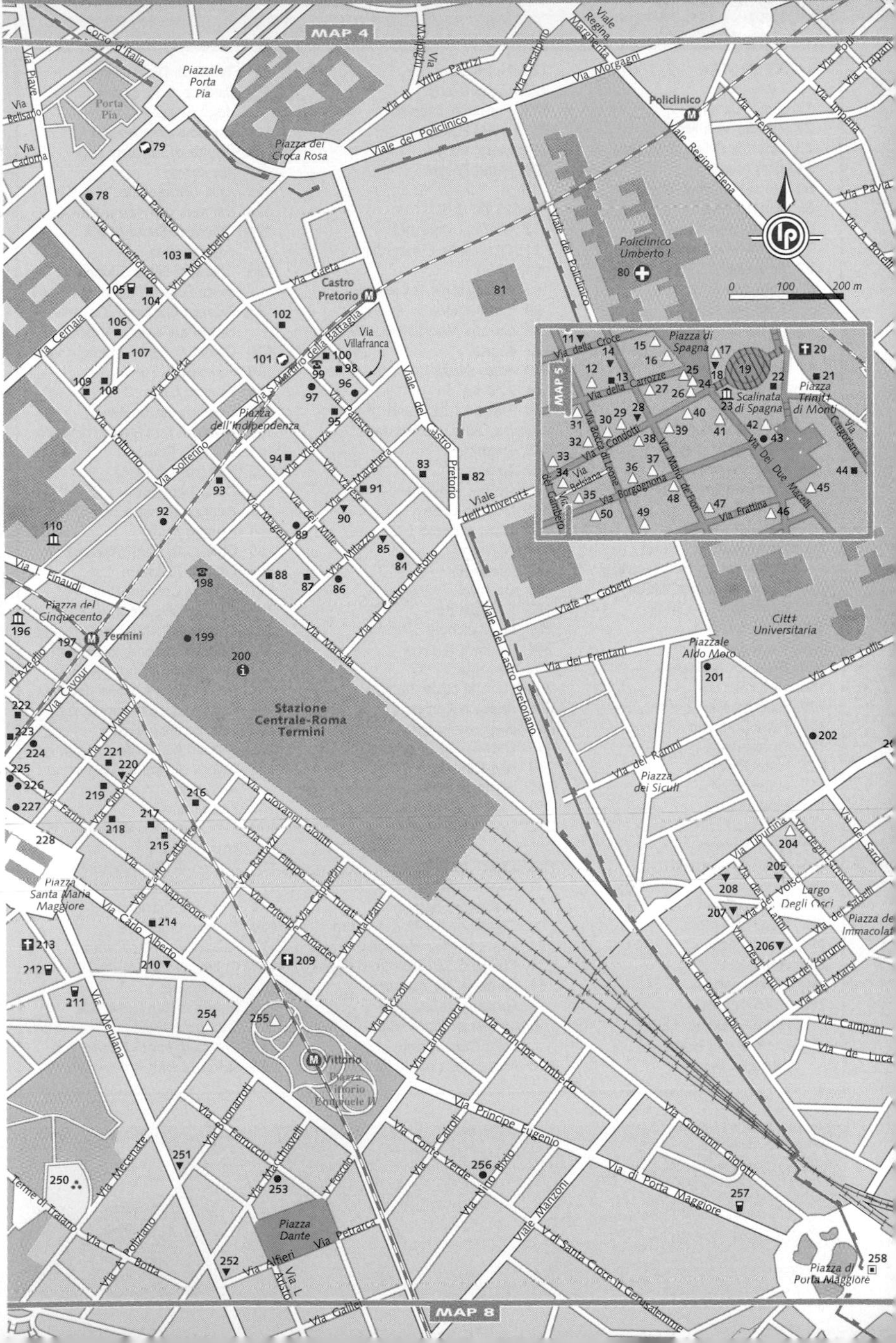

MAP 6

MAP 4

Piazzale
Porta Pia

Porta
Pia

Via
Belisario

Via
Cadorna

Piazza del
Croce Rosa

Viale del Policlinico

Policlinico

Policlinico
Umberto I

79

78

103

105 104

106

109 108

107

Via Palestro

Via Montebello

Via Cernaia

Via Solferino

Castro
Pretorio

102

101 100
99 98
97 96
95

Via Villafranca

Piazza
dell'Indipendenza

94

110

93

92

198

Via Einaudi

Piazza dei
Cinquecento

196

197 Termini

199

200

Stazione
Centrale-Roma
Termini

81

82

Viale
dell'Università

Città
Universitaria

Piazzale
Aldo Moro

201

202

MAP 5

11 14
12 13

15 16

Piazza di
Spagna

17
18 19 22

20

21
Piazza
Trinità
di Monti

25
24

27 26

Via della Croce

Via delle Carrozze

23 Scalinata
di Spagna

31 30 29 28
32
33

34

35
50 49

Via Condotti

Via Borgognona

48

38 39
36 37

40
41

42 43
44

45

47

46

Via Frattina

89

91

90

88 87 86

85 84

83

Via P. Cobetti

Via dei Frentani

Piazza
dei Siculi

Via dei Ramni

Via dei Marsi

204

205

208 Largo
Degli Osci

207

206

Piazza de
Immacolat

222
223
224
225
226
227

228

220
219
218
217
215

216

Via Giovanni Giolitti

209

214

210

213
212
211

Piazza
Santa Maria
Maggiore

254

255

Vittorio

Piazza
Vittorio
Emanuele II

202

250

251

252

253

Piazza
Dante

256

257

258

Piazza di
Porta Maggiore

MAP 8

MAP 6

SALLY WEBB

MAP 6

SALLY WEBB

MAP 7

MAP 5

AURELIO

PLACES TO STAY
2 Villa Bassi
29 Hotel Cisterna
39 Hotel Manara
48 Carmel
56 Aventino & Sant'Anselmo Hotels

PLACES TO EAT
6 Da Lucia
7 FricandÚ
8 Da Otello in Trastevere
9 Da Corrado
10 Casetta di Trastevere
13 La Tana di Noantri
16 Osteria Der Belli
24 Bar San Calisto
25 Paris
26 Pizzeria San Calisto
27 Ripa 12
32 India House
33 La Fonte della Salute
34 Panattoni
35 Pizzeria Popi Popi
36 Pizzeria Ivo
37 Pizzeria da Vittorio
38 Alberto Ciarla
40 Sacchetti
41 Pasticceria Trastevere
43 Frontoni
57 Pizzeria Remo
58 Augustarello
59 Il Gelato di Antonio

60 Trattoria da Bucatino
61 Il Canestro
64 Volpetti Pi"
65 Da Felice
73 Saperi e Sapori
74 Cecchino dal 1887

PLACES OF INTEREST
1 Casa del Sole
3 Fontana dell'Aqua Paola
4 Chiesa di San Pietro in Montorio
12 Museo del Folklore e dei Poeti Romaneschi
14 Basilica di Santa Maria in Trastevere
17 Casa du Dante
19 Chiesa di San Bartolomeo
20 Chiesa di San Crisogono
31 Basilica di Santa Cecilia in Trastevere
53 Basilica di Santa Sabina
54 Chiesa di Santa Maria del Priorato
55 Priorato di Cavalieri di Malta
67 Cimitero Acattolico

SHOPPING
15 Pandora
30 Bibli

44 Standa
62 Mercato di Testaccio
63 Volpetti

ENTERTAINMENT
11 Pasquino
22 Molly Malone
23 CaffÈ Marzio
42 Alcazar
45 San Michele aveva un Gallo
46 Big Mama
51 Teatro Vascello
52 Nuovo Sacher
66 Four XXXX
68 Radio Londra
69 Akab
70 CaffÈ Latino
71 Caruso CaffÈ
72 L'Alibi
75 Villaggio Globale
76 Alpheus (Muccassassina)

OTHER
18 Tourist Information
21 Ospedale San Gallicano
28 Libreria delle Donne: Al Tempo Ritrovato
47 Ospedale Nuova Regina Margherita
49 American University of Rome
50 Ospedale San Camillo

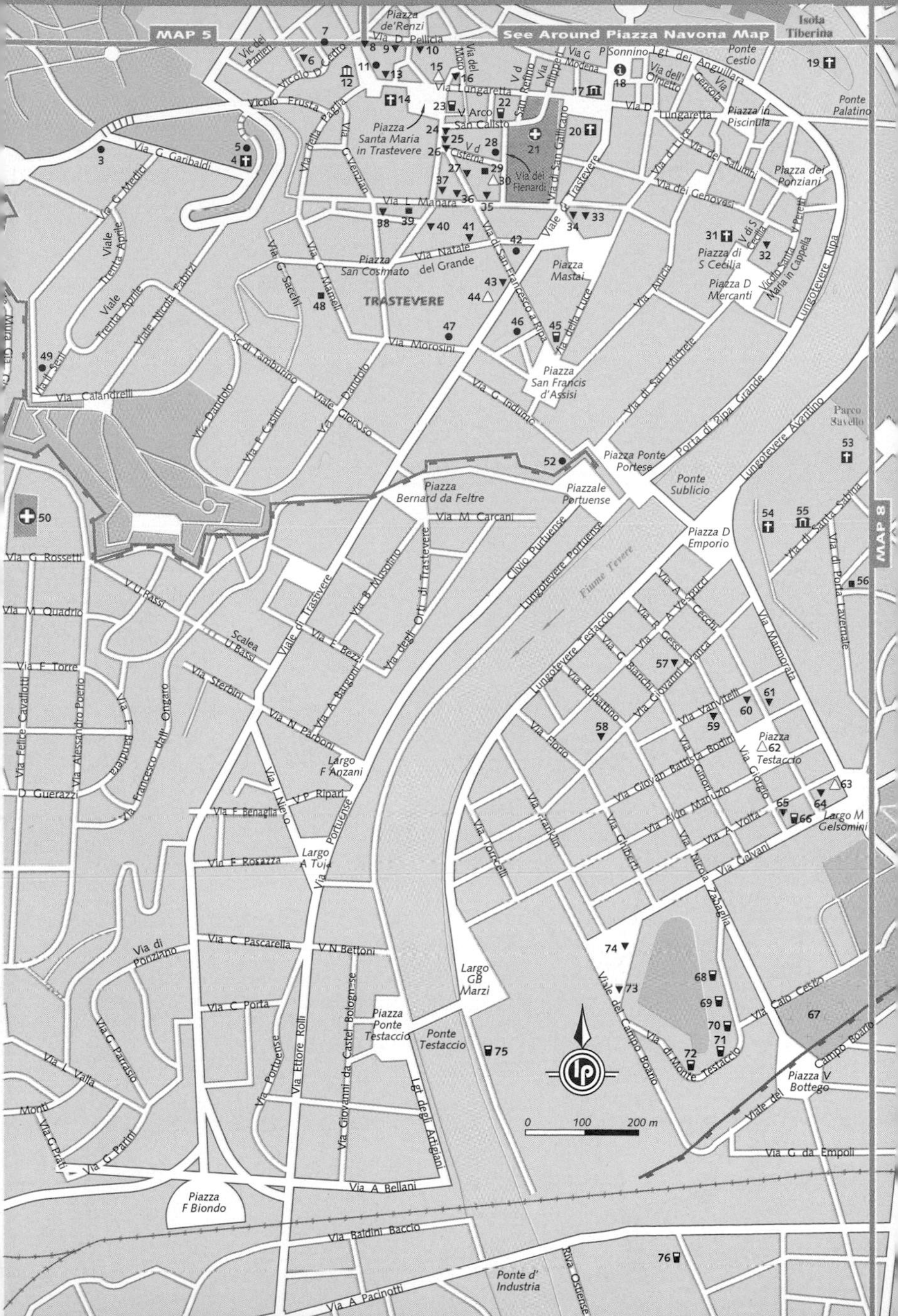

MAP 7

MAP 5

See Around Piazza Navona Map

Isola
Tiberina

Piazza
de' Renzi

Via G
Modena

P. Sonnino

Lgt. dei Anguillara

Ponte
Cestio

19

Ponte
Palatino

Via dell'
Arco

Piazza in
Piscinula

Via della
Lungaretta

Piazza dei
Ponziani

Via de' Salumi

Piazza del
Mercanti

Piazza di
S Cecilia

Piazza D
Mercanti

Via dei Genovesi

Piazza
Santa Maria
in Trastevere

Arco
San Callisto

Via di San Gallicano

Lungaretta

Via L. Manara

Via Natale
del Grande

Piazza
San Cosimato

Piazza
Mastai

TRASTEVERE

Via G. Garibaldi

Via G. Medici

Viale Aurelio Saffi

Viale Trenta Aprile

Viale Glorioso

Via Dandolo

Via Calandrelli

Via di S. Francesco a Ripa

Piazza
San Francis
d'Assisi

Via di San Michele

Parco
Savello

53

Porta di Ripa Grande

Parco
Savello

Piazza Ponte
Portese

Piazzale
Portuense

Ponte
Sublicio

Piazza D
Emporio

54 55

MAP 8

56

Piazza
Bernard da Feltre

Via M. Carcani

Clivio Portuense

Lungotevere Portuense

Fiume Tevere

Lungotevere Testaccio

Via A. Vespucci

Via Luca della Robbia

Via A. Cecconi

Via Giovanni Branca

Via Nicola Zabaglia

Via G. Rossetti

V. U. Rossi

V.M. Quadrio

Scalea
D. Bassi

Viale di Trastevere

Viale Quattro Venti

Via F. Torre

Via Felice Cavallotti

Via Francesco dall'Ongaro

Via N. Piccolomini

Via N. Parboni

Via A. Baroni

Largo
F Anzani

Via F. Ripari

Largo
A Toja

Via F. Benaglia

Via F. Rocazza

Via C. Pascarella

V. N. Bettoni

Via C. Porta

Via di
Ponziani

Via L. Valla

Via C. Parini

Via E. Rolli

Via Giovanni da Castel Bolognese

Via Ettore Rolli

Via Portuense

Piazza
Ponte
Testaccio

Ponte
Testaccio

Largo
GB
Marzi

74

73

Largo M
Gelsomini

Via Aldo Manuzio

Via A. Volta

Via Galvani

Via Nicola Zabaglia

68

69

70 71

72

67

Via di Monte Testaccio

Campo Boario

Piazza V
Bottego

75

Via A. Bellani

Via Baldini Baccio

Via Ostiense

Ponte d'
Industria

Via L. Pacinotti

Piazza
F Biondo

76

Via G. da Empoli

0   100   200 m

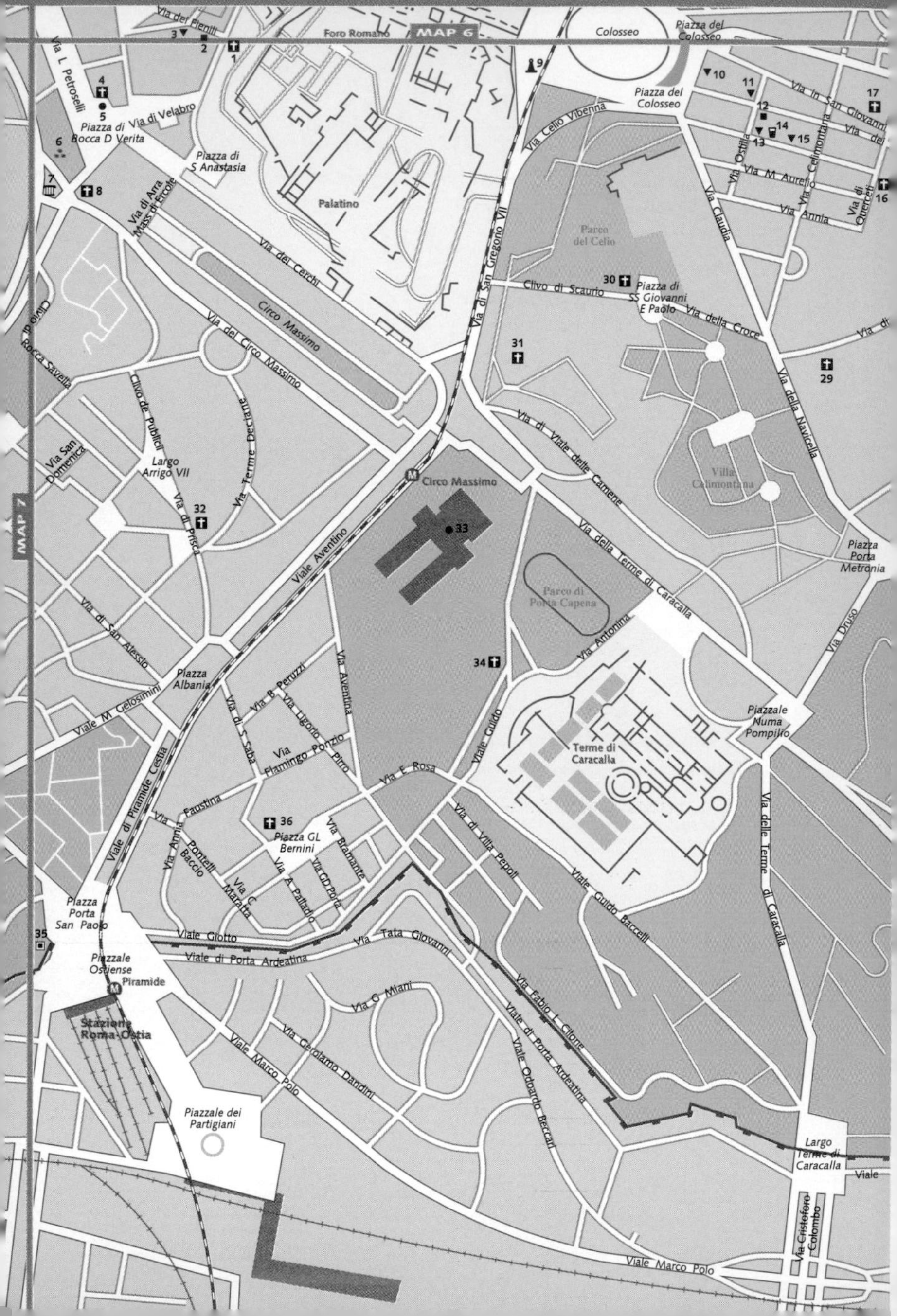

MAP 8

Via dei Fienili

3 ▼ 2

Foro Romano MAP 6

Colosseo

Piazza del Colosseo

Via L. Petroselli

4

5

Piazza di Via di Velabro
Bocca D Verita

6

7

8

Via di Aqua
Mega d'Ercole

Piazza di
S Anastasia

Palatino

Via dei Cerchi

Circo Massimo

Via del Circo Massimo

1 ▼9

Piazza del
Colosseo

▼10 11 17

Via In San Giovanni

12

13 14 15 16

Via M. Aurelio

Via Amba

Via Claudia

Parco
del Celio

Clivo di Scauro

30 Piazza di
SS Giovanni
E Paolo Via della Croce

31

Via di Viale delle Camene

Circo Massimo

33

Parco di
Porta Capena

Via della Terme di Caracalla

29

Via della Navicella

Villa
Celimontana

Piazza
Porta
Metronia

Via Druso

Chiesa

Via Rocca Savella

Via San
Domenica

Largo
Arrigo VII

32

Via di San Alessio

Via di Santa Prisca

Via Aventino

34

Via Antonina

Piazzale
Numa
Pompilio

Via delle Terme di Caracalla

Piazza
Albania

Via M Celosimini

Via P. Peruzzi

Via L Porzio Pirro

Via G
Flaminio Ponzio

Via Aventina

Via F. Rosa

Terme di
Caracalla

Via di Villa Pepoli

Via Guido

Via di
Saba

Faustina

Via
Pontelli
Baccio

36
Piazza GL
Bernini

Via G
Mitella

Via A Pellistri

Via Bramante

Via CD Porta

Via di Porta Ardeatina

Viale Guido Baccelli

Piazza
Porta
San Paolo

35

Viale Giotto

Viale di Porta Ardeatina

Via Tata Giovanni

Via di Fabio L Cilone

Piazzale
Ostiense Piramide

Stazione
Roma-Ostia

Via G. Miani

Via C Miani

Viale di Porta Ardeatina

Viale Oderardo Becari

Via Girolamo Dandini

Viale Marco Polo

Piazzale dei
Partigiani

Largo
Terme di
Caracalla

Viale

Via Cristoforo
Colombo

Viale Marco Polo

MAP 8

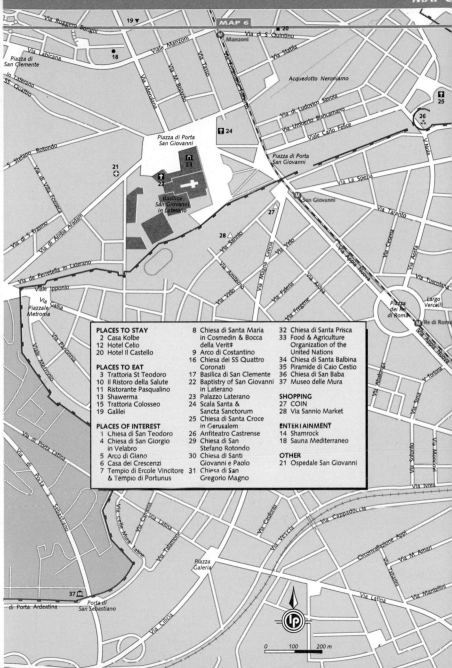

MAP 6

PLACES TO STAY
2 Casa Kolbe
12 Hotel Celio
20 Hotel Il Castello

PLACES TO EAT
3 Trattoria St Teodoro
10 Il Ristoro della Salute
11 Ristorante Pasqualino
13 Shawerma
15 Trattoria Colosseo
19 Galilei

PLACES OF INTEREST
1 Chiesa di San Teodoro
4 Chiesa di San Giorgio in Velabro
5 Arco di Giano
6 Casa dei Crescenzi
7 Tempio di Ercole Vincitore & Tempio di Portunus

8 Chiesa di Santa Maria in Cosmedin & Bocca della Verità
9 Arco di Costantino
16 Chiesa dei SS Quattro Coronati
17 Basilica di San Clemente
22 Baptistry of San Giovanni in Laterano
23 Palazzo Laterano
24 Scala Santa & Sancta Sanctorum
25 Chiesa di Santa Croce in Gerusalem
26 Anfiteatro Castrense
29 Chiesa di San Stefano Rotondo
30 Chiesa di Santi Giovanni e Paolo
31 Chiesa di San Gregorio Magno

32 Chiesa di Santa Prisca
33 Food & Agriculture Organization of the United Nations
34 Chiesa di Santa Balbina
35 Piramide di Caio Cestio
36 Chiesa di San Baba
37 Museo delle Mura

SHOPPING
27 COIN
28 Via Sannio Market

ENTERTAINMENT
14 Shamrock
18 Sauna Mediterraneo

OTHER
21 Ospedale San Giovanni

MAP 6

MAP 7

MAP LEGEND

BOUNDARIES

─ ─ ─ ─	International
─ ─ ─ ─	State
─ ─ ─ ─	Disputed

HYDROGRAPHY

	Coastline
	River
	Creek
	Lake
	Intermittent Lake
	Canal
	Spring, Rapids
	Waterfalls
	Swamp

ROUTES & TRANSPORT

	Freeway
	Highway
	Major Road
	Minor Road
	Unsealed Road
	City Freeway
	City Highway
	City Road
	City Street, Lane

	Pedestrian Mall
	Tunnel
	Train Route & Station
	Metro & Station
	Tramway
	Cable Car or Chairlift
	Walking Track
	Walking Tour
	Ferry Route

AREA FEATURES

	Archaeological Area
	Building
	Cemetery

	Market
	Park, Gardens
	Pedestrian Mall

MAP SYMBOLS

○ **CAPITAL**	National Capital
◉ **CAPITAL**	State Capital
● **CITY**	City
● **Town**	Town
● Village	Village
	Point of Interest
■	Place to Stay
Å	Camping Ground
⊕	Caravan Park
⌂	Hut or Chalet
▼	Place to Eat
▮	Pub or Bar

✈	Airport
⊖	ATM, Bank
⭖	Bike Rental
▲	Castle or Fort
▮	Church
	Cliff or Escarpment
○	Embassy
○	Fountain
⊕	Hospital
▲	Monument
◪	Mosque
▲	Mountain or Hill
⛫	Museum, Art Gallery
←	One Way Street

▯	Parking
★	Police Station
▭	Post Office
△	Shop
❖	Shopping Centre
⛫	Stately Home
	Swimming Pool
▣	Synagogue
☎	Telephone
⬚	Temple
▣	Tomb
❶	Tourist Information
○	Transport
🐘	Zoo

Note: not all symbols displayed above appear in this book

LONELY PLANET OFFICES

Australia
PO Box 617, Hawthorn, Victoria 3122
☎ (03) 9819 1877 fax (03) 9819 6459
email: talk2us@lonelyplanet.com.au

USA
150 Linden St, Oakland, CA 94607
☎ (510) 893 8555 TOLL FREE: 800 275 8555
fax (510) 893 8572
email: info@lonelyplanet.com

UK
10a Spring Place, London NW5 3BH
☎ (020) 7428 4800 fax (020) 7428 4828
email: go@lonelyplanet.co.uk

France
1 rue du Dahomey, 75011 Paris
☎ 01 55 25 33 00 fax 01 55 25 33 01
email: bip@lonelyplanet.fr

World Wide Web: www.lonelyplanet.com *or* AOL keyword: lp
Lonely Planet Images: lpi@lonelyplanet.com.au